Lecture Notes in Computer Science 860

Edited by G. Goos, J. Hartmanis and J. van Leeuwen

Advisory Board: W. Brauer   D. Gries   J. Stoer

Wolfgang L. Zagler   Geoffrey Busby
Roland R. Wagner (Eds.)

Computers for Handicapped Persons

4th International Conference, ICCHP '94
Vienna, Austria, September 14-16, 1994
Proceedings

Springer-Verlag

Berlin Heidelberg New York
London Paris Tokyo
Hong Kong Barcelona
Budapest

Series Editors

Gerhard Goos
Universität Karlsruhe
Postfach 69 80, Vincenz-Priessnitz-Straße 1, D-76131 Karlsruhe, Germany

Juris Hartmanis
Department of Computer Science, Cornell University
4130 Upson Hall, Ithaka, NY 14853, USA

Jan van Leeuwen
Department of Computer Science, Utrecht University
Padualaan 14, 3584 CH Utrecht, The Netherlands

Volume Editors

Wolfgang L. Zagler
Institut für Allgemeine Elektrotechnik und Elektronik, Technische Universität Wien
Gusshausstr. 27/359/B, A-1040 Wien, Austria

Geoffrey Busby
GEC Computer Services Ltd.
West Hanningfield Road, Gr. Baddow, Chelmsford CM2 8HN, United Kingdom

Roland R. Wagner
Inst. for Informatics & Research Inst. for Applied Knowledge Processing (FAW)
Johannes Kepler University Linz
Altenbergerstr. 69, A-4040 Linz, Austria

CR Subject Classification (1991): D.2.2, H.5, H.1.2, I.2.6-7, I.3.6, I.7, K.3-4

ISBN 3-540-58476-5 Springer-Verlag Berlin Heidelberg New York

CIP data applied for

© Springer-Verlag Berlin Heidelberg 1994
Printed in Germany

Typesetting: Camera-ready by author
SPIN: 10479049   45/3140-543210 - Printed on acid-free paper

PREFACE

For the fourth time now the International Conference on Computers for Handicapped Persons is taking place as a successful cooperation between the Austrian Computer Society and 'fortec', the Rehabilitation Engineering Group at the Vienna University of Technology. Again the conference is backed up by several national and international computer societies and related organizations (IFIP, CEPIS, BSC, GI, SI, ACM, IEEE). For me this international cooperation is an indicator for the worldwide importance of and interest in this topic.

The conference has been sponsored by the Austrian Federal Ministry of Environment, Youth and Family Affairs, the Austrian Federal Ministry of Education and the Arts, the Austrian Workers Compensation Board (AUVA), the Österreichische Postsparkasse (PSK), the Federation of Austrian Industrialists, and the Bank Austria.

Following the call for papers more than a hundred experts and research teams have submitted contributions for this conference. For the first time the conference organizers (i.e. the program committee and the organizing committee) decided to split up the contributions into four categories: preconference seminars, conference papers, scientific posters, and short reports that mainly cover ongoing projects and national activities.

After the reviewing process and the subsequent meeting of the program committee, six pre-conference seminars, 79 conference papers, nine scientific posters, and 13 short reports were accepted. This Lecture Notes in Computer Science (LNCS) volume presents all conference contributions except the pre-conference Seminars. The manuscripts for the seminars will be prepared by the seminar speakers as handouts for the seminar participants. In the appendix of the proceedings is a list of the seminars together with the addresses of the speakers.

The editorial is the right place to thank those persons who by their experience and dedication have contributed so much to the preparation of this conference. First of all I want to thank the members of the program committee who have done all the reviewing and by their comments helped to improve quite a number of papers:

A. Arató, Central Research Institute for Physics, Hungary
P. L. Blenkhorn, University of Manchester, United Kingdom
M. Debevc, University of Maribor, Slovenia
F. Destombes, IBM France, Paris, France
J. Ekberg, National Agency for Welfare and Health, Finland
P. L. Emiliani, Consiglio Nazionale delle Ricerche, Italy
H. Funakubo, Shibaura Institute of Technology, Japan
Ch. Galinski, Infoterm, Vienna, Austria
J. Gonzales-Abascal, Euskal Herriko Univ., Donostia, Spain
R. Gunzenhäuser, University of Stuttgart, Germany
J. Halousek, Techn. University of Prague, Czech Republic
K. M. Helle, Work Research Institute, Norway
V. Henn, Universitätsklinik Zürich, Switzerland
J. Klaus, University of Karlsruhe, Germany
J.-I. Lindström, Telia AB, Sundbyberg, Sweden
M. Martin, The Mike Martin Consultancy, United Kingdom
J. Mühlbacher, University of Linz, Austria
H. J. Murphy, California State University Northridge, USA
A. Schneider, Swiss Fed. of the Blind & Vis. Impaired, CH
M. Soede, Inst. for Rehabilitation Research, The Netherlands
A. Spaepen, Katholieke Universiteit Leuven, Belgium
B. Stöger, University of Linz, Austria
T. Vaspöri, Central Research Institute for Physics, Hungary

Especially I would like to thank the two co-chairmen of the program committee: Prof. Wagner (University of Linz, Austria) who has not only been one of the main promotors of this and the past conferences but also made it possible for these proceedings to be published by Springer-Verlag and Geoff Busby (GEC Computer Services and British Computer Society) who in addition to all the reviewing work and despite his physical challenge came all the way from Great Britain to Vienna to join us at the program committee meeting.

Last but not least I want to thank the organizing committee headed by Dr. W. Grafendorfer (Secretary General of the Austrian Computer Society) who dedicated much effort, skill and time to make this 1994 conference possible. I know that for him and for the other members of the organizing committee (Dipl.-Ing. W. Kremser, Dipl.-Ing. F. P. Seiler, I. Sudra) the ICCHP is not just a conference like any other but a meeting that is worth special attention.

"Computers for Handicapped Persons" - for years the conference has sailed under this flag. It is a good and a challenging name. It expresses the belief that computers and computer science can do much in overcoming barriers imposed on persons with disabilities. If we, however, have a closer look at the real meaning of "handicap" the title could be misleading and should be modified. Handicap is defined as the the social result of an inpairment or disability. Therefore, it is our goal that, by using computers in the proper way, the handicaps will be eliminated even if the impairment remains unchanged. The conference title will not be changed in the future, but the true goal is and will be "Computers for Disabled Persons (to leave them) *no longer handicapped.*

Thanks to all the authors who have contributed to this 4th ICCHP. May every paper, poster or seminar be a step further in overcoming barriers and handicaps.

Wolfgang L. Zagler
Program Chair, 4th ICCHP 1994
Vienna University of Technology
July 1994

ACKNOWLEDGEMENT

This conference has been sponsored by

Austrian Federal Ministry of Education and Arts
Austrian Federal Ministry of Environment, Youth and Family Affairs
Austrian Federal Ministry of Science and Research
AUVA – Allgemeine Unfallversicherungsanstalt, Austria
Bank Austria
BCS – British Computer Society
CEPIS – Council of European Professional Informatics Societies
Federation of Austrian Industrialists
GI – Gesellschaft für Informatik, Germany
IFIP – International Federation for Information Processing
NJSZT – John v. Neumann Computer Society, Hungary
PSK – Österreichische Postsparkasse, Austria
SI – Schweizer Informatiker Gesellschaft, Switzerland
TermNet

Held in cooperation with

ACM (SIGCAPH)
IEEE Computer Society

Printed with the support of the Austrian Federal Ministry of Science and Research

CONTENTS

Opening Session

Blindness - Graphical User Interfaces I

Technology and Deafness

Remote Control, Smart Environments

Blindness - Graphical User Interfaces II

Human Computer Interfaces, I/O Devices I

Automatic Control and Robotics

Blindness - Screen Readers

Human Computer Interfaces, I/O Devices II

Short Reports: Activities

Blindness - Access to Documents I

Vision Impairment and Higher Education

Short Reports: Vocation and the Workplace

Blindness - Access to Documents II

Disability and Higher Education

Information Systems on Rehabilitation Technology

Blindness - Access to Math and Software Engineering

Medical and Clinical Aspects I

Speech Impairment - Alternative Communication I

Blindness - New Applications of Sound Signals

Medical and Clinical Aspects II

Speech Impairment - Alternative Communication II

Blindness - Tactile Output Devices

Technology Support in Mainstream Education

Short Reports: Human Computer Interfaces

Short Reports: Education

Technology and Low Vision

Computer Aided Learning, Authoring Systems

Telecommunication and Satellite Navigation

Blindness - Tactile Reading and Writing

Technology and Disabled Children

Late Papers

Appendix

Communications and Information Technology for Persons with Disabilities – The Canadian National Strategy as an Example

Mary Frances Laughton

Industry Canada
Ottawa, Ontario, K2H 8S2, Canada

Abstract: Persons with disabilities have major reasons for use of adaptive systems. These individuals are often handicapped by not having access to traditional forms of communication and information. An individual who is blind cannot read print information. A person who is deaf cannot usually obtain information directly via telephone. An individual with a speech impairment may have the same problem with respect to telephone contact. A person who is in a wheelchair may not have physical access to buildings which house information services and, even if they can get in, their physical limitations may prevent them from using those services without extraordinary assistance. Industry Canada has been involved for a number of years in the development of assistive devices in partnership with a number of Canadian organizations. The search for a global market is always there.

1   Introduction

This paper will report on a series of Industry Canada (a Federal Government department) supported projects to develop communications and information technology (C&IT) tools, systems and services which assist persons with disabilities to communicate with each other and with persons without disabilities. The programme described is called "Communications for Persons with Disabilities."

The right to communicate has been regarded by many as a fundamental right. However, many Canadians are denied access to the normal communications channels due to a disability. The visually impaired cannot fully enjoy television and books without special aids. They need special devices to be able to be fully functional in the workplace. The hearing impaired require captioning to enjoy movies and television. They require special devices to use the telephone. Speech impaired persons have need for augmentative communications tools and languages. Mobility impaired have need for special interfaces to use computers and other communications devices.

The ability to communicate without the need for an intermediary increases independence and will reduce attendant care costs significantly. The ability to easily communicate increases one's self esteem greatly.

2   Background

Canada has always been a world leader in communications. The telephone was invented here and Canada maintains one of the best phone systems in the world with over 97% of households having at least one telephone. Canada had the first domestic communications satellite. Our packet switched network was one of the first. Our radio and television broadcasts are world renowned.

The overall aim of the Canadian strategy is to implement tangible steps that will address the communications needs of Canadians with disabilities in a coherent and pragmatic fashion through cooperation amongst all levels of Government and the private sector.

All Industry Canada activities relating to persons with disabilities are done within the context of the Canadian National Strategy on the Integration of Persons with Disabilities. This is a cross-Government programme designed to increase the integration of persons with disabilities into Canadian society. Communications and information technologies are but one of many tools required but they are a fundamental need!

Industry Canada has been active in the development and implementation of technology and services that improve communications for Canadians with disabilities, but there is much more to do. Many communications problems can only be addressed by fully researching the problem and then developing devices, programmes, tools or whatever is required to meet the needs. There are many activities that go on in Government and other laboratories that could be used to improve communications. Financial assistance needs to be provided to share some of the risk for field testing, trial and other demonstrations. There are a number of private sector and government organizations who are trying to address the C&IT needs of persons with disabilities.

Of great benefit is the ability to get a "critical mass" of devices or systems to be tested to provide the feedback required and to provide the momentum required for full implementation.

In this paper, I will describe the projects ongoing and planned. The partnership aspect with the private sector will be highlighted. The possibility of global markets for these developments will be examined.

In 1993, we completed the first Canadian needs study[1] for C&IT products, systems and services. It also provided a directory of R&D underway in Canada and elsewhere, a listing of conferences and a bibliography. It has been widely distributed and is being used as an awareness raising tool for the programme and as a textbook for special university courses. It is now being revised. It is our hope to undertake the R&D to meet many of the needs identified.

15.3 % of Canadians (4.5 million people) indicated in the 1991 Census that they have some form of disability. Figure 1 shows the breakdown by type of disability.

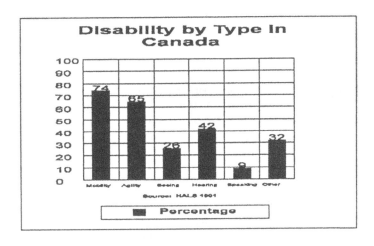

Mobility 74
Agility 65
Seeing 26
Hearing 42
Speaking 9
Other 32

Figure 1

3 Standards

Industry Canada has the responsibility for the development and implementation of C&IT standards. Computer technology has provided persons with disabilities with a means by which they can be more independent in their quest for information. Within computer-mediated communications systems, it is not just barriers between the individual and the information they seek which are broken down; it is also the barriers between people. A person who is deaf may talk to a person who is blind; a person who is both deaf and blind may communicate with the world. An able-bodied individual may discuss issues with people with disabilities without knowing the state of the other individual. The only way that this communication can be ensured is with the adherence to recognized standards. The TTY/TDD telephone for the deaf is first and foremost a standard. The Blissphone project (described later) revolved around the development of an international standard.

4 Process

Each project undertaken is reviewed against several criteria. There is an Advisory Committee of experts which provides guidance to the programme.

1. Is there a user need? The user community is involved in the design of each project and, indeed, is in most cases a partner in the project.

2. Does the project deal with developed or emerging standards? The question of C&IT standards is a central point of each project.

3.   Will the systems developed continue after Government involvement? It is important in any project but especially one in support of people with disabilities that expectations not be created that will not be met. This is the case in each of the described projects.

We produce a report that can assist others in understanding the lessons learned, both positive and negative, in the development process. These reports are available in alternate formats and, by the time this paper will be given, will be available over the Internet.

5   Project Descriptions

5.1   Grocery Product Reader

Needing only simple tools, a computer, a speech synthesizer, a relational database and a standard, the UPC (universal product code), in partnership with the Canadian National Institute for the Blind, a product has been developed to allow people with visual disability to identify their grocery products using a scanner. This product, called ScanTell (a project of Compusult in St. John's, Newfoundland) is now being readied for market and other uses of the technology are being investigated in work situations. It is shown schematically in Figure 2.

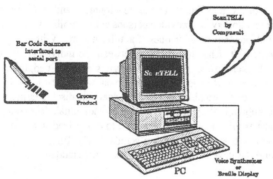

Figure 2

5.2   Newspapers for the Print-Handicapped

It is possible to send a newspaper electronically using a datacasting[1] channel. This did not seem to be an interesting application since the paper copies which we all love so dearly are relatively cheap to produce and people do not generally like to read from a computer screen. However, the transmission of the newspaper via datacasting to the print-handicapped may be ideal. The newspaper is received and stored in a PC. The consumer can then use the numeric keypad to choose which stories should be read to him/her by a voice synthesizer or an alternative braille output device. This enables people with a print handicap to have all the news stories the same as somebody fully sighted.

Since there are 500,000 visually impaired persons in Canada and many other persons with disabilities which make it difficult for them to read a newspaper, a datacasting service is required to distribute the text of the newspaper in order that many of them can all be served.

Similar projects are underway in Sweden, Britain and Japan. In conjunction with the Canadian National Institute for the Blind, an international network of Newspapers for the Blind will be instituted so that information gained in each of the projects will benefit from other's work. A schematic of the system is shown in Figure 3.

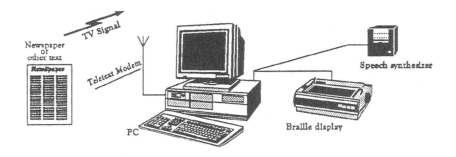

Figure 3

---

[1] Datacasting is the use of electronic means to make data broadly available to geographically dispersed sites at the same time. In the case of this project, the method of distribution is teletext which is the use of the vertical blanking interval (VBI) of a television channel.

5.3   Descriptive Captioning

Descriptive captioning is a means by which the visually impaired can enjoy a television broadcast in the same way the sighted can. The system in use in the United States uses the stereo channel of a TV broadcast to distribute a narrative of the scenes on the screen between the dialogue on-screen.

The Canadian project, in partnership with programme developers, broadcasters and cable companies, is to examine other mechanisms than stereo broadcasting by which the description can be distributed. This includes looking at the use of sub-carriers on the FM sound channel and VBI of the TV broadcasts. Some software will need to be developed to properly synchronize the description and dialogue of the described shows.

Once standards are developed for descriptive video, Canadian broadcasts will be able to be made available across the world and a global network of shared shows will make the lives of the visually impaired more pleasant.

5.4   Home Automation

Home automation systems play a major role in facilitating environments which provide significant independence in many areas of everyday life activities. For instance, these home control systems will allow seniors and persons with disabilities to have integrated control of items such as lights, appliances, TV, VCR, security systems, entry ways, intercoms, telephone and thermostats. Consequently, these automated homes significantly reduce the dependence of these persons on others and, hence, facilitate a substantial increase in the quality of life of these individuals. The desire to obtain or maintain a given level of independence is extremely powerful and, therefore, persons who could potentially increase and/or maintain their independence will vigorously pursue viable avenues that will facilitate their ability to take advantage of automated living environments.

Until recently, most home control systems have been developed in the domain of hobbyists who are interested in controlling various aspects of their home for reasons of fuel efficiency, security or novelty. The major problem with these systems is that the degree of manual dexterity required for their operation made them inaccessible for the use by persons with limited physical movement. For example, most systems used input devices such as keyboards or touch-screens.

The Neil Squire Foundation has developed the Remote Gateway, primarily using simple commercially available components. The device includes a portable remote voice/video terminal mounted on an electric wheelchair, a very functional and efficient method of remote control.

The Gateway presents menu oriented home control information on a compact video screen contained in a portable remote unit. The user uses voice commands to actuate the various control functions and is able to carry out two-way conversations either on the telephone or over an intercom system. In addition, the user can view video information from one or more security cameras. The remote unit communicates to a base unit through a wireless link. The base unit provides the support for the user interface, the voice recognition and the portal into the system.

The fundamental requirements for this product were: user-friendly, voice actuated, visual feedback, portable, highly robust wireless link. Continuing technological advances are increasing the extent to which people can manage their living environments. Recent advances in the automation industry are opening up new applications that were previously not feasible or too expensive. Industry activity suggests that one of the first areas of growth in this market will be for the special needs population. Providing seniors and persons with disabilities greater opportunities to lead autonomous lifestyles has obvious social and economic benefits.

5.5 Jouse

The jouse is a mouth activated mouse emulator that is now being beta-tested by those quadriplegics who have a need for it. This is one of a suite of adaptive switches developed under the programme. It is shown in Figure 4.

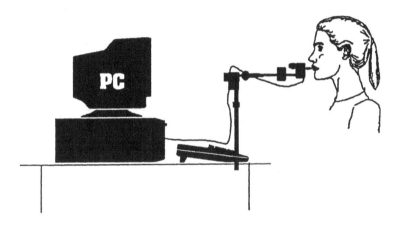

Figure 4

5.6 Bliss

Industry Canada was a partner in developing the BLISSPHONE, a telephone for the speech impaired. There are over 30,000 people in Canada who cannot speak for reasons other than hearing impairment. The causes of their impairment include cerebral palsy, muscular dystrophy, stroke and other neuro-muscular diseases. Currently there are more than 3500 Bliss symbols in use. The symbols are based on a language created by Charles Bliss[2]. The symbols were left in perpetuity to the Bliss Communications Institute which is in Toronto.

We aimed to make electronic communication using Blissymbols available to the largest number who could benefit from their use. Messages can be sent and read using a specially developed programme. An e-mail service is available and there is the possibility of real time "discussion". The aim was to ensure that the coding scheme is recognized internationally and that is now the case[3].

Since Bliss is used in over 35 countries worldwide, the global aspects of this project are always in mind.

6   Conclusions

For many of us, disability is a word that conjures up a picture of a person in a wheelchair. But we don't really stop to think what it means to the person in the chair.

It's not just the issue of putting in wider doors and ramps to make buildings wheelchair accessible. It goes a lot deeper. Disability can mean that you have trouble feeding yourself or that you may have difficulty in making a controlled movement of the hand, foot or head in order to press a simple switch. It can also mean having ideas in your mind that you are unable to express because you can't easily communicate.

We are all disabled to some extent as disability is a continuum. All of us will become disabled simply as a result of the aging process. There is a good chance, therefore, that all of us will at some point need an assistive device.

We hope the Blissphone, the Jouse, the automated house, descriptive captioning, electronic newspapers and many other technologies will give Canadians with disabilities a direct line to the rest of the world.

7   References

1.   Communications and Information Technologies and Persons with Disabilities, Industry Canada, 1993.

2 .   Blissymbols for Use, Blissymbolics Communication Institute, 1980

3.   ISO 8875, 1993

An Intelligent Information System for Blind People – AI Technology and Philosophical Aspects[*]

Thomas Kieninger, Norbert Kuhn[**],

Kerstin Seidenschwann, Werner Weiss

Deutsches Forschungszentrum für Künstliche Intelligenz
Postfach 20 80
D-67608 Kaiserslautern

Abstract. Communication to exchange information is essential for humans. In many fields of communication this has lead to more or less fixed forms that guide or determine the way how people exchange information. This concerns at first a logical layer of the information blocks, i.e., which information has to be transmitted but also a procedural layer describing how the information is send.

A very important domain of communication is the business letter domain. Here, a certain standard has evolved that determines the form of business letters. We distinguish a logical structure and a layout structure that is captured in the international Standard called *Office Document Architecture(ODA*, ISO 8613 [1]).

In this paper we discuss the problem of presenting printed documents to blind people who cannot perceive the information provided by the layout structure of a document. We outline how the ODA Standard can be exploited to allow random access to the logical entities of a printed document. This approach is based on a system that has been developed at the DFKI and which has been described in [5] and which is able to extract the layout information from certain classes of business letters automatically.

1 Introduction

The increasing number of computer applications had strong impacts especially for the office world. Computer based tools are essential in almost any company. They support humans in routine tasks and - what might be even more important - they are a basic means for managing communication among humans, either within the in-house office environment or for communication with other company partners. Computer technology - and in particular computer networks - yield a lot of benefits for business world: information is available on-line, at an

---

[*] This work has been supported by the Stiftung Rheinland-Pfalz für Innovation
[**] phone: (0631) 205-3451, E-mail:kuhn@dfki.uni-kl.de

arbitrary number of different places, and information can be exchanged almost immediately.

For blind people computer technology has substantially improved their communication facilities. Coupling a computer with braille output devices or a speech synthesiser enables blind people to have access to information provided by electronic mail-boxes, electronic bulletin boards or international databases. With an optical scanner and appropriate optical character recognition (OCR-) software even paper bound information can be perceived without the help of seeing people. This technology brought a large amount of autonomy and independence for blind computer users and thus gave reason to assume that it would allow the integration of blind people into an office environment.

Futhermore, there have been efforts to develop integrated computer based products that are particularly tailored for blind people.

A first product of this kind is *ETaB* (Electronic Newspaper for Blind People) which is developed and distributed by the Stiftung Blindenanstalt in Frankfurt/Main (cf. [4]). The subscribers of ETaB obtain a daily version of the Frankfurter Rundschau (FR), a major German newspaper. ETaB already provides different modes of navigation within a newspaper. E.g., a possibility for keyword search is provided. Because up to now there is no common standard used by the editors of newspapers, the FR is the only german newspaper available in electronic form. However, an attempt for such a common standard is underway. This standard will be based on the Standardized Generalized Markup Language (SGML, ISO 8879, [2]) and should allow the integration of other newspapers in the next version of the ETaB system. Also, in the current version of ETaB it is not possible to include graphical portions in the presentation of the paper.

This problem, namely the access to graphical information for blind people is tackled in a large project called Graphical User Interface for the Blind (GUIB) which is sponsored by the European Community within the TIDE (Technology Initiative for Disabled and Elderly People) program ([10]). The objective of GUIB is to provide blind people with access to graphical user interfaces like MS-Windows or X-Windows. Within the project, a certain hard- and software solution has been developed to compensate the visual deficiency of the blind. The results of the project have been published in several papers, e.g. [7] or [6].

However, these systems do not apply for office workspaces. In nowadays offices information is to a large extent still paper-bound. Paper documents contain a lot of information which is in part only relevant at different steps of the document processing. Often they provide information that is not even written down explicitly: the layout structure of a letter guides a reader through a document. It helps finding the recipient or the addressee quickly, or it gives information about the contents, e.g. we might infer that a letter from a company that has a table layout is a bill for something they had delivered.

For blind people it is difficult to perceive this kind of information that is not written down explicitly. In principle, they can have access to printed information by the use of scanners and appropriate OCR-software. But, these tools produce an ASCII representation of a document where the layout and thus the logical information provided by the document is lost. Therefore, within the DFKI project ALV (Automatic Reading and Understanding) a system has been implemented that allows to transform a printed letter into an ODA-based representation. The ODA standard ([1]) is chosen for this purpose because it considers both, the logical and the layout structure of a document.

The project PASCAL 2000[3] at the DFKI now has two major goals. Firstly, we want to exploit this kind of technique and integrate it into an office workspace for blind people. Secondly, in a philosophical part of the project we want to analyze the different impacts and the policies of document analysis tools. Within this attempt we want to integrate blind computer users to obtain feedback for ergonomical demands from the beginning of the system development.

In this paper we first describe the document analysis approach and then discuss the basics for the philosophical aspects. We conclude with a summarizy of these points and give an outlook for our nearest research activities.

2 The Document Analysis Procedure

The purpose of the document analysis procedure is to have as input a printed letter which is then transformed into an electronic version where the logical entities are maintained. A common standard which considers these logical entities explicitly is the Office Document Architecture (ODA).

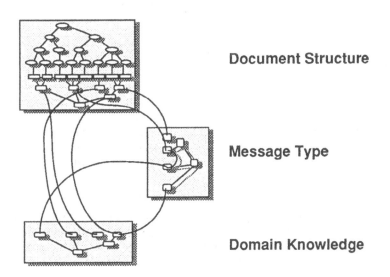

Document Structure

Message Type

Domain Knowledge

Fig. 1. Information Structure for Business Letters

---

[3] The name is dedicated to the French mathematician and philosopher Blaise Pascal (1623-1662)

Figure 1 shows some different parts of knowledge that are important for *understanding* a single business letter. This means that knowledge of these types has to be modeled to be able to understand business documents automatically, i.e. by a computer program.

The graph in the uppermost box of the figure displays the information by the *document content* as its own, that means the content regardless from 'environmental' information. The square boxes in the middle of the graph correspond to content portions of the document. These are text portions that may be cirumscribed by a certain rectangular. Above and below the square boxes we may recognize two disjoint trees that represent two different hierarchies, namely the layout and the logical structure of the particular document. For example, in the business letter the layout objects are pages, blocks, lines, words, etc. while the logical objects comprise elements like sender, recipient, signature, and so on. Via the connection with the content portions we get a mapping of the layout structure onto the logical structure. This process is refered to as *logical labeling*. One central idea in the ALV project at the DFKI has been that the logical labeling is done using only geometrical information, i.e. information od a certain layout object in relation to others. This implies that a hypothesis for a logical label for a particular content portion can be generated before an OCR procedure has started at all (cf. [5]). This approach is very much related to the way that humans perceive a letter. However, as this requires the geometrical information which is only available via visual sensing, this mode of perception is hidden to blind people. Therefor, a first goal in our project is to exploit the existing technique to compensate this deficiency to some degree.

Another type of knowledge that may be useful is the *message type* of a letter. On the one hand this knowledge can be used to understand the logical layout of a letter. For example, in general bills do not comprise a signature, which will make it unconventional to look for it after a letter has been classified as a bill. To classify a letter as a bill we have different approaches. One is to look at the content and the layout of the letter and then come to the result because there are some phrases like 'we have delivered', 'is due till', a.s.o. which make it likely to be a correct guess.

On the other hand, before we receive a bill we usually sent an order to or received an offer from the sender of the bill. Thus, we probably have some background information of the subject of this letter that can be useful in understanding it. This type of information is shown as the *domain knowledge* in figure 1. By this we want to capture all knowledge about processes or about the workflow within an office, a company or in a business correspondence, e.g. the temporal precedence relation between an inquiry, an offer, an order and a bill. If we the dates of a couple of letters are inconsistent according to this relation they are unlikely to fit together into a correspondence. However, if a new document fits in such a chain this gives supporting argument to classify a letter as a bill.

3   An integrated approach: AI and technology-assessment

At the Dartmouth Conference in 1956 John McCarthy presented his vision of an artificial intelligence to the world. Since this birth of a new field in research, a broad knowledge about methods and techniques was composed. The fascination to imitate human cognitive competence, e.g. sensory perception, problem solving or speech and pattern recognition, stimulated constantly the scientific community to increase knowledge and to search for appropriate applications.

The concept of document analysis for paperbound information presented in section 2 is based on AI techniques. Surely, document analysis may have a tremendous impact on the future design of information systems, especially on information systems for blind people. The idea of a supporting communication tool, that enables blind people to work within a modern office environment, is no longer only a benevolent verbal statement; it will become reality in the near future.

Since the original intention of AI is to imitate human cognitive competence on machine processes, this research field is closely connected with anthropological disciplines, e.g. philosophy, linguistics, neurobiology or neurophysiology (cf. [9], p. 1). Therefore, AI projects should be understood as an interdisciplinary approach with the goal to design new communication and information technology as user friendly as possible. The analysis of this interfering framework of different disciplines will help to evaluate the impacts caused by intelligent information systems.

Obviously, the application of AI-techniques bears great potential for the social and functional integration of visually impaired people. Apart from enumerating the hidden chances and the potentials for integration, the enthusiasm should not prevent from also analysing risks for blind users. As shown in figure 3, the multidimensional impact of this technology can be analysed in the light of

- ethical/anthropological aspects as well as
- human factors referring to rehabilitation.

The integration of technology assessment into the system development phase opens the possibility to conciously take into account its amicability towards the human being, society and nature. New technologies' characteristics are hypercomplexity and hyperdynamic which can easily become intransparent for the user. An analysis can show which effects the system has on the self-experience and on the self-esteem of the blind user, if either the computer is a communication partner or if it dominates the user by information abstraction and the information selection process done by the intelligent information system. Part of the human factors that shall be realized is a personality developping work structure as well as a sociotechnical system design. Besides compensating the handicap through knowledge representation the system aims at the integration of blind people into the working world by providing a real workspace.

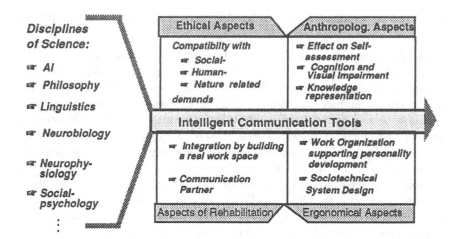

Fig. 2. Chances and risks within aspects of ethics, anthropology, rehabilitation and human factors

Being aware of the ambiguity of intelligent information systems, we have to fulfil an integrated approach of AI-and technology assessment (cf. [8]). Technology assessment can be defined as a systematic analysis, where all impacts and complications, direct or indirect, real or potential, present and future of a technology are defined, evaluated and measured as well as the causeeffect relationships identified. ([3], p. 339) The conceptual decision to assess impacts caused by intelligent information systems must not be misunderstood as a form of "technology arrestment". Rather, this approach will lead to a higher performance of the designed system and greater acceptence by visually impaired users.

4 Conclusion and Outlook

The project PASCAL 2000 is an interdisciplinary project in the fields of Artificial intelligence and philosophy. More specific, it deals with the problem of integrating document analysis tools into an office workspace for blind people.

From the AI point of view its main idea is that paper documents for office communication are arranged in a way that their layout structure corresponds to a commonly agreed logical structure and thereby, supports understanding of the content. This information is destroyed if a document is presented based only on its textual (i.e. ASCII-type) representation. Therefor, we have to use other forms of representation like the one which maintains the logical entities based on the ODA standard for business letters described in section 2. For other kinds of documents (e.g. electronic documents like E-mail letters) other standards can be reasonable assuming that they provide direct access to some kind of logical entities which are directly coupled with content portions of the corresponding document.

The purpose of the project PASCAL 2000 goes beyond dealing with a single document. The overall goal is to exploit such kind of techniques and integrate them into an intelligent office communication system. This system allows random access to single entities of paper bound information and - in that sense - compensates the perceptional deficiency of blind people by using other means of presentation. Then, this person can act as a controller in workflow processes within an office. E.g., the ALV technique can be used to extract an offer from the document data base which corresponds to an order the person is just going to process. We believe that this technology contributes to an enrichment of the field where blind people can work. In general, we will develop plan based, goal oriented query answering mechanisms that enable the system to cope with complex and high level queries for the document data base.

References

1. ISO 8613. Information processing - text and office systems - office document architecture (oda) and interchange format, volume i-iii, parts 1-8, 1988.
2. ISO 8879. Information Processing - Text and Office Systems - Standard Generalized Markup Language (SGML), 1986.
3. B. Bartocha. An instrument for goal formulation and the selection of problems. In M. Centron and B. Bartocha, editors, *Technology Assessment in a Dynamic Environment*, pages 337–356. London/New York/Paris, 1973.
4. Stiftung Blindenanstalt. Elektronische Tageszeitung für Blinde. daily newspaper, Frankfurt a. Main.
5. A. Dengel, R. Bleisinger, R. Hoch, F. Hönes, F. Fein, and M. Malburg. π_{ODA}: The Paper Interface to ODA. Technical Report RR-92-02, Deutsches Forschungszentrum für Künstliche Intelligenz, 1992.
6. K. Fellbaum, K. Crispien, M. Krause, T. Strothotte, M. Kurze, and J. Emhardt. Multimedia interfaces for blind computer users. In E. Ballabio, I. Placenia-Porrero, and R. Puig de la Casa, editors, *Rehabilitation Technology*. IOS Press, Amsterdam, 1993.
7. D. Kochanek. Hypertext system for the blind newspaper reader. In W. Zagler, editor, *Proceedings of the 3rd International Conference on Computers for Handicapped Persons (ICCHP)*, Wien, 1993.
8. W. Rammert. Wie KI und TA einander näherkommen. In *KI*, volume Heft 3, pages 11–16. 1993.
9. VDI Report. Künstliche Intelligenz. Leitvorstellungen und Verantwortbarkeit, 1993.
10. TIDE. Technology inititiative for disabled and elderly people. *Amtsblatt der Europäischen Gemeinschaften*, 1993.

Adapting Graphical User Interfaces for Use by Visually Handicapped Computer Users: Current Results and Continuing Research

Arthur I. Karshmer, Bill Ogden [‡]
Pres Brawner [†], Karlis Kaugars & George Reiswig [†]

Computer Science Department [‡]
Computing Research Laboratory [‡]
Psychology Department [†]
New Mexico State University
Las Cruces, NM 88003 USA
karshmer@cs.nmsu.edu

ABSTRACT. The use of modern computers and software by the visually handicapped has become more difficult over the past few years. In earlier systems the user interface was a simple character based environment. In those systems, simple devices like screen readers, braille output and speech synthesizers were effective. Current systems now run Graphical User Interfaces (GUIs) which have rendered these simple aids almost useless. In no area has this problem become more important than in technologies for the handicapped. What has become enabling technology for the sighted has become disabling technology for the visually impaired. In the current work we discuss new and innovative approaches to permit non-sighted users to interface with GUIs, having the salutary effect of gaining needed access to the most modern computing equipment for a subset of our population that is otherwise excluded from such access.

Using our approach to integrating special interfaces into those already shipped by the manufacturer, the non-sighted user will no longer be isolated from the mainstream of the information world. The net effect of such an interface is to make computing and information resources available to the visually handicapped user at the cost as to the sighted user.

1   Introduction

The need to lend support to visually handicapped computer users has been acknowledged for some time. With the passage of laws such as the Americans with Disabilities Act and similar legislation in other countries, new attention has been focused on a serious societal problem. Delivering new and innovative technologies to visually handicapped students has become a high priority in our society. If attention is not paid to this problem, we are likely to create an underprivileged class in our information based world, not based on the normal delineations between rich and poor, but based on access to modern technologies.

A number of systems have been designed and developed over the years and a few have even made it to market. In somewhat typical projects [31, 30, 15, 16] the philosophical approach taken was to redesign the computing environment's hardware to suit the visually handicapped user. These systems involved the synthesis of technologies uniquely suited to the visually handicapped to provide a more *comfortable* interface without much concern for the bandwidth or the generality of the interface. As a result, such interfaces were suited only for use by the visually impaired. Recent thought has lead us to believe that this was a philosophically incorrect approach. Our current approach is to use a variety of highly organized sounds to enhance, but not alter, already existing visually based interfaces so they will provide a compatible and reasonably high bandwidth communication channel for sighted and non-sighted users on the same hardware/software platform. Thus, our new approach should lead to more economical products for the visually impaired, facilitate interactions between sighted and non-sighted users and enhance the delivery of informational material to the visually impaired.

The Graphical User Interface (GUI) has become the standard in virtually all computing environments available on a broad range of hardware/software platforms available in the domain we call "personal computers." The traditional character based interface has become the exception rather than the norm. From PCs to high-speed workstations to X Terminals, the "dumb terminal" interface is becoming history. While this trend enhances the interface for the sighted, it is yet another stumbling block for the visually impaired. The goal of our current research is to make the GUI available to the non-sighted user.

Recent developments in computer interfaces have made it possible to present ever increasing amounts of information to the user in a visually meaningful form. Window-based and graphical display systems make it possible to display in many windows, and in many forms, large amounts of information. Nearly all of this information is visually presented; only a small fraction is presented via auditory channels. With the rapid advances in, and availability of technology, sound enhanced user interfaces are becoming increasing possible and attractive. Research in many areas has produced results that can be directly applied to the problems of sound enhanced interface design.

Research into computer generated **virtual worlds** [5, 19] has produced the notion of an "audio window" in which a spatial sound presentation system positions sound sources associated with a three-dimensional audio space. "Filtears" are used to emphasize or mute particular audio windows based upon their current activity. Sound generation uses audio signal processing to exploit the psychoacoustic properties of human hearing. The generalization of display systems for three-dimensional acoustic information has been examined in [29], thus providing a reasonable expectation that non-individualized sound based interfaces can be constructed.

In the area of speaking interfaces, the XSpeak system [27] demonstrates that spoken commands can be used to aid in the navigation through a set of windows. Speech input proved to be neither faster nor slower than navigation with the mouse. Playback of digitally recorded speech for fixed text has long been possible; however, high quality text-to-speech synthesis for arbitrary text is also now possible [25].

Considerable research has been done to identify non-speech sounds for use in sound enhanced interfaces [11, 12, 7, 8]. In the Karshmer system, non-speech based sounds are being tested as tools to aid in the navigation of complex hierarchical structures: namely menus. The work by Edwards examined associating sounds with screen objects. Another proposal is to use a system of naturally occurring sounds or 'everyday sounds' to represent actions within the interface [9]. In another interesting work, a musical sound was used to represent the peaks and valleys in the infrared spectrum of a chemical compound [24]. It has also been demonstrated that a rich set of musical variables (rhythm, pitch, timbre, register, dynamics) can be used to establish families of the audio tones equivalent to *icons* [1]. An excellent introduction to this area of research is given in [4].

While researchers have used sound to enhance learning and usability of computer interfaces, the choice of which sounds (pitches) to use has often been made without the benefit of solid empirical data. The frequent implication is that an individual who is not musically trained might not be able to make use of real musical information presented by the interface. There is however, a growing body of research which indicates that even untrained listeners can consistently identify sounds in a given tonal context. Studies have shown positive results in "well-fittedness," indicating the presence of perceivable qualities in sounds from an established context [17, 3].

Further, parallels have been shown between speech and sound cognition [6, 18], with results pointing to the possibility of developing a functional hierarchy of sounds to be attached to an interface/menuing system. The important finding here is that a listener's un-

---

1. The term *earcon* has been suggested to be the auditory equivalent to the now commonplace icon [15].

derstanding of a particular aural event depends heavily on how that event relates to any prior events, and this in turn affects potential future events as well.

The implication for our work is that many of these theories have not yet been fully integrated, explored and tested empirically. We are developing hierarchical sets of context related sounds and attaching them to related features in an interface. By measuring learning and response times for non-sighted users, we expect to show that the appropriate use of such sounds can help visually impaired users learn a system faster and use it both faster and more efficiently than with more conventional systems. The major departure here is that we are embedding our enhancements into already existing visual interfaces (operating systems). The net result of the work will be to extend a common computing environment to a number of groups of users: each having different needs. The interface tools will present no obstacle to sighted users, and indeed may prove to be beneficial to them as well. Our approach will make the delivery of *special* services to *special* users transparent and therefore encourage major manufacturers to move in this necessary direction. In a world of different interfaces for different people, the result was predictable - if the special user group did not represent a significant number of potential sales, the probability of offering such products was dramatically reduced. Hence, special needs have often gone unmet by commercial developers.

In recent work [11, 12, 13] two novel approaches to presenting sound-based tools to visually handicapped computer users were described. One was based on the concept of navigating complex hierarchical menu structures using musical tones. This approach was based in part on work reported by Paap [22, 23]. The second involved the use of directional sound to aid the user in navigating through two- and three-dimensional spaces such as found in the typical GUI. The goal of this work is to demonstrate the feasibility of making the GUI usable by the visually handicapped user.

The current work describes a set of experiments that we have designed to test the ability of users to navigate the graphical *desktop* and hierarchical menu structures using sound. In the remainder of this work we describe our test environment and the methods we will use to gather and analyze the data we need to evaluate our work.

2 Problem Statement & Rationale

The first level interface encountered by the user of a typical GUI (for example the Macintosh) is the what is called the *desktop* (see Figure 1). This is a very common metaphor used in modern interfaces. The desktop is composed of several graphical objects, which can be freely moved on the screen, including:
- A Menu Bar
- Several systems icons on the menu bar (the Apple Menu, the Application Selector, Balloon Help Icon, etc.)
- Various open windows containing icons and/or lists.
- Various icons

While this representation seems quite natural to the sighted user, it presents the equivalent of a mine field to the non-sighted user. Objects on the screen can partially or completely occlude other objects, giving a level of three-dimensionality to the interface. While fully occluded objects are a problem for the sighted user, partially occluded objects further complicate the use of GUIs by the non-sighted. Without special help, such an interface is effectively useless to the visually impaired.

Given the prevalence of GUIs, the use of modern computing in the social environment by the visually handicapped is extremely constrained. It is our goal to design an alternative model of interaction that will serve both the sighted and non-sighted user of the GUI.

To this end we have designed a model of interaction based on the standard GUI which allows the visually handicapped user to navigate the desktop using sound-based information. The desktop is identical to the one used by sighted users, only the navigational cues

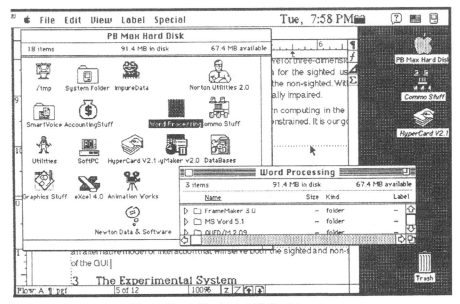

Figure 1 - A Typical GUI Desktop

are different. Navigating through the desktop is the prerequisite step to launching applications needed in the computational process. If the desktop is not accessible, then the underlying applications and other tools will not be accessible.

Generally, we have designed three basic tools to implement and test in order to achieve our goals. These will be described in greater detail in a later section of this work. Briefly stated, they are:

- Navigation of the desktop using a "sound map" and cursor warping[2]
- Navigation of the desktop using sonar vectoring of the cursor
- Sound-based menu navigation.

Given the similar nature of application interfaces to the desktop, our tools will be useful at the application level as well.

2.1 Navigation with a Sound Map

In this system, all items on the desktop are assigned some unique sound which can be selected by the user or by the system. If selected by the system, a combination of speech synthesis and sound generation is used to train the user. At any given instant, the user can request a sound based map of the desktop. As the appropriate sounds are generated by the system, the user on a click of the mouse can be instantly warped to the object just described. Once warped to the proper location, normal mouse click sequences will complete the user's task. The soundmap approach should provide a facile interface with small amounts of training. The interesting questions concerning this interface relate to the use of appropriate families of sounds.

2.2 Navigation with Sonar Vectoring

Consider the desktop as a multi-dimensional collection of various objects, some in front of others. Further, consider the cursor as a sonar emitter and the user as the sonar receiver.

---

2. Warping is the action of placing the screen cursor at a location selected by the system rather than directly by the user. While manufacturers such as Apple frown on this practice, it is critical in special purpose interfaces. Using warping in the special purpose interface has no negative impact on the normal interface.

At any instant the user can receive tonally based vectoring information to indicate the location of the cursor on the desktop and in relation to the various objects on the desktop. The user has the choice of continuous information or periodic reporting. The sonar "ping" returns a variety of information on each report:

- The general location of the cursor on the desktop. For example in which quadrant the cursor is located. Using the stereophonic output capabilities of modern systems, this two-dimensional information can be easily announced to the user.
- The object(s) under the cursor. If multiple objects, the report will indicate both the objects and their depth.
- The objects on or near the current path of the cursor if it is moving. By using a Doppler effect in the ping response, proximity information can be passed to the user.

Once the user identifies that (s)he is on the proper vector, a series of mouse clicks or simple key presses will warp the user to the desired object. Again, at this point standard mouse clicks will do the rest of the job.

2.3   Sound Based Menu Navigation

Given general desktop navigation, one key element needs to be developed to complete the set of tools for the visually impaired user: navigating and manipulating menus. Work in this area is currently underway in the research group. A model of multi-level menu systems has been implemented using HyperCard 2.1[3] which is currently in early beta testing. The model presents up to a six-level menu structure with up to six items on each level. For initial testing, we have restricted the structure to three levels.

Our basic premise is simply "**by use of appropriate tonal cues, computer users will be able to navigate through complex hierarchical menu structures which are organized in an identical manner to those used by sighted users.**" When the final results are in, we expect to answer several practical and one fundamental question. Briefly stated the practical questions are:

- Can menu structures be navigated using verbal cues?
- Can menu structures be navigated using tonal cues?
- What is the difference between the ability of users to navigate such structures using the different clues?
- Do truly non-sighted users have a better ability to navigate these structures than blindfolded sighted users?
- What does all of this imply about how sighted vs. non-sighted people represent and use navigational information?

To test this hypothesis we have developed a test environment that allows us to collect data on a large number of subjects. The subjects fall into two major groups: blindfolded, but sighted, students here at the university and truly non-sighted students at a nearby school for the visually handicapped. Both groups are presented with the same interface.

The interface was developed using the HyperTalk language and runs on any member of the Macintosh family of computers. Snapshots of two levels of the experimental interface is shown in the following figures.

While the menu's structure appears on the screen, the test subject will not be able to see it as (s)he is either blindfolded or truly visually impaired. The control buttons in the lower left corner are used by the experimenter to configure the system. These buttons are disabled once the test session begins.

The subjects are automatically positioned at the top entry (home position) of the menu structure at each level. When given a path to follow they move the mouse up or down

---

3. HyperCard, and its programming language HyperTalk, is an extremely powerful rapid prototyping tool distributed by Apple Computer Corp. Building interface tools with HyperCard allows us to design and test interface concepts in less than 1/10th of the time needed using other programming tools.

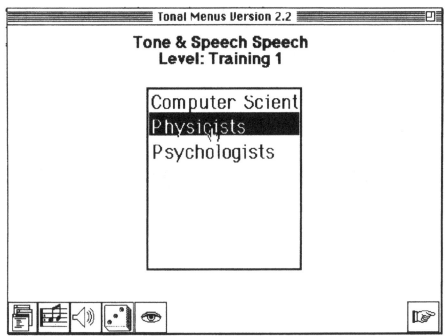

Figure 2 - The First Level of the Test Menu

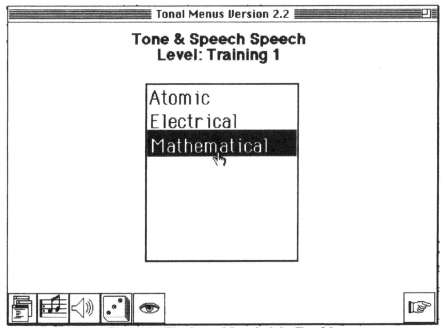

Figure 3 - The Second Level of the Test Menu

receiving auditory cues (either tonal, voice, or both). At any point in the search the user can move down a level by a single click on the mouse. Further, the test subject can request information on the current location of the cursor by clicking with the shift-key held down. Once the test path is given, data are recorded in the areas of total mouse clicks to goal, time to goal and number of help requests made by the subject. In our initial tests, paths are restricted to a width of three and a depth of three.

Two methods have been implemented to help the user keep the cursor within the bounds of the menu. First, if the user strays out of bounds, a special auditory signal informs the subject where (s)he is located in relation to the menu. Second, we have the ability to constrain the movement of the cursor in either the horizontal or vertical direction. Through the use of specially developed HyperTalk XCMDs and XFCNs[4], we are able to *warp* and restrict cursor motion.

The tones generated in each category, each level and each item at each level have been designed to pass on the maximum information concerning the user's location in the hierarchy. Table 1 shows how tones are allocated at the topmost level of the menu structure. Notice that each category at the top level is assigned a specific instrument. As the user progresses down in a category, the instrument remains the same, while the octave and notes vary. This is shown in Table 2. The variability in octaves and notes is as follows:

Table 1: Top Level of Menu Structure

Category	Instrument	Note	Octave
Computer Scientists	Harpsichord	c	4
Physicists	Flute	c	4
Psychologists	Banjo	c	4

Table 2: Level Two of the Structure Under *Physicists*

Menu Item	Instrument	Note	Octave
Atomic	Flute	e	5
Electrical	Flute	f	5
Mathematical	Flute	g	5

as you go down a menu level you also go down an octave; as you go down a menu item at a given level (except the top level) you go down a note. While moving down a menu level, the cursor is automatically placed at the top item in the new level. This acts as a known home position which should aid in the navigation process.

2.4   Menu Navigation Methodology

Two groups of subjects are being used in testing the tonally/verbally based menu system. The first group is composed of a number of university students who are normally sighted. Each subject is blindfolded for the duration of the experiment. The second group is composed of a group of non-sighted students at a nearby school for the visually handicapped

All subjects are given supervised training on how to navigate through the menu system using the tool(s) they will be tested with later. At the end of the training period each subject is given a series of randomly selected paths to navigate. The test paths are presented in the form in which they are expected to operate (tonal, verbal or both). The subjects are

---

4. XCMDs and XFCNs are special purpose routines written to provide HyperCard and other application programs extra functionality. They are called "resources" in the Apple world and can be easily "pasted" into any application.

then asked to navigate to the designated terminal node in the menu structure.

At any point in the navigation process, the subject may request help in one of two ways through simple mouse clicks. First (s)he can ask for a message from the system which elaborates, using the appropriate audible signals, the exact path to the user's current location. The second help command, again a mouse click, automatically returns the user to the top of the menu structure.

Once the actual tests are begun, all movements are recorded in a file which includes the menu moves made and the number of ticks (measured in 1/60ths of a second[5]) since the last action taken. These data are then saved at the end of the test session for later analysis. In addition to timing and pathway data, we also collect biographical data for analysis by such factors as age and gender.

3   Initial Findings in Sound Based Menu Navigation Experiments

To date, the system has been tested on a small number of sighted users wearing blindfolds. We have not yet been able to schedule the truly non-sighted subjects. Our initial findings are consistent with our expectations. They are briefly:

- Constrained mouse motion and warping are absolutely essential in the navigation of menus by non-sighted users. Even with the use of auditory feedback, movement of the mouse in an unconstrained way leads to general confusion and disorientation by the user. While warping is generally frowned upon by the Apple Interface Guidelines, it is essential in special purpose interfaces.
- Navigation using tonal clues proved difficult for our initial subject population of sighted, blindfolded users. We have yet to collect data from truly non-sighted users, and may see some statistically significant improvement in this domain. We feel that the problems in using tonal navigational clues are based on two main factors. First, our users had no previous experience using such data in the assigned task and therefore had difficulty in associating a tone with an object. Second, the tone generating hardware on the test systems was not of the highest quality. The difference in the same note played at neighboring octaves was sometimes difficult to perceive. It could be that our non-sighted population are more adept at using auditory input in their daily lives and will prove more successful at using tones.
- Speech driven menu navigation was, as expected, the most easily mastered technique. All test subjects were able to navigate or test domain with little trouble with a short training period. It seems clear that given constrained mouse movement and mouse warping, that this technique is quite viable.
- The use of the mouse as a pointing device for visually impaired computer users is not optimal. All users found themselves picking up the mouse and moving it in the upward direction on the desk. Because the cursor was warped to the top menu item in each level, all mouse motion was in a downward direction. Users rapidly found themselves running off the bottom edge of the desk. While users were able to cope with moving the mouse upwards, it seems clear that a trackball would be more useful than a mouse. We feel that this is a very minor change in system hardware and could easily be offered as a no-cost option by the manufacturer.

4   References

1. Blattner, M.M., et al., "Earcons and Icons: Their structure and common design principles," *Human-Computer Interaction*, volume 4, number 1, 1989, pp.: 11-44
2. Borenstein, N.S., (1991) *Programming as if People Mattered*, Princeton University Press, Princeton.NJ.
3. Butler, D. "Describing the Perception of Tonality in Music," *Music Perception*, Spring 1989, 6(3), 219-241.
4. Buxton, W., "Introduction to this special issue on nonspeech audio," *Human-Computer Interaction*, volume 4, number 1, 1989, pp.:1-9.

---

5. Naturally, the number of ticks would be recorded in 1/50ths of a second in Europe.

5. Cohen, M. and Ludwig, L. F.,"Multidimensional audio window management," *Int. J. Man-Machine Studies*, 1991, 34, pp. 319-336.
6. Dowling, W. J, and Harwood, D.L. *Music Cognition*, Academic Press, Inc., Orlando, 1986.
7. Edwards, A. D. N. "The Design of Auditory Interfaces for Visually Disabled Users," *Human Factors in Computing Systems (Proceedings of CHI 88)*, ACM SIGCHI, 89-94.
8. Edwards, A.D.N., "Soundtrack: an auditory interface for blind users," *Human-Computer Interaction*, volume 4, number 1, 1989, pp.: 45-66.
9. Gaver, W.W., "The SonixFinder: an interface that uses auditory icons," *Human-Computer Interaction*, column 4, number 1, 1989, pp.: 67-94.
10. Gould, J., (1988) How to Design Usable Systems, In Helender, M. (Ed) *Handbook of Human Computer Interaction*, Amsterdam: North Holland.
11. Karshmer, A.I., Brawner, P. and Reiswig, G., "An Initial Evaluation of a Sound-Based Hierarchical Menu Navigation System for Visually Handicapped Use of Graphical User Interfaces," to appear in a Springer-Verlag Series on Human Computer Interfaces, 1994.
12. Karshmer, A.I. and Oliver, R.L., "Special Computer Interfaces for the Visually Handicapped: FOB the Manufacturer," the proceedings of EWHCI '93, Moscow, Russia, August, 1993.
13. Karshmer, A.I., Hartley, R.T., Paap, K., Alt, K. & Oliver, R.L., "Using Sound and Sound Spaces to Adapt Graphical Interfaces for Use by the Visually Handicapped," The Proceedings of the 3rd International Conference on Computers and Handicapped Persons, Vienna, July, 1992.
14. Karshmer, A.I., Hartley, R.T. and Paap, K., "SoundStation II: Using Sound & Sound Spaces to Provide High Bandwidth Computer Interfaces to the Visually Handicapped," *SIGCAPH Newsletter*, ACM Press, January, 1992.
15. Karshmer, A.I., Davis, R.D. and Myler, H., "The Architecture of An Inexpensive and Portable Talking-Tactile Terminal to Aid the Visually Handicapped," *Computer Standards and Interfaces*, Vol. No. 5, 1987, North Holland Publishing, pp. 135-151.
16. Karshmer, A.I., Davis, R.D. and Myler, H., "An Inexpensive Talking Tactile Terminal for the Visually Handicapped," *The Journal of Medical Systems*, Vol. 10, No. 3, 1986.
17. Krumhansl, C., & Kessler, E. "Tracing the dynamic changes in perceived tonal organization in a spatial representation of musical keys," *Psychological Review*, 1982, 334-368.
18. Lerdahl, F. and Jackendoff, R.," A Generative Theory of Tonal Music," *The MIT Press*, Cambridge, Massachussets, 1983.
19. Ludwig, L. F., Pincever, N., and Cohen, M., "Extending the Notion of a Window System to Audio," *IEEE Computer*, August 1990, pp. 66-72.
20. Norman, D., (1986) Cognitive Engineering, In Norman, D., and Draper, S., (Eds), *User Centered System Design*, Hillsdale N.J.: Lawrence Erlbaum Associates, Inc.
21. Ogden, W., (1986) Implications of a Cognitive Model of Database Query: Comparison of a Natural Language, Formal Language, and Direct Manipulation Interface., *SIGCHI Bulletin*, **18**(2).
22. Paap, K. and Roske-Hofstrand, R., "The Optional Number of Menu Options per Panel," *Human Factors*, 1986,28(4), 377-385
23. Paap, K. and Roske-Hofstrand, R.," The Design of Menus," *Handbook of Human-Computer Interaction*, M. Helander, ed. Elsevior Science Publishers B. V. (North Holland), 1988
24. Peterson, I., "The Sound of Data," *Science News*, Volume 127, June 1, 1985, pp.: 348-50.
25. Sagisaka, Yoshinori, "Speech Synthesis from Text," *IEEE Communications Magazine*, January 1990, pp. 35-41.
26. Schmandt, C., Ackerman, M. S., Hindus, D., "Augmenting a Window System with Speech Input\," *IEEE Computer*, August 1990, pp. 50-56.
27. Schmandt, C., McKenna, M.A., "An audio and telephone server for multi-media workstations," *Proceedings of the 2nd IEEE Conference on Computer Workstations*, 7-10 March 1988, Santa Clara, California, pp.: 150-9.
28. Wenzel, E. M., Wightman, F. L., and Foster, H. S., "A Virtual Display System for Conveying Three-Dimensional Acoustic Information," *Proceedings of the Human Factors Society 32nd Annual Meeting*, 1988, pp. 86-90.
29. Wenzel, E. M., Wightman, F. L., and Kistler, D. J.,"Localization with non-individualized virtual acoustic display cues," *CACM*, March 1991, pp. 351-359.
30. York, B.W. and Karshmer, A.I. "Tools to Support Blind Programmers," to appear in *Visual Programming Environments*, edited by E.P. Glinert, IEEE Computer Society Press (1991).
31. York, B.W. and Karshmer, A.I., "An Overview of T^3 - PBE," *SIGCAPH Newsletter*, ACM Press, Number 41, January, 1989.

Training Blind People in the Use of Graphical User Interfaces

Gerhard Weber[1,2], Helen Petrie[3], Dirk Kochanek[1], Sarah Morley[3]

[1] Universität Stuttgart, Institut für Informatik, Breitwiesenstr. 20-22, 70565 Stuttgart, F.R. Germany

[2] F.H. Papenmeier GmbH&Co., KG, Talweg 2, 58239 Schwerte, F.R. Germany

[3] Psychology Division, University of Hertfordshire, Hatfield AL10 9AB, Hertfordshire, U.K.

Abstract. The need for training of blind people to use graphical user interfaces has arisen since the first access systems became available. Two different approaches on the basis of PC-based tutorial systems are described and their benefits for the blind user are investigated.

1. Introduction

Most new applications like automatic teller machines, word processors, or database retrieval software are designed with a graphical user interface. Still, text-based applications are an alternative, but it is difficult to avoid MS Windows, X Windows or some other graphical user interface (GUI).

For blind users several solutions are developed with a different design of the non-visual user interface. Speech-based, Braille-based, or integrated systems offer access to MS Windows or X Windows with differences in speed of interaction and amount of information being accessible [3].

Tutorial systems have since long been inaccessible to blind users (and still remain) because of the integrated use of text, graphics, pictures, animated scenes and video. In other words: a blind user of the on-line tutorial system which became available with Windows 3.1 cannot perceive the animation provided to explain various selection tasks. As a consequence the tutorial system is of no use to the blind user even if they could benefit most from a tutorial system describing the basic interaction methods used in MS Windows.

2. Training Needs in GUIs

The development of GUIs poses a number of problems for blind users. They must learn new concepts associated with the ideas underlying the philosophy of GUIs, new methods of interaction with a computer, perhaps the use of new hardware. Careful training is required in all these areas if blind users are to access GUI based software most efficiently. Information provided by blind users about such software can be used in two ways. Firstly, it can assist in the development of better interfaces for blind users. Secondly, it can assist in the development of appropriate training programs to train blind users in the use of GUI based applications and operating systems.

For example, in the GUIB project, in order to maximise the usability of the non-visual user interface and to develop appropriate training programs, the first prototype screenreaders for GUIs have been evaluated by blind computer users in two different fashions. Firstly, a laboratory-based evaluation of the interfaces has been undertaken; this required training blind users in the use of the interface and allowed evaluation both of the interface and the training material used. Secondly, the prototype GUIB system was made available to experienced blind users of text-based applications on a permanent, work place oriented basis for longer term evaluation in a realistic setting of use. In both these evaluations, it has quickly been found that this user group needs to learn about the functionality of GUIs and applications in a manner similar to computer novices. Depending on their experience with speech or Braille output they expect either speech-based or Braille-based interaction objects within a GUI.

A recent survey among trainers of blind computer users [8] as well as results from project IRIS which introduced screen readers for MS Windows at the Marburg school for the blind [4]have identified a number of requirements for the requirements for the training of blind computer users in GUIs. These include:

- stepwise introduction of concepts from GUIs
- use of tactile graphics and models
- development of concrete models and metaphors of GUIs
- development of diagnostic tasks which allow identification of specific conceptual problems of the user

GUIs contain many new concepts for blind users. For sighted persons some of the new concepts such as windows, dragging icons have intuitive meaning, but this is less likely for blind users. Therefore it may be helpful to introduce the concepts of GUIs in a meaningful progress. The notion of a "training wheels" version of the interface, where some of the functionality is blocked [1,2] which has been used in training sighted users in the use of complex new interfaces is appropriate here.

3. Tactile Graphical Images

Permanent tactile graphics can be successfully used in the introduction of GUIs to blind users, although clearly they have little role in the normal use of GUIs. For interactive access to wordprocessors, spreadsheet programs, and other GUI-based programs, the current technology of tactile graphical output devices cannot be used efficiently. However, paper-based, solid or layered models are suitable. A teacher can progressively introduce elements of the tactile model and explain them with verbal presentations. A layered, solid model has the flexibility to convey dynamic changes such as window popping up or selection of a menu item.

Pictorial or graphical information can be conveyed as tactile picture or as a written or spoken description. A combination of a tactile picture with such explanation would be a better solution. For this purpose the program EXPLAIN was developed that allows an interactive exploration of tactile images accompanied by descriptions.

From a technical point of view such a combination makes some form of synchronisation through pointing by fingers or a stylus necessary. Several systems have been developed using different pointing devices:

- touch-sensitive screen (infrared technology, [9]),
- paper-based tactile graphics with touch-sensitive pad (pressure sensitive polymers, [7]),
- touch-sensitive interactive tactile display (electromagnetic induction, [5]), and
- paper-based tactile graphics with stylus (electromagnetic induction, [6]).

In any of these systems explanations are linked to a specific area or region of the image which are selected by pointing or by gestural input. Figure 1 shows the basic configuration of program EXPLAIN which is used in project GUIB to aid introduction of GUIs.

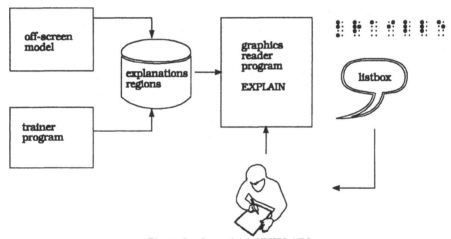

Fig. 1. Configuration of EXPLAIN

The pad has an touch sensitive area at least the size of a standard Braille page and a resolution of 120 * 120 points. Speech output can be either done by a (external) speech synthesiser or using a standard sound card with text-to-speech software.

EXPLAIN consists of two components. The first component is used by an instructor to specify regions on an image and links explanations to this region. Explanations can be structured in levels allowing the trainee to quickly explore the image or get a more detailed explanation of a point of interest. The program facilitates creating of descriptions on the fly as well as loading them form external files.

The second component is used by a trainee who wants to explore an image. After placing the image on the touch pad the user has to identify the image to the program (by name or id number). This will cause the program to load the correct area definition and descriptions. Now the trainee can explore the image. Pressing on a spot will start the linked explanation of the specified level to be spoken. The user can change the explanation level or can repeat it.

Such a system requires a training phase during which explanations are introduced. Figure 1 shows the configuration for the interactive system. The user places a tactile graphics on a touch-sensitive pad and identifies it to the reader program. Through pointing by a stylus or by the fingers an explanation can be retrieved. Output is generated on a Braille display or by speech synthesis. To avoid time consuming preparation of the graphics a snapshot of screen contents can be generated and printed on a Braille printer. Instead of an extensive training phase the contents of the OSM of a particular screen reader can be used as the basis for the generation of verbal explanations.

4. Interactive tutorial system

After the basic concepts of GUIs have been introduced to the user a concrete model application should be used but under strict control of a tutorial program. Such an application introduces the basic interaction objects by using a screen reader with Braille or speech output. The drill&practice tutorial system WINTRAIN for blind users has been developed in project GUIB for this purpose. WINTRAIN appears to the user as a simple text editor.

WINTRAIN is independent of a particular screen reader, nevertheless if required speech output through the Monologue text-speech system can be enabled. In this way the filtering within MS Windows is of dual use: for spoken feedback and for monitoring the completion of tasks. Figure 2 shows this architecture, those parts which are grayed are standard for a screen reader.

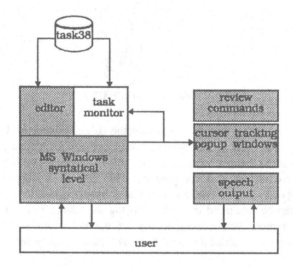

Fig. 2. Dual use of filters for WINTRAIN

The built-in screen reader (with limited facilities for review) generates task descriptions and explains items as well as verbalises windows, menus, buttons, etc. Figures 3 and 4 show a typical scenario in WINTRAIN.

Fig. 3. A task is presented to the user

The user is asked to complete task 38 "select from elements listbox the colour yellow and press the OK button". After pressing "Alt" the menu options are verbalised. As usual in MS Windows the option "Elements" can be selected through mouse, cursor keys or the 'L'-key. A submenu opens with various options including "listbox". Finally the listbox as shown in Figure 4 is presented.

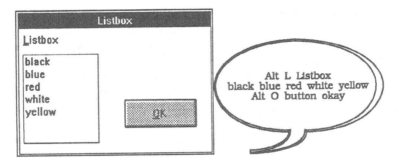

Fig. 4. The user opens a dialogue box

As soon as the user has selected in the listbox the option "yellow" the screen reader announces the closing of the dialogue box, the task monitor announces the successful completion of the task and presents the next task. A tutorial consists of a list of tasks specified in a configuration file. If 50% of the tutorials are successfully completed the next tutorial is started. The following common interaction methods are addressed by the more then 40 tasks:

- menu selection (main menu, popup menu),
- common interaction objects in dialogue boxes (button, radiobutton, checkbox, edit field, listbox, combobox),
- open a file by name and path,
- print a file,
- format a character (font, size, colour, etc.),
- find respectively replace a string,
- read text and move the caret to a specified position within a line of text, and
- resize respectively move the window of WINTRAIN.

This set of tasks reflects the common interaction methods found e.g. in word processors, spreadsheet programs, and other standard MS windows programs. After completing all tutorials the program can be finished including the Windows environment. Thus the user has full control over interaction while working with an Windows application and returns from there to DOS.

Since the training program - unlike to more advanced tutorial systems for GUIs - avoids any animated scenes and graphics any screen reader for MS Windows provides sufficient access to it. An self-explanatory facility is provided further on to help the user in solving his task.

Explanations for beginners should cover
- a short description of the interation method
- a verbal description of the layout of the current window res. the relation among interaction objects
- a verbal description of the layout of windows

By choosing an application from a well known domain (text processing) the blind user is not learning about the application specific operations. Instead they can transfer this knowledge about interaction into the domain of GUIs. While the interaction objects also appear in DOS-based application programs the specific behaviour inside MS Windows can be trained

Several forms of evaluation of these training programs are being undertaken as part of the GUIB Project. For both the EXPLAIN and the WINTRAIN programs, users are given a test of their knowledge of the use of GUI software to measure the usefulness and acceptability on these programs. Users who participate in the WINTRAIN tutorial program are also given a test of their knowledge of the use of GUI software to objectively assess how much they have learnt from the program.

If the above requirements can be included during run-time of the screen reader (and not the tutorial software) a more powerful context-sensitive passive help system can be created (on the basis of the OSM and filtering the user interface) then was originally anticipated.

The limits to this approach are lack of application specific information. In order to overcome this deficit plan recognition together with a model of the user's task can be used. By interpreting such a task model the completion of a particular series of interactions can be initiated automatically as it would be required for an active help system.

5. Conclusions

The benefits of a GUIs will only become available also to blind users if screen readers are designed well enough for successful non-visual interaction. In order to enable blind users to participate in this process they need prototypical screen readers and assistance while learning to interact with an application. This assistance can be provided more easily through flexible tutorial systems. The final paper will refer to feedback given by blind users trying to learn more MS Windows using the presented tutorial system.

Acknowledgements

This work has been supported by the GUIB consortium, a pilot research project of the EEC program "Technology Initiative for the Disabled and Elderly" (TIDE).

References

[1] Carroll, J.M. and Carrithers, C. (1984). Training wheels in a user interface. Communications of the ACM, 27, pp. 800 - 806

[2] Carroll, J.M., Kellog, W.A. and Rosson, M.B. (1991). The task-artifact cycle. In J.M.Carroll (Ed.) Designing interaction: psychology at the human-computer interface. Cambridge: Cambridge University Press

[3] Mynatt, E.; Weber, G. (1994). Nonvisual presentation of graphical user interfaces: contrasting two approaches, in Proceedings of CHI'94, Boston May 26-28, 1994, New York: ACM

[4] Kalina, U. (1993). personal communication, Dec. 14th, 1993

[5] Kochanek, D. (1992). A hypertext system for blind newspaper readers, in Zagler, W. (ed.) Proceedings of the 3rd International Conference on Computers for Handicapped People, Wien: Oldenbourg

[6] Lötzsch, J.: (1993). Audiotaktiler Dialog über Graphiken und Diagrammen insbesondere für Blinde und Sehbehinderte (Audiotactile dialog on graphics and diagrams for blind and visually impaired), in Mehnert, D. (ed.) Elektronische Sprachsignalverarbeitung in der Rehabilitationstechnik, ISSN 0940-6832, pp.153-156

[7] Parkes (1991). Nomad: enabling access to graphics and text-based information for blind and visually impaired and other disability groups, in Proceedings of the World Congress on Technology for People with Disabilities, Washington DC, December 1-5, 1991, pp. 689-716

[8] Petrie, H. (1992). Report on training aspects for blind users in graphics-based environments. Report to the CEC for TIDE Pilot Action Project 103: Graphical User Interfaces for Blind Persons. London: Royal National Institut for the Blind

[9] Weber, G. (1987). Gestures as a means for the blind to interact with a computer, in Bullinger, H.-J. (ed.) Human-Computer Interaction INTERACT'87, Amsterdam: North Holland, pp. 593-595

Artificial Visual Speech
Synchronized with a Speech Synthesis System

H.H. Bothe und E.A. Wieden

Department of Electronics, Technical University Berlin
Einsteinufer 17, D-10587 Berlin, Germany

Abstract: This paper describes a new approach of modeling visual speech, based on an artificial neural network (ANN). The network architecture makes possible a fusion of linguistic expert knowledge into the ANN. Goal is the development of a computer animation program as a training aid for learning lip-reading. The current PC version allows a synchronization of the animation program with a special stand-alone speech synthesis computer via a Centronics parallel interface.

1   Introduction

From the experimental work of Menzerath, together with de Lacerda [1] it is known that the movements of the speech organs are structurally interrelated within the spoken context. The speech organs needed for the formation of upcoming phones, even though currently not engaged, take up position relatively early to their actual use. They produce sound in the course of a fully overlapping phonal coarticulation. The projection of these movements on the speakers face may be seen as *visual speech*. They mostly contain sufficient information to enable hearing-impaired persons to lip-read a spoken text. The visual recognition is largely focussed on the speakers mouth region, especially on the lips. Since lip movements contain most of the visually perceptible information, this paper proposes the modeling of face movements with the help of related lip shapes only.

A realistic appraisal of the research effort leads to necessary limitations due to the high number of influencing factors (e.g. speech specific facial physiognomy, dialect, speed of delivery, sentence and word stress). On one hand, the word material on which the movement analysis is based has to be fixed on a representative subset of the existing phonetic sequences. Thus, the developed motion model is an extension of this subset. On the other hand, the investigation is limited to prototypic speakers.

The smallest speaker-independent units derived from the acoustic signal being semantically distinguishable are the phonemes. The smallest perceptible units of the visual articulatory movements are called visemes. The German language consists of ca. 40 phonemes and 12 visemes [2] .

In order to model visual speech movements, the acoustic speech signal and movement data of prototype speakers were recorded on videotape and analyzed with a workstation. For automatic visual feature extraction in the speaker's face several points on nose and forehead, as well as the lip contours, were marked with a contrasting color. One example frame and the feature extraction is shown in figure 1. The two marked reference points and the set point on the nose refer to the head coordinate system.

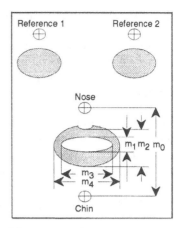

Fig.1. Typical video frame and visual feature extraction.

Those frames fitting best with the subjective impressions for a well pronounced sound were interactively indicated with the help of both the acoustic and visual material by different experts in lipreading; the acoustic phone boundaries - determined with the help of oscillogram, sonagram and playback - limit the scanning range of each wanted frame [3]. In certain cases as, for instance, for the phonemes /h,g,k/, no characteristic frame could be determined.

The proposed set points and contours were localized with the help of an automatic contrast search program. The determined characteristic frames of the text corpus were classified with respect to lip shape and position. The cluster centers compose a set of representative key-frames. In the later computer animation, the given phoneme input sequence is first mapped on a corresponding sequence of key-frames; then, the film is being generated by calculating interim frames within this framework. The linguistic data are at the same time used to control a synchronized acoustic speech synthesis computer. A block diagramm of the analysis-synthesis-system is shown in figure 2.

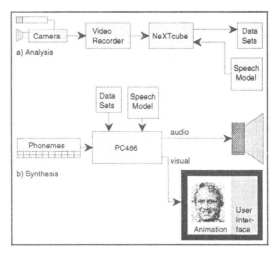

Fig. 2. Analysis-synthesis-system.

2 Key-frame Selection by an Artificial Neural Network

The subject of modeling visual speech and coarticulation effects has been addressed by several authors [4-8] for different languages. The movements are either related to an interpolation between a fixed set of key-frames or controlled by certain visual features. Key-frames may be related to the visemes of the corresponding text. A first order approximation for modeling backward and forward coarticulation effects takes into account the immediate next neighboring phonemes. For this purpose, the phonematic text is split into overlapping diphones and diphthongs are represented by two closely connected single phones, whereas the frames of the second are classified with respect to the first one [7]. This process leads to a deterministic diphone related phoneme-key-frame mapping.

In reality, coarticulation effects extend often far beyond the immediate next neighboring phonemes. A proposed area of influence has strong limits by the need of a finite text corpus.

After establishing a diphone based model, large text corpora with 84 sentences and frequently used German words have been analyzed in order to improve the quality of the motion model. Besides the integration of syllable core-zones or the phoneme representation by a variable amount of key-frames, as proposed in [8, 9], a further step to improve the model is to allow a context depending fuzzy phoneme-to-viseme mapping.

In this case, the feature vectors were classified by means of a fuzzy c-means algorithm [10]. The algorithm generates optimum location of the clusters automatically with respect to a given number of clusters. The representatives of the clusters are again taken as key-frames. In this case, there is no a priori correlation between phonemes and key-frames. For the later visual speech synthesis an ANN has been trained to select the frames with respect to the given phoneme sequence.

The developed motion model consists of a multi-layer neural network; it selects the specific key-frames related to the single phonemes and the surrounding next 3+3 neighbor phonemes. In the later speech synthesis, the film is again generated by calculating interim frames. The general design of the ANN is shown in figure 3.

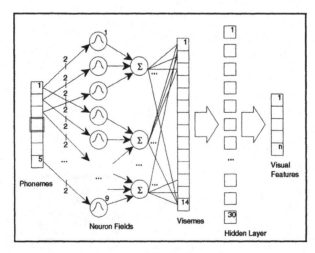

Fig. 3. Design of the ANN for key-frame selection.

In a first step the input sequence of 7 phonemes each out of the set of 41 phonemes is mapped on a set of 14 output neurons by a RBFN with Gaussian distribution functions. Each output neuron represents one viseme. This means that a certain phoneme in its context of 3+3 neighboring phonemes is represented by 14 membership grades to the set of visemes. Linguistic knowledge on the dynamics of the articulation process can be fused in before learning the RBFN, e.g. with methods described in [11].

The viseme neurons are taken as input neurons for a subsequent multi-layer perceptron (MLP) with 30 neurons in one hidden layer. The 5D output vector is pointing to the proposed corresponding feature values. The actual key-frame is selected by using the nearest neighbor method and the Euclidian distance measure.

The network is trained in three steps: i) the phoneme-to-viseme mapping with respect to the visematic system (e.g., since /p,b,m/ belong to the same viseme, a crisp mapping on the /p,b,m/-viseme neuron is proposed when /p,b,m/ are in the center position of the input sequence), ii) the viseme-to-feature-vector mapping with respect to the corresponding training sets, iii) the connected ANN with respect to the given phoneme-to-feature-vector mapping.

The ANN approach allows to i) forecast the course of features for any given input text and ii) refine the so far in the literature crisp phoneme-to-viseme mapping by taking contextual influences into account.

3   Audio-visual speech synthesis

In order to improve the ability of lipreading for hearing-impaired persons, a computer animation program may serve as a language lab for visual speech as described in [7].

In order to improve the diphone based key-frame selection, a motion model that is based on key-frame selection by the described neuro-fuzzy method has again been implemented on a PC, this time with an open amount of key-frames per phoneme. The resulting system is still in the state of pre-testing and experimentation.

The interim frames between the key-frames are calculated by a morphing algorithm. For this purpose, a fixed amount of set points have been interactively placed in each key-frame, serving as a framework for the triangulation algorithm. These set points are related to specific physiological points in the speakers face. For a given phoneme sequence, the interim frames are placed in a grid of equidistant time intervals as indicated in figure 4.

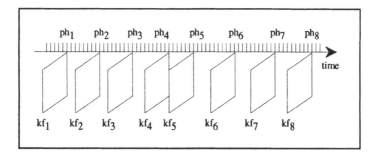

Fig. 4. Selection of key-frames *kf* and calculation of interim frames.

As an exemplary result, figure 5 shows the predicted and the original course of the visual feature m_2 = *height of the outer mouth contour*, referred to an arbitrary maximum value.

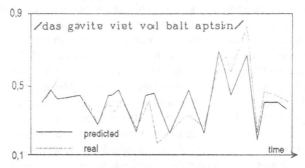

Fig. 5. Predicted and original course of m_2 = *outer height*.

The playback speed of the animation system can be varied in several steps from slow motion to time lapse. The input phoneme sequences are entered by keyboard or mouse and can be combined according to content to form corresponding lessons. The sequence to be depicted from the contents of the chosen lesson can also be selected by a random sequence generator.

The animation system has been synchronized with a stand-alone speech synthesis system which is based on a M68008 microprocessor and some specific hardware devices. For a communication that allows also slow-motion and high-speed speech, the PC as the host computer controls the communication with the speech synthesis computer via a Centronics interface. A block diagram of the speech synthesis computer is shown in figure 6. The speech synthesis uses several diphone based look-up tables.

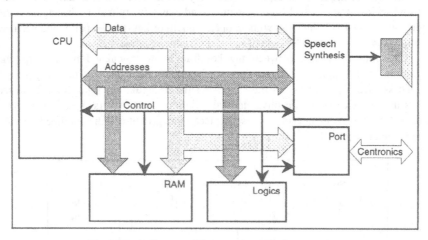

Fig.6. Block diagram of the speech synthesis computer.

Simultaneously with the animated cartoon, a time series of finger signs (dactyls) - correlated with the spoken text - can be presented in an extra window on the computer screen. The speed of the film creates the illusion of moving fingers.

References

1. P. Menzerath and A. de Lacerda: Koartikulation, Steuerung und Lautabgrenzung, Berlin, 1933.

2. G. Alich: Zur Erkennbarkeit von Sprachgestalten beim Ablesen vom Munde (Dissertation), Bonn, 1961.

3. H.H. Bothe and F. Rieger: Lipreading - Analysis and Synthesis on Microcomputers, in: W. Zagler (Ed.), Computers for Handicapped Persons, Proceedings of the 3rd International Conference, Vienna, (1992), 59-64.

4. D. Storey and M. Roberts: Reading the Speech of Digital Lips: Motives an Methods for Audio-visual Speech Synthesis, Visible Language 22 (1989), 112-127.

5. M.M. Cohen and D.W. Massaro: Synthesis of Visible Speech, Behaviour Research Methods, Instruments & Computers, (1990), 260-263.

6. M. Saintourens, M.H. Tramus, H. Huitric, and M. Nahas: Creation of a Synthetic Face Speaking in Real Time with a Synthetic Voice, Proceedings of the Workshop of Speech Synthesis, Autrance, (1990), 381-393.

7. H.H. Bothe, G. Lindner and F. Rieger: The Development of a Computer Animation Program for the Teaching of Lipreading, In: E. Ballabio, I. Placencia-Porrero and R. Puig de la Bellacasa (Eds.), Technology and Informatics 9, Rehabilitation Technology: Strategies for the European Union, Amsterdam, (1993), 45-49.

8. H.H. Bothe, F. Rieger and R. Tackmann: Visual Coarticulation Effects in Syllable Environment, Proceedings of the EUROSPEECH, Berlin, (1993), 1741-1744.

9. H.H. Bothe, G. Lindner, R. Pramanik and F. Rieger: Dynamic Modeling of Visual Articulation Movements, Proceedings of the International Symposium on Nonlinear Theory and its Applications (NOLTA), Hawaii, (1993), 1363-1366.

10. J.C. Bezdek: Pattern Recognition with Objective Function Algorithms, London, 1981.

11. J.S. Roger Jang and C.T. Sun: Functional Equivalence Between Radial Basis Function Networks and Fuzzy Inference Systems, Trans. Neural Networks, Vol. 4, No. 1 (1993), 156-159.

Notational Representation of Sign Language: A Structural Description of Hand Configuration

Jintae Lee

University of Aizu, Aizu-Wakamatsu City, Fukushima 965-80, Japan

Abstract. A universal description method of sign language is the most fundamental requirement in sign language research. Although a number of methods including notations have been invented, few are in substantial use for describing general sign languages. In this paper, we present structural description method of hand configuration based on human hand structure and geometric sign features, and explain with a series of arguments that this method has potential as a universal description method of sign language.

1 Introduction

Although, there are hundreds of sign languages in the world developed in various cultures, there is no agreed way of representing sign language. The question '*Can we develop a compact universal description method of sign language which provides conceptually tractable information of the signs?*' is the most fundamental question in sign language research.

Three main methods can be identified in approaches to sign language representation. The first and the simplest is to use sign image itself. The image can then be edited or digitized to be available for applications. The difficulty is that this scenario involves an explosive amount of data, most of which would probably be useless in any given investigation. Techniques of pattern recognition and scene analysis may be used extract necessary information from the image; however, they have not been developed to this level of practical use.

The second is to describe signs in natural language. The problem is now the reverse of that for imagery: the description may be compact; but actual regeneration of the signs requires a certain amount of knowledge of the natural language. Moreover, natural language descriptions are subject to ambiguity and imprecision in specifying positions, traces, and styles of hand motion.

The third is to describe signs in a notation or symbolic form. This method is the most feasible because it abstracts geometric information of the sign in a more compact and clearer way than the other two.

The expressive power of notation can be exemplified by musical score. Musical score is so well-designed as a description of music that it is used in every process of musical composition: in recording and refining musical ideas, and in performing music.

Argument 1 *As a form of sign language representation, notation is superior to natural language or image in compactness and clearness.*

Our further discussion in this paper is organized as follows: Section 2 surveys conventional sign language notations. Section 3 introduces structural description method of hand configuration. Section 4 gives comparison of the method with other notations. Section 5 concludes this paper.

2 Conventional Sign Language Notations

Two notation systems, Stokoe notation [1] and Honna notation [2], which are known to the general public through books and thus provide sufficient information are chosen to be examined in this section.

2.1 Stokoe Notation

Stokoe notation, the world's first practical notation system of sign language, has been developed in 1964 by William C. Stokoe and his colleagues to describe separate signs of American Sign Language (ASL) by symbols. Analogous with the *phoneme* of natural language, Stokoe named *chereme* (CARE-eem, the first syllable from a Homeric Greek word meaning 'handy') the unit of sign language [3]. Cheremes are instances of three sign aspects which distinguish a sign from all other signs in the language: (1) the place where it is made, (2) the distinctive configuration of the hand or hands making it, and (3) the action of the hand or hands.

Stokoe used fifty-five symbols to describe about 3,000 signs of ASL [1]. A sign is written as TD^s, where 'T', 'D', and 's' represent tab (*tabular*, the place), dez (*designator*, the active hand), and sig (*signation*, the action) symbol, respectively. Signs are written like TD^s_s if the sig actions are combined; that is they are done at the same time. The sig symbols are written side by side (TD^{ss}) if one sig action is done first and a second follows. Two dez symbols (TDD^s) are written if both the signer's hands serve as a double dez.

2.2 Honna Notation

Stokoe notation stimulated researchers of sign language to extend the idea to their own sign languages. In 1984, Honna et al. developed a notation system suited to Japanese Sign Language (JSL) [2].

Honna notation also regards sign language as being composed of three aspects, i.e. hand shape, movement, and location. In Honna notation, however, hand shape is again decomposed into two independent elements, i.e. hand configuration and orientation. Hand configuration is further classified into basic form (H) and transconfigurations (C, B, B', P, A, T, V). Orientation is composed of two directions, i.e. the direction of fingertips (to be exact, it must be the direction of the middle finger when the hand is open) and the direction of the palm. Each direction is one of the six directions: up("↑"), down("↓"), left("←"), right("→"), forward(+), and backward(-). Movement and location are classified into subgroups.

2.3 Review of the Notations

Honna notation is more general than Stokoe notation and can describe hand shapes in JSL and ASL. Unfortunately, however, even Honna notation is probably insufficient as a universal sign language notation because it does not reflect real hand configuration correctly. The finger configurations are defined ambiguously, and constraints of the human hand that exert delicate influence upon hand configuration are not taken into account. Consequently, correct hand shape cannot be deduced from the notation.

Argument 2 *The hand configuration should be described in terms of global features so that the description is not sensitive to local deformation. At the same time, it should be described with reasonable accuracy so that unrealistic hand configurations are not generated.*

"Structural" notation based on anatomical structure of the human hand and structural analysis of signs can overcome the drawback of the conventional notations.

3 Structural Description of Hand Configuration

In this section, we describe a structural description method of hand configuration (hand shape) based on mechanical peculiarities and internal constraints of the human hand. It has been incorporated into the design of "Handnotation" of which we have been working on the development as a general sign language notation.

3.1 Cheremes Concept

We accept Stokoe's concept that cheremes are derived from three aspects of signs, i.e. hand configuration, location, and movement. However, we note the qualitative difference of the three aspects of sign (Fig. 1): Hand configuration and location are static in nature, but movement is dynamic. The number of distinguishable hand shapes is finite, while that of location or movement is finite or infinite. We also believe that movement is nothing but change of static aspects. Therefore, not only change of location but also change of hand configuration is a movement for us.

Argument 3 *Chremes are derived from three aspects of sign: two static aspects – hand configuration and location, and one dynamic aspect – movement. Movement is change of static aspects in a time interval.*

3.2 Hand Configuration Analysis

We take a hand configuration to be a set of feature specifications.

Definition 1. A *configuration* is a set of feature specifications. A *feature spec-ification* is an ordered pair of the form *<feature-name, feature-value>*, where a feature name is an atomic symbol begins with capital letter and a feature value is an atomic symbol in small letter or a symbol indicating a part of the hand or a configuration. When $< f, v >$ is a member of configuration C, we write $C(f) = v$, i.e. C yields the value v for the argument f.

Fig. 2 illustrates the skeleton of the right hand seen from the palmar side. Some terminology and abbreviations in this figure will be used to facilitate our discussion. For example, M(II) represents the metacarpal bone of the middle finger. Joint angle will be represented by the symbol $\theta_\beta^\alpha(\gamma)$, where α is the rotation axis, β the joint, and γ the finger.

Hand configuration (HC) is represented by five finger configurations (FIN(f), f = I, II, III, IV, V) and orientation configuration (ORI):

$$HC = \{FIN(I), FIN(II), FIN(III), FIN(IV), FIN(V), ORI\} \qquad (1)$$

Considering that fingers I, II, III, and IV are planar manipulators [5], FIN(i) (i = I, II, III, IV, V) can be specified by $\theta_{DIP}, \theta_{PIP}$, and θ_{MP} of finger i. If we use the constraint between the joint angles of DIP and PIP ($\theta_{DIP} = \frac{2}{3}\theta_{PIP}$) [5], bending state of a finger can be specified by θ_{MP} and θ_{PIP}.

Although θ_{MP} and θ_{PIP} can have continuous values within the joint angle limits, the bending degree (feature FLEX) can be classified according to singularity:

1. θ has zero value.
2. θ has the maximum value within its joint angle limit.
3. θ has a value between zero and the maximum value.
4. θ is determined by other joint or finger(s).

These four classes are represented as feature values **straight, bent, curved** and **passive**, respectively. The MP joint can move left or right (feature ASIDE) and make the finger contact or cover the next finger. Thus, configuration of finger i is the set of features:

$$FIN(i) = \{MPC(i), PIPC(i)\}, \ i = I, II, III, IV \qquad (2)$$
$$MPC(i) = \{FLEX, ASIDE\} \qquad (3)$$

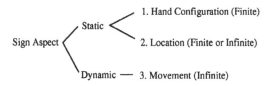

Fig. 1. Qualitative differences of three sign aspects.

I: Thumb II: Index III: Middle IV: Ring V: Little

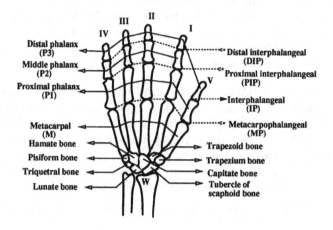

Fig. 2. The hand skeleton seen from the palmar side [4].

$$\text{PIPC}(i) = \{\text{FLEX}\} \tag{4}$$

$$\text{ASIDE} = \{\texttt{no}, \text{CONTACT}, \text{COVER}\}, \text{ where} \tag{5}$$

$$(\text{MPC}(i) \text{ or } \text{PIPC}(i))(\text{FLEX}) \in \{\texttt{straight, curved, bent, passive}\} \tag{6}$$

$$\text{ASIDE}(\text{CONTACT or COVER}) \in \{\text{I, II, III, IV, V}\} \tag{7}$$

The feature CONTACT need not be specified when MPC(FLEX)= bent because the finger inevitably is in contact with its neighboring finger(s) when their MP joints are fully bent (See [5]).

Thumb configuration is more complex to describe since the thumb moves with larger degrees of freedom than other fingers, frequently touching other fingers or the palm. The thumb operates on hand configuration in two ways - by its own configuration or by its relationship with other fingers. When the thumb operates on hand configuration by its own configuration, its configuration is usually at a singular point within the whole configuration space of the thumb. When the thumb operates on hand configuration by its relationship with other fingers, it touches, covers or lies between finger(s).

$$\text{HC}(\text{FIN}(V)) \in \text{T}, \text{ where} \tag{8}$$

$$\text{T} = \{\texttt{ open, closed, stand, fold-in, fold-out}, \text{TOUCH}, \text{INBETWEEN}\}$$

$$\text{FIN}(V)(\text{TOUCH}) = p \tag{9}$$

$$\text{FIN}(V)(\text{INBETWEEN}) = \{\text{F1, F2}\} \tag{10}$$

where p is the place touched and the values of F1, F2 are finger numbers.

Orientation configuration consists of two directions, i.e. the direction of M(II) (DIRM) and the direction normal to the palm (DIRP). It is known that eight directions are adequate to classify directions of shapes on a plane [6]. If we expand the plane into space, all the possible directions become 26. Thus, the value of DIRM is specified as one of 26 unit vectors in our notation. When DIRM is decided, DIRP can have one of eight directions on the plane normal to DIRM.

$$ORI = \{DIRM, DIRP\} \tag{11}$$

$$ORI(DIRM) = e_i, \text{ where } i = 1, 2, \cdots, 26 \tag{12}$$

$$ORI(DIRP) = f_j, \text{ where } j = 1, 2, \cdots, 8. \tag{13}$$

Example 1. The hand configuration of the hand in Fig. 4(a) would be the set of feature specifications as follows:

three =
{<FIN(I), {<MPC, {<FLEX, straight>, <ASIDE, no>}>,
          <PIPC, {<FLEX, straight>}>}>,
<FIN(II), {<MPC, {<FLEX, straight>, <ASIDE, no>}>,
          <PIPC, {<FLEX, straight>}>}>,
<FIN(III), {<MPC, {<FLEX, curved>, <ASIDE, no>}>,
          <PIPC, {<FLEX, straight>}>}>,
<FIN(IV), {<MPC, {<FLEX, passive>}>,
          <PIPC, {<FLEX, passive>}>}>,
<FIN(V), {<TOUCH, IV>}>,
<ORI, {<DIRM, u>, <DIRP, 0>}>}

3.3 Visualization

As it has often been said that a picture is worth a thousand words, pictures can convey meaning in a more intuitive and understandable way than one-dimensional, textual words. Taking this point into account, we created a visual notation in which the information of hand configuration expressed in feature notations can be visualized. The symbols (not all) are illustrated in Fig. 3. They are designed so that the meaning can be understood by their visual form. For instance, the orientation a DIRM symbol means can quickly be understood simply by imagining an arrow located in space. The symbols are written in corresponding places of "sign score" (Fig. 4(b)).

Argument 4 *Symbols in sign language notation must be designed to reveal their meaning in their visual forms.*

4 Experiment

Our method can describe all the manual letters of ASL, JSL, and KSL (Korean Sign Language). Compared with Stokoe and Honna notations, our notation describes more general hand configurations with fewer symbols and more readable

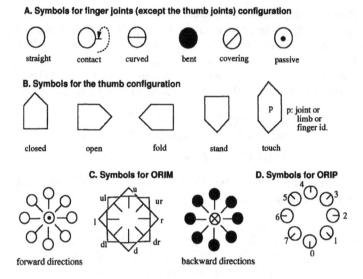

Fig. 3. Visual symbols for specifying hand configuration.

forms (Table 1). Furthermore, its description is more faithful to real hand shapes. For instance, while all the III configurations in their "basic forms" H_{123}(manual letter for "3"), H_{1234}, and H_3 are described identically in Honna notation, we describe the III configuration in the manual letter for "3" as " curved" on MP(III) rather than "straight" considering constraints caused by finger IV (Fig. 4).

5 Conclusion

We presented a structural description method of hand configuration based on anatomical structure and constraints of the human hand. We have shown that this description is compact and can describe more general and precise hand configurations than conventional empirical notations.

There are more works to be done on describing sign movement aspect. As our structural approach to hand configuration description has been very encouraging, we are working to extend it to general sign motion description.

References

1. Stokoe, W.: A Dictionary of American Sign Language on Linguistic Principles. Linstok Press (1976)
2. Kanda, W.: Yubimoji no Kenkyu. Koseikan (1986) (in Japanese)
3. Stokoe, W: Semiotics and Human Sign Languages. Mouton Publishers (1972)
4. Pernkopf, E.: Pernkopf Anatomy, vol. 2., 3 ed. Uran & Schwarzenberg (1989)

Table 1. Comparison of notations.

Notation	Stokoe Notation	Honna Notation	Handnotation
Features	conceptual	conceptual	geometric
Low level unit of description	whole hand	finger	joint
Number of basic symbols	Dez: 19 (Tab: 12) (Sig: 24)	hand config.: 9 hand orient.: 6	4 fingers config.: 6 thumb config.: 7 hand orient.: 26
Describable config.	limited (19)	general but limited in orientation	general
Form	textual	textual	visual
Faithfulness to real hand shapes	weak	weak	good
Constraints	not considered	not considered	considered

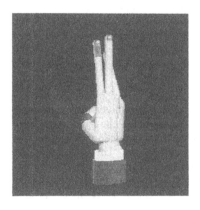

a.

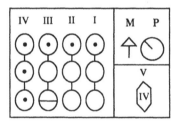

b.

Fig. 4. Manual letter for "3" drawn by the Handnotation interpreter (a), and its notational description (b). III is "curved" on MP by constraints caused by IV.

5. Lee, J., Kunii, T.: Constraint-based hand animation. Models and Techniques in Computer Animation, Springer-Verlag (1993) 110–127
6. Nishida, H., Mori, S.: Algebraic description of curve structure: IEEE PAMI, *14:5* (1992) 516–533
7. Lee, J., Kunii, T.: Generation and recognition of sign language using graphic models: Proc. ACMJ/IISF Int. Symposium on computers as our better partners, World Scientific (1994) 96–103

Further Advances in Real-Time Voice to Text with Steno Interpreters

JONATHAN E. OAKEY

Director Deaf and Hearing Impaired Program
RAPIDTEXT, Inc.
Newport Beach, CA 92660

Abstract. Microcomputer steno-interpreting technology allows the deaf to receive full access to the spoken word. The technology also benefits a variety of disabled people including the dyslexics, brain damaged people, and the deaf-blind. The Rapidtext software on a PC computer translates the stenowriter's output into English words and displays on a computer screen. The spoken English words are converted into text at up to 200 words per minute and displayed on computer screen. The technology also helps international audiences, people speaking English as a second language, and even illiterate people who speak English as their native language.

Needs Justification

Deaf students face communications barriers to completing their university studies and doctoral programs. The deaf cannot relax their eyes while the professors are speaking. Lipreaders cannot easily simultaneously maintain lipreading while looking at the chart, diagram, or poster being illustrated by the teacher. The same problem applies to viewing sign language interpreters. Neither can the deaf look down to write their notes with the same ease as hearing students. Neither can they relax their eyes as a prelude to meditating on important concepts being verbally illustrated by the teacher. If they blink, they may lose a crucial word, or an important phrase illustrating a concept. Lipreaders and signers cannot quickly scan the classroom for other details and still retain mastery of receiving the spoken word. Concentrated eye focus on a moving and floating two inch target (either mouth or hand) at a distance of ten to a hundred feet can be quite taxing to the brain. The level of eye focusing and mental effort is similiar to target competition. That effort is simultaneously superimposed on learning sometimes difficult new information and concepts. The eyes become physically tired after concentrated use as unblinking receptors of information. Hearing students, on the other hand, rely on both their eyes and ears to simultaneously receive doubled sensory inputs of the same information. Deaf people are a visual people. A solution must be found to allow them easy and relaxed access to information. The senses of smell, touch, taste are not suitable for rapid processing of abstract concepts for the deaf. Visual presentation of information is still necessary. Reading is easier than reading lips or signing (especially on abstract or complex subject matter), and happily, reading rates are higher than speaking rates. The solution is found by stretching the spoken information into the past, and simultanously presenting past and present information together within one format. A way has been found to convert spoken information into written information as the words are being said. The solution is analogous to reading a book as it is being typed. The deaf student receives every word accurately and does not miss any words. The deaf student can go back a minute in time to mull over concepts, and relink them to concepts being presented. The student is looking at a full page of the spoken information. He is also free to wander his eyes over to the charts and diagrams, and observe the teacher's expressions and emphasis on key words, and then go back to reread words he may have missed. He is also freed to write notes. He is freed to think. If he is allowed to have control over the keyboard, he can make use of the scrolling function of a word processing program. He can scroll back into the past 10 or 60 minutes, or more.

The dyslexics can be helped by doubling/repeating the same information input through more than one sense. The dyslexics are both hearing and seeing the written information. They may be able to gain increased understanding of the material being presented. A sensory brain retraining effect may be in play to lessen their dyslexity. The deaf-blind is also helped by using this technology combined with screen output braille reader. Normally, the reader machine is plugged into a pc computer. A blind person 'reads' the 'contents' on the monitor screen through his fingers resting on the tactile reader machine. As the steno-interpreter translates the speech into text, the braille reader outputs the text into braille form for the deaf-blind to read. However, the maximum braille output on some tactile readers may be 60 wpm, even though the average speed of both the speaking and steno input is 160 wpm. When the class session is over, the deaf-blind can continue 'reading the class' at leisure, or save it and attend the next class session. Even this slow braille output is better than relying on memory alone. Relying on a tape recorder for recording notes is useless for a deaf-blind. The brain-injured may have short term memory loss. These brain-injured are helped by allowing them to go back in time to refresh their memory and to reconnect their lost thoughts while the speaker is speaking. Depending on the speaker's speed, and the formatting of the text, the visual display allows people to go back up to two minutes into the past without scrolling. If text scrolling is controlled by the reader, more spoken minutes deeper in the past is accessible to the brain damaged listener. This micro-computer based steno-interpreting technology may also open up a new communications channel to bypass other types of brain deficits (defective single or multiple sensory input/information processing) communications channel.

1. Background Review

The average speaking rate of speakers is 160 words per minute. Some speakers speak up to 300 words per minute. Typists, at 60 words per minute, are clearly inadequate to transcribe words being spoken in real time. Stenography offers the solution through phonetic representation. Stenographers use the stenowriter, a phonetic based machine. Fewer strokes are required to represent a word or phrase. The concept is similiar to using macros on the computer to shorten the number of strokes on the keyboard to achieve the same results. The stenomachine's keyboard have fewer number of keys than the typewriter, and the keys are larger. However, the problem is that the output is in steno, which is readable only to trained stenographers. Stenographers laboriously retype into English on an ordinary computer. One hour of live proceedings requires a minimum of an additional five to six hours of typing off-site to make a transcript.

2. Review Solution

The stenomachine keys were wired to send steno signals to a personal computer. Software was written to convert the steno into English words. This is analogous to a computer recognizing the keystrokes on a computer keyboard as representations of letters. This allows for realtime translation of the spoken word into written English words. The entire written text is free of any spelling mistakes, because only complete words appear on the computer screen. However, a stenographer may steno stroke the phonetic equivalent of an English word not yet stored in computer's memory. These visible steno code are called "untranslates". In other words, the untranslate appears whenever the stenographer has not yet entered that word into memory. This memory of stored English words "translates" is called "dictionary", and is a personal dictionary created on disk by the stenographer.

An experienced steno interpreter (my coined terminology to refer to those stenographers trained and equipped with realtime steno translation software and works in a similiar capacity as sign language interpreters for deaf people) has at least a 50,000 general word dictionary stored in memory.

3. Technical Information

There is a less than a quarter second electromechanical lag from pressing a steno stroke to English translation on the screen on AT 12 mz speed computers. It executes faster on higher speed computers. The desirable requirements of a computer are a 486 processor with 40 MB hard drive, DOS 5.0, and a wordprocessing software. A laptop or notebook size computer is suggested for ease of transportation from location to location. For international conventions, the conduct of international scientific/technical/business meetings increases participation and better insightful understanding when the common spoken language among international participants, English, is simultaneously viewed in written form keeping pace along with the speaker.

4. Further Advances

Rapidtext's Rapid Caption software allows the steno-interpreter to send text to a variety of devices, including closed caption encoders, character generators, and the InfoSign, described below (Section 5). Caption encoders and character generators are used to caption a variety of video output devices such those found in television broadcast stations, televisions, videocassette recorders, and RGB video projectors.

The program allows steno-interpreters to control the devices and the format of output directly from the stenowriter. Multiple on-line and off-line scripts can be loaded into memory and accessed instantly as needed. Scripts can be saved as text or printed either in line-by-line mode, or in paragraph form. The program can interface with alternate captioning device, such as a teleprompter, allowing the operator to switch between its ouput and stenographic input. A teleprompter is usually a transparent (to the television camera) screen of prepared text read live by a television anchorman as he looks straight into the camera. A reporter would write the text of his speech into his computer. The text is then loaded into the teleprompter in advance of the reporter appearing live in front of television audiences. Most teleprompters in the USA have now been converted to feed into a caption encoder essentially instantaneously to be transmitted with the rest of the live video-signal being transmitted from the television station. In this way, the news are captioned simply by feeding the reporter's written teleprompter text into the caption encoder. Teleprompter captioning has now become a standard practice in the USA. The problem is that live breaking news, such as a disaster are ad-libbed. The remote reporters reporting into the station live through a satellite feed are also ad-libbing. Live interviews of subjects, or their comments are not pre-written into the script. Jokes and comments between anchorpeople are also ad-libbed and thus goes uncaptioned. So the deaf people are getting essentially the day's old news captioned, but immediate news are uncaptioned. Rapidtext's software has been made to address this problem by allowing teleprompter and live captioning to blend together seamlessly.

Macro recording language allows users to record often used key sequences and play them back with a keypress from the keyboard or steno machine. The program also takes advantage of additional memory found in 386, 486, and Pentium machines. The program can also control two captioning devices simultaneously, and one of these devices can attach to the computer's parallel port (optional converter box required). This is a useful feature, if you wish to have an audience to view the InfoSign, while another audience is viewing a projected video picture with live captions being fed into the video picture.

Both of Rapidtext software now uses windowed interface with on-line help. Dictionaries can be edited on-line. Steno-interpreter can change translation dictionaries in use instantly. This is useful in the case of a speaker speaking about physics using physics terminology, and switching to medical jargon in mid-speech. The steno interpreter can switch from her physics dictionary to her medical dictionary in mid-stream. Access has been improved to decoder functions under the new FCC specification. Macro recording language allows users to record often used key sequences and play them back with a keypress from the keyboard or steno machine. This is useful in the case of a television series where a phrase or a the theme song is repeated on every broadcast.

Developments currently under way include full compatibility with memory intensive, DOS graphical interface applications like WordPerfect 6.0. This reduces need for screen-enhancement software. A feature that allows the steno-interpreter to transcribe proceedings and the user (usually a student) to annotate simultaneously on the same computer without the overhead of multitasking software.

5. LED Display

There has been problems with displaying the text appropriately. The full potential of steno-interpreting technology is not reached with only a computer screen placed on the student's desk. Focusing the eyes from close-up to a distance repeatedly cuts down on the student's understanding and comprehension. The author invented a solution. The seed of the idea was found in a LED display commonly seen in bank lobbies. The words are typically a moving display from right to left. The display is usually only one line. Such display is unsuitable for absorbing complex concepts, and is used only to present simple messages. The author's idea was to convert the LED display into 2 or more lines of text, and made it scroll upwards, for easy reading. The software that is normally used for captioning broadcast, professional, and amateur videotapes was easily converted to be used with LED display.

Captioning creates opportunities that once were almost impossible for the deaf and hearing impaired. You may talk to the deaf author by voice at RapidText™, Inc., where he is the director of the Deaf and Hearing Impaired Program, 230 Newport Center Drive, Suite 250, Newport Beach, California 92660, USA. (714) 644-6500 or by fax (714) 644-5706.

BIOGRAPHY

The author became profoundly and prelingually deaf in infancy from spinal meningitis. He received special training until 4th grade, when he was mainstreamed into regular school. Graduated from regular high school as the top outstanding versatile senior of all area high schools. Majored in Physics at the University of California, and graduated with a degree in Aerodynamics in 1984. He became involved with pc's in 1981. He worked as a director creating a new division based on the author's vision for Climax Computers, a mini-computer manufacturer with PICK operating system, and laser disk photographical storage and retrieval applications. In 1991, he became director and creator of the deaf and hearing impaired program at RapidText™, a stenographic based computer software and peripheral firm.

A Uniform Control Interface for Various Electronic Aids

Christian Bühler, Helmut Heck, Rainer Wallbruch

Forschungsinstitut Technologie-Behindertenhilfe, Evangelische Stiftung Volmarstein
D-58300 Wetter, Germany

Abstract. The operation of technical aids by disabled and elderly people leads to enormous difficulties because users have to deal with different control philosophies and user interface concepts for each technical aid used. Therefore a point of general interest is not only the pure support function of the aid itself, but especially its human machine interface and the interdependencies with further aids used by the same handicapped person. A computer-based user interface management system is presented that allows an assistive person to individually tailored a human computer interface to the user's needs and capabilities which allows the handicapped user to operate very different devices by the same principle and mechanism of control.

1   Computers for People with Special Needs

People with disabilities are often not able to use standard computer hardware and software. Due to various impairments, e.g. physical impairment, mental retardation, or perceptual disorders, they cannot use normal keyboards and pointing devices or they are analphabets or they cannot read text on a monitor screen. But just for handicapped people a computer could open areas of their social and occupational environment. To make the problems clear: what can someone do, who is sitting in a wheelchair, unable to speak and write, and intending to switch on a light or a special TV channel. He can communicate by pointing at pictures (if his communication partner has plenty of practice with this) and ask someone to help him, or he can use a special switch which he can reach from the wheelchair. Both possibilities can be aided by a computer. A computer could aid communication, manage devices in the personal environment, could control a wheelchair or a robot arm. In the European TIDE (Technology Initiative for Disabled and Elderly People) programme [1,2] the need to integrate systems has been broadly introduced.

Thus, handicapped people have special needs in operating computers [3,4]. This comprises not only input and output devices, but also the way of presenting audiovisual information and the complexity/abstraction of information [5]. It is desirable to have aiding devices that help those persons to overcome their handicaps but on the other hand involve as much of the mental, motor and sensoric capabilities of the user as possible. A computer gives the chance to build very individual user interfaces to control the functionality of the computer itself and of external devices.

2 Interface Problems

The normal situation, when a user wants to work with different devices, is generally known. Each device has its own user interface and its own input devices (fig. 1a) [6].

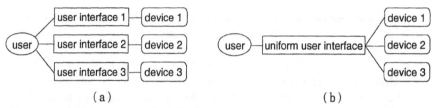

(a)   (b)

Fig. 1. Standard (**a**) versus optimal (**b**) situation when an user works with different devices

For handicapped persons this can mean a new problem: Often it is not possible to use different devices at the same or nearly at the same time. If someone drives a wheel-chair he cannot use a communication aid at the same time, if the only movement he is able to perform is needed for driving the wheelchair. Usually a special device or switch is needed additionally to the wheelchair equipment and it is questionable if this could be operated then. Desirable is one user interface for various devices (fig 1b). For example, a communication aid and a powered wheelchair can be operated via the same input devices and the same monitor program.

In practical use of assisting devices, we encountered another interface problem: in the training situation of handicapped persons in our rehabilitation centre. As described above, the choice of input devices and the electronic aids themself depend on the abilities and needs of the handicapped persons. Every user has his own devices with specific interfaces. This means for a trainer, who e.g. wants to train persons in communicating via symbols, that he has to learn the operation and method of adaption (configuration) of all the communication devices in use. Furthermore, the persons in charge in a residential home for handicapped persons have lo learn all services and all the interfaces they have contact to (fig. 2a).

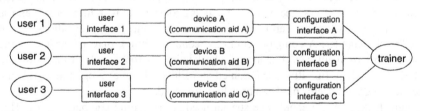

Fig. 2a. Standard situation when a trainer trains several users on devices of the same kind

Additionally, this is not only an inter-individual but also an intra-individual problem: in the case of assisted communication it is possible that someone who begins with a communication aid based on symbols learns more symbols or more complex symbol systems, or he learns to read and to write letters. Seldom the functionality of the communication aid grows as the abilities of its user grows. Usually the disabled person and also his trainer has to change to another communication aid, probably with a different user interface and with another configuration interface.

We found out that the great variety of assistive electronic devices with different human machine interface concepts means a crucial problem for all users, even more for the training staff (occupational therapists, teachers etc.) than for the disabled persons. Often much of the functionality of devices is not used because trainers are not able to or do not have enough time to adapt user interfaces to the users' needs. Here it is desirable, too, that the trainer has only one configuration interface for different devices (fig. 2b) or, respectively, a very flexible system with different user interfaces (fig. 2c).

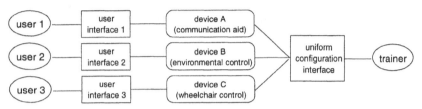

Fig. 2b. Optimal situation when a trainer trains several users on several devices

Fig. 2c. Optimal situation when a trainer trains several users on one device

3   Demand for User Tailorable Systems

From the situation described above, we formulated the demand for a versatile user interface management system (UIMS) for physically / mentally / perceptionally disabled people and their caring persons.

Uniform user interface. From the point of view of a disabled person, the UIMS should enable a very special, *individually adapted and uniform* user interface with
- an *individual* input device out of a *variety* of switches, pointing devices, keyboards etc.,
- an *individual* presentation of information on the monitor screen out of a *variety* of pictures, symbols, texts, colours, windows, menues etc.,
- an *individual* selection/activation method of choices in menues from a *variety* of methods (direct selection, single-item scanning, row-column scanning etc.)

suitable for the use of *several different* electronic aids (the computer included) at the same time. To the user a created user interface should appear uniform (with respect to operation) for all applications.

Uniform configuration interface. From the point of view of a training person, the UIMS should have *one uniform* configuration interface for all the different options of user interfaces and electronic aids.

4 Implementation Model of the UIMS

Figure 3 shows the implementation model of the UIMS. In correspondence with the different users, the trainer configures via the uniform configuration interface individual user interfaces, each of which gives access to different devices in a uniform way of operation.

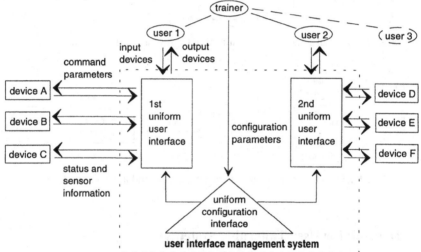

Fig. 3. Implementation model of the UIMS

5 The Configuration Interface

The configuration interface provides the tools for the description of personal configurations for different users. This comprises:
- the choice of input and output devices,
- the way of presentation of the pictures/symbols/text on the screen
  - choice of arbitrary symbols, pictures, scanned photographs or free-hand drawings,
  - size of the symbols,
  - order on the screen,
  - colour of the background and the high-lighting,

- display of text strings related to the symbols,
    - combination of related symbols,
    - organisation of menus,
- the mode of selection of symbols (direct, different ways of scanning),
- timing restrictions for activation of symbols (minimal duration, bolting)
- the assignment of speech output to symbols,
- the assignment of actions to symbols.

Furthermore the inclusion of new pictures/symbols and spoken words or sentences is supported. Necessary configuration input devices are the standard input devices as well as a microphon, a scanner (for scanning photographs or hand-drawn pictures) or an additional PC. According to the requirement that a communication aid has to be adaptable to different kinds of physical impairment, the user interface management system is able to cope with arbitrary input devices, like buttons, switches or pointing devices (mouse, trackball, joystick, touchscreen). Pictures or symbols to be selected are displayed on a colour monitor screen.

6 Applications

Symbol-based communication aids. In the following, examples of user interfaces for various areas are described. At first the case of a basic communication aid for nonspeaking persons [7], e.g. young children, is considered. Because the children cannot read and write, the input is based on graphical symbols, which are monitored on a flat screen and accessed by input devices according to the children's abilities

The delivered objects of the system, here graphical symbols, are in one of three states (passive, selected, activated). A state can be indicated on the screen by several variables: the colour of the symbols or the colour of the background can change, for instance. If a picture is selected, directly or by scanning, it can be activated by a switch and then it can produce two types of actions and a message for output. To each *talking* picture a speech output is assigned. If a talking picture is activated, a corresponding message is sent to the speech output control and the output, preferrable a digitised natural voice for this kind of restricted communication, follows directly. It is also possible to list at first a series of talking pictures in order to build a sentence with several statements and then select and activate a *silent* picture in the very same manner, which triggers the speech output.

Figure 4a shows an example of the screen. A statement composition line is found at the top. Beyond this, one window allows the selection of pictures according to a prior chosen theme. Another small window allows to go to wheelchair or environment control. The selection mode is direct, selection is indicated by a little arrow and a different background colour. Seen in the window on top, the chosen communication theme is "clothes" (selected and activated in the first menu with the other alternatives of "food", "drink", "feelings", etc., whereas every symbol generates other menus or menu hierarchies) followed by the symbols for trousers and jacket with a description of the colour of both ones. At the moment a symbol is selected, which, if it will be activated, leads to another menu with more clothes. At the bottom is a window with symbols, whose actions lead to a new screen ("Neustart" - start again), "undo" the last action ("Löschen" - delete), and control speech output ("OK" - speak listed) sentence. If the speech output should follow ever only after activation of one symbol, the monitor display could be even more simple, e.g. only the larger window in the middle of the just described example.

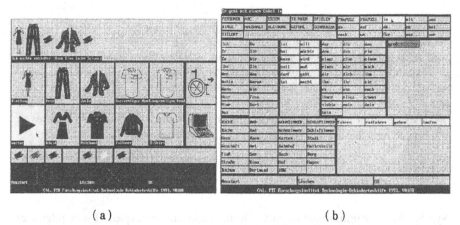

(a)   (b)

Fig. 4. Communication aids with symbols (**a**) and text (**b**)

Text-based communication aids. The same principle can be taken for communication based on text for people who can read and optionally write. Instead of symbols words, morphemes and letters are related, and the output is directed to a synthetic speech generator. A typical screen is show in figure 4b. At the top there is again a statement composition line. Beyond, a window allows the selection of an area of statements in order to monitor just words of current interest on the screen. A subset of the complex German grammar is built in, which permits the generation of grammatical correct statements, e.g. after choosing the subject the visible verbs are correctly conjugated. New words can be easily edited changing to a morpheme and letter screen. In comparison to pure letter editing, the efforts for the generation of statements can be much reduced after suitable individual adjustments.

Wheelchair control interface. For people with multiple and severe disabilities the continuous operation of a wheelchair with the help of a joystick is not suitable. The operation can be eased widely by using direct control in combination with digitally controlled manoeuvres. The above described interface method can be applied for initiating direct and digital control mode and for selecting and monitoring the desired manoeuvre. For reasons of safety, no communication is allowed in parallel, because wheelchair control needs continuous monitoring, but assisted communication is possible nearly at the same time as wheelchair driving and no special device and no special switch is used for communication. As already shown in figure 4a, a general symbol for switching to wheelchair control can be activated. Here objects are related with symbols or text and a wheelchair control activity. Figure 5a shows, as an example, the main menu for the choice of direct and automatic manoeuvres (like turn, side step, etc. or user recorded movements) in a scanning switch mode. At the top window the composing area for commands is found again. In the second window symbols can be chosen. Every activated symbol leads to a new menu display related to this symbol. Here a hierarchy of menus is used to display all possible manoeuvres. The wheelchair movement ends when the switch, which activates the symbols, is triggered again. Then the display shows the beginning of the menu hierarchy again.

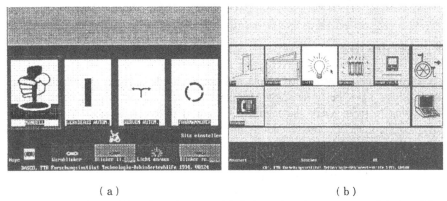

(a)   (b)

Fig. 5. Parts of control interfaces for a wheelchair (**a**) and environment control devices (**b**)

Environmental control. For those people who have problems to access directly their surroundings like doors, windows, TV, alarm, light and so on, environmental control is an important issue for independent living. Environmental objects are adressed via the same selection modes as above. They are related with symbols or text, an environmental control activity and a corresponding I/O line. Figure 5b shows a possible environmental menu, as a result of the activation of the symbol for environmental control shown in figure 4a (third row, last symbol).

7   Implementation

The user interface management system is implemented in the object-oriented programming language C++ for IBM-compatible personal computers (80x86, x>1), either stationary PCs for educational and training purposes (at school or rehabilitation establishments) or on portable or wheelchair-mounted notebooks.

8   User involvement

Before we started this project, there was a request for a versatile communication aid, which came directly from the users, teachers of the special school of our rehabilitation centre. Therefore the users were involved in the project from the very beginning. First considerations led to a small prototype for a communication aid, a principal demonstration of our intentions. Reviewed this, we started the development of the main software in C++. Persons with multiple and severe disabilities tested the selection mechanisms, monitoring adjustment and different types of hierarchies. In accordance to the needs of young persons in the vocational rehabilitation process we specified the environmental control in order to assist their independent habitation. A subset of the desirable wheelchair functionality has been incorporated in the system. This will be extended furthermore. We worked out the demands for wheelchair control based on questionnaires (300 users) and interviews (50 users) [8].

9 Perspective

An adaptable user interface for people with special needs has been introduced. Some applications have been described for special user groups with special needs. According to these needs the interface integrates different devices. We intend to intensify the lines of communication and environmental control. At the present we integrate the wheelchair-mounted manipulator MANUS [9]. We furthermore will consider more feedback information of the system and try to get the same flexibility for system feedback as for the user input.

References

1. TIDE Pilot Action, The Synopses, March 1992, Commission of the European Communities, DG XIII
2. TIDE, 2nd phase Workplan Draft, 1992, Commission of the European Communities, DG XIII
3. Busby, G.: State of the art computer technology. ICCHP 92, Proceedings of the 3rd Intern. Conf. on Computers for Handicapped Persons, pp. 97-100 (1992)
4. H.Gabus, J.C.: JAMES - allgemeine Betrachtungen. Proc. of Congress "Technologie und Handicap", Neuchatel, June 1990, pp. 303-324 (1990)
5. McMillan, W. W.: Computing for Users with Special Needs and Models of Computer Human Interaction. ACM Conference on Human Factors in Computing Systems, CHI 1992 Conf. Proc., 3.-7. May 1992, Monterey USA, Addison -Wesley, pp. 143-148 (1992)
6. Sandhu, J.S.; Richardson, St. (1988): Concerned Technology 1989, Handicapped Persons Research Unit, Newcastle upon Tyne Polytechnic
7. Bühler, Ch.; Heck, H.: CAi - A versatile communication aid for the speech impaired. ICCHP 92, Proceedings of the 3rd Intern. Conf. on Computers for Handicapped Persons, pp. 88-96 (1992)
8. Bühler, Ch.; Schmidt, M.: User involvement in evaluation and assessment of assistive technology. ECART 2, European Conf. on the Advancement of Rehabilitation Technology (1993)
9. Kwee, H.H.: Rehabilitation robotics: softening the hardware. Intern Conf. on Rehabilitation Robotics, A.I. duPont Inst., Wilmington, Delaware (1990)

An Integrated System for Communication and Equipments Control Using Radio Link

Alberto Tronconi, Marco Billi

Consiglio Nazionale delle Ricerche
Istituto di Ricerca sulle Onde Elettromagnetiche
Firenze, Italy

Abstract. In the following we will describe a PC based system which allows motor disabled persons to control devices in a domestic environment. The system will be able to "learn" and reproduce infrared (IR) code from virtually every IR controller currently available, so it can relay on a wide range of commercial devices, now and in the future. The configuration phase will be quite easy, enabling non-experts to perform, without training, the operation needed to adapt the system to user needs. The control code will be sent via a radio link, to allow disabled users to control the desired device without moving around to "see" the receiver. The disabled user will interact with the environment via a highly adaptable iconic interface, designed to be used either to control devices or to send messages to the surrounding environment or to a remote supervising station.

1 Introduction

Disabled people who are unable to control their movements are often unable to use a number of devices in the domestic or working environment, and in some cases even to communicate basic needs or desires.

Our experience in developing communication systems for motor disabled people has lead us to consider the opportunity of using one of the interfaces developed which allows users to control devices in their living environment as well as communicate. We integrated the two features in a unique system capable of acting as a highly intuitive communicator, to send messages either to the local environment or to a remote supervising station and as a means to control a number of devices.

The control system has been designed to comply with three main requirements: to work with a wide range of commercial product now and in the future, to let users operate as freely as possible in a domestic environment, and to interact with the system in a straightforward way.

To achieve these results, we relied on our communication system (MACDIP [1]), which offers a good foundation in terms of flexibility and effectiveness, providing a multimedia editor capable of dealing with photographic image and sound in a friendly way with a highly adaptable and straightforward user interface.

2 The Communication System

We have chosen to assume, as base module, the system named MACDIP (an acronym for Multimedia Ambiental Communication system for DIsabled People) for interfacing and communication, both for its straightforward interaction method and its adaptability to user needs.

The communication process, adopted by MACDIP, consists of selecting an ichnographic representation of the desired issue, causing a message to be emitted to the surrounding environment in vocal form and/or sent to a remote control station.

In order to adapt the system to user needs, operators can rely on a multimedia editor to compose a communication pattern, using multimedia elements like photographic images and digital sound. Operators can grab and choose suitable graphic or photographic images from within the multimedia editor, as well as compose the desired images sequence and link messages to every image into a friendly environment, without specific knowledge.

Furthermore, operators can choose from a number of special input devices and the interaction method to comply with the user's residual skills.

The resulting communication environment will be highly customized, making the recognition process and the interaction with the system as easy as possible.

Relying on the above mentioned features, we added the possibility to the multimedia editor of joining commands to devices to the images while composing the communication pattern. In such a way the user will then be able to control the surrounding environment by choosing the image which corresponds to the desired action, or to send a local or remote message.

3 Structure of the Control System

The control system will consist of hardware and software tools to record useful control codes from different IR controllers, associate a unique identifier to each code, and store them in a file waiting to be used.

While composing the interface, which is done by means of the previously mentioned multimedia editor, the identifier of the desired control code will be joined to a representative image.

When the user selects the icon related to an action, the suitable control code will be retrieved by means of the associated identifier and routed, via the serial port, to a transmitter that sends the code to activate the desired equipment.

In order to overcome restrictions, due to the IR's impossibility to trespass solid object, the transmission relies on a radio link going from the control station to one of the repeaters placed in suitable places throughout the house. The repeater will transform the received code in the original IR signal to activate the target equipment.

4 Recording Commands

One of the main issues we tried to fulfill involves the possibility of employing the control system independent of specific types of controllable devices, so that the user is free to choose the best suited brand or type of controlled equipment.

At present, the most common methods for controlling remote devices in a domestic environment are based on infrared (IR) controllers. Nearly all common electronic equipment (TV set, CD player, etc.) can be handled via an IR controller. The same method is now used to control lights, heating, and other common devices.

Moreover, a number of devices exist, which have been specifically developed for disabled people (e.g. to open/close doors and windows, to handle a telephone, to turn on and off electronic equipments), that can even be handled by an IR controller.

The combination of the wide availability of IR controlled devices and the fact that users are free to use the equipment that best suits their needs led us to design a system that could interact with unknown heterogeneous controlled equipments, using the IR link. Unfortunately an industrial standard on the format of IR commands does not exist, so that they cannot be prestored, but must be recorded by the user.

To solve the problem, we provided our system with a suitable software tool that could control, via the serial port, an IR receiver. The receiver samples an IR control signal and sends the result to the software tool, which stores it in a file. The sampled code will be combined with an identifier (a string of maximum 32 alphanumeric character), the number of target repeaters (explained below), which the code will be sent to, and the duration of the signal in milliseconds.

The user can record all the desired control codes, which can be edited or updated every time s/he desires.

Inside the multimedia editor, a representative icon will be linked to a specific control code identifier instead of a message, so that the chosen icon when selected will be used to perform the corresponding action.

5 Radio Link

Another key issue in developing the control system has been to let users operate in a domestic environment as freely as possible. Since the IR control cannot operate when solid barriers lay between receiver and transmitter, the user would move around to find the right position for activating the chosen device.

This can be difficult or even impossible for people with motor handicaps, so we decided to use a radio link, which is capable of reaching every point of a house, to convey the control code.

This choice would eliminate the purpose of using non-modified commercial equipment, which would require special controlled devices (equipped with radio receiver), so we decided to rely on the radio channel to convey commands and on an IR link to activate the target device.

To achieve such a compromise, we developed an hardware device composed of a radio receiver and transmitter and an IR transmitter, which will act as a repeater, translating the code from the radio to the IR form.

A suitable number of repeaters will be placed in such a way as allow direct control of all the desired equipment, therefore giving the disabled user the ability to control all equipment, regardless of his/her position.

When an user chooses a command the developed software will send it, via a serial port, to an other hardware device (master), that delivers the command via a specific radio protocol to the right repeater. Then the master returns an appropriate code, depending on the success or failure of the command delivery.

6 Radio Protocol

Since in some cases the user could not directly see the result of expected action and since the result of an action can be uncertain when relying on a radio link (eventually affected by noise), we developed a simple protocol to assure the success of IR code delivery.

First of all, when a code has to be transmitted, it is related to the identifier of a specific repeater. Then, the master will send an attention signal, waiting for an acknowledgment. The transmitted signal contains the identifier of the target repeater and that of the transmitting station. If the acknowledgment is not received in 200 ms, the attention signal will be sent again, three times at most. If the replay of the target repeater is lacking, an error message will be displayed to inform the user that a specific repeater does not respond.

In the ordinary operation, the repeater replies with the acknowledgment signals, then the master sends another signal containing the repeater identifier, the selected code and the transmitting station ID. The code will be sent back by the receiver to control the correctness of the transmission. If the code is wrong, it will be sent again until it is received correctly; otherwise a terminating signal will terminate the transaction. At this point the repeater will send the code, in IR form, to the target receiver.

This protocol will assure high error immunity and reduce interference in environments where more than a single user is employing the control system; at present we are developing a more complete protocol to handle collisions.

7 Feedback

In the composition phase, the operator can choose if and how the user must be informed of the progress in code delivery. This can be done using symbolic, text, or phonic messages which state the correctness of a transaction or the type of error incurred.

In some cases, the user has to be aware of what is happening when the system performs an action, even if it will take place in a hidden location. The system does not presently integrate any method to allow direct monitoring of hidden equipment; a common solution can be to use closed loop TV equipment, eventually controlled by our system.

8 Software and Hardware Tolls

As mentioned before, the control system requires software tools to control the recording and delivering phases, and hardware tools to sample IR codes, as well as transmit and receive codes between the control station and a repeater.

We developed the software tool using the Microsoft Visual C++ 1.0, the natural environment of these tools is MS Windows, but the basic communication routine can be used even by software running under DOS.

This feature allows us to maintain the compatibility with the existing DOS systems, like MACDIP, but to be ready for future developments under MS Windows.

The implemented tools have been designed to be as friendly as possible, using on-line help and hints to guide the novice user. As result a very short training period is required: our experience has shown that a two-hour training session is sufficient for an adequate knowledge of the entire system (communication and control).

Hardware tools consist of the IR sampler to capture the IR code, the master, the radio receiver and transmitter, ar.d the repeater. The radio equipment is commercial, while other features of the master and repeater are based on an 8 bit microcontroller (by SGS), which contain the microcode to perform the described protocol and implement the IR receiver and transmitter.

The microcontroller exchanges data with a radio modem, integrated in the circuitry, via a serial connection at 1200 baud; the modem perform an FSK modulation/demodulation to send/receive information to/from the external radio equipment

9 Conclusion

The outcome of our effort is a system that integrates the possibility of controlling a wide range of equipments and communicating simple messages to the local environment in a phonic form, or to a remote supervising station via a radio link.

Both the performed functions (communication and control) will be highly customizable by means of some software tools that allow easy adaptation of the system to user needs on the one hand, and to the controlled equipment and output devices on the other.

Initial laboratory tests show us that the result is an easy to use and effective system that can help people with motor disabilities to better interact with their living environments, without constraints on the type of controlled equipments or the activating process, while requiring a few hardware apparatus installed in the controllable environments.

References

1. A. Tronconi, R. Tronconi, M. Billi, L. Stefani, F. Focardi: A system for basic communication aimed at severe phisically disbled people. Proceedings of 3rd International Conference on Computers for Handicapped Persons, Vienna, July 7-9, 1992

2.   ESPRIT 2431, Home system specification, Commission of the European Communities, DG XIII, 1991
3.   TIDE 2nd phase Workplan Draft, Commission of the European Communities, DG XIII, 1992
4.   C. Bühler: Uniform user interface for communication and control. Proceedings of the 2nd European Conference on the Advancement of Rehabilitation Technology, May 26-28, 1993 Stockholm, Sweden.
5.   R. Bianchi Bandinelli: L'edificio intelligente: stato dell'arte e futuri sviluppi. Atti del 3° Convegno Nazionale "Informatica Didattica e Disabilità", Torino 4-6 Novembre 1993.

AUTONOMY - A Flexible and Easy-to-Use Assistive System to Support the Independence of Handicapped and Elderly Persons

Christian Flachberger, Paul Panek, Wolfgang L. Zagler

fortec - Working Group on Rehabilitation-Engineering
Vienna University of Technology

Abstract. A new assistive system to support the independence of handicapped persons and elderly persons with handicaps is under development at the Working Group on Rehabilitation Engineering at the Vienna University of Technology. This paper describes the concept of the system. To meet the requirements of the very different possible users, high flexibility in supported functions and configuration of the user interface is essential for the concept. So this paper reports about a step towards an all purpose assistive system, usable by very different handicapped persons.

1 Global Aspects

1.1 Some Statistical Remarks on the Situation in Austria and Central Europe

i) According to estimations carried out by the Austrian Statistical Office (Österreichisches Statistisches Zentralamt) it can be expected that the relation between persons in need of care and caregivers will increase by the factor of two until the year 2030.

ii) Within this century the average age for entering employment has risen from 15 to 25 years; the average age for retirement has dropped. [9]

INTERPRETATION: The bottleneck in the field of professional caregiving is likely to become critical.

iii) More than 80% of the care provided in a western community is accomplished by relatives; only 20% is provided by professional care institutions.

INTERPRETATION: If the above mentioned bottleneck narrows down the importance of caregiving within the family will rise.

iv) Though, with respect to age, today more generations are alive simultaneously there is a tendency from the 3-Generation-Household to the 2-Generation-Household even to the 1-Person-Household.

INTERPRETATION: This trend is counterproductive to family provided care.

RÉSUMÉ: This gap will, in the near future, lead to severe social problems which can only be solved by a wide holistic approach. This includes the development of ambulant and mobile services as well as the invigoration of family structures which are in the state of decay for most Central European countries because of changes in society and doubtful family politics.

One aspect of this holistic approach should be the implementation of up-to-date and ergonomic technical aids. At least in Austria there is a considerable gap left between available technologies and the development of the rehabilitation technology market. Many technologies are already existing in principle but are not available for those persons who would need to use them. This has been shown recently ([4], [5], [10]).

1.2 The Family as Caregiver

Within the population which is in need of care and which is nursed by relatives two trends are emerging:

i) Significant increase of elderly disabled persons due to the ageing of the entire population
ii) Increase of (multiply) disabled persons due to improved chances to survive critical situations caused by accidents, illness or complications during birth.

When it comes to caring for family members two major problems arise:

i) Staying at home vs. institutional care:
   Persons in need of care suffer from the feeling to be a burden to their relatives. This is supported by the fact that on the one hand 95% of the population in need of care prefer living at home to institutional care but, on the other hand, are willing to live in an institution if the amount of care they need tends to increase.
ii) Burned-out-Syndrome of caregivers:
   The Burned-out-Syndrome denotes a state of psychical exhaustion caused by permanent overload for the caregiver (the caring relative).

Both problems are stressing the social relations and are leading to a lower quality of life.

2 The Role of Assistive Technology Systems (ATS)

The above mentioned scenario leads to the following tasks and functions an Assistive Technology System (ATS) has to fulfil:

i) Persons in need of care should be able to use an ATS in the full sense of a compensatory device which will widen their abilities by using their residual functions. The extended activity range will lead to more independence and increasing quality of life. These aspects are covered by the *environmental control* functions of the ATS

ii) Improved possibilities for *communication* (Telecommunication as well as person to person communications) widen the social range and increase the number of contact persons.

iii) Ensuring the *personal security* even in the absence of the caregiving person. This makes it possible that persons in need of care can stay alone from time to time.

Common to all three aspects is that they lead to more personal independence of the disabled or elderly person and to a reduction of the load placed on the carers [2]. This mutual relief creates a better climate for the development of interpersonal relations which, in this case, will not be undermined but fostered by the use of technology [8].

3 The AUTONOMY Concept

3.1 System Requirements

- Interaction with the system must be adaptable to the *individual abilities* of the user.
- The functions and specifications of the system must be adaptable to the *individual requirements* of the user [11].
- All assistive functions should be integrated in *one single system* and should be operated via a single user interface.
- *Multiple handicapped persons* with whatever combinations of disabilities should be supported.
- *Elderly people* should be accommodated by an user interface suited especially for aged persons.
- The system *complexity* should be *variable* within a wide range of individual needs.
- The system should be prepared for *expansion* and *shrinking*.
- Installing the system should require the minimum possible effort (e.g. by using wireless communication channels). So it can be used for *short-time applications* as well.
- The *mobility* of the user terminal should ensure comfortable operation for wheelchair users.
- The system should be equipped with a set of *security features* to warrant the safety of the user even in case of system misfunctions (error detection/correction, automatic restart, decentralized system supervision, automatically triggered emergency call in case of function breakdown).

3.2 Examples for AUTONOMY Basic Functions

i) Communication

- Operating the telephone by severely disabled persons. The great importance of this function is shown in the study from M. Ferrario [7].
- Communication via symbol-languages (e.g. Bliss).
- Synthetic speech output for speech impaired persons.
- PC operation by adapted input devices. Thus, the user can access all features of modern information technology like text processing, databases, reading of books stored on CD-ROM, computer games etc.

ii) Environmental Control (Remote Control)

- Remote controlling of lighting, window blinds, air-condition [17] etc.
- Remote controlling of TV/video/HiFi-Equipment and other pieces of consumer electronics.

iii) Safety Functions

- Telephone with emergency call function
- Operating the intercom and the door-opener
- Dead-man's device

3.3 Technical Realization

System Structure. To cover these requirements in an optimal way the following system structure has been designed:

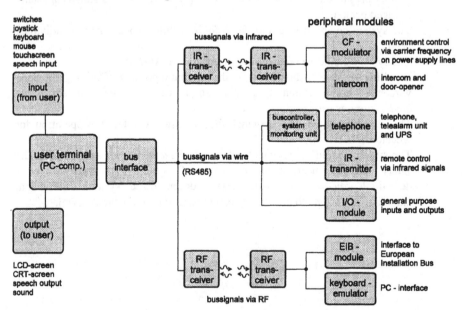

Fig. 1. Example for a system structure of AUTONOMY

The system consists of a mobile user terminal which is linked to the peripheral modules by a bus system. The user terminal can be connected to input/output devices tailored to specific user needs (e.g. input devices [3] like special switches, joysticks, standard or modified keyboards, touchscreens and output devices like LCD or CRT screens, speech output or soundboards). The user terminal has to handle the entire interaction with the user. To ensure optimum adaptation to the user needs and abilities the software has to be highly flexible and must be variable by configuration in a wide range. For this reason the user terminal is made up by a PC-compatible microcomputer (e.g. embedded PC). The PC itself is concealed.

The various peripheral modules are responsible for carrying out certain functions and for linking to other systems. They can be considered as building blocks which can be combined according to the demand of the user. Functional transparency of these blocks is important, as shown in the work of I. Craig and P. Nisbet [6].

The link between the user terminal and the peripheral modules is established by a serial bus. Data transmission can be accomplished by wire (RS-485), via radio or infrared light - or by a combination of these means.

A watchdog feature is implemented in the user terminal. System errors are detected and cause the processor to reboot. In addition to this, the telephone-module which is responsible for emergency calls performs periodical system checks. A lasting and not amenable system break down is recognized by the telephone module in a decentralized manner and triggers an emergency call.

The Software Concept "AUTOSOFT". The flexibility of the AUTONOMY user interface also calls for a maximum of variability in the area of software. To reach this degree of flexibility the following strategy has been used:

Fig. 2. The software concept "AUTOSOFT"

While A. Tronconi et al. distinguish two different phases in the utilisation of their system [16], we decided to distinguish two very different programs building up the AUTONOMY-System.

The essential program for establishing the user interface is hardcoded but imports all information about the composition of the user interface, about the functions to be supported etc. from an extensive data base.

This data base is set up and modified by using a configuration program. Implemented in the configuration program there is a test-mode by which the system operation can be simulated. This allows for immediate testing of a configuration without leaving the configuration program.

Nevertheless, modifications of global parameters like the timing of input devices can also be accomplished during the execution of the user program.

Menues and Icons. The basic structure of the user interface is composed of a number of hierarchical menues. These menues are defined during the configuration procedure (using the configuration program) and filled with functional elements. Every functional element consists of a part defining the user interaction (a graphical symbol, a piece of text, a phrase to be spoken by the synthesizer etc.) and a second part determining a function (execution of a list of commands, moving to another menue etc.). As the functional elements are mainly represented by their graphical symbol on the screen they will be called icons even if their manifold features reach far beyond the characteristics of usual icons (graphic symbol assigned to a certain function).

Structure of an icon:
- name
- graphic symbol
- text beneath the graphic symbol
- function (list of commands to be executed)
- speech pattern (for the speech recognition system) *)
- piece of prerecorded speech *)
- piece of text for the speech synthesizer *)

*) options

Functions. The functions are assigned to an icon as a list of commands. During the configuration all commands to be executed by activating the icon are entered into this list (e.g. "increase TV volume", "telephone off-hook", "open door", "move to another menue"). The link between the commands (which are entered as plain text) and the codes necessary to address and activate the peripheral modules is accomplished via a special command file.

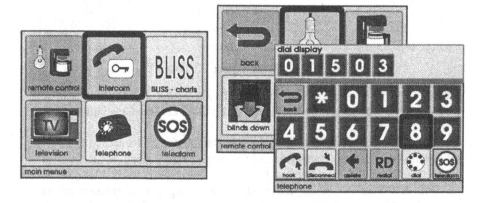

Fig. 3. Some examples for user specific screen menues of autonomy

Events. Events are things that happen in the periphery and which are reported to the user terminal (e.g. "The telephone is ringing"). Similar to the icons the reaction of the system to the occurring of an event can be defined by a command list. The advantage of this concept is that functional links can be established. For example: If the telephone is ringing the system can automatically display the menue necessary for operating the telephone; at the same moment the volume of all sound sources (TV, HiFi) will be reduced to a level not disturbing the telephone conversation. This will, in some cases, lead to significant time savings for the user.

The versatility of the "AUTOSOFT"-Concept. The versatility of the "AUTOSOFT"-concept can best be demonstrated by the following examples:

Example 1: Environmental Control (remote control). Within one single menue remote control functions for different devices using different transmission channels can be combined at will. For consumer electronic products remote controls reduced to the essential functions can be realised.

Example 2: Telephone control. In addition to the icons for functions like "hook", "dial" etc. any number of direct-dialling keys or even an extensive telephone directory can be installed where the command to dial a certain number is assigned to the corresponding icon.

Example 3: Picture communication (symbolic communication). The concept of icons perfectly supports picture communication. During the configuration step words or phrases are assigned to appropriate icons (e.g. using Bliss symbols). In order to be able to compile longer sequences of text and to edit this text before activating the speech output, the configuration of any icon allows options for immediate execution of the commands or storing the icon in an editor.

It should be mentioned that even a combination of symbols for picture communication with telephone operation is possible. By this means persons who are both, mobility and speech impaired, can get access to the telephone.

Example 4: Simulating a PC keyboard and a mouse. Part of the AUTONOMY-System is a peripheral module which emulates the PC keyboard and the mouse. By assigning commands for the simulation of keystrokes to certain icons AUTONOMY can be used to access any PC. As the keyboard/mouse emulation is accomplished by external hardware, problems with compatibility are a priori eliminated.

4 Special Aspects of the AUTONOMY System

4.1 Ergonomy and different levels of users

One of the main goals of the AUTONOMY project is the creation of a system with a maximum of ergonomic design in order to cover the very heterogeneous needs of the users (according to [11], [14], [1]). To achieve optimum adaptation to individual user needs the AUTONOMY system offers a variety of possible configurations for the user interface and the user program.

From interviews with prospective users of the future system it became evident for the project team that the ergonomy of the configuration program is a prerequisite for the ergonomy of the user program

The AUTONOMY system distinguishes (with reference to the work of Dag Svanæs et al. [15]) three groups of users:

- Level 1 users (L1U): Persons with special needs
- Level 2 users (L2U): Therapists, family members etc.
- Level 3 users (L3U): Experts, installers

The L1U is the end-user of the system which has been tailored to his/her personal needs and abilities. The L2U has a profound knowledge about the L1U's needs and abilities and is ready to work out a configuration which as much as possible fits the requirements. For setting up the configuration data he/she will use the configuration program. The role of the L3U is the initial installing of an AUTONOMY system in a way which enables the L2U to perform the individual adaptations without in-depth knowledge.

The L2U is supported by the configuration program which offers a MS-Windows-like intuitive user interface. Furthermore the present system configuration is graphically displayed for on-line testing of possible variations. It is assumed that the L2U because of his/her importance in configuration optimization will play an essential role concerning the user acceptance of the entire system.

4.2 Multiple handicaps

AUTONOMY will offer assistance for different types of functional impairments:

- *Visually impaired persons:* Persons with low vision will profit from the variable icon size (the number of icons to be displayed can be selected). In extreme cases only one single icon will be displayed on the entire screen. For blind persons an acoustic user interface can be configured. The names of the selectable icons will be announced by speech synthesis.
- *Mentally retarded persons:* They will use simplified procedures. For example a telephone call can be established by selecting an icon showing a photography of the person to be called without the necessity of knowing any details of operating a telephone.
- *Persons suffering from dementia:* Persons whose abilities are tending to decrease will profit from the system's flexibility. The system not only can be expanded to meet increasing needs or abilities, if necessary, a shrinking is also possible.
- *Persons with speech impairments:* They will use the speech output (text to speech synthesis or digitally recorded speech) for communication.
- *Persons with language impairments:* They will be assisted by the implementation of BLISS-Symbols.

- *Persons with motor impairments:* They will be offered various methods to control the AUTONOMY-System with a single switch and so on.

In case of multiple handicaps more than one of these functions can be implemented at once into the system.

4.3 System logbook and evaluation

All system-user interactions as well as other events which occur during the use of the system can be recorded. The evaluation of these recordings can offer valuable information for:

- the therapist about possible optimisation of the personal system configuration and about therapeutical progress achieved by using the system (progress in training).
- the system engineer about the acceptance of the implemented user interface during real application.
- the scientist to gain new knowledge about user interface design for persons with special needs.
- the technician for eliminating weak elements of the system during test applications (recording the history preceding system failures).

The logbook-recording is a background job which does not show up on the common user interface. It goes without saying that activating the logbook-function must be agreed upon with the L1U.

5 Future Aspects

Presently the here described assistive system called "AUTONOMY" is under development by the Working Group on Rehabilitation Engineering at the Vienna University of Technology. One of the next steps will be the manufacturing of several prototypes and the evaluation of the entire system. A co-operation with a support centre for physically and multiple handicapped persons is planned.

In care giving and rehabilitation the classical goals "warm", "well fed" and "clean" are superseded by the goal of helping the person in question to regain or keep a maximum of independence. Assistive technology has to fit into this concept. Thus the implementation of assistive technology like AUTONOMY must be part of the therapeutical program and must not be done in isolation. Only if therapy, medical treatment, social environment, barrier-free design and assistive technology work together in an optimum way comprehensive care and rehabilitation will be successful. This fact has been shown by Marcia L. Scherer in the "Matching Person and Technology (MPT) Model", described in [13].

Besides evaluating the concept of "AUTONOMY" in ergonomic, technical and social manners, one goal will be the development of a model for an all-embracing program of rehabilitation based on a holistic approach including assistive technology. This will be done in co-operation with the support centre for physically and multiple handicapped persons and its experts (e. g. occupational therapists).

References

1. Baeyens, J.P.: Introduction to and Summary on (Home) Health Care (Technology), in: Bouma, H. and Graafmans, J.A.M. (Eds.): Gerontechnology, Amsterdam: IOS-Press, 1992, 395-399.

2. Bogman, J.A.M.: The Application of (Innovative) Technology in the Care for and Service to the Elderly and the Disabled, in: Bouma, H. and Graafmans, J.A.M. (Eds.): Gerontechnology, Amsterdam: IOS-Press, 1992, 367-371.

3. Brandt, Åse: Control of Computers for People with Physical Disabilities, in: Zagler, W. (Ed.): Proceedings of the 3rd International Conference on Computers for Handicapped Persons, Vienna: Oldenbourg, 1992, 71-76.

4. Brandt, Å.; Seelen, B.; Biilmann, Z.: Why don't hospitals use electronic communication aids for patients who are severely motor impaired and who can't speak?, in: Proceedings of the Second European Conference on the Advancement of Rehabilitation Technology, Stockholm: Swedish Handicap Institute, ECART, 1993, p.1.3.

5. Carruthers, St.; Humphreys, A.; Sandhu, J.: The Market for R.T. in Europe: a Demographic Study of Need, in: Ballabio, E.; Placencia-Porrero, I.; Puig de la Bellacasa, R. (Eds.): Proceedings of the 1st TIDE Congress (Technology for the socio-economic Integration of Disabled and Elderly people), Amsterdam: IOS-Press, 1993, 158-163.

6. Craig, Ian and Nisbet, Paul: The smart Wheelchair: An augmentative Mobility 'Toolkit', in: Proceedings of the Second European Conference on the Advancement of Rehabilitation Technology, Stockholm: Swedish Handicap Institute, 1993, p.13.1.

7. Ferrario, Massimo: Experimentation for a counselling, personalizzation and training aids and technical devices for a personal and / or housing autonomy for quadriplegic people, in: Proceedings of the First European Conference on the Advancement of Rehabilitation Technology, Hoensbroek, The Netherlands: ECART, 1990, p.6.1.

8. Helle, Kari Marie and Tiller, Hanne: Needs of the disabled and solutions by computer technology including human, social and financial aspects, in: Tjoa, A.M.; Wagner, R; Zagler, W. (Eds.): Proceedings of the Second International Conference on Computers for Handicapped Persons, Vienna: Oldenbourg, 1990, p.123-128.

9. Lehr, Ursula: Langlebigkeit verpflichtet zur Prävention und Rehabilitation, Vortrag gehalten im Zuge der Rehabilitations-Herbsttagung, Tiroler Verein zur Förderung sozialmedizinischer Betreuung und Rehabilitation, Innsbruck, Oktober 1993

10. Martin, M.: People with Special Needs as a Market, in: Tetzcher, St.v. (Ed.): Issues in Telecommunication and Disability, Luxembourg: COST 219, Commission of the European Communities, 1991, p.55-60.

11. Read, R.F: Client Evaluation and Equipment Prescription, in: H. Murphy (Ed.), Proceedings of the Fifth Annual Conference: Technology and Persons with Disabilities, Los Angeles: Office of Disabled Student Services, California State University, Northridge, USA, 1990, 553-564.

12. Read, R.F.: Technology Delivery is a Technology, in: H. Murphy (Ed.), Proceedings of the Fifth Annual Conference: Technology and Persons with Disabilities, Los Angeles: Office of Disabled Student Services, California State University, Northridge, USA, 1990, pp. 565-578.

13. Scherer, M.J.: Living in the State of Stuck - How Technology Impacts the Lives of People with Disabilites, Cambridge, MA: Brookline Books, 1993.

14. Stewart, Tom: Physical Interfaces or "Obviously it's for the Elderly, it's grey, boring and dull", in: Bouma, H. and Graafmans, J.A.M. (Eds.): Gerontechnology, Amsterdam: IOS-Press, 1992, 197-207.

15. Svanæs, D.; Lundälv, M.; Poon, P.: The Specification of a Versatile Communication Aid and Writing Tool, in: Proceedings of the Second European Conference on the Advancement of Rehabilitation Technology, Stockholm: Swedish Handicap Institute, ECART 1993, p.P.III.

16. Tronconi, A.; Tronconi, R.; Billi, M.; Stefani,L.; Focardi, F.: A Multimedia Communication System for Severe Physically Disabled People, in: Proceedings of the Second European Conference on the Advancement of Rehabilitation Technology, Stockholm: Swedish Handicap Institute, ECART 1993, p.P.III.

17. Zegers, L.E.: Integrated Applications for the Home, in: Zegers, L.E. (Ed.): Home Systems, Proceedings of the European Conference on Integrated Home Applications, Amsterdam: RAI Congress Centre, 1991, p.1.1-7.

The project "autonomy" is going on in co-operation with
Legrand Österreich Ges.m.b.H.

Screen Reader/2 - Programmed Access to the GUI

Jim Thatcher

Interaction Technology
Mathematical Sciences Department
IBM Research
Yorktown Heights, NY 19598

Abstract: In this paper I will describe the Screen Reader/2 personality, that is the 'look and feel' of Screen Reader/2. As I do that I hope to give the reader an introduction to the Profile Access Language (PAL), which is one of the most important components of Screen Reader/2. This PAL introduction will not be formal, in the sense of careful syntax and semantics; I want to get across the idea of PAL so that one might want to program in the Profile Access Language to access the Graphical User Interface (GUI) of OS/2 and of Windows applications running under OS/2.

1. Introduction

IBM Screen Reader/2 is the only access system that gives blind computer users access to OS/2, DOS and Windows applications (running seamlessly). It is the only screen reader to have a fully programmable interface. Screen Reader/2 has grown over nine years in response to the demands of users in IBM and outside who needed the function for their work, education and home environments.

2. Basic Screen Reader/2

Screen Reader/2 for OS/2 is a follow-on to the DOS based product that was released in January of 1988 and upgraded two times since. Two things about IBM Screen.Reader distinguish it from all other screen access software; the separate 18 key keypad and its total programmability. On the latter count, the power of the programming language, PAL, is a significant distinguishing feature.

2.1 The Screen Reader/2 Package

Screen Reader/2 for OS/2 consists of an 18 key keypad, a keypad cable, some audio cassettes, some hard copy documents, and two diskettes with on line documentation and software. The keypad is attached through the mouse port. If such is not available, there is an adapter card for the keypad that can be used instead.

The software can be grouped into roughly five sections.

1. Screen Reader executables and dynamic link libraries.
2. Configuration files and utilities.
3. Installation utilities.

4. The PAL compiler and profiles.
5. On line documentation.

The keypad is used as an input device to Screen Reader/2 to request information from the display or to change settings in the speech environment. There are literally hundreds of states that effect how Screen Reader/2 responds.

Screen Reader/2 responds or speaks as the result of a user request through the keypad or because of some *autospeak*. In both cases the nature of the response is determined by the current Screen Reader/2 state and the PAL profile that is active. The important point here is that everything that Screen Reader/2 does is a consequence of some profile code written in the Profile Access Language.

2.2 The Role of Profiles

Profiles both define the basic screen reading environment, the Screen Reader/2 personality, and they are also used as add-ons to tailor that basic environment to specific applications when that is desirable or even necessary.
This aspect of Screen Reader is often misunderstood. The application specific profiles are developed for making applications easier to use. Everything that is done in application specific profiles could be done without them (probably), but with more effort (probably a lot more effort).

The simplest example of the desirability of an application specific profile is when the application has a status area in which, say, error messages are displayed. Using the keypad and standard core requests, the Screen Reader/2 user can read that area to find out about any messages without a special profile. With an application specific profile, however, that area can be monitored and automatically read. In addition, a simple application specific key sequence could be defined to read the status area.

There are about 30 applications specifically supported by the Screen Reader/2 product. These profiles are supplied for OS/2, DOS, and Windows applications.

Whether considering application profiles or the base Screen Reader profile, it is crucial also to understand that Screen Reader's behavior is completely determined by the current active profile or profiles.

2.3 Sessions

There is one base or core profile, called srd2.kpd. This profile textually includes the sub-profiles for the edit facility, mouse movement, icons, scanning, etc. These are all conceptually and syntactically part of the base profile.
The way this base profile works is that it is loaded and active when Screen Reader/2 is started. This base profile and any environment settings that might be determined by it, define what we call *default* Screen Reader/2 *session*.

Whenever a new profile is added to (we say *pushed on*) the base profile, i.e., the default session, that action creates a new Screen Reader session associated with the foreground process. You can save settings in that session, you can push another profiles for that session. When the process is killed the session goes away.

To illustrate this session concept, just imagine that there are two sessions, the default session and a new session created by pushing a profile for, say, the System Editor. Then you could be in *spell format* (where everything is spelled) in the System Editor session, and *text format* (normal reading) in the default session. Then any time you switched from the default session to the system editor session, you would switch from text to spell format and conversely.

2.4 The Nature of Profiles

A simple example will help to illustrate the use of PAL and the idea that any Screen Reader/2 response can occur as a result of a keypad entry or some event that triggers an autospeak.

Example 1

```
include 'srd2.inc'
Var TimeWatch: AutoHandle;

{1} Msg ( 'it is ', DateTime( DT_HOUR ), ' o clock' );

AutoSpeak TimeWatch
    Watch DateTime( DT_HOUR ) Do
    Msg ( 'it is ', trigger , ' o clock' );
```

The file srd2.inc has definitions of constants like DT_HOUR. The third line of PAL code above gives meaning to the 1 key, {1}, of the screen Reader Keypad. When this fragment is active and the 1 key is depressed, the message 'it is 9 o clock' is spoken. This line of PAL Code is executed when the 1 key is pressed. On the other hand, the autospeak with handle TimeWatch, watches the value returned by the function DateTime(DT_HOUR) which, the reader might have guessed, is the current hour. When that changes, then the body of the autospeak is executed. That body is also a message statement (Msg sends its arguments to the attached serial device). The value of the reserved variable, *trigger*, is the value that triggered the autospeak, in this case the current hour. So at the moment the hour changes to 9, the message 'it is 9 o clock' is announced, just like pressing key 1.

2.5 Basic Review Requests

Screen Reader has many standard review requests programmed into its base profile (os2core.kpd, included in srd2.kpd mentioned above). Each of these requests is tempered by the *Mode* and *Format* setting.

There are two reading 'modes,' called *cursor* and *pointer*. In cursor mode all reading requests are relative to the application cursor; in pointer mode all requests are relative to Screen Reader/2's own 'pointer' (called the review cursor by some screen reading packages). Because other screen readers do it differently, it is important to emphasize that there are many reading requests and all of them work in either pointer or cursor mode. The request is the same sequence on the Screen Reader keypad, like {2} for current line. Depending on the current mode, that will be the cursor line, or the line containing the Screen Reader/2 pointer.

There are five reading formats called *text*, *pronounce*, *spell*, *phonetic*, and *ASCII*. In text format Screen Reader tries to read as if reading a book. In pronounce format, punctuation is also announced. In spell format, all words are spelled and in phonetic format everything is spelled using the international phonetic alphabet. In ASCII format you hear the ASCII value of each character.

Again, I want to emphasize that all the basic requests are available and the result of each depends on the current format setting. There are shortcuts, however. For example, it is unlikely you really want ASCII format, so a key sequence is defined to give the ASCII value of the current character, and none to switch to ASCII format. Similarly, another sequence is defined to spell the current word with out changing the active format.

Here is a list of some basic review requests.

- Read the entire window or read from current position to the end.
- Read the current, previous, next sentence, line, word, or character.
- Move pointer to cursor, to top left, to bottom left, or to right edge.
- Spell the current, previous or next word.
- ASCII value of current character.
- Current character in Phonetic alphabet.
- Search for a string, search again, or search from bottom.

This list could be expanded, but such detail becomes tedious. There is a separate, though related, list which is important in portraying the Screen Reader/2 personality. As I mentioned above there are many components of the Screen Reader/2 state that can be set by the user, and in fact, can be different in different Screen Reader/2 sessions. The ways these state components are set is not so important as is the following illustrative (certainly not exhaustive) list.

- Mode cursor or pointer.
- Format: text, pronounce, spell or phonetic.
- Ignore capitalization or not.
- Announce spaces or not.
- Treat entire screen as single line (wrap) or not.
- Announce line numbers while reading or not.
- Use the dictionary or not.

The following are GUI specific.

- Hear drawing noise or not.
- Include icons or not.

Having just listed a sampling of Screen Reader/2 core requests, now I want to give a sample how some of these appear in PAL. Remember that we are not detailing the syntax and semantics of PAL. I believe that the examples will, for the most part, be self explanatory. The following examples are exactly as they appear in the profile, os2core.kpd, shipped with Screen Reader/2.

Example 2

```
{0A}  'read entire screen'
      Save( Wrap); Set( Wrap, on);
      Get(1, 1); Say(line);

{1}  'previous line'
     Get( row-1, 1); Say( Line);

{6}  'next word'
     Get( Nextword); Say( Word);

{*C}  'Ascii value of current character'
      Save( Format); Set( Format, Ascii); Say( Char);
```

A key definition in PAL is a key or key sequence in braces, followed by an optional comment used for help. After that is a sequence of PAL commands.

Only four Screen Reader/2 commands are used in the key definitions in example above. The *Save* command saves one or more components of the Screen Reader/2 state. Any saved component is restored automatically at the end of the command sequence.

The *Set* command sets a component of the state. In the statement sequence for {0A}, *Wrap* is set to *on* which means the entire view is treated as one line. The format is set to ASCII in the command sequence for {*C}.

The *Get* command positions a local pointer to a position specified by its arguments. When a command sequence is started, the local pointer is assigned the cursor position if in cursor mode, and the pointer position if in pointer mode. The local pointer's coordinates are always given in two read-only variables, *row* and *col*. The local pointer gets updated throughout a command sequence and is assigned to the Screen Reader/2 pointer at the end of the sequence if in pointer mode.

The *Say* command is used to send text from the display to the synthesizer (or other device). Depending on its argument, Say works on a line (or whole screen if wrap is on), word or character.

2.6 Editing

The Screen Reader/2 edit facility provides for feedback as the user moves the cursor and types. The edit facility is in fact another profile, and a rather complex profile at that. I don't want to explore the design of that profile here. (Neither do I want to discuss the question of whether or not the edit facility functions should or should not be built in at a lower level in Screen Reader/2.)

Instead I will mention the 5 major feedback options in the edit facility.

- **Line Browse.** With Line browse, every time the cursor moves one position to a new character, that character is spoken; when the cursor moves horizontally a word at a time, the word is spoken, and when the cursor changes row or the line changes as in a scroll, the new line is spoken.
- **Flush.** With flush turned on, each new edit facility response cuts of (stops) the previous response,

The Default edit settings are line browse and flush. In addition there are three echo settings.

- **Character echo.** Echo each character as typed.
- **Word echo.** Echo changed words as the space is typed at the end of the word.
- **Line echo.** Echo changed lines when move to new line.

There other options in the edit facility that can make life easier under some circumstances, including a margin indicator and a column browser.

3. Navigating around the Graphical User Interface

Almost all OS/2 and Windows applications respond to keyboard input as a substitute for mouse input. As a simple example, the window list (the list of running programs) is displayed using the right mouse button on the desktop, or using the keyboard combination Ctrl + Esc. One can highlight an item in a list by using the mouse and single click, or by moving to the item with the arrow keys. The item is invoked (or opened) using a double click with the mouse or by highlighting the item and pressing enter.

In general, a blind user navigates around the GUI with the keyboard. During that navigation, Screen Reader/2 provides constant feedback.

3.1 The Concept of View

Under the default settings, Screen Reader/2 always restricts reading to what it determines to be the main window and all text and icons contained in that main window. Because the word 'window' is over used, we call that rectangle the Screen Reader/2 *view*. As the user switches between applications, or between main windows, Screen Reader/2 automatically adjusts the view to the current main window.

Besides adjusting the view; Screen Reader/2 automatically announces the window title when the main window or application changes.

Once the view has been established, the view is treated very much as if it were a text window. All the text in that view is sorted by baseline into a certain number (*view.rows*) of distinct rows and each row is assumed to have the same number (*view.cols*) of 'columns' namely the maximum character length of the rows.

We believe that this simplifies access to the graphical view, though it is not always an accurate reflection of what is displayed. Our experience has been, with many users of Screen Reader/2, that this filtering of the displayed data is a help for review and that no significant information is lost.

The characters in the first 'column' cannot be expected to be seen to be lined up vertically as they are in a text screen. There is no implication about vertical positioning even of different rows. One 'row' might be huge and take up most of the view, with the remaining rows crammed in a small font at the bottom of the view, like, say, footnotes. One block of text could have a baseline just above a block to its right. These would be considered distinct rows.

Two blocks of text could be the same font, size and style and have the *same* baseline and still be on different 'rows.' This happens when the text occurs in separate windows. And the reason we put text in different windows into distinct rows is because, almost certainly, one wants to be read the text of those windows separately.

All the information that is ignored by this row-column access of the view is available to the user. This includes:

- The pixel position of each character and its size (*char.left*, *char.bottom*, *char.right*, *char.top*).

- The font, pitch, style and color of each character. (*char.font*, *char.pitch*, *char.style*, *char.color*).

- The pixel size of the view and its position on the desktop. (*view.top*, *view.left*, *view.bottom*, *view.right*).

- The identity of the window containing the text, the *window handle*

By calculations in PAL (we have not found reason to use these in basic profiles).

- Whether one row or column truly lines up below another.

- The amount of white space between rows.

• The amount of white space at the beginning and end of rows.

The reason the view is set as it is by Screen Reader/2 is that conventional review requests would be utterly confusing without it. Successive lines or blocks of text might come from different main windows and make no sense at all. As with most function and default operation of Screen Reader/2, the user can have it both ways. With standard requests, the user can make the whole display (or *desktop*) the view, or only the contents of a single push button.

Views are determined by the windows. A view always includes all child windows contained within a specified window. Thus the view determined by the desktop window includes everything displayed; the view determined by a push button is just the button text or icon. Pushbuttons are windows in the technical sense (except in the case of some Windows applications written by MicroSoft).

Views are not the only way of restricting reading. Viewports are rectangular regions within a view, to which reading can be constrained.

3.2 Using Controls within a View

A *dialog* is one kind of main window that does not fit well into the row and column format described above. Dialogs typically consist of several windows (in the technical sense, again) which allow the user to enter data and make choices. The individual windows (buttons, entry fields, static text fields, check boxes) are called **controls**. The user makes choices with the buttons, entry fields and check boxes; the prompts or headings are provided with by the 'static text.'

A sample will help. In the OS/2 Enhanced editor, a search dialog appears when you want to search for and possibly replace text in a file you are editing. At the top of the dialog are two entry fields. The first has the prompt (or name) 'search' and the second has the prompt 'replace.' You type in the string you want to search for in the first entry field and press enter.

These two entry fields and their prompts actually comprise four windows in this view, and four rows as well. As you move to them, however, with the standard tab-key movement, you hear 'search entry blank' and 'replace entry blank' respectively. When the data is put in the entry field, then the editing functions of Screen Reader/2 can be used.

Because of the feedback from Screen Reader/2 to the user, there is little interest in what rows and columns are involved, or the fact that the sighted user might say that the prompt and the entry field data appear to be on the same 'row.'

Continuing with this example, below the entry fields is a box (looks like a window and is called a group box) with a heading 'Options.' That box contains five check box controls which consist of small squares (about one-quarter inch) which may or may not have check marks in them. Each has text immediately to the right of the small square. These are used to select options such as 'ignore case,' or 'change *all* occurrences.'

As the user tabs into this area the and arrows around the check boxes, Screen Reader/2 responds with

'Group box options check box ignore case checked'

or

'Group box options check box change all occurrences not checked'

It is standard in the GUI to toggle the check state of a check box with the space bar. Hitting the space bar when on the ignore case check box, results in the announcement

'Group box options check box ignore case not checked'

from Screen Reader/2.

Finally, at the bottom of this dialog is a group of six *push buttons*, things like 'Find,' 'Change,' and 'Cancel.' When the user tabs to this group of buttons, and arrows around there, the information, is presented in a form similar to that for check boxes:
'push button find'
'push button cancel'

3.3 Mouse Actions and other Tricks in Screen Reader/2.

There is no doubt that not using a mouse with the graphical user interface is a disadvantage. It is quicker to do some things with a mouse than with the keyboard equivalents (when those keyboard equivalents are known). The worst part of this is probably the fact that help panels are written with the mouse user in mind. They often do not include the the keyboard alternatives.

Screen Reader/2 has done some things to make this situation better. One of the most important features is our *switch list*.

A mouse user brings a window to the foreground by moving the mouse to any part of that window and clicking with the left mouse button. If that window is totally obscured, either other windows must be moved, resized, minimized, or closed; or the mouse user can use the keyboard equivalent if they know what it is.

From the keyboard, Ctrl + Esc brings up the list of open programs. Then the Screen Reader/2 user can scan that list one at a time, or pres the first letter of the title, until the item is found and then open the folder or start the program by pressing Enter. This is a significantly longer activity than moving the mouse and clicking.

The Screen Reader/2 user can identify up to 15 windows (in the default case) and when they want to switch to one of their favorite windows (whether obscured or not) they just enter the number of the window preceded by the simple chord 89 on the keypad. Movement between a collection of standard windows becomes easier than the same task for the (sighted) mouse user.

The OS/2 2.1 desktop covers the entire display. On it are icons for programs and program folders and other objects like printers. To open (start) one of these objects the mouse user must find it, and double click. Other windows that are open are very likely to obscure one or more of these icons, and the only option here for the mouse user is to close, move, resize, or minimize some of the open windows. This is often a problem for the sighted user, but it would be a disaster for the blind user.

Screen Reader/2 solves this problem with an alternative desktop which is a normal folder object and can be brought to the foreground just like other folders. In particular the Screen Reader/2 switch list can be used, to make the desktop the current view.

As the last subject in this section, mouse actions (left and right button, click and double click) can be preformed with Screen Reader/2 at any time.

Think of the Search Dialog for the Enhanced Editor described in the previous section. As we discussed there, the normal use of that dialog is to tab or arrow key to the required spot, enter data, or change options with the space bar, and then press enter to carry out the action. An alternative is available for any application.

Using a couple of basic Screen Reader/2 requests from the keypad, the blind user can perform a mouse single click (chord 23 then 4) or double click (chord 23 then 5). So when the Screen Reader/2 user reviews the contents of dialog and is reading, for example, the 'ignore case" checkbox, a single click (using the keypad) will change the check state of the check box from checked to non-checked or conversely.

4. Some Technical Constructs in PAL

In this last section I will describe a couple of the unique and powerful features of the Profile Access Language. Continuing in the spirit set in the first section, I will not stress the detailed syntax of PAL, but instead illustrate the ideas with PAL code and descriptive text.

4.1 Autospeaks and Procedures

In the first section, *Example 1* showed how an autospeak could be defined to announce the time when the hour changed. The watched expression in that case was a function (DateTime) which returns the current hour.

This idea, watching a function or procedure, is key to a very powerful concept for Screen Reader/2; but some history first.

Ten years ago, when Screen Reader was a research project called *PC SAID*, we did have programmable autospeaks, but only to watch specified screen positions, and somewhat later, numeric expressions. In its early days, this was far ahead of anything else that was available or planned in the screen access area.

Lets review how the autospeak construct works. The syntax (roughly) is:

AutoSpeak Syntax

```
AutoSpeak <autohandle>
    watch <expression>
        do <Command Sequence>
```

The *autohandle* is a variable needed to query the state of the autospeak, and to turn it on or off. It is not important for understanding this discussion. The expression is just that, any expression in PAL. So you can watch a part of the display as in the original PC SAID autospeaks by watching, for example,

```
Display( 23, 67, 4)
```

to watch row 23, column 67 for 4 characters.

Then *Command Sequence* is any PAL sequence of commands.

The way this works is that the expression is evaluated periodically, say every tenth of a second. If that value changes (and stays changed for some specified time -- a detail that won't bother us) then the autospeak body (the Command Sequence) is executed. As indicated in the time example in Section 2.4. there is a convenient system variable, *trigger*, which contains the value of the expression that triggered the autospeak.

All of this is pretty much the same as has been available since the days of PC SAID; the syntax has been cleaned up and there are some conveniences. But what is truly new here is the fact that PAL for Screen Reader/2 has user-defined procedures that return values, and, of course, these can be parts of expressions. This is a major functional change, significantly increasing the power of the autospeak feature.

Why is this powerful? Because *in principle* it makes the autospeak construct universal, that is, one could, *in principle*, design and code an autospeak to announce whatever was desired based on the information that Screen Reader/2 knows to be on the display.

There are dozens of examples of procedures which are watched by autospeaks in the profiles shipped with Screen Reader/2. These are generally used to search for something, either in the given view, looking for some special indication, or sometimes in another view.

There are important simplifications implied by watched procedures also. It is good practice in profile development to write a procedure to obtain information from the display (from the view) and to use that procedure in a key sequence (for review) as well.

A prototypical use of this idea is checking for a highlight bar in a text based application running under the OS/2. This is a requirement for working with some DOS applications running under OS/2, but generally not for the OS/2 GUI applications.

Think first of a single row (say row 3) across the top of the display, with menu items on that row which are highlighted by changing the background color when accessed with F10 (usually) followed by arrow keys.

In this case the procedure (called *action*) to be watched checks row three and returns the column of the highlight if there is one and returns zero otherwise.

Example 3

```
proc action returning integer is
var place : integer;
    get ( 3, 1 );
    Get( diffattr,
         (char.color bitand &hff00),
         &hff00, +);
    if rc = 0 then place := col;
    else place := 0; endif;
    return place;
```

The key command in the procedure above is the Get command for finding colors (attributes). This is, in fact the most complex command in PAL. The first argument is a reserved word; you want to find the same or different attributes (*sameattr*, or *diffattr*, respectively). The second is argument is the attribute to be compared using the third argument as a mask. The forth argument tells whether to go forward to backward.

In our case we are to find the first occurrence of a color which is different from the current attribute (*char.color*) in the second byte (the background), and go in the forward (+) direction.

The return code (*RC*) will be set to zero if the search was successful, and non zero otherwise. Therefore the procedure returns the column where the different background was found it it was found, and zero otherwise.

Now if we watch this procedure with an autospeak it looks like this.

Example 4

```
var a: autohandle;

autospeak a watch action do
    if trigger <> 0 then
        get( 3, trigger); say( field);
    endif;
```

This autospeak results in the procedure *action* being evaluated periodically, and if action finds a highlighted item, the return value is non-zero and the body of the autospeak will announce the highlighted item because *say(filed)* speaks from the current position to the end of field, where a field is a contiguous sequence of character positions with the same attributes (color).

The application on which I am testing these examples uses the the same highlight for lists of elements inside boxes. When an action item is selected (with enter) the action item is no longer highlighted, and some other item is.

With an simple change in the procedure, *action*, all these highlight items can be announced, For this the *wrap* switch needs to be used (see *Example 3*) to search the whole view for a highlight. Then only minor modifications are needed in the autospeak as well. The following presents the completed example.

Example 4

```
var r, c: integer;

proc action returning integer is
var place : integer;
   Save ( wrap ); set ( wrap, on );
   get ( 3, 1 );
   Get ( diffattr,
       ( char.color bitand &hff00),
       &hff00, +);
   if rc = 0
      Then c := col; r:=row; place := row*25+col;
      else place := 0; endif;
   return place;

var a: autohandle;

autospeak a watch action do
   if trigger <> 0 then
      get ( r, c ); say ( field );
   endif;
```

4.2 Autospeaks and Events

As I indicated in the preceeding section, the expressions that autospeaks can watch provide a great deal of power over what was available for Screen Reader/DOS. There is another addition for ScreenReader/2. Autospeaks can watch *events*. Unlike expressions, which must be evaluated periodically, events are generated by Screen Reader/2, or even another process, and those events trigger the execution of the body of the autospeak.

Here is an extremely simple example of an autospeak on EventCursorChange that does a lot of what the edit facility (Section 2.6) does. It certainly does not do all that the edit facility does.

Example 5

```
var Edit : autohandle;
var r, c : integer;
```

```
autospeak Edit
    watch EventCursorChange Do
    if r <> crow then   -- row changed
        get ( crow, 1 ); Say ( line );
    elseif if abs( c - ccol) = 1 then   -- one col change
        get ( crow, ccol ); Say ( char );
    else Say ( word );
    endif;
    r := crow; c := ccol;
```

The idea of this edit autospeak is to say the line if the cursor line changes; the character if only one column changes, and the word where the cursor lands if the change is more than one column. The variables r and c are used to save the previous values of the cursor row and column which are contained in the read-only variables, *crow*, and *ccol*, respectively.

The following is a list of events available for programming access to OS/2 and its GUI.

EventCursorChange. A cursor being created, deleted, or moved.

EventDeviceIn. Input from the synthesizer or brialle device.

EventExternal. Another process can generate this event. Sample illustrative code is included with ScreenReader/2.

EventIndexIn. An index marker returned to Screen Reader/2 causes this event.

EventKeyPressed. Key pressed on the keyboard.

EventMouseMove. This event occurs when the mouse moves.

EventPointerChange. Whenever the Screen Reader/2 pointer changes, this event occurs.

EventProcessChange. Whenever the current process changes, this event occurs.

EventSelectorChange. A selector being created, deleted, or moved causes this event.

EventShiftChange. A shift key being pressed causes this event.

EventScroll. When window scrolling is detected.

EventSpinButton. Whenever a spin button control is used to change a value.

EventViewChange. This event occurs whenever Screen Reader/2 changes the view.

Acknowledgement

Screen Reader/2 is the result of the efforts of many people. The author has had a project in the Mathematical Science Department of IBM Research for almost 10 years and several people have worked on that project. The Special Needs Organization of the IBM PC Company is the organization responsible for making a research project into a product. They took PC SAID and made IBM Screen Reader. Many people have been involved there as well, developers, planners, and writers. Fran Hayden is one of those writers and she has been invaluable in making this paper more readable. Finally there are users. Those individuals both inside and outside IBM provided both the direction and motivation for the Screen Reader/2 effort.

Bibliography

1. Adams, F.R., Crepy, H, Jameson, D.H. and Thatcher, J.W., "IBM Products for Persons with Disabilities," IEEE GlobeCom '89. November, 1989. (1990) 496-502.

2. Adams, F.R. and McTyre, J.H., "Screen Reader: An Audio Access System," ICAART Conference Proceedings, Montreal June, 1988.

3. Boyd, L.H., Boyd, W.L., and Vanderheiden, G.C., "The Graphical User Interface: Crisis, Danger and Opportunity," **Journal of Visual Impairment and Blindness 84** (1990) 496-502.

4. Emerson, M.R., Jameson, D.H., Pike, G.G., Schwerdtfeger, R.S., and Thatcher, J.W., "Screen Reader/PM - GUI Access by blind computer users," Proceedings, World Congress on Technology, December, 1991.

5. "IBM Independence Series Screen Reader, Reference," The IBM Corporation, Amonk, New York, 1989.

6. Jameson, D.H., "PC SAID: Computer Access for the Vsually Disabled," M.Sc. Thesis, Trinity College, Dublin, Ireland, 1986.

7. Mynatt, E.D., and Weber, G., "NonVisual Presentation of Graphical User Interfaces: Contrasting Two Approaches," *Proceedings*, CHI '94., April, 1994.

8. Schwerdtfeger, R.S., "Making the GUI Talk," **BYTE**, 118-128 (1991).

9. Thatcher, J.W., "How to make OS/2 Talk and Why. Access to OS/2 with Screen Reader/2," To Appear, Proceedings OS/2 World Conference, July, 1994, Santa Clara, CA.

10. Thatcher, J.W., "Screen Reader/2 - Access to OS/2 and the Graphical User Interface" Submitted, ASSETS '94 (Sponsonsered by SIGCAPH - Computers And the Phiysically Handicapped), October, 1994.

Designing an OffScreen Model for a GUI

Dirk Kochanek

Universität Stuttgart, Institut für Informatik
Breitwiesenstraße 20-22, D-70565 Stuttgart
F. R. Germany

Abstract. Blind or visually impaired people get access to computers by using a screen reader. A screen reader is a special access program that operates on a database modelling the user interface and presents it in an appropriate form to the user. While in textbased user interfaces this database is fairly simple for graphical user interfaces a more sophisticated design is necessary. This article describes the design issues of such a database as well as an overview of a complete architecture of a screen reader system.

Introduction

For a long time access to GUIs was neither considered necessary nor possible [1]. This was on one hand caused by the high price of machines able to run GUIs. On the other hand the obstacle built up by presenting text as graphics (pixels) seemed to be insuperable.

With the advancement of technology and the accompanying breakdown in prices the use of GUIs became more and more popular. This trend is also reflected by today's applications. A survey among leading software producers conducted in 1992 has shown that 30% are only producing GUI-based software. 93% are producing some GUI-based software while only 27% plan to have text-based alternatives to the GUI version [2]. These figures show the strong need for suitable adaptations of graphical user interfaces for persons who are blind.

The complexity of a GUI due to its graphical nature is putting an additional mental load on blind users. Using a GUI brings also some advantages. All applications running on a GUI will mainly use interaction objects provided by the interface. For consistency interaction objects share the same lock and feel. This uniformity can not be achieved easily in textbased applications.

Screen Readers

A screen reader is a special program giving access to computer systems that are otherwise inaccessible to blind or partially sighted users. It will present its output in a form appropriate for the users.

A screen reader operates in two modes: tracking mode and review mode. In tracking mode the screen reader follows every change occurring in an application. These changes can be caused by an external event (i.e. arriving mail) of by actions taken by the user (i.e. keyboard). In review mode the user can explore the screen independent from applications currently running. The user has to therefore either explicitly enter a special review mode using the standard keyboard or implicitly by using dedicated keys or a separate keyboard.

Different media can be used to convey the information to the user. Synthetic speech is a quick and cost effective solution while refreshable braille is a more expensive medium but offers a unsurpassed notational precision. 2D or even 3D nonspeech sounds can convey information about status of positions that are otherwise difficult to present. Although most screen readers are designed to use only one output medium users will benefit from combining two or more.

The Pixel Barrier

Access programs for textbased applications are usually driven by events such as keyboard actions and changes of the screen content. Keyboard actions can be detected by hooking into the keyboard service of the operating system. Changes of the screen content are either detectable by hooking the video service of the operating system or by constantly monitoring the video (refresh) memory. Video memory is used as a form of database for retrieving text from the screen.

Access programs operating on a GUI rely on events that have to be filtered within the GUI. Monitoring changes of the video memory is, compared to a textbased UI, a time consuming task due to the vast amount of data that has to be compared (> 256K for a GUI vs. 4K in a textbased UI). On the other hand the video memory is no longer an easy source for text retrieval because text is no longer stored as character/attribute pairs. Instead every character is broken into several pixels. These pixels are points of different colour and intensity.

This „pixel barrier" can be overcome by introducing a virtual screen copy (VISC). The VISC is a database for information about every single pixel to what character it belongs to. This information can be gained in two ways. First by intercepting the process when a character is broken into pixels. This can for example be done by modifying the video driver. Second in reversing the pixel process by applying OCR techniques to either the video memory or directly to the video signal. While the last method has the advantage to be completely independent of the operating system and GUI it is difficult to achieve high accuracy and/or good performance [3] [4] [5].

The second problem that comes up when adapting a GUI is its use of high level interaction objects such as windows, menus, buttons and listboxes. Since the VISC will contain only information on a lexical level such objects are difficult to detect or discriminate. Several applications running concurrently are causing another problem. Windows of such applications can overlap making text hard to read. One solution would be to restrict the scope of presentation to the active application. Since the VISC is lacking such syntactic information as windows dimensions overlapping windows can not be separated.

Instead a database that modeling this structure is required. Such a database is then called offscreen model or OSM. It is also advisable to incorporate information kept in the VISC into this database.

Interaction objects

The elements of a GUI are called interaction objects. Basic objects are windows, a rectangular region with a frame around it, and icons, a symbol for a minimised application. Other interaction objects allow the selection of items from a list. In case the list has a fixed number of items the object is called menu, for an undefined number listbox. Actions or settings can be triggered by various forms of buttons. We can distinguish between pushbuttons, checkboxes, radiobuttons etc. Objects containing descriptive text are called labels or statics while those with changeable text are called text- or editfields. Settings within a certain range can be represented by sliders or scrollbars.

While the appearance and mode of operation of a class of interaction objects vary between GUIs the standard functionality of a class as such remains the same.

Design issues

When designed carefully an OSM should be suitable for different GUIs. This means it should be independent of the underlying operating system and/or GUI. It should be furthermore invariant from the source of information. So it should not matter whether text is retrieved by means of OCR or a modified video driver.

Taking care of these design issues a screen reader operating on an OSM will to a high degree be independent from the GUI. To simplify development and maintenance of a screen reader another level of abstraction can be introduced.

Sources of Information

Since the OSM is a specialised database the question rises how to fill its entries. Two methods of filtering text were already mentioned above (OCR and modified video driver). The source for syntactic information is the GUI itself. By using so-called hooks it is possible to get access to internal information within the GUI. This is a „legal" method since hooks are provided by the manufacturer of the GUI. On the other side access is somehow restricted since the hooks are often not designed to filter information for an OSM.

Another possible way is by directly modifying the GUIs' executable by means of patching. Patching can be prohibited due to security reasons since it changes pointers to functions which is in most operating systems an illegal since impossible operation because GUI and filter run in different address spaces. In systems with lower security like MS-Windows 3.1 where patching is possible however it allows access to nearly every piece of information that is considered necessary or has otherwise to be deducted from other sources in a more or less complicated way.

To simplify development of applications more and more user interface toolkits are used. By modifying or extending such a toolkit events for the screen reader as well as all necessary information to keep the OSM up-to-date can be deducted. Although this filter approach is only valid for new applications build with such a modified toolkit it is a very promising way since the information available is of first hand.

OSM

Nearly all GUIs are internally using a tree-like structure to represent interaction objects and their dependencies. Therefore it is only logical to choose a nth tree as basic data structure for the OSM since a tree best maps the internal structure. It also implicitly incorporates parent-child relations between interaction objects and is also independent of the type of information kept in one node.

The screen reader needs to perform certain operations on the OSM. These operations can be identified by the following methods:

instanciate: create and destroy a node in the OSM tree (fig. 1 a)

update: fill resources of a node. This can be either done by some set-value function or by directly querying the filter module.

retrieve: read resources of a node. The screen reader has to retrieve information in order to present a node.

navigate: allows movement in the tree. This can either be done by structure (parent-child / previous-next) as well as by position (screen layout) (fig. 1 b)

traverse: loop / for-each function that performs a given action/function (i.e. search). Possible processing orders are top-down and bottom-up in prefix as well as in postfix sequence.

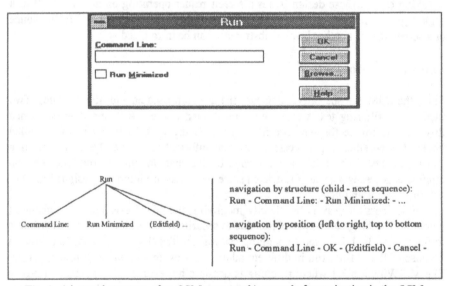

Fig. 1. a) internal structure of an OSM segment. b) example for navigation in the OSM

Different interaction objects have to be represented in the OSM. Although a common object for all possible interaction objects could be used a better solution is to have unique objects for each type of interaction objects. Different objects may have the same appearance. For example an application based on the Athena widget set will use XawButton as its button class while another build for Motif will utilise XMButton. This results in the need to map classes of interaction objects in the GUI to the class internally used in the OSM. Such a mapping should not be directly coded into the OSM source code. Instead it should be handled in a more flexible way i.e. by an alias list.

While different node types in the OSM already contain the information what object they model each node needs to hold additional information in so-called resources. Resources can be devided into three groups:

organisatorial:	an unique Id, the node type, pointers to "close" relatives, information source id
common:	position (x, y, z) and dimension of the object, its name, the widget (class) name of the object within the GUI
individual:	i.e. status of a button, formatting properties of a label or fontsize used in a textfield.

Since different classes of interaction objects most likely use different resource names a mapping mechanism similar to the one for classes is necessary.

Filter module

In order to have a uniform interface between the OSM and its sources of information all requests and their corresponding replies should be bundled in a separate module. This separation will make the OSM independent from changes in the filters as long as the quality of information remains the same. The filter module is also responsible to pass events that possibly cause changes in the OSM to it or the screen reader.

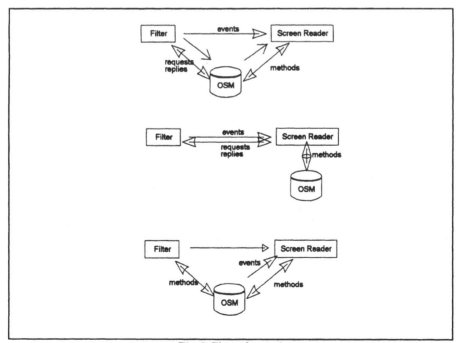

Fig. 2. Flow of control

Fig. 2 shows the flow of control in different OSMs and screen reader systems using filters. In a) the screen reader is triggered by events coming either directly from the filter module or through the OSM making the separate connection between filter and screen reader obsolete. Depending on internal rules update methods of the OSM are called. The OSM will then request necessary information from the filter and fill resources with the replies. Upon successful update the screen reader can then present the changes according to the chosen presentation model.

In b) the update will be more tightly controlled by the screen reader. Requests to the filter are issued by the screen reader. The resources in the OSM are filled with information extracted from the replies by using set-value calls. Although this gives a better control over what is updated it contradicts the separation between the screen reader and the internals of the GUI. This separation is broken because the screen reader has to deal with actions such as class mapping that should be a clear task of the OSM.

When a modified toolkit is the source of information the flow of control follows the one shown in c). Every change in the state of a filtered application is controlled by functions of the toolkit. The toolkit (filter) can therefore keep the OSM updated at every moment. From there on following the flow of control like in a) the screen reader will ask the OSM to update interaction objects. Since the OSM is always up-to-date this update will immediately report success.

Models of presentation

Depending on the quality of information available to the screen reader through the OSM and the output medium/media being used different presentation models can be used.

In case the OSM contains only lexical information a list-based presentation is most likely to be used. A hierarchical or spatial presentation is possible if lexical as well as syntactic information is available.

List-based or hierarchical models can be used with either speech or braille while the spatial model is only suitable for braille or a combination of speech and multi-dimensional sound or a combination thereof.

Conclusion

The proposed architecture has proven to be suitable and useful to give blind users access to three different platforms and GUIs. A working system for MS-Windows and X_windows has been developed in project GUIB. Future work is investigating the architecture of filters in NextStep. The increasing awareness by developers of GUIs of users with special needs will hopefully result in better integration of filters. Standardisation of interfaces in future releases or new developments of their products may improve the completness of an OSM.

Acknowledgements

This work has been supported by the GUIB consortium, a pilot research project of the EEC program TIDE (Technology Initiative for the Disabled and Elderly). I would like to thank my colleagues within the consortium as well as A. Vogel and M. Brandner for their work in X-Windows and NextStep.

Literature

[1]   Boyd, L.H., Boyd, W.L., and Vanderheiden, G.C. (1990): 'The graphical user interface: crisis, danger, and opportunity', Journal of Visual Impairment and Blindness, 84, 12, pp. 496-502.

[2]   Gill, J. (1993): Acces to Graphical User Interfaces by Blind People, RNIB, London, ISBN 1-85878-004-7

[3]   Schwerdtfeger, R.S.: Making the GUI talk. BYTE, Dec. 1991, pp.118-128.

[4]   Gunzenhäuser, R. and Weber G. (1994): Graphical User Interfaces for Blind People, in: Proceedings of 13th World Computer Congres, Hamburg August 28 - September 2, 1994, Elsevier,Amsterdam, in print

[5]   Harness, S., Pugh, K., Sherkat, N., Whitrow, R. (1993): Fast Icon and Character Recognition for Universal Access to WIMP Interfaces for the Blind and Partially Sighted, in Ballabio, E.; Placencia-Porrero, I.; Puig de la Bellacasa, R. (eds.) Rehabilitation Technology, IOS Press, Amsterdam, pp. 19 - 23.

Screen Reader for Windows Based on Speech Output

Paolo Graziani[1] and Bruno Breschi[2]

1 - I.R.O.E. "Nello Carrara" - C.N.R., Via Panciatichi 64
I-50127 Firenze
2 - IDEA I.S.E. s.n.c., Via S. Francesco d'Assisi 65
I-50046 Poggio a Caiano (PO)

Abstract. A so-called "screen reader", enabling blind persons to access the Windows environment, is presented and discussed. It is based on synthetic speech used to present information related to the graphic user interface and organized into a database. Some remarks will be made concerning the comparison between Braille and speech presentation.

1 Introduction

Transitory Braille and synthetic speech represent the alternative displays for blind people in accessing personal computers.

These two modalities present different characteristics, their advantages and disadvantages have been topics of much discussion. According to a widely accepted opinion, Braille presentation is considered more powerful and preferred by experienced Braille readers, while speech output should be reserved to blind persons who have difficulty in reading Braille.

Another criterion of choice would be represented by the cost of these technologies: a Braille display costs about ten times that of a screen reader based on speech output. This consideration would also lead to the conclusion that those who choose the speech synthesis are forced into doing so for economical reasons.

By analyzing this problem, this classification of blind computer users and of performances of technical aids does not appear entirely accurate. In fact, we can find a number of blind persons who prefer speech synthesis even though they are good Braille readers since, once they become practiced users, they appreciate the superior possibilities of effectiveness in interacting with the machine, and their hands free from reading tasks.

The initial preference of a Braille display has to be considered a prejudice caused by greater familiarity with this modality and the consequently easier approach to the machine by means of this method. The speech synthesis does in fact require more training and often presents, at the beginning, some difficulties in comprehension. However, this does not mean that the final result is less suitable or less effective.

Many view speech synthesis as a sort of "sonic Braille", i.e. a mere transduction of the same information, usually presented on a Braille display, into a audio modality, requiring the same approach for reading it. Also, the common name of "screen readers", used to indicate programs for accessing the computer through synthetic speech, appears inspired by this incorrect concept.

The term "screen reader" evokes the idea of a line by line presentation of the screen contents, like Braille displays generally do, and not of an intelligent selection of the various pieces of information according the needs and the class of the textual information, much like what is performed by the sophisticated speech program developed for the DOS environment in the last decade.

Incidentally, it should be observed that we utilize the name "screen reader" in the title of this paper only to use a generally accepted term, even if it appears much less adequate in Windows environment than in DOS.

In fact, the approach followed in developing the so-called "screen reader for Windows", in most cases, is not related to the graphic presentation of objects on the screen but on their logical concatenation, which is the relevant part of the information.

Only the access to the text displayed in an application window, such as a word processor, presents a problem similar to that of the corresponding application for DOS, but also in this case the "reading" does not necessarily consist of the line by line translation into voice.

2 The "Off screen model"

The GUIB project [1] approach to the problem of accessing MS Windows by blind persons is based on the reconstruction of the graphic user interface environment and the set of objects presented on the screen into a data structure, conceived in the form of a database, in which the relevant information is represented by the logical relationships among the elements, regardless their real graphic presentation. This is called "Off screen model" [2].

The database is automatically updated corresponding to the events of the environment through a system of filters contained in the runtime modules linked to the user interface. An appropriate language, called ERL (Event Response Language), has been developed by the project to collect, request, organize and provide the necessary information related to the events and the objects represented in the database.

A variety of solutions to the problem of effective access to this data structure have been developed by the project. The more general and effective solution is based on a multi-media presentation and interaction set consisting of integrating a large transitory Braille display, a speech synthesizer, a sound processor and a touch pad emulating the mouse.

Other less expensive solutions are under development to ensure different possibilities of access with a high level of effectiveness as well.

In this paper, a solution based only on the speech output is described, which is currently under development at IROE-CNR, in cooperation with a sub-contractor:

IDEA-I.S.E. We will utilize the experience of the development of a screen reader for DOS, called Parla [3], which is one of the most diffused in Italy.

3 The screen reader for Windows

Two operating phases are provided for the screen reader: a "Tracking" phase, in which a real time voice feedback is produced in relation to the keyboard or mouse actions, and a "Review" phase, in which a large number of commands are available for an off line exploration of the environment and to set a number of flags and parameters for the speech synthesizer and the screen reader itself.

A "hot key" allows switching between these two phases.

This organization is similar to that of the most sophisticated screen readers for DOS. Such a similarity also regards the interaction with the text contained in the "client area" of an application or the items of menus and listboxes.

In fact, in the Tracking phase, any cursor or selection bar movement is followed by the program and the character, word or line pointed to are automatically uttered, according the user's choices. This ensures control of any text editing operations or the selection of items in the other cases.

More specifically related to the problem of interaction with the software architecture of Windows environment are the possibilities of vocal feedback during the navigation through the tree of applications and the objects of the user interface such as buttons and dialogboxes. According to the user's choices, some pieces of information are automatically spoken in Tracking phase when one of these objects is selected or when a window is opened, under the action of a key or the mouse.

Also, runtime error or request messages for confirmation of a command can be uttered automatically.

The main differences with a screen reader for DOS concern the Review phase. Due to the complex environment and to its reconstruction in form of database, commands of exploration of such an environment are conceived to navigate along a number of directions inside the tree of objects, regardless the position of each object on the screen.

In other words, the database is considered to be a sort of hypertext distributed in a multi-dimensional space. This allows the blind user to realize the structure of the tree of objects much better than a trivial exploration of the graphic presentation in which the objects appear to be projected onto a two-dimensional space, and consequently their images often result overlapped.

Incidentally, we can observe that the analysis of the graphic layout would be very difficult without a panoramic vision.

In order to obtain an effective organization of the Review phase, it has been divided into four sub-environments: Navigation, Search, Text and Parameters.

The Navigation sub-environment is devoted to the exploration of the tree and its elements. a number of couple of keys are devoted to move along the different directions. For example, in the tree: up/down (parent to first child and viceversa), right/left (among children), jump to the top, to the bottom, to the beginning or the end of the sequence of children; inside a dialog box: rotation among listboxes, comboboxes, edit-fields, buttons; in menus: horizontal and vertical lists of items.

Text environment is devoted to the exploration of a text, line by line, word by word, character by character.

Search environment allows the user to search for a specified piece of information, such as a string inside a text, an item inside a menu or a listbox, the name of an application, a specified button etc..

Finally, Parameters Environment allows the user to select different operating modalities of the screen reader and of the speech synthesizer. A number of flags and switches are provided for these needs.

In addition, some special commands are available to produce artificial actions of the mouse, such as the movement up to a specified object, followed or not by a single or a double click. This represents the generalization of the "cursor routing" function provided from the screen readers for DOS and makes this screen reader for Windows a powerful tool for a blind person.

In fact, the possibility to replace the use of the mouse with artificial actions, controlled directly in Review phase, solves one of the main problems for the blind user in using the Windows interface. The mouse is not a suitable pointing device for a blind person because of the difficulty in realizing quickly the absolute position of its pointer on the screen. Usually, a blind person prefers to perform the same actions by means of key strokes. The real-time vocal feedback ensured in Tracking phase allows to follow the effect of the various keys for the interaction with the user interface.

The "generalized cursor routing" allows the user to obtain the same results with an alternative procedure, which can be more effective than the sequence of keystrokes in the Tracking phase.

In fact, this utilizes the powerful features of exploration of the Review phase in order to understand the logical layout, to individuate the appropriate action and to produce it directly, avoiding the repetition of a sequence of actions in Tracking phase.

We can observe that, in most of the interaction acts, the user does not know how or where an object is displayed on the screen. Even in the case of menus, the concepts of "horizontal" and "vertical" are not important. The blind user is free to imagine the environment in a different spatial distribution. The same occurs when a text is read, if the user is only interested in the content. (When we are listening to a radio-news or to a "talking book" recorded on cassettes, we do not relate what we hear to the written text that the speaker sees).

Only in some specific cases does the spatial distribution of a text result important, and the user needs to be able to perceive such a distribution. For example, in a spreadsheet or in a word processor, it can be necessary to verify the format of the page.

Usually, this is the case in which a Braille display results more effective than a speech output. However, the potential disadvantage of the speech can be compensated by appropriate functions to transform the spatial position into different pitches or even by producing a sophisticated stereo-phonic effect [4].

4 Conclusions

The possibility of an effective man-machine interaction based only on the synthetic speech as an alternative display for the blind has been demonstrated in textual presentations in DOS environment. A large number of blind persons successfully utilize the personal computer with speech output.

The new challenge is the possibility of a similar approach to the graphic user interfaces.

In this paper we have presented a potentially satisfactory solution which requires careful evaluation and probably some additional development. However, the first results appear encouraging.

This opens good perspectives for an effective and rather inexpensive solution to the problem of new barriers produced by the technical development in the computer field.

5 Acknowledgement

This work has been supported by the GUIB project (Textual and Graphic User Interfaces for Blind persons), in the framework of the EEC program TIDE (Technology Initiatives for Disabled and Elderly people).

References

1   Emiliani P.L. "Graphical User Interfaces for Blind People"; in Proceedings of ECART2 Conference, Stockholm, Sweden, ISBN 91 88336 19 0, 1993.

2   Kochanek D.: "Designing an OffScreen Model for a GUI"; in Proceedings of the 4th ICCHP, Vienna 1994.

3   P. Graziani: "Programma PARLA: Ausilio tiflotecnico per l'accesso al personal computer IBM-compatibile per mezzo della sintesi vocale", Report TR/ESI/08.93, IROE-CNR, Firenze 1993 (Italian language).

4   Crispien K., Würz W., Weber G.: "Using Spatial Audio for the Enhanced Presentation of Synthesised Speech within Screen-Readers for Blind Computer Users"; in Proceedings of the 4th ICCHP, Vienna 1994.

The New Wireless LinguControl

Walter Schmitt, Werner Zang

Klinikum RWTH Aachen, Fachhochschule Aachen, Germany

Abstract. Persons who do not have the use of their limbs are isolated from daily functioning in society. It has been found that pathologies like traumatic injuries of the spinal cord or diseases of the neuromuscular and central nervous system do not affect the function of the user's tongue. LinguControl is a tongue activated communication controller and was presented at the 3rd ICCH. The intraorally worn thin plate with encapsulated sensors was connected by cable with an extra-oral smart box having computing means. *The New Wireless LinguControl* version is an intraoral assembly with telemetric based transmitting of the tongue position to the microcomputer operated controller. The embodiment of the controller includes software for decoding the received signals and for converting them into infrared control signals to manipulate environmental devices.

1 Introduction

The number of disabled people is increasing in the general population. Some of these persons may have suffered traumatic injuries of their spinal cord, such as during automobile accidents or sport injuries, progressive neuromuscular diseases, such as multipe sclerosis and the like.
Rehabilitation technology offers a great amount of communication devices:

Mouthstick controller, a device clenched in the users teeth, leads easily to detorisation of teeth and oral occlusion. Additionally , a mouthstick controller requires a high degree of mobility to accomplish specific tasks.

Voice recognition systems require good articulation and volume. In many cases the speech articulation and volume of quadriplegics is hampered.

Single switch controlled devices require an action of breathin, chin movement and this like. A single switch controller does not achieve the desired speed to handle modern communication systems.

To have a near-normal lifestyle, there is a need for faster and more aesthetically acceptable communications controller. The New LinguControl is a universal intraoral lingually activated communication controller, that can be used by a large number of persons having limited mobility, to operate various devices.

2 Method

Eleven sensors are integrated in a 2mm thin smooth plate, which covers the hard palate and a part of the vestibule of the upper jaw. The basis for the plate is *Bioplast*, a biocompatible material used in dentistry. Two kind of sensors, an optical and a mechanical sensor were developped to fufil the selection criteria for intraoral applications. Furthermore *The New LinguControl* (Fig.1) includes   intraoral electronics for encoding the sensor signals and a radio-based transmitting assembly (Fig. 2).

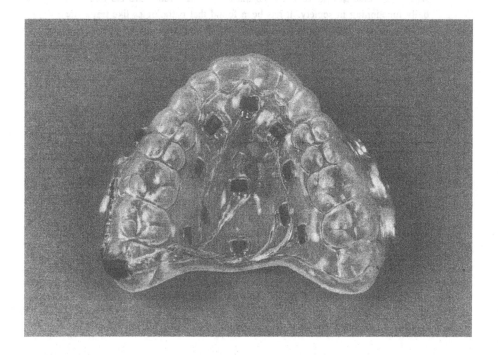

Fig. 1   The New Wireless LinguControl plate

Fig. 2   Diagram of intraoral electronic device

The extraoral controller includes a receiver for decoding the encoded signals.
A Mikrocomputer then forms a set of instructions and sends commands to the operating devices by infrared remote control (Fig.3). While using the cable connected LinguControl version, the user had to touch one of the eleven sensors with his tongue to activate a control command. Comparing it to the new radio-based version, while using the optical sensors, there is an important additional function. Here the tongue don't has to touch the sensors any more. By meassuring the reflected radiation of all eleven light barrier sensors, the telemetry transmits the intraoral positon of the tongue to the microcomputer operated controler. That means, that every position of the tongue in the mouth can be controlled by the eleven sensors. The next step is to programm tongue positions and to transform them into commands. This is done by the software *LinguLearn*.

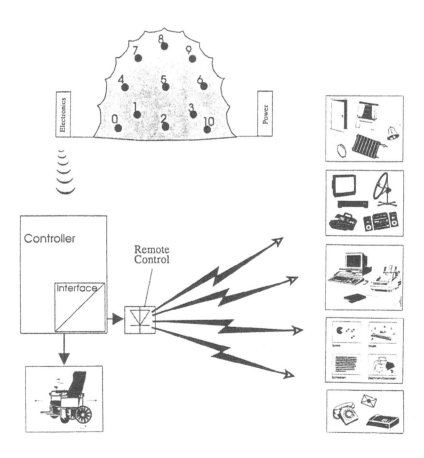

Fig. 3 Diagram of the New Wireless LinguControl system

For programming the system, the user has to touch a reproducable position in the mouth. The intensity of the radiation of the eleven sensors marks this position and the data is fixed in the controller. Howmany commands can be programmed depend of the mobilility of the users tongue and the users demands (Fig.4).

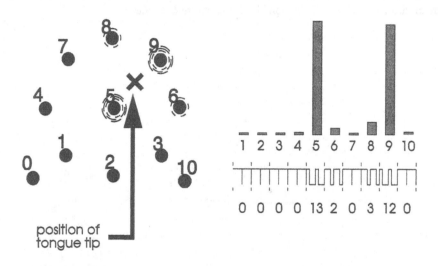

Fig. 4 Reflected light intensity and code of transmitted data for position of tongue tip

3 Results

While *The New Wireless LinguControl* System needs more intraoral electronics, a clinical study was realized to find out, where to place the electronic components. The study has shown, that there is enough space in the vestibule of the maxilla.
The dental plate is quickly accepted by the user in the same manner as other dental prothesis. To run the LinguControl system, the microcomputer operated smart box can be fixed at the wheelchair and powered by the wheelchair energy system. That makes the user independent from any outside cable connection. Error-free activation of the functions is learnt in the shortest of time.

While sitting in the wheelchair, the remote control intercom-phone and the PC-Fax-Modem make modern information exchange accessible. LinguControl can instruct the telephone to send and receive calls; phone numbers may be stored and redialed automatically.

Television sets, videorecorders, videocameras, satellite dishes or hi-fi receivers, compact disc players and many more electronic entertainment devices can be switched by the universal IR remote control.

Basic and special functions of the particular device can be programmed into LinguContol, depending on the users individual desires. LinguControl replaces the computer keyboard as well as the computer mouse with wireless remote control.

The system is independent of special interface software. It works with simple text editors as well as with complex programms. It opens up more fascinating and creative applications of computers. Music can be composed, changed and repayed in full orchestral sound. Colored graphics cam be painted. Last, but not least, skill or adventure games may be played alone or in company.

4 Discussion

The LinguControl system is aimed to return the user to independence in as many social and vocational areas as possible.

For this to be achieved any of the descriebed applications can be implemented.

Wheather driving an electric wheelchair, working on a computer or controlling domestic environment - LinguControl offers a multitude of possibilities.

The initial clinic results with regard to application and handling of the tongue controlled manipulator are more than satisfactory. The microcomputer controlled intraoral sensorfield provides an ideal means for the social and occupational rehabilitation of handicapped persons via application-oriented programs.

Ultimately, the range of the tongue controlled manipulator convers not only para- and tetraplegics, but all those, whose extremities fail to fulfil their biomedical functions.

The FeelMouse:
Making Computer Screens Feelable

W. Kerstner, G. Pigel, M. Tscheligi

Vienna User Interface Group University of Vienna
Lenaug. 2/8, 1080 Vienna
{gp, mt}@ani.univie.ac.at

Abstract. The FeelMouse supports the user by providing tactile and force feedback to the user. Depending on the object the user points to the force necessary to press the mouse button differs. With more or less resistance the user perceives harder or softer objects or objects which jut out more or less from the virtual computer surface. If the force is switched continuously a vibrating object is generated. In addition to "normal" usage the FeelMouse can be used to enable the work with GUI´s also for visually impaired people.

1. Introduction

Unless the usefulness of tactile feedback in comparison with visual feedback still has to be fully explored [2,3,4,9,10,13], there is some evidence for the integration of this form of communication. In [15] an attempt has been made to investigate the effectiveness of tactile feedback, using a computer mouse. The study shows that tactile feeback can provide an enhancement to visual stimuli for sighted individuals. For the visually impaired, the tactile feedback has the potential to become a partial substitute for visual stimuli.

Motivated by these results several universitary and non-universitary research institutions have worked on the development of tactile input devices mostly based on a computer mouse. All of the input devices described below combine tactile feedback with a pointing device. Some of them even provide force feedback. The tactile feedback of the multi-modal mouse [1] is provided by a needle which is pushed out of a hole in the mouse button directly under the user's finger. The tactile feedback of the multi-modal mouse is binary, i. e. either the needle stands out from the mouse button or it does not. This mouse has force feedback, too. However, it affects moving the whole mouse device, but not pressing the mouse button.

Another mouse input device with tactile feedback [6] has vibrating items on the left and right side of the mouse. Whether the left or the right or both items vibrate, depends on whether the mouse pointer is located to the left or right side of an object on the screen. The vibration frequency depends on the distance between mouse pointer and object. This mouse input device therefore simplifies positioning. As an improvement, the inventors tried to represent a part of the screen on the mouse button. For example the mouse button is a 8 by 3 matrix where every field represents one pixel of the screen. The user can thus feel a tiny part of the screen as a relief on the mouse button. Again, there is no force feedback intended to affect pressing the mouse button.

Hewlett Packard works on a computer system providing tactile and vibrational feedback on several kinds of input devices [7]. This computer system is basically based on stylus and touch screen as input devices although the same principle seems to make sense for mouse input devices, too. The feedback may be a continuous or pulsed vibration. The frequency and amplitude may be varying according to the selected position. The tactile feedback given when a user selects a soft function key may be different from that given when an icon is selected. For certain items, e.g. buttons, the feedback may be such that a physical click is both heard and felt by the user. Texture can only be felt if the user's finger or stylus is moving across the surface of the device. Therefore textural vibration is zero if the finger or stylus is stationary. The speed of moving the finger or the stylus is a parameter which is used to generate the feedback.

IBM works on a mouse ball-actuating device with force and tactile feedback [8]. The mouse utilizes a ball that rotates (rubs against) two shafts orthogonal to each other. In general these are only used for position sensing. For force feedback small electromagnets are attached to these X- and Y-axes. A host computer will provide a signal to the mouse when force feedback is desired. The signal determines the amount of current to be applied to the magnets to determine the resistance against moving the mouse along each axis. At full force, the mouse cannot be moved and the shafts act as a brake. Smaller resistances create various "feels". Different forces on each shaft allow movement in a specific direction. A momentary increase in resistance may act as a tactile indication to a user that an event has occurred. Actively changing the force feedback can provide an apparent "groove", or path of least resistance, which may assist the impaired. Tactile feedback may be provided as a "clicker", which can be felt and heard by the user. The click can occur once when stepping over a grid or as a continuous buzz when entering an illegal zone. A complex clicker can be implemented to simulate rolling the mouse over surfaces of various roughness.

As an alternative approach the JoyString [14] is a "T"-form handle which is mounted on three wires on each end. The wires are used to provide force feedback. Sensors on the end of each wire measure with how much force and speed the user twists the handle. These data are transmitted to the computer. Thus it is possible to move and steer for example robots. Special devices on the end of each wire can make it more difficult or at least impossible to pull a specific wire. This force feedback can be used to stop the user's interaction in a certain direction, if, for example the robot bumps against the wall.

A special kind of the VPL DataGlove [5] is able to give tactile feedback to the user. Small piezoelectronic items beneath the fingertips of the gloves provide a tactile feelable tingling (20 to 40 Hz sinus). This simulates the touching of virtual objects. The intensity of this impression (according to the force the object is grabbed) can be varied by changing the frequency of the piezoelectronic items.

However all the devices mentioned so far are either too sophisticated and expensive for the common user or too limited in the feedback they can provide. The FeelMouse (see also [11], [12]) is the first device which provides tactile and force feedback with a reasonable tradeoff between cost and performance.

2.   A New Approach: The FeelMouse

The FeelMouse is a mouse interaction device which gives the user tactile information and force feedback through changing the force which is necessary to push down the mouse button by a lifting magnet.

Usually users keep holding their fingers on the mouse button while interacting with the computer. Therefore, they feel the changing force as a kind of resistance which grows or falls. As every object may have a corresponding value of force, the resistance conveys the impression of touching objects of different softness. When the force is high enough, the finger is lifted up, when the force falls, the finger is lowered again. This gives users a three dimensional impression of the objects. They feel objects which jut out more or less from the virtual computer surface. The user therefore can recognize edges, borders, shapes or states of different objects.

By changing the resistance of the mouse button the force feedback is generated. This resistance is different for different objects or operations initiated by some screen elements. Some objects or operations may even be so "hard" that it takes much effort to push down the mouse button. This makes it possible to restrain users from selecting operations with protected objects or to prevent them from selecting operations, without any undo-possibilities and maybe terrible effects, if chosen in the wrong moment.

Depending on the application the required maximum force has to be high enough to generate an adequate number of graduations of force. The number of graduations has to be fixed, so that the difference in force can be clearly distinguished. It would seem useful if these graduations were logarithmic rather than linear. It would then be possible to recognize each of them more easily, as the next level of resistance is twice as strong as the previous (Fig. 1).

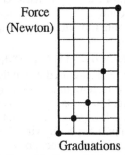

Fig. 1: Logarithmic graduations of force

In a usual mouse, the distance between the lowest (pressed down) and highest (not pressed down) position of the mouse button is very short. In the FeelMouse, there is a small lifting magnet attached beyond the mouse button. It is therefore possible to vary the distance as well as the resistance of the mouse button. On the one hand, the user should be able to feel the force long enough to recognize the changing graduation. On the other hand, the resistance perceived by the user should be as springy as possible. For both purposes it is important to keep the force upright over the total distance.

When the lifting magnet is activated, the magnet's anchor is pulled into the magnetic field. The force necessary to push the anchor out again will decrease the more the anchor is pushed out. In the above mentioned case a very strong magnet is necessary, as the force should not decrease beyond a certain resistance.

Another possibility is, to use a magnet with reverse behavior. This means, that the resistance remains constant or is even increasing, the more the anchor is pushed out of the magnetic field. This can be shown as magnetic lifting force curve as in fig. 2.

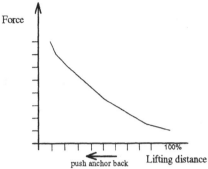

Fig. 2: Reverse magnetic lifting force curve

3.   Making GUIs Feelable

How can the tactile feedback of the new device be explored to make the structure of a GUI feelable? The FeelMouse as a new device allows communication between man and machine in two directions at the same time. The information the computer gives to users is primarily tactile feedback based on input manipulations of the users. The users feel this feedback as a certain amount of force at the mouse button. As different objects or functions have their distinct amount of force, users can already recognize the object when they point at it. Besides, they can recognize whether a certain operation might be allowed for this object or not.

What distinguishes the FeelMouse from conventional mouse input devices on the application side is, that it generates a three dimensional image of the flat visual appearance of the GUI. Moreover it adds different tactile attributes like softness or roughness to the elements of the GUI. These are the basic thoughts when improving existing elements (i.e. objects and functions) of window management systems.

A very important objective in designing GUIs is to exclude as many potential sources of error as possible. In order not to tempt the user, only those functions should be offered which are valid for the very context. In menu boxes valid functions often are black, invalid ones are grayed out. This is an adequate visual distinction. But how can the visually impaired users be supported by this mechanism?

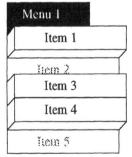

Fig. 3: Visual and tactile different menu items

Menu entries seem to be nothing else but buttons, combined in groups having similar functionality. An other way to distinguish valid from invalid functions is to add tactile attributes to these buttons. When a real button gets pressed, one has to use more or less effort to overcome the resistance of the button. By assigning differently high resistances to different states it is possible to recognize the state - valid or not - by simply pointing at the button. Fig. 3 shows menu items, which can be distinguished visually (color) and tactily. The force is shown as differently high levels of 3-D representations of the button.

A valid menu item (button) can therefore be selected (pressed) with normal effort, i.e. the force necessary to press the FeelMouse-button is on the average level. Invalid items cannot be selected, because the resistance of the FeelMouse-button is very high. This means for the user that this function cannot be carried out in this particular context. The high resistance of the FeelMouse-button symbolizes a kind of lock to the user, although the button could be pressed using very high effort.

If the resistance depends on whether the function can be carried out or not, it is also possible to provide no resistance for invalid menu items instead of a very high one. This means, if the very function does not exist for a particular context, there cannot be a button for it.

As another example for the utilization of the special features of the FeelMouse in human-computer interaction a dialogue box, which is a combined interaction technique for selecting multiple elements of a selection set, can be applied. All input parameters for a certain function are combined into a clearly arranged box, where users can easily manipulate them for their purposes. After changing the parameters, the box must be closed explicitly. Therefore there are often two buttons with different effects. When selecting the button often called "O.K." or "Done" the dialogue box is closed and the function will be carried out with the selected parameter. The other button is mostly called "Cancel" and selecting it closes the box without carrying out the function.

A severe problem seems to be a selection of the "O.K" button by mistake. This happens, when users only have visual feedback. Expert users do interactions faster than windows are drawn on the screen or even automatically, without looking at the screen at all. That means that they possibly click buttons without reading their labels, just knowing where to click. Moments of thoughtlessness - also with non expert users - can therefore cause severe troubles, especially when the UNDO-function cannot be applied.

In order to focus one's attention to a potential error before it happens, it is necessary to make differently severe effects of buttons feelable. Users are able to feel the difference, for instance of the "O.K." and "Cancel" button, before they even select one of them. The force necessary to select the "O.K." button may then be much higher than the force for pressing the "Cancel" button. If users expect the normal resistance of the one, but in fact feel the high resistance of the other button, they will certainly think twice before carrying out the action.

An even more impressive form of reminding the user is to cause a striking tactile impression by rapidly changing the force of the resistance so that a vibration is generated. This is possibly the most impressive form of reminding the user of critical interactions.

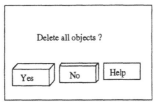

Fig. 4: Dialogue box with tactile buttons

Fig. 4. shows different buttons of a menu box. The more the three dimensional view of a button juts out from the box, the harder it is to press the FeelMouse button in order to select the appropriate function. Force feedback even makes it possible to exclude unauthorized users from selecting special functions. If the resistance of the FeelMouse button is maximum, it is equivalent to a lock, as described in fig. 4

A first approach to make graphic objects feelable is to transmit the visual represented three-dimensional appearance through tactile feedback to the user's haptic channel. Differently high elements produce differently high resistances of the FeelMouse button. This results in a realistic feelable impression of a tactile profile of the GUI. If one imagines the mouse pointer on the screen to be the virtual finger of the user, one may also think of a pixel of the screen as the mouse button. In this case it is possible for users to feel a single pixel and therefore to make very exact manipulations.

When users move the cursor across objects, they can feel their edges and surfaces. Fig. 5 shows lines on a surface. Along the inserted mouse move path, the user can feel the lines standing out from the surface like a relief (fig. 6a) or like being imprinted in stone (fig. 6b). In both cases it is very easy for the user to realize if the cursor points exactly to the object or not.

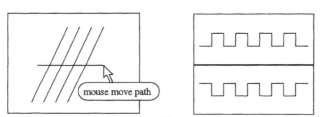

Fig. 5: Graphics example   Fig. 6a,b: Tactile profiles of mouse move path

Fig. 7 shows a simple text editor with a GUI. It allows saving, quitting and inserting text at an arbitrary position by moving the cursor. How can the new interaction techniques provided by the FeelMouse be applied to make the functionality supplied by this editor feelable?

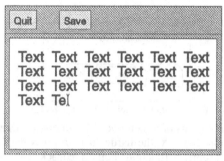

Fig. 7: Tactile user interface

"Quit" of course is a most critical function, which should not be selected accidentally, especially if the work has not been saved before. Therefore the feedback of the mouse consists of a vibrating button with a high amplitude. If there exists the danger of losing previous edits, the mouse button should also require very high force to be pressed. "Save" only is a useful action if there have been made changes to the text before. Therefore the function should be realized by the user by the high mouse button. If saving the edits makes sense there should be medium force required to press the button, if not, there should be no force resistance at all as nothing happens if a document with no changes is saved. To allow the visually impaired users to detect when they are moving the cursor into the area where text can be edited, the border of the text edit area must be feelable by a very high mouse button when crossing it. When the mouse is moved across a written word its button should vibrate with medium amplitude and low frequence. When reaching the end of the text and therefore clicking with the mouse button places the cursor correctly to append text, the mouse button should vibrate with high frequency to indicate the "hot spot". In this way a graphical interface could also be used by heavily visually impaired persons.

4. Conclusions

Visually impaired can be assisted in the use of computers in many different ways. One can enlarge certain areas of the screen depending on necessity. Research and development of voice interaction with the computer has come a long way. But research in the field of tactile input devices shows the importance of tactile cues for visually impaired persons. The FeelMouse has added to these support systems for handicapped computer users by providing tactile and force feedback. The FeelMouse makes it easier to orientate oneself on the screen by means of feeling. Computer users are now able to form a three dimensional image through the FeelMouse button on the objects on a two dimensional screen. Further research with the FeelMouse will include improved prototypes with a better magnet than used in the current prototype. User studies will clear up the still unsolved question of how many graduations of force a user can distinguish. It has to be taken into account that visually impaired persons probably have a better developed tactile sensitivity than non impaired users.

Despite of the many still unsolved questions experiences have shown that the FeelMouse is a valuable low cost input device for easier and more efficient interaction between man and machine.

References

[1]   Akamatsu M., Sato S.: *The Multi-Modal Integrative Mouse - A Mouse With Tactile Display*. ACM CHI'92 Poster and Short Talks, p. 60.

[2]   Bach-y-rita, P., *Tactile vision substitution: past and future*, International Journal Neuroscience, 1983, Vol. 19, pp. 29-36.

[3]   Collins, C. C., Madey, J. M. J., *Tactile sensory replacement*, Proceedings of the San Diego Biomedical Symposium, 1974, 13, pp. 15-26.

[4]   Craig. J. C., *Tactile pattern perception and its perturbations*, Journal of Acoustical Society of America, 77 (1), January 1985, pp. 238-246.

[5]   Foley J., van Dam A., Feiner S., Hughes J.: *Computer Graphics, Principles and Practice*. Addison Wesley, 1990, p. 355.

[6]   Göbel M.: *Eingabevorrichtung mit taktilem Feedback*. Offenlegungschrift DE 41 40 780 A1, 1992, Deutsches Patentamt.

[7]   Hewlett Packard Comp.: *Input device with tactile feedback*. WO-A1-92/00559, 1992. PCT.

[8]   IBM: *Mouse ball-actuating device with force and tactile feedback*. IBM Disclosure Bulletin vol. 32, no. 9B, p. 234, New York, 1990.

[9]   Jansson, G., *Tactile guidance of movement*, International Journal Neuroscience, 1983, vol. 19, pp. 37-46.

[10]   Kaczmarek, K., Bach-y-rita, P., Tompkins, W., Webster, J., *A tactile vision-substitution system for the blind: computer-controlled partial image sequencing*, IEEE Transactions on Biomedical Engineering, vol. BME-32, No. 8, Aug. 1985, pp. 602-608.

[11]   Penz, F., Kerstner, W. The feelmouse. In WWDU'92 Work With Display Units, Abstractbook from the Third International Conference on Work With Display Units, September 1-4, Berlin, 1992, p. P-22.

[12]   Penz, F., Tscheligi, M. The FeelMouse: An Interaction Device with Force Feedback. In INTERCHI'93 Adjunct Proceedings: Bridges Between Worlds. ACM, 1993, pp. 121-122.

[13]   Stark, L., Neurological control Systems: Studies in Bioengineering, 1968, pp. 297-337, 348-399

[14]   Tello E.: *Between Man and Machine*. Byte Sept. 1988, p. 288.

[15]   Terry J. A., Hsiao H.: *Tactile Feedback In A Computer Mouse*. Proc. of the 14th annual northeast bioengineering conference, 1988, Durham, NH, US, p. 146.

Unexpected Benefits of Voice Type Computing

Douglas R.Bowes

Special Education Technology British Columbia
Victoria British Columbia V8R 4C5, Canada

Abstract. Six of seven grade school students using Voice Type Voice Data entry systems experienced a variety of unexpected learning. Improvements in speech, breathing patterns, stamina and overall communication were noted in six of the participants. This paper looks at the partnership that produced this result as well as case synopsis for six of the users

1 Introduction

The Voice Project is a cooperative study among British Columbia schools and students, IBM Canada, and Special Education Technology -British Columbia (SET-BC) . Funding for the specialised equipment was provided by the Woodward foundation. IBM Canada provided technical and equipment support , SET-BC provided equipment, technical administrative and travel support and a speech therapist/technology consultant for research design and student training/support.

The objective of the project was to put Voice Input computing technology (Voice Type™ voice data entry) into British Columbian schools so that students with disabilities have the opportunity to produce their written work independently. The secondary objective of the project was to learn what adaptations had to be made to the equipment, to student training and to work environment so that users with speech disabilities could use it as an effective education tool.

Seven Computers adapted using M-ACPA™ speech recognition cards and IBM Voice Type™ Software were offered to students participants with physical handicaps in all regions of British Columbia. Students using the above configured computers can cause any keyboard command to be entered into the computer by using their voice . The student merely dictates his written work into a microphone and the computer transcribes it into a word processing (database or spreadsheet) document .

2 Objectives:

2.1 To allow the student participants to produce their written communication and written school work independently

2.2 To make the necessary adaptations to software, hardware and training methods so that students with specific disabilities could use this technology effectively and,

2.3 To examine if any improvements in oral communication (speech) occurred as a result of using Voice Type.

3 Measurement and Achievement of Objectives

The seven students in this project have a variety of disabling conditions including cerebral palsy, muscular dystrophy, and ALS (Lou Gerhig's Disease) and come from Elementary and Junior High Schools across the province. All of the participating students have great difficulty producing their written work without assistance, and most have significant speech difficulties that affect intelligibility.

All of the students increased their ability to produce written work significantly. Most of the students tripled their WPM output with one improving by 25%. Other benefits included increased speech intelligibility and endurance (see case studies).

4 Case Studies

Student S: As well as tripling her WPM, she used the Voice Type as an adjunct to speech therapy for the correction of a lateral lisp. The strategy involved using Voice Type to reinforce correct production of her /s/ & /z/ sounds. A Voice Type training session would follow a speech therapy session. If her speech production was good, the Voice Type would recognize the word, if not she had to delete it and repeat it "correctly' for the computer to understand. Initially, this approach yielded some good results, however, the effort required to do both speech therapy and Voice Type training in a short period of time proved to be too physically demanding for this student participant. This student carried on with Voice Type successfully, but probably has not made any permanent changes to her speech patterns. It is felt that the trial period was not long enough to successfully test the Voice Type as a therapy adjunct. (other potential Voice Type user have indicated that they are interested in exploring this approach)

Student K: This student increased her output from 7 to 23 WPM. Her ability and desire to produce written communication are demonstrated through her perseverance (as well as through the efforts of her school based team) in relearning the system after a severe deterioration in her health. Her illness required emergency medical treatment which caused a memory loss that resulted in her inability to use the Voice Type system upon return from hospital. This student and her team worked hard and soon relearned the system. K, a grade 6 student has recently written a short book 32 pages on her love of horses. Speech is only a peripheral issue for this student as her disability only had a marginal effect on intelligibility.

Student L: As well as tripling her WPM, L could use the Voice Type as an interpreter for those who couldn't understand her speech patterns. (The Voice Type understood her speech when others did not.) The computer had to be trained to ignore random respiratory noises that she made and the Voice Type rejection threshold had to be altered. The physical effort of speaking make it difficult for her to use the Voice Type for lengths of time greater than 20 minutes. Her use of the product is being reviewed by her school based team.

Student S2: Voice Type increased his output by 5 WPM. He felt that the 5 WPM did not justify his continued use of the Voice Type. He is striving to improve his adapted access on a regular keyboard. He feels good having explored the possibilities of Voice Input computing and is confident that he will do better with an adapted keyboard

Student A: Increased his output from 8 to 22 WPM and continues to use the system. Student A is a new addition to the program and little data is available at this time.

Student J: This student's breathing patterns were so inefficient (shoulder clavicular) that initially he lacked the breath and stamina to even begin training the computer. Amplification of his voice proved to be ineffective as it also amplified environmental and respiratory noise. Initial training sessions were also limited to 10 minutes because the student's stamina and endurance were low. Modified training sessions involved lying the student on his back to diminish the effects of gravity and inhibit his shoulder clavicular breathing. Diaphragmatic breathing patterns were taught while training the initial Voice Type vocabulary. Modifications to the Voice Type parameters include increasing the word duration and decreasing the rejection threshold. As well as being able to produce his written work when using Voice Type, this student can monitor his speech and breathing patterns as a function of how well the computer understood his speech patterns. If the computer doesn't understand, then he has to modify his breathing patterns. J increased his WPM from 4 to 12.

Student J2 had the most difficulty with the system. J2's education to date had him placed in special needs classes. Because of severe motor and vision difficulties, reading was well below his junior high placement. Instead of Word Perfect, this student used IBM's Primary Editor Plus as his Word Processor. J2 proved to have a very low literacy level, probably because of his poor speech, low vision and lack of attainable challenges. Training started with Dolch Vocabulary lists. Sight Vocabulary showed a significant increase during the initial stages of his participation.

This student transferred to another school district in the fall of 1993 and ceased using Voice Type because of a lack of trained support in his new district.

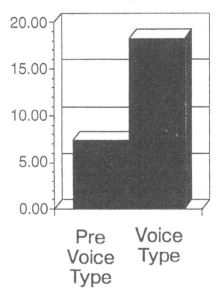

Average Change in Quantity of Written Output (WPM)

Benefits of Project

In Canada It is a fair assumption that jobs in the year 2000 and beyond will require much more technical savvy than jobs held by previous generations. As Canada turns from resource based industry to technical and manufacturing industries, employers will be looking for a new type of worker. More important than an individuals physical ability will be their intellectual skills and ability to interact with technology. Students participants in this project have access to technology that can make them competitive in the classroom and the workplace. This technology and it's future iterations will allow employers access to some great minds that might not otherwise be considered for employment because of the physical limitations of their bodies.

Change in Quantity of Written Work (WPM by student)

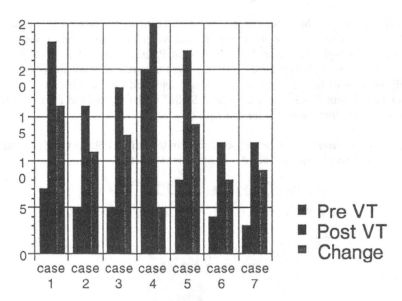

On average participating students using Voice type more than tripled their written output compared to previous methods using adapted computers. All but one of the students acquired the skills necessary to produce their written work independently.This was achieved by modifying word pause, rejection thresholds, posture, seating, breathing patterns and the training routines. Beyond increasing the amount of their written work produced independently, some of the student participants demonstrated an improved speech intelligibility and increased stamina (breathing and speaking).

Benefits of the Project to the educational institutions

Any school benefits when a project helps them realise their goal of of helping to make their students independent members in the community. By participating in the project the participating schools helped to remove a barrier to independent learning for their students. Most of these students used an adult scribe to produce their written work prior using the Voice Type system. When the student participant wasn't using the Voice Type system teachers and other students were encouraged to explore its potential for use with the student participant's classmates. Learning Disabled students and English as a second language students also made use of the equipment.

to the students The opportunity for student participants to participate more completely in their education is a goal that is more readily attainable because of Voice Type. Most students indicated that technology like Voice Type will be a significant factor once they graduate and seek employment.

to the teachers Any learning tool that serves a student through their school experience and leads to independent learning is welcomed by teachers. One of the first things a student is taught in school is how to write. This valuable learning and communication tool is denied to those students whose bodies cannot allow them to use a pen or pencil. The Voice project allowed these students to use Voice Type as an electronic pencil to write easily and intuitively for the first time in their lives.

to the parents Every parent wants to see their child succeed. None are more committed to the success of their child than the parents of a student with a physical handicap. The Voice project has helped to remove one obstacle to success for their child and offered a larger measure of independence for that child.

to society One of the great minds of this century is trapped inside a barely functioning body. Steven Hawking's insights into the nature of space and time would not be known today if computer technology was not adapted to allow him to communicate his ideas with the world. This project has allowed seven students another way to communicate their thoughts with the world . Time will tell if the their words will be heard as far and wide as Steven Hawking's.

Development of Long Term Relationships between business and Education

SET-BC and IBM Canada are now exploring the use of Voice Type 2 as a written communication platform for secondary and post secondary students in British Columbia. Preliminary data suggests that the new training module for Voice Type 2 significantly cuts down on the amount of training for users of Voice Type. SET- BC is now actively using a number of IBM products in BC schools for Visually Impaired students, physically challenged and speech Impaired students. SET-BC is exploring a project with GUS Robotics and IBM Canada to produce a made in Canada VOCA (Voice Output Communication Aid) for the speechless around the world. A prototype has been produced and trials are beginning at this time.

Robot control methods using the RAID workstation

Håkan EFTRING

CERTEC, Center of Rehabilitation Engineering

Lund University, Sweden

Abstract:

CERTEC intends to develop an autonomous grasping function, making it easier for physical disabled people to control robots, but first user requirements have to be studied.

Therefore, user trials have been carried out on the RAID workstation (Robot to Assist the Integration of the Disabled) at the Rehabcentrum Lund-Orup in Höör, Sweden, see fig. 1. This paper will describe the control methods used in these trials as well as the results of the trials.

Fig. 1: The RAID workstation.

1. Introduction

The flexibility of a pre-programmed robot is sometimes too low from the user's point of view, because the disabled user can only perform pre-programmed tasks.

One way to increase the flexibility is to control the robot in manual mode. Unfortunately, controlling a six-axis robot in manual mode is often very time consuming and increases the cognitive load on the user. The most difficult part, when controlling the robot in manual mode, is to control the final, small grasping movements of the robot arm.

An autonomous grasping function can hopefully decrease both the cognitive load on the user and the time needed to grasp an object. The user would then only have to move the robot gripper to the vicinity of an object and then start the autonomous grasping function.

Additionally, an autonomous grasping function will make it possible to program the robot without teaching accurate positions. This will make it easier for disabled users to program the robot themselves.

Before an autonomous grasping function is developed, it is important to study the user requirements. The following questions will be discussed in this paper:
- How close to an object can the users manually control the robot gripper within a specified time limit and by using different control methods?
- At what distance do the users want to start the autonomous grasping function?
- How much help do the users get from a TV monitor showing the robot gripper from a different angle?

User trials have been carried out on the RAID workstation (Robot to Assist the Integration of the Disabled) at the Rehabcentrum Lund-Orup in Höör, Sweden. The RAID workstation is described in [1]. This paper will describe the control methods used in these trials as well as the results of the user trials.

2. Control methods

At the user trials two tetraplegic users controlled the RAID workstation in various ways. Both users are able to use a mouse emulating joystick to control the cursor on the screen and to control the robot in manual mode. The users click with the joystick by pressing it down. One of the users controls the joystick with his chin, see fig. 2.

Fig. 2: One of the users controlling the joystick with his chin.

2.1. Automatic Mode — Shelf Number

During the RAID project only pre-programmed tasks were used and the user addressed a book by its shelf number. For example, if the user wanted to move a book from shelf number 11 to shelf number 12, the following menu alternatives were selected:

Menu 1: "BOOK"
Menu 2: "FROM SHELF 11"
Menu 3: "TO SHELF 12"

One of the aims with the following user trials was to educate the users in different robot control methods. During the user trials the menu tree in appendix A was used. Here, the user can move a book, by using two different addressing methods: Shelf numbers or book titles. The task above would require the following menu alternatives in these trials:

Menu 1: "SHELF NUMBER"
Menu 2: "FROM SHELF 11"
Menu 3: "TO SHELF 12"

2.2. Automatic Mode — Book Title

In the first part of the trials, the users also addressed a book by its title. A very simple database was updated automatically when the robot moved a book. For example, if the user wants to move the green binder to an empty shelf, the following menu alternatives are selected, see appendix A:

Menu 1: "BOOK TITLE"
Menu 2: "GREEN BINDER"
Menu 3: "TO EMPTY SHELF"

The database will find the shelf number of the green binder and an empty shelf, where it places the binder. If more than one shelf is empty, the robot will place the binder in the shelf with the lowest number.

The users were shown what happened when a book was borrowed and returned to another shelf. In this case the database was incorrect, which caused the robot to make a grasp in the air. To be able to grasp the moved book, the users had to update the database using the "NEW POSITION" alternative in the main menu, see appendix A.

2.3. Manual Mode

In the second part of the trials the users controlled the robot in manual mode. Manual mode was needed to be able to grasp a binder positioned on a table outside the book shelf, see fig. 3.

Fig. 3: Manual mode was needed to be able to grasp a binder
positioned on a table outside the book shelf.

To control the robot in manual mode, the users tried both the joystick for continuous movements and an xyz menu for incremental displacements of 25, 10 and 2 cm. In these manual modes, the users only had to control the position of the robot (x, y, z), not the orientation (yaw, pitch, roll).

Instead of x, y and z, the user was prompted for left/right, away/here and up/down, all relative to the user, see the menu tree in appendix A.

When using a two-degree of freedom joystick, the user had to switch between controlling the robot in the xy plane and along the z axis. The joystick manual mode is included in the French MASTER 2 system, which was used during these trials.

The robot starting position was: (200, 660, 1150)
The position of binder 1 was: (440, 730, 765)
The position of binder 2 was: (440, 590, 765)

This means that the robot gripper was 240 mm to the right and 385 mm above the two binders, from the user's point of view. The distance between the centres of the two binders was 140 mm. The distance to the user was approximately 2 metres. A technical description of the book gripper can be found in [2].

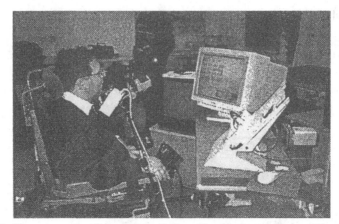

Fig. 4: A video camera was directed towards the table with the two binders. The view was displayed on a TV monitor standing beside the computer monitor during the trials.

A video camera was directed towards the table with the two binders. The view was displayed on a TV monitor standing beside the computer monitor during the trials, see fig. 4.

When the video camera was turned on, the users could see the table, the binders and the robot gripper from the side view, helping the users when controlling the robot along the away/here line.

2.4. Manual Mode and Autonomous Grasping

In the third part of the trials a simulated autonomous grasping function was invoked by the users, when the gripper was in the vicinity of a book, see fig. 5. The distance from the gripper to the book was measured when the users invoked the autonomous grasping function.

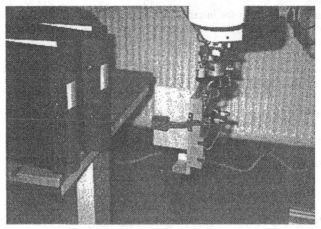

Fig. 5: A simulated autonomous grasping function was invoked by the users, when the gripper was in the vicinity of a book.

3. Results

3.1. Automatic Mode — Shelf Number

It was difficult for the users to see the shelf numbers of the books. One of the users would like to have a small piece of paper attached to the screen, to be able to remember the shelf numbers of the books. The database has this function, acting like a small piece of paper inside the computer.

3.2. Automatic Mode — Book Title

The users liked this way of addressing a book, because they did not have to see the shelf numbers of the books.

When a book was borrowed and returned to the wrong shelf, causing the robot to make a grasp in the air, the users wanted to correct the robot by addressing the book by its shelf number instead of its title. This just temporarily solved the problem. The database was still incorrect. The users did not ask how they could update the database, but they were shown how to do it.

3.3. Manual Mode — XYZ Menu

The time to control the robot from the starting position until a binder had been grasped was approximately 8 minutes, using the xyz menu. 75 % of this time was due to the menu response time, i e the time delay before the robot movement had started and before the new menu had appeared on the screen.

The time to grasp a binder was reduced to approximately 4 minutes when the users repeated the trials. The users began to remember the displacements to select in the menus.

The TV monitor did not reduce the grasping time. One of the users wished to have the video camera mounted above the table, showing the top view of the binders.

3.4. Manual Mode — Joystick

Using the joystick to control the robot, the time to grasp a binder was 2 minutes down to 1 minute. The time the users had to wait for the menus was approximately 25 % of this time.

3.5. Manual Mode and Autonomous Grasping

The gripper position just outside the back of the binders is 100 mm to the right of the grasping positions. Therefore, the positions, where the users invoked the autonomous grasping procedure, are measured to the following binder positions:
Binder 1: (340, 730, 765)
Binder 2: (340, 590, 765)

Using the xyz menu, the users started the autonomous grasping function when the distance to the back of the binders was approximately 50 mm. The time to reach this position was approximately 3 minutes. 75% of this time was menu waiting time.

When the users used the joystick, they first had 40 seconds to move as close to the back of the binders as they could. The final distance was 50 to 90 mm with an average of 75 mm.

When the users only had 20 seconds to move the robot, the final distance was 60 to 160 mm with an average of 95 mm.

The approximate grasping times when controlling the robot in manual mode are summarized below. The grasping times are presented in minutes and seconds (rough positioning time + fine positioning time = total grasping time).

Including menu delay:
XYZ Menu: 3:00 + 5:00 = 8:00
Joystick: 0:40 + 1:20 = 2:00

Excluding menu delay:
XYZ Menu: 0:45 + 1:15 = 2:00
Joystick: 0:30 + 1:00 = 1:30

4. Conclusions

The TV monitor, showing the robot gripper from another angle, did not reduce the grasping time. The reason for this could be the difficulties to distinguish the gripper clearly from a messy background, but when the TV monitor was turned off the users were unsure of themselves. Tests with the camera mounted above the table and on the robot arm should be carried out.

The users liked the simulated autonomous grasping function, mainly because of the reliability of this function compared to manual mode, but also because of the short grasping time:
13 seconds (including menu delay)
6 seconds (excluding menu delay)
However, a real autonomous grasping function will probably be slower.

The autonomous grasping function should be able to find and grasp an object from a distance of 100 mm. This position could be reached by the users in approximately 30 seconds using either xyz menus or a joystick.

When objects are smaller than binders and positioned closer to each other, the autonomous grasping function could have difficulties to find the correct object. Further user trials should be carried out with objects of different sizes.

5. Acknowledgements

I would like to thank the RAID partners for developing the RAID workstation, the Swedish foundation "Stiftelsen för bistånd åt vanföra i Skåne" for funding this project and last but not least the users for their participation.

References

[1]   J L Dallaway, R D Jackson
        RAID — A Vocational Robotic Workstation
        Proceedings of ICORR 92,
        Keele University, UK, 1992.

[2]   G Bolmsjö, H Eftring
        RAID, Robotic end-effector developments
        Proceedings of the 1st TIDE Congress,
        pp 108-112, Brussels, Belgium, 1993.

Håkan Eftring
CERTEC / LTH
Lund University
Box 118
S - 221 00 LUND
SWEDEN

E-mail: Hakan.Eftring@certec.lth.se

Appendix A

The following menu tree was used during the user trials:

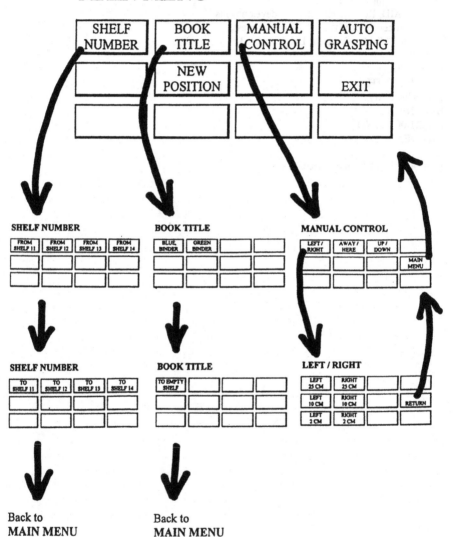

MAIN MENU

SHELF NUMBER | **BOOK TITLE** | **MANUAL CONTROL**

Back to **MAIN MENU**

Back to **MAIN MENU**

The ultrasonic navigating robot, WALKY

Håkan Neveryd [1,2], Gunnar Bolmsjö [2]
[1]CERTEC, Center of Rehabilitation Engineering, Lund University, Sweden
[2]DPME, Dept. of Production and Materials Engineering, Lund University, Sweden

ABSTRACT
A mobile robot system is being designed to work in a chemical laboratory environment for people with physical disabilities. We have found that chemical laboratories are good workplace alternatives to the office environment (see BACKGROUND). The main requirement for the workplace is to keep the work meaningful after the workplace has been robotized. The reasons for working with a mobile robot system are numerous:

- high flexibility for the disabled (the possibility to move between different workstations).
- only small changes in the physical environment are necessary.
- possibilities for the disabled and the non-disabled to use the same laboratory equipment.

BACKGROUND
The aim of this project is to get injured people back to work earlier and to increase employment possibilities for the disabled, including severely disabled. Earlier attempts to design service robots for the disabled in Sweden have been for the office environment. People with disabilities are neither more nor less interested or competent in administrative work than people without disability. We have also found that a laboratory could be a good working environment. We have found three different work-stations which are suitable for robotization:

- microscoping, for example cell exami-nation, cell and chromosome counting.
- blood group determination.
- culture analysing.

THE DESIGN OF THE MOBILE ROBOT SYSTEM
The mobile robot system consists of the following main components:

- Mobil base, Labmate
- Robot, Scorbot ER VII
- Sensor system
- Wireless radio modem
- Communication computer
- Local network

The outside dimensions of WALKY's base are 700 x 750 mm and the height is 1350 mm (when the elbow is in the upper position).

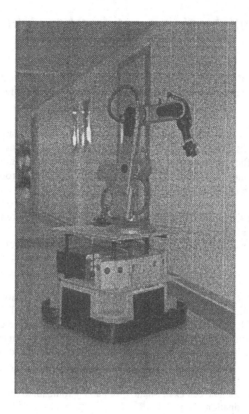

Fig 1   The ultrasonic navigating robot, Walky

SENSOR SYSTEM
It is possible to connect 3 interface boards to the sensor system. To each interface board 8 ultrasonic and 8 infrared sensors can be connected .
The task for the sensors in this project is to measure distance. The infrared sensor technology has difficulties with:

* Sensitivity to ambient temperature
* Relatively directional
* Narrow and non uniform field of view

And the ultrasonic sensor technology has difficulties with:

* Object must be non porous
* Very directional (10°-30°) with incident angle less than 15°
* Temperature sensitive
* False detection

In the beginning of the project we have chosen to only use ultrasonic sensors.

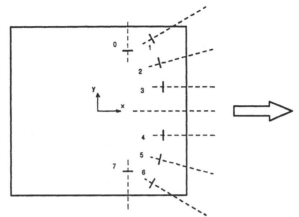

Fig 2   TheWALKY's sensor positions

The WALKY's sensor positions are a modified variant of the IPAMAR[1] mobile robot. The IPAMAR is a mobile autonomous robot (MAR) developed at the Fraunhofer Institute for Manufacturing Engineering and Automation (IPA) for carrying parts and products between the work cells of a factory.

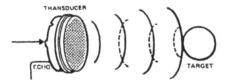

Fig 3   The Polaroid transducer

Ultrasound sensing, based upon the speed of sound, depends upon producing a high frequency; sound wave (above 20 kHz), transmitting the sound wave, and then measuring the time interval from the sound burst until a reflection returns from a target surface. A problem with ultrasonic sensors is that the speed of sound is a function of temperature also relative humidity.

The speed of sound varies only slightly with humidity, max 0,35% at 20°C.

The speed of sound in air is determined from the following relationship:

$$v_c = 331.4 \cdot \sqrt{\frac{T}{273}}$$

where T is the ambient temperature in degrees Kelvin and v_c is the speed of sound in m/s. If the temperature changes 28°, the variation of the speed of sound is 5%.

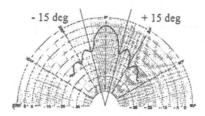

Fig 4   Typical beam pattern at 50 kHz

The Polaroid ultrasonic sensor [2] has full angle beam width (Figure 4) of 50 kHz at approximately ± 15 degrees. The sensor is capable of detecting the presence and distance of objects within a range of approximately 27 cm to 10,7 m.

SCENARIO

The functionality of mobile systems can be described by the following scenario.

The operator is sitting by his/her workplace. He/she would like to fetch an object from another workplace. Through his/her computer the operator commands to the mobile robot system to go a predestined position at the other workplace. (The communication between the computer and the mobile robot system is handle by a wireless network.) If there isn't any obstacle between the start and end position, the mobile robot system drives directly to the end position.

If there is an obstacle, for example a chair, the mobile robot system drives in front of the chair. The sensor system gives enough information, for the mobile robot system to find a way around the obstacle. If there isn't any way around the obstacle the mobile system drives back to the start position.

Should any person obstruct the mobile robot system, it stops immediately due to information from the sensor system. If the sensor system would fail, the emergency system stops the robot system by physical contact between the person and the bumpers on the mobile base.

When the mobile system reaches the end position, the specified object is identified and grasped. Object identification is required, when the environment is unstructured. The grasping of the object and the transportation of the robot arm can be controlled by either pre-programmed routines or direct control. Also, a combination of pre-programmed routines and direct control will be possible.

SAFETY

When the evaluation of tasks has been done to select the meaningful work tasks which should be left after the robotization, the following research and development work remained:

- Safety.
- User friendliness.

The safety aspects should be solved by the sensor system [3]. If an object enters:

- *the ignored zone*, nothing happens.

- *the obstacle detection zone*, the speed is slowed to 70% of the normal speed.

- *the reflex zone*, the speed is slowed to 50% of the normal speed and WALKY tries to avoid obstacle.

- *the safety zone*, a signal is transferred from the sensor to the controller of the mobile base. The base stops immediately. If this system fails, the bumpers on the Labmate stop the vehicle on contact.

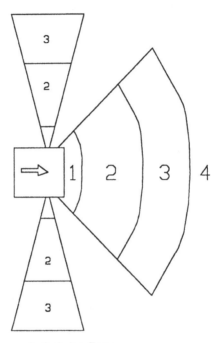

1ı Safety Zone
2ı Reflex Zone
3ı Obstacle Detection Zone
4ı Ignored Zone

Fig 5   The detection zones

USER INTERFACE

The program moves the robot base with the aid of information from an Autocad drawing which describes the space in which the robot base can be manoeuvred. The drawing contains walls, doors, furniture and other objects which can limit the movements of the robot base.

The Autocad file must be in the DXF format, Autcad's format for file transfer between Autocad and other programs, where the drawing is defined as a set of Autocad primitives: Line, Circle, Point, PolyLine, Arc and Solid. The program stores the drawing as a list of these primitives.

When the drawing is read, it is shown in a window within the main program window on the screen. To complete the initialization before the program is ready to use, the synchronization must be done. The synchronization connects the co-ordinate system of the robot base with the co-ordinate system of the program, so that the program knows where in the drawing the robot base is.

When the initialization is done, the user can move the robot base in two ways – either with the arrow keys on the keyboard or via the menus. When navigating the robot base from the menus the user points on the drawing shown on the screen with the mouse, where he or she wants the robot base to be moved. The program then calculates the best path to that point and moves the robot base according to that path.

The program is written in C++ for the Microsoft Windows graphical environment and uses the ObjectsWindows package included with the Borland C++ compiler.

ACKNOWLEDGEMENTS

The financial support under contract number 91-0414 of the Swedish Work Environment Fund is gratefully acknowledged.

REFERENCES

[1] Kacandes, Langen, Warnecke, A combined generalized potential field/ Dynamic path planning approach to collision avoidance for a mobile autonomous robot operating in a constrained environment, Proceedings of an International Conference of Intelligent Autonomous System, 11-14 December 1989 Amsterdam, The Netherlands

[2] Biber, Ellin, Shenk, Stempeck , The Polaroid ultrasonic ranging system, Presented at the 67th AES Convention, 31 October-3 November 1980, New York, USA

[3]Dietriche, Gelin, Ploix, Lambert, Mal-blanc, Assisted guidance device for electric wheelchair, The 1992 International Con-ference on Rehabilitation Robotics, 15-16 September 1992, Keele University, Staffordshire, England

Håkan Neveryd
CERTEC/LTH
Lund University
Box 118
S-221 00 LUND
SWEDEN
e-mail: hakan.neveryd@certec.lth.se

Prof. G. Bolmsjö
Dept of Production and Material Engineer-ing/LTH
Lund University
Box 118
221 00 LUND
SWEDEN
e-mail: gunnar.bolmsjo@mtov.lth.se

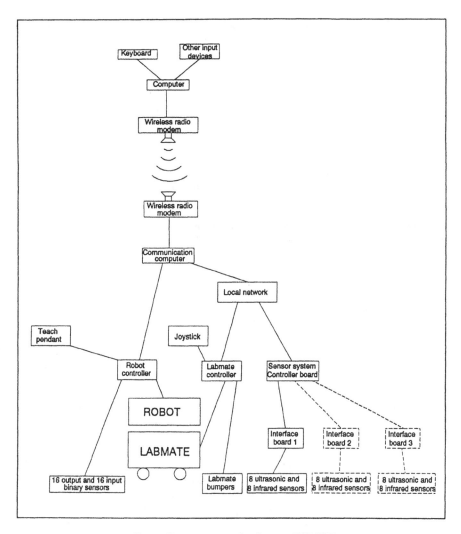

Fig 6   Diagram over the design of WALKY

NavChair: An Example of a Shared-Control System for Assistive Technologies

Simon P. Levine[1,3], David A. Bell[1,2], and Yoram Koren[2,3]

Rehabilitation Engineering Program, Dept. of Physical Medicine and Rehabilitation[1];
Dept. of Mechanical Engineering[2]; and Graduate Bioengineering Program[3]
University of Michigan

Abstract. The NavChair assistive navigation system was originally conceived as an application of mobile robot obstacle avoidance to a power wheelchair. In this system, the user shares wheelchair control with obstacle avoidance and other navigation components. The philosophy of shared control has important implications for the design of these components. This paper discusses the development of navigation methods for the NavChair guided by design criteria for shared control systems.

1 Introduction

Human-machine systems in which control of a function is allocated between the user and machine can be termed shared-control systems. Such systems have the potential to achieve desired outcomes which neither the user or machine could achieve independently [18]. Adaptive shared-control systems go one step further by adapting the machine, over time, in response to changing human behavioral characteristics and/or environmental features. Adaptive shared-control systems offer a promise of significantly increased function for individuals who require the use of assistive technologies [11,16].

The NavChair assistive navigation system is being developed to safely improve the mobility of people with motor, sensory, cognitive, and/or perceptual impairments that limit their ability to operate a power wheelchair [13,8,12]. The NavChair control system is designed to avoid obstacles, travel safely through doors, and provide other forms of navigation assistance under the direction of the wheelchair user. It is an example of an adaptive shared-control assistive technology system.

The NavChair's shared-control architecture allows users to remain in high-level control while benefiting from the improvements provided by the navigation capabilities [3]. The user indicates the desired direction and speed of travel while various navigation routines modify the user's command, if necessary, to provide improved navigation and safety through a combination of changing the direction of travel and slowing the chair.

Adaptability allows the NavChair to perform well under a wide variety of conditions and is incorporated into the NavChair through the employment of different operating modes. For example, the NavChair has a standard obstacle avoidance mode for operating in open environments, a wall following mode, a door passage mode, and a close approach mode. Some of these are mutually exclusive (i.e. obstacle avoidance and close approach) while others are not (i.e. obstacle avoidance and wall following).

An example of automatic mode selection demonstrates how adaptive shared control can improve system performance. Figure 1 illustrates a situation in which the NavChair performs mode selection in response to a change in user behavior. In this case, environmental variables are not sufficient to determine mode selection because the presence of a door doesn't necessarily imply that the user wishes to travel through it. The decision to change modes must be based primarily upon observations of user behavior.

Fig. 1. Mode Selection: Frame (1) shows the NavChair approaching a doorway. One of two outcomes is possible: either (2a) the NavChair performs door-passage behavior, or (2b) the NavChair performs an avoidance maneuver. These two behaviors correspond to two modes of operation, door-passage and obstacle avoidance, that cannot be performed simultaneously.

Two methods are typically used to perform real-time adaptation in human-machine systems: 1) manual user control of machine adaptation where the user selects the NavChair's control mode or 2) automatic machine adaptation based upon observations of environmental variables. Neither of these approaches is fully successful in the NavChair system. Manual mode selection undermines the primary benefits of the NavChair for some of the potential users who do not have the ability to control an additional input. Automatic machine adaptation based only upon environmental feedback is not always successful because it neglects the intention of the user [17].

Our attempts to understand adaptive shared control in the NavChair have lead to general design criteria for adaptive shared-control systems [5]. These criteria include the requirements that adaptive shared-control systems should:

1) model human-machine performance in order to adapt system operation;
2) provide smooth system performance that is stable, comfortable, and intuitive for the user; and
3) include a means for continuously adjusting the degree of influence allocated to the each machine control component vs. the human user.

The first criteria has been satisfied in the NavChair system through the development of a new method, called "Stimulus Response Modeling" (SRM), which is used to automatically determine the most appropriate mode of operation [4]. The primary advantage of SRM over traditional user modeling techniques is that SRM can be applied to the majority of human-machine systems in which user goals can not be measured directly. SRM operates by maintaining a model of user responses to known stimuli and using model parameters as feedback about the user for machine adaptation. Thus, SRM requires that the system must be able to measure disturbances in control loops that involve the user; either measurable external disturbances need to be available for this purpose or the system must be able to apply disturbances that do not interfere with system performance.

Original testing with SRM in the NavChair used a small joystick perturbation (briefly offsetting the resting joystick position from zero) as a stimulus. An autoregressive model relating user joystick responses to these perturbation stimuli was continually updated using recursive system identification [10,14]. Stimulus-response model parameters provided direct, quantitative information about current user behavior. We have also observed that stimulus-response model parameters reflect changes in user control related to intention. Preliminary results of SRM testing with two subjects operating the NavChair system have demonstrated that a single response can be used to differentiate between driving in an open room vs. a hallway with 80 to 94% accuracy [4] and that this accuracy increases to nearly 100% as data is accumulated over time.

In order to provide an effective means for implementing control decisions based on SRM modeling, navigation routines for different modes which satisfied criteria 2 and 3 had to be developed. It became apparent during the development of the NavChair that the obstacle avoidance method initially employed, called the Vector Field Histogram (VFH) method, did not adequately satisfy these requirements as discussed below. This paper describes a new method (MVFH) for assisted navigation in the NavChair system that satisfies these requirements and reports on tests which compares NavChair performance under the control of the VFH vs. MVFH navigation routines.

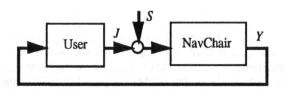

Fig. 2. Stimulus Response Modeling: Observations of responses to an applied stimulus, S, are used to model the behavior of the user. The stimulus perturbs the motion of the wheelchair, Y, which evokes a response in the joystick command from the user, J.

2 Navigation Methods

The VFH obstacle avoidance method was originally employed because of its success in autonomous [15] and tele-autonomous robot control [6], which is similar in many ways to the control of the NavChair [4]. A detailed description of the VFH method for this application has previously been presented in the literature [7]. Briefly, VFH performs obstacle avoidance calculations in four steps:

1. Sonar readings are accumulated in a two-dimensional grid that represents the probable locations of obstacles around the wheelchair;
2. Obstacle data is reduced into a polar histogram (h) which is a measure of obstacle density versus direction of travel;
3. The polar histogram is searched for a safe travel direction (t) closest to the joystick direction (j)
4. t is modified slightly by an amount proportional to a virtual obstacle repulsive force.

Figure 3 illustrates the behavior of VFH in the scenario from Figure 1. VFH selects a direction of travel (t) that is closest to the desired direction (j) and in which the polar histogram is below the safety threshold value (m). This method allows the NavChair to insure collision-free travel while giving the user high-level control of wheelchair motion.

 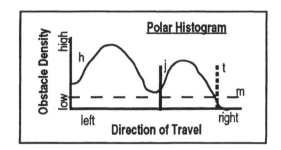

Fig. 3. VFH Obstacle Avoidance in the scenario from Figure 1. The left figure shows the certainty grid around the NavChair; the right figure shows the polar histogram at the same instant, where: j is the desired direction of travel, as indicated by the user with the joystick (solid arrow); h is the polar histogram representing obstacle densities in each possible direction of travel; m is the safety threshold value; t is the actual direction of travel selected by VFH (dotted arrow).

The presence of a human user in the NavChair control loop constrains the design of NavChair components. Design criteria 2 requires that obstacle avoidance provide "intuitive" control for the user. Unintuitive control increases training time and reduces the ability of the user to adapt to unusual circumstances. "Intuitive" control implies, among other things, that the user must feel that the wheelchair's responses to input are rational and predictable. One of the great strengths of the VFH method in autonomous and teleautonomous systems robots is actually a drawback from this standpoint. VFH allows relatively fast travel through cluttered environments by avoiding obstacles with only a minimal reduction in speed. However, this behavior is perceived by a wheelchair user as sudden and unpredictable changes in direction. This perception reflects the invariable degree of influence of VFH; it cannot give the user more or less control in different circumstances. This problem typifies the difficulties experienced in applying robotic obstacle avoidance to the NavChair.

2.1 MVFH Navigation

In response to these difficulties, a new navigation method, Minimum VFH (MVFH), was developed that is consistent with our design criteria for shared-control systems. Because it was developed for use in human-machine systems, the design of MVFH provides a broader range of navigation assistance than the obstacle avoidance provided by VFH. MVFH uses the same certainty grid and polar histogram as VFH, but calculates speed and direction of travel differently. MVFH performs navigation calculations in four steps (as illustrated in Figure 4):

1. Sonar readings are accumulated in a two-dimensional grid that represents the probable locations of obstacles around the wheelchair;
2. Obstacle data is reduced into a polar histogram (h) which is a measure of obstacle density versus direction of travel;
3. The sum (s) of the polar histogram (h) and a weighting function (w) is minimized to find a safe direction of travel (t);
4. Wheelchair speed is reduced by an amount that depends on the distance to the nearest obstacle in the path of the wheelchair.

 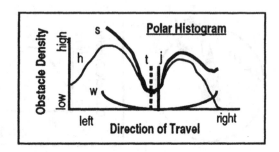

Fig. 4. MVFH Obstacle Avoidance in the scenario from Figure 1. The left figure shows the certainty grid around the NavChair; the right figure shows the polar histogram at the same instant, where: j is the desired direction of travel, as indicated by the user with the joystick (solid arrow); h is the polar histogram representing obstacle densities in each possible direction of travel; w is the weighting function: a parabola centered on the desired direction of travel (j); s is the sum of h and w; t is the actual direction of travel selected by MVFH at the minimum of s.

The first two MVFH steps are identical to those of the VFH method. In step 3, MVFH trades obstacle avoidance against the goals of the user by optimizing a combined function of obstacle avoidance performance and user goals. The shape and steepness of the weighting function, w, controls the degree to which MVFH can influence wheelchair motion: when w is a steep parabola compared to the polar histogram, MVFH can modify the target direction only slightly; when w is relatively flat, MVFH can deviate from the target direction by a large amount, if necessary. Therefore, changing the steepness of w changes the influence of MVFH in providing navigation assistance. With more influence, MVFH causes the wheelchair to go around obstacles with little decrease in speed, while a low degree of influence allows the user to force MVFH to travel close to obstacles and through doors. Therefore, NavChair control modes can be changed by adjusting the steepness and shape of w.

Unlike VFH, MVFH does not guarantee that the wheelchair will always move in an obstacle-free direction. Therefore, a collision prevention routine (step 4) slows the chair by an amount proportional to the square root of the distance to the nearest obstacle in the direction of motion. This routine smoothly decelerates the wheelchair to a stop a specified distance from obstacles.

3 MVFH vs. VFH Testing

MVFH was compared to VFH by evaluating NavChair performance in terms of the following quantitative measures:

- average speed -- m/sec.
- jerkiness -- RMS average of the portion of the motor command above 10 Hz.
- average obstacle clearance -- The average distance from the side of the wheelchair to the nearest obstacle.
- collision risk -- collisions and near misses per s.

System performance with obstacle avoidance is related to eight parameters. These obstacle avoidance parameters were set to produce optimal system performance for VFH and MVFH, as measured by the variables above.

3.1 Hallway Test

Five tests were performed in a u-shaped hallway with two right-angle turns. This segment of hallway was selected because it contained difficult trap situations typical of modern buildings: smooth walls, a segment of glass wall, and doors barely wide enough for passage. The course was approximately 30 m in length and 2 m wide. Tests 1 and 2 evaluated VFH obstacle avoidance, while tests 3 and 4 used MVFH. In tests 1 and 3, a blindfolded user employed a strategy of pointing the joystick towards one of the walls (at about 45°) thereby traveling along that wall while moving down the hallway. In tests 2 and 4, the user's strategy was to point the joystick straight ahead and to travel down the middle of the hall. In all tests, the user was instructed to move the joystick in a different direction if the NavChair stopped moving, such as in corners. In test 5, an experienced user covered the course as rapidly as possible without obstacle avoidance.

Table 1 compares the results of these tests and shows that MVFH equals or surpasses VFH in terms of every performance measure recorded. In particular, notice that MVFH is as fast as VFH and that its motion is smoother. No collisions occurred using either method. These results suggest that the NavChair system allows a blindfolded person to operate the wheelchair safely at about half the speed of an experienced user.

Table 1:	VFH		MVFH		User
Hallway test number:	test 1	test 2	test 3	test 4	test 5
speed (m/s)	0.73	0.78	0.77	0.78	1.62
clearance (m)	0.44	n/a	0.45	n/a	n/a
jerkiness	0.95	0.68	0.58	0.55	n/a
collisions	0	0	0	0	0

Table 1. Four measures of performance are compared for a blindfolded user using obstacle avoidance and an expert user in the smooth hallway course. These results indicate that the blindfolded user is able to travel safely at about half the speed of the experienced user traveling without obstacle avoidance. MVFH slightly outperforms VFH.

3.2 Door Passage Test

Figure 6 compares experimental results of door-passage success for the original and Minimum VFH methods. Ten trials were made at door widths from 0.65 to 1.2 meters. The ratio of successful to attempted door passages was recorded for each width. Success was defined as passage without the need for user intervention. MVFH is more successful at door passage than VFH because it allows the NavChair to move closer to obstacles (the doorposts) and because it naturally tends to center the chair as it approaches the doorway.

4 Discussion

Many human-machine system components are developed as autonomous machines. However, design criteria for human-machine system components are substantially different than for autonomous systems. An awareness of the differences in design philosophy between autonomous and shared-control systems is necessary for the development of the best possible rehabilitation technologies and to allow autonomous components to be integrated into effective human-machine systems.

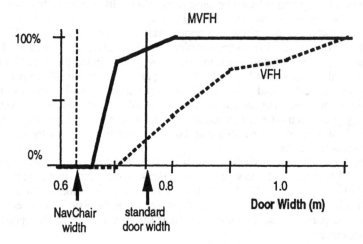

Fig. 6. Door Passage Test Results: Percentage of successful door passage versus door width for VFH (dashes) and MVFH (solid). Two vertical marks provide scale: 1) dashed: the NavChair is 0.63 m wide; and 2) solid: standard doors are 0.76 m wide.

The design criteria presented above guided the development of MVFH, a new method for assistive navigation, and SRM, a method of modeling changes in user behavior for adaptive shared control. MVFH provides: 1) relatively fast, safe and effective obstacle avoidance; 2) a variable and controllable degree of influence on wheelchair motion; and 3) safe and effective door passage.

SRM allows the full adaptive capabilities of MVFH to be utilized by adapting the influence of MVFH in response to changes in user behavior. SRM models operator behavior in real time for adaptive shared control [4]. Model accuracy increases as data from past times steps is accumulated. For every application, a specific level of accuracy will be required within a specified time to make the implementation of adaptive shared control successful. Rich (i.e., high-power, high-bandwidth) stimuli provide optimal model accuracy, but can negatively impact system performance. Research is being planned to evaluate how stimulus characteristics influence the speed and accuracy of the modeling process. In the NavChair system, we have been able to use the action of MVFH in tests with five subjects as a 'naturally occurring' stimulus that does not degrade system performance at all (in fact, it enhances system performance by providing assistive navigation functions). The MVFH action was found to be a sufficiently rich external stimulus to adequately model the user and thereby allow effective adaptive shared control.

The design criteria presented here were developed in the context of the NavChair system. However, this discussion may benefit other researchers who are experiencing similar difficulties in other human-machine systems. For example, an ability to design systems capable of seamless human-machine adaptive shared control might allow a communication system to automatically configure itself to optimally fit a user's changing abilities or strategy. As another example, an ability to model changes in driver behavior in real time could allow a car to adapt the efficiency/performance settings of its transmission to meet the current needs of the driver. These and many human-machine systems stand to benefit from this research in adaptive shared control.

Acknowledgments The NavChair Project is funded under grant B630-DA from the Department of Veteran Affairs Rehabilitation Research and Development.

References

1. Arai, F., T. Fukuda, Y. Yamamoto, T. Naito, T. Matsui. "Interactive Adaptive Interface Using Recursive Fuzzy Reasoning." IEEE VRAIS '93 1993: 104-110.
2. Bell, D. A., J. Borenstein, S. P. Levine, Y. Koren, and L. A. Jaros. "An Assistive Navigation System for Wheelchairs Based upon Mobile Robot Obstacle Avoidance." 1994 IEEE Conf. on Robotics and Automation 1994.
3. Bell, D. A., S. P. Levine, Y. Koren, L. A. Jaros, and J. Borenstein. "Design Criteria for Obstacle Avoidance in a Shared-Control System." RESNA '94 1994: 581-583.
4. Bell, D. A., S. P. Levine, Y. Koren, L. A. Jaros, and J. Borenstein. "Shared Control of the NavChair Obstacle Avoiding Wheelchair." RESNA '93 1993: 370-372.
5. Bell, D. A., S. P. Levine, Y. Koren, L. Jaros and J. Borenstein. "An Identification Technique for Adaptive Shared-control in Human-Machine Systems." Proc. of the 15th Annual International Conf. of the IEEE Engineering in Medicine and Biology Society 1993: 1299–1300.
6. Borenstein, J., and Y. Koren. "Tele-autonomous Guidance for Mobile Robots." IEEE Transactions on Systems, Man, and Cybernetics 17(4) (1991): 535-539.
7. Borenstein, J., and Y. Koren. "The Vector Field Histogram — Fast Obstacle Avoidance for Mobile Robots." IEEE Journal of Robotics and Automation 1989.
8. Borenstein, J., S. P. Levine, and Y. Koren. "The NavChair--A New Concept in Intelligent Wheelchair Control for People with Multiple Handicaps." CSUN's Fifth Annual Conference on Technology and Persons with Disabilities 1990.
9. Browne, D. "Adaptation and Operator Models" Position Paper for the CHI+GI '87 Workshop on Operator Models 1987.
10. Eykhoff, P. System Identification: Parameter and State Estimation. New York: Wiley. 1974.
11. Hancock, P. A., and M. H. Chignell. "Adaptive Control in Human-machine Systems." Ed P. A. Hancock. Human Factors Psychology. New York: Elsevier Science P. 1987. 305-346.
12. Jaros, L. A., D. Bell, S. P. Levine, J. Borenstein, and Y. Koren. "NavChair: Design of an Assistive Navigation System for Wheelchairs." RESNA '93 1993: 379-381.
13. Levine, S., Y. Koren, and J. Borenstein. "NavChair Control System for Automatic Assistive Wheelchair Navigation." RESNA 13th Annual Conference 1990.
14. Ljung, L. Theory and Practice of Recursive Identification. Cambridge, MA: MIT P. 1983.
15. Manz, A., R. Liscano, and D. Greene. "A Comparison of Real-time Obstacle Avoidance Methods for Mobile Robots." Experimental Robotics June, 1991.
16. Schönpflug, W. "Coping Efficiency and Situational Demands." in G. R. J. Hockey, ed., Stress and Fatigue in Human Performance. 1983: 299-329.
17. Schweighardt, M. F. "Using the Context of Interactions to Adapt to Users." Proceedings of the Human Factors Society 34th Annual Meeting 1990: 346-351.
18. Sheridan, T. B. "Telerobotics." Automatica 25(4) (1989): 487-507.

Using Spatial Audio for the Enhanced Presentation of Synthesised Speech within Screen-Readers for Blind Computer Users

Kai Crispien[1], Wolfgang Würz[2], Gerhard Weber[3]

(1) Institut f. Fernmeldetechnik
(2) Institut f. Kommunikationswissenschaft
Technische Universität Berlin
(3) F.H. Papenmeier GmbH&Co KG, Schwerte &
Institut f. Informatik, Universität Stuttgart
email: crispien@ftsu00.ee.tu-berlin.de

Abstract. In order to enhance the presentation of synthesised speech output within GUI-based screen-readers for blind computer users, a spatial audio processing system, based on head-related transfer function processing technology is used to apply virtual acoustic positioning to synthesised speech. The spatial audio processing system and methods for generating spatial auditory displays are introduced. A procedure for the integration and synchronisation of an external speech synthesiser to the system is described. Finally, some prospects for the use of the enhanced speech output facilities of the system are given.

1 Introduction

Until recently, human-computer interfaces have consisted mainly of textual information represented by ASCII-coded characters. Blind computer users can access these command line-based interfaces by using a *screen-reader* software which usually reads the text displayed on the screen and provides information to either a synthetic speech synthesiser and/or a tactile text display, consisting of refreshable Braille modules. The introduction of graphics-based user interfaces, referred to as GUIs (Graphical User Interfaces), has raised various problems for blind computer users, since access to these human-computer interfaces requires enhanced methods and design of non-visual computer interaction.

One approach for enhancing the auditory representation within screen-readers for GUI systems is the spatial presentation of audio information, represented by auditory interaction objects, referred to as "auditory icons", or synthesised speech output [1, 2]. The spatial presentation of audio information can provide orientation and navigation aids within the user interface, since the position of interaction objects, text components or pointing devices becomes determinable for non-visual users, exploiting the human perceptual ability of auditory localisation.

For the representation of continuous text, appearing for example in word processing or spreadsheet applications, spatial positioning of synthesised speech output can enhance the immediate understanding of the text layout and enables improved interaction methods. Additionally, non-verbal audio components can be used to identify text attributes and to assist pointing in text-based applications.

2   GUI-based Screen Readers

Blind users have learned since nearly a decade to work with speech synthesisers for access to text-based application programs running on PCs. Especially in North America work places for blind users have been equipped with a synthesiser and a screen reading program (or simply called screen-reader). In contrast, Braille displays are read actively by the fingers while speech output allows the user to be passive.

For access to graphical user interfaces a verbalisation of the graphical interaction objects like windows, menus, buttons, icons has to be generated by a dedicated screen-reader program. The screen-reader relies for this on a model of the visual interaction objects which is called an *off-screen model* (OSM, see [3]). While an OSM is hierarchically structured such a model can also consist only of lines of text and is flat. We then call this model a *virtual screen copy* (VISC).

The screen reader handles two activities:

- tracking of changes on the screen and reporting about these changes through appropriate verbalisation to the user
- assist the user in review the contents of the screen (receptively the OSM or VISC)

The spatial information describing the size, position, overlapping of interaction objects can be presented on a large Braille display appropriately (see [4]). For speech-based screen readers current solutions only make use of the hierarchical model of an OSM. During tracking the screen reader selects one node in the OSM which is active. During review the user traverses through this hierarchy in order to gain an overview on the windows contents or the complete screen. The spatial relation among interaction objects is currently not properly communicated, res. absent in the OSM. As long as interaction remains keyboard based such an approach can be suitable but many applications are operated more easily with a mouse or other pointing devices. Recent research has found that pointing is also suitable for blind users if non-verbal acoustic feedback is used (see [5]). In order to provide an understanding of the spatial relations within the user interface it is proposed to apply a spatial acoustic representation to verbal and non-verbal auditory interaction components. This, can improve for example the use of pointing devices since positions of interaction objects become determinable through direct perception of acoustic locations.

3   Spatial Audio Processing

Conventional stereophonic recordings, monitored with headphones, only provide a relatively poor auditory locational performance. The perceived position of a sound source usually appears along an axis through the middle of the head. This phenomena is known as the so-called "inside-the-head" localisation [6].

This is based on the fact, that even though *interaural temporal* and *intensity differences* (ITD, IID) appropriate to an external source are present, the direction-dependent reflection and refraction effects of the head, outer ear (pinnae) and shoulders are absent in the recording. Many studies suggested the importance of these effects, acting as a direction-dependent frequency filter within the human auditory system. Especially for the determination of sound sources in the median plane (in front, above or behind of the listener), where ITDs and IIDs are not present, these spectral distortions of the head and body provide the primary cue for the human auditory localisation system [6]. Therefore, an appropriate model of the human acoustic system, such as a dummy-head with microphones embedded in its artificial ears, can simulate a close approximation of the natural listening impression within a three-dimensional spatial sound field. Providing an improved *externalisation* or *outside-the-head* listening impression, if monitored with headphones.

With the introduction of powerful signal-processing technology in the 1980s, a technique for the computational simulation of spatial sound presentation with headphones was investigated (see e.g. [7, 8]) and led to the development of a number of real-time processing systems. In general, these systems use a collection of *head-related transfer functions* (HRTFs), usually derived from measurements of a sound stimulus placed in certain appropriate directions around a listener. The stimuli are measured with probe microphones placed in the outer ear of either individual human subjects or dummy-heads, resulting in a pair of specific impulse responses for each direction. These HRTFs then can be convoluted with an audio signal in the time-domain, performing as direction-dependant filters. In order to achieve real-time performance, finite-impulse-response (FIR) filters are used for the fast convolution process. HRTF processing thus represents a linear system that is a function of sound source position.

Applying this processing method to an audio signal, monitored with headphones, produces a perception of spatially located sound sources in a *virtual* three-dimensional acoustic free-field[1]. Motion of sound sources can be achieved by interpolation between certain transfer functions. Head motions of the listener, which form another important cue used by the human auditory system, can also be integrated in the simulation process.

---

[1]An acoustic free-field is defined as an reflection-free acoustic field. A sound source is not superimposed by any sound waves reflected from boundary surfaces, like in a reverberant room (diffuse-field).

Therefore, the head position has to be transmitted and updated continuously using a "six-freedom-of-choice" position-tracking device mounted on top of the headphone. Present systems offer different numbers of channels that can be independently *spatialised* for azimuthal and elevational directions. These systems are used so far in aviation and aerospace applications [9], enhanced radio-communications, musical recording and mixing [10] and auditory displays for man-computer interaction [11].

3.1 The Beachtron™ HRTF-based Audio Processing System

Due to the fact that HRTF processing, carried out in real time, requires extensive processing load, systems available so far have been highly cost-intensive and not affordable for applications in the rehabilitation area. Only recently, in 1993 a cost-effective system became available on the market, namely the "Beachtron" system from the pioneering American manufacturer Crystal River Engineering, Inc..
This system combines a high quality digital sound processing device for PCM recording and playback of sounds and a musical instrument synthesiser with a HRTF processing-engine. Additionally, external audio sources can be applied to the system.

The Beachtron system consists of a ISA bus-based plug-in board which is capable to process two independent sound sources in real time. The boards are cascadable, thus up to sixteen individual spatialised sound sources can be presented simultaneously. Monitoring is carried out with a conventional, high quality headphone (Sennheiser HD540). Except the headphone, no additional external hardware is required for the generation and spatialisation of sounds.

The system uses the processing method described before (figure 1). HRTF filters are obtained from measurements of one female subject (subject SDO) which participated in the experiment of *Wightman* and *Kistler*, 1989 [see 7, 8]. This subject showed the most accurate performance for either free-field or simulated headphone-based localisation of sound sources among all participants in the experiment. It was found that different persons are able to adapt to this subject's HRTFs and can perform acceptable accurate sound localisation[12].

The distance of sound sources is simulated by an "atmospheric absorption" model which attenuates higher frequencies. The degree of attenuation depends on the distance through which the sound travels in the atmosphere. This results in a lowpass-filtered or "muffled" characteristic of distant sound sources. Motion of sound sources, res. head motions - monitored by an additional position-tracking device, are processed by using an interpolation algorithm between the four nearest stored transfer functions.

™ The Beachtron is a registered trademark of Crystal River Engineering, Inc., 12350 Wards Ferry Road, Groveland, CA 95321, USA; Phone: (209) 962-6382, Fax: (209) 962-4873.

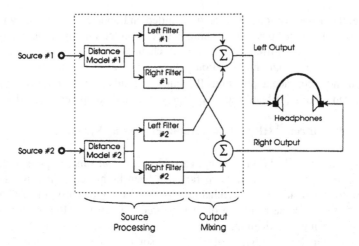

Fig. 1: Spatialisation processing in the Beachtron system.

3.2 Generation of a Spatial Auditory Display with the Beachtron System

In order to generate a spatial auditory representation of the computer screen with the Beachtron system, such as the auditory part of a screen-reader, *auditory objects* can be generated by attaching a specific sound representation and an auditory position to a screen object. Sound representations can be either any PCM waveform sound (8/16 bit, 44.1 kHz), a preset-based synthesiser sound or synthesised speech, generated by an external speech synthesiser. The position of an auditory object within the virtual acoustic free-field is described by a three-component vector [x, y, z] (see figure 2).

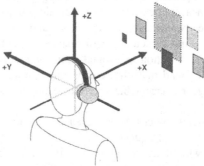

Fig. 2: Conceptual illustration of a spatial auditory display.

Due to the fact, that such a virtual spatial representation of auditory objects is not restricted to physical dimensions (as it would be the fact, if monitored with a loudspeaker system), a spatial mapping between the visual representation of the GUI (computer screen) and the auditory representation can be carried out which is suitable for an optimised representation of the auditory display.

Therefore, a geometrical projection has to be applied which transforms the 2D rectangular screen-position into a virtual 3D auditory position. In order to make maximum amount of the facilities of the human auditory localisation system - which does not perform linear for all directions [6], an extended projection can be chosen. A projection of the screen plane to an cylindrical shape seems to be a good mapping, since the elevational plane, where sounds are usually localised more inaccurately [6], can be extended above and under the listener's position.

In our approach, currently mainly positions on the frontal hemisphere of the listener are used for the mapping of screen contents to the auditory display. The back hemisphere can be used for the presentation of extraordinary events in the human-computer interface, like e.g. on-line help information. The third dimension (X plane) of the auditory display, appearing as acoustical distance information, can be used to represent background processes or inactive interaction objects, e.g. a file transmission process or overlapped windows.

4   Enhanced Representation of Synthesised Speech

4.1   Spatial Representation of Synthesised Speech

In general, speech synthesisers devices provide speech output by text-to-speech conversion of ASCII-coded character strings. Textstrings, usually transmitted to the device via the serial port, are examined for phrase and word components which can be spoken, res. commands for the control of the device. Common control parameters are: speech timbre, pitch, speed, word prosody, etc..

Although, a larger number of speech synthesisers are available only a few devices supply multilingual text-to-speech conversion. A well known device in Europe is for example the "CompactVoxBox" by the Swedish manufacturer Infovox. This device offers text-to-speech conversion for up to ten different European languages. Additionally, the CompactVoxBox provides a software-based facility, called *indexing* which enables the possibility of sending index commands to the text-to-speech converter at specific locations in the text which are transmitted back to the screen-reader. Therefore, indexing can be used for the control of the asynchronous behaviour of the speech synthesiser within an application program. An *index-string* consist of an *index-identifier* (e.g. ASCII 'ctrl-A') and an *index-marker* consisting of a three-position digit (e.g. '001'). If a textstring is passed to the speech synthesiser, containing one or multiple index-strings, the text-to-speech unit returns the index-markers on the serial port during speech output. The index marker is transmitted back immediately after the succeeding regular text part has been spoken.

In order to achieve spatial representation of the speech output facilities of a screen reader the speech synthesiser is applied to the external input connector of the Beachtron board.

Static text components, such as window or icon titles, menu text, etc., can be *spatialised* by attaching their screen position to the Beachtron system before the specific text string is transmitted to the speech synthesiser via the serial port. The incoming synthesised speech signal is then processed spatially and appears at the specified acoustic position.

For the spatial representation of continuous text, like. e.g. text edited in a word processor, the spatial acoustic position of the text position has to be updated continuously. This requires a mechanism which synchronises the speech synthesiser to the spatial acoustic processing system. Therefore, a string handling procedure concatenates text parts (e.g. single words or characters) delimited by white-space characters (e.g. blanks, tabs, etc.) with an index-marker. These index-markers contain the column position (e.g. 1-80) of the specific text parts (see figure 3).

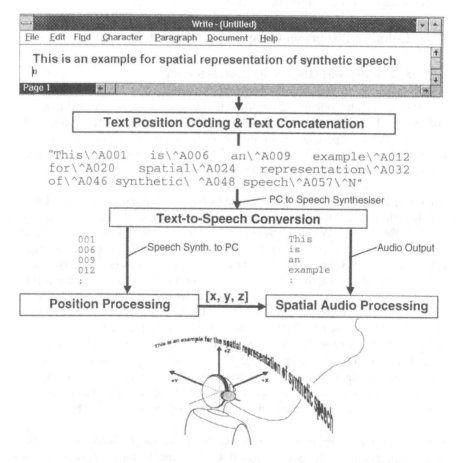

Fig. 3: Mechanism for the spatial representation and synchronisation of synthesised speech.

The concatenated text string is then passed to the speech synthesiser and processed by the text-to-speech unit. If an index-marker is returned from the text-to-speech unit the index-marker, contains the column position of the successive text part which is used for the computation of the spatial acoustic position of the speech output.

Beside the spatialisation of text, also the asynchronous behaviour of the speech synthesiser is taken into account, if for example the speed of the speech output is slowed down by the user. The mechanism therefore provides a synchronised, closed-loop between the speech synthesiser and the spatial acoustic processing system which updates the azimuthal acoustic text position continuously (figure 3). Vertical positions of different lines within the text are processed by using the line-feed character (ASCII '\n') as an incriminator for the elevational acoustic positions.

4.2   Interaction with Spatially Represented Speech

Spatial representation of speech output the assists the user to identify the position of spoken text parts in relation to the visual representation on the screen. This can enhance the immediate understanding of the text layout within a word processor and other text-based applications. An example for the use of this information is the representation of multi-column text as used in documents, tables or spreadsheets.

The synchronisation between screen and audio-output has some useful implications, especially in the combination with the use of pointing devices. On a technical level, it is now possible to synchronise the caret cursor or mouse pointer and the acoustic speech-position.

During tracking of the mouse pointer movements, spoken feedback can be handled in two different ways (see [13]):

- the currently spoken item is interrupted; a new item is pronounced immediately when reached
- the currently spoken item is completed; instead of speaking a new item a non-verbal sound is produced

Synchronisation of the speech output with pointing enables the user not only to follow passively the screen-reader, but provides the opportunity to interact actively with the text components through pointing.

Additionally, non-verbal sounds can be controlled by the synchronisation mechanism. Non-verbal sound components then can be used for conveying additional information during text-based interaction as for example text attributes like bold, italic, underlined, etc. text styles or highlighted text, commonly used in hypertext applications (such as e.g. the MS-Windows help facility).

Therefore, one digit of the index-maker can be used for the coding of specific text attributes within the indexing mechanism, described in section 4.1.

A typical scenario for a hypertext-based interaction with the system is for example, that a non-verbal sound is started if a highlighted text part is read by the speech synthesiser. This "hypertext-sound" keeps on playing in the background until the speech synthesiser has finished reading the highlighted text part. Through the presentation of the non-verbal sound in parallel to the speech information the user becomes able to monitor the specific highlighted text information and to navigate in the hypertext system by activating the hypertext through keyboard- or pointing device-based interaction.

5 Conclusions

This paper has proposed a method for the enhancement of synthesised speech output within GUI-based screen-reader programs. Synthesised speech is represented at within a virtual spatial auditory display, processed by a spatial audio-processing system. The location of the spatially represented speech are computed from text positions derived by the screen-reader program. The mechanism also provides a synchronisation between the screen-reader and the asynchronous speech output. This can assist pointing and the control of non-verbal audio information for the communication of text attributes, which can enhance text-based interaction for blind computer users.

Acknowledgements

This work has been supported by the GUIB project ("Textual and Graphical User Interfaces for Blind Computer Users"), a pilot project of the EEC program TIDE ("Technology Initiative for the Disabled and Elderly"). Thanks to Prof. Dr.-Ing. Klaus Fellbaum and Andreas Korte at Technical University of Berlin for their support.

References

[1] Edwards, A.,& Mynatt, E.: Mapping GUIs to Auditory Interfaces. UIST '92: The Fifth Annual Symposium on User Interface Software and Technology, Monterey, California, ACM Press, New York, 1992.

[2] Crispien, K.,& Petrie, H.: Providing Access to GUI's Using a Multimedia System - Based on Spatial Audio Presentation. Audio Engineering Society 95th.Convention Preprint, New York, Oct. 1993.

[3] Schwerdtfeger, R.S.: Making the GUI talk. BYTE, Dec. 1991, pp.118-128.

[4]   Mynatt, E.;& Weber, G.: Nonvisual presentation of graphical user interfaces: contrasting two approaches. in Proceedings of CHI'94, ACM Press, New York, 1994.

[5]   Petrie, H., Heinila, J.,& Ekola, H.: A Comparative Evaluation of Computer Input Devices for Blind Users. in Proceedings of ECART 2, Stockholm, Sweden, May 26 - 28, '93, ISBN 91-88 336/19/0, 1993.

[6]   Blauert, J.: Spatial Hearing: The Psychophysics of Human Sound Localizaton. Cambridge, MA, MIT Press, 1983.

[7]   Wightman, F. L.,& Kistler, D. J.: Headphone Simulation of Free-Field Listening. I: Stimulus Synthesis. J. Acoustic Society of America, Vol. 85, Febr. 1989, pp. 858 - 867, 1989.

[8]   Wightman, F.L,& Kistler, D.J.: Headphone Simulation for Free-Field Listening II: Psychophysical Validation. J. Acoustic Society of America, Febr. 1989, pp. 868-878, 1989.

[9]   Wenzel, E. M.: Three-Dimensional Virtual Acoustic Displays. in Blattner, M.M., & Dannenberg, R.B., (eds.): Multimedia Interface Design, ch. 15, pp. 257 - 288, ACM Press, New York, 1992.

[10]   Gierlich, H. W.,& Genuit, K.: Processing Artficial - Head Recording. J. Audio Engineering Society, Vol. 37, No. 1/2, 1989.

[11]   Ludwig, L., Pincever, N.,& Cohen, M.: Extending the Notion of a Window System to Audio. Computer, 23, pp. 66 - 72, 1990.

[12]   Wenzel, E. M., Arruda, M., Kistler, D. J.,& Wightman, F.L.: Localization Using Nonindividualized Head-Related Transfer Functions, J. Acoustic Society of America, July 1993, pp. 111-123, 1993.

[13]   Weber, G.: Modelling interaction of blind people using graphical user interfaces. Vogt, F.H. (ed.): in Proceedings of 12th World Computer Congress, Personal Computers and Intelligent Systems, Information Processing '92, Elsevier Science Publishers B.V.(North Holland), pp. 39-46, 1992.

Multimodal Concept for a
New Generation of Screen Reader

Nadine Vigouroux, Bernard Oriola

IRIT-URA-CNRS 1399
Université Paul Sabatier
118, Route de Narbonne
F-31062 Toulouse Cedex
Phone: +33 61 55 63 14, Fax: +33 61 55 62 58
e-mail: vigourou@irit.fr

Abstract. One aim of this research is to explore how the selection of output modality and information presentation can be used to allow more appropriated access to electronic document by visually impaired persons. This paper shows how multi-modal interfaces can decrease certain difficulties linked with the visual disabilities. At IRIT our work consists in representing and developing multimodal access for the electronic document consultation. A representation space of output modalities is proposed in the goal of defining a multimodal user interface management system.

1. Introduction

Traditional interfaces are designed to allow direct manipulation of textual entities or graphic objects. They are typically command-oriented, completed with mouse to provide direct manipulation. An ordered set of manipulation is required to perform a given action. This requires familiarity with the system interface and the text processing functionalities. This fact is increasing instead of making them available for visually impaired persons (VIP).

The problem of having access to electronic documents (Eds) like newspapers, specialised magazines, books, ... [14, 23] by VIP, is completely renewed by the introduction of multimedia workstations [16] and multimodal interfaces [2, 18, 6, 1].

This paper presents the features of audio modality and the needs to define a modality model in order to specify a multimodal user interface management system (MUIMS). We will focus here particularly on the aural consultation of EDs by VIP. To perform this aural consultation, we need multimedia workstations provided with speech synthesis and/or speech recognition systems also as other communication devices such as adapted keyboards, mouse, adapted printers or displays, ... The users of these workstations can be disabled people like motor handicapped or visually impaired persons.

Years ago, Braille writing, allowing text access to the visually impaired, already realised an important progress. But this communication medium is still limited.

Indeed, only 10% of the visually impaired can read Braille. More over, they can only have access to a few transcribed and Braille printed texts, which are often old because the transcription takes a lot of time, while every day an important quantity of books, magazines and newspapers are published.

Recently, new progresses [25] have been possible thanks to the text-to-speech synthesis which allow reading of electronic information. The emergence of applications reading the contents of a screen offers the possibility to the blind to peruse and subsequently to converse with computers, to write programs or to read electronic texts [8]. We can list here the screen editors Edivox from Elan Informatique [7], Sonolect from Club Micro-Son, IBM Screen Reader [11], ...

But these aural devices are not yet sufficiently integrated in MUIMS, a fact which still restricts their scope. The paragraph 2 aims for a taxonomy of the modality concept. In paragraph 3, we focus on the aural modality features. The paragraph 4 describes our multimodal access system of EDs. Then, we lay the foundations of a referential space for the multimodal output presentation of EDs.

2. Taxonomy

Taxonomy of multimodal systems from an engineering point of view are emerging [12, 15]. First we should aim for a terminology that it is clear. Given that music, beeps, written and spoken natural language may be called *modalities*. These modalities are representational modalities. Each of this modality can be characterised by a set of features which serves to identify modalities from one another. These features are assumed for represented information: linguistic/non-linguistic, static/dynamic, and metaphoric/non-metaphoric.

For instance, the same linguistic information may be represented in either the graphical, sound or touch medium but the choice of the medium has influence on the perceptual qualities [10]. So perceptual modality qualities must be taken into consideration for the multimodal human-computer interfaces.

This paper reports first considerations from work undertaken on the modality concept for VIP. This concepts must be integrated in research on the information representation and exchange capabilities of multimodal interfaces. Since the beginning of the nineties, designers of interactive human-computer interfaces started to use increasing numbers of different, input/output modalities for the expression and the exchange of information between systems and their users.

Our intention is to propose a model of information-exchanging between user and system during **task performance in context**, defining the **input/output modalities** which constitute an optimal solution to the representation and exchange of the information.

Obtaining the modality model requires investigation in the following area:
- the study of aural modality,
- the definition of a conceptual and taxonomic space problem for analysing each type of mono- or multi-modal output representation (a),
- the integration of (a) in the human-computer interaction design.

3. Aural Modality

Speech recognition and speech synthesis are technologies of particular interest for their support of direct communication between user and computer.

3.1. Speech Input

The usability of Speech Recognition System is increasing. Speech will become an important component of the computer interface in dictation, report generation, automated telephone services, commands, ... For more information, see [21].

With regards to the technology thus involved, both technological advances, proper, and user behaviour toward this technology, make it reasonable to contemplate it as the possible interactive mode in various areas of voice applications [9].

There are some opportunities for using:
- shortcut rather than accessing a file by crossing many levels of hierarchical menus, a user can say "OPEN FILE" for example,
- information retrieval systems graphical user interfaces are awkward for specifying constraint based retrieval,
- preferable to keyboard in difficult situations because of free hand task.

CNET [25] experiments on using speech input as a means of running input/output voice servers, so to show that users now tend to prefer voice to keyboard interaction. More and more, speech input is favoured over DTMF telephone keyboards.

3.2. Sound Output

Different outputs based on sound modality may be used in the auralization of the human computer interaction such as speech synthesis, sound and/or music cues.

Speech synthesis offers an output channel in cases where visual displays are either not possible, insufficient or awkward. The constraints, set by voice-response systems, depend upon the latter types. There are two sorts of voice synthesis systems: the encoded speech systems and the text-to-speech systems.

The first ones yield a very good restitution of voice, with natural tone and prosody since they correspond to a digitised voice recording but takes a lot of place on the hard disk. To give an idea, when digitised through this method, a daily newspaper will require some 64 MB (with a 24 KB adaptive coding) [26]. For this reason, and because this kind of technique requires a numeration phase (long time consumable), the text-to-speech systems are preferable in the case of short-living documents of variable length.

The currently available text-to-speech systems include a grapheme-to-phoneme transcription module [24] that actualises technological and linguistic compromises, yielding an acceptable pronunciation for some 90% of the words making up a simple text. But this average drops sharply when tackling either technical texts, or small ads, telex, that involve acronyms, abbreviations, foreign words and/or linguistic exceptions. A good intelligibility of this type of texts demands considerable improvement of their pronunciation. In general, supplying lexicons of exceptions and/or abbreviations may afford a solution within the context of specific applications.

In order to overcome such limitations, an environment for the pre-processing of linguistic texts has been developed: TEXOR [4], a system operating on the ortho-graphic string to be synthesised. This system uses both lexical and phonological knowledge, a set of morpho-orthographic rules and a bi-class grammar.

Not only a high quality voice speech synthesis is important for text comprehen-sion but also all the spatio-temporal features and typographical characteristics con-tributed to intelligibility.

It is why sound modality can be released under different forms: sound, music or speech. In this context, Karsmer & al. [13] have demonstrated the advantage of using systems of music notes and chords, in order to make available menus of inter-active systems for visually impaired persons.

3.3. The problems posed by an exploration in sound

We now give some characteristics that will be taken into account in a multidimen-sional sound space. Using a sound component as a means of feed back information requires that the following characteristics are to be respected:
- *access:*
  the aural information units are received sequentially, whereas visual entities are grasped (semi-)globally; the eye being able to scrutinise at once several elements of a structure ;
- *perception:*
  sound **restitution is but partial** as contemporary text-to-speech synthesis systems do not take into account all the semantic information that is associated to a linguistic statement (for more information, see [4]) - namely, the morpho-dispositional and typographical properties. Numerous studies have demonstrated the importance of morpho-distributional representation with respect to memorisation and understanding [27] ;
  the sound modality is **perceptible**, even if the operator is not in front of the source or awaiting information. Introducing the sound modality into process-ing control systems such as remote surveillance goes to show the intrinsic in-terest of this type of modality.
  Both of these latter points raise fundamental questions about communication theory and Searle-type language acts ([22, 19]).
- *nature of the modality:*
  sound is volatile, as opposed to text data or to static image, both of which are enduring. So, memorisation increases largely the cognitive load of the user. That's why we need to provide the user with redundant information by differ-ent output channels: aural, tactile and kinaesthetic.

4. Multimodal interface for electronic documents

We have chosen to put on our interface for VIP the greater number of the technical devices available at the present time:

- As input devices, the user has the possibility to use, in addition to the standard keyboard, a Braille keyboard and a speech recognition system ;
- As output devices, he has, in addition to the screen and the computer buzzer, a text-to-speech synthesis and a Braille display.

Our remarks will be more particularly turned towards the multimodal output devices. For more details concerning the different functionalities of our IODE system see [17, 18].

Reading a document has two phases; the first one concerns the choice of the text to be read and the second one the reading itself. These two stages determine two well distinguished behaviours:

- The navigation through the different menus is more pleasant on a Braille display than with the text-to-speech synthesis. As a matter of fact, it is possible to peruse a menu entry reading only a few letters while the synthesis will read it on its integrity which soon becomes boring.
- During the text consulting itself, the advantage of having two output media is constant. Nevertheless, we need not duplicate the information on each device but use at best the different features of the two communication modes.

For the users (young and using computers) the text-to-speech synthesis modality allows quickly to peruse a text because Braille reading is slower. It is then indicated for the text reading itself.

However, Pring and Rusted [20] have demonstrated that we memorise much more easily a fact if we have *"seen"* it tactile rather than only listened. We extend this conclusion to the VIP: they memorise better the things they read in Braille.

These facts lead us to propose that it is useful, maybe absolute necessary to relieve the cognitive load of the user spreading over the Braille display a certain number of information in order to punctuate the text with written marks. These can be structural and/or typographical information on the text read out or messages like the header for example.

On the other hand, words or sentences can be not well pronounced by the speech synthesis. That is the case for acronyms, abbreviations, foreign words, ... [4]. A Braille restitution will take off the ambiguity. The enrichment of this modality co-operation with a third aural dimension the computer buzzer or any other acoustic event [13] allows the VIP to mentally represent a certain number of marks like a change of paragraph or page, ...

All these establishments have lead us to define a model of multimodal output presentation based on the features of aural and tactile modality.

5. Towards a model of multimodal output representation

An interface is said to be multimodal [5] when it allows the use of different input/output communication channels.

Our work on the output representation and generation relies on the remarks and the conclusions of [12], exclusively devoted to the problems of a multimodal inter-pretation (axe: user to system).

The characteristics of the interfaces including several input devices have defined a reference space for the interpretation, namely the axis: modality usage and association of several knowledge sources in the interpretation mechanism. Our purpose here is to demonstrate the validity of this reference space and its extension for the output representation and generation. This reference space is defined according to the following axis (at the state of the model): modality usage, fission axis, output granularity and abstraction level.

- **The modality usage axis** reveal the temporal disposability of the output devices. The use is sequential, when, at a given time, only one output media can be used for output production. In the opposite case, we talk about parallel or simultaneous usage of media. For example, noises and speech constitute two kinds of aural information perceived by the aural channel. The transmission of the message from the system to the user can be spread over several channels in a simultaneous (parallel) or sequential way.

- **The fission axis** represents the possibility of the distribution of the message from the task to the user under different output representations. The lack of fission characterises the fact that the message has only one output mode. For example, we can consider the transmission of a message for the user in its tactile or aural form. If there is no semantic link between the different forms, they are said to be independent. On the other case, they are said combined.

- **The output granularity axis** takes account of the output discretisation level.

- **The level of output representation and abstraction axis** defines the degree of transformation of the message to send to the user. These abstraction levels depend on the state of the task and of the interaction; for example, a vocal message can be synthesised word by word in its totality relatively to its meaning in the task domain.

We can see here that the output multimodality problem space permits the classification of an output multimodality system. It also allows to account for the use of the output modalities. For example, during the system use, we can observe that a modality is not relevant in a synergetic use and a very great usability in an exclusive usage.

6. Conclusion

A given system can only allow one kind of multimodality. Another one can be hybrid and permits, depending on the **contexts, several types of multimodality**. In that case, the generation model must be able to decide dynamically on the appropriate strategy according to **the state of the task and to the user**. It is obvious that the implementation of this kind of output multimodal generation needs further research on the strategies of the users during their consultation task like in the MUIMS.

References

1. Y. Bellik, D. Teil: A Multimodal Dialogue Controller For Multimodal User Interface Management System, Application: A Multimodal Window Manager, In Proceedings of InterCHI'93 Proceedings, Amsterdam, (1993).

2. D. Burger: La multimodalité: un moyen d'améliorer l'accessibilité des systèmes informatiques pour les personnes handicapées. Dans ERGO.IA '92, pp. 262-277, (1992).

3. J.M. Carrol: Creating a Design Science of Human-Computer Interaction, in Interaction with Computers N° 5, 1, pp.3-12, (1993).

4. D. Cotto: Traitement automatique des textes en vue de la synthèse vocale", Thèse d'Université Toulouse III, (1992).

5. J. Coutaz, S. Balbo: Applications: a dimension space for user interface management systems. In CHI'91, ACM Publication, pp. 27-32, (1991).

6. A. Dufresne: L'importance d'un accès multimodal aux ordinateurs pour le non-voyant. Dans Le Curseur, vol II, n°1, pp. 1-4, Canada, (1993).

7. Elan Informatique: Vocalix Dos. Dans Aides techniques pour les déficients visuels, 1991.

8. J. Engelen, B. Bauwens: Large Scale Distribution of Text Information: The Harmonisation and Standardisation Efforts of the TIDE-CAPS Consortium. In Proc. of the European Conference On The Advancement of Rehabilitation Technology Ecart 2, pp. 27.1, Stockholm, (1993).

9. Joint ESCA-NATO/RSG10-Tutorial and Workshop - Applications of Speech Technology, Lautrach, Bavaria, 16-17 September, (1993).

10. Y. Hatwell: Images and non-visual spatial representations in the blind. In Non-Visual Human-Computer Interactions, Eds D. Burger, J.C. Sperandio, Colloque INSERM / John Libbey Eurotext Ltd, Vol. 228, pp.13-35, (1993).

11. IBM, Screen Reader: Système de synthèse vocale au service des non-voyants et des malvoyants. Dans Document Publicitaire, (1991).

12. Compte rendu des ateliers: Interface Multimodale et Architecture Logicielle. TELECOM Paris 93 S 004, pp. 9-45, (1992).

13. A.I. Karsmer, R.T. Hartley, K. Paap: Using Sound and Sound Spaces to Provide High Bandwidth Computer Interfaces to the Visually Handicapped. In SIGCAPH Newsletter ACM Press, N° 44, pp. 1-10, (1992).

14. D. Kochanek: A Hypertext System for the Blind Newspaper Reader. In Proc. of the 3rd Int. Conf. on Computers fro Handicapped Persons, pp. 285-293, (1992).

15. L. Nigay, J. Coutaz: A Design Space for Multimodal Systems: Concurrent Processing and Data Fusion. In Proceedings of InterCHI'93, pp. 172-78, (1993).

16. C. Lu: State of the Art:Publish It Electronically. In Byte, pp. 94-109 (1993).

17. B. Oriola, D. Cotto, G. Pérennou, N. Vigouroux:Consultation de documents électroniques pour les personnes handicapées de la vue. Dans Conférence "L'interface des mondes réels et virtuels", Montpellier EC2, pp. 489-500, (1992).

18. B. Oriola, G. Pérennou and N. Vigouroux: An Oral Input-Output Interface for the Reading of Electronic Newspapers by the Visually Impaired. In 1st TIDE Congress, Brussels, (1993).

19. E. Pascual, J. Virbel: Connaissances linguistiques et morpho-disposition-nelles pour le contrôle de la décomposition structurelle des documents. Dans Colloque national sur l'écrit et le document, CNED, Actes dans Bigre, 80, pp. 217-224, (1992).

20. L. Pring, J. Rusted: Pictures for the blind: an investigation of the influence of pictures on recall of text by blind children. In British Journal of Developmental Psychology, 3, pp. 41-45, (1985).

21. A. Rudnicky, G. Hauptmann, K.F. Lee: Survey of Current Speech Technology. In Communication of ACM, Vol. 37, N°3, pp. 52-57, (1994).

22. J.R. Searle: Les actes du langage. Hermann, Paris (1972).

23. F.P. Seiler, N. Vigouroux, M. Truquet, P. Bazex, C. Decoret: Access To electronic Information for Visually Impaired Persons. Seminar Day, 4th ICCHP Vienna, (1994).

24. C. Sorin: Synthèse de la parole à partir du texte: état des recherches & des applications. Dans Deuxièmes journées nationales du GRECO-PRC, CHM, Toulouse, pp. 131-146, (1991).

25. C. Sorin, D. Jouvet, M. Toularrhoat, C. Gagnoulet: Commande vocale et synthèse à partir de texte pour les services vocaux: l'expérience du CNET. Dans Conférence "L'interface des mondes réels et virtuels", Informatique 93, Montpellier EC2, pp. 305-310, (1993).

26. U. Strempel: Presentation of different types of Talking Newspapers with Special emphasis on ETAB. Stiftung Blindenanstalt Frankfurt am Main, Allemagne, (1990).

27. B. Thon, J.C. Marque, P. Maury: Le texte, l'Image et leurs Traitements Cognitifs. Dans Colloque Interdisciplinaire du CNRS, "Images et Langages" Multimodalité et Modélisation Cognitive, pp. 29-39, Paris, (1993).

Auditory Extension of User Interfaces

Andrea R. Kennel

Institut für Informationssysteme, ETH Zürich
CH-8092 Zürich, Switzerland

User Interface

Users communicate with computers via the user interface. Internal objects in computer systems like files, windows, menus and messages are represented in the user interface by different symbols, which are perceived and interpreted by the user.

Today most symbols in the user interface are visual symbols. Blattner [1] and Gaver [2] demonstrate that also auditory symbols can be used. If the screen is overloaded or the user is performing a task where he cannot always watch the screen, auditory symbols are helpful. For visually handicapped users the advantage of auditory symbols is obvious.

Auditory Symbols and Point of Experiments

The perception of auditory symbols is complementary to the perception of visual symbols. A visual symbol exists in space and over time, an auditory symbols exists in time and over space [2]. Therefore auditory symbols are a useful addition to visual symbols. They can be described by the parameters: characteristic; volume; pitch; duration.

Depending on its duration an auditory symbol represents a internal object continuously or instantaneously. For a continuous representation the status of the internal object is represented during its whole existence by an auditory symbol with a flexible duration. For an instantaneous representation only the beginning of a status is represented by an auditory symbol with a short fix duration.

Which and how many auditory symbols can be distinguished by the user? - Which are the minimum and maximum duration of auditory symbols? - For these and other questions ergonomic rules have to be found by user testing. Therefore we are developing a user interface framework, which allows to add and exchange interface symbols in a easy way.

References

1   Blattner, M., Sumikawa, D. & Greenberg, R. Earcons and icons: Their structure and common design principles. Human-Computer Interaction 4 (1989), 11.

2   Gaver, W. The SonicFinder: An interface that uses auditory icons. Human-Computer Interaction 4 (1989), 67.

AUDITORY EXTENSION OF USER INTERFACES

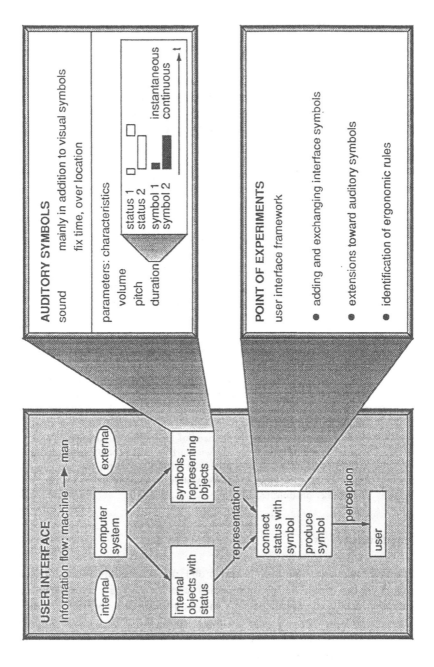

An Attempt to Define Fully-Accessible Workstation Levels of Accessibility

RJ Cooper
Adaptive Technology Specialist
Capistrano School District
San Juan Capistrano, CA, USA

Jeffrey C. Senge
Computer Access Coordinator
California State University at Fullerton
Fullerton, CA, USA

Contact information:
24843 Del Prado #283
Dana Point, CA 92629 USA
Voice: 714-240-4853 Fax: 714-240-9785
Email: rjcoop@AOL.com or jsenge@fullerton.edu

The development and adoption of defined and standardized 'fully accessible workstations', which serve the needs of a great percentage of persons that require non-traditional access to computers, is a goal of all facilities that consider meeting the needs of persons with disabilities. Although the needs of every person with a disability are unique to that individual, it is possible to develop standards based upon relative incidence and probable need of technology assistance. These standards would provide a known starting point for those facilities wishing to begin technology access assistance programs, and structured upgrade paths for those facilities wishing to expand their services to cover other disabilities.

1 Introduction

The authors suggest adopting a series of Fully-Accessible Workstation (FAW) standards, that would define those assistive technology aids necessary to provide computer access to various persons with non-traditional abilities. In the United States, at present, various groups are implementing technology access programs with a need to specify which type of product will address which type of disability, and relative need and necessity of each disability.

"Almost 1 in 11 full-time freshman (8.8%) enrolled in college in 1991 reported a disability. Since 1987, this was a considerable increase when the proportion was about 1 in 38 freshmen (2.6%)." [1] FAW accessibility must address prevalence and need, which are inversely proportional. Visual and learning disabilities comprise 25% of those freshmen listing a disability, while orthopedic disabilities comprise only

14% [1]. The need for assisted technology access is high for those with severe visual impairments, low and as yet unproven for those with learning disabilities, and high, once again, for those with severe orthopedic disabilities. Naturally, the greatest number of people with disabilities have moderate disabilities, which dictate less need, while the fewer number of people with disabilities have severe disabilities, which dictate greater need. That is, those with moderate disabilities have less of a need for technology access assistance while those with severe disabilities have a greater need. This applies to both computer course/work and to that course/work which can only be accomplished via computers by a person with a severe disability. As an example of the former, most English Composition course/work is executed via word processing; this can be considered computer coursework. An example of the latter may be researching a particular subject which requires physically locating, and manipulating numerous reference materials. This process simply cannot be performed manually by a person with severe disability. This person requires not only technology to perform the research, such as on-line reference databases, but technology assistance to access the technology which allows the research to proceed.

The precedent for such a system of Level definitions exists in the MPC (MultiMedia Personal Computer) Levels set by MicroSoft, IBM, Intel, and others. These Levels dictate what equipment is necessary for a computer company, or value-added reseller, to label their product MPC Level One or Level Two. This pseudo-certification addresses hard disk space, processor type and speed, sound capabilities, CD-ROM inclusion, and several other components. That is, one works along a continuum of possible devices employed in a home workstation, from very basic, to very high end, capable of handling any type of application.

This paradigm can easily be applied to workstations for persons with disabilities. After traditional keyboard access is considered inappropriate by either the end-user, care-giver, or facilitator (employee, technology specialist, or other person at the facility in question), one works along a continuum of devices and aids, from slightly assistive to greatly assistive. As the facility gathers more adaptive devices for the workstation, it becomes more capable of handling persons with a greater variety of disabilities.

These standards can be applied to any computer platform, and are not specific to brand. Adaptive devices for almost all computer types are now made commercially and available internationally. For the purposes of this paper, the authors will limit themselves to the two main platforms, the Macintosh by Apple Computer, and a PC, which is any computer that is IBM 80x86 or Pentium compatible.

In most cases, the authors are referencing a specific product by a specific company, but brand names and company names are omitted for academic reasons. The intent is to specify device capability, rather than product promotion. Should readers wish to receive references on specific devices, they should contact the authors.

2 Methodology

A continuum of physical abilities (for persons with DISabilities) and devices that address those abilities will now be presented. Beginning with those with the most moderate handicaps the list will ascend to those with the greatest challenges. This will take the form of specifying the physical abilities of the user, and the possible device and capabilities of the adaptive device.

For those persons that can access the keyboard, and can move a mouse, but cannot click the mouse while holding it steady:
1) A trackball which allows the user to move a ball within its cradle, remove his/her hand from the ball, and click with a different motion entirely is recommended.
2) An external switch, operated by another motion, other than the ball manipulation is recommended. This switch is hard-wired to emulate the mouse-click.
3) A second external switch is hard-wired to a button on the trackball which performs a 'drag-lock', that is, activating this second switch causes the computer to believe the user is holding down the primary click, thus performing the drag function.
4) This device shall be known as a Switch-Adapted Mouse device.

For persons that can access the regular keyboard but cannot control the mouse sufficiently:
1) A trackball might be appropriate.
2) A joystick that emulates the mouse might be appropriate.
   a) This device shall be known as a Joy-Mouse.

For those persons that can access the keyboard, but cannot manipulate the mouse at all:
1) There are free programs available for both platforms that allow certain keys to move and click the mouse, so that all mouse functions can be performed by keyboard. Macintosh computers include these programs with their systems, while the corresponding utilities for PC's are available free from IBM.
2) These utilities shall be known as Mouse-Keys.

For those persons that have gross control of their hands but cannot access the traditional keyboard or mouse:
1) A slightly larger keyboard with 'keys' that have greater separation than the traditional keyboard, is recommended. This keyboard is also 'definable' so that it can be customized to a person's needs, physically, and software-wise. This keyboard is simply plugged in where the normal keyboard is usually plugged in, and the normal keyboard can still be plugged in tandem with it. This keyboard can also perform mouse functions by keystrokes.
2) This device shall be known as an Oversize Keyboard.

For those persons that have limited vision:
1) Several 'magnifying programs' exist which enlarge any portion of the screen selected by the user. The Macintosh ships with the program CloseView for this purpose. Similar programs are available for the PC.
2) These programs shall be known as Screen Magnification Software.

For those persons that can hear but cannot see the screen at all:

1) Numerous software programs exist for the PC and one is available for the Macintosh which give a blind person complete access to user-selectable auditory monitoring of both text-based and Graphic-User-Interface screens.

2) These programs shall be known as Screen Reading Software.

For those persons that can operate a pointing device but cannot access a normal keyboard or an oversize keyboard:

1) An On-Screen Keyboard program allows a person that can use a joystick, mouse, or a trackball, to move a cursor/arrow and click the button, in order to select keystrokes. Mouse moves can be handled directly through the appropriate input device or through appropriate keys on the on-screen keyboard.

a) These programs shall be known as On-Screen Keyboard Software.

2) There exists a variety of pointing devices. The best known is a mouse, of course, with a trackball and joystick also well known. On the Adaptive Technology market, there are several devices available for persons that can move another part of their body, most frequently their head, to control an on-screen cursor that tracks the movement of the controlling appendage.

3) Several of these on-screen keyboard programs allow the user to select keystrokes by simply by keeping the cursor over an on-screen key or function for a preset time.

a) This function shall be known as Dwell-Selectable.

For those persons that can operate a single switch, with a voluntary and consistent motor movement, but cannot access any of the above:

1) Some type of screen scanning is called for. With this method, the user clicks an appropriate external switch or input device to initiate an indicator which moves through the user's possible actions/selections, until the user activates their input device to send the desired selection to the host application. The following scenario illustrates this approach.

A horizontal line appears across the width of the screen, at the top of the screen. This line descends down the screen until it reaches the desired vertical location and the user clicks a second time. A finger appears at the left edge of the line and begins moving horizontally until it reaches the desired horizontal location. The user clicks a third time to select that location, just as if a traditional mouse mover moved the mouse directly to that location, and clicked. Double-clicks, drags, and menu bars are handled similarly. Text entry may be performed via an On-Screen keyboard by this same method, only restricting the area of screen scanning to the Keyboard area to increase speed of input.

3 Corroboration

The results of a survey concerning this matter will be disbursed at the conference. The body currently being polled are members of Project EASI, Equal Access to Software and Information, an international collaborative effort of professionals in higher education, representatives of several Fortune 500 companies, and developers of adaptive aids. One of the missions of Project EASI is to assess and evaluate the technology status of workstations as it currently relates to access and information. From this assessment and dialog, solutions are sought. Both authors of this paper are members of Project EASI. It is hoped that survey results of up to 100 members will be compiled and analyzed. These results, along with the authors' specifications, will define EASI/FAW Levels.

4 Conclusions

In deciding what part of its budget to allocate to assistive devices, a facility could compile data on prevalence and need relative to the populations it wishes to serve. After prioritizing the workstation needs as dictated by the compilation, the facility could simply cross-reference its needs with the FAW Level sequence to help isolate possible assistive aids. Further research would be necessary, by the facility, to decide between brands and features of products at a certain level, but it is hoped that many manufacturers would adopt the standards also, so as to make the facility's comparison efforts easier.

Each level specified herein would need to be further defined and possibly divided into sub-levels, as features become accepted as standards, or remain product features. That is, the primary features of a product apply to its Level assignment, whereas the secondary features of a product might be considered Preferences, which are available with most software. It will be quite difficult, without complete manufacturer agreement, to separate these two. A certain manufacturer might claim that their feature is really necessary to address a certain Level, whereas another manufacturer might claim that it is their feature that defines the standard at that level. Some sort of governing peer group would be necessary to make certification decisions, Level definitions, and guideline adherence.

Given the above paragraph's success, and acceptance of the theme of this paper, a committee within a group such as Project EASI could begin work on logistics. The following steps might form a desired sequence of activity.
1) Fully specify, along a continuum such as that presented here, all major assistive item groups and the disabilities they address.
2) Define those features of each item that form the basis of that Level.
3) Specify those items, of all items made, that conform to that Level specification.
4) Inform manufacturers of their inclusion or exclusion, and specify rationale.
5) Choose certain model sites and assist in implementation.
6) Publish articles in appropriate publications reporting creation of Level standards.
7) Produce FAW Level booklets specifying guidelines and criteria for facilities wishing to replicate model sites.

As an example of the difficulty facing such a project, the following quotations are presented from an E-mail letter attempting to negotiate/work out a compromise with the Computer Access Bill facing California legislators during mid-May, 1994. The authors of this E-mail attempted to facilitate a compromise between needs and funds availability, and found that insufficient definitions existed to reach a compromise. [2]
"...this study shall include...an assessment of the degree to which students with disabilities are currently able to use the computers in each open lab."

"An accessible computer is one that has been modified to contain hardware or software that makes it usable by a visually, mobility or hearing impaired student."

"This is accomplished primarily by consulting with individual students about the computer hardware and software accommodations they need, and providing access to adaptive computers..."

"We need to agree on a chart of what is needed for the computer station...and what an accessible station should look like. We do not need several chefs cooking this brew. We need consensus among us and especially among the high tech center program managers."

One can easily ascertain, from these quotations, the need for acceptance of this paper, or its theme. If one of the largest post-secondary school systems in the world, the California State University system, is having difficulties such as quoted above, then it is time to consider standardization such as those proposed herein.

5 References

1. C. Henderson: College Freshmen with Disabilities: A Statistical Profile. In HEATH Resource Center of the American Council on Education. Washington, DC.

2. California State Department of Rehabilitation: E-mail letter distributed to all University of California and California State University campus administrators

Graz Brain-Computer Interface (BCI) II[1]

J. Kalcher, D. Flotzinger, S. Gölly, Ch. Neuper, G. Pfurtscheller

Institute of Biomedical Engineering, Department of Medical Informatics,
and Ludwig Boltzmann-Institute of Medical Informatics and Neuroinformatics,
Graz University of Technology, Brockmanngasse 41, A-8010 Graz/Austria

Abstract. This paper describes the new setup of the Graz Brain-Computer
Interface (BCI) system II, which is based on on-line classification of EEG
patterns to determine which of three kinds of movement is planned by a
subject. This classification can be exploited for on-line control which may
constitute a great help for handicapped persons in the future.

1 Introduction

Theoretically, the thoughts of a person should be reflected in the person's brainwaves
and therefore be measurable by electrodes on the person's scalp. In practice, several
groups have shown that such 'thoughts' as mentally answering 'yes' and 'no' [1],
intention to move a joystick [2] or planning of hand movement [3, 4] can be
discriminated based on the recorded EEG with surprising accuracy. These findings
have led to the idea to exploit the EEG for control in cases where other means of
control are either impossible, e.g. in cases of handicapped persons, or infeasible, e.g.
if both hands are occupied.

A system which uses EEG to build a communication line between the brain and
an electrical appliance has become known as a Brain-Computer Interface (BCI).
Several teams all over the world are currently working at such systems [5, 6]; this
paper describes the work done in Graz, a system which is mainly based on the
discrimination of various types of movement planning [7, 8].

2 Experimental Paradigm

The basic idea of the Graz BCI system has already been outlined in previous
papers[7]. The Graz BCI I was a one-dimensional cursor control system which could
discriminate between left and right hand movement planning whereby in the initial
session the subject had to press a microswitch with either the left or right index
finger. The cortical areas involved in these two kinds of movement planning are
primarily the left and right sensorimotor hand areas; the corresponding electrode
positions overlying these areas are C_3 and C_4 (international 10-20 system) [3].

[1] Supported by the "Fonds zur Förderung der wissenschaftlichen Forschung", project P9043
and "Forschungsförderungsfonds für die gewerbliche Wirtschaft" project 2/312..

To increase the dimensions of control, additional EEG patterns have to be found which are discernable from left and right hand movement. Studies of foot and tongue movement showed that these two kinds of movement can indeed be discriminated from left and right hand movement, especially in the movement planning phase [8] (see Fig. 1). Therefore, the additional movement type 'foot flexion' was built into the Graz BCI which, due to several changes in the recording scheme and experimental paradigm, is now called Graz BCI II.

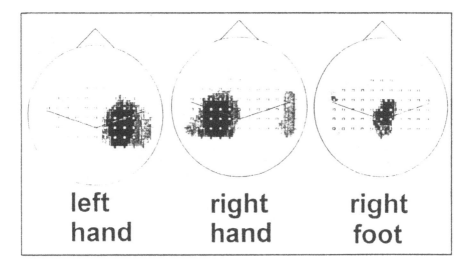

Fig. 1. Topographic maps display alpha power decrease during planning of hand and foot movement. "Black" indicates cortical areas with large power decrease. The electrode positions and the approximate location of the central sulcus are indicated.

The basics of a trial of the Graz BCI II are shown in Fig. 2. The subject is seated in a comfortable chair looking at a fixation cross on a monitor 1 meter in front of the subject's eyes. One second after an acoustic warning stimulus ('beep') a cue in the form of an arrow, pointing either left, right or down, appears and indicates to the subject that as soon as the arrow vanishes (after 1250 msec) he should either press a microswitch with his left index finger, his right index finger or move the toes of his right foot upwards (dorsal flexion), respectively. A 1-second period starting 250 msec after presentation onset of the cue is classified into one of the three movement tasks and the corresponding classification of the system is fed back to the subject either as correctly identified ('+'), undecided ('o') or wrong classification ('-').

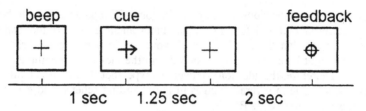

Fig. 2. Experimental paradigm of the Graz BCI II

A PC486 with a DSP-board records and classifies the EEG and provides the feedback to the subject. Three bipolar EEG channels are used for on-line classification: C_3-C'_3, C_z-C'_z and C_4-C'_4 (see Fig. 2). The signals are sampled at 64 Hz, whereby the features extracted from the 1-second period of EEG and presented to the classifier are comprised of four power estimates, each representing 250 msec, per EEG channel. These power estimates are calculated by squaring each sample and then averaging over 16 samples. The 12 features (3 EEG channels times 4 power estimates) are offered to a classifier which calculates both a classification and a measure describing the certainty with which the classification was obtained. Depending on this quality measure and the correctness of the classification, the system provides a feedback to the subject in the form of a small or large '+' if the classification is correct and the quality measure is in medium or large range, respectively, a small or large '-' if the classification is incorrect, and 'o' if the quality measure is very small.

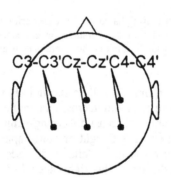

Fig. 3. Positions of the electrodes on the scalp

Four subjects (1 female and 3 male students aged between 23 and 27 years) participated in four experimental sessions on different days within 2 weeks. Each session lasted about 1.5 h and comprised four blocks of 60 trials each with 5 min breaks between blocks. In the first session, data were collected for the creation of the classifier and therefore no feedback was provided. In the following sessions 2 and 3, the classifier was used to discriminate the 3 kinds of movement out of the movement planning phase and to give feedback to the subject as described above. In session 4 no physical behavior took place, using the same stimulation procedure as in the first sessions, the subject was asked to concentrate on left hand, right hand or foot movement. In this session the classifier was applied to EEG data during mental activity and provided feedback about discriminability of three different mental states.

3 Classification Method

The classifier built into the Graz BCI II system is a Learning Vector Quantizer (LVQ) [9, 10]. Its classification speed and ease of use in the Graz BCI I system have suggested its further use in on-line EEG classification of more than two categories.

Basically, a LVQ is a nearest-neighbour classifier whereby a labelled codebook is generated such that for each training example the nearest codebook vector is of the same category as the given example. Thereby, LVQ tries to optimize the representation of the training examples by the codebook vectors (also known as Vector Quantization) and at the same time to minimize the classification error. The labelled codebook is generated using an iterative learning procedure where in each iteration a randomly selected training example of known classification is compared to the codebook and the two closest codebook vectors are found. Depending on the class labels of the given example and of the two codebook vectors the latter two are updated by either pushing them towards the example (if the class labels are identical to the known classification of the example, correct classification) or pushing them away from the example (for a detailed description of the algorithm see [9, 10]. The overall aim of this learning algorithm is to increase the probability of correct classification the next time the given example is presented.

Extensive off-line analyses have shown that only a very small number of codebook vectors is needed to provide satisfactory performance. usually 3-4 codebook vectors per category suffice. Searching twelve (4 codebook vectors times 3 categories) 12-dimensional vectors for the nearest codebook vector is an extremely simple and fast form of classification.

The quality measure of the classification can be obtained by not only searching for the nearest codebook vector but also for the nearest codebook vector of a second category. By comparing the distances of these two codebook vectors it can be determined whether the given example lies near a class boundary, in which case the distances to the two codebook vectors d_1 and d_2 will be very similar, or whether the given example clearly belongs to the category of the closest codebook vector, in which case distance d_1 will be much smaller than d_2. Therefore, the quality measure can be computed as

$$qu(d_1, d_2) = 1 - \frac{d_1}{d_2}.$$

It is obvious that this formula will provide values close to zero if the distances d_1 and d_2 are about the same and values close to one if distance d_1 is much smaller than d_2.

'A6'	big +	+	o	-	big -
Session 2	21,7%	37,5%	21,7%	16,7%	2,5%
Session 3	25,0%	34,6%	23,8%	13,3%	3,3%
Session 4	20,8%	24,2%	24,2%	24,6%	6,3%

'B9'	big +	+	o	-	big -
Session 2	20,0%	21,7%	15,4%	30,4%	12,5%
Session 3	18,8%	23,3%	15,8%	28,8%	13,3%
Session 4	12,9%	20,8%	22,5%	28,8%	15,0%

'A1'	big +	+	o	-	big -
Session 2	22,9%	27,5%	18,8%	23,3%	7,5%
Session 3	20,0%	21,3%	20,8%	26,7%	11,3%
Session 4	19,6%	24,2%	20,4%	21,3%	14,6%

'B8'	big +	+	o	-	big -
Session 2	10,4%	27,9%	21,7%	33,3%	6,7%
Session 3	21,7%	25,0%	13,8%	29,6%	10,0%
Session 4	14,2%	26,3%	24,6%	26,3%	8,8%

Table 1. On-line performance (%) of four subjects in three sessions.

4 Results and Discussion

The on-line performance for the last three sessions (the first was used for training the classifier) of each subject are given in Table 1. All subjects showed more than random on-line performance (random performance in 3 categories would be 33,33% correct).

From Table 1 can be seen:
> (i) There are always more trials classified correct (+) compared with incorrect (-).

(ii) About 20% of the trials are not classified into any of the 3 classes. This number depends on the threshold used and is a potential for further improvement.

(iii) In the first "mental" session (session 4) for three subjects the majority of trials were correctly classified

These results are far from optimal but they show for the first time that after only 4 sessions a discrimination between 3 different EEG patterns is possible. It has to be kept in mind, that the systems of Clark and Tizard [1], Hiraiwa et al. [2] and Wolpaw et al. [5] were all designed for a 2-class discrimination problem and none of these systems were applied to 3 classes.

There are different possibilities for further improvement:

(i) Selection of the optimal frequency band with the largest EEG reactivity. For the parameter estimation not only the alpha but also the beta band can be used.

(ii) Selection of the optimal electrode positions. It was shown recently, that classification results depend on the location of the electrodes [11] whereby the optimal positions are not the same for each subject. Such electrode positions should be selected in a pre-experiment, where the EEG is recorded from a large number of electrodes.

(iii) Increase the number of sessions.

5 Conclusion

The design of the Graz BCI is based on mental preparation of different kinds of movement. It was shown, that 3 "movement patterns" can be differentiated in an on-line experiment within fractions of a second. It is planned to extend the Graz BCI to 4 classes, whereby the 4th class can be e.g. visual imagination.

There are, however, still a number of problems to be solved in relation to optimize the performance of the system. Among these are the improvements in the experimental paradigm including a more effective feedback, the estimation of more specific EEG parameters and improvements in the learnable classifier. As already mentioned, a very important task is also the selection of the optimal electrode positions.

References

1. Clark C.R., Tizard J.: Single-trial analysis of scalp electrical fields using artificial neural networks. Proceedings of 3rd Int. Congress on BET Amsterdam, 1992.
2. Hiraiwa A., Shimohara K., Tokunaga Y.: EEG topography recognition by Neural Networks. Engineering in Medicine and Biology, pp. 39-42, 1990.

3. Pfurtscheller G., Berghold A.: Patterns of cortical activation during planning of voluntary movement, Electroenceph. and clin. Neurophysiol., Vol. 72, pp. 250-258, 1989.
4. Pfurtscheller G., Flotzinger D., Mohl W., Peltoranta M.: Prediction of the side of hand movements from single-trial multi-channel EEG data using neural networks, Electroenceph. and clin. Neurophysiol., Vol. 82, pp. 313-315, 1992.
5. Wolpaw J. R., McFarland D., Neat G. W., Forneris C. A.: An EEG-based brain-computer interface for cursor control, Electroenceph. and clin. Neurophysiol., Vol. 78, pp. 252-259, 1991.
6. McFarland D. J., Neat G. W., Read R. F., Wolpaw J. R.: An EEG-based method for graded cursor control, Psychobiology, Vol. 21, No. 1, pp. 77-81, 1993.
7. Pfurtscheller G., Flotzinger D., Kalcher J.: Brain-Computer Interface - a new communication device for handicapped persons, Journal of Microcomputer Appl., Vol. 16, pp. 293-299, 1993.
8. Pfurtscheller G., Flotzinger D., Neuper Ch.: Differentiation between finger, toe and tongue movement in man based on 40-Hz EEG, Electroenceph. and clin. Neurophysiol., Vol. 90, pp. 456-460, 1994.
9. Kohonen T.: The Self-Organizing Map, Proceedings of the IEEE, Vol. 78, No. 9, pp. 1464-1480, 1990.
10. Flotzinger D., Kalcher J., Pfurtscheller G.: EEG Classification by Learning Vector Quantization, Biomedizinische Technik, Vol. 37, No. 12, pp. 303-309, 1992.
11. Flotzinger, D., Pregenzer, M., Pfurtscheller, G.: Feature Selection with Distinction Sensitive Learning Vector Quantisation and Genetic Algorithm Proceedings of IEEE conference on Neural Networks (ICNN 94), pp. 3448 -3451, 1994.

Human-Computer Interfacing for the Severely Physically Disabled

A.D. Cherry*, M.S. Hawley#, M. Freeman** and P.A. Cudd*

*Dept. Electronic and Electrical Engineering, University of Sheffield, Sheffield, S1 3JD
**Philippa Cottam Communication Clinic, Dept. of Speech Science, University of Sheffield, Sheffield, S10 2TA
#Dept. Medical Physics, Barnsley District General Hospital NHS Trust, Barnsley, S75 2EP

Abstract. Human computer interfacing issues and the need for design standards for switch operated integrated rehabilitation systems are discussed. Input methods and compatibility problems are summarised. Formulae for access times to menu structures for a number of single switch selection methods are given. Quantitative comparisons are given for example selection processes. It is concluded that row column scanning is fastest for small selection sets. Advantages and disadvantages of the use of multiple switches for input are indicated.

1 Introduction

Rehabilitation integrated systems are in their infancy, in the future as they mature they offer the potential to meet the electronic device control needs of a broad range of disabled people. The latter electronic devices can support some or all of the following functions: mobility, communication and environment control, and especially when computer based, education and employment. The potential for computer based integrated systems to benefit disabled children is significant because there is easier and greater scope for the system to grow with the child than with Rehabilitation Systems of the past.

The important features which are offered by a properly designed integrated system are: appropriateness to a large target population; an user interface that can be optimised to the individual's needs and abilities, including the adaptability to cater for the changing needs of the user; safe operation; a comprehensible and functional setting up procedure. Other factors are cost, robustness and compactness. On most of these points, integrated systems based on portable computers appear to show considerable promise.

Designed integrated/semi-integrated systems are emerging[1,2], but agreed design standards are not yet in existence. Words+[3] produce a suite of applications that can be used together as an integrated system. However, the user is restricted to using software from that company and would have difficulty using it with other software successfully. A major advantage of using Words+ software is the availability of free upgrades for life. Prentke Romich[4] build stand alone communication aids which can be enhanced to provide environmental control and computer keyboard emulation. A number of systems are evolving[5,6] but these are not yet sufficiently established to be widely used for the development or provision of integrated systems. The advent of

Microsoft Windows has established a better software design environment for the PC. It should be noted that other platforms with similar graphical user interfaces offer this advantage, e.g. Apple Macintosh platforms.

The Sheffield and Barnsley Rehabilitation Research Group have developed integrated systems designed for severely physically handicapped people using a number of switches for the input device[7,8]. More recently systems based on fully PC compatible computers, e.g. BASIS[9], have offered colour displays and the option for use of pointing devices for input.

This paper discusses some of the factors that must be considered in the development of switch user interfaces for integrated systems. Many switch users operate their computer by use of mouse and/or keyboard emulators. The use of an icon and switch based user interface, i.e. BASIS, has caused the authors to reconsider the suitability of standard input device emulators for generic applications.

2 Input Methods

For users with insufficient motor control to use a standard computer keyboard and/or mouse, a number of alternative devices exist. They generally fall into one of three categories:

- **Alternative keyboards.** These range from keyboards with alternative layouts to expanded keyboards with either large or very tightly-packed buttons, or, switch operated emulators. Usually the application software will use its standard keyboard interfacing.
- **Mouse emulators.** Touch screens, track balls, head pointers etc. come into this category. Usually the application software will use its standard mouse interfacing.
- **Switches.** Switches of varying size and required operating force are used. They require dedicated switch driven interfacing.

Depending on which of these alternatives is being used, the method of connecting them varies. Alternative keyboards usually connect to the keyboard port. Mouse emulating devices usually connect to the serial port, often requiring a driver in addition to the mouse driver. The situation for switches, however, is more complex. Unlike the keyboard or mouse, there is currently no standard means of connecting switches to a computer. Typical switch connection techniques are as follows:

- Switches are hardwired in parallel to the buttons on a mouse.
- A switch in circuit between a common line and a handshaking line on the serial port.
- A switch in circuit between a common line and a handshaking line on the parallel port.
- A dongle is connected to a standard port, the switches are connected to the dongle. This provides transparency (e.g. a 'through' printer port) and software copy protection .

2.1 Software compatibility of integrated systems using switch input

If a switch user wishes to use just one switch-driven application, no problems should occur. Increasingly however, computers are being used as the basis of integrated systems with a number of both assistive and 'standard' applications needing to be controlled from the switches. Each application may have a different switch interface, and indeed require a different port connection. Applications not designed for switch use usually require a keyboard and/or mouse emulator to function. With such an emulator, switch presses are transformed by the emulator to key presses or mouse operations to create input that the application can accept. Problems associated with using multiple applications can be eased in environments such as Microsoft Windows, but compatibility between the applications' switch inputs is still not guaranteed. A typical integrated system may consist of products from two or three different sources and the above problems can still exist. The user is then left with the following choices:

- A carer may have to move the switch connection for the user;
- The user may have to use a compatible but possibly inferior application;
- Technical assistance may have to be sought, the problem may or may not be solvable by local expertise. If not, one or more of the applications would have to be re-designed.

Clearly none of the above are satisfactory solutions. The first two points result in the user having an inferior integrated system. The third point may require great effort and take too long. The problems are exacerbated if these multiple applications control a speech synthesiser, infra-red sender and wheelchair. With desktop computers the required extra ports can be added via an expansion card, but notebook computers, used commonly by wheelchair-bound users have little or no means of expansion.

2.2 Standardisation

The well specified user interface in modern environments, such as Windows with its 'feel of similarity' across applications, is a step forward in potentiating access to applications for disabled individuals. However, it does not go far enough. The philosophy behind many of the commercially available graphical user interfaces includes the tenet 'the user should need to know a minimum, preferably nothing, about the computer hardware to use the computer', leading to the trend that more and more of the low-level system operation, such as the code that interprets the incoming signals from the mouse, is difficult to replace. Access to the low-level system operation is of fundamental importance to Rehabilitation system developers. The authors would argue that commercially available user interfaces should hide all unnecessary hardware related aspects to facilitate ease of use, but that the blocks of code handling the user input and feedback be replaceable, i.e. make these blocks separate applications. For switch input, generic software standards that interpret the input and possibly a standard hardware port are needed. The exact nature of the hardware standard is not so certain because this could also be specified for the PCMCIA interface and/or the serial, parallel, PS2, keyboard or perhaps games ports.

The future requirements for the hardware standard are not sufficiently understood due to safety issues and the possibility of needing adaptive interfaces.

The M3S bus project[6] proposes a standard hardware interface to which all assistive devices belonging to an integrated system would be attached. As this interface would have to be incorporated into all new equipment including computers its general acceptance could take a long time. Also, following its rationale fully implies even providing each switch with an M3S interface. Ultimately, international standards and approaches are desirable for this technology to mature. The open system approach offered by Comspec[5] is to be welcomed. Just like other rehabilitation development, standards should be derived from the needs of the users. The needs of the users will determine the required human computer interface which in turn will specify the requirements for the software and hardware. In considering the definition of the standards, the goal should be maximising functionality for the user. It often looks as if software is written with too much emphasis on the provider; of course, if systems do not have a simple set up procedure, they are unlikely to be supplied. Integrated system and general assistive devices developers should aim to at least provide clearly specified hardware/software interfacing information.

3 The Human Computer Interface

Two of the most important factors of the human-computer interface are the method of presentation of information to the user and the efficiency with which the user is able to achieve tasks.

3.1 Presentation of information

It is generally agreed that icon-based interfaces are more effective than purely textual ones. This has lead to the wealth of graphical user interfaces currently used. In a rehabilitation context, the use of symbols in complex selection tasks in communication aids is common. It is possible to view the use of symbols in an integrated system as an extension of this. As a result, the BASIS system developed by the authors employs icons for presentation of information to the user. Colour screens are able to convey more information than monochrome and so are suitable for more complex set-ups, and, for systems for children and those with perceptual or cognitive difficulties. Figure 1 defines the various parts of a menu. An item is in the case of BASIS a picture (icon) depicting the control to be initiated.

The style of highlighting in menus where items are selected via scanning is important. Items or groups of items highlighted should not be obscured or their picture quality degraded by the highlight itself. If this is the case, the user may have to remember the function of the items obscured, possibly requiring too great a cognitive demand. Showing an item has been selected is important, especially in some control applications where it may not be obvious the action has been initiated.

The presentation and organisation of the selection sets will affect operating efficiency. When designing an interface, the cognitive and perceptual demands of the interface must be taken into account. The choice in communication applications between dynamic menus and those using multi-meaning symbols is currently the subject of debate. Each method is supportable in BASIS and is of use in particular

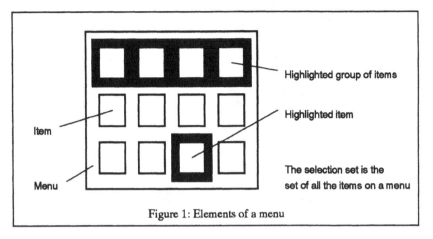

Figure 1: Elements of a menu

situations. However, the BASIS system was designed to work with the principle of dynamic displays. This method produces the lesser cognitive load on the user since selection depends on recognition and does not greatly load the user's memory. Since BASIS is primarily aimed at children, a lower cognitive loading is appropriate.

3.2 Selection Processes with switches

Making switches send key presses via a keyboard emulator is not always efficient. A keyboard emulator offers the user the choice of any of the keys available on the keyboard during the selection process, whereas an effective generic switch user interface would only offer the choice of selecting the relevant commands at any given point in time. This would include all of the keys of a keyboard when that was appropriate.

BASIS supports a number of different input selection devices, including mouse emulators and switches. Most switch controlled applications give a choice of a small number of scanning methods. Currently the provider and user have no means of deciding which is the best selection method; they are often chosen according to the provider's preferred method. The results below compare the efficiency of some different scanning selection processes. The scanning methods compared were :

A. **Row-column**.

B. **Binary division** - split selection set in half and scan, on selection split remaining items and scan, this continues until the required item is left

C. **Single division & row column** - binary divide the selection set once, proceed with row-column scanning the remaining half.

D. **Double division & row column** - binary divide the selection set twice, proceed with row-column scanning.

Figure 2 shows an example of scanning method C.

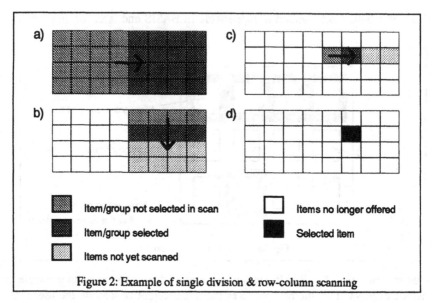

Figure 2: Example of single division & row-column scanning

Average times for selection were calculated for each of the methods with a number of menu sizes ranging from a 2x2 to a 16x8 matrix . The average times were calculated assuming one-switch input with a 1 Hz timer moving the scan highlight. In this theoretical test, the following assumptions were made:

- scan always starts from the same position (i.e. top left option offered);
- all items have equal probability of being selected;
- user knows menu layout and required item is correctly selected first time;
- selection is made as soon as that item is highlighted.

The table below shows the formulae derived for the average time to access an item using each scanning method. It also shows the number of switch presses required to select an item. n_x and n_y are the number of items on the menu page horizontally and vertically respectively.

Type	Average access time	Num. switch presses
A	$\frac{1}{2}\left(2 + n_x + n_y\right)$	2
B	$\frac{3}{2}\log_2\left(n_x + n_y\right)$	$\sqrt[3]{n_x n_y}$
C	$\frac{16 + n_x + n_y}{4}$	3
D	$\frac{10 + n_x + 2n_y}{4}$	4

For menus with $n_x \leq 6$ and $n_y \leq 6$ items, row column scanning is with the above assumptions the fastest access method. For menus larger than this, division methods

C and D have significant time advantages. For menus with $n_x \geq 8$ and $n_y \geq 8$, method D is fastest. Binary division (method B) is always slower than the alternatives and has the added disadvantage of requiring many switch presses to select a particular item.

This study indicates that row column scanning is fastest for single switch operation of a small menu of items. Extension of this study to other scan methods, dynamic displays and larger numbers of switches is in progress.

There are few rehabilitation aids which currently allow input from more than two switches. It is apparent that employing a greater number of switches could increase selection efficiency. Using switches in non-scanning selection methods and the fact that multiple switches may be utilised to associate the desired action with the switch positions could be advantageous. A disadvantage is that the physical and cognitive limitations of a user may preclude the use of more than one switch. However, the possibility of more efficient access for some makes it worthy of further study.

Short term and long term adaption of the display may also help to improve efficiency. Short term adaption is temporary reorganisation of the items presented in a menu dependent on current usage. At a simple level this could entail presenting to the user only those items that can follow the currently selected item. Short term adaption could also take into account the user tiring over the course of a day allowing them to change from their favoured switch selection mechanism to a less demanding and slower one. Long term adaption involves establishing a pattern of selections and introducing more efficient selection routes where appropriate.

4 Conclusions

A very important part of any proposed electronic aid is the Human-device interface, generic rehabilitation integrated systems require sophisticated background interfacing. User interfacing is needed that allows flexible configuration and appropriate support of communication, control and software tasks. The required flexibility in future integrated systems and their user interfaces implies that there is still much research and development to do. The latter development must include 'system' configuration tools that enable rehabilitation aid providers to supply and support systems.

Currently not enough is known about the human computer interfacing of integrated systems for disabled people to provide an optimally functional aid. The authors have identified that only limited quantitative data exists on efficiency of switch accessing methods and to a lesser extent on visual feedback. Most study of human computer interfacing in this context has been for communication aids[10,11]. The work presented throws some light on efficiency of switch use for a static display. This work is being extended to more complex systems. As has been highlighted by the above discussion, standards need to be established both for hardware and software aspects of computer based integrated systems. Any standards proposed should not stifle innovation. Modern graphical user interfaces for the able-bodied market offer significant improvements in terms of access to standard applications through such packages as Switch Access to Windows[12]. Although many of the software applications specifically developed for the rehabilitation market have yet to be implemented on Microsoft Windows, this process should speed up since compilers will be available shortly which do not require knowledge of the workings of the Windows environment.

Current computer user interfaces and environments are still limiting because most are tied to a particular software application, hardware or fixed user interface operating environment. The challenging next step is to allow an individuals interfacing requirements to be specified to re-configure the standard user interface for computer systems. The authors would argue that individual user interface configuration is achievable if the concept behind the human-computer interfacing of state of the art user interfaces is extended. It is the intention of the authors to investigate this.

References

1. Bühler C, Uniform user interface for communication and control, Proc. Ecart 2 Stockholm, pp. 22.3, May 26-28 1993
2. Redmond B., Allen R., Bullock R, Mobile Communications and Environment Control for Wheelchair Users (MECCS), Rehabilitation Technology, ed. E. Ballabio, IOS Press, Amsterdam, pp. 65-69, 1993
3. Words+ Inc., PO Box 1229, Lancaster, CA 93534, USA.
4. Prentke Romich Company, 1022 Heyl Road, Wooster, Ohio 44691, USA.
5. Lundälv M., Svanæs D, Comspec - towards a modular software architecture and protocol for AAC devices, Rehabilitation Technology, ed. E. Ballabio, IOS Press, Amsterdam, pp. 55-59, 1993
6. van Woerden J.A. et al., A safe and easy to use integrated control and communication method M3S, Rehabilitation Technology, ed. E. Ballabio, IOS Press, Amsterdam, pp. 75-79, 1993
7. Hawley M.S., Cudd P.A., Wells J.H., Wilson A.J., Judd, P., Wheelchair-mounted integrated control systems for multiply handicapped people, J. Biomedical Engineering, vol. 14, iss. 5, pp. 193-198, May 1992
8. Cudd P.A., Hawley M.S., Inexpensive PC-based integrated control systems for severely physically disabled people, Proc. 14th Ann Int. conference of the IEEE Engineering in Medicine and Biology Soc., Paris, pp. 1648-9, 1992
9. Hawley M.S., Cudd P.A., Cherry A.D., Implementation of a PC-based integrated control system for children, to be published in J. Biomedical Engineering, vol. 16, iss. 5, May 1994
10. Rosen M.J., Goodenough-Trepagnier C., Modelling Reciprocal Tapping Performance Of Neurologically Disabled People For Prediction Of Communication Rate, Proc. ASME, pp, Nov. 1987
11. French, L.E., Reddy, N.P., Communication and errors in single switch controlled auto-scanning communication aids, Annual International Conference of the IEEE Engineering in Medicine and Biology Society, vol. 13, iss. 4, pp. 1837-8, 1991
12. Head P., Poon P., Morton C., Colven D., Lysley A, Switch Access To Windows 3 (SAW) - A New Concept In Emulation Techniques, Proc. Ecart 2 Stockholm, pp. 22.2, May 26-28 1993

Day and Assessment Training Technology Centres

Geoffrey Busby MBE. D.UNIV (MIDDX) MA FBCS CEng
GEC Computer Services Ltd,.
Great Baddow, Chelmsford
ENGLAND

Abstract. Modern technology affords opportunities to severely physically and sensory disabled people that previously would have been out of the question. In this paper I am not going to discuss the opportunities mentioned above, time doesn't permit, but rather the environment of my concept of the ideal environment in which such opportunities can be explored. Essentially it's a description of a planned Centre which I am hoping to set up in S.E. London.

Mission Statement

To provide Outreach Centres across the UK where people with disabilities and those, in or entering disability professions, will be afforded the opportunity to reach their full potential.

A full range of activities will be offered through the medium of computer technology. Such activities will enable people with disability to undertake programmes of recreation rehabilitation, learning and computer applications, allowing people with disabilities to liberate their latent skills.

In short every Compaid Outreach Centre will aim to secure the lasting economic, social and physical regeneration of its surrounding locations with particular reference to empowering people with disabilities.

Objectives

* Be centres of excellence where people with all types of disability can, through the use of technology, reach their full potential.

* Be centres where people with disabilities can come to try out technical solutions in order to ascertain which is best for them.

* Be centres of excellence in disability awareness.

* The centres will provide respite care.

* A vehicle for students/practitioners to gain practical experience.

* Provide relief for carers.

* Be a resource to local commerce.

Services Provided

* Day attendance with access to recreational and rehabilitational use of computers.

* Short courses on work related use of computers and related technology.

* Employment counsel and advice.

* Professional assessments measuring the potential of adaptive technology.

* Formal, qualification-led, courses related to computing, and employment.

* Office services (document production etc).

* Computing and IT consultancy.

* Basic care services.

* Training of trainers/carers.

Choice of Location

The first Centre will be in East London. There are a few organisations in England, similar to the proposed Centre, however on a first survey, none exists to service East London, or more generally the densely populated area of S.E. England. In addition the Royal London Hospital is the London and S.E. Centre for head injuries and their treatment - this being the type of activity which the centre can work with. Moreover at the current time there is an over-supply of business premises in the East London area, which should enable the proposed Centre to find attractively priced (or even free) space.

Many of the larger commercial, and governmental, organisations based in East London, have a positive policy on disability, and on employment/disability issues. These organisations are a source of both funding, volunteer resources across a range of skills and a natural outlet for clients who wish to progress into mainstream employment.

Relationship to Europe

In the middle term, as project activities grow, and the Centre is seen to be establishing a national reputation. The accessibility of East London to City Airport becomes relevant as it opens up one of the ways by which the Centre would grow its European and International reputation.

Physical shape of centre

The two diagrams appended show firstly, the concept of how the Centre will work, and secondly, a detailed layout of the facilities.

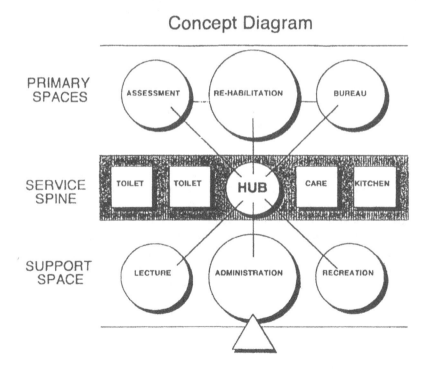

Concept Diagram

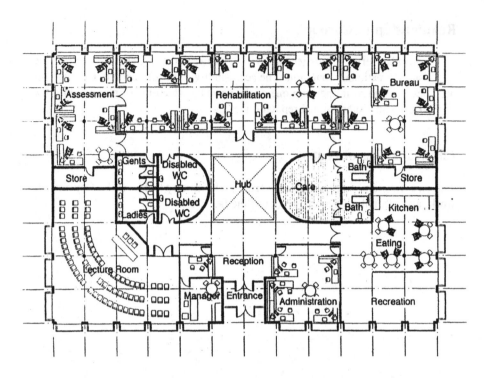

From the diagram you will see that I intend to offer three main areas of service which, I believe is necessary to make up the whole.

Some of you may be surprised to see the high level of care we intend to offer, the reason for this is two fold. Firstly in Great Britain since 1992 there has been a philosophy of integrating people with all types of disability into the community. This system, "Care in the Community", has suffered from our Government failing to recognise the financial expenditure required. Secondly the outcome has been unfortunate for many people, particularly those with mental illnesses, who have found themselves residing in inappropriate accommodation without any assistance and close relations/friends of physically disabled people are finding themselves taking on an increasing care roll. I therefore hope the services offered at the Centre will overcome part of this problem while at the same time introduce such clients to technology and possibly awaken their awareness to their own potential.

The North America Association of Rehabilitation Programs in Computer Technology Seeks to Network with Other Training Programs

Dr. Robert J. Leneway, D.P.A.
ARPCT President, STIRC
Plainwell, MI 49080 U.S.A.

Abstract. A North American Association of Training programs in Computer Related Areas hope to connect with other worldwide forums and training and placement programs also interested in working with persons with disabilities.

1 Introduction

The Association of Rehabilitation Programs in Computer Technology (ARPCT) is an organization of 59 computer related training programs in the United States and Canada for adults with disabilities. Founded in 1978, ARPCT is dedicated to improving the communication and operations among and between member training programs. It's purpose is to promote and support communication between and among programs designed to train and place persons with disabilities in areas of computer technology and information processing. It also provides assistance for the establishment of new computer training and job placement programs for persons with severe disabilities. The ARPCT would like to extend our North American networking to training programs for persons with disabilities and the students and staff that they serve in the E.C. and elsewhere.

The ARPCT member training programs range in size and are currently located in a variety of American and Canadian settings. They range from single curriculum programs with 15 students and staff in a small town Goodwill Industry training program, to large state wide programs with 300 or more students and many different types of computer related curricula, such as computer programming, CAD, PC office skills and LAN Administration. But all programs are guided by volunteer business advisory committees, and all train and place persons with disabilities in some type of computer related occupation.

2. The ARPCT Program

The Association of Rehabilitation Programs in Computer Technology was established so that each member program would be represented on the ARPCT Board of Directors. The members meet twice per year, once in the fall for a national leadership conference and once in the spring for a training conference. The semi annual conferences have provided a way to foster the exchange of information, reports and idea sharing. However, with advances in computer online networking, opportunities for other training programs and interested persons throughout the world to also network with ARPCT members are now much more possible. There are four standing ARPCT operating committees including: Program Operations, Communications, New Programs, and Conference Planning. The Program Operations Committee provides coordinated information curriculum, adaptive technology and accommodations, screening and selection of participants, evaluation of student training, Business Advisory Council roles, support services, and hardware and software issues. A New Program Committee is charged with the development and sharing of information to promote the establishment of new computer training and placement programs for adults with disabilities. The Communication Committee fosters organizational communication through a newsletter, VIEWPOINT and developing an on line communication network. These 59 training programs along with nearly 500 other job training and education programs and the IBM corporation have formed the network to help ensure that adults with disabilities and/or those who are disadvantaged are provided access ramps to the informational super highway. This consortium is known as Project ACCESS and includes (ARPCT), the IBM JTC, another 114 U.S. vocational training program for adults who are disadvantaged and 300 programs who are members of the America Association of Adult Continuing Educators (AAACE). Another 85 program members of the International Association of Business, Industry and Rehabilitation (I-NABIR) are currently in the process of joining this consortium. This network is dedicated to improving telecommunication and information on behalf of the training and employment of persons with disabilities and/or who are disadvantaged. It is estimated that the ACCESS programs have a potential membership of over 20,000 U.S. and Canadian members including adults with disabilities, and/or those who are disadvantaged, business supporters and professional staff who are involved with the consortium's program throughout the United States and Canada.

3. IBM Partnership

This consortium aided by a generous equipment donation from the International Business Machine (IBM) have negotiated a contract with one of the leading on line electronic U.S. networking services, America Online. Through America Online, each of these 500+ training programs are linking together in a nation wide education and training telecommunication network for persons with disabili ties and/or who are disadvantaged. Through America Online, Access members also have free part access to the Internet. Each of the ACCESS members are dedicated to providing greater opportunities for persons with disabilities and/or those who are disadvantaged; to live and work independently. ACCESS provides a telecommunication forum for the exchange of information in areas such as: curriculum, adaptive technology, telecommuting, legislation, funding, and other disability related issues. In addition par ticipants are able to write, post resumes, conduct business background searches, communicate directly with employers and network with others on employment and independent living issues anywhere in the world. Next year professional development and student courses are proposed to be offered on line. This is only the beginning for all the promise and potential that the telecom munication media has to offer.

IBM has already made PCs, printers, and modems available to many of the programs. Most of the others programs have their own. Many of the adult learners have access to computers with modems. Some of the programs have internal Local Area Networks connecting all users within a local program. IBM has also agreed to contract America Online for basic monthly connect fees for the ARPCT and JTC programs for the disadvantaged.

4. Conclusion

Future planning is needed to pursue new emerging concepts includ ing such areas as: teleconferencing, InterNet access, extension to other related international job training programs, curriculum sharing, national job matching, small business start up, home bound education, accommodation information, on line literacy training, professional development, etc.

We now hope to connect with other worldwide forums and training and placement programs also interested in working with persons with disabilities. Persons interested in establishing an internet connection, please contact either Vicky Olson e-mail Volson@aol.com or Bob Leneway Leneway@aol.com for more information.

Disability and Rehabilitation Database
in Chinese Language

Li Quankai and Guo Ming

China Rehabilitation Research Centre , Beijing, China

Abstract. Disability and Rehabilitation database collected articles published
in China 's journals , newspapers , papers in conference and laws which were
relevant to   rehabilitation and related areas. These were   in Chinese and
published from the year of 1949 to 1993. The DR database collected 35,000
records.

1 Introduction

Although the number of databases made in China probably exceeds 10,000, the
number of dababases relevant to any one field is substantially less. For a number of
field , databases have been made .   To the best of our knowledge, no such database has
been made for the field of rehabilitation.

The records published in 400 journals , 100 newspapers, conference papers and
laws on a specific field are collected in DR database.

The purpose of this communication is to provide a database which might help
individuals 's searches for information relevant to rehabilitation in China.

2 Method

CDS/ISIS   (Computerized   Docurrment   Service/ Integrated Set of Information
System) was used to make RD database. The operating enviroment: (1) Main memory
of 1MB, hard disk more than 40MB. (2)286   and above   PC IBM and
compatable.Struturing data design of the database consisted of 4 files : FDT(field
definition table),FMT (format) , FST (field select table) , PFT (print format table).
Once the four files were produced , the database was generated.

The first step to make the database was to select out 400 journals and 100 newspapers
and then marked out every article which was relevant   to rehabilitation.These
journals and newspapers seem to indicate a wider range of coverage, including titles from
such fields as orthopaedics,physical therapy ,   prosthetics and orthotics, physiology,
bilological engineering,   special education, base-community rehabilitation, disablility
law and etc.

The second step was to fill worksheet .   The worksheet consisted of 30 fields
which had been definited in FDT. The most important fields were Chinese thesaurus,
provisional headings.   Chinese thesaurus   were standard vocabulary terms   that
described the concepts covered in DR database records. Chinese thesaurus allowed

users to retrieve all references to a particular topic, even if different terminology was used in the records. Each record contains several Chinese thesaurus. These thesaurus were found in the two CT fields : Major CT and Minor CT. Used the CT field abbreviation to search both CT fields. Used the MJCT field abbreviation to find all records in which the term is a major topic . Used the MICT field abbreviation to find all records in which the term was a minor topic. All CT appeared in the CT fields. Major CT were marked with an asterisk. Since CT was not enough to cover the field of rehabilitation, provisional headings were added from Mesh (Medical Subject Headings) which were translated into Chinese and some special words we collected in our dailywork before. The third step was to input all these datas on worksheet into format in the database.

When these research was performed, a database in dBASE III named Periodicals China Base on Disc was completed by an information institute. We decided to implant records we needed from PCBD to DR database.Firstly , searched out the records relevant to rehabilitation in PCBD. Secondly, changed all these selected records from dBASE III format to ISO 2709 format. Thirdly, changed ISO 2709 format to CDS/ISIS format and implanted to DR database.

3 Result:

35, 000 records are collected in this database. Users can search for articles, laws , papers relevant to rehabilitation published in China from 1949-1993. Every search consists of two major parts : FINDing the records and SHOWing them on the monitor.After users show the records on the monitor, users can print records and/or transfer records to floppy or hard disk.

Users can type in a search at the FIND prompt, or users can select term(s) from the INDEX or word(s) and/or phrase(s) from a record displayed through the SHOW function and automatically have the system search. Type a single word in any combination of upper and lower case letter. Further narrow the search by using specially indexed limit field. Using a " limit field", the system searches only in the specified field. For example, database might have a field for publication year which has been designated as a limit field. This enables users to perform a search for a specific publication date. For the fastest search, search on the words exactly the way it appears in the INDEX.

Index collects CT, PT, authors's names , titles, journals and showed occurrences in the database . CT, PT can be corrected through their occurrences in the future. PTs with high occurrences might be CT in the future work . It might help indexing the documents of rehabilitation. Through database analysis, the results we can get include: (1) The process of rehabilitation development from 1949-1993 by the difference among the numbers of documents in each year. (2) Review of conditions of rehabilitation in every clinical fields. Core journals of rehabilitation are identification through database analysis.

4 Discussion

Two points, however, should be noted . First , the articals which we collected in DR database is an indication of relevant articles , not necessarily the degree of relevance or the quality of those articles. Second, Documents in fields of rehabilitation scattered in medical , clinical, engineering and social fields. Although we had done our best to collect these documents, it is far from complete with respect to the literature of rehabilitation.

Individuals , hospitals and institutes seeking informations relevant to rehabilitation, therefore, may find the database of use.

References

1. Richard W. Bohannon (1991), Core journal, of Rehabilitation : indentification through index analysis. International Journal of Rehabilitation Research 14,pp.333-335

2. Keith Andreus (1993). Writing for medical journals. Clinical Rehabilitation 1993:7,pp.91-98

Toward a Single Global Market for Assistive Technology

Joseph P. Lane

Rehabilitation Engineering Research Center on Technology Evaluation and Transfer
Center for Assistive Technology, University at Buffalo, Buffalo, New York, USA

Abstract. Public and private sector programs in North America parallel programs underway in the European Communities. Pursuing a single global market for assistive technology will reduce duplication, leverage resources, and accelerate progress toward our shared goals. This paper presents a rationale, reviews relevant programs in North America and invites participation in a global effort.

1 Introduction

The European Community established the Technology Initiative for Disabled and Elderly People (TIDE) in 1991. TIDE's major objectives are to improve the EC's environment for pre-competitive research and development in assistive technology, and thereby increase the technology's value and accessibility. To this end, TIDE established the concept of a single EC market for assistive devices. TIDE is implementing the single market concept through research and development projects on specific technologies and applications, along with supporting projects on broader issues such as standards and information distribution.

2 Need for a Single Global Market

The EC has many reasons for promoting a single market in assistive technology. Some are:
1) The number of persons *aging with disabilities* is increasing due to reduced mortality rates for persons with developmental disabilities and degenerative diseases. Emergency and trauma medicine enables people to survive injuries that were previously fatal.
2) The number of persons *aging into disabilities* is increasing due to the general increase in average life spans, and the aging of the post-World War II population cohorts.
3) The costs of dependent care continue to escalate, making the costs associated with preserving independence relatively attractive. Sustaining independence through assistive technology is a cost-effective option for a portion of persons with disabilities and the elderly.
4) The marketplace for assistive technology is fragmented. Marketers, clinicians and consumers have difficulty finding each other. Marketing costs inflate retail prices, but consumers make sub-optimal decisions without good information. Cost reimbursement and product liability issues remain significant disincentives for marketers and consumers alike.
The circumstances driving TIDE's programs are equally compelling to the rest of the world community. In North America, the United States and Canada are funding programs, and consumer and professional organizations are active. Defense-based industries are exploring technology transfer options, but they encounter the long-standing barriers to estimating

market sizes and product revenues. The market's climate remains uncertain as funding, reimbursement, regulation and liability problems persist. A single market approach would focus North America's resources and prompt policy reforms.

In the Far East, Japanese industry/government research centers explore assistive technology, because Japan faces significant issues in eldercare and building access. Russia as yet lacks adequate capital to educate their health professionals, but they recognize the need. Countries is Southern Asia, Africa and South America are considering the civic and economic value of "appropriate" assistive technologies -- those designed for local production and support. Asia and the Southern Hemisphere need a single market approach to effectively translate and apply the installed base of assistive technology from nations in the Northern Hemisphere.

3 U.S. Programs with Global Application

3.1 Federally-Sponsored Research and Development

Many federal agencies fund programs in assistive technology. The Department of Education's National Institute on Disability and Rehabilitation Research (NIDRR) funds sixteen Rehabilitation Engineering Research Centers, and thirty-six Rehabilitation Research and Training Centers. These centers conduct research and development, and information dissemination on specific disability or technology areas. NIDRR also funds the state Technology-Related Assistance projects, mandated to provide consumers with information and referrals on assistive technology devices and services.

The Department of Veteran Affairs operates the Technology Transfer Service to evaluate and fund prototype devices useful for disabled veterans. The DVA has four regional Rehabilitation Research and Development Service centers, where DVA medical researchers collaborate with university faculty on device development. The National Institutes of Health's National Center for Medical Rehabilitation Research funds research on functional impairments and outcomes. The National Science Foundation operates the program, Engineering Senior Design Projects to Aid the Disabled, which supports student engineers at twenty universities in the design and construction of customized assistive devices.

In addition to these targeted programs, sixteen federal departments support over six hundred research and development laboratories. Members of the Federal Laboratory Consortium (FLC) volunteer to collaborate with private companies and state and local governments. Participating laboratories are organized into six geographic regions. Locator services provide information on their program interests and resources. Federal laboratories sponsored by the Department of Defense, the Department of Energy and the National Aeronautics and Space Administration (NASA), are all now evaluating the field of assistive technology as an application area for their advanced materials, products and systems.

3.2 Private Sector Development and Application

The Electronic Industries Association's Assistive Devices Division is developing design standards for devices with electronic components. The National Association of Medical Equipment Suppliers is collaborating with RESNA to improve the quality of marketing information. Manufacturers and suppliers of assistive devices are partnering with researchers, clinicians and consumers to improve the exchange of products and information. The U.S. government supports private sector activity by having federal agencies allocate money to fund the Small Business Innovation Research program, where small businesses in the private sector compete to provide research and development support. These small businesses often seek partnerships with outside firms to secure needed expertise for projects.

3.3 Professional Organization Information Dissemination

Professional organizations in the U.S. have much to offer. For example, RESNA as an inter-disciplinary society, sponsors special interest groups in technology transfer, information networking and international applications. The professional associations in occupational therapy, physical therapy, speech and hearing, and special education, all have assistive technology concentrations. The American Society on Aging is addressing assistive technology and home modifications for older persons. The Institute of Electrical and Electronic Engineers now has a division for rehabilitation engineering. These organizations all have international chapters, improving opportunities for global cooperation.

4 Summary

We all need a single global market for assistive technology. This review shows the wealth of expertise and resources that remains largely untapped between nations. Developed countries could readily identify existing products, share prior research and focus available resources. Developing countries could emulate the best practices in knowledge transfer and technology transfer. A single global market would decrease overhead costs for marketers and decrease access costs for consumers -- making more resources available without additional investments. Producers and consumers have much to gain, and nations have little to lose by establishing a single, global market. Let the dialogue commence with a global vision.

Acknowledgment: The RERC-TET's work is supported by the National Institute on Disability and Rehabilitation Research, U.S. Department of Education.

Using Structure Within Electronic Documents to Make Editors more Accessible

Nick Ayres, Tom Wesley

University of Bradford
Department of Computing, Bradford, BD7 1DP, United Kingdom
Email: t.a.b.wesley@bradford.ac.uk

Abstract. This paper describes on going work within the CAPS Consortium—Communication and Access to Information for People with Special Needs, a European Union funded project in the Technology Initiative for Disabled and Elderly People (TIDE) Programme—that is examining ways in which *structure* within electronic documents may help make those documents more accessible to people with print disabilities. The work concentrates on the production and editing of documents by people with visual impairments and considers how structured editors may be useful to them. A structured editor has been designed to test the ideas, and this is described in the paper.

1 Introduction

The main work of the CAPS Consortium (Communication and Access to Information for People with Special Needs, a European Union funded project in the Technology Initiative for Disabled and Elderly People (TIDE) Programme) is directed to developing methods to increase the access to information for the print disabled [1]. People with print disabilities include the blind, the deaf–blind, the partially sighted, the dyslexic and those with motor impairments which make it difficult to physically control paper documents.

Accessibility to documents is not just about acquiring information for reading—it also involves the production and editing of documents. Problems are evident here in a number of ways. The first is the creation of a visually interesting document that is often necessary for sighted colleagues. The second problem is created by the limitations imposed upon a visually impaired person by the internal model used by many word processors or editors, and the display of information in a visual or WYSIWYG manner.

Most editors treat the text of a document as a linear character string. By doing so, limitations are placed on the operations that may be performed on documents. For example, documents must be scrolled through in a linear order to reach a particular place. If an electronic document has structure explicitly encoded within it, then additional functionality may be added that is potentially of use to people with print disabilities.

By structure is meant a description of the parts of a document in terms that are independent of the appearance of a document. Thus a document has headings, footnotes and sections, rather than pieces of text with a roman type face indented by a centimetre. When structure is created for electronic documents most existing editors specify that individual documents conform to a set of rules. For example, it may be required that a footnote can only appear in a paragraph, and not in a heading. This set of rules is often called a generic document.

A further problem is related to the explosive growth of the graphical user interface (GUI). It is well understood that this poses severe access problems for people with visual impairments. Considerable research and development is underway to provide access to the *interface*. However, the growth of GUIs is encouraging the growth of visual presentation methods in *applications*. Structured editors will therefore rely heavily on visual displays of structure. Where this involves actual graphics, this will make it particularly difficult for people with visual impairments to gain the advantages available through the use of structured editors.

The present work has a number of aims. Firstly, to examine what features of structured editors may be of benefit to people with print disabilities. Based on this understanding, it should be possible to produce a set of guidelines to be used in various ways. Potential users may be made more aware of how they can use certain techniques, and hence ask for these in applications, and make choices based on this information. The guidelines should provide information for software producers so that accessibility is built in to their products. Finally the procurers of software within companies will gain assurances that visually impaired people will continue to be able be productive in the commercial office environment, even if this is totally using graphical user interfaces.

2 Existing Editors and Techniques

In order to clarify how structure could be useful for people with print disabilities, the literature was examined and a number of structured editors were investigated. Full details are presented by Ayres [2]. A number of papers on existing editors and related issues were particularly helpful; these are listed in [3].

Overall, two disadvantages of many of the editors were apparent. Firstly, they were aimed at people who had both a high technical background and also an awareness of the underlying format. Secondly, often few concessions to usability had been made. However, a number of techniques were discussed which could be of use to the print disabled.

2.1 Selection of Document Units

Probably the most useful set of techniques are those that allow the selection of a subset of the parts of a document for display and editing. When displayed, these subsets are often called 'views' of a document. Particularly interesting is the document overview, whereby the subset in some way shows the overall organisation of the document. This subset is usually the set of section headings. Conceptually it is possible to use this overview to move the insertion point around the document quicker than having to scroll through the complete text, but this seems to have been rarely implemented.

The overview concept may be extended so that different criteria may be used to select the document units displayed. Examples might be displaying only paragraphs with a particular style or displaying only the lists within a document. This could make it relatively easy to find specific places within a document when such information is known. Instead of positive selection criteria, it is possible to have negative selection criteria. Text may be hidden if it meets some criteria, otherwise it is displayed. This mechanism may be used to hide footnotes from the main text of a document.

Having decided which parts of a document to display, editors vary on how the parts are displayed. There are two approaches—display views simultaneously in different windows, or sequentially on request in the same window.

The selection of parts of a document may be used for other purposes than display. Some editors provide a mechanism to select complete units for operations such as cut and paste. This should speed up performance since the units do not have to be selected by scrolling through the complete text.

2.2 Creation of Visual Appearance

Structure is frequently used for the automatic creation of the visual appearance of printed or displayed documents. This presupposes a set of rules that describe transformations from the structure to the visual appearance. In the workplace it is becoming common to have guidelines for the ways in which documents are displayed, that is a corporate style. For example, it may be specified that headings should be in a particular typeface at a particular size. It may possible within structured editors to encode these rules so that a user rarely needs to specify directly the look of a document, but only its structure. If visually impaired writers are able to manipulate the structure, then they may never need to create directly the visual appearance of a document.

2.3 Automatic Creation of Document Content

Within many types of documents, there exists content that could be created automatically. These include numbering schemes such as section numbers and footnote numbers. In some cases such as tables of contents and running headers, the text used is often the same as headings. These could be created automatically if an editor was aware of the rules for creating text. This kind of capability is found to a limited extent in one of the subsets of the Open Document Architecture (ODA), FOD36 [4].

Structure may be used to perform automatic numbering of units such as footnotes and sections. While this could be done after editing, numbering can produce useful information to a user about structure within a document. When used as feedback, the interactive numbering system does not have to be the same as that for the final printed document.

2.4 Feedback Provision

There are two types of feedback that may be useful—firstly, feedback about the structure created, and secondly, the use of text from structural units to give audio feedback to visually impaired users. Editors use a number of different schemes to provide feedback to the user about the structure that they create. This is often visual in nature, such as different fonts or graphical symbols. Some editors use text labels placed at the start and end of a unit. If the editors were based upon a markup system such as the Standard Generalized Markup Language (SGML), then these labels could be the same as that used in the underlying representation, which makes them relatively hard to use.

One of the conclusions of this study is that structure may be used to give meaningful audio feedback to users with visual impairments about operations that they perform. An acknowledged feature of good application design is the use of consistent feedback about operations [5]. There are few things more annoying than the lack of an indication of the result of an operation. For the majority of users, feedback is in visual form and is immediately obvious. Visually impaired users may have to actively check the results of operations to confirm their success. If text associated with specific units, or the name of units operated upon (such as 'footnote'), is given as audio feedback, then visually impaired users will have more immediate feedback about the results of the editing operations.

2.5 Bookmarks

A common technique used by structured editors is the bookmark although this is not strictly a feature of structured documents themselves, rather a feature of the editing process. As the name suggests, a bookmark is a mechanism to mark places within documents as being of special interest. At least one system [6] allows a user to give names to bookmarks, which are displayed in a separate window. Users can select the name in order to move to the bookmark or move sequentially through a document to the next or previous bookmark.

2.6 Creating Structure

Most structured editors are awkward in the way in which they allow users to indicate the structure in a document. For example, many editors force a user to create a section before being able to create a section heading; an easier technique would have the creation of a section heading signal the creation of a section. This type of awkward interface may be the result of the perceived need to cater for more than one generic document, that is to provide a very general interface. If generic documents are carefully designed, than some of the awkwardness within editors may be removed. As described later, in the current work limitations have been placed on the generic documents handled within the editor in order to remove some of the difficulties for users.

2.7 The Styles Mechanism

Early word processors allowed users to specify that particular pieces of text should have properties such as being bold or italic when printed. It was soon realised that when text fulfilled a certain semantic function, for example, a heading, it would often have a set of properties associated with it. Word processors then started to attach a name to this set of properties so that the set could be applied to text in a single operation. This bundling of properties is called the style mechanism [7].

Conceptually styles may be associated with either individual characters, words or paragraphs. Microsoft Word for the Macintosh, for example, has styles that are associated with a complete paragraph, but not with individual characters within a paragraph.

While examining existing structured editors, it became clear that if constraints are placed upon the rules that a structured document must obey, and styles are associated with structural units, then the styles mechanism may be used to indicate structure within a document. This is being used to a limited extent within the CAPS editor.

3 The CAPS Editor

Within the CAPS Project, a prototype structured editor is being produced in order to examine how people with a visual impairment could benefit from some of the ideas discussed in the previous sections.

3.1 FOD26

FOD26 [8] is a subset of the Open Document Architecture (ODA) standard [9]. Ayres [10] and Ayres and Wesley [11] have discussed the way ODA may be of value to people with print disabilities. FOD26 provides a relatively simple set of structural types that can be used to test the usefulness for the print disabled of many of the features of structured editors. These include footnotes, sections, automatic numbering of sections and footnotes, styles, alternative textual descriptions of graphics and the automatic generation of a description of how a document will appear visually when printed. This latter capability can be extended with the commercial toolkit produced by the ODA Consortium [12] which also provides a PostScript converter.

As the current investigation is attempting to create general guidelines for the use of structured editors by people with print disabilities, it was decided to use the FOD26 subset of ODA, rather than any proprietary word processor. Quite apart from the difficulty of accessing the internals of proprietary systems, the use of an ISO standard such as ODA allows the investigation of general methods, rather than any particular implementation. The results of the investigation should be valid for structured editors as a whole, and do not depend on the penetration of ODA in the market place.

Recognising that most people use a word processor as an augmented typewriter, it was decided to concentrate on a relatively small number of concepts that are as close to normal usage as possible. It was therefore decided to place limits on the structure within FOD26 that the editor can handle. The style mechanism is being used to input structure. As markers for the start of sections 'inbuilt' heading styles are being used. There are precedents for this in the Word/ODA converter that has been produced by Bull [13].

3.2 Non–structure Design Decisions

There were a number of non–structure design issues that had to be made. The ODA Consortium Toolkit can only be used with graphical user interfaces X–Windows on UNIX or MS Windows on PCs. Given the current lack of an effective screen reader for X-Windows, it was decided to base the editor under Windows. However, the state of Windows screen readers leaves much to be desired, so it was also decided to avoid the use of a mouse and that all commands should have hot keys, thus eliminating use of pull down menus.

3.3 Document Views

It was decided to have a number of views of a document. These are the complete document, without footnotes—the normal view; a headings based view—overview and a footnote view that displayed only footnotes. These are displayed as separate windows and switching between views uses a key combination.

The heading overview, besides giving an overall impression of the document organisation, can be used to perform operations on complete sections. By selecting one of the headings, an operation such as cut and paste of complete sections can be performed easily without having to scroll through large amounts of text. The heading is used for audio feedback.

The normal view has a number of interesting features. Structure can be used to ease movement through a document. For example, the insertion point may be moved sequentially from heading to heading. The heading text is also used in this case as feedback. It is possible to move the insertion point to the start or end of paragraphs, in which case the first five or last five words are used as feedback. As a further aid to navigation within a document simple bookmarks are being implemented. While these are not directly visible to a user, it is possible to place and move sequentially between them. This aids quick movement between different places in a document when it is necessary to consult one place while editing text in another.

3.4 Feedback

In both the normal view and overview, content is generated to produce feedback about structure. A simple algorithm is used to create section numbers which are displayed within the view to give further feedback about how the sections are organised in the document. This algorithm, used principally to aid the user during document editing, may be different from the one produced when the document is finally formatted and printed.

Another form of feedback is the display of textual labels for units. Examples of this are the use of the name of the style associated with a paragraph, and the placing of the word 'footnote' in the normal view as a place holder for an actual footnote.

4 Conclusions

Much effort is placed into making previously created documents accessible for people with print disabilities. However, there are a number of circumstances, such as the work situation, where the accessibility of documents must be considered to include their creation and editing.

The usual model of an electronic document as a character string places limitations upon the editing process; the use of structure adds potential extra functionality that should be able to increase the accessibility of documents for people with visual impairments.

This paper has described some techniques used in existing structured editors that may be adapted for people with a visual impairment. A structured editor that is specifically aimed at testing the use of these techniques has been designed and is being implemented, in order to produce a set of guidelines that may be used within commercial editors.

Acknowledgement

This work has been partly funded by DGXIII of the Commission of the European Union, under its Technology Initiative for Disabled and Elderly People (TIDE) Programme. The other CAPS partners are the Royal National Institute for the Blind (UK), Sensotec BV (BE), Infovox (SE) and the Handicap Institute (SE).

References

1. Full details of the CAPS Consortium can be obtained from the Coordinator, Professor Jan Engelen at the Katholieke Universiteit, Leuven, Belgium. The Consortium maintains an ftp site, gate.esat.kuleuven.ac.be in the directory /pub/CAPS and its sub directories, which provides access to its latest public documents.
2. N. Ayres: Structured Editors—Existing Systems and Techniques Report. CAPS Internal Report, August 1993. Obtainable from the Coordinator [1]
3. D.D. Chamberlin, H.F. Hasselmeier, A.W. Luniewski, D.P. Paris, B.W. Wade, M.L. Zolliker: Quill: An Extensible System for Editing Documents of Mixed Type. In: 21st International Conference on System Science. Hawaii: 1988, pp. 317–326

   Complexity in Structured Documents: User Interface Issues. In: R. Furuta (ed.): International Conference on Electronic Publishing, Document Manipulation and Typography EP90. Gaithersburg: CUP 1990, pp. 79–91

   ISO/IEC TR 10037 (E) 1991 Information technology—SGML and Text–entry Systems—Guidelines for SGML Syntax–Directed Editing Systems. International Organisation for Standardisation

   M.D.P. Leland, R.S. Fish, R.E. Kraut: Collaborative Document Production using Quilt. In: Conference on Computer Supported Cooperative Work. Portland Oregon: 1988

   V. Quint, I. Vatton: Grif: An Interactive System for Structured Document Manipulation. In: J.C. van Vliet (ed.): Text Processing and Document Manipulation. Nottingham: CUP 1986

   V. Quint: Systems for the Manipulation of Structured Documents. In: J. Andre et al. (ed.): Structured Documents. CUP 1989, pp. 39–74

   V. Quint, I. Vatton: Combining Hypertext and Structured Documents in Grif. In: D. Lucarella et al. (ed.): Proceedings of the ACM Conference on Hypertext. Milano: ACM Press 1992, pp. 23–32

   A. Vercoustre: Structured Editing—Hypertext Approach: Cooperation and Complementarity. In: R. Furuta (ed.): International Conference on Electronic Publishing, Document Manipulation and Typography EP90. Gaithersburg: CUP 1990, pp. 65–78

   J.H. Walker, R.L. Bryan: An Editor for Structured Technical Documents. In: J.H. Miller (ed.): Protext IV. Boston, USA: Boole 1987, pp. 145–150

   J.H. Walker: Supporting Document Development with Concordia. Computer 23, 48-55 1988
4. ISO/IEC DISP 11182 1992 Information Technology—International Standardized Profile FOD36 – Office Document Format – Extended document structure – Character, Raster Graphics and Geometric Graphics content architectures – Part 1: Document Application Profile

5. A. Dix, J. Finlay, G. Abowd, R. Beale: Human Computer Interaction. Prentice Hall 1993, pp. 131–145
6. J.H. Walker: The Role of Modularity in Document Authoring Systems. In: ACM Conference on Document Processing Systems. Santa Fe, New Mexico: 1988, pp. 117–124
7. J. Johnson, R.J. Beach: Styles in Document Editing Systems. IEEE Computer 23, 32–43 1988
8. ISO/IEC DISP 11181-1 1991 Information Technology—International Standardized Profile FOD26 – Office Document Format – Enhanced document structure – Character, raster graphics and geometric graphics content architectures – Part 1: Document Application Profile. International Organisation for Standardisation
9. ISO 8613 1988 Information processing—Text and Office systems—Office Document Architecture (ODA) and Interchange Formats. International Organisation for Standardisation
    H. Brown: Introduction to the Office Document Architecture. In: J. Rosenberg (ed.): Multi–media Document Translation ODA and the EXPRES Project. Springer Verlag 1991
10. N. Ayres: ODA—State of the Art Report. CAPS internal report, February 1993. Obtainable from the Coordinator [1]
11. N. Ayres, T. Wesley: Open Document Architecture—An Opportunity for Information Access for the Print Disabled. In: The 3rd International Conference on Computers for Handicapped Persons. Vienna 1992, pp. 556-561
    N. Ayres, T. Wesley: Automated Braille Production from ODA Documents. In: European Conference on the Advancement of Rehabilitation Technology, ECART 2. Stockholm: 1993
12. ODA Consortium Toolkit, ODA Consortium, Avenue Marcel Thiry 204, B-1200 Brussels
13. Bull ODA Product Set Users Guide, Bull SA, March 1992

Distinguishing Pattern-Types in Printed Documents

Georg Lokowandt, Waltraud Schweikhardt

Institut für Informatik

Universität Stuttgart, Germany

Abstract. Reading machines and other devices have helped a lot in integrating blind persons into society. Simultaneously the progress and widespread use of desktop-publishing systems lead to documents that are hard to recognise for current reading machines. Nevertheless, access to printed documents is required by most blind persons. In this article we show a possible structure of an improved and flexible system for document recognition. It will be capable of processing any printed document, for instance a letter or a musical score as well as diagrams or line drawings. Special emphasis is put on correct and efficient distinction of categories of documents. Requirements for distinction are shown and an suggestion for an implementation is presented. It will perform this classification in a fast and flexible way. Also, the suggested method can automatically as well as interactively classify the type of a document. Afterwards the contents of the document can be displayed in an appropriate style. The blind users also have the possibility to interactively define new classes of documents if required. The prototype of this system is currently being implemented at our institute.

Motivation

To read the contents of a printed document without the help of a sighted person, blind people can fall back on computerised equipment. For most computers, there are OCR (Optical Character Recognition)-systems available, that provide the possibility to read out recognised text. But many documents can not be processed to be adequately represented for the blind. Especially documents, that are not composed of a character set, like graphics and diagrams, can not be processed by today's OCR-systems. In these cases the content of the document has to be read with the Optacon, copied on swelling paper or analysed with similar devices. As shown in Figure 1, ways to process an unknown document, which are available today (OCR, Optacon and swelling paper) share the problem, that non of these devices is capable of processing every content of a document. If help by a sighted person is not available or not wanted because of privacy considerations, the document analysis is a very time-consuming process.

Our goal is to develop a system to support the blind in reading and exploring any printed document on their own. The program should appear like an expanded OCR-System. Graphics shall be represented in a reasonable way.

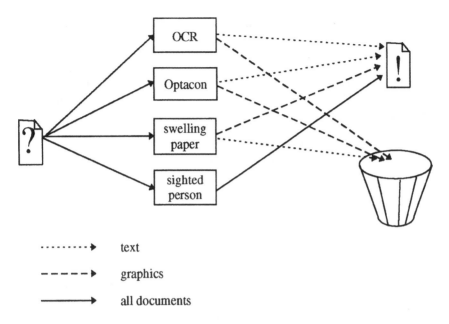

Figure 1: Current Ways of Understanding the Contents of a Printed Document

Basics

Experiments have shown that many documents which include graphics can be understood without big difficulty if they are presented in the proper magnitude or if only some aspects are shown at a time. It is difficult, but not impossible for blind persons to determine a suitable magnitude on their own. If the document shows an unknown item in an unknown format the examination will take several iterations. First the right face of the page and the correct orientation have to be determined. Afterwards, most of the participants of our tests tried to find text passages and read them, in order to conclude the contents of the whole document from what they read. By understanding the text, most people were able to relate the document to a specific topic. If the tested persons were familiar with this topic, they also knew of some classes of documents that are usually used to present this information. By putting the document in one of these categories, it is easy to decide whether to proceed with the analysis. Also the decision what tools are to be used to process this kind of document is made after the classification. For example in a document showing a musical score it is searched for other tokens than in a document showing a pie chart or a diagram. While the tactile copy of a diagram can be used to get the required overview, the position of each note is essential for reading a score. Therefore an Optacon is the better choice for getting the details of a score. To select the right tool for further processing and therefore to understand the contents of the printed document requires a correct classification of the document.

A blind user will classify a document according to its semantic characteristics. A program, however, does not have this ability. On the other hand, many syntactic features of a printed document can easily be determined. The existence of lines and their arrangement, the usage of colour or the usage of text that is emphasised by changing its background colour, can be determined by well-known algorithms. Classification of this kind resembles to the classification performed by a sighted person. A sighted person is able to recognise the use of colours as well as the use of lines and coloured areas at a glance. Experience helps to classify a document according to its visual syntactic features before reading it. We therefore believe, that syntactic features are sufficient for classification of printed documents.

Reflections on Current Recognition Systems

It has been suggested to use neural nets or fuzzy-logic controllers to perform the classification. Also rule-based systems are applied to the problem of document classification and document analysis. Usually the whole process of document recognition is divided into two phases, the *feature extraction* and the *contents recognition*. In the first phase syntactic features are extracted and in the second one, the contents of the document are extracted by application of neural nets or fuzzy controllers. Without a separate phase of document classification these approaches are only capable of processing a small number of document classes. Usual OCR-Systems can only process text and another program has to be used to process for instance musical scores. The classification phase is implicitly performed by the user who has to know which program to use. There is another disadvantage that follows from feature extraction being a separate step. A fixed set of routines for feature extraction has to be used for every document. Afterwards, a fast and flexible method is used for recognition. The less features are extracted, the less time is required but the less documents can be recognised correctly. The number of features extracted therefore depends on the time that might be spend during feature extraction and the accuracy required for the recognition process. If this approach is generalised on arbitrary printed documents, the number of required algorithms for feature extraction and therefore the recognition time, rises. An additional disadvantage of this approach depends on the requirement, that every algorithm must compute useful results for every document. When the extraction algorithms are generalised to process a wider variety of document classes, they usually get more complicated and require more computation time.

Suggested Solution

Our approach suggests to merge the phase of *feature extraction* with the new phase of *document classification*. Whenever a feature of the document is extracted, the document should be classified according to this feature. When the class of the document is determined with an acceptable amount of certainty this phase should be ended and the *recognition phase* should begin.

To allow a program to perform the classification, three groups of routines have to be implemented:

- routines to extract relevant information,
- routines to administer document classes,
- routines to control the classification.

When the computation of all relevant syntactic features can be expressed by algorithms, an important step towards automatic classification will be done.

Another step has to be the definition of appropriate document classes. This goal, however, will never be achieved completely, because new document classes can and will be developed at all times. Nevertheless, there is a small number of general document classes which are sufficient for processing most of the documents. Obviously, these basic classes must be provided from the beginning. To work quickly and efficiently, additional document classes can be defined on demand. In order to do this, the system must be open to new document classes. The blind users should be able to perform these additions on their own.

This concept of an expandable class structure and a few general classes helps to integrate the intelligence of the user to recognise and perform necessary additions. Therefore our program itself does not need to integrate components for acquiring knowledge and ends up in a less complex result.

The last part of the classification system are the routines that control the classification. They use the extracted features to assign a given document to a defined class of documents. This is a typical problem of decision finding which is not easy but not unsolvable. Attention has to be paid that the whole classification is performed within a reasonable time for interactive work.

Terms

Document Classes

A class of documents is a set of documents that share a set of common features. Each document is an instance of a hierarchy of document-classes, but only the most specialised class is called the class to which the document belongs or the *type of the document*. For each class there is an arrangement of specialised routines to extract the contents of documents of one kind. Also there are routines to represent the information to the user. Examples of classes of documents are:

- raw text
- business forms
- mathematical formulas
- line drawings
- music charts
- composed documents.

This enumeration can easily be continued to any length. Some users might want to distinguish between a *business letter* and a *private letter*, while other users might want to use the document class *petri-net*.

Explicit Information

This kind of information consists of all characters, symbols, graphical lines etc. with all their attributes as size, font etc. Also the layout of the document may be included. It resembles to syntactic information. This information is extracted in the analysis-phase.

Implicit Information

This term stands for all kinds of information that are extracted during the classification process. We could also call it meta-information because this information describes the class of a document and not its contents. For example, a text containing formulas has a mathematical content, although this meaning needn't be expressed anywhere in the printed text.

Implementation

The whole process of document recognition is divided into several phases. These phases are described in the following sections.

Document Classification

Before the explicit information within the document can be extracted, the class the document belongs to has to be determined.
The routine to solve this task uses an expandable decision tree, as shown in Figure 2 and initialises a list of attributes, that characterise the document after its way through the decision tree. The algorithm controlling the classification passes every document trough this tree. At every node it is decided which branch has to be taken. Each node within the tree contains the algorithm which has to be applied next and the branch which has to be taken after the algorithm has extracted another syntactic feature of the document. This feature is added to the list of attributes.
When a leaf is reached, the classification phase is completed and the type of the document is determined. If the document, however, does not belong to any of the known types, all implicit information that has been extracted, is presented to the user. Since the classification would end without a result, the user must be able to interfere into the classification process.

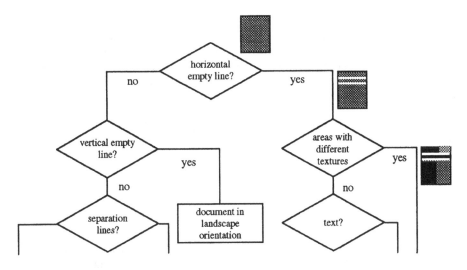

Figure 2: Decision Tree for the Document Classification (part)

Often a document is composed of several areas with different patterns. In these cases the analysing algorithm can divide the document. Afterwards, the analysing algorithm can call the classification routine again for every area. The decision tree in Figure 2 shows a leaf to handle a document in landscape-format. In the analysis-phase, the contents of the document will be turned to portrait-format and afterwards be processed as any new document.

Phase of Analysing

During the phase of analysing, the information, which is comprised in the document is represented in an internal data-structure adequate to the document type. Plain text is represented by ASCII-Characters, control characters for font, sizes and other attributes. All text attributes have to be recognised and stored within the internal data structure as well as the layout of the printed text. This information is required as a whole in order to enable the blind and sighted to work together. In general, the internal data-structure should be suited to hold all information that is required to work with a document of the specific class. In addition all information that is required to cooperate with a sighted person should be stored. The analysis is performed by a set of special routines which call a library of general image processing routines.

Representation of Results

When all information that is included in the document, is extracted and converted into the internal data-structure, the representation of this information is started. For each class of documents, there is a special routine to control the presentation. All these routines can use a library of general dialogue-routines. This library manages a set of input and output devices. Output devices we use primarily are a Braille-display, a speech output device, a pin matrix device and a text- as well as a Windows screen. According to the used output device, we want to use the cursor routing keys, the keyboard, the pin matrix device or a mouse for the input. Several of these devices should be used simultaneously or on their own. In order to store the results of processing a printer and files must also be supported. For the analysis only devices which can be used interactively should be used.

Building up the Decision Tree

The classification of documents as described above requires a decision tree that holds the information on how to perform the classification. During the usual classification the decision tree is unchanged. Whenever a new class of documents is defined and whenever a new algorithm for the extraction of syntactic features is implemented, the tree has to be rebuild. The time that is spend during this process doesn't matter because it is performed seldom and doesn't require any user interaction. Therefore we can apply all algorithms for extracting syntactic features on every available document. Afterwards a clustering-algorithm calculates the significance of every syntactic feature for the distinction between document classes. The quotient of significance and runtime of an algorithm determines its position within the decision tree. The fastest algorithm with the most significant results is put at the root of the tree while the slow algorithms are positioned near the leafs.

Summary

In this paper, we introduce our strategy to split the process of recognising a printed document into two phases. We always start with a classification phase which is followed by an analysis phase, if the document's type has been determined. Since we also consider composed documents, it is possible that a further phase of classification will be necessary for a part of the document later on. We believe that our system will finally process almost any printed document in an adequate manner. By storing and presenting explicit as well as implicit information, the user gets the possibility to understand and influence the recognition process in case of errors. The described scheme requires and promotes interactive work.

Literature

Nadine Baptiste, Monique Truquet
    A Complete Solution to Help a Blind Musician to Access Musical Data
    Proceedings of the ECART 2 Conference, Stockholm, Sweden, May 26-28, 1993
Inhao Chang, Murray Loew
    Pattern Recognition with New Class Discovery
    Proceedings of the CVPR Conference, June 3-6, 1991 pp. 438-443

Alan Y. Commike
  Syntactic Pattern Classification by Branch and Bound Search
  Proceedings of the CVPR Conference, June 3-6, 1991 pp. 432-437
Andreas Dengel
  Automatische Visuelle Klassifikation von Dokumenten
  Ph. D. Dissertation an der Fakultät Informatik, Universität Stuttgart, 1989
Gaby Glanzman, Bernhard Arnolds and Uwe Koch
  Evaluation of Text Scanners (Reading Machines) available for general use at the
  University Library, Freiburg
  Proceedings of the ECART 2 Conference, Stockholm, Sweden, May 26-28, 1993
Wolfgang A. Kreissl
  Interaktives Erkunden gedrucker Dokumente
  Diploma thesis Nr. 794, Institut für Informatik, Univ. Stuttgart, 1991
Urs Mueller, Markus Schenkel
  Improving Reading Machines for the Blind with Interactive Document Segmentation
  Computers for Handicapped Persons
  Proceedings of the 3rd International Conference, Vienna, July 7-9, 1992 pp. 363-372
Martin Recker
  Erstellen einer tastbaren Orientierungsseite zu gedruckten Dokumenten
  Diploma thesis Nr. 717, Institut für Informatik, Univ. Stuttgart, 1990
Waltraud Schweikhardt
  Interaktives Erkunden tastbarer Grafiken durch Blinde
  Bullinger, H.-J. (Hrsg.), Software-Ergonomie `85,
  B.G. Teubner Stuttgart, 1985, pp. 366-375.
Waltraud Schweikhardt
  Bildschirmtext - ein Rechnerunterstütztes Kommunikationsmittel auch für Blinde
  Hansen, H. R. (Hrsg.), GI/OCG/ÖGI Jahrestagung 1985
  Springer-Verlag 1985, pp. 691-701.
Waltraud Schweikhardt
  From Printed Media to Tactile Documents
  Workshop „New Problems and Future Solutions for Man Machine Interaction"
  Stuttgart, Dec. 16-17, 1991
Wolfgang L. Zagler, Johann Haider, Peter Mayer, Franz Peter Seiler and Michael Busboom
  Technology for Supporting Mainstream-Education
  Proceedings of the ECART 2 Conference, Stockholm, Sweden, May 26-28, 1993

Structuring Documents: the Key to Increasing Access to Information for the Print Disabled

Bart Bauwens, Jan Engelen, Filip Evenepoel

Katholieke Universiteit, Leuven
Kardinaal Mercierlaan 94, B-3001 Leuven, Belgium
Email: engelen@esat.kuleuven.ac.be

Chris Tobin, Tom Wesley

University of Bradford
Department of Computing, Bradford, BD7 1DP, United Kingdom
Email: t.a.b.wesley@bradford.ac.uk

Abstract. There is a growing conviction that the Standard Generalized Markup Language, SGML, can play an important role as an enabling technology to increase access to information for blind and partially sighted people. This paper reports on mechanisms that have been devised to build in accessibility into SGML encoded electronic documents, concentrating on the work done in the CAPS Consortium—Communication and Access to Information for People with Special Needs, a European Union funded project in the Technology Initiative for Disabled and Elderly People (TIDE) Programme—and by ICADD, the International Committee on Accessible Document Design. The CAPS follow on project, HARMONY is briefly described.

1 Introduction

The main work of the CAPS Consortium (Communication and Access to Information for People with Special Needs, a European Union funded project in the Technology Initiative for Disabled and Elderly People (TIDE) Programme) is directed to developing methods to increase the access to information for the print disabled [1]. People with print disabilities include the blind, the deaf–blind, the partially sighted, the dyslexic and those with motor impairments which make it difficult to physically control paper documents.

A previous paper [2] has indicated that one of the significant limiting factors for the print disabled is the difficulty they face in accessing the predominant form of information provision, which is almost entirely oriented to printed and other visual forms. The proportion of information easily accessible to the print disabled is very small. This is so for two main reasons:

- provision of information in forms suitable for the print disabled is regarded as a peripheral activity in comparison to provision for normally sighted persons;
- the means to produce information in forms suitable for the print disabled, such as braille, large print or synthetic speech, are slow, manually intensive and divorced from the initial information creation and distribution processes.

CAPS believes that a vital factor in creating the environment for such improvements is to develop methods in which the provision of information for the print disabled is, as far as possible, an automatic supplementary process related to the normal information creation processes. Technologically, this can-be achieved through application of the developments of *standardised structured electronic documents.*

Electronic documents are the key to linking into the commercial information production processes, as increasingly these processes are electronically based; and to the transformations required to make the information accessible to the print disabled.

The importance for the print disabled of *structure* in electronic documents can be realised when it is considered how the normally sighted reader obtains a significant amount of information from the layout of a document—titles in bold, bulleted indents, emphasised sections in italics. These are crucial when browsing through a large document. To make this information available to aid the print disabled user to browse—or navigate—within a document, the structure needs to be defined explicitly within the electronic document.

However, the transformations into forms accessible for the print disabled are, in many cases, non–trivial and this points to the need for *standardised* structured electronic documents. Having once made the transformations for *standardised structured* documents, significant amounts of information can rapidly be made available to the print disabled as the use of such standards grows in the commercial world.

An important document system standardised by ISO, the International Standards Organisation is the Standard Generalized Markup Language (SGML) [3]. The CAPS Consortium has recognised the potential of this standard for increasing the access to information for the print disabled, and Engelen and Wesley [4] have given a general account of this potential. The use of SGML as an internal format in the publishing industry is growing rapidly as publishers recognise the value and power of using a truly international standard for encoding their electronic documents.

A major part of the CAPS Project is devoted to developing methods whereby SGML is used at the heart of a generic model for dramatically improving the access to information for the print disabled. Within the current phase of the Project, which will complete at the end of 1994, a Pilot Electronic Library is being set up. Access will be provided interactively using synthetic speech on both an adapted work station and also through the home telephone using a voice response system with high quality real time text to speech. In addition, the provision of information through the off line production of braille and large print versions is being investigated.

This paper describes the techniques that the CAPS Consortium has devised to incorporate accessibility into SGML encoded documents.

2 An Overview of SGML

The complexity of real world documents is often not fully understood. SGML, in creating a standard for the description of such documents, is therefore, itself complex. A useful practical technical description is by van Herwijnen [5], while perhaps the easiest general guide is in the Text Encoding Initiative (TEI) Guidelines [6]. This overview draws particularly from the latter.

SGML is an international standard for the description of marked up electronic text. More exactly, SGML is a *metalanguage*, that is, a means of formally describing a language, in this case, a *markup language*. Historically, the word markup has been used to describe annotation or other marks within a text intended to instruct a compositor or typist how a particular passage should be printed or laid out. As the formatting and printing of texts was automated, the term was extended to cover all sorts of special markup codes inserted into electronic texts to govern formatting, printing, or other processing. Generalising from that sense, *markup* is defined as any means of making explicit an interpretation of a text.

By *markup language* is meant a set of markup conventions used together for encoding texts. A markup language must specify what markup is allowed, what markup is required, how markup is to be distinguished from text, and what the markup means. SGML provides the means for doing the first three; application programs which process the markup are written with an understanding of what the markup means.

2.1 Characteristics of SGML

There are two characteristics of SGML which distinguish it from other markup languages: its emphasis on descriptive rather than procedural markup and its document type concept.

Descriptive Markup. A descriptive markup system uses markup codes to provide names to categorise parts of a document. Markup codes such as <para> simply identify a part of a document as a 'para'. By contrast, a procedural markup system defines what processing is to be carried out at particular points in a document. In SGML, the instructions needed to process a document for some particular purpose (for example, to format it) are sharply distinguished from the descriptive markup which occurs within the document. Usually, they are collected outside the document in separate procedures or programs.

With descriptive instead of procedural markup the same document can readily be processed by many different pieces of software, each of which can apply different processing instructions to those parts of it which are considered relevant. For example, a braille conversion program can apply appropriate rules for the correct formatting of paragraphs in the various national literary braille codes.

Types of Document. Secondly, SGML introduces the notion of a *document type*, and hence a *document type definition* (DTD). Documents are regarded as having types, just as other objects processed by computers. The type of a document is formally defined by its constituent parts and their structure. The definition of a report, for example, might be that it consisted of a title and possibly an author, followed by an abstract and a sequence of one or more paragraphs. Anything lacking a title, according to this formal definition, would not formally be a report.

If documents are of known types, different documents of the same type can be processed in a uniform way. This separation of the definition of the document *type* from the document *instance* is a key feature for our purposes. If a particular DTD can be made accessible, then all document instances are made accessible.

2.2 Defining SGML Document Structures: the DTD

A DTD is expressed in SGML as a set of declarative statements, using the syntax defined in the standard. The DTD defines what markup is allowed, the major unit of markup being an *element*. A fragment of a DTD for a publication of bibliographic information might be:

```
<!ELEMENT publ  - -    (date, title, sec1+) >
<!--            Publications have a date to identify this occurrence
                along with the title; the title is followed by at
                least 1 but typically many sections. -->
<!ELEMENT sec1  - -    (heading, ((data, sec2*) | sec2+ )) >
<!ELEMENT sec2  - -    (heading, ((data, sec3*) | sec3+ )) >
<!ELEMENT sec3  - -    (heading, data) >
<!--            Sections may be nested to three levels. Each section
                has a heading followed by a mixture of subsections
                and data. -->
```

As can be seen from the comments embedded within the fragment, the DTD defines the properties of a set of document instances. Thus, the DTD is a formal, parsable specification of the structure of a class of documents. However, SGML imparts no semantic significance to the elements defining the structure, such as 'heading' or 'title'. Of course, it is good practice to name elements so that they can generally be understood; however, the semantic significance is generally incorporated in the application programs which process SGML documents. This process can be illustrated diagrammatically:

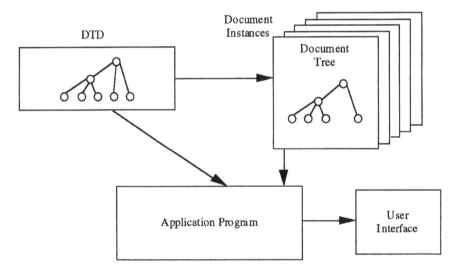

in which an application program, guided by the DTD, delivers a set of document instances to a given user interface. For our purposes, it is important to observe that the application program is likely to provide the information without consideration of accessibility for people with print disabilities.

3 SGML Associated Specifications

3.1 General Principles

There is a need to add extra information to DTDs to enable access for people with print disabilities to documents conforming to those DTDs. CAPS has called this extra information, *Associated Specifications*. An accessible application model is shown diagrammatically:

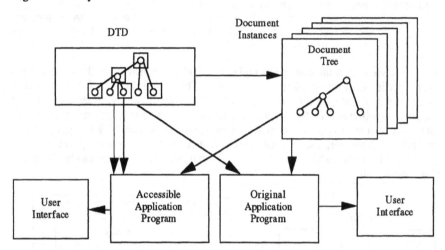

This model shows a number of fundamental features. Firstly, Associated Specifications, in the form of SGML conformant syntax are added to the DTD, *not* to the document instances. Thus, a whole class of documents is made accessible, without the major resources required to edit individual documents. Secondly, the Associated Specifications are added to the DTD—nothing is removed; thus, the original application program can be used without modification. This conforms to the principle that accessibility should be a by–product of the normal production processes. Finally, it should be noted that no new document formatting standards are needed—the Associated Specifications can be fully defined in SGML.

CAPS recognised the following main design principles for Associated Specifications which should allow:

- the transformation of electronic documents to a variety of accessible formats, such as braille, Moon and large print;
- the possibility of associating a text string with each element class that would ease the understanding of the meaning of the element class for an end user during interactive use;
- the addition of extra text that would normally be generated in the ink print version so that it may also occur in accessible versions;
- elements with the same generic identifier to have different treatment depending upon their context or relative position in the document;
- interactive operations that use the structure, such as overviews using headings and navigation through a document from heading to heading;
- multiple languages—any product that is to be distributed across Europe or wider

must be able to cater for an arbitrary set of languages.

In developing the concept of Associated Specifications, CAPS has worked closely with ICADD, the International Committee on Accessible Document Design [7]. This Committee, a non–profit organisation, incorporated in the State of New Hampshire, has the aim of developing techniques and raising awareness to enable documents to be made available to persons with print disabilities at the same time and at no greater cost as the print enabled community enjoys. Not surprisingly, given the common nature of both the needs and the potential technological solutions, the approaches taken by CAPS and ICADD have converged. CAPS in addition is gaining advantage from the legislative push being provided by ADA, the Americans with Disabilities Act.

In a remarkable development, ICADD has managed to have its mechanisms for accessibility incorporated into a new ISO Standard DTD for Electronic Manuscript Preparation and Markup [8]. This is, as far as is known, the first time that disability issues have been directly incorporated into a standard for *commercial* use. If, as seems likely, publishers start using the standard, accessibility will be automatically built in to any document instances that are produced.

3.2   The Basic Mechanism

The Associated Specifications developed by CAPS are fully documented in [9] and described in [10]. They are a superset of the ICADD mechanism detailed in [8], in which a number of fixed SDA (SGML Document Access) attributes are used to map an arbitrary DTD into a simple fixed ICADD DTD. In this paper it is only possible to sketch briefly the technical details.

The Base Tag Set. The complexity of real world documents means that DTDs used commercially are complex, and define many elements. The Book DTD defined in ISO 12083 has, for example, about 150 elements. Given the relative simplicity of the formatting available in braille, ICADD defines a simple set of 22 elements which can guide the production of accessible forms. A group of elements (h1 through h6) is used to define a hierarchy of headings; another group contains 'inline' elements such as b (bold), it (italics), lang (language). These elements may occur within, for example, the text of a paragraph and indicate another type of processing, for example, a lang element will switch the language.

Simple Mappings. One of the four fixed SDA (SGML Document Access) attributes is named SDAFORM:

```
<!ATTLIST   sectitle   SDAFORM     NAME    #FIXED   "h1">
```

In this example, the attribute SDAFORM indicates that wherever a <sectitle> element occurs, it should be mapped to an h1 element.

One can declare simple context–sensitive mappings as follows:

```
<!ATTLIST   section   SDARULE     NAMES   #FIXED   "title h1">
<!ATTLIST   chapter   SDARULE     NAMES   #FIXED   "title h2">
```

This example defines two rules: the first is intended to be used within section elements, the second within chapter elements. Within sections the title will be mapped to h1 headings, while within chapters the title will map to h2 headings. Complex mappings can be defined by more advanced techniques: if title appears in a chapter within a part, map to an h2; if the chapter is not in a part, map to an h1.

The third and fourth SDA attributes, named SDAPREF and SDASUFF, enable the replacement of start–tags (SDAPREF) or end–tags (SDASUFF) by specified text, for example:

```
<!ATTLIST  author    SDAPREF    CDATA  #FIXED  "Author name:">
```

3.3   Interactive Applications

Transforming the Original DTD. CAPS accepts that for non–interactive processes such as braille or large print on paper the transformation of a document so that it conforms to the simpler ICADD DTD seems acceptable. However, for interactive processes this loss of structure is *not* acceptable. For interactive applications, users may require much of the original document structure, and need to interpret or view it by means of its Associated Specifications.

Interactive Explanations. Users of interactive applications may need contextual information about where they are in a document. By keeping the original structure, this information could be provided by means of the element names of the SGML document. However, this is not appropriate—users should not be confronted with abbreviations for elements as declared in the DTD, which are designed for automatic processing by SGML aware applications. CAPS has therefore defined, for interactive applications the attribute, SDAEXPL, to explain element names. The following example associates with an element called npinfo the text "Newspaper Information":

```
<!ATTLIST  npinfo    %SDAEXPL;    "Newspaper Information" >
```

4   HARMONY

As the current CAPS Project draws to a close, the work will be continued in a new EU TIDE funded project, HARMONY, Horizontal Action for the Harmonisation of Accessible Structured Documents [11].

One of the main CAPS results is the development of the CAPSNEWS DTD as an interchange format for electronic newspapers for the print disabled [12]. However, despite the technological progress, CAPS has recognised that the effort so far allocated to ensuring the wider acceptance—particularly by major publishing companies—of such developments and standards has been inadequate.

HARMONY will address the non technological barriers to the growth of electronic newspapers for the print disabled. Its main objective is "to increase the *quantity and quality* of information accessible to print disabled people—especially in daily newspapers—by stimulating the publishing community via a process of involvement, lobbying and standardisation, and by encouraging them to adapt their existing electronic production systems to make use of appropriate new document structuring concepts." It will also maintain a technical watch on developments in the SGML area so that they may be used as soon as possible for the print disabled.

Acknowledgement

This work has been partly funded by DGXIII of the Commission of the European Union, under its Technology Initiative for Disabled and Elderly People (TIDE) Programme. The other CAPS partners are the Royal National Institute for the Blind (UK), Sensotec BV (BE), Infovox (SE) and the Handicap Institute (SE).

References

1. Full details of the CAPS Consortium can be obtained from the Coordinator, Professor Jan Engelen at the Katholieke Universiteit, Leuven, Belgium. The Consortium maintains an ftp site, gate.esat.kuleuven.ac.be in the directory /pub/CAPS and its sub directories, which provides access to its latest public documents.
2. J. Engelen, J. Baldewijns: Digital Information Distribution for the Reading Impaired: from Daily Newspapers to Whole Libraries. In: The 3rd International Conference on Computers for Handicapped Persons. Vienna, 1992, pp. 144–149
3. ISO 8879 : 1986 Information processing—Text and Office systems—Standard Generalized Markup Language (SGML). International Organisation for Standardisation
4. J. Engelen, T. Wesley: SGML—A Major Opportunity for Access to Information. In: The Seventh International Conference: Technology and Persons with Disabilities. CSUN Los Angeles, 1992, pp. 593-598
5. E. van Herwijnen: Practical SGML, Second Edition. Kluwer, 1994
6. A Gentle Introduction to SGML. In: C. Sperberg–McQueen, L. Burnard (eds.): Guidelines for Electronic Text Encoding and Interchange. 1994. Up to date information can be obtained from L. Burnard, Oxford University Computing Services, 13 Banbury Road, Oxford, OX2 6NN.
7. The latest information about the International Committee on Accessible Document Design (ICADD) can be obtained from the President, Michael G. Paciello, 110 Spit Brook Road, Nashua, NH. USA 03062, phone: +1 603 881 1831, Email: Paciello@Shane.Enet.Dec.Com.
8. ISO 12083 : 1993 Information processing—Text and Office systems—Electronic Manuscript Preparation and Markup. International Organisation for Standardisation
9. CAPS Deliverable D1, Development of SGML Associated Specifications, August 1993 and Addendum to Deliverable D1, November 1993. Obtainable from the Coordinator [1]
10. B. Bauwens, J. Engelen, F. Evenepoel, C. Tobin, T. Wesley: SGML—An Enabling Technology for the Reading Impaired. In: SGML Europe '94. Montreux: Database Publishing Ltd, Swindon, UK 1994
11. Full details of the HARMONY Consortium can be obtained from the Coordinator, Professor Jan Engelen at the Katholieke Universiteit, Leuven, Belgium
12. European Interchange Format, CAPSNEWS DTD, Version 2.0, November 1993. Obtainable from the Coordinator [1]

Study Center for Visually Impaired Persons
Supportive System for Blind and Partially Sighted Students at the University of Karlsruhe/Germany

Joachim Klaus

Studienzentrum für Sehgeschädigte
der Universität Karlsruhe
Engesserstrasse 4
76128 Karlsruhe
Tel.: 0721 - 608 2760
Fax: 0721 - 697377

Abstract:

In 1987 a pilot project was started at the University of Karlsruhe dedicated to involve new communication technologies for visually impaired students and the sighted world. This supporting system for blind student led after five years of model development to a Study Center for Visually Impaired Students, which offers equal chances to these handicapped students in steps towards university, in living, learning and examinations inside the university system as well as in steps towards labour market.

1. Introduction

In April 1993 the former pilot project "Computer Science for the Blind" at the University of Karlsruhe was institutionalized. It is now called "Study Center for Visually Impaired Persons". From autumn 1987 until spring 1993 the pilot project had been financed by the Federal Ministry for Education and Science (Bonn) and the Ministry for Science and Art Baden Württemberg. The project´s aim was to lead visually impaired persons to study courses and to according profession which were scarcely accessible to them before. This is made possible by

- new technical working aids with special programmes for visually impaired users which have partly been developed at the University of Karlsruhe

- the offer of intensive pedagogical and psychological counselling and care

- specific support concerning study and exam regulations

- further integrative offers like mobility training, university and municipal sports and cultural programmes.

Due to the original offer to support visually impaired persons studying Computer Science and Industrial Engineering, those two study courses are the main subjects being studied but they are complemented by subsidiaries of other faculties.

There is also a close cooperation between the Study Center and the school of Industrial Computer Science at the Fachhochschule of Karlsruhe where visually impaired students are now enrolled, too,

2. Technical Supporting System

With the help of modern information technology the blind and partially sighted students gain access to the relevant study literature. Special hard- and software like Braille display, voice output, scanner, large print or print enlargement systems, Braille printer etc. make printed media available to them. The technical support can be divided into the following parts:

1. The technology available within the rooms of the Study Center enables the blind and partially sighted students to quickly and directly exchange e.g. texts, diagrams and drawings among each other or with sighted fellow students. The study literature which is transferred into electronic form is available on diskette and via the local network.

2. At present there are three decentralized work stations for visually impaired students, one at the university library, one each at the library of the Department of Computer Science and Industrial Engineering which offer the possibility to independently scan printed literature. Further decentralized workstations shall be set up in order to make it possible to work and learn at the same places as their sighted fellow students.

3. For studying an adequate personal technical equipment at home is absolutely necessary. It consists of a powerful personal computer with respective assistive devices as well as a portable unit for taking notes during lectures or seminars. In general this equipment is granted by the relevant Social Security Office for the duration of the studies.

4. Via a speech server which can be operated by phone some services of the local network and a voicemail function are made available for the students to be used from the outside.

3. Student assistance

Textbooks, lecture notes, exercise papers etc. are usually only available in black print, that means blind and partially sighted students have only limited access to that literature. Each term up to 25 student assistants therefore transfer texts into electronic form or generate tactile graphics.
The student assistant is assigned to a lecture - not to a visually impaired student - and is responsible for the correct and timely transfer of the relevant literature into electronic form. In general every third or fourth week during term the so-called student-assistant meeting is held which is attended by the student assistants as well as by visually impaired students and employees of the Study Center. Current questions concerning the transfer of the literature, text lay-out or the organization of the student-assistant programme are discussed at these meetings.

4. Counselling and Care

The close cooperation between the Study Center and the concerned faculties as well as the Center for Information and Guidance (zib) - the Student Counselling Center at the University of Karlsruhe - aims at encouraging the visually impaired prospective students to take their interests and leanings into serious consideration when choosing their courses especially with regard to their future job qualification.
Therefore intensive counselling and guidance is offered to visually impaired students of secondary education and those doing the Abitur (school-leaving exam) while they are still at school. Every November an Information Day is held for students of the school years 11 and 12 in connection with a general Open Day organized by the university for school leavers.
Furthermore, an Orientation Unit over several days is scheduled in May for visually impaired students preparing to take their school-leaving exam. During these days information is given on the study courses themselves and on the support provided by the Study Center. At the end of this Orientation Unit, the prospective students should be able to make up their minds about whether they feel up to the study requirements. During terms regular meetings are held in order to give the visually impaired students the possibility to exchange experiences among themselves and with the members of the university (lecturers, fellow students, administration). A network of institutions (Center for Information and Guidance zib, student organization of the individual departments, subject counselling, Psychological Advice Center) offers the corresponding assistance in case of questions and difficulties relating to studying as well a to personal problems.
In cooperation with the university administration, industrial companies, Institutions of the Civil Service and the Center for Information and Guidance special possibilities are offered by the Study Center to visually impaired students of qualifying in an effective way for the labour market (e.g. by arranging periods of practical training in industry at home and abroad, application and interview trainings and a special Open Day for industrial companies.

5. Library

The Study Center has its own library which is incorporated into the network of scientific libraries. Due to its being a reference library the holdings can´t be borrowed as a rule. They comprise the study literature transferred into electronic form for the visually impaired students (i.e.

diskettes, tactile graphics), its black-print editions, manuals of hard-
and software as well as literature on subjects relating to handicapped
in general and to visually impaired persons in particular.
The study literature transferred on diskette does not fall under the
regulation of the reference library; these media can be borrowed by
visually impaired students of the University and the Fachhochschule of
Karlsruhe.
In addition visually impaired students of other universities may borrow
study literature available in electronic form at the Study Center via
interlibrary loan. A current catalog of the holdings may be ordered.

6. University and City of Karlsruhe

The campus of the university directly borders on the Center of Karlsruhe. The local condition facilitates the visually impaired students´
orientation on the campus and in the city. A tactile street map for visually impaired persons and a mobility training plan of the university
campus are available. The students have access to nformation on the
scientific and cultural activities at the university campus and in town
via the local network. Local newspapers, the Student´s Offical
University Journals, are available on diskette. Thus, an intensive
network of institutions and cooperation are set up to provide equal
chances to the visually impaired students.

7. International Cooperation

During the pilot project phase an international exchange and communication system was established. From 1990 - 1993 a COMETT II-
Project was dedicated to the objective of "Integration of Visually Impaired Students into Work by their Completing Practical Training in
Europe". A Europe wide network between universities and national and
international companies was established. The VIPPRA "Visually Impaired Persons Practical Training", an electronic data base provides
information about

- Companies which offer practical trainings for visually impaired
  students

- students` reports about their personal experience with their
  practical training

- general and specific news in this field.

A TEMPUS-Joint European Project (1991-1994) aims at opening university education for visually handicapped students and the improvement of their learning, living and vocational integration in the Czech and Slovak Republic. In the meantime Study Centers - comparable to the one in Karlsruhe - have been established at the Technical University of Prague and at the Comenius University of Bratislava. We are waiting for the approval of two follow-up applications within the TEMPUS II programme

- "Software Engineering in Market Economy" with a possibility of the integrated study for visually handicapped students at the Technical University of Prague

- "The Improvement and Development of Conditions for Integration of Visually Disabled Persons in Education - Creation of a System for the Preparation of Teachers, Counselors, and Itinerant Teachers acting in/for Integrated Settings" at the Comenius University of Bratislava.

After giving support to build up comparable Centers at the Technical University of Dresden/ Germany and the University of Linz/Austria the Study Center at Karlsruhe now works on a student exchange programme with the University of New Orleans, the Oregon State University and the Queen's University of Kingston (Canada). The first blind student is about to begin his studies abroad.

The pilot project and the activities of the Study Center demonstrate the highly positive way in which modern computer technology and electronic communications can offer new chances in life and at work for handicapped persons and open ways of integration and human normality.

References:

Joachim Klaus, Ute Lehnerer
Integration von Sehgeschädigten Studierenden und
Hochschulabsolventen in die Arbeitswelt
(COMETT II-Project)
Karlsruhe, 1991

University Studies of Visually Handicapped Students
Seminar - TEMPUS II - Project
Prague, 1992

New Study and Vocational Possibilities for
Visually Handicapped Students
Seminar -
TEMPUS II - Project, Bratislava, 1993

Joachim Klaus, et al.
Abschlußbericht des Modellversuchs
"Informatik für Blinde - Studium für Sehgeschädigte
in Informatik und Wirtschaftsingenieurwesen"
-Final report-
Bonn, 1994
(being published in "Bildung und Wissenschaft" des Bundes-
ministeriums f. Bildung und Wissenschaft)

Support Centre for Visually Impaired Students

Ludmila Moravcikova

The Faculty of Mathematics and Physics, Comenius University,
Bratislava, SLOVAKIA

Abstract. The paper deals about problems, achievements and prospect of building the support Centre at the Comenius University in Bratislava. The support Centre of academic studies for the blind and partially sighted has been built within the project TEMPUS JEP 2423 "New Study and Vocational Possibilities for Visually Handicapped Students" at the Faculty of Mathematics and Physics since September 1992. The basic role of the Centre is to secure conditions for the integrated study of visually handicapped students at Comenius University and enable them to acquire education in the fields that have not been attainable before
...

1 Introduction

Our Centre has been built thanks to contacts with the Union of the Blind and Partially Sighted in Slovakia and with Mr. Mamojka, who have helped us to join the project TEMPUS. Slovakia was the part of Czechoslovakia, so the first idea was to build one Centre at the Technical University of Prague and the second one at our University. Centres in both cities have been cooperating since their establishment and also after the country was divided into two states.

The coordinator of the project is the University of Karlsruhe, where they have been realizing a pilot project, "Informatik für Blinde" since 1987. The main difference between the German and our Centre is in the scope of work. While the German Centre has focused its support mainly on future mathematicians, experts on informatics, and the students of industrial engineering, our Centre intends to promote studying in all fields according to their interest.

Since the Centre should work with modern computer equipment, special peripherials and software, the decision was made to place the Centre at the Faculty of Mathematics and Physics.

2 The Main Achievements

2.1 The Technical Equipement

The Centre is situated into two rooms, one of them is for sighted people who prepare study material for their handicapped colleagues and the second is for handicapped students. The technical equipement of the Centre is:

- local Novell network with eleven computers and monitors of a different dimensions
- for blind students
  - eighty cell Braille line
  - two voice outputs
- for partially sighted students
  - VGA reader
  - colour reader
  - programme LP DOS
- for sighted people transforming study material into appropriate form for handicapped people
  - OCR system with scanner
  - Braille printer
  - dictaphones.

2.2 The Staff of the Centre

The staff of the Centre consists of five members:
- coordinating person
- technical person
- pedagogical and psychological councellor
- technical councellor
- the manager of tutoring system

Only pedagogical councellor has fulltime job in the Centre, other members of the staff are university teachers of informatics and they work in the Centre only partially. Non of us has had previous experiences with handicapped people. At the beginning we went through study visits in Germany, Great Britain, Canada and USA, where we learnt how to use special devices for the blind, how to handle blind people and which kind of services are necessary for the successful study of visually handicapped students at university.

We organised a conference in Bratislava and a workshop in Mala Lucivna about motivation and preparation of handicapped students for university study, integration and counselling services at school and university. Both meetings were a good opportunity for Slovak specialists who are involved in work with visually impaired people to exchange their experiences with foreign colleagues.

2.3 Activities Aimed at Visually Impaired Students

In the last academic year, two blind and three partailly sighted students studied at our university. They studied journalistics, law, pedagogics, history and mathematics.

They have received aid through preparation of study material, courses for electronic compensatory techniques and pedagogical - psychological counselling.

Before the blind students started to study at the University, they had gone through the mobility training and courses on special technical equipment (Eureka) by specialists from the Union of the Blind and Partially Sighted and courses on special computing in our Centre. They had already learned type-writing at high schools but they had not any experiences with computers. We trained them to use computer and special devices (Braille line and printer, voice output), the basic skills for using MS DOS and word processor (Word Perfect 5.1). Then we have been continuosly providing them with counselling about technical equipment of the Centre when it was needed. The counselling was provided also for partially sighted students, teachers from special schools for visually impaired students and for students of educational study (future teachers).

The essential condition is that visually impaired students should have studied scientific literature at their disposal in parallel with their fully-sighted peers. To accomplish that the Centre has been compiling and providing needed study materials (lecture notes, books, exercises) in the digital form, which was easily transformed into the Braille or large print, or displayed on the Braille line. This kind of work has been done by students from our faculty. I must appreciate that in current difficult economical situation, the main motivation for them was possibility to work with technique of high quality and learning of new technology. We are making use following technologies:

- 1. Transformation of the printed text into digital form using OCR system: scanner - computer - recognizing software (Recognita). Then we can print the text on Braille printer or it can be read through the Braille line or voice output. We can transform the digital information into form usable by Eureka using special software.
- 2. Text of the low quality, which is difficult to recognize by recognizing software, has been typed by students on computers.
- 3. Great amount of study material is recorded on audio-tapes. Unfortunately, our blind students prefer listening the tapes to using computers because of their undeveloped computer literacy. This fact implies two kinds of problems:
  First, it is more difficult to find students of our faculty who are willing to record audio-tapes than students willing to use computers.
  Second, it is more expensive to store data on audio-tapes than on flopy-disks. In future we plan to use multimedia systems to transform analogue information to the digital form.

Great problem for us was to find students of similar study fields, who would have been preparing study materials of individual subjects. The reason of that was that not all handicapped students could live together with their schoolmates because of unsuitable accomodation conditions, so they lost contacts with them.

2.4 External Activities and Cooperation

Except of activities mentioned above we went on in trying to map the situation in Slovakia for the future interest and plans of visually handicapped secondary school students in academic study. While making the survey of the situation in Slovakia, we have established contacts with teachers and pupils in special schools in many research institutions and faculties, whose competence and knowledge is related to our problems and thus we need their cooperation.

It would be naive to think that the Centre would work properly if we did not focus our activity also on wide circle of population. It seems it will be a long-term process of teaching not only the academic public to accept handicapped students, communicate with them, understand their needs and demands and form a proper psychological climate for their study and life.

There has been a trend in the education of the blind to concentrate (and somehow separate) them into special schools and institutions in our country and elsewhere in Europe. Such primary schools are located in the towns of Levoa and Bratislava.

All the achievements mentioned above wouldn't have been received without support of many institutions. On behalf of all I would like to appreciate the university's attitude towards the project. Especially the financial support in a present difficult economical situation was very helpful.

I must mention a cooperation with Slovak Blind and Partially Sighted Union too. The cooperation is very important for us. People from the union have helped us to understand better needs of blind and we have solved together a few technical problems concerning the adaptation of special devices for Slovak national environment.

The cooperation with the Western partners - German, English and Czech - has been very good. Clear rules, equivalent position of all partners and large indepedence in concrete decisions are main features of our cooperation.

3 Conclusions and plans for the future

The integrated education in Slovakia nearly does not exist. Conditions for study and living for visually impaired people allow them to choose only from one or two possible properly supported choices. The only solution of this situation is the establishment of a properly supported system of integrated education acting parallel with the special education, with increasing role and responsibility towards higher level of education. But there is a great lack and an urgent need of qualified staff and support services for the integrated education. Opening of the Centre at Comenius University in November 1993 was the first step to the really integrated education which needs to be followed by other concrete measures. Two years experience within the project opened new horizons, needs and demands.

Because our TEMPUS project will finish this year, we have applied for the next one. If it is accepted we plan to go on through the following activities:

- 1. The establishment of the Distributed Network of Support Services for Visually disabled University Students (Expanding of the activities of the Support Centre at Comenius University as a coordinating body of the network including distance study, implementation of new communication and computer technology for remote provision of services, creation of the research and production unit for the tactile graphics). The network will consist of the main centre and three local centres at universities over the country. We have already opened first contacts with the universities in Bansk Bystrica, Koice and Nitra. Later, other local centres could be created according to the incidence and demands of visually disabled students.

In this activity will participate also our western partners:

- National Council for the Blind of Ireland will participate in the establishment of distributed network of support services for visually disabled university students including the distance study.

- The main role of the Royal National Institute for the Blind would be in the training and support infrastructure development.

- Loughborough University of Technology will guide the establishment of a research and production unit for tactile graphics by advising on appropriate technology.

— 2. Establishing new possibilities for preparation of professionals for integrated education and rehabilitation of visually disabled persons (postgraduate courses for educational counsellors and/or itinerant teachers, basic courses for mainstream teachers, courses for professional instructors of social rehabilitation).

This activity will make use of the outcomes of others activities - in the field of informatics, adaptive technology and tactile graphics.

The best place to realize this activity is at the Department of Typhlopedology at Faculty of Pedagogics because of its influence on future teachers and experts.

— 3. Development of new courses supporting integrated education for future mainstream teachers of sciences and informatics and development of intensive courses for pre-school training (both in primary and secondary education). Courses should be focused on technologies of developing educational computer microworlds with specially adapted graphics for partially sighted students as well as for non-handicapped students to understand problems of handicapped in modern integrated school. New educational activities should be "children centred" contrasted to more traditional "teacher centred" activities. Corresponding in-service training should be developed for teachers of elementary and secondary schools.

To succeed in this effort we decided to make extensive use of the newest implementation of Logo language, called Comenius Logo for Windows. Logo is a creative environment developed specially for children to support their logical mind and common sense abilities by making them solve simple problems - they are planning, decomposing problems into subproblems, and combining partial results into final solutions. The Logo environment has all promises to support "children centred" teaching/learning activities and has been successfully used in both mainstream education and special education for mentally disabled, for handicapped children etc. throughout the world. Its new implementation, Comenius Logo for Windows is extremely powerful implementation which stresses easy visualization of activities (by letting objects move all over the screen, by popular turtle graphics using multiple parallel turtles etc.).

We plan to focus the courses around developing small projects (Logo microworlds) which will illustrate the way handicapped children have to make the communication, to learn, to entertain. We believe that graphical and multimedial features of Comenius Logo environment are suitable for developing, implementing, and evaluating such microworlds, and for learning the educational principles of such applications. Moreover, we plan to develop a course devoted to the ways the special technology for the handicapped is used. This course should make use of new developments of active learning environments, which may positively influence traditional special education.

At the beginning of May we applied also for COPERNICUS project together with partners from Scotland, Finland, Austria and Hungary. A title of the project is: "Remote Service Provision for People with Disabilities" and it seems to be a technology demonstrator project based on a multimedia training system for visually handicapped using internet, modem and ISDN links.

- 1. In this project we plan to extend our services to allow students throughout Slovakia to participate in the educational process via telecommunication's links, concentrating on text based services such as "talking books".
- 2. We would like to adapt the new technology, which is successfuly used in some western countries, for our national environment and develop needed software products for IBM PC and SUN Unix computing systems or for special electronical equipement and computers for the blind.
- 3. We have some experiences with hypertext systems and we plan to develop applications, which could enable visually impaired people to use and efectively manipulate multimedia information.

Many suggestions for these activities come from Slovak Blind and Partially Sighted Union which will also participate in all of them as a representant of interests of visually disabled people, they will use its long time experience in provision services to visually disabled people and they will transfer gained knowledge and experience to the general visually disabled community.

There is much more to run across - problems and successes. We must go on to achieve many interesting results, which I am sure will be of interest for both of you and us. Cross your fingers.

References

1. Mendelova, E.: The problems and prospect of building the Centre at Comenius University, New Study and Vocational Possibilities for Visually handicapped Students, Proceedings, The International Conference, January 31 - February 2, 1993, Bratislava
2. Waczulik, J.: Tempus JEP 2423: New study and vocational possibilities for visually handicapped students, Individual Institutional Report, Comenius University Bratislava, Academic year 1992/93

3. Blaho, A., Kalas, I., Tomcsanyi, P.: Comenius Logo: Environment for teachers and Environment for learners, Proc. of the 4th European Logo Conference, Suppl. pp. 1-11, Athens

Educational Endeavour "Computer Science for the Blind"
State of the Art and Experiences in Supporting Visually Handicapped Students

Roland Wagner
Bernhard Stöger
Klaus Miesenberger

Department of Computer Science, Johannes Kepler University, Linz, Austria

Abstract. This report wants to show our experience and line out the state of the art of the Educational Endeavour "Computer Science for the Blind" at the University of Linz. First we will show that supporting visually handicapped at University is a task for Computer Science. After that we will have a look at the social background of a handicap. Special notice we will be given to education and integration. Taking these basic intentions into account we will then focus on the services offered at our university.

1 Introduction

In 1991 the institute for Computer Science at the University of Linz, Austria, started to support visually handicapped students by offering special services for the integration in normal courses of studies. The chances opened up by new information technology and the necessity to use them in practice in a socially reflected way led to such an engagement at our institute. The goal is to make the integration into different courses for studies - not only computer science - at our university possible. A program for reducing the extra work of visually handicapped was to be established.

2 The Computer as a Useful Tool and a Starting Point for Integration

The benefit of information technology for the handicapped, especially for the visually handicapped, is quite obvious. There are many examples which show the practical advantages of these new devices and the new software. Especially this conference shows such possibilities. The computer supports the presentation of the information of (approximately the same) processes for different kinds of accesses (e.g. visually, audible, tactile) at the man-machine interface. The special situation of every user (education, style of working, task, ..., and also the special needs of visually impaired) can be taken into account by this multi-media power. This independence of the output media offers a link for integration into real processes for the visually handicapped. The wide-spread and increasing use of computers shows the possibilities, the necessity and responsibility of supporting the integration.
According to this we want to point out the necessity of a close relation of such an edeavour to computer and/or other technical sciences or practical work: The

complexity of normal computer systems, the higher complexity of computer systems adapted for visually handicapped with special devices and software, new developments and changes in the way of using the computer (e.g.: Graphical User Interfaces, Networking, Hypertext, Electronic Publishing, ...), the ongoing initial role of the computer as a useful tool for handicapped people - these and other facts show that a close link between integration and theory and practice of information technology is undeniable. The development of new systems for handling several tasks, which can be seen as a general goal of computer science, offers a great chance for handicapped people by opening up a way of access by adapting the man-machine interface. This is and will be a task for computer science and practical work. It is an important experience of our work that high technical knowledge is the basis for supporting the integration of visually handicapped.

3 The Social Process of Developing a Handicap and the Importance of Education and Integration

This technical progress must not make us forget the fact that a handicap is a social construct built up by our conventional views and judgements based on handed down social values which are often more prejudices than justified judgements. Like any other social process a handicap has to be treated by looking at the social background first. The handicapped person, the environment, the professionals as well as the "not concerned" have their roles in this play which we learn during socialisation.

We have to be aware of the fact that a physical shortcoming is not the same as a handicap. By concentrating only on the new technical aspects of treating the physical shortcoming as the most conspicuous and noticeable fact of the situation we neglect the social roots of a handicap. Being fascinated by the possibilities for the medical problem we often tend to believe in an "efficient" technical solution for the whole situation and neglect the social circumstances. One of the most important experiences of our work shows that concentrating exclusively on the technical aspects of using the computer can only treat the medical and technical aspects of the physical shortcoming. The enormous amount of possibilities for a technical support extended and still extends the gap between chances of technology and realisation in social programs. These tendencies can lead to situations which confirm the "gettho-situation" of the handicapped.

There are also people who work with handicapped persons in practice but are not willing or able to bring the technical chances into use. Being uninformed about or distrustful of new developments some people are not aware of the enormous possibilities of computers. Chances for independence and integration are withheld from the handicapped.

These two extreme tendencies should show what we think is most important for us today: We have to concentrate on social, pedagogical and didactic aspects, when deciding when and how to use the computer for the support of visually handicapped. We have to enable a better use of these possibilities for visually handicapped and try to make people understand and feel that also a visually handicapped person can be a worthy member of our society- not *because* of using a computer but supported by this tool -. The social context of a handicap invites us to take new technologies as a starting point. We have to reflect this social background by offering a program for the use of technical possibilities.

Education plays an important role in this context because of its still growing importance for participation in all kinds of processes within society. Learning has become a task for lifetime. For visually handicapped education is even more important: Managing the normal environment is more complex for the visually handicapped because of the reduced or non-visual approach to the visually arranged world. Faster changes in society increase this complexity. The traditional image of visually handicapped as being "inefficient, dependent, helpless, etc." causes disadvantages in taking part in educational programs as well as the deficit in access to education strengthens the underrating image - a vicious circle and self-fulfilling prophecy -. We are convinced that teaching skills in using the computer can offer a way out of this situation. This knowledge is of high appreciation within our society. The ability to apply computers to independent self-help and to several conventional tasks opens up a chance for more understanding and being accepted as a worthy member in society.

Another basic question is: Why integration? Is it not better and more efficient to treat the special circumstances in special situations? As pointed out above this is only a biased technical and medical view. I want to point out an other important aspect of integration, especially in the field of education: Apart from the general social situation, which make integration a undeniable task anyway, there is also a more social, pedagogical argument: Every social process, group, institution, etc. has its own way of interaction and communication. For participating it is necessary to become familiar with this special behaviour. Such a "secret curriculum" based on special opinions, special vocabulary, ideologies, norms, values, behaviour and so on is built up and transmitted, often without the users being aware of. In their special institutions and situations handicapped people can not learn these special signs of conventional social processes; they behave in their own way which is often strange and unfamiliar. To acquire this "information" it is necessary to have the opportunity of integration. Integration to the highest possible level is indispensable for an adequate technical as well as social qualification.

4 Program of Support and Accompanying Activities

The considerations stated above show the background of the endeavour in Linz and reflect on some experience of our work. Although the situation of visually handicapped people in Austria has improved considerably over the past decades, only a small minority among the visually handicapped with outstanding talent and devotion have managed to graduate at university. To improve this situation and following the example of the university of Karlsruhe, Germany, the University of Linz began to open university education to a wider range of visually impaired people in 1991. Beyond that we want to describe our program of support.

It is intended that the endeavour in Linz eliminates to a large extent the enormous amount of extra work which rely on the conventional, visual oriented teaching methods. The basic concept is to support visually handicapped students during their integration in conventional courses of studies and into everyday life at university.

The university has to impart scientific and practical knowledge in an understandable and usable manner. This task has to be fulfilled by selecting, preparing and presenting suitable contents and examples for *all* students who have the permission and are willing to study. The access to the official as well as to the "secret curriculum" should help the students to become members of society with academic titles and obligations. In order to make managing this task also possible to visually handicapped students the Institute of Computer Science took the initiative to built up a special service centre with a specific educational, technical as well as scientific task. Let us now have a look at our main activities:

4.1 Special computer equipment, information services

According to the students´ special needs computer equipment is available at the university campus. Students are supported in two ways:
First of all, they can use adapted computers at several locations at the campus. Up to now four stations are accessible for the students. An additional fully equipped station will be put up this year. Because students take part in different courses we have to pay attention to configure these stations as flexible as possible to be able to move them from one location to the other. All stations are situated at, let me say: "strategic locations for integration" (libraries, programming laboratory, seminar rooms, etc.). If the "strategic location" changes, the station changes its location, too. All "strategic locations" are accessible 24 hours a day.
Secondly, every student has his or her private equipment which is adapted to the special needs of each student. This equipment has to be a portable one. Students can use their equipment at home but they can also rely on all functions of modern word processing when using the prepared digital studying material in the lectures. It enables them also to take notes during a lecture and to give presentations. There is also the possibility to use them at "strategic locations" by connecting them to the network of the University. It is praiseworthy that in Austria public institutions pay the cost of this privat equipment. We want to point out that these possibilities of working at the conventional locations is indispensable for our concept.
Each of these stations can be used as a local PC or can be connected to a local network, which is integrated into the network of the university, which has a gateway to the Internet. The local network facilitates the management of the stations (e.g. on-line trouble shouting, support of users, installation of software), offers a powerful tool of communication (mailing, access to study material and other information) and makes the supply of special features such as special local information sources (digital newspaper, register, timetable of public transport, information about sportive and cultural events, menus, video text, BBS, CD-Rom, etc.) and access to Internet resources possible. This technical background is the basis for our support.

4.2 Accompanying program

Before entering the courses. For a successful start it is necessary to support the first steps at university. To reach this target, we do the following:

Computer Camp: The idea to organise a computer camp goes back to the fact that visually handicapped children and youngsters should also have the opportunity of support in using the computer in scholl and everyday life. Such a project supports the transfer of knowledge in using the computer. Such projects offer a good chance for the visually impaired children and youngsters to learn to deal with their situation by using the computer, to feel and learn how to play an active role in an integrated groups and thereby to build up a positive sense of identity. The sighted can take up the possibility of interacting with the visually handicapped and can build up a positive image of the visually handicapped, an image with less prejudices. It is important to gain a lot of useful experience for our work with this project. For our work at the university such projects also offer the possibility to support the preparations for a way to university at an early period.

In 1993 we realised the First Integrating Computer Camp. 24 visually handicapped and sighted children and youngsters took part in the camp. In 1994 an international organisation team is working to realise the First International Computer Camp in Austria. Especially for a small country like Austria such connections open the door to a larger international community of visually handicapped. In the following years the idea of a Computer Camp should become a fixed part of our work.

Counselling about studying possibilities and necessities: Counselling youngsters to find an orientation and a decision what they should do after leaving school gets more and more difficult. Therefore different institutions offer a special support in Austria. For visually handicapped their is a special institution offering counselling for entering the labour market. Till now there is no special counselling for visually handicapped people who want to go to university. Therefore we started a counselling program this year (for students in the last two years before leaving school) in co-operation with the Students Counselling Centre of the university and the Austrian representation of students. We have prepared and are still preparing information which is published by different institutions and pass them on in digital form. During personal counselling we concentrate on technical preconditions and knowledge. For students who are interested in studying in Linz we organise information days and orientation units for preparing the first steps at university.

First steps at university: Visually handicapped students who want to join a course of studies in Linz are supported when doing the enormous amount of organisation and bureaucracy at the beginning. We help them with the organisation of a mobility training, finding a room, acquiring the personal equipment, etc. We support the integration into conventional orientation courses offered for all students. We also offer courses in handling the equipment and information resources. To handle this tasks it is necessary to start the preparations as soon as possible. The difficult situation at the beginning makes such an intensive support necessary to form the preconditions for integration. We reduce such efforts step by step to prevent overprotection and to lead the students on a way to independence.

Accompanying the study process.

Preparing material for study: The most serious and also obvious obstacle for a visually handicapped student is restricted access to written material. Since, as mentioned above, these people can work well with a computer, the material (sets of lecture notes, books, folios, contents of the blackboard, exercises, examination questions, etc.) has to be presented in digital form. We employ special tutors to do this work. These tutors are senior students with profound knowledge in the field of the lecture which they are allocated to. The tutors are allocated to a lecture and not to the student or to us. Obviously their work is strongly dependent on the form in which the particular material is presented:

a) The material is already available in digital form. In such a case the tutor's task is to reformat, to number and to structure the material with a wide-spread word processing program. The tutor should work out a structure which makes a general overview, a better and faster orientation and moving through the text possible.

For blind students this seems to be the only possible way, as presenting material in Braille needs a high a amount of paper. Only the most important parts of a material are printed in Braille. The students can also use a Braille printer to make outputs for themselves.

The digital information also has striking advantages for partially sighted students, because of the possibility of producing printed outputs which are adapted to their special needs and to use screen enlarging software or speech output for an alternating, not tiring access with the computer.

Graphics also have to be embedded into the text. Tutors have to produce simplified tactile graphics with additional explanations for the blind students. All graphics are numbered and collected in a map; references to the numbered graphics are made in the text. For the partially sighted students the graphics also have to be adapted and integrated in the digital as well in the printed version.

It is an important experience that two or often more versions of every material have to be made to cope with the special needs of the students. Therefore the digital form of a material is indispensable. We also want to point out the importance of using a wide-spread and well known software for presenting the material in order to facilitate co-operation and integration.

Our biggest problem in this context is the access to the material in digital form to facilitate our work. Theoretically, every person who prepares printed material uses or is able to use a computer for this work at out university and therefore a digital source exists. In practice, however, we often fail to get such a digital original since the authors or publishers are often not willing to pass it on. We hope that this access will be facilitated in future. Extensive public relations work in- and outside the university has to be done to make authors, publishers and also the public become aware of this disadvantage. As a first step one publishing house is willing to hand over all scientific books in digital form if one exists and the author consents.

New developments in the field of publishing (e.g. hypertext systems) and teaching (e.g. Computer aided lectures) offer a great chance for an access to the material in digital form but there are also tendencies to a more graphic oriented presentation which confronts us with new tasks. We make several scientific efforts to test such new systems which are used at the university due to the possibility of an access for visually handicapped students.

b) The material is presented in printed form: For partially sighted students sometimes an enlarged copy of print material is suitable. Mostly we produce a digital version which is of advantage for both the partially sighted and the blind students. The tutors use a high-resolving scanner together with teachable OCR software to convert the material into digital form. Then the process can continue as described in a). Like in a) there is the problem of getting the permission for preparing a digital version of the material.

c) The material is presented in hand-written form: There is no other way but typing the whole hand-written text and then to proceed as in a).

d) The material contains mathematical symbols: Mathematical symbols represent an additional difficulty. There is the need for an ASCII representation of mathematical formulae. We have decided to use the source code of the mathematical word processing program TEX, since this is well known to many people working in the fields of mathematics, physics, computer science etc. Students able to read TEX source enjoy the additional advantage that whenever they need to produce mathematical texts in printed form, then the ideal tool for this task is at their hand. While the TEX source itself presents mathematics to a totally blind student in a readable form, partially sighted students cannot be expected to read formulae in this notation. However, since the TEX package contains a previewer that lets "TEXed" formulae appear on the screen as they would appear in a book, using TEX satisfies both groups of clients. If we get material in TEX, the tutors have to "simplify" the source (not the contents) by deleting unnecessary layout instructions. Printed as well as hand-written material has to be brought into TEX by hand.
In addition we make a scientific effort to facilitate the production of suitable TEX sources in co-operation with the Research Institute for Symbolic Computing (RISC) at our university.

The material should be available at our network BEFORE the lectures. The visually handicapped student should have the opportunity to use the material in the lecture. It has to be pointed out that the success of the support of a lecture highly depends on the will of the lecturer. Problems, which are often said to be a mistake of our work, are caused by the style of education (no material, no preparation of the lectures, etc.) which makes our support difficult. Because of the necessity of a change in their educational style the lecturers tend to prefer "extra" situations for the visually handicapped, which seem to be more "efficient" in the sense pointed out above. One of the most important points in our work is making people understand the concept of integration and their own responsibility. Unfortunately we cannot offer a complete solution to all problems in access to material. To provide support in difficult situations our tutors hold repetition sessions in which they answer questions of the students resulting from their inability to follow the presentation. It is important to say that this does not mean that we reduce the requirements for studying or that we are an excuse for the lecturers. This is a necessary task for an equal access and no overprotection.

Counselling and care: The students are obliged to organise their lectures with the lecturers themselves. If problems occur we offer support. To facilitate this process in general we organise meetings and visits at the lecturers to give them a better understanding of our goals. The students also have to arrange their conditions of examination. In general they have more time or can take the exam in verbal form. If necessary we invigilate the exam because of its longer duration. To support the self-organisation of the lectures and the integration into them, a special "social-skill-training" is organised. The students can participate voluntarily in such courses which are held by professional psychologists. We are not responsible for the organisation of their studies but it is necessary to support them in case of questions related to studying or personal problems based on the social background and social circumstances of handicap.

First steps into working life. The over all goal of the endeavour is the integration into working life. To make this transition easier we build up contacts to industrial companies, to civil services as well as to job centres, visit different institutions to present how visually handicapped people fulfil their task and organise periods of practical training.

The endeavour is accompanied by an interdisciplinary research program and a supervision system for the stuff. We are also in close co-operation with the universities of Karlsruhe and Dresden which offer similar programs. The exchange of experience and co-operation in several fields (e.g. exchange of students and tutors) should be strengthened.

5 Conclusion

The necessity of such an endeavour at university was expressed best by one of our students. He said that the mere fact that there is an institution which takes care of the special situation of the visually handicapped students facilitates studying as lecturers and the other stuff gets to know that they have to be aware of their responsibility towards these people. We have to say that "equal access" can and does not mean "equal efforts". The students have to care for themselves, a fact which may make higher efforts necessary. Integration should also look for conditions, which avoid overprotection. The visually handicapped should have the opportunity to learn to handle their situation, not only for managing their job at university but also in everyday life. Like all the other students they should have the opportunity to learn their lesson in self-organisation and independence.

Ten students, four of them are blind and six are partially sighted, use the support of our endeavour. They are studying Computer Science, Law and Business. Another crucial feature of our university is that people with no university qualifications can obtained the right to study by attending a year's foundation course. We also support this course. However, we are sure that it will help many blind and visually impaired people who had, until now, no chance of obtaining a university qualification. In future we will try to build up the organisational framework to be able to support all courses of studies held in Linz.

Modellversuch "Informatik für Blinde"

Bernhard Stöger, Klaus Miesenberger

Department of Computer Science, Johannes Kepler University, Linz, Austria

Studying in Linz. The University of Linz is a campus: Institutes, student homes, classrooms etc. are arranged on or around the campus. The vast pedestrian zone and the immediate connection to the public net of traffic are a particularly advantage to the visually impaired.

Technical Equipment. New technology opens to the visually impaired independent and efficient access to information and, therefore, to teaching materials also. At the University of Linz, this technology is available, trained, and maintained:
Adapted computers are available at the most important locations of the university. They are linked into a local area network, which by itself is connected to the university LAN and, therefore, gatewayed onto international networks. Two magnification reading devices, one swell paper copying machine, and two printers (one for normal print and one for Braille) supplement the equipment. For learning at home and for working in class (reading, writing, presenting) it is necessary for the students to have personal, preferably portable, equipment available. The personal workplaces can also be linked to the network.

Preparation of Studying Materials. The kernel of support activities is the digital preparation of all studying materials such as books, lecture notes, overhead sheets, exercises, contents of the blackboard and so forth, by tutors who are students in an advanced semester. Materials that are already present in digital form are converted to a format suitable for the vision impaired. Materials present in printed form are processed by a scanner.

Initial and Accompanying Support. Informational days, support in the initial phase at University, special examination conditions (e.g., oral exams instead of written ones, and/or prolonged examination time), meetings with lecturers, practical training in industry, consulting and tutoring for education-related or personal issues are offered to make integration possible.

Educational Consulting. As a special service, educational consulting for the vision impaired - independent of the particular place Linz - is offered. In particular, the technical possibilities of support for the vision impaired can be covered. In cooperation with the Austrian Student Association and with the psychological department of the University, finding decisions shall be supported profoundly.

Modellversuch "Informatik für Blinde", University of Linz, Altenbergerstrasse 69, A-4040 Linz, Austria; Tel.: +43 732 2468 9232, Fax - 9322; E-mail: info@mvblind.uni-linz.ac.at

Johannes Kepler
Universität Linz

Visually Handicapped Students at University

Program of Support at the University of Linz

Technical Sciences **Social and Economical Sciences** **Law**

Technical Support

WAN

special office (LAN)

screen enlarging system

scanner

braille display

speech output

braille printer

Adapdation (integration) of computers at different locations (libraries, labs) at the campus

FIRST STEPS INTO WORKING LIFE (CONTACTS TO COMPANIES, PRACTICAL TRAINING)

COUNSELLING AND CARE (TUTORIALS, MOBILITY TRAINING, ...)

INFORMATION, TECHNICAL SUPPORT, PREPARING MATERIALS FOR STUDY

Modellversuch "Informatik für Blinde", Universität Linz, Institut für Informatik
Altenbergerstraße 69   A-4040 Linz
Tel: +43/732/2468/9232 Fax: .../9322   E-mail: info@mvblind.uni-linz.ac.at

Cottage Industry at NewLink

K.M.S.Barnes, R.W.Jotham, C.I.G. Sherman

Department of Adult Education, University of Nottingham

Abstract. This paper outlines the design and development of a computer communication system for an education and training project for people with physical disabilities in the East Midland Region of England. The emphasis is not merely upon the technical development itself but upon the need of technical developments for people with physical disabilities to be created with consideration being given to the social context in which these individuals live. If such considerations do not take place there will be an increasing number of people with physical disabilities who do not have access to these new forms of communication.

1 Introduction

The Department of Adult Education at the University of Nottingham has been delivering courses in Information Technology to people with a physical disability for 7 years. It has a special project in this area called the NewLink Project. At present this consists of a federation of training projects and proto-enterprises in the East Midland region of England. The project has received funding from national and local government, the Leverhulme Trust, the British Council, the Gulbenkian Foundation and the European Social Fund including the Horizon and Euroform initiatives.

The project is currently delivering education and training to approximately 300 people each year. There is no charge for physically disabled adults and all courses incorporate the use of computer technology. The courses offered range in content from office skills to music composition.

2 The Social Context

Through this work it has been found that at present the high cost of Rehabilitation Technology (RT) has led to a polarisation of IT users with a physical disability. The vast majority have little or no access to IT, whilst a small minority have been able to obtain the latest technology by using private funds or applying to charities etc. This minority are also those most likely to have benefited from a better education, who are therefore likely to obtain employment; consequently they are more capable of earning enough to purchase further RT products. This is a further manifestation of the situation described on page 14 of the March edition of the Commission of the European Communities, TIDE 1993-1994 Workplan.

> *These consumers, particularly disabled people of working age are caught in a vicious circle whereby a lack of RT provision, training and high prices, means that they are not enabled to contribute to the community by working.*

It is evident from the factors mentioned above that, what is needed is the creation and successful distribution of training and products that will go some way to off-setting this historical situation.

This context has formed the backdrop for the research that has been carried out alongside the courses offered by the NewLink Project. One such piece of research has been sponsored by the Leverhulme Trust and has attempted to assess the applicability of computer communications to the lives of physically disabled adults. This research has moved through a variety of stages and has attempted a number of different applications of computer communications. Perhaps the most significant of these has been the development of a simple system based around IBM PC compatible computers which enables tele-working and incorporates tele-training. This work has always had the intention of extending the services offered to adults with a physical disability in their homes and has been conducted under the general name "Cottage Industry At NewLink" (CIAN).

3 CIAN the System

The development of this system had its beginning in the setting up of Bulletin Board System (BBS) in August 1990. It was linked to a number of other Bulletin Board Systems around the world, on the FIDONET network. These links were paid for by the Chatback Trust, which is a charity set up to assist disabled people.

As the various implementations of the BBS were tested, a number of regular informal discussions with a variety of disabled individuals were held. The topics covered ranged from the possible activities that could be assisted by CMC, to what sort of equipment was best to buy. From these discussions it was decided to create a system that would allow people with a disability to work and train from home without incurring any extra cost to them.

To keep the cost of the system to a minimum it was decided to write our own controlling software, and to use a shareware program for the communications. The controlling software would present a simple user interface which would then use the communications software to carry out the necessary phone calls etc.

The first steps in writing the software for this system started in August of 1991 and took about four months to complete. This was followed by initial tests of the whole system at the end of 1991. In early 1992, new problems emerged, which were eventually resolved and in November 1992 the system was installed in several users' homes and more tests were carried out. In January 1993 the system was released to the NewLink-Nottingham workshop for the reception of work done at home by workshop members.

A further extension to the system, that will enable the dissemination of training materials from centres to individuals in their home has been considered. This has been partially designed and implemented but it seems to be being overtaken by the rapid changes in telecommunications systems that is occurring at the present time.

The East Midland region of England is being covered by an independent cable operator called Diamond Cable. As part of this service they offer some novel services that are of particular interest to the NewLink Project as a whole. The current plan for the NewLink Project is for between three and five centres to be linked together by a Diamond Cable service. In the first instance, this will enable cheaper inter-centre telephone communications and, the data on these systems will be transferred by traditional analog equipment ie: modems.

Each of these centres will use the existing CIAN system and act as a HUB to a selection of people in their locality. This HUB will both, supply them with work/training materials and, collect from them the work they have produced on their home computers. This will allow tutors or job allocators to be at any of the centres and for the work/training to be carried out by a wide pool of individuals spread out across the area, whilst the running cost of the operation is minimized.

Through this link there will be access to various electronic services. The most significant connection will undoubtedly be a link to the Internet.

4 The Future

The possibilities for the future extend well beyond the speed limitations imposed by this medium. Direct digital connections will be possible between each centre using ISDN technology. This will allow high rates of data exchange and thus bring new services such as video-conferencing and distance training etc.

At present NewLink is making cautious plans to enter this arena. We are concerned that our developments are accessible, affordable and transportable. The accessibility must place them into a particular educational and social context. The affordability must take into consideration the typical incomes of individuals and projects that work with people with physical disabilities.

The dream is that NewLink will significantly contribute to the inclusion of as many people with a physical disability as possible into the ever growing world of computer communications, and that this will assist them in being more fully included in society.

Bibliography

Barnes, K., R. W. Jotham, C. I. G. Sherman. 1994. Information Technology Training and Community Enterprise for people with a disability: Computer-Mediated Systems for Training and Enterprise. Submitted to the Journal of Microcomputer Applications.

Brodin, J., M. Magnusson. 1993. Videotelephony and Disability: A Bibliography. Department of Education, Stockholm University.

Jotham, R. W. 1992. The Impact of Computer Technology on the Vocational Situation of Disabled People. Computers for Handicapped Persons. Proceedings of the 3rd International Conference.

Wells, R. 1992. Computer-Mediated Communication for Distance Education: An International Review of Design, Teaching, and Institutional Issues. ACSDE, The Pennsylvania State Uni.

Telework for Handicapped People: an Experience

Marco Zampiceni

Development and Vocational Training, Fondazione pro Juventute don Carlo Gnocchi
Milano, Italy

Abstract: The goal of the courses organized by Fondazione Pro Juventute in collaboration with A.S.P.H.I. (The Association for the Development of Information Technology Projects for the Handicapped) in computer software applications programming, is to secure employement to young disabled people and more than 80% of those qualifying find a job. The remaining 20% isn't able to find a job, usually owing to geographic origin and degree of autonomy. The interest of Fondazione Pro Juventute Don Carlo Gnocchi and A.S.P.H.I. in the concept of telecommuting fits into this framework.

1. Introduction.

The Foundation Pro Juventute Don C. Gnocchi has worked for several years in the sector of professional training for those with motor disability and in particular, in collaboration with A.S.P.H.I., has for twelve years implemented training courses in computer software applications programming for medium to large data processing centres. The goal of these courses is to secure genuine employment and, even with the difficulties connected with the economic situation, the achievement of employment by ex-students has to this date been satisfactory: more than 80% of those qualifying are engaged in the world of work. The remaining qualified ex-students, who are not employed, owe this situation to the coming together of two different problems:

a) *geographic origin*: The course collects students from all the national territory, even, that is to say, from small villages in areas not particularly economically developed.

b) *the degree of autonomy:* It is equally obvious that a limited personal autonomy, especially relative to primary needs, acts as a powerful brake on every attempt to gain employment in the absence of structures or initiatives adequate to overcome such obstacles.

The interest of the Foundation and of A.S.P.H.I. in the concept of telecommuting (working at home via a telecommunications link) fits into this framework.

While being conscious of the difficulties of relationship that such a way of working presents, we maintain that telecommuting can offer at least a partial answer to the primary need "to be of use". In 1992 we had the occasion for an initial experiment.

2. Parties Involved in the Experiment.

DC.R. is a disabled youth who qualified as a programmer in the year 1991-2.

The co-existence of objective logistical difficulties - those of geography (he lived in Foggia, in the South of Italy), and of serious physical difficulties (spastic tetraparesis), combined with a personal capacity acquired and demonstrated during the entire passage of the course made him seem the ideal candidate for this experiment.

NETSIEL is a medium-sized company belonging to the Finsiel Group. It was established in Bari in 1988 with the object of producing quality software components to supply to other operators in the sector which would assemble them and integrate them into finished systems for the end-user market. Today it has 310 employees with a high level of education and qualifications.

S.I.P. is the provider of the Italian telephone service. It was interested in the experiment and supplies the means to establish a data transmission link between NETSIEL(Bari) and DC.R.(Foggia).

A.S.P.H.I. (The Association for the Development of Information Technology Projects for the Handicapped) is a non-profitmaking association which aims to pursue the active integration of disabled people into society with the help of information technology and telecommunications.

The Foundation Pro Juventute Don Carlo Gnocchi is one of the most important institutions for rehabilitation in Italy (Institute of Scientific Care and Research).

3. The Working Environment.

From the technological point of view working activity will be carried out using: a Personal Computer and an printer which are the property of DC. R., an emulation card SDLC-3270 and the associated software made available by Netsiel and a modem made available by S.I.P. S.I.P. will implement a dedicated line between Netsiel and DC. R. Netsiel will supply the computing power and the mainframe IBM/MVS application development software necessary for the production of modular software in COBOL-CICS-DB2.To transmit messages DC. R. will have at his disposition an electronic mail function already in use in the company. Netsiel undertakes to give DC. R. the didactic support used in the company for basic training courses which is necessary to complete the training he has already received.

The output will regard some software components which can be assembled together to make part of an automatic procedure for the internal use of the company.

4. The Organization of the Experiment.

On the 16th March 1993 S.I.P. activated the direct digital link (4800bps) between the Netsiel establishment at Bari and DC. R.'s home at San Severo (Foggia).

Netsiel commissioned (according to article 2222 of the Italian Civil Code) the software components subsequently and separately. During the experiment the company guaranteed technical support which DC. R. made use of by means of the pre-arranged communication channel for all clarification of the work being carried out.The company, in agreement with the worker, also carried out the monitoring of the various phases of the experiment to supply data concerning the connection times and the type of activity carried out (coding, testing, communication etc.).

5. Final Considerations.

"RESULTS ACHIEVED
(...) From this point of view, the following aspects are considered to be:
negative: the absence of continuous monitoring of the state of progress of the work made it impossible to carry out accurate rescheduling, and hence created dead times which influenced productivity throughout the entire period of the experiment.The lack of a direct, continuous and in person relationship with the programmer in the training phase slowed down the rate of learning.
positive: The efficiency of the tools used both for the software development phase and for communication between interlocutors.The compliance of the components with the specification supplied to the programmer.The efficiency of the communication channel. The entirely satisfactory quality of the products developed.
CONCLUSIONS.
The experiment has demonstrated that because of the time necessary to carry out the work a direct digital link is not an economic solution.
To achieve a correct cost/performance relation the experiment carried out suggests the use of products which permit operation in a stand-alone mode, simulating mainframe systems on workstations, together with the used of a non-dedicated connection. It seems desirable to organise periodic attendance of the interested party in the company, for example on the occasion of training activity. This could form a basis to encourage a more real integration into the company. From the systems/technical point of view the experience seems capable of being perfected and susceptible of further development. From the point of view of work organisation it is necessary to structure differently the feeding of work to the programmer, arranging a plan of activity for a longer period (three - six months) with periodical checkpoints.
The possibility of establishing a regular contract of employment is obstructed by the absence of any regulations governing a telecommuting relationship."

"DC. R. CONSIDERATIONS
(...) In the first place, I have to say that, on my side, there has been the greatest satisfaction with this experiment, as you already know. In fact, despite all the problems that the experience has little by little posed, in some ways I consider myself a normal worker. When you informed me that the tests of one of my programmes had had a positive outcome it gave me the greatest satisfaction.I also felt that I was charged with great responsibility since a successful outcome could bring about the extension of telecommuting to other people with problems similar to mine. I think (but you are better judges of this) that I have acquired greater competence during the year. I am naturally very appreciative of the accessibility and above all of the patience with which you have clarified my every doubt.
Finally, I hope that at the next meeting it will be decided to follow up this experiment. (...)"

AbleProfessionals: A Recruiting and Accommodation Service for Atlanta Employers

by
J. Hunter Ramseur, M Ed., C.R.C., and
Lee S. Gardner, M.S.; and Darcy S. Painter
Center for Rehabilitation Technology, Georgia Institute of Technology,
Atlanta, Georgia, USA

Abstract

In the 1990s and beyond, businesses face increasing demands for a competitive edge in the global marketplace. Nations also face similar global economic pressures. It is clear that effective, efficient use of human and technological resources are key factors for national economic survival as we enter the next millennium. One measure of human resource efficiency in a society is the percentage of its members who contribute to the economy. The society's technological resources, in the form of accessible computer tools integrated into the workplace, can enable the contribution of a larger percentage of its members. This paper presents a business being started in Atlanta, Georgia, USA, that assists corporations in hiring people with disabilities by offering to locate and recruit quality candidates and provide complete, cost effective accommodation service including design, and installation of office technology to enable them to be effectively employed.

The Shortcomings of Traditional Hiring Processes

When corporations or businesses decide to do the right thing and hire a person with a disability, they often are penalized. This is because the traditional approach to hiring people into a corporation is based on assumptions about the average person that are violated when the issue of hiring a person with a disability is considered. The problems that the recruitment and accommodation of people with disabilities pose for traditional human resource organizations can be costly and complex. To hire a person with a disability corporations must frequently go to great lengths to locate and recruit their perspective employee as well as coordinate any accommodations that are necessary in computer equipment, office furniture or building architecture. These activities drive up the cost of hiring a person with a disability and add a significant technical challenge to the process in the form of the computer tools and office accessibility issues that must be addressed if people with disabilities are to be able to work. These factors combine to create the perception that hiring a person with a disability is too much additional work and is too risky. Doing the right thing is deemed too complicated, too expensive and the legal risks are too great. The end result is that very few people with disabilities are hired by employers.

For corporations to offer people with disabilities opportunities to work commensurate with their qualifications and potential, the problems of technical expertise, proper equipment and accommodations must be solved. The cost and time investments on the part of the corporate employer to hire people with disabilities must come closer to the well known, commonly accepted costs of hiring traditional employees.

The AbleProfessionals Solution

The Center for Rehabilitation Technology, Inc. (CRT, Inc.), at the Georgia Institute of Technology in Atlanta, Georgia has devised a practical solution to the problems of locating, recruiting and arranging the computer accommodations of people with disabilities. This new business venture is called AbleProfessionals "The Place to Find Qualified Professionals with Disabilities". The AbleProfessionals name comes from a line of more than a dozen office tools called The AbleOffice which are marketed worldwide by CRT, Inc. These tools are designed to assist people with disabilities to function productively within a standard office environment. AbleOffice products feature universal design and work for both the disabled and general populations. They are complementary office tools that give people with disabilities the abilities to access files, store and use books and manuals, open mail, use the telephone, and access computers and printers. Products are modular and fit neatly in with modular office decor. In the past three years, more than 90 AbleOffice systems have been installed at locations in 24 states in the US as well as three foreign countries.

'One Stop Shopping' Approach to Recruiting, Employing and Accommodating

When an employer confronts the problems with computer technology, office equipment and architectural barriers and considers bringing a person with a disability into their company anyway there are a thousand unanswered questions. Questions like, "can we cope with the accommodations this new employee will require," "can we afford the accommodations for this person;" and "will this person fit in at our company, will they understand and accept our corporate culture?" Questions on another level include, "what if this person doesn't work out?", "will that failure be our fault?", "will we end up with a legal problem?" Traditionally employers have to seek answers to these questions from different experts in various locations. What happens is that employers' good intentions are penalized with having to spend additional time and money trying to get help in their endeavor to hire the person needing the accommodation.

The AbleProfessionals solution is to offer a business service team that provides 'one- stop shopping' expertise to:
- locate, recruit and coordinate employment of quality, qualified people with disabilities and
- screen candidate clients for qualifications, quality and suitability and
- provide complete, cost effective accommodation service over the long term.

AbleProfessionals Provide Continuing Technological and Accommodation Support to Their Clients over the Long Term

Part of the original contract agreement AP makes with the employer will concern long term technical and accommodation support for any clients that are hired under the agreement. This clause is intended to ensure that once the client is successfully employed that they continue in their employment despite changes in their physical condition. With changes in their physical abilities AP would bring back the experts in accommodation from CRT to re-adjust or re-design any accommodation that the employee needed as a result of a change in the employee's abilities.

The other part of the long term support has to do with new capabilities in office equipment or computer technology. AP would be responsible for keeping its clients continuously informed about advancements in technology. When one of the advancements solved a technical problem for an AP client, AP would take the responsibility for acquiring and installing that equipment. An example of this with regard to the computer systems analyst with the vision impairment concerns the limitation of the screen reading software to handle Windows based operating systems and applications. Currently the screen reading software does not accommodate Windows. When the technology breaks through and Windows can be handled by screen reading software, or in some other fashion can be translated into sound AP would take the initiative and ensure its clients with vision impairments got the word and were able to take advantage of the new technology.

Conclusions

AbleProfessionals is founded on the premise that the employment potential of people with disabilities increases with the growing incorporation of computer technology into the business world. All that need be done is to bring the people with the technical know-how together with the employers who have the vacancies and the people with disabilities who have the education, experience and the need for the job and the accommodation they require to do it - AbleProfessionals will take care of the rest. This arrangement permits each participant to leverage the competencies of the other two parties in this agreement. Each party is able to avoid the costly option of vertical integration. In other words, the corporate human resource staffs of the organizations that sign up with AbleProfessionals are liberated from the tasks of recruiting, placing and accommodating people with disabilities. They can out source the task to AbleProfessionals who will complete it at a lower cost and higher value-added than the buying corporation can. The cost of the technology may be lower because AP will be coordinating the acquisition of the computer equipment working the best deals and substituting less expensive technology where possible. Further, AbleProfessionals offers a flexible menu of services to its corporate clients. Corporations can choose the services they want to contract for. This flexibility is useful if a business wants to contract for AP services for an existing employee, who because of changing circumstances needs a different piece of equipment, or who needs a different accommodation because of changing business practices on the part of the corporation. AbleProfessionals would assist in researching, acquiring, installing and training the employee to use their new equipment.

„NewsReader" - A Comfortable Digital Newspaper and Bookreading System

Dipl.-Ing. Peter and Wolfgang Resele
Communications Laboratory[1]

The project "NewsReader" is aimed at the development of state-of-the art digital newspaper and bookreading systems for blind people. The key concepts in "NewsReader" are digital transmission from the source (the publisher) to the reader, a user interface that is based on extensive reader surveys and an object-oriented approach to software development. Currently, the "NewsReader" reading system already enables blind people of all ages to read a variety of document types like newspapers, magazines and books. Available output devices include speech synthesis, braille and screen enlargers. Field trials showed that the user interface can be mastered within about 10 minutes for simple tasks like the reading of a newspaper article. While a menu-driven approach, together with a minimum number of only four keys, allows also computer-illiterate and computer-sceptical persons to use the system with minimum effort, a set of powerful functions is available to the advanced user.

1. Background

The aim of project „NewsReader" is to make all kinds of printed media, particularly newspapers, available to the handicapped, and especially the blind people. While most blind people still very much depend on special braille editions, audio cassettes, or relatives and friends who read for them, recent developments in the publishing industry as well as the rapid spread of personal computers allow more sophisticated means of access. Nearly all printed media are prepared on computers, and in principle, the direct transfer from the publishing house to the personal computer at home is technically feasible. Once stored in the memory of the personal computer, the documents - newspapers, magazines, books, etc. - can be easily accessed with artificial speakers (voice synthesis), electronic braille displays, or large-character displays for the visually handicapped. Since the delivery done via existing telecommunication networks (in its simplest form, the telephone), it is fast and cost-effective, and therefore allows the daily, up-to-date access to newspapers. As an additional benefit, the navigation (identification of interesting articles) can be supported with powerful search functions not available to the reader of the paper copy.

Widespread acceptance is truly the main goal of „NewsReader" - to be the reading system that can be used and is used by everybody, from the five-year old to the over-70 year old (the majority of blind and visually-impaired people is over 50 years old!). Many technical problems, especially in the area of the user interface, have been solved to reach this goal and hide the technical complexity from the reader. The field trial with

1. Communications Laboratory, Dipl.-Ing. Peter Resele, Hugo Wolf Gasse 10, A-8010 Graz, +43 (316) 38 66 71, e-mail: p.resele@ieee.org

the prototype version of the system showed that this goal has been achieved, that the system is very quickly mastered by the young as well as the elderly, and that it is very well accepted.

2. Project Goals

The main goals for the system have been defined as follows:

The reading program must be

- comfortably to operate (reading newspapers and books should be a pleasure!)
- very simple to learn, yet also support advanced features
- *must not rely on any computer-knowledge or knowledge of the keyboard*
- must be able to support all kinds of newspapers, magazines and books
- must run on standard computer hardware (PC)

The declared aim is to get the largest possible readership, and to support not only the computer-specialists but also the computer-illiterate and even the computer-sceptics. This, and the definition of the user interface, is a main difference to earlier trials in this direction.

3. System description

The function of the whole system is shown in figure 1. The raw data from the newspaper are transferred from the computer in the publishing house via telephone modem into a computer which is part of our network. In this computer, called „server", the raw data (full text of the articles) is processed, indexed and converted into the format which is understood by the reading software at home. From the server, the data is fetched via a distribution network, which can be anything from a simple telephone modem to a satellite link. Initially, distribution is done via the telephone network. The data transfer is *done fully automatically* (at the press of a button), so that the reader does not need to know anything about the technical process which is involved.

As soon as the newspaper is stored in the computer at home, the blind reader can comfortably and easily select the various parts (politics, sports etc.), read the headlines of the articles, and select the interesting ones for reading. Possible output options include braille on a braille display, artificial voice (speech synthesizer) and enlarged screen display.

4. Reading software („NewsReader")

Over the past years, several versions of a reading program have been developed and tested successfully, which culminated in the first commercial release in April 1994. A major feature of the program is its carefully designed user interface, which has been used by a variety of people in a very short time. It has an object-oriented design and has been implemented in C++ from the very beginning, resulting in a very flexible structure of the whole system which allows rapid extensions for new features and applications.

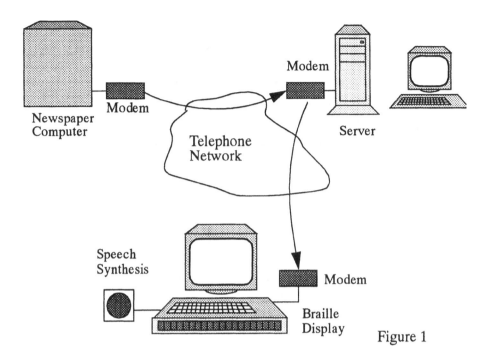

Figure 1

4.1 User Interface

Input

The first, simple user interface is operated with a very small set of keys (4-10 keys). *Only four keys are sufficient to operate all standard functions of the NewsReader program.* They can be mapped to any key on the keyboard (see figure 2 for the standard mapping, which takes into account easy grasping of the keys). Most users, who have never used a computer keyboard before, are able to master them in very short time. The keys are defined for very generic functions (next page, previous page, next article, previous article) and do not depend on any typical computer function keys. It must be possible to execute all major reading functions, like selection of a newspaper, selection of subjects and articles, adjustment of the systems parameters like the speed of the artifi-

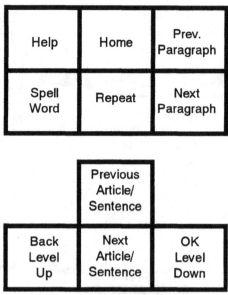

Figure 2 : Standard - Keyboard

cial speech and so on. Also the navigation within the selected document is made as comfortably as possible.

As an alternative for computer-sceptics and elderly people who are usually deterred by a full computer keyboard (even if they only need a small number of keys), an off-the-shelf "console" of a video game has been adapted as an input device (figure 3). Since it is very small and light-weight, it is also useful for more demanding users when reading on the couch or bed.

For more advanced users, several additional functions are available with the full alphanumeric keyboard. Indexed access (the user types an index keyword and the system looks up all relevant articles) as well as full-text search, where the user can search for one or more phrases in the system, are possible. Other more sophisticated input methods like speech recognition should be easily possible using commercial speech recognition software.

However, the main goal of the input interface is to make simple tasks like browsing a paper or a book as comfortably as possible, while still offering more sophisticated functions - which are also more difficult to master - for advanced users.

Output

For output, three types of interfaces are supported:

1. Braille displays (all displays that support automatic cursor routing)

2. Speech synthesis (currently four different speech synthesis systems are supported)

3. Enlarged letters on the screen (any commercial screen enlarger can be used)

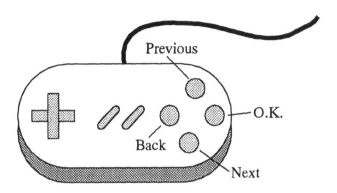

Figure 3: Easy input pad

In the development of the database interface, use of existing developments in the market will be made as much as possible.

4.2 Automatic Reception of Data

The fully automatic transmission of newspaper and other data from the distribution centre to the reader is one of the most important features of any system that wants to be used in true daily operation. For telephone transmission, a number of commercial software packages exist which allow the exchange of data using a so-called telephone modem and a suitable mailbox-program. However, these software packages can only be operated by non-handicapped users or the "experts" among the blind. Therefore, the development of a special module, which automates the process of connection establishment, transmission/reception and handling of errors, has been developed and used with much success. As an additional feature, it is also able to display the progress of the data transfer in a form which can be read by the users, i.e. voice or braille.

5. Distribution Network

The network, mostly built with off-the-shelf components, allows the automatic dissemination of data, access control from the outside, verification of the callers, accounting and generation of charging information as well as remote network management. Initially, a network with three nodes in Austria is being set up. The so-called servers store a variety of newspapers, books and other up-to-date information. Also old newspaper issues are available, again something not easily available to sighted readers. Special consideration will be given to methods which can protect the rights of the information providers, i.e. the publishers and prevent users from unauthorized copying.

The access network is the part of the network which transfers the information from the publisher to the processing server. This part of the network will necessarily be operated by ourselves and will consist of dial-up telephone connections between PCs at the printing houses and our own premises. Since only one transmission is made every day, the cost of a phone call does not matter so much.

On the other hand, the distribution network must bring the information to all subscribers, which may be several thousand in the real operation. Currently, the distribution is also done via modem and in future possibly ISDN. For a low to medium number of users, this has been identified as the most cost-effective means of transmission, with the additional advantage of cheap off-the-shelf hardware that can also be used for other purposes. This may be extended to other distribution methods in future, as soon as the they become commercially feasible.

6. Transformation of data

The internal data formats used by the publishing houses for typesetting are very different and all unsuitable for the reading system. Therefore, before the dissemination of data to the end users, a lot of data processing is necessary. Currently, such automatic "converters" have been developed for two Austrian newspapers. In the development of the necessary processing software, a cooperation with the „Modellversuch Informatik für Blinde" in Linz, Austria has recently been established.

7. The Electronic Library becomes reality

With the version 1.8 of NewsReader, powerful functions have been integrated that allow the comfortable reading of all types of electronic books, e.g. fiction and lecture notes. Several types of "table-of-contents" are available and bookmarks can be set and cleared by the reader, as well as shared with others. It was important for us to realise that books are not just another type of newspaper, but something very different in the way they are used. This is taken into account by the user interface. Currently, a small but quickly growing number of very different titles is available like lecture notes, large fiction books, cookbooks and others.

7.1 Bookmaker

An important tool that is given to every user is "Bookmaker", a software package that allows to prepare/convert electronic book titles into the NewsReader format. Together with any RTF (Rich Text Format) compatible word processor (like Microsoft Word), fully structured NewsReader books can be easily prepared and distributed. This is very useful especially to education and university environments, where a large number of important teaching material is prepared internally and is typically already available in RTF format. As soon as they are available in NewsReader format, they can be read by everybody who has the reading software installed, in all possible output formats, comfortably, and within very short (learning) time.

8. Conclusion

One of the most important goals for NewsReader is its general availability to an as large as possible community of readers and information providers[1]. From the very beginning, it was not designed as an "academic exercise" but as something that is really useful to a large number of people, who up to now do not have any means for reading newspapers, books and magazines on their own. This aspect (free choice of information without involving others) turned out to be most important for the readers. From November 1993 to April 1994, NewsReader has been tested in a highly successful field trial in several regions in Austria, during which a newspaper was made available on a daily, up-to-date basis. A general service is currently being started. The system proved to be highly stable and reliable already during the first year of operation, which we regard as a proof for the object-oriented concept. The experience of the first readers (from seven-year to seventy-year old) was enthusiastic, and it encourages us to continue on this path into new areas.

9. Acknowledgements

The authors would like to gratefully acknowledge the help from Dipl.-Ing. Bernhard Stoeger and Mag. Klaus Miesenberger ("Modellversuch Informatik fuer Blinde" in Linz), Klaus Martini from the Austrian Society for the Blind, and various people at the Odilieninstitut in Graz. All gave us very important comments on the initial versions of our system and taught us - patiently - to see with the eyes of the blind.

---

1. The NewsReader system is being made available to interested parties under special licensing conditions.

Digital Talking Books -
a Report from a Practical,
Ongoing Project

Kjell Hansson, Lars Sönnebo* and Jan Lindholm*

The Swedish library for Braille and talking books (TPB)
* Labyrinten Data AB

Summary: This project aims to develop a new system for storing and retrieving talking book material using digital technology. The project shows how radically new means of information access can be put to work using a digital talking book system based on standard personal computer technology.

1   Introduction

In 1992, TPB was granted funds from the Swedish Ministry of Education to investigate how new technology could be used to give students new and better means to access talking book information.

A three-year project was initiated to evaluate the possibilities of digital technology for talking books. The first year was to be spent on getting general and unbiased information about suitable technology. During the second year, the project was to enter a more pragmatic stage, intending to actually create practical results, that could serve as a basis for demonstration and real-world testing.

This report describes some of the results from the project.

The project focused on human voice as the main information carrier for the talking book, rather than speech synthesised from machine-readable text by a text-to-speech synthesiser. Other projects at TPB have been investigating the latter technology from the student's point of view.

1.1   The Preliminary Survey

The first year of the project aimed at taking a close look at which technology was available, and what could be achieved by using it. The result was a survey of both methods for processing and storing voice data as well as suitable media for digital talking books.

The report is available to all interested. A full version is available in Swedish, and an abridged version is available in English.

1.2 Some Starting Points

After the preliminary study, it was decided that the project in its second year should concentrate upon some of the most interesting results from the preliminary survey, and from these build a prototype digital talking book system, suitable for demonstration of access principles, voice coding techniques etc. The system could also be used as a basis for practical testing at a later stage.

Before starting the second year of the project, some basic goals and standpoints were stated:

- When choosing a storage/distribution media for a digital talking book system, it is desirable to use one that is widely spread and used for other purposes, well standardised and one that will be available for a long time. CD-ROM was chosen as media for the project

- The system should be based on a standard PC, to allow the student to use the computer for other tasks, e.g. word processing, information retrieval and reading with synthetic speech etc. The PC would also be a good platform for the software development and for testing of necessary peripheral equipment.

- Standard computer technology was to be used as much as possible. We therefore decided to use the platform offered by the Multimedia Extension under Microsoft Windows, running on an IBM-compatible PC.

- The base for the system should be a general data structure that allowed for easy future expansion with new data types, new data formats etc. The format specification should be made open for other talking book producers and system developers to make their own implementation. This was seen as important, since it would be highly beneficial if a commonly adopted standard could be established amongst libraries, even in different countries. Such a common standard would make interlending services possible.

- The system should be capable of storing vast amounts of material, so that long recordings should be possible to store on one media unit. The output quality of the voice recording should be good, comparable with the quality offered by standard audio cassette systems.

- The system should be expandable in the future in terms of storage media, distribution methods, data format for voice recording etc.

- The system should give the user fast, random access to the book's material. The material should be structured in much the same was as a normal printed book, to allow the user to read the talking book in a similar way to a normal, printed book. The response of the system should be fast, without long delays before they desired material was played back, no matter which part of the material was requested.

2 Our PC based Talking Book System

The following is a brief description of the PC-based talking book system that has been developed during the second year of TPB's talking book project.

2.1 Some unique aspects of the system

The uniqueness of the system being developed in the project can be summarised by the following properties:

- Using digitised human speech as the information carrier gives much better voice quality than in systems using synthetic speech.

- Voice data is treated in comparatively small units, allowing common database-type techniques to be used for storage and retrieval of data. Furthermore, the data can be organised in a structural and hierarchical manner, resembling the original printed material. This renders random access to any part of the material, from the section (chapter, part etc.) down to the sentence (phrase) level.

- Since the system is not restricted to a particular kind of storage media or device, technology advancements can easily be integrated in future versions.

- The system uses standard computer technology as its hardware base, which will help keeping costs for playback equipment down, as well as simplifying system development. The use of a standard personal computer as the core of the system will allow for integration with other computer applications.

- The system is open, constructed upon a foundation of common computer standards and methods, which will be published, so that other developers may implement their own solutions.

2.2 General System Description

The system uses digitised human voice recordings, stored in a compressed (coded) data format on CD-ROM media. CD-R technology is used as the main production system, since a library such as TPB mainly makes a very small number of copies of each talking book. Nothing hinders mass-production of talking books from a master, though.

The data representing the voice recordings are divided into small data blocks called "phrases", using an automatic pause-detection system in the recording software. The phrases are organised into "section", which in turn are organised into a hierarchical structure, resembling the printed book's table of contents. The material can be accessed from software as a database-like structure.

The voice data is stored in compressed format on the CD, allowing a standard CD-ROM disc to hold 15-50 hours of continuos speech, depending on voice coding technique and required output voice quality. The system allows for new compression/decompression technologies to be added as they become available, allowing higher voice quality and/or more hours of recording on each CD-ROM. Our system currently uses ADPCM-type coding and decoding.

The user reads the book with a specialised software, currently running under Microsoft Windows. The reading software will have a fully talking interface, using digitised voice.

The reading system consists of a standard IBM-compatible PC (a 486 SX or better), equipped with a standard CD-ROM XA and photo CD-compatible drive, a 16 bit audio card and the playback software. The PC can be complemented with a speech synthesiser and screen reading software, to give the user access to other Windows applications.

Beside the audio data, the data structure also allows for the book's original text (and, if desired, its illustrations) to be placed on the media in machine-readable form, sharing the same structure as the voice recording. Thus, the text could be viewed on screen or accessed via a speech synthesiser if desired.

2.3   User Interface Functionality

While designing the first version of the user interface for the reader, the goal has been to give the user access to the recorded material in a way similar to a sighted user, reading a normal printed book. The underlying data structure was created with this in mind, and the user interface is therefore mainly a continuation of the book's structure.

The reading is controlled from a hierarchical structure, resembling the original book's table of contents (ToC). Each item in the talking book's ToC is a "section", made up of a collection of "phrases" (voice data blocks). A section has a certain level in the ToC's hierarchy, which determines when and in what order its phrases are read back.

To select which part of the book to read, the user simply selects a section from the Book's ToC. As section headings are selected, the section's title is read back, using the appropriate phrases from the recording. The titles of the sections in the ToC are also shown on screen for sighted or partially sighted users.

After selecting the starting point, playback can be started at the desired position by a play command. The user can also jump forward or backward in a section by phrase, by phrase group (as defined by the producer) or by page. The latter relies on page breaks which have been placed in the section by the producer, based upon the page layout of the printed book.

The book can be read in continuos mode, section by section or it may be read phrase by phrase, page by page etc. Skipping between phrases, groups etc. within a section is a quick and easy process, giving the reader convenient "skimming" abilities.

Pauses made in the recorded material are interpreted in the recording process and stored as tokens rather than voice data of zero amplitude. This saves storage space, but more importantly, it gives the reader /user control over pause length, thereby controlling an important aspect of the reading. Together with the fast random access to the material even on low level (phrases), the system gives the user a very quick retrieval system, especially compared with sequential access as on a standard magnetic tape recording. To allow for even faster reading, the system offers "intelligent time compression" (ITC), which gives higher playback speech rates compared to the original recording.

In addition, the data structure makes it easy to implement special features in a PC-based system such as user notes, marking of phrases for later retrieval, bookmark placement etc. Such data is stored as a "user book" on the PC's local hard disc.

The playback voice quality is good, comparable with results from ordinary compact cassette recordings. Such a good quality can be retained with the current data compression technique, even for books of 20-25 hours in length. Longer recordings can be stored on a single CD-ROM with reduced voice quality, using the current compression technology. As an alternative, extremely large talking books can be split up onto two or more CD's, where each CD-ROM will be treated as a separate book.

2.4   The Producer's Perspective

The data structure allows for recording of data in arbitrary order. Recording is done phrase-by-phrase, where each phrase represents a sentence or paragraph in the original, printed material. Phrases can be corrected, inserted, deleted or moved. The producer can also group related phrases together and insert page breaks between phrases, following the printed book's layout, thus simplifying the user's access even to highly complex material.

The silence-detection system relieves the recorder from having to keep in time with a moving tape. There is no need to manually enter record mode - the reader just starts talking, This recording process should mean less stress and also make editing much easier than on tape.

The recorded material is stored on a large hard disk, and can be transferred to MO (Magneto-Optical) or tape media for backup or for transfer to another system, e.g. a system for proof-reading.

After recording all material for a section, a section file is created. All the section files making up a talking book are organised on their highest level by a "book file". The book file and section files can be transferred to a CD-ROM image using CD-R equipment or to a master for production in larger scale.

The multi-session capability of today's CD-R devices allows for more than one book on a CD-ROM, which can be recorded one at a time.

The intention behind the recording tools that have been, or will be developed by our project, is that the person who is the recorder should also be able to edit the material as well as produce the distribution media.

A streamlined production system can give very cost-effective talking book production, compared to the methods commonly used at present.

3   Project Status Autumn 1994

A prototype PC-based talking book system was finished in early May 1994. The system was capable of demonstrating the general principles for data structure and user access. Basic recording tools were created to create the talking book material for the demonstration. A CD-ROM disc containing demonstration material, taken from several publications was accompanying the system.

The original intention was that the project should be reported and finished in its third year. Since the project has been very successful and have come up with remarkable and practical results, we are now trying to get founding to prolong the project. The third year will then be spent on turning the prototype system into a fully working system.

More work is needed to achieve a stable and fully working system. For example, on the recording side, streamlined tools are needed and the user interface for the reader needs to be proven and developed according to user's needs and demands.

The prototype system set-up will be copied and distributed to several students for field testing, probably during the autumn of 1994. A set of CD-ROM titles will be created, containing appropriate literature for the testers.

The continued project will aim to create a fully working complete talking book system, ready for mass production. To do this, we will work together with the test users as well as some of today's producers of normal talking books. Their demands and opinions will be collected and the result will be implemented in the system. It is estimated that by the end of 1995, a version 1.0 of the system will be presented.

New voice coding/decoding techniques will be tried for the system in the future, giving better voice quality and/or higher compression rate then the algorithms currently used.

During the next stage of the project, we will also try to interest other talking book producers in Sweden and other countries in the digital talking book format that has been developed in the project. Hopefully, this format can form a common base for future production systems, so that talking books can be interchanged between different libraries.

4 Future Plans

4.1 Standardisation

It is highly desirable that digital talking books can be shared amongst different libraries, services and production systems in various countries. The project will therefore make serious efforts to promote the general data structure to all who are interested in creating a digital talking book system . The data format will be open, so that different producers can implement their own tools . Alternatively, our software tools could be made available to other libraries.

The data structure of our system is advanced enough to cope with the most complex publications, but may equally well be used also for material of a simpler structure, for example fiction literature. In those cases, the material could simply be stored in a small number of sections, representing the parts or the chapters in the book. Thus, our data structure will be usable as a standard for all kinds of digital talking book material.

4.2 Building Purpose-built Equipment

The current system is based around a personal computer, since the computer gives many advantages to the student. The core of the system may however be implemented in a specialised computer-system, resembling a stand-alone unit, much like a normal compact disc player. Such a machine could still give the user many of the features found in a PC-based system, of course without features like making notes in relation to the recording etc. With such a device, the digital talking book standard could be used by today's average talking book reader, and so the positive aspects of digital talking book technology could be spread to a wider range of readers.

Since production of talking books with the aid of digital technology seems likely to be rather cost-effective, there is even a chance that talking books may be a competitive distribution media for information, even aimed at sighted users. If a suitable talking book playing device can be made available at a competitive price, today's producers of commercial talking books might be interested in the new technology created by this project.

The Electronic Kiosk
Accessing Newspapers with Electronic Media

Arnold Schneider, Cleto Pescia
Swiss Federation of the Blind and Visually Impaired

Contents

1. Abstract

This paper presents a project which has been initiated in Switzerland in 1992 to provide people who are blind or visually impaired with daily newspapers. At present newspapers in Italian and German language are available. Articles are sent to a host computer from where the readers can download the files they want to read. An especially developed reading program enables the reader to select the articles of his or her interest.

2. Introduction

As everywhere in the world blind people in Switzerland were thinking about a suitable way to access printed information sources with electronic media. The focus was put on daily papers, because this kind of information cannot be made available with tape recordings or in braille. We had knowledge of the project in Sweden [1], the research activity of TIDE [2], the project in Frankfurt Germany and of the project of the Italian Association of the Blind. They started in 1992 a project in which "La Stampa di Torino" was sent as ASCII file over a TV channel (Teletext or Videotext depending on local designations of the technique allowing the transfer of text information over a TV channel).

The blind people in the Italian speaking region of Switzerland had access to this innovative information source and after a short time they decided to start a local project. Using a TV channel is a complicated organizational problem and the transfer is very slow. So they decided to use a private host computer for data transfer from the editing office to the blind readers. On October 15, 1992 the "Edicola Elettronica" (the electronic kiosk) opened its electronic doors. All those blind people equipped with a PC and an appropriate output medium (speech synthesizer or braille display) could access two local newspapers every day. In addition they also could access "La Stampa di Torino" and 3 monthly magazines. Today about 30 persons are using regularly this service. For those who could not afford the cost for the required equipment, a special funding project has been started.

This beautiful and very valuable realization has motivated members of the Swiss Federation of the Blind in the German and French speaking areas of Switzerland to extend the electronic kiosk to their language and region. The break-through was reached end of 1993 when the "Neue Zürcher Zeitung" (NZZ), one of the most important papers published in German language in Switzerland accepted to make their issues available to blind readers in an appropriate form.

3. Information acquisition and preparation

The data files which contain the articles of an issue are collected by the editing office and sent via modem as one package to a host computer of EuroCom, a specialized company located in Lugano. The format of the data files usually varies from paper to paper, for the wordprocessing and document management systems used by the various publishers differ from one another. However, most papers use some kind of "mark-up language" to catalog the data for their internal needs, and therefore it is possible to easily isolate the relevant information about an article, like, for instance, the topic it belongs to. For each paper a special filter program is triggered as soon as the data files have been stored on the EuroCom host. This program processes the paper's data, filtering out the unnecessary information in a first step and then generating the electronic kiosk version of the paper. Each article is given a classification code, so the information can be grouped in 12 to 15 topics. This classification allows an easy selection of matter of interest in the reading program. Index files are generated in order to give fast access to a specific piece of information.

4. Distribution

The articles and index files are compressed before they are made available to the readers, in order to minimize transfer time and cost. Using a special communication program, the readers can dial in the system and download those parts of the paper they are interested in. The selection process happens off-line, before the actual connection takes place. This reduces the overhead of information to be exchanged during a connection, and helps in keeping the transmission costs low. The full transfer of an NZZ issue (about 180 to 250 KB) takes 4 to 5 minutes at 9600 bps and costs less than 1 Swiss Frank per day.

5. The on-line reading program

This program has been especially developed in order to provide an easy and comfortable access to the text files transferred to the user over the telephone line. This program is menu driven and specifically designed to be used with speech synthesizers (simple presentation, full word menu items). At the top level about 12 topics are proposed to the user, e.g. home events, foreign events, culture, sports, tourism etc. Having selected one of these topics, the user obtains the list of articles pertaining to the chosen topic. The user can navigate with the cursor keys and select an article with the ENTER key. The article is then presented according to the selected reading mode. There is a "page by page mode" as in standard text editors, and there is a "continuous reading mode" especially designed for users of speech synthesizers. The whole article is sent as a continuous data flow to the output channel. The user can listen to the text output without the need of hitting a key after a fixed number of lines; but he may stop and restart reading at any time by hitting the space bar.

In addition the program offers a library function. All transferred issues can be stored and accessed later through a menu. Individual articles can be extracted from an issue and stored in a special archive directory.

6. Statistics - Graphs and Comments

The electronic kiosk has undergone beta testing in the period from April, 1 to June, 30, 1994. Only a few comments can be reasonably made based on the statistics gathered during these 13 testing weeks. The graphs are illustrated on last page.

Graphs No. 1 "No. of Calls in Each Test Day" shows an erratic behaviour of callers. As we will see in the following graph, this is due mainly to the fluctuating interest of readers in newspapers depending on the day of the week. Graph No. 2 "Daily Frequency of Calls" reveals a peak interest on Monday (over 120 calls), a still intense but somewhat lessened interest from Tuesday through Thursday (around 110 calls a day), and a definitely declining interest with the approach of the week end (from 95 to 70, to 38 calls from Friday through Sunday).

A tendency which is independent on the special test conditions, is probably the "Hourly Frequency of Calls" during the day, as depicted in Graph No. 3. As it probably happens to sighted people, the preferred moment to buy the newspaper is in the early moment. In fact, Graph No. 3 shows the maximum peak of over 80 calls between seven and eight o'clock. We meet the second peak just before lunch (47 calls between 11 and 12 o'clock) and after lunch (57 calls between one and two PM). The third major peak is found in the evening, from eight to eleven o'clock, with 37 calls between eight and nine, 51 calls between nine and ten, and 42 calls between ten and eleven PM. But speaking in general, and except for the around-noon peaks, the peaks correspond basically with the low-tarif telephone time, which in Switzerland goes from 5 to 7 PM and from 9 PM to 8 AM. However, newspapers are downloaded during the whole day. Only from one o'clock in the night to five o'clock in the morning there has never been a hook up.

7. Evolution of the project

The next goal is to obtain a similar result in the French speaking area. Discussions are progressing and we hope to have access to a weekly magazine in a very short time. The main problem is in general at the operational level. Not all editing offices are preparing the articles in a way which allows relatively simple extraction of pure ASCII files. There is also the problem to define the people who are responsible for the data transfer to the kiosk host computer.

With a growing group of users of the electronic kiosk more requirements for the reading program will arise. The Swiss Federation of the Blind is prepared to sponsor further developments in this field. The leading staff is convinced that this project is a very significant contribution to the social and cultural integration of visually impaired people.

8. Graphs

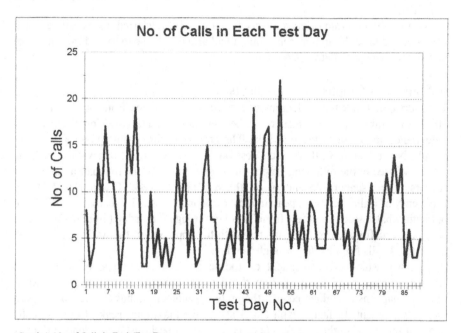

Graph 1. No. of Calls in Each Test Day

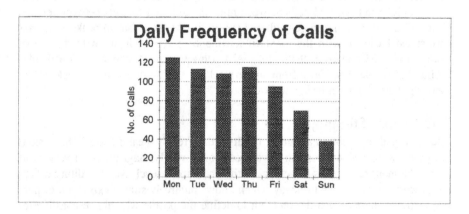

Graph 2. Daily Frequency of Calls

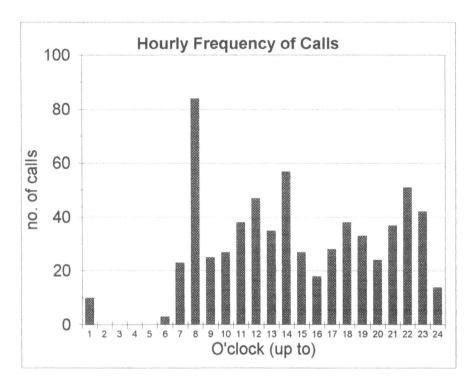

Graph 3. Hourly Frequency of Calls

References

[1] Henryk Rubinstein and Aleksander Ratz: Radio-Distributed Talking Electronic Newspaper for the Blind - an Everyday Service; procedings of the World Congress on Technology, December 1-5 1991, Washington D.C.
[2] TIDE: "Technology for the socio-economic Integration of the Disabled and Elderly People".: Project CAPS: Communication and Access to Information for Persons with Special Needs, final report December 1991 - March 1993.

Students Support Services at a Scientific University

Claude DECORET
Laurent DE BERTI

University CLAUDE BERNARD LYON1, Bât. 305
43 Bd du 11 Novembre 1918
69622 VILLEURBANNE CEDEX
tel : (+33) 72 44 82 79   fax : (+33) 72 43 11 60
email : decoret@chitheo1.univ-lyon1.fr, deberti@chitheo1.univ-lyon1.fr

Abstract. In this paper, we intend to describe the functioning of the services for handicapped students at our university. Details of functioning are given which show The co-ordination role of the Handicap Mission between teachers, students and administration. Links between the Handicap Mission and research and development laboratories teams, librarians, etc. are essential for diminishing handicap and facilitating studies in the framework of integration. This last point has specific aspects in a scientific university.

1. Introduction

The access of study for handicapped persons at the university level is theoretically facilitated with the extensive use of microcomputers and related technologies such as adaptive technologies[1]. More and more materials are on electronic format and those materials seem to be more and more accessible by handicapped persons. The second trend is not obviously irreversible, as for instance the tendency for Graphical User Interface G.U.I. [2] , source of difficulties for blind and Visually impaired people. Due to these trends or/and general evolution of our developed societies, the number of handicapped students is growing slowly and most universities have created services for facilitating a two-directions communication [3] (teacher-student, student-teacher) on the basis of technological availability and in many cases helping to solve problems of mutual comprehensivness. Does it means for the long term a full insertion of persons with differences or their exclusion from the main stream? Nobody can pretend have the answer, which nevertheless is "capital" for our society [4] and we have to be aware of the dangers of uniformity [5]

2. General situation

2.1 In the world and especially UNITED STATES

Students support services are of different kinds depending generally from the historical origin. For instance, at Baruch College [6] CUNY (City University of New York) already in 1977, existed a service devoted essentially to computer science and aptative technology. This service was shared by the 17 colleges of the CUNY. Visually impaired students could come in a room with many computers equipped with Braille terminal or voice synthetizer. Since lots of university have created disabled student support services more or less successfully in regards with the number of disabled students which is 2.83 % in California [7]. Associations such as AHEAD aim to develop experiment exchange, to help them some books were published [8,9]. In England, where the central organisation, Royal National Institute for the Blind (R.N.I.B.), is very developed, a central service exists [10] and has a booklet, in various format, designed to inform students , giving them counselling for their attitudes, right and difficulties to overcome, and it is logical that each university more or less refer to this central English service. In USSR, in 1983, existed also on a central basis, a service of this kind to help disabled students, and referring here to visually impaired, as an example, blind students in mathematics or computer science could find somebody to read specialized papers (program listing, e.g.). At the same period, in France, due to individual needs or initiatives, some experimental services were created as in the university Paris VI and in the university Paris VII, known as the "Relais Handicap" or an inter-university service in Lyon the FIDEV (Formation Informatique pour DEficient Visuel) .

Since, more and more handicapped students pursue studies at university level in many countries, and in parallel, many services have been created and developed. So that it is difficult to have an overview [8,9].

2.2 In FRANCE

In France, for example, each university (about 90) have at least a representative in charge of supporting handicapped students and the ministry have a special services to co-ordinate their actions. In our area, the Rhone-Alps region, three locations have developed services, each one with a special feature, university of Savoy (Chambéry) with more experiment in the field of problem of hearing, universities of Grenoble in the field of motor impaired students and universities of Lyon in the field of blind and Visually impaired student. Mutual exchange of experiments is constant to avoid specialisation and concentration of students with the same impairment in the same universities. The three universities of Lyon (LYON III, juridical and language studies, LYON II, human science studies and LYON I, science and medical studies) develop services and moreover a common resource centre exist for producing material for blind and Visually impaired students and teachers. Our concern in this paper is with the university LYON I and specific questions of scientific studies for handicapped people.

3. Local situation

What people are registered as handicapped students in our university UCBL (University CLAUDE BERNARD LYON1) ? At this point, we have to make the difference between handicapped and impaired people, for if all buildings would be accessible by wheelchairs[11], there would be no handicap for people obliged by their impairment to move in wheelchairs. But if impairment is not retained as the unique criterium, we have to appreciate the difficulties of each person entering the university to pursue studies when these difficulties are due to some inadequacy between what they have to do and what they are able to do without various support to be furnish by the university. It is to be said that mental diseases are not taken into account. So, facing such questions, what services are qualified to perform that appreciation? The response is made through a synergy between medical service for students, the handicap commission, the mission and concerned teachers. We will define the role of each one in what follows. First is to be mentioned that the work is facilitate by a recent legal "circular" from the ministry date: march 1994) which gives the legal procedure to for asking as handicapped students and define the disposition to be taken for passing exams.

3.1 Prevent medical service for students.

This service , which is inter-university in our town, is the only one qualified to give the right for a student to pass exams with the special dispositions displayed in the ministry "circular". These dispositions consist of giving the third-time (the right to have a third-time more than the duration time for other students and prescribing means to diminishing handicap (the right to use adaptive devices, to be helped by qualified persons, to pass exams in a separate room, etc. depending the case of handicap.

3.2 The Handicap Mission (M.H.).

This service consists of Claude DECORET, a secretary also blind and a CES, that is a sighted people half-time without special qualification and two computer science engineers in charge of adapting technologies for the special needs of handicapped students in a scientific and medical university. One (Laurent DEBERTI) is full-time as making his military service and the other fifth-time employed by the CNRS. The M.H. is qualified to manage the money allocated by the university or by the minatory (special disposition for deaf students) and needed for passing exams and for following studies all along the year. At this point, students supported by the service are not only the ones being the benefit of the third-time for exams. We will describe below more precisely the various ways of working of the mission. The M.H. by various means and in close collaboration with the commission handicap works to make known by students its existence and the services available.

3.3 The handicap commission.

It is composed of all handicapped students by definition. There are about 40 handicapped students on 24000 students.

4. Supports available

4.1 On the campus

4.1.1 The M.H. The role of this Mission is to co-ordinate actions, supports and information, promote research. The office of the M.H. is located near the main entrance of the campus. There, students finds documentation on their rights, procedure for third-time right, etc. They may have advises and inquiries concerning accessibility of studies, summer stages, after studies employment opportunities, etc.

4.1.2 The university library. It manages in closed collaboration with the M.H. a room equipped with various devices, accessible at opening hours for handicapped customers. Moreover, a person is present two hours a day to help eventually students in the uses of devices. The equipment is Visually impaired and blind oriented facilities and consists of what it could be expected, that is, computer, with voice synthesiser (French and English) Apollo, a Braille printer INDEX, a screen reader, an ordinary printer, an electronic magnifier, a scanner READING EDGE.

There also, students have the opportunity to connect to the network and enter the world of INTERNET. They have some hours of teaching and then they receive an electronic address. The M.H. have created its own WWW public server (http://www.univ-lyon1.fr/fb/ch/ch.html)

4.1.3 towards teachers. At the beginning of the university year, teachers concerned by having an handicapped student is usually taught by this student how to manage with him. As soon as possible at the beginning of the year, the M.H. recommends students to take contact with their teachers. Then, teachers find complementary inquiries at the M.H. and plan with it the support to be done, as pedagogical sustainments, if needed, assistance for passing exams, note takers for deaf.

4.1.4 administration services. The M.H. is a kind of administrative service closely related with other services. It is directly depending of the university president. The M.H. does not replace other services which act regularly towards handicapped students as regular students. Special disposition concern the registration form, on which students can specify if they are asking for a third-time to pass exams

4.2 resource centre

This centre was created several years ago especially for blind and Visually impaired students and is shared by the three universities of Lyon. An agreement between this centre (FIDEV) and the university LYON1 that the FIDEV provides Braille formatted text of Exams and transcribes Braille copies from students to normal print. The FIDEV has also a MINALTA for making raised drawings which at the disposal of students and teachers on their site. These two points (Braille and raised draws) are very important for scientific studies because it needs very skilled people (Braille mathematics at high level) and knowledge of what is to transform or not to obtain a raised draw from a printed paper.

5. Commission handicap.

At the beginning of the university year, the M.H. organises a meeting of handicapped students, known as such from preceding years or asking for third-time. At this meeting, students are informed on the procedure to be followed for obtaining third-time. There, they can make acquaintance and exchange experiences, discuss problems, and they are informed of the various means offered by the university and they can ask for new means to be found for their own needs. A reduced commission is formed (6 to 8 people) to follow current affairs with the M.H. The reduced commission meet about each 3 weeks and the large commission three times a year. Very often, a new students is a new experiment for him, for teachers and for the M.H. because our university offers a large range of studies in physics, chemistry, biology, medicine, pharmacy, mathematics, computer science, etc. We take care, as much as possible, of classroom day-life, to find or suggest solutions when questions arrived, practical and sometimes psychological. For instance, chemical studies for blind are not withdrawn, because examples are known of blind professionally active in chemistry as theoreticians or documentalists. Motivated students are generally successful in their study and it is often the case because they are looking themselves as pioneering in their field. They are spontaneously ready to promote scientific studies among handicapped scholars and so, participate to various meetings in schools or are present to give inquiries at the time when scholars comes to university to know what the university offers as study (one special day is reserved for such a visit, each year). They are also present when students come to take inscription at the university at the end of the year.

6. results and future

As it can be seen in this paper, most aspects of insertion of handicapped students are very similar at whatever university[12]. Nevertheless, some aspects are specific to scientific studies such as physic, chemistry, biology, etc. relative to human science, juridical, language , etc. studies. To my point of view, the differences are essentially related to the question of specific writing and speaking of formulas[13], drawings, etc. and the questions of technical practices, such as in chemistry for instance. These questions are particularly sensitive in the case of blind and Visually impaired students So, in what follows, I will emphasises examples in this field.

First of all, the aim of university studies is not only to obtain diplomas but above all to find a job[14]. The consultative role of the M.H. with its background experience is primordial as well as for students as for teachers. It must take into account professions or jobs already known as available for disabled people, it must also take into account the growing and to be enhanced facilities for new professions and jobs due to technical progress and due to diversification, evolution and changes of working places. So a reasonable part of new experiment is to be kept in mind when counselling a student or a teacher group. It usually concerns the degree of adaptations needed to obtain the required knowledge level. For instance, what is the degree of practical knowledge to require for a blind student in chemistry, concerning practical experiments with manipulations of chemical products, when the purpose of such studies is to find jobs in documentation or theoretical work on computer or even teaching jobs. It is a hard question for teachers who have eventually to deliver the same diploma as for other and who have to adapt experiment when possible or to control the level of knowledge acquisition when the handicapped student works as specific help in a team (most often for practical experiments students work by two or three, due in general to the lack of available places).. These questions are very general, answers are very diversified depending on many factors, because the degree and type of handicap vary for almost each disabled student, the degree of imagination of teacher, and his/her good will, the availability of adaptive means at the university (such adaptation are often very expensive). It must be said that the good will is the most efficient way to overcome difficulties and are compensate by a rigorous control of acquisition of knowledge. In not rare cases, teachers let me know that they are impressed by the simplicities of adaptation needed, students are no so handicapped as we thought before knowing them and furthermore they may have a dynamic role for other students in the same classroom, perhaps due to their need of help and consequently facilities of communications.[15]

7. Concerning to blind people, question of transcription

As many universities, transcriptions are made by hand in most cases. A paper copy for exams are given to the resource centre (FIDEV). At this centre, people , there are people knowing perfectly well Braille mathematical signs (French code), there are blind people among them. They can do the work of transcription and reversibly when Braille copies are given to them. The main problem is to obtain paper copy in time, teacher are sometimes reluctant to give their exams subject (or to prepare) too long before. As it is explained before, it is possible to perform raised drawings, electronic schemes, etc. often with adaptation of the drawings to take into account that the touch with fingers is sometimes very different from the view in affording and transmitting information. Such changes are often made in agreement with the concerned teacher (what to suppress, transform or emphasised, or enlarge).

Concerning special signs, as mathematical ones, we are aware that number of teachers write their exams and courses on computers [16]. They use word processor facilities for such signs and a growing number write in an special language named TeX, especially in mathematical and physic departments of the university. Here, the question of automatic transcribing occurred and a research and development little programme is developing to transform TeX into mathematical Braille. Similar work seems to have been done for transferring TeX towards files readable by synthesised voices. The M.H. pilots this programme.

Reference

1.   ORIOL-PARIS Nathalie, These de doctorat d'economie, Univ LOUIS
      LUMIERE LYON II, 29 juin 1993,
      Insertion professionnelle des aveugles: du marche du travail au processus de
      production.
2.   Project Archimede C.S.L.I. (Centre for the Study of Language and Information)
      Standford University

3.   "Journée Nationale de sensibilation et d'échanges sur l'accueil des étudiants
      handicapés à l'Université."
      Claude Bernard Lyon I University - January 18, 1990
4.   Albert Jacquart, Eloge de la difference ...
5.   Peter Muhlhauser : Sauver Babel (sauvguard Babel) , courrier de l'U'NESCO,
      French braille editon, no64 marh 1994 p68
6.   Baruch College
      17th Lexington ave
      1010 New York NY

7.   Jeffrey C. Senge : Print accessibility for print disabled students in postsecondary education
     CSUN 1994

8.   Karin J. Spencer : From access to equity, ressource manual for service providers
     AHEAD, Colombus Ohio.

9.   Directory of college facilities and services for people with disabilities
     Thomas and Thomas ORYX Press
     3rd edition 1991

10. RNIB at Peter Borogh College

11. "Journée nationale de sensibilisation et d'echanges sur l'accueil des étudiants handicapes à l'Université" Claude Bernard Lyon I University - January 18, 1990 p. 63

12. READAPTATION, n°407 Febbruary 1994 "Les Etudiants handicapés" published by ONISEP 168, bd Montparnasse 75014 Paris (France)

13. T.V. RAMAN, "Audio System for Technical Reading" presented to the faculty of the graduate School of ornell University in partial Fullfilment of the Requirements for the degree of Doctor of Philosophy ; May   1994

14. ZAID L. VOGEL J. "Insertion professionnelle des personnes handicapées en France",
     Informations techniques n°4 (C.R.E.A.I.), Nantes, Octobre 1985.   10p.

15. HERNANDEZ C. "Handicaps handicaper ?", Edition sociale (compte-rendu du Colloque nationale : handicaps, société, libertés, le droit de vivre différent, libre te heureux), 1978. pp. 9-28

16. This book, Seminar on Access to Electronic Information for Visually Impaired Persons. part 3.1

ASSISTIVE TECHNOLOGY IN US HIGHER EDUCATION:

THE UNIVERSITY OF WISCONSIN-WHITEWATER EXPERIENCE

John D. Truesdale and Connie Wiersma

University of Wisconsin-Whitewater

Abstract. The advent of the personal computer age has significant implications for the lives of individuals who happen to have disabilities. It also has significant implications for the system of service delivery of computers and other assistive technology. New paradigms of service delivery may be needed to take full advantage of the power of technology systems. It is suggested that the introduction, training and use of computers is most effective when it is part of a comprehensive, multi-disciplinary team approach and based on the philosophies of human development and independent living.

1 Introduction

At the Third International Conference on Computers for Handicapped Persons, Scherer (1992) pointed out the need to use a model of service delivery which would assure the successful introduction and use of assistive, educational and workplace technologies. According to Scherer, "...the integration of technology into a setting is a complex and multi-faceted task.". Our experience tends to confirm Scherer's position. It is essential to take into consideration the environment in which you are working, the individuals with whom you are working, the future environment(s) in which those individuals will be working, and match the technology to the present and future needs of the individual.

2 Environmental Context

The University of Wisconsin-Whitewater (UW-W) established a formal program to provide services for students with disabilities during the 1970-71 academic year. At the time UW-Whitewater initiated its program to serve students with disabilities, there were few such programs in existence nationally. UW-Whitewater adapted its service delivery from the program to serve students with disabilities at the University of Illinois. The Illinois program was started in 1947 to provide services for disabled military veterans It followed the medical model and provided comprehensive, multi-disciplinary services such as the various medical specialities, allied health professions, therapeutic recreation, counseling, transportation services, and personal care services. With a record of educational and vocational success with disabled veterans, the program soon attracted civilians with disabilities from around the United States. These students also experienced the same degree of success as did the veterans. It was presumed that the success of these students could be attributed in large measure to the program model.

3 Needs of Students with Disabilities

A common belief in United States higher education is that college students usually drop out because of academic failure. However, it is estimated that fewer than 15% of all student drop outs result from academic dismissal. Decisions to withdraw most often relate to personal, social or financial problems (Hackman & Dysinger, 1970; Noel, 1985; Pantages & Creedon, 1978) In addition to the stresses of entering into an entirely new life experience, students with disabilities are often confronted with many new challenges that are not faced by their nondisabled peers. For example, it may be quite traumatic for a student to move from his/her home and a supportive community network and family members as care givers to a residence hall where virtually everyone is unknown and care givers are available on an hourly basis. That individual may now be called on for the first time to be self-directing and self-managing. They may lack sufficient life experience to feel competent in addressing these issues in addition the transition issues faced by all students.

The multi-disciplinary team bridges the gap between family and campus by thoroughly evaluating student needs and making recommendations for equipment, environmental modifications, physical training, health care, mobility needs, arranging for personal care needs and so on. The efficacy of the comprehensive, multi-disciplinary approach is partially reflected in retention data for students with disabilities at UW-Whitewater. Between 1985 and 1992, the average rate of retention of students with disabilities on our campus was 75%. This was significantly higher than the retention for the student body as a whole. This has occurred in spite of the ever increasing severity of disabilities presented by our students. Computers have played a significant role in permitting us to maintain this level of retention.

4 Computers in a Multi-Disciplinary Environment

Our initial venture into adapted computing occurred in 1989. We set-up a WANG AT 286, with only 640 mb of RAM to provide limited services to students who were blind or otherwise print impaired. We purchased and loaded a braille conversion program and a screen reading program. We attached a braille printer, a laser printer, an OCR scanner, and a DECTalk to this machine. We used every slot in the machine and every available byte of RAM to operate this system. The machine did not have the capacity to use a screen enlarger, or we would have loaded that also. We also learned, during this process, that compatibility is a major concern. When we investigated hardware, software, and adapted equipment and asked manufacturers questions about whether their product would work on our system or our network, we were frequently told that they really did not know--that we would have to try it to find out. This situation has improved over the past several years, but we still often find ourselves operating under the trial and error method.

Our center opened in 1990 with four DOS-based and four Apple Macintosh computers. The eight machines were linked together via a Novell Network. These machines and the network were of the same type being used in the "main" computer lab on campus. The same basic software programs used in the main lab were made available in the adapted computer lab. A laser printer was attached to the network to provide for quality output.

The Assistive Technology Coordinator was given responsibility for the overall functioning of the lab and to arrange for the delivery of services. Basic equipment purchased included easily adjustable furniture, which probably provides access to more people than any other single adaptation available, a screen enlarging program, alternative "mice", including the "headmaster" and keyguards. Access issues were and continue to be addressed on an individual basis. The students participate in this process. They "try-out" various pieces of equipment or configurations and decide what works best for them. Simple accommodations, such as placing the keyboard on the tray of a student's wheelchair, especially in situations where strength, reach and range of motion are at issue, are solutions that are often preferred over expensive equipment. One student found that placing the keyboard on a music stand next to her wheelchair, and typing using a dowel stick with some "goop" on one end and a pencil with an eraser provided her with all the access she needed to operate the computer. Her arms were crossed and "frozen" across her chest, her hip and leg joints were frozen so that she was positioned nearly lying down in her chair. But she could use her fingers and was able to type very rapidly. She also became a Macintosh "whiz" and served as supervisor/scheduler/trainer for the student workers in the facility. When she graduated and left school, she took her knowledge and "solution" with her and is gainfully employed by Hilton Hotels in Chicago. Naturally, she uses a computer to perform her work tasks.

4.1 Organization of services

Assistive technology services are divided into several components: general computer usage, assessment of needs, training, advocacy for obtaining equipment, assistance with set-up and training on individual systems, assistance with trouble-shooting and/or having equipment repaired, and outreach.

Interrelated to the general lab operations is the assessment of needs and the provision of training. Students with personal care needs undergo a pre-enrollment evaluation. This includes an informal evaluation of their computer-related needs. After they arrive on campus, a formal technology evaluation is completed. Students have the opportunity to work extensively with the computers and adaptive equipment in an attempt to determine what hardware and software will best meet their needs. Many students have received assistance from our staff to identify the equipment and software they need based on their functional needs, academic major and vocational choice. In most cases we have been able to identify resources to purchase that equipment. We frequently provide a copy of the evaluation and rationale for the equipment to help them justify the purchase. Once students receive their equipment, we assist them with set-up and training needs as may be necessary..

Unfortunately, over the years, we have seen too many students who have participated in technology evaluations (elsewhere, of course), had equipment recommended and purchased for them, but failed to fully utilize it when received. There appears to be a gap, at least in our area, in providing for training and support services for the individuals, including repairing equipment when it does not work properly. A young woman, who entered our University this past fall had her own laptop computer with the program, Words+, for augmentative communication. She had the computer and the program available to throughout her secondary education.

Unfortunately, the computer did not have sufficient memory to run the speech program. The result was that she simply did not use it.

We assist our students to set up and learn to use their adapted hardware and software so that it is functional. It can be very frustrating to students when their equipment is not adequate to meet their needs or when it does not work properly. A young man, who needs to use his computer for all of his writing needs because he has no arms, was referred to an evaluation center to determine what computer technology would best meet his needs. Unfortunately, the equipment recommended was not adequate. The evaluation center had recommended the purchase of a voice-activated system that the manufacturer stated should be used as an evaluation tool or for students in their first or second year of high school. Other equipment included a CD-ROM and a scanner. However, the computer had only enough memory to load the voice program, but not enough to operate the voice program and the various software programs that he needed to actually do his work. We have attempted to help him correct these problems. More memory will be purchased for his system so that he can at least run his programs. He will have to "live" with the second-class voice-activated system and make the best of it, at least for the present time. In the meantime, the academic year ended before his system was even made operational, even though he received his equipment near the beginning of the first semester and we worked closely with him during the entire academic year.

Our center also serves our students by assisting them with maintenance concerns, including obtaining repairs or replacement parts. A well-meaning agency purchased a laptop computer for a student who had experienced a traumatic brain injury. However, they failed to purchase the software needed to use the computer. The student came to the Assistive Technology Center for assistance in selecting appropriate software to use on her machine. It was determined that she planned to use the computer to do word processing. We had this student use a laptop from the Center loaded with the program Word Perfect in the Windows version. The student used different types of "mice", deciding on a "standard mouse" rather than the clip on track ball that came with the computer. We modified the program and streamlined her access to it as we worked with her. She came in almost daily for the next two months to learn to use the computer, initially sitting in the office of the Center coordinator to receive assistance when needed. Due to a short term memory loss, it was necessary to repeat some instructions over and over until she had "learned" them. Some instructions were also written out for her to use. Finally, we were able to recommend software and a mouse for her to use on her own computer. The recommended items were purchased and her system was configured by us. The mouse provided by the vendor did not work on her machine, so arrangements were made by ATC staff with the vendor to obtain the correct item. Additional training was indicated to become functional. Further, it was discovered that her machine would need more RAM (memory) to run the software efficiently. Once received, ATC staff installed the card and the student now uses her computer regularly and is progressing nicely with her academic course work. Ever increasing numbers of students have their own computers and equipment and are in need of support services to keep it working properly. Most services are delivered by the Coordinator of Assistive Technology and student workers. However, we frequently consult with other professionals in our department, the computer lab staff from the main lab on campus, manufacturers and vendors. Information is also obtained from attending conferences and training sessions.

The final area of our services involves outreach. Students from classes at the University, such as business education, have toured our lab to learn more about meeting the needs of students with disabilities in the area of technology to better prepare them for teaching at the secondary level. Individuals from the community are welcome, and do come to our center to learn what is available that might be helpful to their children or a family member who has a disability. We are willing to share what we have learned with others who are working in this field, and to also gather information and learn from others in forums such as this conference.

4.2 Areas of concern

We know that we must make contintuing education a priority, as technology is changing almost faster than our ability to apply it. It is often difficult to draw the line and say, this is what we are going to purchase or learn how to use when we know that by the time we have done so, that particular item may have become obsolete.

We see tremendous possibilities for persons to access computers through voice-activated systems. We took delivery of our voice-activated system in April of this year. We purchased the entire system for less than the voice-activated system alone cost just last year. The learning curve is a bit steep, but for many of our students it is the only method currently able to provide them with computer access. At this time, these systems work with DOS-based programs and "Windows". As users migrate to the Windows environment, visually impaired users may be at a disadvantage unless DOS-based adaptations are ported to the Windows environment.

For those with speech impairments, using technology may greatly enhance the ability to communicate. Access is still an individual matter, where input and output methods are basic considerations and we must continue to find ways for persons with disabilities to be included as new technology becomes available.

4.3 Conclusion

We believe that college students with disabilities in the United States benefit from a multi-disciplinary approach to the provision of services. The philosophy of service should follow that of the Independent Living model or other developmental approach with an emphasis on behavior or performance by the individual. Assistive technology is a very important service component for students with disabilities. It is strongly recommended that expertise be developed on or near a campus that focuses on knowledge of the various disabilities, knowledge of the various computers and software applications, knowledge of adaptive hardware and software appropriate for each disability, teaching students how to use their hardware and software, and, the provision of follow-up services to assure efficient use of their system.

References

Hackman, R. & Dysinger, W. (1970). Commitment to College as a Factor in Student Attrition. Sociology of Education, 43, 311-324.

Noel, I. (1985). Increasing Student Rentention: New Challenges and Potential. In I. Noel & R. Levitz (Eds.). Increasing Student Retention. San Francisco: Jossey-Bass.

Pantages, T. & Creedon, C. (1978). Studies in College Attrition: 1950-1975. Review of Educational Research, 48, 49-101.

Scherer, M. J. (1992). Psychosocial Influences on Computer use by Persons with Disabilities: A Preliminary Model and Theory. In Zagler, W. (Ed.). Computers for Handicapped Persons. Vienna: R. Oldenbourg.

Leadership and Technology Management (LTM)
The Strategic Management of Technology
in a Consumer-Driven Environment

Harry J. Murphy

Founder and Director
CENTER ON DISABILITIES
California State University, Northridge

1 Introduction

The CENTER ON DISABILITIES at California State University, Northridge (CSUN) has designed a new training program, "Leadership and Technology Management (LTM)," to begin in the Summer of 1994, with the purpose of identifying and training leaders in the area of 'system change', i. e., putting more technology in the hands of more people with disabilities. The LTM is funded in part by a grant from the U. S. Department of Education to the California State Department of Rehabilitation (DR) and by the CENTER ON DISABILITIES at California State University, Northridge (CSUN). DR in turn has contracted with the CENTER ON DISABILITIES at CSUN for this training program.

The LTM Program is designed to increase the availability and utilization of assistive technologies among persons with disabilities through "systems change" activities. The LTM Program will assist managers from human service agencies to effectively take leadership roles in designing strategies to put more technology into the hands of more persons with disabilities.

Participants will gain greater insight into current and new technologies, visit model programs, and develop a personal "Action Plan" to initiate systems change activities within their own organization. LTM graduates agree to be a continuing resource to the Program and to serve as mentors to others. The LTM provides a solid grounding in understanding, developing, and utilizing leadership skills to manage a consumer-driven, technological environment.

A limited number of California residents are awarded full scholarships (including tuition, transportation, expenses) to the LTM. Others - including those from other countries - may enroll at a cost of $795 per person, with each individual being responsible for their own travel and expenses.

2 Program Objectives

The LTM Program has set the following objectives: (1) to provide perspective, concepts, and tools to anticipate opportunities and challenges presented by the rapid growth of technology and demand for system change; (2) to provide managers from a wide range of human service agencies with a shared understanding of the dynamics of system change; (3) to develop a long-term support network of LTM graduates around the common commitment of integrating more assistive technology into the lives of more individuals with disabilities; (4) to identify and evaluate exemplary processes for bringing technology to unserved and underserved populations; (5) to identify and disseminate funding streams that provide opportunities for people with disabilities to acquire technology; (6) to develop a personal Action Plan designed to bring about system change within an organization, and (7) to apply new and emerging technologies to the needs of individuals with disabilities.

3 Class Composition and Schedule

A typical class is limited to twenty (20) decision-makers from a wide variety of human service organizations with a commitment to the long and difficult process of system change, i. e., providing more assistive technologies for more people with disabilities. This small class size permits a hands-on, interactive learning environment which encourages a high degree of individual participation, team building, and the exchange of knowledge and experience by class members themselves.

The program begins on a Sunday afternoon with an Orientation and an initial team-building exercise and continues from 9:00 AM - 5:00 PM for the next five days, concluding on Friday afternoon. There are also several evening sessions.

3.1 LTM Resource Building

During the week-long workshop, all class members will have the opportunity to learn and share through participation in dynamic group activities which encourage integration, application, and synthesis of leadership knowledge and skills.

3.2 Field Trips

At the mid-point in the LTM course (Wednesday), LTM participants spend the day in the field. These site visits provide a 'reality check,' a look at 'what is' as well as 'what should be.' LTM participants will visit technology programs and conduct candid interviews with administrators of model programs in order to see how other leaders address the major issues within the LTM curriculum. An evaluation of programs visited and a debriefing of the day's experiences take place over a dinner meeting.

3.3 Action Plan

Each participant is required to develop and submit a personal "Action Plan" within 30 days of completion of the LTM Program. This Action Plan -- grounded in each individual's own organizational setting -- will identify and evaluate the opportunities and challenges to initiating or improving assistive technology services to individuals with disabilities. Each plan will contain general goals, and specific steps to be taken toward systems change.

3.4 The Application Process

Each candidate for the LTM Program will complete an application and be interviewed by LTM staff. Each LTM participant agrees to attend all sessions, submit a personal Action Plan within 30 days of completion, and serve as a long-term resource to others with a commitment to putting technology into the hands of more people with disabilities. A Certificate of Completion is jointly awarded to all who meet these requirements by California State University, Northridge's CENTER ON DISABILITIES and the California Department of Rehabilitation.

A limited number of full scholarships (tuition and expenses) are available to qualified California residents under the "Technology-Related Assistance to Individuals with Disabilities Act" (the "State Tech Act grant").

3.5 Participation from Europe and Elsewhere

LTM training is available to anyone outside the state of California on a tuition basis of $795 per person, with each individual being responsible for their own travel, per diem, etc. Individuals may apply for the LTM. It is also possible for a single organization to contract with the CENTER ON DISABILITIES for an LTM workshop and send 20 people from just one organization for training in either northern or southern California. Each training program is tailored to the individual needs of each group of trainees.

For further information:

Harry J. Murphy, Ed. D.
Founder and Director
CENTER ON DISABILITIES
California State University, Northridge
18111 Nordhoff Street
Northridge, CA 91330 - 8340
Phone: (818) 885-2578 Voice/TDD/Message
FAX: (818) 885-4929
EMail: HMURPHY@VAX.CSUN.EDU
CompuServe: 71740,2745

The Leadership and Technology Management (LTM) Program is funded in part by a grant (H224A30008) from the U. S. Department of Education to the California State Department of Rehabilitation, and a contract between the California State Department of Rehabilitation and the CENTER ON DISABILITIES.

Multimedia information system on assistive devices

R.Andrich

SIVA, Fondazione Pro Juventute Don C.Gnocchi IRCCS
Milano, Italy

Abstract. A computerised information system with multimedia capabilities is described which supports a network of technical aids information and advice Centres in Italy. The system is currently used by 58 Centres disseminated throughout the Country, mainly run by Local Health Authorities of the National Health Service, and by 10 Centres abroad. The distribution medium is the compact disk CD-ROM. A number of other services (monthly telefaxed bulletins, training programmes, help desk) are provided along with the quarterly distribution of CD-ROMs.

1   Background

Information on the available assistive devices and related aspects (manufacturing, distribution, legislation etc...) plays a substantial role in the whole process of delivering appropriate technology for rehabilitation and independent living. For such purpose a number of specialised computerised information systems have been developed in many Countries, like most European Countries, USA, Canada, New Zealand, and some of them have a long lasting tradition.
SIVA launched in 1981 its own information system, which has been in use since then within SIVA's technical aids information and advice Centre.
Over the years a continuous improvement of the information system software and contents was carried out by SIVA's multidisciplinary team, on the ground of the advances in informatics and of the direct experience of providing information and advice to a wide variety of clients.
In 1988 decision was taken to move the system from a centralised approach (mainframe DEC VAX 11/750, also made available for remote access through modem and dial-up telephonic line) to a decentralised approach based on Personal Computer, responding to a highly increasing demand by Local Health Authorities (in Italian "USL"), Regional Governments, Associations of disabled persons involved in community services.
In 1992 the system entered its multimedia stage, by starting to manage pictorial information (pictures of technical aids) complementing textual information.

2   Design criteria

On the ground of the previous experience and after getting deeper insight into the information needs of rehabilitation professionals, the data bank management system was completely rewritten for implementation onto the most widespread Personal Computers.

Advantage was taken by the most recent available techniques and programming languages. The most remarkable improvement consisted in associating pictorial information on products (technical aids) to factual data.

The possibility to get on the screen the picture of a given technical aid in addition to textual information had always been deemed of immense value when choosing a technical aid for meeting a need of a disabled individual. Until recently this possibility was hampered by the cost of the needed equipment in terms of either hardware or distribution media. Now the economic threshold has been overcome and an effective solution has been implemented.

That brought about the need for adopting a new distribution medium with suitable data storage capabilities (the compact disk CD-ROM), thus making the information system a powerful tool for assisting the rehabilitation professional in the choice of the most appropriate technical aid.

3   Description of the system

The current version of the computerised information requires a DOS (rel.6) compatible Personal Computer based on at least a 386 processor, equipped with:
- 4 Mbytes RAM memory
- SVGA colour screen able to display 256 colours
- 550 Mbytes CD-ROM drive
- at least 25 Mbytes available in the hard disk.

The files format complies with DBIII format and the software management system was written by SIVA in Clipper language (release 5.1) for running directly in MS/DOS environment. The software interface is highly user friendly, its use does not require any informatics skill, its concept is especially addressed towards rehabilitation professionals.

The following retrieval functions are offered by the main menu:

NATIONAL FILE (read only)
A   technical aids
B   manufacturers, suppliers, retailers of technical aids
C   associations, research centres, relevant institutions
G   guide to technical aids classification
L   legislation concerning disability

P arrangements for funding technical aids or house adaptations

N the Ministry Official List of assistive devices entitled to free-of-charge provision

B literature concerning tech.aids and accessibility

LOCAL FILE (read/write)

I saving clients' records

R retrieving client's records

S statistics concerning clients' profile

Pict. 1 - SIVA CD-ROM

The data bank contains about 19000 records in the whole: almost 6000 of them describe products (technical aids), about 7000 describe commercial or non commercial organisation, the remaining ones refer to legislation, literature, explanations and miscellaneous.The data bank also includes:

- a guide to the selection of technical aids, based upon the ISO 9999 International Classification of Technical Aids, which allows the user to navigate through terminology and get suggestions on points to consider when choosing a technical aid.

- the official national register of technical aids, listing those devices and orthopaedic appliances which can be provided by free of charge by the USL

- a special utility for keeping record of the counselling services given to the clients, based upon standardised forms which can be easily filled in. This facility includes also the possibility to record a follow up form which is generally sent to the client after some six months. Processing such data provides also statistics of the users profile, their impairments and pathologies, raised questions and proposed solutions.

- a on-line user manual, accessible whenever pressing key F1.

Searching on technical aids (function "A"), for instance, is possible by specifying up to 14 retrieval parameters (e.g. model, classification, thesaurus, sizes, functional limitation etc...), raising to 23 when searching on complex products like for instance wheelchairs (e.g. seat size etc...). At the end of a search the description of the retrieved products can be displayed on the screen or printed according to various formats. A typical product description shows up to 50 parameters including identification data, factual data, freetext, and a colour picture.

4 Updating, management and distribution

The production, the updating and the distribution of the data bank is carried out by a team which includes 2 experts in technical aids, 3 documentalists, 1 technician, 1 computer analyst/programmer, plus co-ordination and clerical support. In the whole the dedicated manpower is the equivalent of 6 full-time workers.

Pictorial information concerning each product is taken from pictures provided by manufacturers (or from commercial catalogues), through a colour scanner or video-camera (Screen Machine rel.2) and commercial scanning or video-grabbing software. A minimal amount of graphic manipulation is then performed in order to comply with a set of consistency rules so as to ensure that the resulting image be understandable and informative for a rehabilitation professional. Each picture constitutes a file record which is stored onto a large-size-memory hard disk in FLM format (each file contains the pictures of all products belonging to a common brand name), from which it is converted into a PCX file with relevant links with the associated textual records everytime a new CD-ROM is prepared.

The system is designed for quarterly distribution through compact disk CD-ROM whose mastering is performed by a service agency. In order to have the whole information system implemented onto a single compact disk and fully usable with widespreads VGA colour screens, decision was taken:

- to limit the palette to 256 colours
- to have just one picture per product
- to have the image as large as possible on the screen so as to improve intelligibility and appreciation of details. Such compromise has been experienced as excellent between image quality, speed of screen presentation (almost instantaneous), required mass-memory (100-150 Kbytes for each picture).

Now compression techniques are being experienced in order to be able to manage more than one picture per product.

In retrieval stage access to the picture is provided by pressing an appropriate function key after textual information relevant to the given product is displayed.

5   The information/advice centres network throughout Italy

Assisting the client in the appropriate choice of a technical aid is a highly professional task. Therefore SIVA's Data Bank is mainly addressed at rehabilitation services and re-source Centres, where experts are expected to be prepared to act as counsellors to disabled clients. Up to now 58 centres (scattered throughout 12 out of the 20 Italian Regions) are accessing the system and thus take part in this network. However their number is rapidly increasing. Most of them have been set up inside Rehabilitation Units of Local Health Authorities: the remainder are information and Resource Centres set up by Municipalities, Associa-tions ad Universities. 14 of them are concentrated in the Region of Lombardy and 10 in the Region of Campania, in the frame of special projects aimed at providing every

Pict.2 - SIVA network

Local Health Authority with a specialised information office able to deal with all matters concerning technical aids.

Subject to an annual subscription, Siva provides the data bank and updates it every fourth month by mailing of a new compact disc. Every update is a new version of the whole package (data and software) which supersedes the old one.

The subscription also includes a monthly bulletin which reports on relevant initiatives (congresses, courses, important news) in the field of disability and rehabilitation. In order to responding to the need for fresh and quick information on such events the bulletin is telefaxed: a cost-effective solution for that was found through an external agency which provides a computer-assisted fax dispatching system.

In addition to that, SIVA offers specific training programmes addressed at professionals of the local information Centres, concerned with a global approach to counselling on the choice of technical aids with the support of the data bank. A permanent help desk is ensured on the phone which assists the data bank users in installation problems and in conceptual data retrieval difficulties. One-and-half day training sessions are also offered to help the data bank users in improving their skills in searching on the system.

6   Links with the European HANDYNET System

SIVA has been involved in the development of the European information system HANDYNET since its inception in 1986, together with a number of research and rehabilitation Institutions in other European Countries.

Now it is appointed as the national responsible for Handynet data collection and distribution in Italy. Through a purpose-made software interface data are transferred from SIVA information system whenever requested by the European Commission and reformatted so as to comply with the Handynet standards. The Handynet CD-ROMs and the related multilingual retrieval software are then distributed to all the Information Centres belonging to SIVA network, thus providing a powerful possibility to search for technical aids available on all the Common market.

Pict. 3 - The Handynet CD-ROM

7   Discussion

The current version of the information system benefits of 13 years of experience in idevelopment, management, distribution and direct use as a tool for supporting information and advice service delivery on technical aids. International discussion, exchanges and research were also carried out concerning this topic within the framework of the EEC Handynet project.

Whenever an improvement was carried out concerning the data bank structure or software, a field test was performed by direct observation and collection of opinions among the data bank users, who now range to about 240 professionals. The information system has proven to be a substantial tool for rehabilitation professionals and technicaids advisers; moreover, the possibility to access pictures is felt by them as a decisive step forwards.

But it has also been confirmed that the potentialities of the Data Bank can be exploited fully only in the hands of persons showing a solid background in the field of technical aids. That encouraged SIVA to design and experience training programmes aimed at reinforcing such knowledge and introducing well-defined methodologies of Technical Aids Counselling assisted by an information system.

A 100 hours training curriculum is now provided to professionals of the Centres who wish to take part in the SIVA cooperation network of Technical Aids Centres. That ensures a common commitment to quality of information service delivery and suggests a possible model applicable also in other Countries.

References

Andrich R.: The provision of technical aids in Italy: present situation and new models. In: Lorentsen O. (ed.): Rehabilitation Engineering. Proceedings of the UN/ECE REHAB-2 Workshop (Fagernes 12-15/5/91). Amsterdam: IFMBE 1992, pp. 73-87

Andrich R.: Educational programme for professionals and information providers. In: Technology and Accessibility. Proceedings of the ICTA international conference (Hoensbroek 12-13/11/91). Hoensbroek: Lucas Stichting 1992, pp.70-75

REHA – A Multimedia System to Learn About IT-Systems for Disabled Persons

O. Rienhoff, H. Wittchow

Institute of Medical Informatics, University
Marburg, Bunsenstrasse 3, 35033 Marburg, F.R.G.
FAX: +49-6421-28-8921

Abstract. In the last five years R&D activities in the field of information-technology-support for disabled persons have boomed. However, despite many impressive pieces of technology no breakthrough to a broad usage of this technology has happened. In this context an interdisciplinary working group at the Institute of Medical Informatics worked on the didactic- and presentation concept of Reha, a multimedia learning system, orientated towards three main target groups for information technoloy for the disabled: physicians, medical students, and patients. The concept was transformed into a demonstrator.

The program offers information and explanations about certain diseases. From there is a direct branching to the IT-aid part of the program to introduce a corresponding IT-aid that seems to be suitable.

1   Silent Market

In the last five years R&D activities in the field of information technology support for disabled persons have boomed. Not only that the European Union has formulated and carried out a major R&D program (TIDE) under its telematics activities but many research institutes, hospitals, rehabilitation institutions, medium and large enterprises have invested into the sector.

However, despite many impressive pieces of technology, despite some equally famous users like Stephen Hawking, no breakthrough to a broad usage of this technology has happened. Patients and doctors often do not know about existing possibilities. As a consequence, not enough consumer requests are made to establish a regional, national or European market and consequently prices for appropriate equipment are high and distribution of products is slow and hesitating.

The Mid Term Report to the Third Framework Program of the European Union regards the TIDE program as not too successful due to the fact that the market is extremely fragmented and that mainly small enterprises have been active in R&D work.

The results of the booming R&D activities are presented at more and more conferences and fairs. But as long as the market stays silent no cash flow will back up the further advancement of the technology. In this case an upswing can be expected and the possible impact of the new technology for disabled persons may be limited.

In this context, the Institute of Medical Informatics at Marburg University was looking for a booster for the slowly evolving consumer market.

2   The REHA Booster

The medical market is primarily driven by health care providers who prescribe drugs or sometimes medical equipment. In most countries of Europe physicians play this role. To a limited degree a similar function is related to other health care professionals like nurses for home care or e.g. orthopaedic shops. Despite efforts to a more active role of patients or disabled persons the key to a more effective use of information technology for disabled persons lies in the hands of physicians and other health professionals.

However, from studies it is known that many health professionals have kept a distance to information technology. In most European countries they do not get any serious introduction into medical informatics during their medical training. A good example for this distance is the distribution of computer systems in private physicians' offices. It is only higher in those European countries which have a governmental promotion policy (e.g. the UK.). If one further realizes that the development of IT support for disabled persons is still very much in its early development it becomes immediately clear that the key prescribers of this technology do never learn about the impressive results which can be achieved already today.

Therefore, a tool is needed to effectively inform: practising doctors, medical students, other health professionals, and patients about general possibilities on the one hand and about specific products on the other.

As the development of such an information tool needs a substantive investment effort and a continuous updating activity, in 1993 a concept for a multimedia learning system was derived: REHA.

REHA tries to utilize as many existing information sources as possible, e.g. the database Rehadat which is provided by the Institut der Deutschen Wirtschaft. Reha is also based on some of the most commonly available software tools like MS-Windows® and Toolbook®. An interdisciplinary working group at the Institute at Marburg worked for six months on the didactic- and presentation concept of REHA and transformed the concept into a demonstrator which was presented at the CEBIT fair at Hannover in March 1994. The demonstrator has all key functions of the REHA concept and is exemplified for the field of IT support for persons with limited eyesight.

The curricular modules are organized in three layers. The top layer is a general layer which contains all information about REHA and how to use it. The intermediate layer contains all information modules regarding various types of disabilities and correspondingly various types of information technology to overcome shortcomings caused by the disabilities. The bottom layer is a medical technical encyclopedia which contains all specific terms which are used in the modules above.

3   REHA - the Principal Structure

Fundamentally, the program puts the various modules to the user's disposal as shown below.

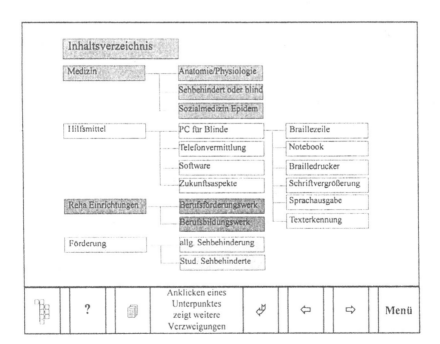

Contents of the module (translation of figure)

Medicine	Some different types of disabilities are shown here including typical diagnoses and their possible etiology. They are consolidated with information and statistics being part of social medicine.
IT-aid	Due to the possibilities of various different media, the user can get a very realistic demonstration of IT-based aid, whose categorisation follows the rules of the standardised ISO-classification.
Database	Some examples are made available for the learner. With the help of these examples they can practise to make searches in the database REHADAT.
Supportive measures	Information about specialised institutions of rehabilitation and supportive measures are given to the user of REHA.

It is worth mentioning that no previous knowledge is expected to work with the different modules. Using the advantages of a multimedia system different media have been used whenever it seemed reasonable. In addition to text information pictures, picture sequences, demonstrations, sound and simulations (e.g. using a Braille-keyboard) are used to fulfil every type of learners' expectations as there are auditive, visual, haptic and intellectual types of learners. Information that are foreign to the subject but imperative as well, e.g. those of the sector of informatics, are explained and illustrated or shown as a demonstration to make learning come alive.

4   The Curricular Design of REHA

The curricular design of REHA is orientated towards its three main target groups: physicians, medical students, and patients. With respect to the target groups, different paths through the various system modules are recommended.

The program allows practising doctors two different possibilities to use it:

- as a learning program for the target groups: physicians, students and patients
- as an explanation aid within a confidential talk between a physician and a patient, during a medical consultation or treatment episode

The access to the program will be basically different in the two cases. In the first case the access will be dominated by interest, that means the user is intrinsically motivated while, in the latter, the access will go straight up to the patient's problem.

The **physician** can give some information and explanations about a certain disease the patient is suffering from. The medical part of the program allows to show corresponding pages at the physician's disposal. Following, there is a direct branching to the IT-aid part of the program, so the physician may introduce an IT-aid that seems to be suitable.

It is not necessary to describe the course of access usually taken when **other health professionals** use REHA, because it is similar to the way described above.

To **medical students** the program REHA offers a new and different approach to the topic disability. Pure medical knowledge may immediately be completed by information about IT-aid. There are "buttons" on the pages of the medical part of REHA that offer a branching to corresponding pages of the IT-aid part of REHA. The buttons carry icons with a high stimulative nature suggesting sound-, picture- and video-information. As a supplement there is a "personal experience part" to the medical module: with this typical multimedia function medical students can personally experience disabilities, e.g. how patients, suffering from retinopathia pigmentosa perceive their environment. The students ought to have experienced it themselves because this possibility may lead to a more emotional affinity to the topic disability.

5 The Didactic Layout of REHA

The didactic layout is following the general principles of the design of multimedia systems in the teaching context (see literature). All modules follow in their layout a set of rules valid for the entire system.

5. 1 Structure of the Program

- The program is not split into definite chapters or learning units (like in a book), so the work with the program can be organised in a very individual way.

- The program does not have to be worked through sequentially, it can be interrupted at any time. This individually adapted shortest sequences of time can be used for learning.

- To fulfil the various expectations of the main target groups with their different background knowledge, REHA offers an encyclopedia function as a constant feature to look up unknown terms. A simple click on the unknown term inserts a spiral pad on the right part of the screen and without leaving the actual page the user gets further explanations to the searched term.

5.2 Using the Program

- Neither a manual nor much time is necessary to work with REHA as it is easy to handle with a mouse. Only four buttons will let you move through the program.

  There are three more buttons to make the work easier: With a click on the "?" - button the user can ask for on-line help which supplies extensive additional help. After a click on the "structure button" the structure of the main parts of the program are shown, details can be requested. A mark shows the actual position, there is no danger to get lost in hyper space.
  A click on the "▤" - button will branch to a page that contains an index on its left part. Choosing one of the listed headwords an explanation of the headword is shown on the right part of the page. Supplementary an offer is made to branch to the corresponding page of the program which deals with the topic. This facilitates the access to the program led by headwords and is therefore very fast.

  All the buttons are activated with a simple mouse-click. They have got the same function, same appearance and same position on the screen throughout the entire program.

- Within any text further information can be offered: On the screen are special areas with a short hint of the topic and a special symbol to show whether further information is available as sound, picture or video information. The information to which part of the program the module is branching is withhold from the user intentionally. The choice of the special area shall entirely be based on the interest of the user. The program supports such "free explorations". There is no necessity for the user to remember complex return routes, with the help of the "↺" - button the skip back to the last branching is possible.

- The layout was unified for all modules. For an easier orientation a different colour was chosen for the background of each of the four modules (medicine, IT-aid, database and supportive measures). The reddish background for example automatically indicates that your position is somewhere in the medicine module.

- The headings of chapters, text information and pictures have got their fixed position on the screen.

- Single pictures of film/audio-sequences are at least presented for six seconds. Sequences must be started by the user, they never start automatically. In this way it is avoided that two sources overlap and may thereby disturb each other. According to this the screen is presented in grey while sound information is presented. The principle is to allow concentration on one medium only.

The interface to the Rehadat database which holds actual information about products is being programmed now. For the demonstrator it was acceptable to have some dummy frames in the system to show the principle and receive user reactions.

The Rehadat interface will be the first example of interfaces to other systems. REHA can only survive if it can utilize databases which are maintained by commercial organizations.

6   REHA - Hardware and Software Requirements

6.1 Software Requirements:

- DOS 3.1 or higher
- Microsoft Windows 3.0 or higher
- ToolBook® 1.5 (Asymetrix Corporation)

6.2 Hardware Requirements:

The recommended minimum system configuration to run Reha and ToolBook® is:

- A personal computer with at least a 16MHz 80386 SX processor
- 2MB RAM (4MB recommended)
- 1.4MB (31/2") disk drive
- A hard disk with min. 10MB of free disk space
- A monitor and graphics card for VGA or VGA Plus
- A Windows-compatible mouse
- An MCI-compatible audio subsystem, such as the SoundBlaster Pro board

7   Test of REHA

The exhibition of the REHA demonstration at the CEBIT was part of a first testing phase in which physicians, medical students, and visitors of the fair were asked to comment on the system. This led to a revision of the first version in April and May 1994. REHA 1.1 has in the meantime attracted the interest of two health insurance companies in Germany after being demonstrated to them in the current version.

A major validation phase is prepared within the department to test the demonstrator, its curricular design and the handling of the system with groups of medical students from the Medical School. These tests will lead to a revised version 1.2 which also shall include the functioning interface to the actual Rehadat database. Version 1.2 will be the basis of horizontal extensions of REHA into other areas of human impairment.

Literature

SCHAUB, M. (1992). Code X: multimediales Design. DuMont Buchverlag, Köln.

EULER, D. (1992). Didaktik des computerunterstützten Lernens: praktische Gestaltung und theoretische Grundlagen. Bildung und Wissenschaft Verlag, Nürnberg.

HANNAFIN M. J. & PECK, K. L. (1988). The Design, Development, and Evaluation of Instructional Software. Macmillan, New York.

FRIEDRICH, H. & MANDL, H. (1990). Psychologische Aspekte autodidaktischen Lernens. In: Unterrichtswissenschaft 3, 197-218.

ISSING, L. J. (1988) Wissenserwerb mit Medien. In: H. Mandl & H. Spada (Hrsg.): Wissenspsychologie. Psychologie VerlagsUnion, München-Weinheim.

WEIDENMANN, B. (1986). Psychologie des Lernens mit Medien. In: B. Weidenmann & A. Krapp (Hrsg.) Pädagogische Psychologie. Psychologie VerlagsUnion, München-Weinheim.

Introducing Voice Control - Widening the Perspective

Ian French, Philip Halford*, Jill Hewitt, John Sapsford-Francis

University of Hertfordshire, Hatfield, Herts, England, AL10 9AB
Telephone: 44 707 284766 Fax: 44 707 284303 email: comrirf@herts.ac.uk

*Compris Consulting Ltd, Studio II, 2 Beverley Gardens, London, HA7 2AB.
Telephone: + 44 (0) 81 424 2477 Fax: + 44 (0) 81 424 2479

Abstract. This paper describes the development of a multimedia tutorial system which is designed to encourage more people to use voice controlled systems. A three part tutorial takes a user through a first introduction at an exhibition or assessment centre, an intermediate learning level designed to improve performance in using speech controlled systems and finally an application oriented tutorial designed to accelerate learning to 'expert user' status. The system is designed to be used in hands-free mode right from the first access by a new user, thus giving the disabled user more independence of use throughout their training, hence minimising the need for third party assistance.

Keywords. Speech Controlled Systems, Hands-Free Operation, Tutorial System, Multimedia Tutorial.

1   Introduction

The SHELVS project (Self Help Learning for Voice Controlled Systems) is jointly funded by ESRC and the DTI. This is a collaborative project with partners from academia and industry which aims to fulfil the training needs of many people with disabilities who could benefit from the use of voice controlled systems.

There are currently a wide range of commercial speech recognition systems which provide an alternative to keyboard input, but usability problems with these systems mean that they do not attract as many users as they could and that the users often do not exploit the full potential of the systems. Most systems require some keyboard input during the tutorial and training stages, and often have error recovery routines, which, although very powerful, are daunting to a new user. In addition they do not address the very real difficulty that many users have in adapting to the idea of talking to a machine, compounded with the extra burden of learning to use a computer and its applications. The SHELVS system addresses these problems by providing a tutorial management system which allows the user to progress from new user to expert status at their own pace and under their own voice control, thus doing away with the need for expensive consultancy and able-bodied assistance.

In the following sections, we discuss the rationale behind the system, including the results of a questionnaire of existing users, the overall system design and the evaluation programme.

2   Rationale

Commercial speech recognition systems such as the DragonDictate and its derivative the IBM Voicetype record impressive data entry rates of up to 60 words per minute and recognition rates of up to 97% correct (Baker, 1989), and can be operated by experts without recourse to the keyboard. However it is apparent that, particularly for new users, there are still significant usability problems. New users have to undergo a fairly lengthy training period, and typically require the services of a consultant for at least a half to one day before they can begin to use the systems on their own. They need to learn the International Communications Alphabet for when they have to spell words, they need to know how to recover from errors and they need to understand how to build and use macros (single word commands that instigate a series of actions or keystrokes). Typically before they can begin to use a system such as DragonDictate they will have to train and remember 204 command words. All of these factors can be seen as a considerable disincentive to a disabled user who is assessing the relative merits of a voice controlled system against the more traditional switch input device, even though the eventual performance rate of the speech system will outstrip other input modalities.

We set up a simple trial in which an expert, a novice and a new user of IBM Voicetype all tried to input the same text. The expert was a system trainer, the novice had undergone the initial training and had learned the International Communications Alphabet and trained all the command words, and the new user had trained some command words and had some knowledge of error recovery procedures gained through watching other users. The results are given below:

> **Expert:** 59 utterances created 120 words of text (using macros). 4 errors, no use of keyboard, 38 words per minute, recognition rate of 91%
> **Novice:** 42 utterances created 28 words of text, 14 errors, two uses of keyboard, 8.5 words per minute, recognition rate of 67%
> **New User:** 44 utterances, created 15 words of text, 29 errors, three uses of keyboard, one word left wrong, 3 words per minute, recognition rate of 34%

In our opinion, the expert was inputting text at the maximum rate possible for the system (operating on a standard 486 compatible PC). She could only have achieved a better data entry rate by the extensive use of macros. The progress of the novice and the new user was slow enough for us to abandon the trial before all the text had been input. In both their cases, it was essential for the keyboard to be used by the experimenter to correct errors caused by the system consistently misrecognising a command word. If they had been on their own and unable to use the keyboard they would have been unable to progress.

This trial reinforced the opinions of the expert regarding the difficulties faced by new users, and serves to show that there is a need for a user centred approach in designing tutorials and applications for voice controlled systems.

3   System Overview

The SHELVS system is being developed through an incremental prototyping approach (Vonk, 1990) with an emphasis on user involvement throughout the design and implementation. Throughout the project we have been building on experience gained in earlier developments of speech based systems. A main focus of the ISDIP project at Hatfield (Tough, 1990) was to provide a word processor that allowed hands-free operation even in compounded error situations. Results from this research point to the need for a good error recovery dialogue commensurate with the user's expectations (Cheepen, 1990) and more closely related to a human to human conversation than a conventional keyboard operation, even when a restricted vocabulary is used (Zajicek & Hewitt, 1990).

The system being built will provide tutorials at three levels:
- Sampler - to introduce and demonstrate voice controlled systems
- Primer - to allow controlled learning of important aspects of voice controlled systems
- Practitioner - to teach effective use of a voice controlled system for a variety of applications

These are described in detail in sections 3.2 to 3.4

3.1 User Requirements

In order to establish the user requirements for the tutorial system we sent out a questionnaire to recent purchasers of DragonDictate and IBM Voicetype systems. We also elicited the opinion of a voice system consultant. Further requirements were identified as a result of the first prototype evaluation and we expect to further refine the requirements specification as a result of future prototype evaluations.

3.1.1 User Questionnaire

A questionnaire was sent out to 48 recent purchasers and 20 responses were received. The results indicated a wide range of usage patterns and ability levels and showed some degree of dissatisfaction with the systems, they are recorded in some detail in (French et al, 1994). Thirteen people reported problems with the system, the most significant being poor word recognition and incompatibility with Windows (all users had DOS versions of the systems). Twelve people suggested improvements to the system, with the most significant being the need for compatibility with Windows, an improvement in speed and a strong preference for English as opposed to American spelling.

3.1.2 Usability Criteria

In keeping with our usual practice in following a user centred design approach, we drew up usability criteria for the three main parts of the system. These took into account the analysis of existing users and the perceived requirements of new users. They provided a framework for the design of the system and its subsequent evaluations. An overview of these criteria is given in the table in Figure 2, they should be considered in conjunction with the system description in the next section, since different criteria are used for different parts of the system.

Criteria	Sampler	Primer	Practitioner
User attitude	Priority 1	Priority 1	Priority 2
Learning Time	Priority 1	Priority 2	Priority 2
Performance	Priority 1	Priority 1	Priority 1
Error Rate	Priority 1	Priority 2	Priority 3
Retention	Priority 3	Priority 2	Priority 1
Flexibility	Priority 5	Priority 3	Priority 2

Figure 2 Usability Criteria and their priorities for the three parts of the system
(Priority 1 = high and 5 = low)

3.2 The Sampler System

This has been designed for an interaction of 10-15 minutes duration and is intended to be used in exhibitions and show-rooms. Its purpose is to allow users to explore the potential of voice controlled systems, to allow users to evaluate informally the suitability, for them, of voice controlled systems and to introduce users to the whole tutorial system.

The system starts with an introductory video loop showing how to engage with the system (...put on the headset microphone, with assistance if necessary) and from this the user is able to select speech or keyboard control. If speech is chosen, a selection of six words (<UP>, <DOWN>, <LEFT>, <RIGHT>, <SELECT> and <QUIT>) are trained which is sufficient to take the user through the rest of this level.

Navigation around the sampler is achieved using direct spatial mapping, this is shown in figure 3. When the user utters one of the control words (<UP>, <DOWN>, <LEFT> or <RIGHT>) the input focus is moved to the relevant button and further information about the option they have selected is given in the space adjacent to that button. The button is activated when the user says <SELECT>. Saying <QUIT> at any point will take the user to the top level of the system.

The user is able to choose between two or three introductory videos detailing the functionality of the application, how speech recognition works and examples of (good and bad practice in) speech recognition. These can be controlled by voice.

This level also incorporates different types of games that the user can play under speech control. One of these games is shown in figure 4. This is a simple maze game in which the user moves a ball (top left) through the maze to a man (bottom right) at the end. The control words to move the ball are the same as used in the navigation in the system, but the user is not required to say <SELECT> after each movement. During the game, the user can say <QUIT> to exit from the game. The purpose of this and other games is to give the user a chance to practice the vocabulary they have learned so far, and to establish if speech is a viable medium for them to use (if for example they have a disability that effects the pronunciation or consistency of their speech).

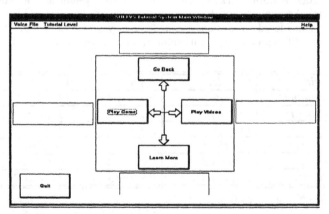

Figure 3 Sampler Screen showing a Directional Spatial Metaphor for selecting system functions

3.3 The Primer System
The Primer system is intended to be used in assessment centres, rehabilitation centres, homes, exhibitions and show-rooms. Its purpose is to allow users to gain the necessary familiarity with a number of speech recognition essentials that apply

across the majority of voice controlled systems. These essentials include use of the international communications alphabet to spell words, use of numbers and specific commands. The Primer system also introduces users to environmental control using voice controlled systems.

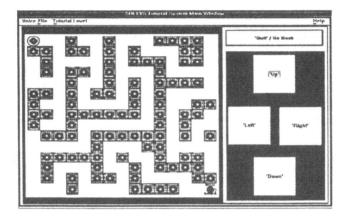

Figure 4 The Maze Game

This part of the system has been designed for a session of about 30 minutes duration, but it is envisaged that users will return for several sessions to reinforce their learning and to cover different aspects of the tutorial. It follows that any words trained by the user during this session will be saved for subsequent use both in this and the Practitioner tutorials. Navigation around this part of the system will be performed in the same way as in the Sampler level. Selection of one of the options at this level will instigate training of the words required.

To allow the user to practice the international communications alphabet a hangman game has been implemented, this is shown in figure 5. The utterence of one of the letters of the alphabet causes the button containing that letter to be disabled. After a couple of tries at guessing words by spelling, the button array shown at the bottom of figure can be made invisible, thus helping the user learn the alphabet.

3.4 The Practitioner System
The Practitioner system is intended primarily to be used in the home, but it may also be used in rehabilitation centres and assessment centres. The purpose of this system is to provide users with an orientation to the DragonDictate system and help users to learn the commands and interaction sequences that will allow them to use the system efficiently.

The functionality of the Practitioner will depend to a certain extent on what is provided by DragonDictate with their Windows product (due for release in Spring 1994). The complement of DragonDictate with our own tutorials will provide a complete and usable set of tutorials.

3.5 Dialogue Design
An important principle in the design of the system was that it should be operable by speech even before a user had trained any words. To achieve this end, a "bootstrapping" dialogue has been designed. In addition, the system must cater for

existing users who have already trained the initial vocabulary, by loading the appropriate voice files. The Dialogue given in Figure 6 shows how both these requirements have been catered for. The diagram is in USE format (Wasserman et al.)

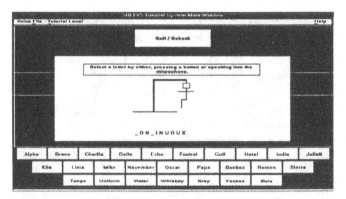

Figure 5 The Hangman Game

From the start state there is a timeout which passes to a video loop showing how to engage with the system. A message on this screen will tell the user to do anything (keypress, mouseclick or utterance) to engage with the system. The new user then has the option of selecting the Sampler by pressing on a button (taking them to the Message 1 Sampler screen), or by saying "Select Sampler". As they have not yet trained any words, the system will only be able to look for an approximate match for the utterance "Select Sampler" - the degrees of freedom for the recognition will be set very high. Once presented with the Sampler Screen (message2 Sampler in the diagram), the user will be asked to say "Yes" to continue with speech input or "Exit System" to go back to the start. These two words are of sufficiently different length and profile that the system should be able to distinguish between them for most users. A user who has already enrolled with the system will need to establish their identity so that it can load their voice files. They will say a (trained) codename, which, if recognised by the system, will be followed by a request for them to input their password, by spelling one letter at a time. The degrees of freedom on recognition of the codename will be very small to minimise the risk of the system mistaking a new user for an existing one. A further security check is given by the need to input a password, since it would be problematic if a user was allowed access to someone else's voice files.

4 Evaluation

In the early stages of the project the development team established links with related product vendors and were able to accomplish two goals to assist the team in the evaluation:

    i) to verify the current use profile of the prospective market. i.e. what existing users were using their system for and for how long etc...

    ii) to establish a speech-control-fluent user group who were willing to evaluate our products for us.

Prior to field trials of the system, a Hallway and Storefront evaluation was undertaken. This was primarily needed to establish whether the first draft of the system was apt for use by people without the use of keyboard. The team were also keen to see whether the users could use the metaphors adopted in the system to control the application i.e. the sequence of training the utterances and using the games in the first (Sampler) level of the system rather than getting in a total

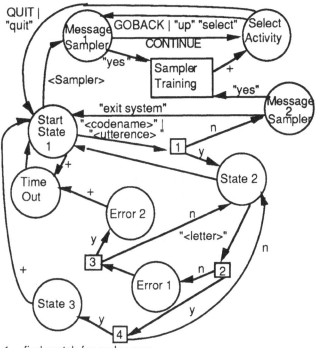

1 = find match for codename
2 = find match for password
3 = increment failure, count test for > limit
4 = Password complete?
State 1 = "<name>" enter password or stay silent to exit"
State 2 = "Voice files loaded for <name>"
State 3 = "Password Accepted"
Error 1 = "Error, please repeat"
Error 2 = "The system isn't recognising your voice,
        please re-enter as a new user or seek assistance"
Message 1 = "Say YES to select speech"
Message 2 = "Say YES to select speech or EXIT SYSTEM to return"

Figure 6 A Bootstrapping Dialogue

muddle. The chosen scenario was a busy canteen area at the University to see how the system would cope with a high level of background noise to simulate an exhibition environment. The team designed a path for the user to take that led the user into the system gently and used a variety of interaction objects supported by MS Windows. This introduced them to a well balanced subset of the system elements. When the users had completed their session with the system, they were de-briefed immediately using a set of screen images that were seen in the interaction, and were asked for their opinion on usability and clarity and for comments on the screen and system layout. In addition to this, the team used a

Mediator system to capture the interaction on video tape discretely rather than obtrusively using an external camera unit. The initial findings from this primary evaluation session were as follows:

- all of the users found the experience using speech positive and were encouraged rather than discouraged to try to use other speech systems
- some of the users found the training of the words confusing
- the initial vocabulary which included <right>,<left> and <quit> was found to be too tight phonetically and led to misrecognitions
- one of the games that was used in the system was considered too difficult to play in the short timescale allocated
- some of the users wanted more on-screen instruction to assist them with the decisions on the screen.

At the moment the team are digesting the corpus of information amassed from this evaluation and are planning the next prototype of the tutorial which will be evaluated by our established user base.

5   Conclusions

Existing speech recognition systems, although powerful, still present users with considerable usability problems. New users require a long learning curve before they become proficient in their use, and even long-term users have problems with recognition and error recovery. The systems cannot be used without recourse to keyboard, at least in the initial training stages. We are building a three-level tutorial system which will address these problems. An initial Hallway and Storefront evaluation indicated a number of interesting problems, but it showed that the main purpose of the Sampler system - to encourage new users to want to progress in the field of speech controlled computing - was a marked success.

6   References

Baker, J. 1989, "Large Vocabulary Speech Recognition", Speech Technology, April/May

CheepenC. 1990 The pragmatics of friendliness and user-friendliness, International Pragmatics Conference, Barcelona.

French, I, Halford, P, Hewitt, J, and Sapsford-Francis, J, 1994 "Developing Hands-Free Tutorials for Speech Controlled Systems in a Windows Environment", Computer Science Technical Report Number 195

Kay, P. 1991, "Speech Controlled Graphics on a Macintosh", in Independence through Technology, 7th Annual Conference, The BCS Disability Programme, Leeds: BCS, 45-50

Tough, C. 1990 "The Design of an Intelligent Transparent Speech Interface",

Vonk, R, 1990, "Prototyping", Prentice Hall

Zajicek M. & Hewitt J. 1990, "An Investigation into the use of error recovery dialogues in a user interface management system for speech recognition", in INTERACT'90 D. Diaper et al. (Editors), Elsevier Science Publishers B.V. (North Holland)

Mathtalk: The Design of an Interface for Reading Algebra Using Speech

Robert Stevens and Alistair Edwards

Department of Computer Science, University of York, York, UK YO1 5DD

Abstract. The problems that a visually disabled person has with reading, writing and manipulating standard algebra notation are characterized in terms of *speed, control* and *external memory*. The Mathtalk program has been developed to enable the listener to read algebra notation in a quick and active manner, that overcomes some of these problems. Prosody has been added to the synthetic voice output to resolve grouping ambiguities, decrease mental workload and improve memory for the presented notation. Browsing functions and the associated command language allow the listening reader to shift his or her attention to any part of an expression. To make most effective use of the *speed* and *control* afforded by Mathtalk, an *audio glance* is provided that should allow planning of the reading process. The development and evaluation of Mathtalk has led to the proposal of a set of design principles that should facilitate the production of other, similar user interfaces for the reading of structured information. Further work includes the development of Mathtalk in the TIDE Maths project. As well as reading, the problems of writing and manipulation need to be tackled.

1 Introduction

This paper describes the design and evaluation of the interface to Mathtalk. This is a PC based system that aims to enable blind people to gain a quick and active reading of standard algebra notation, using speech and non-speech audio. Algebra and other related notations are the most common form of expression in both mathematics and sciences, which are both subjects of great importance. The ability to use such notations in a quick and effective manner has the potential to enhance the employment and educational prospects of many visualy disabled people. This work will be extended to cover the writing and manipulation of a wider set of Mathematics in both speech and Braille as part of the European Tide Maths project.

Standard algebra forms the core of most notations used in mathematical, scientific and technical disciplines. It is used both to manipulate and to communicate mathematical concepts. Printed algebra notation gives a persistent record of these ideas, thus making many mathematical tasks easier by affording an *external memory*. The external memory allows a sighted reader to *control* the information flow with speed and accuracy. This control makes the sighted reader the *active* partner in the reading process. As well as enhancing memory for an individual, this external memory can support communication between mathematicians, as the spoken word may in other disciplines.

A blind user does not have the luxury of a piece of paper and must use either braille or recorded speech. A tape recorder is a poor interactive tool [1]. Using a tape recorder is a slow and inaccurate process. Mathtalk is an attempt to improve the usability of spoken algebra. Spoken mathematics is often ambiguous and symbol names are inconsistent. The speech signal is transient and thus great demands are made upon human memory. In addition, the The listener is passive and frequently loses concentration, making the reading task more difficult. The listener is not truly a reader: to be so the listener must be the active party in the interaction and become what Simpson [13] calls the *listening reader.*

The Mathtalk program seeks to provide both a useful external memory and the means to control information flow to make the listening reader an active reader. The design, implementation and evaluation of the Mathtalk program has given rise to a set of design principles that can be used to enhance the reading of complex information by blind people. The following sections describe these design principles in more detail.

2 How to Speak Algebra notation

The first question that needs to be answered is 'what information to present?' Printed algebra notation presents only the syntatic elements of an expression. The syntax primarily presents the grouping within an expression. It is the reader, using his or her knowledge of mathematics, algebra and any other surrounding text, who parses and makes any mathematical interpretation. This is the first principle for the design for an aid to read algebra: The aid should only present the elements of the algebra notation, it is for the reader to make any mathematical interpretation.

2.1 Resolving Grouping Ambiguities

After deciding what information to present, a decision must be made on how to present that information. The spatial cues within a printed expression group items together and help to indicate how they should be parsed [9]. In print that the fact that $x^n + 1$ is parsed differently to x^{n+1} is obvious. The eyes can be used to move through an expression in such a way that these cues can be used to facilitate parsing. As a result of the transient speech form providing no external memory and control being poor, the utterance 'x to the n plus 1' is potentially ambiguous in that the scope of the superscript is not made explicit. The auditory display must be enhanced to avoid grouping ambiguities and facilitate parsing in an manner analogous to printed algebra.

Using Lexical Cues One method of preventing grouping ambiguity is to use special words or phrases (*lexical cues*) inserted into the utterance to delimit the scope of syntactic groups. Chang [7] proposes set of rules for speaking mathematics, both consistently and unambiguously. Chang offers several levels of mathematical information in the types of lexical cue he uses. A Mathtalk option applies a subset of Chang's rules that are consistent with the minimal level of syntactic interpretation offered to the reader.

An example that covers many of the syntactic types used by Mathtalk is shown below:

$$x = \frac{-b \pm \sqrt{b^2 - 4ac}}{2a} \tag{1}$$

This is spoken as:

> x equals the fraction, numerator negative b plus or minus the square root of the quantity b squared minus four a c denominator two a.

The notion of *simple* and *complex* syntax can be introduced to guide the speaking of an algebra expression. A complex item is one in which more than one term is grouped together by an explicit parsing mark or spatial grouping in the printed form. For example, parenthesised sub-expressions are complex items. A complex fraction has more than one term in either numerator or denominator. Superscripts, like fractions, can be either simple or complex. It is to delimit complex items that lexical cues are used. This notion of simple and complex will arise throughout the discussion of the Mathtalk program.

Thus, the use of lexical cues can avoid any grouping ambiguity in a spoken algebra expression. Evaluation of this style of presentation revealed some problems. The addition of lexical cues makes an utterance much more verbose. The large amount of spoken material is difficult to parse, retain and integrate. The use of lexical cues often invoked the suffix effect [2], causing the content of complex items to be lost. Evaluation of mental workload [8] showed this style of presentation to be very demanding and frustrating [16].

Using Prosody in Spoken Algebra Synthetic speech is a much impoverished signal compared to human speech. The speech component known as prosody is often missing. Prosody can be thought of as the non-verbal information content of speech [10]. An example of the latter phenomenon may be seen in the following sentences: "The last time we met / Robert was horrible" and "The last time we met Robert / was horrible". The slash indicates where a prosodic cue, usually a pause, can be inserted to completely change the meaning of the utterance. As the grouping structure of an algebra expression is known, appropriate prosodic cues could be ascribed to the syntactic junctures to indicate grouping instead of lexical cues.

For the Mathtalk program we derived a relatively simple set of prosodic rules from the analysis of a series of spoken algebra expressions. These prosodic cues agreed with and enhanced those derived from earlier research [17, 11]. These rules cover the core of algebra notation presented by Mathtalk, and should be capable of being extended. A simple expression such as $3x + 4 = 7$ is divided into terms by pauses; the start of each new term is also indicated by a pitch rise; multiplication is indicated by verbal juxtaposition and the imminent end of the expression is indicated by a sharp pitch fall. The complex part of the expression $3(x + 4) = 7$ is grouped together by a pitch fall, increased speed and no internal pausing. So, despite having the same lexical content, the prosodic structures are radically different.

These rules have been implemented in the Mathtalk program. Evaluation of the use of prosodic cues in comparison with lexical cues reveals several interesting improvements [16]. Listeners indicate an overall preference for the prosodic cues. Using prosodic cues instead of lexical significantly improved both apprehension of syntactic structure and retention of content. The absence of lexical cues probably reduces problems due to the suffix effect. The prosodic cues, particulary the pauses, chunk the utterance into meaningful subunits facilitating parsing, integration and retention in short-term memory. The prosodic cues can be thought to have the same effect as the spatial parsing cues present in print (see [9]).

This use of prosodic cues to make the spoken presentation more usable is one of the design principles of Mathtalk. However, enhancing the auditary display and making the presentation more usable is not enough to enable active reading by a listener. With both prosodic and lexical cues, recovery of structure and retention of content fails with greater *complexity* and length of expression. A full utterance will often overwhelm a listener and more importantly the listener is still the passive agent in the reading process.

3 Active Reading by Browsing Algebra

Visual reading is an active process because the reader has fast and accurate control over the information flow. This level of control needs to be given to the listening reader to make him or her a truly active reader. Mathtalk provides a series of browsing functions and the means to control them, that should enable this active reading.

A default reading strategy is provided. This is a left-right movement through the expression, revealing a term at a time, under the control of the reader. In each term the simple items are spoken in full. Any complex items are folded or hidden and simply refferred to by their type. When a complex item is encountered, the next stage of the default strategy is to move into that item and successively reveal the contents.

The principle behind *folding* means that complex items are hidden from view and referred to only by their type. moving through the expression $3(x + 4) = 7$ at the top-level reveals the items 3, 'a quantity', = and 7. The sub-expression is referred to by its type label: 'A quantity'. Other reading moves can be used to explore the sub-expression or to reveal the whole item without exploration. This folding of complex items helps the reader maintain control of the information flow, aiding integration and retention.

There are two vital components needed to make successful use of the browsing: Planning and directing their use. How Mathtalk enables the listening reader to plan his or her reading strategy is dealt with in the next section. As well as the default reading style, , access to any part of an expression must be given in an unconstrained manner, that allows review of the expression and modification of the reading style. The reader controls these browsing functions with a command language. The nature of the notation and associated browsing leads to a necesarily complex interface. Yet, The reading process is of primary importance and any method of em controlling the information flow that is mediated externally, unlike visual reading, must intrude into the reading process as little as possible. The means of controlling the reading process, issuing commands and recieving feedback about moves made must be as transparent as possible so that the reading process is supported rather than disrupted.

Matthalk's command langauge is a combination of **actions** (e.g. current, next and previous) and a series of syntatic **targets** (e.g. expression, term and item). An action word is combined with a target word to form a command. At present a mnemomic mapping to the key-board is used to issue commands. For example, to move to the next term the action **next** and target **term** are issued as the keyboard command **nt**. This makes the issuing of commands swift. Together with the wide coverage of the browsing gives the reader both fast and accurate control of the information flow.

By adding browsing functions to the user interface the reader may become the active agent in the reading process. The reader's method for directing the browsing must allow for adequate control in the reading process. Yet, the method of control must not intrude into the reading process itself. The command language uses a relatively small number of *action* and *target* words that can be combined to cover the large range of possible browsing moves. The speed and accuracy given by such a command language should go some way to mitigating the effects of the transience of the speech signal. Browsing may be more effective to refresh a reader's memory by giving easy access to any part of an expression, rather than relying on remembering the material recently heard.

The commands fall naturally into a spoken form and thus fit neatly into the speech based nature of the interface. The command language will be mapped to input by voice recognition. In the near future the control aspect of Mathtalk will be evaluated for ease of use, learning, predictability and effectiveness.

4 Planning the Reading Process

As well as allowing control in the reading process, the external memory allows a sighted reader to plan his or her reading process. To develop an appropriate reading strategy, the listening reader also needs to have some high-level information complexity of the expression. With only browsing, the reader has to read the expression to find out the complexity. Thus planning is not possible. The print memory allows the reader to skim the expression quickly and note the salient features that determine its complexity. The auditory display needs a similar facility.

Speech was rejected as a means of providing this audio glance. A non-interpretive description of an expression's complexity would be too long. A glance should be a quick overview. Work on *earcons* [3, 5, 4] provided a method to use non-speech audio for this glance, giving a very quick, non-interpretive overview of an expression's structure.

Earcons are abstract, structured sequences of sound that may be used within a computer interface to represent objects or events to the user [3]. The parameters that describe earcons are similar to those that describe the prosodic component of speech. Parallels between guidelines for earcon construction [4] and the rules for algebraic prosody mean there are many similarities between the two forms of information. The concepts of earcon structure and prosodic cues have been combined in *algebra earcons* to provide an audio glance to facilitate planning in reading algebra.

In algebra earcons each syntactic item is represented by a different musical timbre. Prosodic rules are then combined with the algebra syntax to give structure to the sounds. A full set of rules for generating algebra earcons have been developed for Mathtalk [15]. Evaluation of the earcons has shown that listeners can recognise even very complex expression structures from listening to an algebra earcon. Subsequent evaluation has shown that people retain a useful mental representation of an expression after hearing an algebra earcon. This representation may vary from an idea of the complexity to a very detailed view of the target expression. When integrated with the other components of Mathtalk, this representation should be useful in providing information to plan the reading of the expression. A good representation of the expression could be used to help resolve grouping ambiguities in the spoken forms of the expression and provide a cognitive framework for the reading process.

Algebra earcons are capable of providing the information needed to plan reading of an algebra expression. The rôle of algebra earcons could be extended. An audio glance could provide orientation and navigation information for the listening reader. The use of musical timbres to represent syntactic types could be exploited. The same timbres could be used as background sounds, that are played while the reader is within that syntactic environment. The onset of such background sounds is noticed by the listener, but fade into the background [6]. The listener can then sample such sounds to determine the current environment, and again notice the switching off of the sound as he or she leaves the current environment.

5 Discussion

The Mathtalk program gives blind readers a truly active reading interaction with algebraic material. The design principles derived from this work will be applied to other potentially complex information, such as programming languages. This work also has a wider significance for the design of non-visual interfaces. The ability to read such material in a quick and active manner has the potential to enhance educational prospectus of many blind people.

The design principles derived from the Mathtalk program are based on solving the problems of *control* and *external memory*. Once a decision has been made on what level of information to present, such design decisions can be made. The transience of the speech signal is mitigated by the addition of prosody, to ease retention, and giving quick and accurate access to any part of an expression, via browsing. Prosody can also replace the rôle of spatial grouping in printed form, preventing grouping ambiguity.

The control aspect of reading is enhanced with addition of the browsing functions and associated command language. This allows the reader to maintain control over the information flow and shift attention to any part of an expression. This ability will allow completely unambiguous reading of an expression, which is not entirely possible with an uncontrolled full utterance.

To make full use of the potential control a reader needs to plan his or her use of the browsing functions. *Algebra earcons* are provided to give an audio glance at an expression. This glance at least gives the reader an idea of the expression's complexity and in the best case provides a framework into which details can be fitted and that can help resolve grouping ambiguity.

Each major component of the Mathtalk system will have been evaluated for its effectiveness in tackling a particular problem of reading algebra using speech and sound. The whole Mathtalk system will then be evaluated. Such evaluation is necessary for the development of usable interfaces that mediate such complex tasks as the reading of algebra. It is not enough to enable presentation of information, that material has to be able to be read in an active, effectivce and efficient manner.

The work on the Mathtalk program has fed into the European Tide Maths project. This project seeks to produce an algebra work-station for the reading, writing and manipulation of algebra notation. This takes a multi-media approach, using Braille, enhanced visual display, speech and non-speech audio to give a presentation suitable for many visual conditions and tastes. The work to be carried out at York includes methods for writing and manipulating algebra; use of non-speech audio in navigation and orientation, extending the work on algebra earcons; enhancing the work on algebraic prosody.

Acknowledgements

We would like to thank John Local, Department of Linguistics, University of York for his help in the investigation of algebraic prosody. This work was supported by SERC grant 91308897.

References

1. F. Aldrich and A. Parkin. Improving the retention of aurally presented information. In M. Gruneberg, P. Morris, and R. Sykes, editors, *Practical Aspects of Memory 2: Current Research and Issues*. Chichester, England: Wiley, 1988.

2. A. D. Baddeley. *Human Memory: Theory and Practice*. Lawrence Erlbaum Associates Ltd, 1990.

3. M. Blattner, D. Sumikawa, and R. Greenberg. Earcons and icons: Their structure and common design principles. *Human Computer Interaction*, 4(1):11–44, 1989.

4. S. A. Brewster, P. C. Wright, and A. D. N. Edwards. An evaluation of earcons for use in auditory human-computer interfaces. In *INTERCHI'93*, pages 222–227. ACM Press, Addison-Wesley, 1993.

5. S. A. Brewster, P.C. Wright, and A.D.N. Edwards. A detailed investigation into the effectiveness of earcons. In G. Kramer, editor, *Auditory Display: The Proceedings of the First International Conference on Auditory Display*. Addison-Wesley, 1992.

6. W. Buxton, W. Gaver, and S. Bly. Tutorial no. 8: The use of non-speech audio at the interface. In *CHI'91 Conference proceedings, Humantems*. ACM Press: Addison-Wesley, 1991.

7. L. A. Chang. *Handbook for Spoken Mathematics (Larry's Speakeasy)*. Lawrence Livermore Laboratory, The Regents of the University of California, 1983.

8. S. G. Hart and C. Wickens. *Workload assessment and prediction*, pages 257–296. New York: Van Nostrand Reinhold, 1990.

9. D. Kirshner. The visual syntax of algebra. *Journal for Research into Mathematics Education*, 20(3):274–287, 1989.

10. E. Lehiste. *Suprasegmentals*. MIT Press, 1970.

11. M. H. O'Malley, D. R. Kloker, and B. Dara-Abrams. Recovering parentheses from spoken algebraic expressions. *IEEE Transactions on Audio and Electroacoustics*, AU-21:217–220, 1973.

12. K. Rayner and A. Pollatsek. *The Psychology of Reading*. Prentis Hall, 1989.

13. P. J. Simpson. Enhancing text to synthesized speech systems for the blind. In *Proceedings of the IEE Colloquium on Special Needs and the Interface*, January 1993. IEE Digest no. 1993/005.

14. R. D. Stevens. principles for the design of systems for reading complex information by visually disabled people. Internal report, 1993.

15. R. D. Stevens. Rules for the construction of algebra earcons. Internal Report, 1994.

16. R. D. Stevens, P. C. Wright, and A. D. N. Edwards. Prosody improves a speech based interface. Unpublished, 1994.

17. L. A. Streeter. Acoustic determinants of phrase boundary representation. *Journal of the Acoustical Society of America*, 64:1582–15:1 92, 1978.

A Method of Access to Computer Aided Software Engineering (CASE) Tools for Blind Software Engineers

Paul Blenkhorn and David Gareth Evans

Technology for Disabled People Unit, Systems Engineering Group,
Department of Computation, UMIST, Manchester, M60 1QD, England.

Abstract. This paper proposes a technique to allow blind software engineers to access the information held in Computer Aided Software Engineering (CASE) tools. Such tools support systems analysis and design methods that typically encode information as hierarchically structured two-dimensional graphs. The paper discusses the problems that blind engineers face in accessing this type of information by considering the structure of system models built in one Software Engineering notation, namely Hatley-Pirbhai Real Time Structured Analysis. It introduces a long established, but not widely used, notation, N^2 charts, which provide an equivalent tabular encoding for many software engineering notations. This style of presentation is used, together with talking touch tablet, to provide an interactive means for blind software engineers to access full system models.

1 Introduction

Many blind people work in the computer industry; the programming of computers is very largely text based and there are many well established methods for blind people to interact with text-based computer applications. However, there is very much more to developing a piece of software than simply writing the computer program. Software programs can be extremely complex and they are often used in safety-critical applications, for example in the control of aeroplanes, where failure in the software part of the system can have catastrophic effects. To control the complexity of the software program and to fully analyse its function, software-based systems are subjected to rigorous development methods. Such methods are termed Software Engineering methods.

When complex software systems were first developed, development methods consisted of a set of stages that resulted in a set of largely text-based documents. However, the problem with such methods is that natural language is a rather imprecise way of specifying definite concepts and that for complex systems these documents grow to considerable size, thus maintaining internal consistency in such documents is a formidable task. In the 1970s Software Engineering methods developed, initially for complex information systems, which specified the requirements and design of the system in, chiefly, graphical forms. The most significant method to be developed (in terms its of usage within the software industry) is Structured Analysis. This is used to capture system requirements and carry out high level system design. Structured Analysis methods are widely used in a number forms, e.g. Yourdon [9], Hatley-Pirbhai [3] and Ward-Mellor [8]. These methods are broadly similar, and use notations to represent the developing system, which are almost identical. Over the past few years a set of similar methods, the Object-Oriented Software Engineering methods, have been developed (e.g. [2, 4, 7]); these share common goals with the Structured Analysis methods and the graphical notations to capture a system's requirements and to specify its design have strong similarities.

These methods are supported by a variety of computer-based tools (Computer Aided Software Engineering (CASE) Tools) supplied by a wide variety of vendors. These tools support the capture of the graphical models and carry out consistency checks to ensure that model is consistent with the set of rules specified by the development method.

The adoption of Software Engineering methods and the use of CASE tools presents a difficult problem for blind software engineers. The system analysis and design information is encoded in a two-dimensional graphical form making it extremely difficult for blind engineers to use standard methods of computer interaction. Moreover, as the next section describes, the information is presented in a hierarchical structure, the traversal of which is controlled by mouse-based 'point and click' techniques. In this paper we propose a method by which blind software engineers may access the information held in the graphical notations used in software engineering and show how this information is encoded. The proposed technique is currently under evaluation by the Technology for Disabled People Unit.

2   Software Engineering Notations

Initially we have chosen to restrict our work to the analysis phase of one of the Structured Analysis methods. The method chosen is the widely used Hatley-Pirbhai Real Time Structured Analysis method [3]. This method is used to analyse the requirements of the software and to carry out the high level design of the system. This particular method is chosen as it is popular and is supported by a number of CASE tools. The notation it uses is very similar to that of the other Structured Analysis methods and the technique presented in this paper is appropriate to the others. It is thought that object-oriented methods may also be handled by this technique, however they are somewhat different in detail to those described below.

The Hatley-Pirbhai Real Time Structured Analysis method is supported by a graphical notation, known as data flow diagrams (DFDs), which are used to describe the behaviour and the design of the system under development. A DFD presents a view of part of the system by dividing it into a number of processes that communicate with one another through data flows. A typical data flow diagram is shown in Fig. 1.

The circles (or "bubbles") on this diagram are processes; these take input data, process it and create output data. Data is routed from process to process through the directed arcs (the lines with arrows); these are named to describe the data that flows between the processes. The vertical bar is used to indicate a control specification associated with the DFD. Control information is routed into the control specification through a set of directed arcs, which are represented by broken lines. These carry control information; i.e. they transmit, to other processes, the current state of the processes in the system. Control specifications are used to control the system by generating new control flows and by enabling and disabling the processes on the DFD, i.e. turning them off and on. Data stores are represented by parallel lines and have a name associated with them. These store persistent data in the system and are written to, and read from, by processes through unnamed data flows. Flows (both control and data) that do not have both ends connected to processes are connected at the immediately higher level in the hierarchy of DFDs.

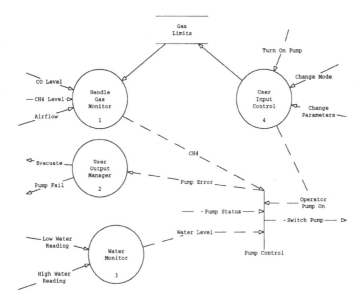

Fig. 1. A Typical Hatley-Pirbhai Data Flow Diagram

DFDs are connected into a hierarchy to form a complete model that represents the behaviour and design of the system. The hierarchical connections are formed by process refinement. Each process represented in a DFD at one level of the hierarchy can have its behaviour described by another DFD in the next layer of the hierarchy. At the top of this hierarchy there is a DFD with single process on it, which is connected by data flows to externals. These are elements at the boundary of the system, which provide input stimuli and accept output responses. This is called the context diagram because it sets the context for the system under development by describing the interface between it and the outside world. The decomposition of a system from context diagram is shown in Fig. 2. Processes are decomposed in this way until they are identified as being primitive, i.e. they are deemed simple enough not to warrant further decomposition. Their behaviour is described by a text specification, called a process specification, written in a language similar to a standard programming language. The control specifications are not decomposed in the same way as the processes but have their behaviour described in a table or as a state transition diagram. Control specifications can be handled by the techniques proposed in this paper, however, due to space limitations these are not discussed further here. All data and control flows are described by text entries in a list called the Data Dictionary.

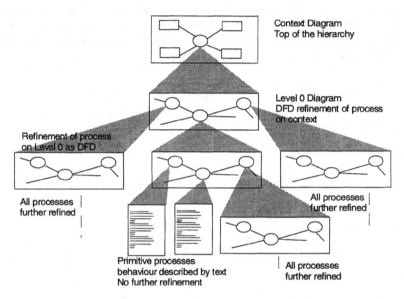

Fig. 2. The Hierarchical Structure of a Structured Analysis Model

When using a CASE tool, a sighted software engineer accesses the model of the system by moving up and down through the hierarchy. This is generally supported by the CASE tool in an interactive way, typically pointing to the process using a mouse pointer and clicking the mouse button will show the internal decomposition of the process, either as a DFD, or if primitive as a text specification. Data dictionary information is also accessed through this point and click mechanism.

Allowing blind software engineers to interact with captured Structured Analysis models requires: that the text be converted into a suitable media (here we use speech); and that the DFDs are redrawn, so that the notation *elements*[1] (i.e. processes, stores and control specifications) and *flows*[2] can be easily located and their associated text delivered. The notation used in the method proposed here is based upon N^2 charts, which are described below.

---

[1] In this paper the term *elements* is used to refer, collectively, to processes, stores and control specifications.

[2] *Flows* is used here to refer collectively to data flows, control flows and the connections to data stores.

3 N^2 Charts

There is an equivalent tabular form of any DFD; this is called an N^2 chart [5, 6]. These are not widely used in the software engineering industry, which generally favours more graphically based notations. The N^2 chart is a matrix with the *element* names running down the major diagonal. *Flows* between two *elements* are shown in the rectangles where the row and column of the connected *elements* intersect. Entries in the same row as an *element* are the outgoing flows from that *element*; entries in the same column are incoming data flows into the *element*. *Flows* that are connected at a higher level are placed on the N^2 chart to connect with a special *element* entry called the 'Upper Level'. The N^2 chart equivalent of Fig. 1 is presented in Fig. 3.

Upper Level	CO Level CH4 Level Airflow		Low Water Reading High Water Reading	Turn On Pump Change Mode Change Param -eters	Pump Status	
	Handle Gas Monitor				CH4	
Evacuate Pump Fail		User Input Manager				
			Water Monitor		Water Level	
				User Input Control	Operator Pump On	Writes to Gas Limits
Switch Pump		Pump Error			Pump Control	
	Reads from Gas Limits					Gas Limits

Fig. 3. N^2 chart equivalent of Fig. 1.

N^2 charts form the basis of the proposed method of access. Using a generic form of these charts and a talking touch window an evaluation system has been developed that allows a blind engineer to navigate through the full hierarchy of a Structured Analysis model.

4 The Evaluation System

The evaluation system is shown in Fig. 4. It consists of a UNIX workstation, which runs the Teamwork CASE tool and some custom software. A Touch Window and a speech synthesiser are connected to the workstation by serial lines. The user interacts with the system and interrogates the model by using the Touch Window. Most user actions cause the custom software to interrogate the database of the CASE tool by using a set of procedures provided in the Teamwork/ACCESS package [11]. In response to a user action, speech is generated that describes the selected portion of the model.

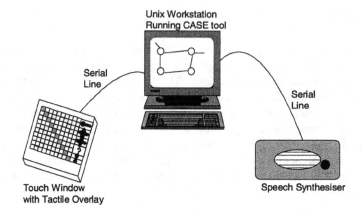

Fig. 4. The Architecture of the Evaluation System

The touch window is overlaid with a tactile diagram [10] that has the layout of a generic N^2 chart and a number of control areas to allow the user to move through the hierarchy. Thus, a blind engineer can locate significant areas on the chart by tactile means, select an area on the chart and have the associated text spoken to him/her. This is a particular instance of using "Talking Tactile Maps", which are described in [1]. The overlay is shown in Fig. 5.

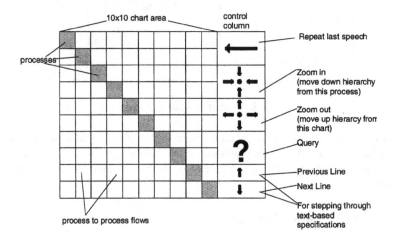

Fig. 5. Tactile Overlay for the Touch Window

The tactile overlay is divided into two parts; a generic 10x10 N^2 chart, which takes up most of the area, and a control column, which has a number of fields used by the engineer to control access to the information.

The N^2 chart encodes a DFD with the *elements* situated on the main diagonal of the matrix. To enable the engineer to find these elements these boxes are textured and are shown as being shaded in Fig.5. Depressing one of these boxes will cause the system to speak the name of the element. For example, *"Process name is: Handle Gas Monitor."*. The other boxes represent the connection, via *flows*, of the *elements*. These boxes are not textured but the dividing areas between the boxes are raised. Depressing one of these boxes will cause the name of any connecting *flows* to be spoken; for example *"Flow name is: Water Level."*.

The control column has six fields. The first field (top right) has a horizontal arrow imprinted on it; depressing this field will cause the last text string to be repeated. This is a typical feature of talking tactile maps.

The second field is used to move down the hierarchy. Depressing an *element* square and then this field will cause the system to move to the refinement of that *element*. If the *element* is a process, this will cause either a new DFD to be accessible by using the N^2 chart or give access to the text based process specification. When entering an *element* refinement, the system speaks the name of the refined *element*, indicates the its type, and gives parameters (such as number of elements on a DFD or number of lines in a process specification). The second field is also used in conjunction with the *flow* boxes to give access to the data dictionary entry for each connected *flow*.

The third field is used to move up the hierarchy. Depressing this field will cause the current N^2 chart to be replaced by its parent and the name, type and parameters of the upper level diagram to be indicated.

The query field, indicated by a question mark, is used by the engineer to obtain information about the connections to any given *element*. Depressing this field and then an *element* square will cause the system to list all flows into and out of the *element*. This facility saves the user from having to search in every field in the matrix to determine the connectivity of an *element* and the topology of the whole diagram.

The last two fields, indicated by an up arrow and a down arrow, are used when reading textual specifications. Depressing these fields causes the next or previous line of a text specification to be read. This is used when accessing process specifications and data dictionary entries.

A 10 x 10 N^2 chart imposes a limitation on the complexity of DFDs that can be accessed by the user. This limits the total number of processes, data stores and control specifications on a DFD to 9 (the tenth entry is used for specifying interconnections with the higher level diagram). In many cases this limit of 9 is perfectly acceptable; many software engineering texts suggest that the number of processes on a diagram should not exceed 7 for it to be readable. However, in practical situations this limit of 9 will often be exceeded. When the 10 entries on the N^2 chart are exceeded, the system supports enquires about the other processes, stores and control specifications via the keyboard. If the number of additional elements is not too great, it is hoped that the chart will still be readable. The number of entries in a given N^2 chart is governed by the resolution of the Touch Window and the size of the user's finger. Larger N^2 matrices could be used if the user were to accept smaller matrix entries.

5   Conclusions and Further Work

A practical evaluation system has been developed and this will be tested by a number of blind software engineers.

Further work involves the somewhat more difficult problem of allowing blind software engineers to create Structured Analysis models.   Firstly these will be supported by the engineer creating a series of N^2 charts using the Touch Window, tactile overlay and the keyboard.   This will create a representation wholly in N^2 charts.   As noted above, these are not commonly used in the software engineering industry and a method of creating standard, CASE tool readable DFDs, which sighted users can read, will be investigated.

Acknowledgements

The authors would like to acknowledge the work of Andrew Brook who has developed the prototype evaluation system as part of his undergraduate degree in Software Engineering from the Department of Computation at UMIST.   He has contributed greatly to the ideas contained in this paper.

This project has been carried out within the Technology for Disabled People Unit at UMIST. The authors would like to acknowledge the grant funding for this unit by both The Guide Dogs for the Blind Association and the UMIST Millennium Fund.

References

1.   P. Blenkhorn, D.G. Evans: A System for Reading and Producing Talking Tactile Maps and Diagrams. Ninth Annual International Conference, Technology and Persons with Disabilities, Los Angeles, March (1994)

2.   G. Booch: Object-Oriented Analysis and Design With Applications. Benjamin/Cummings (1994)

3.   D.J. Hatley, I.A. Pirbhai: Strategies for Real-Time System Specification. Dorset House Publishing (1987)

4.   I. Jacobson: Object-Oriented Software Engineering. ACM Press (1992)

5.   R. Lano: A Technique for Software and Systems Design. North-Holland Press (1979)

6.   P. Loy, Y. Strapp: DFD's [sic] vs. N^2 charts. ACM Sigsoft Software Engineering Notes, 18, A16-A17 (1989)

7.   J. Rumbaugh et. al.: Object-Oriented Modelling and Design. Prentice-Hall (1991)

8.   P.T. Ward, S.J. Mellor: Structured Development for Real-Time Systems. 1, 2, 3, Yourdon Press (1985)

9.   E. Yourdon: Modern Structured Analysis. Prentice-Hall (1989)

10.   Tactual Graphics: Research and Resources. Aids and Appliances Review, The Carroll Center for the Blind, 14 (1984)

11.   Teamwork/ACCESS User Manual, Hewlett Packard (1989)

Automatic image processing in developmental testing of visual-motor integration

M.C.Fairhurst, N.Higson, C.Clar

Electronic Engineering Laboratories, University of Kent,
Canterbury, Kent CT2 7NT, U.K.

R.Bradford, W.Clark, E.Pringle

Mary Sheridan Centre, Kent and Canterbury Hospitals NHS Trust,
43, New Dover Road, Canterbury, Kent CT1 3AT, U.K.

Abstract. Figure copying and related tasks are commonly used in the evaluation of perceptual and motor-perceptual functioning, yet there are many potential difficulties associated with the administration of such tests and their objective assessment. This paper describes a study, based on the Beery Developmental Test of Visual-Motor Integration, which investigates the use of automatic image analysis techniques to implement and evaluate figure copying tasks, and which can afford the opportunity for the extraction of further characteristics of drawing execution which are of potential significance in assessing performance.

1. Background

The evaluation of neurological functioning is important in the monitoring and assessment of a variety of clinical conditions, and a range of cognitive and perceptual tests have been developed over the years in order to achieve this [1,2,3,4,5]. The assessment of perceptual and motor-perceptual ability in children with learning difficulties has in recent years been accorded a higher priority than hitherto with the increasing awareness of the problem of dyspraxia, the incidence rate of which is estimated to be of the order of 6-7%, and may be greater [6].

Although many forms of testing may be considered in investigating perceptual-motor functioning, the difficulties in applying many traditional testing procedures generally relate to the severe demands they place on available resources, both in terms of the time taken for their administration and/or the requirement for specially trained clinical staff, the stress often induced in the patient by the procedures involved, and the unsuitability of the tests for regular or repeated performance. Even more importantly, the evaluation of test results can often be very subjective and inherently unreliable. Figure copying and related tasks in particular, however, suggest an approach to the evaluation of perceptual and motor-perceptual ability which is potentially very suitable for computer-assisted implementation and which might be able to provide interpretation on a widely accepted basis [7].

This paper will describe an approach to perceptual testing which utilises image analysis techniques to provide the framework for the implementation of a computer-based testing and evaluation system suitable for routine clinical use. The results of some initial experimentation with a prototype system are described and discussed.

2. Developmental testing

A widely used test adopted for developmental assessment of children is the Beery Developmental Test of Visual-Motor Integration [8]. This test has been designed to assess the developmental maturity of 5 to 11 year old children in relation to their visual, fine-motor and visual-motor development.

The test consists of 24 geometric shapes of increasing complexity, starting with single lines and simple shapes such as the circle, square and triangle, and proceeding to more complex combinations of shapes and three-dimensional representations of shapes. The shapes are displayed on the top half of a sheet of paper (three shapes to a page) and have to be copied by the child in boxes underneath the target shapes. The copying task requires the child to combine his/her ability accurately to perceive a given form with the ability accurately to reproduce it, and hence is an indicator of visual-motor integration. However, it also allows the identification of children with pure perceptual or pure fine-motor difficulties - a child drawing confidently but inaccurately may be suspected to have principally perceptual problems, whereas a child obviously struggling with the execution of the drawing but giving other evidence of correctly perceiving the shape will be suspected to have mainly fine-motor difficulties.

The shapes comprising the test were originally chosen on the basis of large studies of children's copying behaviour, and a review of their ability in drawing and copying as determined through studies of the literature. These studies were also the origin of the establishment of age-equivalents for each score, giving an indication of which shapes a child should be able correctly to reproduce at a given age.

The individual shapes are scored according to strictly defined criteria in an all-or-nothing manner (i.e. no partial marks are given). The scoring is graded according to difficulty (i.e. score 1 or 0 for the easiest shapes, up to 4 or 0 for the most difficult), and a composite score is calculated at the end and converted to an age-equivalent score.

Although a widely used and well established standard test, the Beery test is nevertheless vulnerable to many of the difficulties outlined above. In particular, questions concerning the issue of objectivity in scoring (allowing for inconsistencies in the interpretation of the scoring rules) and the problems of administering and scoring the test, detract from its overall effectiveness as an evaluative tool.

For these reasons, work is in progress to investigate the use of automated evaluation of testing procedures such as that instantiated by the Beery test. The aim is to use computer-based acquisition and analysis of the test data and the subsequent automated scoring of the test results. In this way, the power of computer-based processing can be exploited to remove many of the difficulties encountered with this type of testing and, as will be seen, can also potentially enhance the effectiveness and diagnostic capabilities of the testing procedure.

3. The testing environment

The task domain requires a subject to generate line drawings (by copying target shapes) which are subsequently to be analysed according to pre-defined scoring rules. In order to enable computer-based acquisition of the drawing the target shape is copied by the subject on a graphics tablet which is interfaced to a microcomputer. This allows the acquisition of the drawing data as a stream of coordinate mappings, and the analysis of this data, in real time. The general system infrastructure is illustrated in Figure 1.

Figure 1

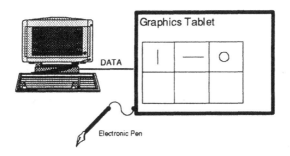

Figure 1

A principal advantage of this data acquisition environment is that, although complete data capture can be readily achieved, there is no interference from the subject's viewpoint with the normal procedure involved with standard pencil-and-paper execution of the test. The system uses an electronic pen which can also generate hard copy in the traditional way. The pen may be an integral wired-in device or, depending on the choice of tablet, can be wire-free, and the task execution is thereby achieved in an entirely familiar fashion.

4. Preliminary results

Initial trials have been carried out to establish the viability of the approach proposed. The complexity of the geometric shapes to be analysed varies considerably, becoming progressively more complex as the test proceeds. Figure 2 shows the first and last shapes in the sequence to illustrate this point.

Figure 2

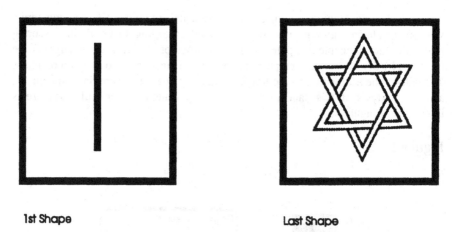

1st Shape   Last Shape

Appropriate image processing algorithms have been designed to analyse the drawings produced and recorded during computer-based administration of the test. For some shapes these require the direct extraction of relevant features from the images produced, while for the more complex shapes more extensive knowledge-driven procedures for interpretation of the defined scoring rules are required.

A test was carried out in which 15 children (aged between 5 and 12 years, and referred to an assessment centre dealing with learning and coordination difficulties) were tested with the system, their drawing data being acquired on-line while hard copies of the test output were simultaneously obtained. The test output was then scored both by the occupational therapist administering the test (from the hard copy output) and by means of the computer-based automated implementation of the scoring rules (from the tablet data).

Figure 3 shows the results obtained in initial testing. It can be seen that the majority of target shapes show a complete convergence between automated scoring and the human expert scorer. The discrepancies observed in some instances are due largely to the current lack of sufficient data to allow adequate implementation of the scoring rules (this is the case, for example, with shape 23), while in other cases the variability of the data obtained leads to atypical or unpredictable patterns, a situation which requires refinement of the scoring algorithms to increase their robustness. Current work is seeking to refine and enhance the algorithms to improve their sensitivity, power and reliability in dealing with such problem cases.

Figure 3

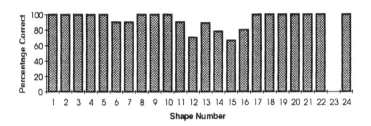

5. Further refinement of computer-based testing

Although a principal aim of the work reported here is to increase efficiency and objectivity of testing through the automation of evaluative procedures, a further potentially highly significant benefit arising from the exploitation of the automated testing environment described here should be noted. In its present (pencil-and-paper) form the test focuses on the extraction of information from each test sample only of static features of the test drawing, features related to the finished drawing and observable solely from the overall visual appearance and broad characteristics of the child's output. Related research reported in recent years [9] strongly suggests that further very important information about performance is likely to be found in the dynamic features of the output, features which characterise specifically the actual physical execution of the drawing. In particular, the dynamic information gathered may allow a more detailed analysis of the mechanisms of a given child's impairment. Although this is the subject of continuing research, it is valuable to indicate an example of how such additional information might be considered.

Since the computer-based data acquisition environment allows the on-line monitoring of task execution, information about dynamic characteristics such as pen velocity can be readily measured. In order to demonstrate the potential value of such measurements, Figure 4 illustrates the use of pen velocity profiles, showing the mean score obtained by the five fastest drawers, the five slowest drawers, and the five drawers exhibiting intermediate velocity profiles in the tests described above. Although no formal analysis has been carried out here, it is nevertheless possible to hypothesise that very low pen velocities correlate with difficulties in drawing execution and that very high pen velocities are indicative of difficulties in coordination or carelessness (thereby generating lower age-equivalent scores), while an appropriately balanced velocity profile correlates with higher levels of achievement.

Figure 4

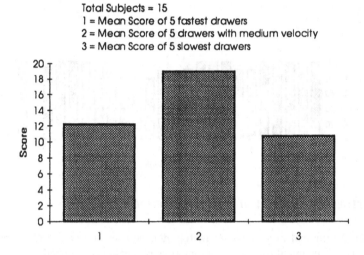

Total Subjects = 15
1 = Mean Score of 5 fastest drawers
2 = Mean Score of 5 drawers with medium velocity
3 = Mean Score of 5 slowest drawers

There are clearly also many other such dynamic factors which may prove to be relevant and important, particularly those concerned with constructional strategy (stroke sequencing, directionality, and so on) or other behavioural characteristics. Issues such as this clearly require more thorough investigation, but do appear to point to the potential value of the principle of extracting hitherto unobservable performance characteristics such as those related to dynamic execution.

6. Conclusion

This paper has described a new approach to the administration of standard testing procedures for the evaluation of perceptual and motor-perceptual functioning. The testing procedures proposed exploit computer-based image processing techniques to improve objectivity and efficiency in the testing process while, as an added advantage, offering the possibility of allowing the extraction of additional dynamic characteristics of performance which might provide further important diagnostic information.

Although only a preliminary study is reported here, the results presented are most encouraging, justifying the further work which is presently in progress.

7. References

[1] Anastasi,A.: Psychological Testing, Macmillan, New York, 1968

[2] Ackrill,P., Barron,J. et al: A new approach to the early detection of dialysis encephalopathy", Proc. EDTA, 16, 659-660, 1979

[3] Miller, E.: Abnormal Ageing, John Wiley and Sons, London, 1977

[4] Pearce,J. and Miller,E.: Clinical Aspects of Dementia, Bailliere Tindall, London, 1973

[5] De Renzi,E.: Disorders of Space Exploration and Cognition, John Wiley and Sons, New York, 1982

[6] Brenner et al: British Medical Journal, (iv), 259-262, 1967

[7] Ilg and Ames: Child Behaviour, Harper, New York, 1955

[8] Beery,K.E.: The VMI-Developmental Test of Visual-Motor Integration Administration, Scoring and Teaching Manual, 3rd Revision, Cleveland: Modern Curriculum Press, 1989

[9] Fairhurst,M.C., Smith,S.L. and Potter,J.: Computer-assisted analysis of visuo-spatial neglect in stroke patients, Proc. 3rd Int. ICCHP Conf., 157-165, Vienna, July 1992

Computer Neuropsychological Training in Mentally Retarded Children

Enrico Castelli, Geraldina Poggi, Cristina Ferraroli, Vittoria Trebeschi

Scientific Institute Eugenio Medea
Bosisio Parini, Como , Italy

Abstract. Informatic tecnology can be the right answer to deal with some neuropsychological troubles of children. The goal of this study is the application of computer programs as a possible strategy in rehabilitation of children with cognitive problems. Four programs were selected to stimulate various basic brain functions: problem solving, categorization, logical sequence and spatial thought. The programs were tested on a group of 20 mentally retarded young subjects matched with a comparison group of 20 like subjects trained with ordinary techniques. The computer trained group showed a significant improvement in tests involving attention, motivation for learning and problem solving abilities. These results, in our opinion, would confirm the usefulness of specific software as a rehabilitative method in dealing with cognitive problems of children.

1 Introduction

In the last years personal computer has been used as a major tool for the traitment of many kinds of disabilities, including the cognitive disorders (1, 3, 6, 8, 9)..
The aim is, in the latter case, at stimulating the residual abilities of the disabled subjetcs in order to exploit such competencies at the best or (if the patients are children) at furthering their development (1, 2, 6).
Even though the literature on this topic is quite rich, the researches specifically directed to the problem of mentally retarded children are very few: surprisingly, because the mentally retarded possibly could take great advantages from this kind of rehabilitation.
As our Institute is dealing, for many decades, with the problems of mental retardation and learning disabilities,we are researching even in this field: a recent study, still in advancing, is summarized as follows.

2 Rationale

Some different programs (software) have been selected in order to stimulate specific intellectual functions as sequencing, selecting among multiple choices,classifying and performing spatial tasks (1, 2, 4, 5, 7).

The real goal is the increasing of the child's abilities in using particular information-processing strategies through a number of facilities which enable him or her to perform a task.

The hypothesis was that a goal-oriented training would allow these subjects to reach higher performances,if compared with those of a control-group treated with the traditional, not computerized, rehabilitative techniques.

It is worth noting that we emphasize rather the concept of strategy than the issue of the neuropsychological competency. We will see that even motivation has its own weight.

3 Materials and Methods

Four programs were selected suited to a MS-DOS based personal computer; this choice was justified by the low cost of this machine and its large diffusion.

The first program, Sequence, requests the correct rearrangement of a succession of images. It displays four pictures, each representing one step of a logical sequence, in a random order. The child has to arrange the sequence, pointing to each picture in the right order. The program gives feedback by playing an animation that confirms the passage leading from one step to the next.

The second program, Matrix, requests logical selection from a group of objects. It displays in the left side of the screen an object and in the right side a set of pictures. The child has to choose the picture among those displayed in the set that logically matches the right image. Acoustic and visual feedback are given.

The third program, Claxi, stimulates the children's ability to classify plane figures following different criteria.It displays in the left top corner of the screen fifteen figures, with a maximum of three different colours, shapes and sizes. In the half bottom corner of the screen there are three empty boxes.The child has to draw one figure at a time in one of the three boxes, according to a given classification criterion. Feedback is given following the criterion which has been used by the child himself, not to discourage him.

The fourth program, Views, stimulates spatial thought, requiring the correct matching between two different points of view: downwards and forward. It is actually based on a well known Piaget's test. It display the surface of an island on whose coasts are various landmarks (e.g. some trees, a train, a city etc.). A sailboat appears in the sea surrounding the island. The frontal view of each landmark appearing on the island (as it can be seen from the current sailboat position) is displayed inside a bottom-screen frame. The program can either change the frame of the content, asking the child to move the sailboat where such a view is possible, and the content itself that represents the view from the boat. Visual feedback is given.

These programs were tested on 40 selected children, ranging in age from 6 to 14 years (10y.7m. $\pm$ 2y.10m.), suffering from learning disabilities as a consequence of inferential and logical impairment (depending on a condition of mental retardation), free from sensory disorders or severe emotional problems. We selected only children with Total Intelligence Quotient (TIQ) at the Wechsler Scale (WISC-R) ranging from 50 to 80.

All the subjects underwent psychometric tests in order to assess attention level, learning motivation and problem solving abilities. We used also ordinal scales: Raven's Standard/Coloured Progressive Matrices (PM) test - for the assessment of inferential and logical abilities - was administered.

The 40 children were then randomly divided into two groups of 20 subjects, matching for age and TIQ. The subjects belonging to the first group attended 50 training session, 45 minutes each, twice a week, using the selected programs; the subjects of the second group attended 50 training session, 45 minutes each, twice a week, using ordinary techniques (handy training equipment). At the end of the period all the subiects were re-tested with the same battery of tests.

4 Results

The psychometric tests undertaken by the children before and after rehabilitation showed a statistically significant increase (sign - test, $p < 0.05$) of the attention level at the end of the training in the computer trained group (6 positive differences, 14 ties) compared with the not significant increase in the control group (2positive difference, 18 ties) (fig. 1). In a similar way, motivation for learning significantly increased ($p < 0.05$) in the computer treated group (8 positive difference, 12 ties) and did not significantly change in the control group (1 positive difference) (fig. 2). Problem solving abilities increased in both of the groups , but the difference was statistically significant ($p < 0.05$) only in the computer treated group (7 positive difference, 13 ties vs 3 positive difference, 17 ties in the control group) (fig. 3).

Results in the PM test did not show any statistically significant change in the computer trained group (85.6 ± 15.6) before rehabilitation (b.r.); 87.9 ± 15.6 and after rehabilitation (a.r) .

The change in the control group was larger (82.8 ± 30.2 b.r; 89.3 ± 3.3 a.r) even though a statistically not significant. A t-test comparison between the PM scores of the computer trained group and of the control group before and after rehabilitation was not significant.

5 Discussion

From the outcomes of our study, it seems that the use of specific softwares in training retarded children is more effective if compared with that based on the traditional ordinary techniques.

Undoubtedly the weight of motivation must be considered: working with the computer may be playful and fun and possibly promotes the children's interest.

Yet the improvement of attention and problem-solving capacities has been proved: it is quite unlikely to consider such an improvement the mere effect of a higher interest.

Possibly interacting and working with the PC compels the retarded child to deal with algorythms, to build mental representations, to process analysis/synthesis tasks and consequently to become more proficient in using strategies that the PC can facilitate.

So the better performances by the computer-trained subjects in the problem-solving tests can be easily (but not completely) explained.
Indeed extensive work still has to be done both in order to understand the actual processes underlying the outcomes and to create a wider range of programs.
We also believe that it is necessary to find new procedures enabling the children to train themselves, actually using the PC as an inanimate but powerful therapist.

6 References

1) Castellan .N.J.(1993) Evaluating information technology in teaching and learning *Behavior Research Methods, Instruments & Computers* 44, 6

2) Castelli. E. , Piccinelli P. , Borgatti R. , Reni G. , Moretti M. ,(1991) Facilitazioni informatiche per lo sviluppo di competenze neuropsicologiche nel grave disabile motorio. *Saggi* Anno XVII, 1 ,31-36

3) Corradini E. ,Tressoldi PE . ,Pellegrini A. , Ciot C. , (1993) L'analisi del software educativo finalizzata ad una programmazione riabilitativa mirata. *Edizioni La Nostra Famiglia*

4) Fedrizzi E. , DalBrun A. , Rivala A. , Schiaffino A. , Fronticelli G. Castelli E. , Belloni G .(1993)Indicazioni e limiti all'uso del personal computer per il grave tetraplegico in età scolare. *Giornale di Neuropsichiatria dell'età evolutiva.* 13, 2, 129-140

5) Ferlazzo F. , Conte S. , Gentilomo A. , (1993) Event - Related Potentials and recognition memory : the effect of word imagery value . *International Journal of Psychophysiology* 15 , 115-122 .

6) Merteus D. M. , et al (1992) Combining Cognitive learning theory and computer assisted instruction deaf learners . *American Annals of the Deaf.* 137, 399 - 403

7) Ross.F. L. (1992) The use of Computers in Occupational Therapy for Visual - Scanning training . *American Journal of Occupational Therapy* 46, 314 -322

8) Skinner A .D. , Trachtman L.H.(1985) Use of a computer program in cognitive rehabilitation . *American Journal of Occupational Therapy.*, 39 ,7, 470-472.

9) Weiss.P.(1990) The integration of Computers into the occupational Therapy Department . *American Journal of Occupational Therapy* . 44, 6, 527-534.

FIGURE 1

ATTENTION LEVEL
(difference after-before rehabilitation)

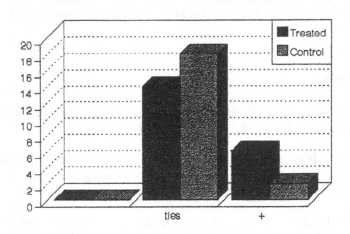

FIGURE 2

MOTIVATION FOR LEARNING
(difference after-before rehabilitation)

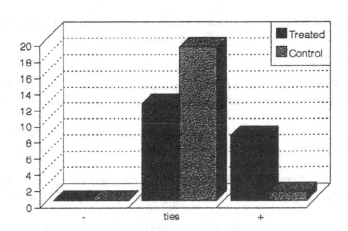

FIGURE 3

PROBLEM SOLVING ABILITIES
(difference after-before rehabilitation)

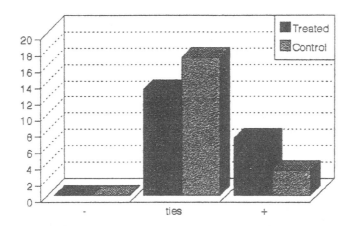

Computer Training in Cognitive Remediation of the Traumatic Head Injured

Dr. Jack Rattok, Executive Director

Transitions of long Island
LIJ Medical center
Manhasset, NY 11030

Traumatic head injury is distinct from other forms of disability in that the impact is direct and multiple upon the physical, emotional, and cognitive functioning of the disabled person. While therapies dealing with the physical and emotional aspects of the disability have been in existence for a relatively long period of time, cognitive remediation has not been available for victims of head trauma, and has remained mainly within the province of special educators working with the neurologically impaired child.

Research in cognitive remediation with stroke patients was begun at Rusk Institute, NYU Medical Center in the early 1970's and expanded into cognitive remediation with the traumatically head injured in the early 1980's. (Rattok, J., Ben-Yishay, Y., Thomas,J. L., Ross,B. 1981). Diller and Gordon (1981) in a summary article describing issues in cognitive remediation with neurologically impaired adults, indicate that there has been relatively little work done in the area.

Until 1984, the majority of cognitive training was done using paper and pencil tasks, and simple educational tools such as cubes and cards, which derived from special education techniques. Some researchers recognized the potential inherent in using computers for cognitive remediation, but they were expensive, used mainly for research in the area, and not in common use as training tools. In 1984, when the less expensive personal computers appeared on the market, training became computerized and is currently a common tool for cognitive remediation in rehabilitation facilities.

Computerized training has many technical advantages over the remedial tools which preceded. A variety of input devices: keyboard, joy stick, mouth, trackball, etc. can be selected to suit the needs of a disabled person. Visual devices (monitors) can be color or monochrome and appear in different sizes and shapes, enabling flexible adaptation to a patients visual needs. The computer is accurate, consistent, and stores a large amount of information in small space. Since it is a new and popular tool, it appeals to patients as an instrument of remediation.

Since cognitive training is not the purview of any single professional discipline, a variety of therapists have adapted these computerized tools to their use. While the physical and emotional aspects of head trauma are attended to by specific areas of medicine and psychology, cognitive remediation services that employ computer software are rendered by neuropsychologists, speech therapists, occupational therapists, special educators. Our survey showed that cognitive rehabilitation services are generally provided by: speech therapists (40%); occupational therapists (30%); neuropsychologists (10%); cognitive technicians (20%). Cognitive technicians represent a newer form of service. They are individuals trained in the implementation of specific exercises (mainly through use of the computer) and their work is a technical follow-up and reinforcement of the domains dealt with by the other disciplines cited. However, there remains question as to whether the currently used computer software proves effective in remediating the cognitive-intellectual malfunctions experienced by traumatically head injured patients.

The software that is currently available covers four major domains of cognitive remediation: (1) eye-hand coordination; (2) basic attention; (3) basic academic skills; (4) problem solving.

Computerized eye-hand coordination tasks are games such as "Pac-Man" and "Space Invaders." Basic attention tasks are generally made up of packaged software developed out of cognitive psychology (Ben-Yishay, Piasetsky, and Rattok, J. 1987. Basic academic skills training consists mainly of software developed for schools by special educators and the majority contain drill exercises in reading comprehension and arithmetic. Problem solving techniques are usually based on material designed to advance the problem solving capability of school age children. In sum, currently available software is geared mainly toward augmenting basic cognitive skills.

Most publications available concerning software for cognitive remediation consist of non-critical lists of the software available and their sources (Kreutzer, Hill, and Morrison, 1987). Some publications review software and give the reviewer's impressions, but have no base in research (Lynch, 1985.) Others dissect software technically and provide a thorough description of the software, but have no theoretical orientation and do not present outcome measures. A few papers dealing with training outcomes have been published, (Kerner, and Acker,1985). These papers are not comprehensive nor numerous enough to allow any conclusions about the efficacy of computer software for cognitive retraining.

In recent years more and more publications start to appear, researching and organizing the various elements that are necessary to produce comprehensive products to remediate various aspects of cognitive deficits (Rattok 1992, Rattok and Ross 1992, Kaufman and Rattok 1992).

As personal computers became widely available in the mid-1980's, it became evident that they could serve to replace these costly and commercially unavailable electronic devices, and had important applicability as a more accurate and efficient tool to replace the use of paper and pencil tasks. Objections that "the computer will replace the clinician" in the decision-making process were soon dispelled. Professionals began to use computers and came to understand them as an elaborate tool, rather than an intellectual entity.

Recent findings indicate that for some psychological testing the patient tends to be more honest and provides the right information to the computer screen then to the clinician. (Fillon, 1990)

The main advantage of computerized psychological testing with the Head Injured involved the Visual perceptual difficulties experienced by this disabled population. Most common inventories (MMPI, SCL, CPI) usually cram hundreds of questions onto a few pages and employ computerized answer sheets that confuse and overload patients with visual and perceptual demands. In order to maximally control for perceptual malfunctions we computerized the tests so that each question appears clearly by itself on the screen together with the answer choices. The computer automatically records both the answer and the time that it takes to answer each question. This arrangement yields the ability to score performance more accurately than the usual pen and pencil administration.

Example (Rattok, & Ross, 1993): The PENN Inventory for Post Traumatic Stress Disorder (PTSD) was administered to Head Injured subjects. It consists of 26 sets of statements. In each set, the subject must choose the statement that best describes his situation. In order to maximally control for perceptual malfunction we computerized the tests so that each set of questions appears clearly by itself on the screen. The computer automatically records both the answer and the time that it takes to answer each question. This arrangement is more suitable for the head injured with various cognitive disorders (Rattok & Ross, 1986), and also yields the ability to score performance more quickly and accurately than the usual pen and pencil administration. All subjects were tested in individual sessions in order to assess their functioning on the PENN Inventory.

The paper and pencil version displayed 10 sets of questions per page and was so confusing that most of the subjects in the experiment refused to participate.

Fig 1. Exemplified the way the questions were presented on the Computer screen.

The outcome is presented on the secern immediately (Fig. 2) and includes normative comparison to other population. Similar capacities make the actual cognitive training exercises more successful then their pencil and paper counter part.

Visual exercises that involve complex pictorial presentations can not be part of a training program without adequate software. An example for such an exercise can be seen in Fig. 3. The picture on the screen is the normal picture, the picture in Fig. 4 was scrambled and the patient has to rebuild it (the original screen is in 640 X 480 resolution 256 colors).

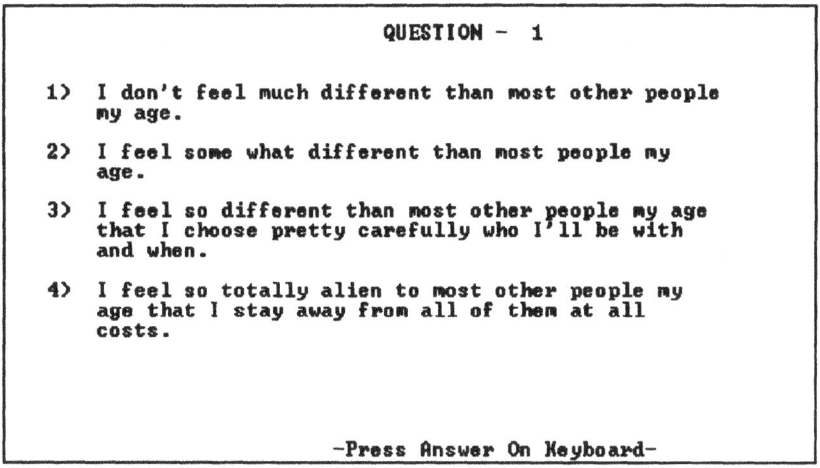

QUESTION - 1
1) I don't feel much different than most other people my age.
2) I feel some what different than most people my age.
3) I feel so different than most other people my age that I choose pretty carefully who I'll be with and when.
4) I feel so totally alien to most other people my age that I stay away from all of them at all costs.
-Press Answer On Keyboard-

Fig. 1 Item screen (PTSD)

SCORE
60
45
35
30
15
0
48.0
15.3
28.2
55.2
Client
Non
Psy
PTSD
PRESS <R> TO RETURN TO MENU <P> FOR PRINTOUT

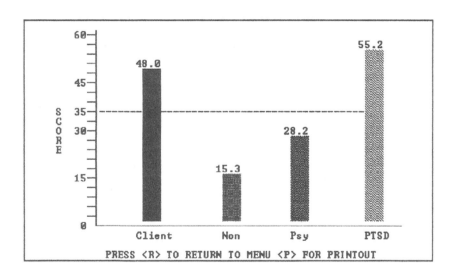

Fig. 2 Score screen (PTSD)

Fig. 3 New York skyline unscrambled

Fig. 4 New York skyline scrambled

Hardware Consideration

Numerous amounts of special hardware for the physically disabled is available, however a big part of this hardware is not useful for the head injured since in addition to the physical disability they acquire cognitive (intellectual and severe memory deficits) disability and thus can not learn how to use the sophisticated systems available for them.

In the early 1980's most software for cognitive retraining was written for the Apple II line of computers. With the reduction of cost most clinical settings moved to use IBM and IBM compatible (MS DOS) computers. At the time the Apple line moved to the Macintosh model. The majority of the software is written by professional providers that come mainly from the medical and paramedical fields (not computer specialists). Most of this software written in the late 80's into the nineties is written for the Intel Microsoft combination (MS DOS) and it is hard currently to find a choice of software for cognitive retraining operable on the Apple Macintosh line. Our discussion on hardware choice will center on the IBM and IBM compatible computer.

CPU.

The current trend in the software for cognitive retraining shows a move toward using the Windows environment for the new programs coming out. Thus choice of CPU today has to conform with adequate hardware that will support this environment. Currently it means at least 486SX processor running on 25 Mhz with 4 Mbytes of memory, 170 Mbytes hard disk drive and a SVGA capable of running 640x480 with 256 color monitor.

We would like to indicate that some providers keep a few old 8086 computers since early software was written without use of timed delays and work correctly on the old 8086 CGA computers, but run too fast on the 386 and 486 machines. Check the software that you buy and don't buy it if you do not have one of the old machines available.

Monitors.

Patients suffering from head injury usually have multiple visual problems and thus need a screen presentation that is relatively large. However, the majority of them also have visual scanning disorders (spatial neglect) and thus will omit some information presented on a big monitor. If the clinic has more than one system for cognitive retraining buy various sizes; 12", 14", 15", and 17" will be most adequate. If only one system is available the popular 14" will do.

Input Devices.

Most head injured patients experience (at least in the first year post their injury) motor control and coordination difficulties, thus the use of regular keyboards is inadequate. Special keyboards for the disabled are available to compensate for this problem. For our clinic, we found most versatile the Intelkey keyboard manufactured by Unicorn Engineering. Usage of non keyboard input devices like a mouse stylus etc, can be problematic. The input device that we found to work well is a trackball (the bigger the better) since in using a trackball it is enough to be able to coordinate two to three fingers rather then the whole hand (as is necessary with a mouse).

Audio Devices.

Speech therapist working with the head injured are using successfully microcomputer equipped with an audio board to improve communication skills of their clients. The majority of the software was written geared toward propriety, or the Covox standard. The general standard that govern the audio boards in the MSDOS market today, is the AdLib Sound Blaster standard some boards are capable of handling multiple standards. Unless a therapist is using only one specific software package, make sure that the audio board installed in the cognitive retraining system is a multi standard board.

Printers.

The printer seems to be the least problematic part of the system. We noticed that with the lack of normal eye hand control in these patients, printers using continuous feed paper are hard to handle. If you want your patient to be as independent as possible use a cut sheet feeder (most inkjet printers are capable of handling regular noncontinuous printer paper and are a good choice for cognitive retraining systems.

Multimedia Devices

The capacity of multimedia devices seems to be very promising and probably will augment the quality of cognitive training. Unfortunately current scientific literature of cognitive rehabilitation does not address this topic. Therapist who would like to experiment with multimedia systems should install MPC level 2 systems. Such system will include double speed CD-ROM, 16 bit sound card, and speakers.

References

Ben-Yishay, Y., Piasetsky, E. B., and Rattok, J. (1987). A Systematic Method for Ameliorating Disorders in Basic Attention. In Neuropsychological Rehabilitation, Meir, M. J., Diller, L., and Benton, A., L. (Eds.). Livingstone, London, p. 165-181.

Diller, L., and Gordon, W.A. (1981). Intervention for cognitive deficits in brain injured adults. Journal of consulting and clin. Psychology. 49, 822-834.

Fillon, M. Face to Face or Interface. Information Week, 281, New York, 1990.

Kaufman B., Rattok J. A Computerized Training program to Facilitate Word Retrieval. A paper presented in: Technology and Person with Disabilities. University of California, Northbridge, 1992

Kerner, M.J., and Acker, M. (1985). Copmputer Delivery of Memory retraining with Head Injured Patients. Cognitive Rehabilitation. November, 26-31.

Kreutzer, J.S., Hill, M.R., and Morrison, C. (1987). Cognitive Rehabilitation Resources for the Apple II Computer. NeuroSience Publishers, Indianapolis.

Lynch, B. (1985). Captain: Cognitive Training Series. Software review. Cognitive Rehabilitation. November, 32-34.

Rattok, J., and Ross, B. The Use of Personality Inventories with the Traumatically Head Injured. Journal of Clinical and Experimental Neuropsychology, Vol. 10, January 1987.

Rattok J. Computer assessment of three dimensional visualization. A paper presented in: Technology and Person with Disabilities. University of California, Northbridge, 1992.

Rattok J., Ross B.: A Practical Approach to Cognitive Rehabilitation. NeuroRehabilitation, An Interdisciplinary Journal, Vol. 2, No. 3, 1992.

Rattok J., Ross B. Post Traumatic Stress Disorder (PTSD) in the Traumatically Head Injured (THI). Journal of Clinical and Experimental Neuropsychology, Vol. 16, March 1993.

Rattok J., Ross B. Cognitive Rehabilitation. In: Silver, Yudofsky, & Hales (Eds.) Psychiatric Aspects of Traumatic Brain Injury. American Psychiatric Press, Washington D.C, 1994.

Computer Utilisation for Speaking Re-education

Radu V. Ciupa, Alexandra A. Ciupa, Emil Simion

Technical University of Cluj-Napoca
3400 Cluj-Napoca, Romania

Abstract. The purpose of the research was to study the problems which exists in the speech analysis domain and to work out a system through which speaking ability regained for this kind of patients was facilitated as far as speed, quality and reduction of useless staff in the educational process are concerned. The device was conceived and carried out with a double-aimed role: -a computer interface, for the analysis of the quality of uttered words and the display on a video screen of the results of comparison in graphical form proper for the usual feedback related to pronunciation correctness and, -a system of auditive feedback carried out with the same aim.

1 Introduction

The loss of speaking ability, the difficulties encountered during the speech learning of the handicapped children, mainly those having a poor hearing or with acquired deafness are a source of serious psycho-social disbalance for the patient.

The purpose of the research was to study the problems which exists in the speech analysis domain and to work out a system through which speaking ability regained for this kind of patients was facilitated as far as speed, quality and reduction of useless staff in the educational process are concerned.

The main objectives aimed during speech analysis are the following [1]: a) an efficient codification of voice signal in order to transmit or record it, b) synthesis of voice signal; there could also be synthesised vocal messages with predetermined content that have been recorded after a more or less short treatment, c) recognition of speech as an essential base (as well as the synthesis) in the development of a system of man-machine dialogue.

2 Background

In its simplest form, direct codification consists in the representation of each sample of signal or of its spectrum irrespective of all the other samples. By speech compression it may be considerably reduced the volume occupied by the spoken signal thus adapting it to the diminished perceived volume of an auditory handicapped. In the system of parameter compression, speech is submitted to an analyser in order to extract a number of essential parameters. With their help, speech is then recognised or restored by a complementary synthesis operation.

The considerable development of micro-electronics enables now a very complex numerical treatment of the signal, even in the real time. The numerical representation can be made both in the time and frequency domain. The latter frames the sub-band coding (SBC) system too [1]. This coding system consists in dividing the signal spectrum in a certain number of sub-bands of width B_k be they equal or not. The whole made up from them reconstitutes the original spectrum, in principle. The minimal sampling frequency is $2B_k$.

The signals supplied by each filter (Fig.1) are quantified so as to equally distribute the quantifying noise as function of frequency for a certain binary rate. The quantification must be finer the lower bands in order to maintain the formants structure and fundamental component. The signals are encoded (with Adaptive Differential Pulse Code Modulation), multiplexed and transmitted.

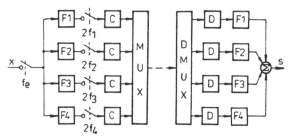

Fig. 1. The sub-band coding system

The decomposition in sub-bands is obtained with a set of filters which constitute the main system element and which can be also met in the receiver where the vice-versa process, that of de-coding takes place. As each filter presents a non-null transition zone, two consecutive bands cross each other in order to avoid lacks in spectrum re-covering. A re-make of the spectrum of each sub-band after re-sampling is the consequence of this operation.

3 Development

The solution we chose takes into account the double aim of the device, i.e. that of auditive feedback or interface for systems provided with visual feedback. The block diagram is presented in Fig.2 [2].The information received from the external loudspeaker is applied to the input amplifier I.A. (Fig.3). Diodes D_1 and D_2 are protection diodes; if the input signal amplitude exceeds 0.6V the mass short-circuiting takes place and the protection of IC_1 is the results. The potentiometer P_1, ensures the control of the input level amplitude. R_1 limits the signal coming from the microphone. C_1 is a DC separation condenser. Condenser C_4 and resistance R_6 constitute a low pass passive filter. Condenser C_5 plays the part of a DC separator between the input amplifier and the analog/digital converter. The amplified signal is passed through a passive filter RC and reaches the input of the analog/digital converter.

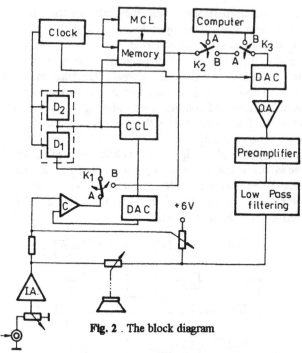

Fig. 2 . The block diagram

The comparator C, the displacement register of 2 bits D_1, D_2, a digital/analog converter (DAC) and its Control Logic (CCL) are also parts of its structure. The actual bit from the latch D_1 is stored in the internal memory of the device (M=6x64 kbits) at each clock tact.

Some technical characteristics of the memory unit components: maximum access time-150ns, read/write cycle-300ns, read/modify/write cycle-345ns. Due to the multiplexing of 16 address bits in the 8 address pins a high storing density is allowed. The two address level are ensures by the two TTL clocks: Row Address Strobe (RAS) and Column Address Strobe (CAS). After one reading or a valid read/modify/write cycle, the information is maintained on D_{out} through the CAS transition in 0. The Data Output is brought back in a state of high impedance by the returning of CAS in 1.

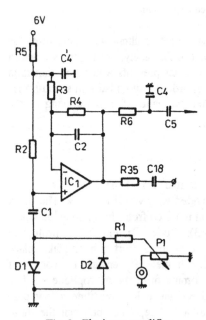

Fig. 3 . The input amplifier

The circuit can maintain the information at the output by keeping CAS in 0 while RAS is used for refreshing (RAS - only cycles). The refresh takes place simultaneously with the development of RAS only cycles or ordinary cycles read/write through those 128 $A_0...A_6$ address combinations during 2ms. The memory clock generator for the memory control logic (MCL) and displacement registers of 2 bits is given by an astable provided with invertors.

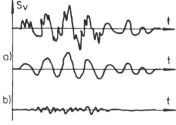

Fig. 4 . The signal oscillogram

The analysed signal oscillogram as well as the low (a) and high (b) frequency components can be seen in Fig.4. As the variation of the fundamental tone of the speaker causes a change in the spectral frequencies, when designing the filters, it has been taken into consideration a certain type of patient, having his fundamental tone round 100 Hz. Each filter may be introduced in, or taken out from the circuit with the help of a potentiometer which can also diminuate, more or less the signal from the respective spectral region. Thus we may provide an artificially amplified or attenuated signal in certain frequency bands compared to the normal signal, a fact necessary in certain cases of poor hearing. Being assured the necessary synchronism between MUX control and scanning frequency on the horizontal, the output of each filter will be selected at a given moment and on a well established period of time within a TV line. In this case the length of the vertical bands that appear on the display is proportional to the amplitude of the corresponding spectral components. This relation of proportionality is carried out by the comparator block COMP to whom there are applied a multiplexed signal at the measure input and a saw-tooth voltage at the reference input. The syncrogenerator block provides a set of auxiliary TV signals necessary for a proper operation of the TV monitor. The complex video signal results from adding the useful signal to the auxiliary TV signals in the adder-formative block, in which the required levels of these signals are also set.

Three types of programs have been elaborated, namely: acquisition of speech parameters, learning the typical parameters by a speaker and recognition of the learned phonemes. For the duration of speech, the acquisition program undertakes a set of values of the detected voltages at the output of filters every 2ms. Then, by mediating the sets of adjacent values in time, a numeric sample of the frequency characteristic is obtained. Based on these acquired values there has been tested the codification by delta modulation. In any case, sub-band coding is more complex then the adaptive delta modulation [3].

4 Results

The device was conceived and carried out with a double-aimed role: - a computer interface, for the analysis of the quality of uttered words and the display on a video-screen of the results of comparison in graphical form proper for the usual feedback related to pronunciation correctness and - a system of auditive feedback carried out with the same aim.

The process of speech re-education of the clinical cases showed the fact that a repeated pronunciation of model-words or words uttered by patients is beneficial due to a better concentration of the patient and his affective-volitive involvement in regaining a proper speech. More than often, especially patients of an educated extraction behaved as inhibited or refractory patients due to either their embarrassment because of an incorrect utterance in front of strangers -be they re-educators, medical staff or their comparison to little children learning to speak. The proposed system offer the patients the possibility of comparing their pronunciation with the correct one, thus eliminating the physical participation of the medical staff for longer periods of time during their logopaedic treatment.

References

1. R. Boite, M. Kunt: Traitement de la parole. Lausanne, Presses polytechniques romandes, ch.3.2, pp.55-59, ch.3.5, pp.89-100, 1987
2. R. Ciupa: Method and device for speaking re-education. Proceedings of the VI th Mediterranean Conf. on MBE, Capri, Italy, vol.II, 1297-1300, (1992)
3. J.L. Flanagan: Speech coding. IEEE Trans. Com-27, no.4, 710-736, (1979)

The Effectiveness of the Intonation Meter for Teaching Intonation to Deaf Persons

Gerard W. Spaai[a, b], Dik. J. Hermes[a], Esther S. Derksen[b] & Paul A. Kaufholz[a, b]

[a] Institute for Perception Research/IPO, Eindhoven, the Netherlands
[b] Institute for the Deaf/IvD, Sint-Michielsgestel, the Netherlands

Abstract. Prelingually, profoundly deaf speakers frequently experience problems in generating a proper intonation. For this reason several attempts have been made to improve their intonation with the help of visual intonation-display systems. A system has been developed, called the Intonation Meter, in which visual feedback of intonation is given as a continuous representation of the pitch contour containing only the perceptually relevant aspects of the intonation pattern. Two exploratory studies were carried out to determine the effectiveness of the Intonation Meter for teaching intonation to prelingually profoundly deaf children aged 6 to 18 years. The results indicate that the Intonation Meter can be an effective tool for teaching intonation to older children, i.e. children of nine years and older. Furthermore, younger children (i.e. 6-7-year-olds) receiving intonation training progressed well, irrespective of whether or not the Intonation Meter was used.

1 Introduction

Many investigators have reported on the problems that prelingually, profoundly deaf children have with pitch control [1-3]. The characteristic difficulties include abnormally high pitch [1, 3] and a lack of linguistically relevant pitch variations resulting in unnatural intonation patterns [2]. A better production of pitch contours is important because it contributes to speech quality [3] and speech intelligibility [4].

It is difficult for deaf speakers to learn to control the pitch of speech for three main reasons. First, deaf speakers may not have sufficient residual hearing capacities to perceive the auditory cues necessary for the control of pitch. Secondly, other feedback modalities, such as tactile and proprioceptive feedback, play no or only a minor role in pitch control [5]. Finally, the major variations in pitch are determined by the action of the cricothyroid muscle [6], which means that it is impossible to give visible cues on the underlying physical mechanism of intonation. Thus, a process-oriented approach in which the attention of the pupil is focussed on the processes responsible for the production of pitch cannot be applied for teaching intonation. Therefore, to help profoundly deaf speakers acquire better pitch control, various researchers have developed sensory aids that extract the pitch from speech and display it visually [7, 8]. They allow for a product-oriented approach for teaching intonation to deaf speakers in that they can circumvent the disrupted auditory feedback loop by providing information on pitch via the visual channel.

Although visual intonation-display systems may be useful in teaching intonation to deaf speakers, they are not widely used in schools. One factor that may have contributed to this is that little is known about the effectiveness of these systems in teaching intonation to prelingually, profoundly deaf persons. Another important factor that may have contributed to the absence of widespread use of visual display systems in schools is that, in these systems, pitch was measured and fed directly back to the deaf speaker without post-processing the pitch contour. Two problems arise when speakers have to interpret an unprocessed pitch contour. The first problem arises from the fact that the interpretation of the displayed pitch contour is hampered by the interruptions during unvoiced parts which are at variance with the continuously perceived course of pitch. The second problem relates to the presence of many perceptually irrelevant pitch variations, also called micro-intonation, which may distract attention from the perceptually relevant pitch variations. In order to solve these problems, a system has been developed, called the Intonation Meter, that gives visual feedback on intonation as a continuous representation containing only the perceptually relevant pitch variations. This results in the so-called stylized pitch contours [9]. This means that unvoiced parts are interpolated and the course of the pitch contour is approximated by a small number of straight lines without the perceptually relevant properties being affected. This representation of the pitch contour is intended to facilitate the interpretation of the visual feedback of the intonation contour [9].

The apllicability of the algorithms for measuring pitch and stylizing the pitch contours was evaluated for speech utterances of deaf speakers and their speech therapists in a study reported by Spaai [10]. It was found that the algorithms for measuring pitch and stylizing pitch contours performed satisfactorily and needed no further adaptation for application in speech training situations of deaf speakers.

In the following sections two explorative studies will be presented that were carried out to determine the effectiveness of the Intonation Meter for teaching intonation to prelingually profoundly deaf children. In the final section the results will be discussed and suggestions will be given for increasing the effectiveness of the system for teaching intonation to prelingually, profoundly deaf children.

2 Study 1: The Effectiveness of the Intonation Meter for Teaching Intonation to Deaf Children Aged 14 to 20 Years

2.1 Design and Procedure

Two groups of profoundly deaf students practised intonation. The first group, the *control group*, practised intonation with the help of regular means. This group received speech training using mainly auditory input via personal hearing aids. The second group, the *experimental group*, received speech training using auditory input and the Intonation Meter to provide visual feedback on pitch. Typically, when a student was working with the system, an example of a pitch contour was produced by the speech therapist and displayed on the upper part of the screen of the Intonation Meter and then had to be imitated on the lower part. While imitating, direct unprocessed feedback was given by means of real-time pitch measurements. After the conclusion of the whole utterance, the stylized contour was also calculated and displayed. Progress in learning of both groups was compared with that of a third group, the *reference group*, which did not receive any extra practice in intonation.

Progress in learning was measured as differences in intonation tests that were conducted prior to training and at the end of the training period. These tests were based on the Fundamental Speech Skills Test [11]. The intonation test was conducted without sensory aids except for the students' personal hearing aids. The students' productions were tape-recorded and a speech therapist who was experienced in listening to and evaluating the speech of deaf children rated the recordings. For this explorative study results are reported for: 1) the production of appropriate average pitch in words and sentences; 2) the production of pitch variations in long vowels and syllables.

2.2 Training Sessions

The experimental group and the control group practised intonation three times a week, each session lasting about 15 minutes. This was done over a four-month period. Generally speaking, speech training focussed on the remediation of an inappropriate average pitch and, to a lesser extent, on the production of variations of pitch in vowels and syllables. Practice consisted of four groups of activities: pitch-awareness training, auditory discrimination and identification of pitch contours, imitation of pitch contours and production of pitch contours without the benefit of the teacher's model.

2.3 Subjects

Twelve prelingually, profoundly deaf students from a secondary school for special education at the Institute for the Deaf in Sint-Michielsgestel, the Netherlands, participated in the experiment. They had been educated according to the 'oral reflective method'. The age of the subjects ranged from 14 to 20 years. All the students had hearing losses greater than 90 dB ISO bilaterally. They produced pitch contours that were perceived by their speech therapists as 'relatively flat', reflecting a monotonous voice. Also, in some cases, their pitch appeared to be too high for their age and sex. The subjects were matched in groups of three as closely as possible in terms of their age, residual hearing, school performance and speech skills. After the subjects had been divided into three groups, one subject dropped out. The numbers of children participating in the control condition, the experimental condition and the reference condition were three, four and four, respectively.

2.4 Apparatus

Use was made of the Intonation Meter, which is capable of providing unprocessed and stylized visual feedback on intonation. The core of the Intonation Meter consists of an AT386 computer running under DOS with a 80387 co-processor extended with a TMS320C25-based Digital Signal Processor board (DSP), a 80 Mb hard disk, a VGA colour monitor and an audio interface. This audio interface is connected to two input microphones, one for the speech therapist and one for the deaf child. Speech input is amplified and low-pass filtered by the audio interface with a cut-off frequency of 2500 Hz. The output of the audio interface is then fed into the input of the DSP board, which is capable of analysing the speech signal. Analysis implies the computation of pitch and amplitude via the method of subharmonic summation. The unprocessed pitch measurements are displayed in real-time. Immediately after the speech utterance, the stylization based on the raw pitch measurements can be calculated and displayed [9].

2.5 Results

Average Pitch. Fig. 1 shows the percentages of acceptable ratings in the pretest and the posttest for the average pitch in isolated words (22 items) and sentences (12 items). The data are presented for the experimental group, the control group and the reference group. It is immediately apparent that the experimental group made more progress than the reference group and the control group. Furthermore, the control group performed better than the reference group.

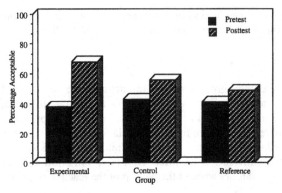

Fig. 1. Average ratings of the mean pitch. The percentages of acceptable judgments are plotted for the experimental group, the control group and the reference group. The appropriateness of average pitch in isolated words (22) and sentences (12) has been rated. The data are presented for the pretest (dark bars) and the posttest (light bars).

Pitch Variations in Vowels and Syllables. Fig. 2 shows the percentages of acceptable ratings in the pretest and the posttest for the production of variations in pitch in long vowels (135 items) and syllables (18 items). The data are presented for the experimental group, the control group and the reference group. The results clearly show that the experimental group made most progress (64%). The control group and the reference group also showed progress but the magnitude of improvement was not as large: the percentage of acceptable judgments increased by about 17%.

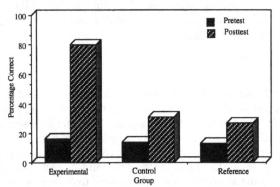

Fig. 2. Average ratings of the production of pitch variations in vowels (135) and syllables (18). The percentages of acceptable judgments are plotted for the experimental group, the control group and the reference group. The data are presented for the pretest (dark bars) and the posttest (light bars).

2.6 Discussion

The results of this study showed that children who received intonation training by means of both regular methods and the Intonation Meter showed more progress in the production of appropriate average pitch and the production of pitch variations in vowels and syllables than a matched control group that practised intonation merely by means of regular methods and a reference group that did not receive any extra intonation training. Moreover, the differences in progress between the control group and the reference group were limited, illustrating that teaching intonation to a profoundly deaf person by means of regular methods is an extremely difficult task. The children who participated in this study could probably be characterized as having more impervious phonatory problems owing to their age. Furthermore, it is hypothesized that intonation training is more effective when it is initiated after an intonation problem arises. This may prevent the development of incorrect speech habits which are difficult to remediate. Generally speaking, this implies that intonation training should be commenced at a very young age [1]. This hypothesis is in agreement with the results of studies on second-language learning that showed that teaching the intonation of a foreign language is more effective with younger children than with older children. However, it is unknown whether a visual intonation-display system can be used for teaching intonation to young deaf children. Young children may be unable to relate the visual representation of the pitch contour to the corresponding speech signal or to integrate the visual representation of speech with the orosensoric and the residual auditory representation of speech.

3. Study II: The Effectiveness of the Intonation Meter for Teaching Intonation to Deaf Children Aged 6 to 11 Years

3.1 Design and Procedure

A single-subject A-B-A-B withdrawal design was used to assess the intervention effects, i.e. the effects of intonation training by means of regular methods (A-phase) and the effects of intonation training by means of regular methods involving the use of the Intonation Meter (B-phase). This design typically involves a baseline phase followed by a treatment phase. Then the treatment is withdrawn, and this is followed by a return to the treatment phase.

Each phase included 9 experimental sessions: successively, a test session, three training sessions, an intermediate test session, three training sessions and a final test session. Experimental sessions were conducted three times a week with the experimental group. This was done over a four-month period. Each training session took about 10 minutes. For each phase a specific set of intonation patterns was trained and tested using speech materials varying from vowels to syllables and simple words consisting of two or three syllables.

A test session lasted about 5 minutes. Children were instructed to imitate a certain intonation pattern on a specific vowel, syllable or word that was produced by the speech therapist. The students' productions were tape recorded and were rated by a listener of normal hearing experienced in listening to and evaluating the speech of deaf children. A dichotomous scoring system (acceptable/unacceptable) was used to grade each response.

Initially, in the *Introduction Phase*, the deaf child received some pitch-awareness training. Furthermore, some time was allotted to auditory discrimination and auditory identification of pitch contours where training focussed on the acoustical signal using the student's hearing aids while eliminating cues from speechreading and other modalities. Following this, children were assigned to a Baseline Phase or a Treatment Phase. Both phases are described below.

Baseline Phase (Phase A). In the Baseline Phase intonation was only trained by means of regular methods. For instance, a pitch contour was produced on a vowel or syllable and the child was instructed to imitate this. Information on pitch was also presented via some visual activity of the speech therapist, e.g. raising or lowering the hand to indicate the pitch level. No visual or tactile sensory aid was used in the Baseline Phase. Besides imitation of pitch contours produced by the speech therapist, intonation training involved the production of pitch contours without the benefit of the teacher's model.

Treatment Phase (Phase B). In the treatment phase, intonation was trained by means of both regular methods (see the Baseline Phase) and the Intonation Meter to provide visual feedback on intonation.

3.2 Training Sessions

Generally speaking, speech training focussed on the production of intonation patterns in vowels and syllables. Furthermore, some time was devoted to the production of intonation patterns in words. On average, about 18 items (intonation patterns in approximately 6 vowels, 10 syllables and 2 words) were practised in each phase.

3.3 Subjects

Six prelingually, profoundly deaf pupils from the primary school for special education at the Institute for the Deaf in Sint-Michielsgestel, the Netherlands, participated in the experiment. All the children were being educated according to the 'oral reflective method' [21]. The age of the children ranged from 6 to 7 years and from 9 to 11 years, respectively. All the children had hearing losses greater than 90 dB ISO bilaterally. The mean pure-tone average was approximately 108 dB in the better ear, ranging from 92 dB to 130 dB ISO. All the children produced pitch contours that were perceived by their speech therapist as 'relatively flat', in that linguistically relevant pitch variations were absent.

3.4 Results

The results showed that the 9 to 11 year-olds progressed more under treatment conditions than under baseline conditions whereas the 6 to year-olds progressed well irrespective of whether or not the Intonation Meter was used.

Here, the results are presented for only two subjects since they are representative for their age groups. Figure 3 shows the experimental results for Subject 1, one of the children aged 9 to 11 years, and Figure 4 shows the results for Subject 2, one of the children aged 6 to 7 years. Both figures show the percentages of acceptable ratings for the production of pitch variations in vowels, syllables and words in the initial test, the intermediate test and the final test for the different phases.

Figure 3 shows the results for Subject 1. On the basis of visual inspection of the results it can be concluded that the performance gains, as determined by the differences between the scores of the initial tests and the scores of the final test, are greater under treatment conditions than under baseline conditions.

As for Subject 2, it is clear from Figure 4 that performance gains under baseline conditions were comparable to those under the treatment conditions. Furthermore, it was found that, irrespective of the phase in which the subject was practising the production of intonation patterns, the subject progressed well.

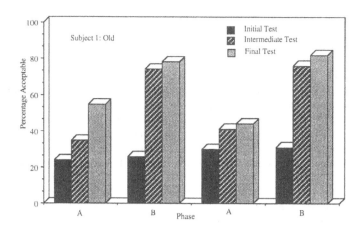

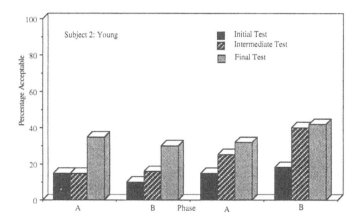

[12]. Tahta et al. [12] studied the abilities of 5 to 15 year-old monolingual English schoolchildren to replicate the intonation of a foreign language. Performance in the production of intonation patterns remained steadily good for the 5 to 8 year-olds and then dropped rapidly from 8 to 11 while the 11 to 15 year-olds showed comparably poor performance. This can possibly be explained by the fact that younger children have better *rote-memory ability* ,i.e. the ability to retain associations between stimuli and responses, than older children. Another possible explanation for the absence of a differential training effect in the case of the very young children is that they are not yet capable of relating the visual representation to the corresponding speech signal.

Foremost in clinical intervention is the need to generalize skills from more structured, imitative tasks to everyday situations. At present it is not known whether children with 'prosodic difficulties' easily transfer skills learned through intervention using elicited imitation to real-life communication situations. Long-term research is necessary to determine whether the intensive use of the Intonation Meter in regular speech training can result in improved control of intonation in connected discourse. This type of research is also necessary to verify the hypothesis that stylized pitch contours are more efficient in teaching intonation than unprocessed pitch contour representations.

5 References

1. C.M. Beijk, B.A.G. Elsendoorn: A comparison of fundamental frequency of deaf and hearing children aged 14 to 20 years. ESCA Workshop Speech and Language Technology for Disabled Persons. Stockholm, May -June 1993.
2. N.S. McGarr, M. Osberger: Pitch deviancy and the intelligibility of deaf children's speech. Journal of Communication Disorders 11, 237-247 (1978).
3. R.B. Monsen: Acoustic qualities of phonation in young hearing-impaired children. Journal of Speech and Hearing Research 22, 270-288 (1979).
4. D.E. Metz, N. Schiavetti, V.J. Samar, R.W. Sitler: Acoustic dimensions of hearing-impaired speakers' intelligibility: segmental and suprasegmental characteristics. Journal of Speech and Hearing Research 33, 467-478 (1990).
5. P. Ladefoged: Three areas of experimental phonetics. London, University Press, 1967.
6. R. Collier: Physiological correlates of intonation patterns. Journal of the Acoustical Society of America 58, 249-255 (1975).
7. K. Youdelman, M. MacEachron, A.M. Behrman: Visual and tactile sensory aids: Integration into an on-going speech training program. Volta Review 90, 197-207 (1988).
8. N.S. McGarr, J. Head, M. Friedman, A.M. Behrman, K. Youdelman: The use of visual and tactile sensory aids in speech production training: A preliminary report. Journal of Rehabilitation Research and Development 23, 101-109 (1986).
9. G.W.G. Spaai, A. Storm, D.J. Hermes: A visual display for the teaching of intonation to deaf persons: Some preliminary findings. In: W. Zagler (ed.): Proceedings of the 3rd International Conference on Computers for Handicapped Persons. Wien/München: R. Oldenbourg 1991, pp. 480-488.
10. G.W.G. Spaai: Teaching intonation to deaf persons through visual displays. In: B.A.G. Elsendoorn, F. Coninx (eds.): Interactive Learning Technology for the Deaf. Nato ASI Series F, Volume 113. Berlin: Springer Verlag, pp. 151-163.
11. H. Levitt, K. Youdelman, K. Head: Fundamental Speech Skills Test. Colorado: Resource Point Incorporation 1990.
12. S. Tahta, M. Wood, K. Loewenthal: Age changes in the ability to replicate foreign pronunciation and intonation. Language and Speech 24, 363-372 (1981).

Application of Artificial Intelligence Methods in a Word-Prediction Aid

Nestor Garay-Vitoria and Julio González-Abascal

Laboratory of Human-Computer Interaction for Special Needs
Informatika Fakultatea. Euskal Herriko Unibertsitatea
649 postakutxa; 20080 Donostia. SPAIN
E-mail: acbgavin@si.ehu.es; julio@si.ehu.es
Telephone: +34 43 21 91 81; Fax: +34 43 21 93 06

Abstract. Word-prediction appears to be a good aid to enhance message-composition rate for people with physical disabilities. Usually word-prediction is based on statistical information (mainly on word frequencies). Hit rate can be enhanced by trying to imitate the behaviour of a human interlocutor (who uses syntactic and semantic information). In this paper some new approaches based on Artificial Intelligence methods are presented. Advantages of syntactic and semantic analysis in relation to bare statistical methods are studied. Furthermore, the integration with human-computer interfaces for disabled users is also described.

1 Introduction

In the last few years several devices to assist people with severe speech and motor disabilities in personal communication have been developed in different countries. Even though most of them have supposed an enhancement of disabled people communication possibilities, the speed achieved remains far lower than that of a normal dialogue. The rate of an oral conversation can be estimated at 150-200 words/minute, whilst the writing rate of a user who has some motor problems tends to be much slower (in the order of 2-10 words/minute) [2].

Word prediction is an interesting choice to speed up writing composition. Basically, prediction or anticipation lies in trying to guess what a user is going to 'say' next, just as a human interlocutor normally does. The feasibility of obtaining good results in word prediction is due to the excellent balance existing between the average word size and the reachable hit ratio. This is based, to a great extent, on the large amount of redundancy and the high quantity of information (statistical, morphological, syntactic, semantic...) accompanying words [3, 4].

Depending on the kind of information used to make predictions, different types of predictors can be distinguished. Predictors by frequencies use purely statistical information, whereas syntactical predictors add syntactic information, and semantic predictors operate with semantic categories.

In the next section some general notions about how our predictors operate and the methods we apply for our study are presented. Later, some Natural Language processing techniques and their application in word prediction will be discussed.

2 Revision of the Notions

We have implemented a system which emulates the behaviour of a user to evaluate the performance of distinct type of anticipators: a process which reads words from a 'trial text' and sends them to the predictor character by character emulating the behaviour of a user. The predictor receives what is sent by the user and stores the information relevant for prediction. Then, depending on the strategy, it sends the user the most likely words or, where appropriate, informs the user that it is impossible to make a prediction. The user, depending on the case, will accept or reject the proposals given by the predictor. If a proposal is accepted, the user computes the improvements so far, and the predictor updates the dictionary. The predictor can also update the lexicon if the user produces words that were not included. The functioning of these predictors is shown in Fig. 1

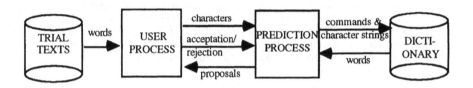

Fig. 1 Predictors functioning

This way data about the performance of each proposed predictor can be obtained and some comparisons working under the same conditions can be made.

In a previous project, two strategies of word-prediction using purely statistical information have been developed. The first method uses word frequencies to make its proposals, taking into account only the current word. Each time the user inputs a character, the predictor proposes the most frequent word (or words) which begins with the last characters typed. The system has to memorise the words last proposed but not accepted in order to avoid repetition. Basically, the entries of the dictionary are composed of the words and their associated frequencies. In order to properly adapt the system to the user the frequencies associated with the used words are updated. This first approach has a great computational speed, but results are not very satisfactory because the context is not taken into account (words are seen as isolated entities within the conversation).

The second approach tries to avoid this problem by placing words into a wider unit: the current sentence. Each word plays a role (specified by the syntactic category) within the sentence. A table was formed with information about the probabilities of each syntactic category following any other category, and also the likelihood of a category starting a sentence. The behaviour of this approach still based on statistical criteria: the category of the preceding word is stored, and the predictor looks into the table for the most probable categories to follow the current one. Using the beginning of the current word, the words stored in the dictionary with related information to their category and frequency are obtained. The predictor makes the proposals, combining adequately the values of the entries of the table and the frequencies of the lexicon. Basically, an entry of the lexicon is composed of the word, its frequency and

its syntactic category. The personalisation occurs by changing the word frequencies in the dictionary and the entries of the table. This approach maintains a satisfying speed of operation. More details about these prediction systems can be found in [4].
Both predictors have been implemented in C language and are part of a human-computer interaction system for disabled people developed in our Laboratory. They are very useful to make comparisons with the newly proposed methods.

3 The Chart Bottom-up Technique

Charts are used in a bottom-up parsing method to analyse sentences in Natural Language [1, 8]. This technique works with a Natural Language grammar defined by rules in the manner:

$$LEFT ->[RIGHT]^+$$

That is, the left compound constituent is decomposed into one or several constituents which appear on the right of the rule. The bottom-up parser uses the rule to take the sequence of symbols and to match it to the right-hand side of the rule. Then, it identifies them as the left symbol. Matches are always considered from the point of view of one symbol, called the key. To find rules that match a string involving the key, the parser looks for rules that start with the key, or for rules that have already been started by earlier keys and require the present key either to complete the rule or to extend it.
A record of the state of a bottom-up parse is kept in a structure called a *chart*. This structure is a record of the relative positions of the words in the sentence and the new structures derived from the sentence. The chart also stores the rules that have matched previously but are not complete: they constitute the active arcs on the chart.
This method is very adequate for our goals because it is not complex, it adds low computational load and it allows a reasonably good natural language analysis.

4 Syntactic Word-Prediction Using Charts

This technique for syntactic analysis of sentences can also be applied in word-prediction. The goal is to make use of the information provided by the syntactical structure of the sentence. This information allows a more accurate selection of the possible words to be proposed.
The procedure is as follows: each grammatical rule in the chart has an associated weight, which depends on its frequency of use. To weigh each rule a lexicon that contains words associated with their frequency, syntactical category and other morphological marks, if existing, such as gender and number, was previously built.
To completely escribe any natural language a large amount of rules must be defined as there are many different kinds of structures and sentences (e.g.. active, passive, interrogative, affirmative, negative, imperative, ...). Keeping in mind that our purpose is to obtain a high hit rate within a short time, a complete grammar would be too complex from the computational point of view, and hence too slow [5]. Moreover, this approach seems to be excessive, because some rules add very little information due to their low frequency. For this reason, a partial grammar containing the most representative rules (from the statistical point of view) was defined.
This type of anticipator takes into account syntactical and statistical information. The syntactic information is accessed by using the active arcs on the chart (that is,

the partially completed rules) and the position of the current word in the sentence. Looking at the active arcs pointing to a word, the most probable syntactic categories are obtained, according to the previously defined grammar. The probability of each category depends on the weights of the active arcs and their associated rules.

While the user is writing a word "W", the predictor proposes the most frequent word (or words) belonging to the most probable syntactical category of the current position in the chart and having the same beginning as "W". As more than one arc can be active simultaneously, the statistical weights of the different arcs are crucial to determine the most probable category. Due to the syntactic knowledge obtained, proposals are given with the most appropriate gender and number, depending on the considered rules.

The operational way with the first word in the sentence must be different, because there is not an active arc. In this particular case, an array with the probabilities of the syntactical categories beginning a sentence is used. A combination of the entries in this array (that is, the weights of the categories beginning a sentence) and word frequencies is used to give proposals.

Tailoring of the anticipation method to the individual user is done by updating the word-frequencies in the dictionary and the weights of the rules (or the entries of the array with the probabilities of the syntactic categories in the case of the beginning of a sentence). To include new words in the lexicon all the information needed must be provided either when the new word appears or later. In this last case, the new word is set aside into a special category until in a particular session someone adds the complete information. When new words are accepted in the lexicon some problems arise. The most important one is the appearance of syntactic ambiguities. In our case, this problem can be solved by creating special categories for the ambiguous cases involving more than one single category.

5 Semantic Prediction Using Grammars.

5.1 Antecedents

An interesting approach to semantic prediction is mentioned by Hunnicutt in [7]. A semantic classification of the words is made. This classification can have several levels and which may include some generalisations and inheritances.

A possible implementation of this approach is to build a lexicon as a knowledge base in which each word is interconnected with some others depending on their meaning. This approach allows access to the base by meanings or by clues, such as the number of syllables, intermediate letters, etc. These characteristics are very useful if the user suffers from amnesia, aphasia or anomie [6]. However, the increase of the complexity of this approach can represent a problem. This is a direct consequence of the dictionary's structure and the related working procedures. For this reason the access time can experience a great increase. There is another problem if new words appear, because the words in the base are interrelated. The special sessions to categorise new words will be longer and very complex, because a great portion of the data base will have to be changed.

5.2 Our Approach

We tried a different approach to the semantic prediction, similar to the one designed for syntactic prediction. The difference is that now semantic categories of the words are defined, and a semantic grammar is built. The procedure is the following: with regard to the categories, semantic information related to the theme of the conversation is linked to each word. In relation to the grammar, the syntactic approach is enriched with semantic categories. That procedure narrows the field of feasible words, which should enhance the hit ratio. Thus, we can model the conversation taking into consideration which themes are treated, and in which context they are suitable. The defined grammar covers the proposed modelling of the conversation. Entries of the dictionary are similar to the preceding approach, adding to the syntactic category the semantic one. User adaptation is done in the same way as in the previous approach.

Results for people with limited conversation possibilities may be better than the ones obtained with statistical prediction [4], but they will be close to the results of the syntactic approach, because they present the same behaviour. With this approach a new problem arises. It is a direct consequence of the modelling of the conversation: when new topics are treated, the hit ratio is expected to decrease, because of the lack of semantic information.

A promising possibility for prediction taking into account semantic information is the use of neural networks. In a neural network approach, neurones can reflect the stage of the conversation, and the connections between neurones reflect the weights of the transitions at this stage. A transition happens if the identified word appears. This seems to be the most "natural" approach, because it is similar to the way people make predictions. An advantage of this approach is that, whilst the previous semantic approaches may be constrain-limited, this one can manage non-constrained conversations, and can learn from the experience.

6 Integration of the Predictor in Human-Computer Interfaces

All these predictors are intended to be integrated in some different interfaces designed in our laboratory for severely motor and speech impaired people. These interfaces have a scan based input: matrixes containing different options are scanned sequentially and the user selects the element (character, word, sentence...) pressing one or more buttons when this element is highlighted. Inside these matrixes a place is reserved for the words offered by the anticipator. An important parameter to be tuned up is the number of words that the predictors offered, because the time (and sometimes the number of keystrokes) needed to accept or reject a proposal, depend on the number of proposals received. When this number increases, the hit ratio also increases, but more time is needed to make a selection. So, to obtain the best results a balance between the number of proposals issued each time and the increment in the effort to make a selection should be reached.

If only one proposal is made a new possible procedure is possible, namely explicit rejection. That is, the user must explicitly accept or reject the proposed word. When the hit ratio is very high, this method considerably enhances communication speed, because the selection effort is minimised. Otherwise, continuous rejections can make this procedure very boring. Explicit rejection is not possible when more than one proposal is made, because the selection of one of the words implicitly supposes its acceptation.

In our study four cases have been tested: predictors which offer one, five and ten proposals with implicit rejection and one proposal with explicit rejection (ER).

7 Comparison of the Results

Two standard Spanish texts, as seen in figure 2, have been used to compare the results of the implemented anticipatory methods. Four prediction methods (word frequencies, syntactic with automaton, syntactic chart and semantic-based chart) are compared. In figure 3 text A and in figure 4 text B are used.

Text	Size (in characters)	origin
A	994	colloquial language
B	2444	colloquial language

Fig. 2 Characteristics of the trial texts

To test the behaviour of the predictors saving percentage is taken as a figure of merit. Saving percentage is the savings in the number of keystrokes obtained when the predictor is used, in comparison to the production of the same text without any prediction method.

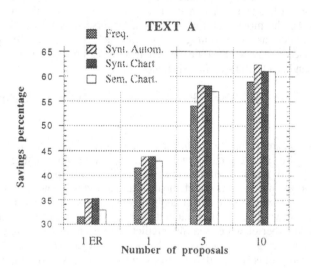

Fig. 3 Results with text A

To make comparisons, the method of prediction by frequencies is taken as a model. This method gives low results, but the needed computational effort is minimal. According to its results the semantic prediction method using grammars follows. Nevertheless, results are worse than expected because the number of the sentences which do not fit the defined semantic grammar is too large in relation to the number of sentences fitting it.

The other two approaches are very similar, considering only the results. But the needed computational effort is greater in the syntactic prediction using grammars.

In both texts, as can be seen in figs. 3 and 4, the savings percentage increases with the number of proposals. But, when the number of proposals increases, the acceptation protocol has to be more complex and therefore slower. Only in some applications a large set of proposals is useful.

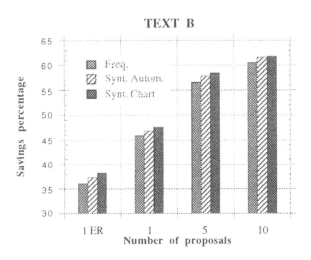

Fig. 4 Results with text B

8 Conclusions

In this paper we have shown two new methods of anticipation based on techniques of Artificial Intelligence, such as the *chart* bottom-up technique (used in the Natural Language Analysis). On the one hand, syntactic approaches appear to offer the best results, compared to the prediction using frequencies that need a low computational effort but obtains worse results. On the other hand, the implemented semantic approach produce results between those of the prediction using frequencies and the syntactic predictions, but is constrained to a narrow model of the conversation. If this model changes, the performance of this method decreases quickly.

Our proposal is to use syntactic prediction using grammars, since this approach works with a reasonable computational cost and produces a high hit ratio, and therefore a reasonable enhancement of the communication speed. Furthermore, some possible solutions for problems detected in this approach have been proposed.

370

Acknowledgements

This work has received financial support from the Department of Economy of the local government "Gipuzkoako Foru Aldundia". Furthermore, Nestor Garay-Vitoria holds a doctoral grant from the Department of Education, Universities and Research of the Basque Government, to whom the authors would like to acknowledge its support.

References

1. James Allen: Natural Language Understanding. Benjamin Cummings Publishing Company. (1987)
2. Norman Alm, John L. Arnott and Alan F. Newell: Prediction and Conversational Momentum in an Augmentative Communication System. Communications of the ACM. Volume 35, Number 5 (May 1992). Pages 46-57.
3. Arnott, J. L., Pickering, J. A., Swiffin, A. L. and Battison M.: An Adaptive and Predictive Communication Aid for the Disabled that Exploits the Redundancy in Natural Language. Proceedings of the 2nd International Conference on Rehabilitation Engineering (Ottawa, Canada. 1984) pp. 349-350.
4. Nestor Garay and Julio González-Abascal: Using Statistical and Syntactic Information in Word Prediction for Input Speed Enhancement. Information Systems Design and Hypermedia. Proceedings of the BIWIT-94. Biarritz, France (February 1994), pp. 223-230.
5. Craig W. Heckathorne and Dudley S. Childress: Applying Anticipatory Text Selection in a Writing Aid for People with Severe Motor Impairment. IEEE MICRO, June 1983. Pages 17-23.
6. Sheri Hunnicutt: Input and Output Alternatives in Word Prediction. STL-QPSR 2-3/1987. Pages 15-29.
7. Sheri Hunnicutt: Using Syntactic and Semantic Information in a Word Prediction Aid. Proc. Europ. Conf. Speech Commun. Paris, France. September 1989, vol. 1, pp. 191-193.
8. Kepa Sarasola: Natural Language Processing (in Spanish). Notes of lectures Academic Course 1989-1990.

Speech Therapy, New Developments and Results in LingWare

Wolfgang Grießl, F.J. Stachowiak

c/o Phoenix Software, Küdinghovener Straße 98, D-53227 Bonn,
(0049)(0)228/97584-0 (Tel.), (0049)(0)228/07584-18 (Fax)

Abstract: LingWare/STACH is a permanently extended multimedia program for computer assisted language and speech therapy, which includes besides the therapy programme an author system for creative and extensive use. A short example of one of the more than 2000 exercises is given.

Since two years LingWare is extended: new soundcards, foreign versions, features to support home based therapy. The principles are outlined.

The German Federal Ministry of Research and Technology provided financial support to carry out a randomized multicenter study on the efficacy of LingWare/STACH as a form of supplementary therapy in addition o the language therapy provided by a speech therapist. A detailed description of the study and the results is given.

1. Speech Therapy with LingWare/STACH

LingWare/STACH was developed since 1985 and used is in a randomized multicentric study. The therapy system, in the meantime in clinical use at more than 400 facilities, is able to synchronize graphics (e.g. scanned pictures of daily situations), written and spoken text (by means of a soundcard)), thereby allowing the presentation of interactive exercises on the monitor.

For instance patients learn the correct use of prepositions from a multiple choice set of prepositions which fits in the sentence accompanying a picture. After the exercise desired is selected, the first picture in a series of pictures appears (e.g. a man is standing on a ladder). The sentence *The man ist standing ... the ladder* enters the screen from the right (Figure 1).

The multiple set of prepositions is given at the top of the screen. The instructions in dialogue line ask the patient to move the cursor to the correct preposition. The patient controls the movement of the cursor by a joystick, mouse, trackball or the cursor keys. The dialogue line alerts the patient to an incorrect answer. This is fortified by speech output: *Sorry incorrect!* The dialogue line ask to try again.

When the correct preposition has been chosen, the complete sentence is shown along with the corresponding speech output. In the case of erroneous performance the computer can provide cues in a form of easier tasks, e.g. the presentation of a situation in which the prepositons are visually represented or a naming task, etc..

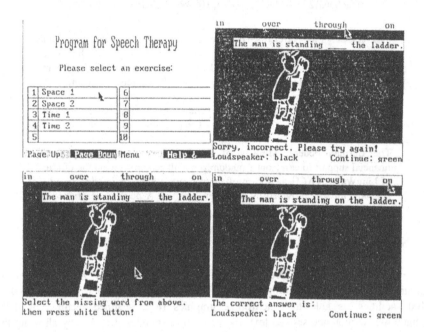

Figure 1: Exercise example

There is a total of more than 2000 exercises, based on 20 different open exercise schemes. The exercises comprise language modalities such as naming, dictation, sentence structure, comprehension, sound discrimination.

2. Home Based Speech Therapy

A lot of patients would be able to work with a therapy computer at home - without the permanent support by therapist. Some requests must be fulfilled by the system to offer *home based computer therapy* in addition to the conventional therapy:

The responsible therapist must be able to construct subsets of the total amount of exercises according to the special need of the patients. We introduced in our system the feature of *therapy plan*. Once a set of therapy plans is constructed, each therapist is responsible to assign a well suited therapy plan to each patient.

Different user interfaces must be available for therapists and patients - according to the special needs of each user group. We introduced in our system the subsystem *user managment*. A therapist as a user has now available all the powerful facilities of the system (author system, user management, statistics, therapy management, etc.), a patient as user only *sees* his assigned exercises in his therapy plan.

It must be possible to copy the patients exercises onto a random access medium. Using his volume, each patient can do his *homework* outside the clinical institution, for example at home. Now our system is able to copy therapy plans onto floppy discs. The statistical data of each patient are stored also on that floppy disc - the *statistical analysis* can be done by the therapist in his clinical institution. To decrease the system cost for patients version, the newer versions of LingWare/STACH now support the worldwide available soundblaster card.

To increase the patients motivation again it should be more easier to include private therapy material in the computer-based speech therapy: pictures of holidays, hobbies, family, friends, etc.. The newest version of our system now supports the use of *video cameras* together with videoblaster adapters. The standard material which comes with the system is now stored on a CD-ROM, the new private material is stored on harddiscs or floppies.

3. Evaluation of Computer Assisted Speech Therapy

The German Federal Ministry for Research and Technology (BMFT) supported a study examining the effects of supplementary computer assisted speech therapy performed with the LingWare/STACH system as a supplementary form of training.

The purpose of the study was not to compare computer assisted training to therapy performed by a professional speech therapist. The computer was considered to be a tool of speech therapy. The question examined was: Is the computer-based therapy effective as a form of supplementary speech therapy? The patients were devided into two groups: one group received one hour of conventional therapy per day and the other received 30 minutes conventional therapy and 30 minutes of supplementary computer assisted speech therapy per day.

As the literature (Baso, 1987) had stated that effects of speech therapy are almost impossible to show, if the patients have not been treated daily for a period of at least 6 weeks. The study embodied a six-week training period, i.e. thirty hours of language training between pre- and post-testing with the Aachen Aphasia Test Battery (AAT). The patients were assigned randomly to one of the two experimental groups, using a strict randomization procedure. The effect of spontaneous remission was controlled by including only patients with at least four months post-onset.

2 therapy groups	speech therapy versus speech therapy plus supplementary computer training
Length of treatment	6 weeks
Length of study	24 months
Multi-centric	12 centers involved
Grouping	randomized
Stratification	according to center and degree of severity
Testing	pre and post therapy
Scale	AAT, Token Test, evaluation of spontaneous language

Figure 2: Study concept

Other exclusion criteria were double sided brain damage and progressive brain damage such as senile dementia, etc.. Biometric procedures put together groups which were comparable in age, sex and other factors. The study was limited to patients who reached the second part of the Token Test, meaning, that they had at least a minimum of language capacity.

It is clear that this study, which for statistical reasons has to include at least 150 patients, would answer the general question on the supplementary computer training as far as this was possible with standardized testing procedures such as the AAT. It is generally recognized, that the AAT is a relatively crude instrument in that it measures performance in language modalities such as repetition, naming, language comprehension, etc., but does not measure other factores relevant to therapy such as verbal short term memory, the speed of language processing and attention as well as linguistic factors such as syntactic and semantic areas of language competence and performance. Furthermore, it does not measure communication abilities except in Part 1 (Spontaneous Language). Nevertheless, we hoped that the AAT would show at leat tendencies of the effects of supplementary computer training.

4. The Study Population

156 aphasic patients were recruited for this study. Everyone gave her/his written consent to participate in the six-weeks training and for the data to be analyzed. Almost all the patients were in-patients at rehabilitation centres during the participation in the study.
77 patients received conventional speech therapy, 79 conventional speech therapy plus supplementary computer training. The patients did not work independently at the computer; a therapist or trained volunteer was present at each session to assist the patients in selecting exercises and operating the programme as far as necessary. The data was recorded automatically by the computer.

Inclusion Criteria	Exclusion Criteria
Aphasic, according to AAT	Age > 75 years
Duration of illness > 6 months	Bilateral lesion
	retrogade anterogade amnesias
	progredient illness
	not reaching the second part of the Tokentest
	Score of < 6 on the Tokentest
	Inability to work with a computer

Figure 3: Selection criteria

Ten patients dropped out due to illness or technical difficulties at one of the participating centres, respectively. One patient dropped out at his own wish, as he did not enjoy this form of training.

5. Results

All of the patients were routinely examined with the AAT. Therapist and examiner were usually not identical. The *Biometrisches Zentrum Aachen* (BZA) controlled the data collection and carried out the statistical analysis. Figure 4 gives an overview of the raw scores reached in the subtests of the AAT.

The scores are given for both groups and for the subtests: Tokentest, Repetition (Nachsprechen), Written language (Schriftsprache), Naming (Benennen), Oral and written comprehension (Sprachverständnis). Every dot stands for a patient and shows the number of points more or fewer achieved in the post-test as compared to pre-test scores. For instance the highest score (25) in the subtest repetition for the computer group shows that this patient improved by 25 points over the pre-test score. The lowest score (-15) shows that this patients score worsened by 15 points following the 6-week training. Altogether this figure shows that most of the patients scored above the zero line, demonstrating that most patients showed improvements in the AAT following therapy.

The clearest differences were in written language and naming, which were also the focal points of the computer training programme.

The AAT (see Huber et al, 1983) gives criteria for establishing an improvement as being significant for an individual patient. According to these criteria the results were evaluated for each individual patient: Figures 4-7 show how many patients from each syndrome group showed significant improvements in the five subtests for the computer group and the conventional groups, respectively. Thus in comparison, 10 of 20 Broca aphasics in the computer group and 5 of 29 Broca aphasics in the conventional group showed significant improvements in the Tokentest.

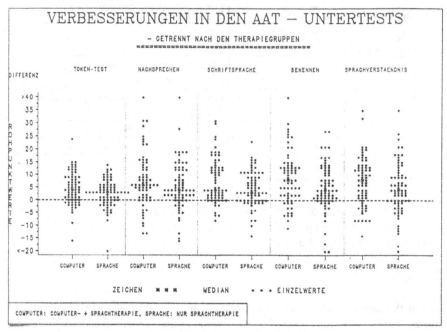

Figure 4: Improvements in the AAT - Subtests

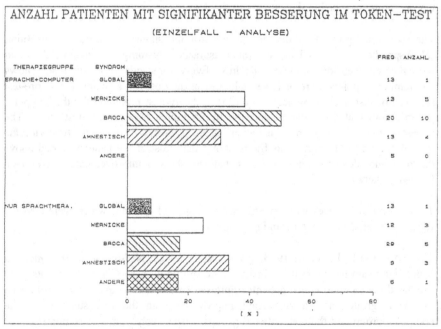

Figure 5: Improvements in Tokentest

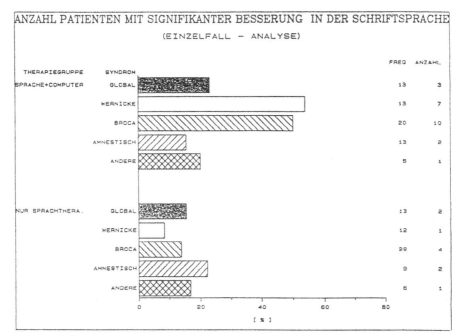

Figure 6: Improvements in written language

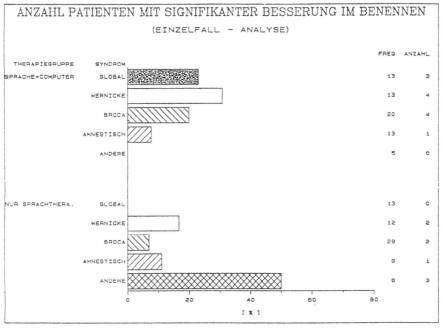

Figure 7: Improvements in naming

Figure 6 shows the high proportion of Broca's and Wernicke's patients with significant improvements in the subtest for written naming in the computer group. Here single case analysis clarifies the results obtained by simply comparing the raw scores in Figure 4.

The evaluation of spontaneous language in the AAT also showed better effects for the computer group. A difference of 45.3% as compared to 30.4% (percentage of patients who improved by at least one point on the AAT for communicative behaviour) was observed.

6. Discussion

It must be emphasized that progress in therapy was not measured by the material trained, but with a standardized test measuring performance in certain language modalities. Practically speaking, this corresponds to a generaliziation effect to untrained material.

If the results are summarized, we first see positive effects of speech therapy in general and secondly effects of supplementary computer training focusing on naming and written language. This is especially true for Broca and Wernicke aphasics and more for women than for men.

A post hoc study with 17 patients also showed, that the same amount of training received over a period of 12 weeks did not achieve the same effects. These speaks in favour of a cost-reduction effect.

Taking into consideration the wide acceptance of the programme by patients and therapists and the supplementary effects combined with potential effects from a six-week stationary treatment, the results are promising.

7. References

Basso, A. (1987), "Approaches to Neuropsychological Rehabilitation: Language Disorders" in: M.J. Meier et.al. (eds.): Neuropsychological Rehabilitation. Edinburgh, Churchill Livingstone, 294 - 314.)

Grießl, W, (1994), "LingWare-Therapiesystem", User Manual, Phoenix Software GmbH, Bonn

Grießl, W., Stachowiak, F.J., "Computer Assisted Speech Therapy" in: W.L. Zagler (ed.): 3rd ICCHP, Wien, 1992

Huber, W., Poeck, K., Weniger, D. & Willmes, K. (1983), Aachener Aphasie Test (AAT). Göttingen, Hogrefe

Projective Display of Document Information by Parametric Sound Beam

Yoshimichi Yonezawa, Hideki Nonaka,
Kazunori Itoh and Masami Hashimoto

Department of Information Engineering
Faculty of Engineering, Shinshu University
500 Wakasato Nagano-shi 380 JAPAN

Abstract. For the input work of sentences by the blind, the location information of cursor is necessary. We have tried to display document information by the sound(voice). The sound we used is secondary one derived from parametric array driven by an ultrasonic range signal. We got the movable sound source using the sound and projecting it on the wall just like torch light. The basic characteristics show the possibility of the document information display by this method.

1 Introduction

The key-in work is thought to be hopeful work for the blind because they can work as fast as the non-visually handicapped people when they've got used to the work(by training). The system they use is usually make to support the work by the function of tactile one-line braille display or voice confirming system. But, there is no system which transfers the information of two dimensional layout of key-inned document and position of cursor realtimely to an operator, though it is an ordinary function of CRT.

The new system we tried can cover the lack of functions above mentioned by the sound with positional or vocal information. Because the sound source position in free space can be recognized (localized) easily by hearing the sound, there is a possibility to display images by the sound if we make sounds or voices correspond to colors or characters respectively and move the sound source in space. We tried to make sound beam, to project it on the wall and to deflect the beam and got a reflected movable sound source. The sound beam was made by using parametric array effect[1,2].

2 Principle of Parametric Array

The parametric array effect we adopted is caused by a nonlinear characteristic of air for acoustic pressure. And for example, an ultrasonic wave (primary) of 40 KHz modulated by 1 KHz sine wave in amplitude makes the secondary one corresponding to 1 KHz wave along the way of propagation of primary wave in air(Fig. 1).

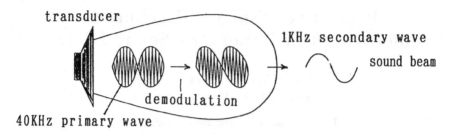

Fig. 1 Principle of parametric array

In this case, the generation points of the secondary wave are localized in the pattern of phased array and then beam-like sound pressure distribution of secondary wave is realized. If we use a voice signal as modulator one, we can get a voice as a secondary wave beam.

We tried to make movable sound source by projecting the beam on the wall (screen) and deflect it two-dimensionally, because the projected and reflected sound is heard as if there is a sound source on the wall. The beam is deflected by two axial servo mechanism controlled by computer(Fig. 2).

3 Localization Characteristics I (1 Dimensional)

The transducer used for this system is piezoelectric type and a matrix array of transducers (4x4) is used for primary sound source. The secondary wave derived from parametric array effect has characteristics in frequency as shown in Fig. 3. The frequency range shows that display sound can be voice or any audible sound. Really, we can hear and message and music from reflective sound source on the screen.

To evaluate the display method, two kinds of screens were made and one dimensional accuracy of localization of the reflective sound (white noise) was measured. Fig. 4 shows the two kinds of screen, one is plane and another is a part of ellipse with two focuses, – one at listener and another at primary sound source (transducer). Fig. 5 is the lattice pattern on the screen used for evaluation of the system, and the listener was asked to answer the recognized position by the x,y number of lattice on the screen when the direction of the sound beam is changed on-dimensionally one after another randomly.

Fig. 6 shows the result of the experiment for two kinds of screen. The size of the plotting mark shows the rate of the correct answer for every position as shown under the figure. If the display point is recognized perfectly, the largest marks (10/10) are arrayed on the inclined straight line. These results show that higher answer rate is shown on the elliptical screen.

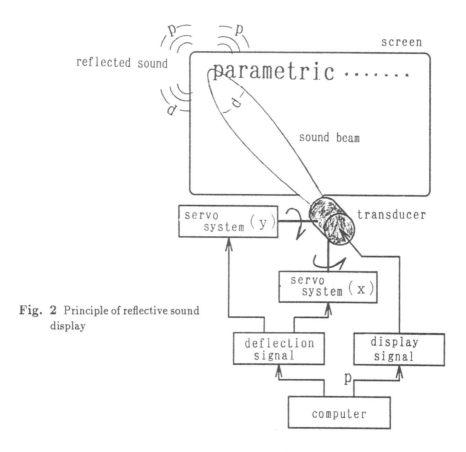

Fig. 2 Principle of reflective sound display

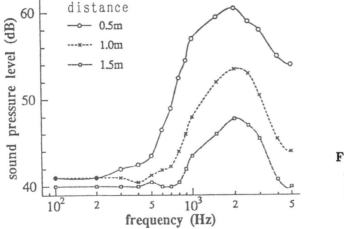

Fig. 3 Frequency characteristics of parametric array

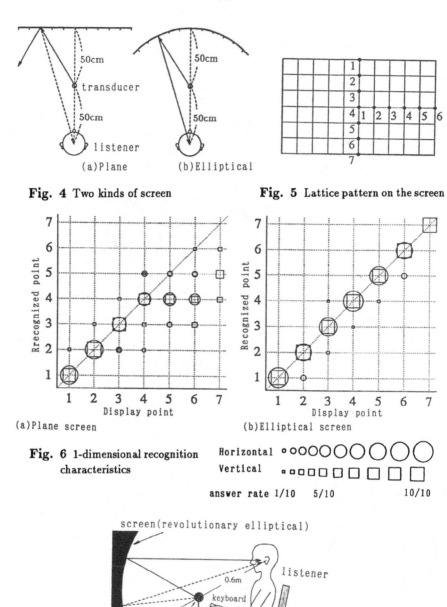

Fig. 4 Two kinds of screen

Fig. 5 Lattice pattern on the screen

(a)Plane screen

(b)Elliptical screen

Fig. 6 1-dimensional recognition characteristics

Horizontal

Vertical

answer rate 1/10   5/10   10/10

Fig. 7 2-dimensional screen and listener

4 Localization Characteristics II (2 Dimensional)

A two-dimensionally curved screen was made to evaluate the two-dimensional location accuracy. The curved surface of revolutionary ellipse was made based on the result of one dimensional localization accuracy measurement. By this screen any sound beam projected on the screen comes back to listener as shown in Fig. 7.

The localization accuracy is also measured and shown in Fig. 8. The size of round mark shows the rate of correct answers obtained by 1/4 screen (right under, 5x5 points) as shown under the figure as example. And the size of an inner circle shows pure correct answer rate respectively and that of the outer one corresponds to the answer rate including the case when the point designated by the listener is the neighboring point. The dark circle shows the case of correct answer rate under 40To improve the recognition rate, diplejs (30mm in diameter) are carved on the surface of screen to disperse the reflective beam in 50 degrees (Fig. 9). This makes the wave front of reflective sound more natural and easier to listen to. The result in Fig. 9 shows the improvement in localization by this method.

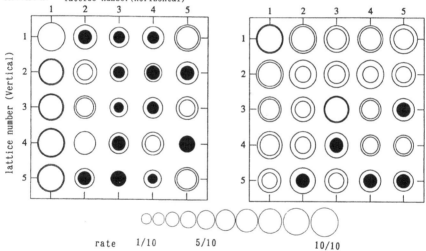

Fig. 8 Localization rate of the flat screen

Fig. 9 Localization rate of the screen with dimples

5 Conclusion

A movable sound source was made by formation of audible sound beam by parametric array, by projection on a wall and by deflecting the beam two-dimensionally. The screen was formed by the elliptical curve and dimples are added on the screen for better localization.

The movable sound source on the screen can emit voice and any defined special sound (cursor, comma etc.) with locative information. This function is just like CRT and can be a great support for the key-in work of visually handicapped people.

References

1. P. J. Westervelt, "Parametric acoustic array", J. Acoust. Soc. Am. 35, 535-537 (1963)

2. M. Yoneyama, J. Fujimoto, Y. Kawamo and Sasabe, "The audio spotlight: An application of nonlinear interaction of sound wave to a new type of loudspeaker design", J. Acoust. Soc. Am. 73, 1522-1536 (1983)

Synthesizing Non-Speech Sound to Support Blind and Visually Impaired Computer Users

A. DARVISHI, V. GUGGIANA, E. MUNTEANU, H. SCHAUER

Department of Computer Science (IfI)
University of Zurich, Winterthurerstrasse 190, CH-8057 Zurich, Switzerland

M. MOTAVALLI

Swiss Federal Laboratories for Material Testing and Research (EMPA)
Uberlandstrasse 129, CH-8600 Dubendorf, Switzerland

M. RAUTERBERG

Usability Laboratory, Work and Organizational Psychology Unit
Swiss Federal Institute of Technology (ETH), Nelkenstrasse 11, CH-8092 Zurich, Switzerland
Tel: +41-1-632 7082, email: rauterberg@rzvax.ethz.ch

Abstract. This paper describes work in progress on automatic generation of "impact sounds" based on physical modelling. These sounds can be used as non-speech audio presentation of objects and as interaction-mechanisms to non visual interfaces. In this paper especially we present the complete physical model for impact sounds "spherical objects hitting flat plates or beams." The results of analysing of some examples of recorded (digitised) "impact sounds" and their comparisons with some theoretical aspects are discussed in this paper. These results are supposed to be used as input for the next phases of our audio framework project. The objective of this research project (joint project University of Zurich and Swiss Federal Institute of Technology) is to develop a concept, methods and a prototype for an audio framework. This audio framework shall describe sounds on a highly abstract semantic level. Every sound is to be described as the result of one or several interactions between one or several objects at a certain place and in a certain environment.

Keywords: non speech sound generation, visual impairment, auditory interfaces, physical modelling, auditive feedback, human computer interaction, software ergonomics, usability engineering, material properties

1   Introduction

The following sections describe the background about using computers by blind computer users and the development of graphical user interfaces and their impact on this group of computer users. Subsequently two approaches for presenting non visual interfaces will be described. A short description about using non speech audio in different applications follows, two basic strategies for creating non speech audio and our approach to automatic generation of non speech audio are introduced. At the end this paper describes some steps which are carried out and those which are supposed to be done by the end of the project.

2   Background

For much of their history, computer displays have presented only textual and numeric information to their users. One benefit of this character-based interface, was that users who were blind could have fairly easy access to such systems. Users with visual disabilities could use computers with character-based interfaces by using devices and software that translated the characters on the screen to auditory information (usually a synthesised human voice) or/and tactile terminals and printers. One of the most important breakthrough in HCI (Human Computer Interaction) in recent years was the development of graphical user interfaces (GUIs) or WIMPs (Windows, Mice, Pointers). These interfaces provide innovative graphical representations for system objects such as disks and files, and for computing concepts such as multitasking by windows. GUIs are not powerful because they use windows, mice, and icons. Rather it is the underlying principles of access to multiple information sources, direct manipulation, access to multitasking, and intuitive metaphors which provide the power [Mynatt-91]. Since the mid 80's, the computer industry has seen a remarkable increase in the use of GUIs, as a means to improve the bandwidth of communication between sighted users and computers. Unfortunately, these GUIs have left a part of the computing population behind. Presently GUIs are all but completely inaccessible for computer users who are blind or severely visually-disabled. Today, there are some commercial products which are able to convert textual information on the screen of GUIs into synthetic speech, however they are absolutely insufficient. This is due to the fact that historic strategies for providing access for these users are inadequate [Boyd-90, Bux-86]. Today, there exists no simple mapping from graphical window based systems into the auditory or tactile domains.

3 Models for Non-Visual Presentation of GUIS

Based on different models there are two approaches for presenting information from GUIs in non visual forms [Crispien-94]. They are being investigated in two projects (see below). Both projects present prototypically information about graphical applications and also graphical computer environments in non visual form. These applications make use of on-screen graphical mechanisms (such as buttons and scroll bars) to control the application, and the environments provide an abstraction for the basic objects in the computer system, such as data files, directories, etc., and the basic computer operations, such as copying and deleting. The following diagram illustrates two strategies of deriving an audio/tactile perceptual manifestation of an interface display. Conceptual and perceptual mapping can be carried out either directly (e.g. a room environment representation - first approach) or indirectly (by using the visual model - second approach) [Gaver-89].

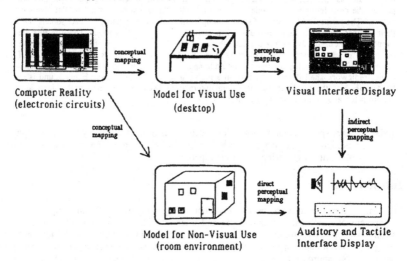

Fig. 1. Two different mappings between computer world and user world

4 First Approach: Hierarchical Presentation of Interface Objects

The Mercator project [Mynatt-93] is an example for this approach. Its aim is to provide access to X-Windows and Unix workstations for computer users who are blind or severely visually impaired. The interface objects (such as icons, windows etc.) are organised in a hierarchical tree structure which can be traversed using a numerical key path. The primarily output modality is audio (synthetic speech and non speech audio) and since recently Braille output. The Mercator project uses the so-called "Audioroom" metaphors and spatial sounds to simulate the graphical computer environment.

5   Using Non-Speech Cues in the Mercator Project

The interface objects in the Mercator environment are called AICs (Auditory Interface Component). The type and attributes of AIC-objects are conveyed through auditory icons and so called "Filtears". Auditory icons are sounds which are designed to trigger associations with everyday objects, just as graphical icons resemble everyday objects [Gaver-89]. This mapping is easy for interface components such as trashcan icons but is less straightforward for components such as menus and dialogue boxes, which are abstract notions and have no innate sound associated with them. An example of some auditory icons are: touching a window sounds like tapping on a glass pane, searching through a menu creates a series of shutter sounds, a variety of push button sounds are used for radio buttons, toggle buttons, and generic push button AICs, and touching a text field sounds like an old fashioned typewriter.

6   Second Approach: Spatial Oriented Approach

The GUIB (Textual and Graphical User Interfaces For Blind People) is an example for this approach [see Crispien-94]. GUIB uses concepts and methodologies of visual interfaces and translates them into other modal sensories primarily Braille and also audio. Some special devices are built for input and output. Spatial 3-dimensional environments and auditory icons are also integrated.

7   Non Speech Audio

Non speech audio is being used in many fields including:

- Scientific audiolization [Blattner-92]

- User interfaces [Gaver-86] such as:

  - Status and monitoring messages.

  - Alarms and warning messages [Momtahan-93].

  - Audio signals as redundancy information to the visual displays to strengthen their semantics.

  - Sound in collaborative work [Gaver-91]

  - Multimedia application [Blattner-93]

  - Visually impaired and blind computer users [Edwards-88].

Just as with light, sound has many different dimensions in which it can be perceived. Visual perception distinguishes dimensions such as color, saturation, luminescence, and texture. Audition has an equally rich space in which human beings can perceive differences like pitch, timbre, and amplitude. There are also much more complex "higher level" dimensions, such as reverberance, locality, phase modulation, and others. Humans have a remarkable ability to detect and process minute changes in a sound along any one of these dimensions [Rossing-90]

8   Generation of Non Speech Audio

There is an increasing world-wide interest for generating and fast processing of audio data in many areas, especially for non visual interfaces. In principal there are two different ways of generating and processing audio data:

(1) digital recording, storing these audio data (sound samples), searching and playing them synchronously when needed;

(2) modelling audio data on a highly semantic level through extraction of relevant parameters of sound, storing the parameters that need a low rate of storage, generating audio data through these parameters.

We present results to go the second way [Rauterberg-94].

Every sound is to be described as the result of one or several interactions between one or several objects at a certain place and in a certain environment. Every interaction has attributes, that have an

388

influence on the generated sound. Simultaneously, the participating objects, which take part in the sound generation process, can consist of different physical conditions (states of aggregation), materials as well as their configurations. In themselves also have attributes, which can have an influence on the generated sound.

The hearing of sounds in everyday life is based on the perception of events and not on the perception of sounds as such. For this reason, everyday sounds are often described by the events they are based on. First, a framework concept for the description of sounds is presented, in which sounds can be represented as audio signal patterns along several descriptive dimensions of various objects interacting together in a certain environment. On the basis of the differentiation of purely physical and purely semantic descriptive dimensions, the automatic sound generation is discussed on the physical, syntactical and semantic levels.

To be seen as physical descriptive dimensions are the sound pitch, frequency, volume and duration; as semantic dimensions, the differentiation of the interacting objects concerning their physical condition (state of aggregation) solid, liquid and gaseous has resulted.

Within the scope of this research project, we shall especially look for possibilities to describe the sound class "solid objects," in particular the class of the primitive sounds "knock" ("strike", "hit"), because this class of sounds occurs very frequently in everyday life and many blind persons orient themselves through auditory landmarks in everyday life, the interacting objects can be easily and well described by their material characteristics and the knowledge of solid-state physics and acoustics can be used. The generation of "impact sounds" based on physical models provides new possibilities to synthesise sounds for parametrized auditory icons [Gaver-93] especially for presenting objects and interactions in non visual interfaces.

In next sections we describe an experiment and the corresponding physical model for comparing the natural frequencies. The last section describes some phases of the project that are not carried out so far and still should be done in the next phases.

9 Experiments with Plates and Beams

We have investigated and modelled the sound patterns: "impact of a solid spherical object falling onto a plate or beam". A laboratory experiment (see fig. 2) was carried out to examine and optimise the derived theoretical model with the sound of a real impact. The experiments were done in an sound-proofed room.

Six different spheres (tab. 2) with different radii and one glass sphere were dropped from three different heights (tab. 1) on six different plates and beams (tab. 3). The signals were digitised via a DAT- Tape. 252 sound sequences (7 radii * 3 heights * (6 plates + 6 beams) = 252) were recorded. Hence some parameters which were derived from the theoretical model could be changed and examined.

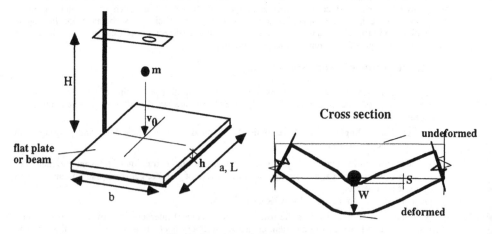

Fig. 2. Experimental Device

Height (H) [cm]	100	50	5

Tab. 1.: Heights

Name	g	s1	s2	s3	s4	s5	s6
Material	glass	steel	steel	steel	steel	steel	steel
Diameter [mm]	14.1	7.5	8.0	9.0	10.0	12.0	14.0
Mass [g]	3.65	1.72	2.09	2.98	4.07	7.02	11.16

Tab. 2.: Spheres

Material	h plate [mm]	h beam [mm]	density [kg/m³]	Poisson's ratio	elasticity [Pa]
steel	2.96	2.96	7700	0.28	19.5E10
aluminium	3.98	3.98	2700	0.33	7.1E10
glass	7.94	7.94	2300	0.24	6.2E10
plexi	3.80	3.90	1180	-	-
PVC	6.00	6.12	-	-	-
wood	8.06	8.06	-	-	-

Tab. 3.: Properties

10 Physical Modelling of Thin Plates and Beams

The physical description of the behaviour of the plate's oscillations following the impact with the sphere provides variations of air pressure that we are able to hear. The natural frequencies of our small spheres are usually not in the audible range, therefore we don't care for the time being about this. However, we are concerned to include in our simulations the essential influence of the interaction on the impact sound.

How does the sound arise? The sphere hits the plate or beam and stimulates vibrations with the natural frequencies. These oscillations are transmitted to the medium as variation of pressure. The human ears receive these pressure waves and we interpret them as sound. The natural-frequencies of our small sphere are too high and they overtake the threshold of audibility. Thus, for the beginning we don't take them into consideration in our physical models.

General Notations:

E = Young's modulus σ = Poisson's ratio   w = displacement
D = bending stiffness ρ = density   h = thickness
I = moment of inertia ρ' = mass per unit length   L = beam's length
a,b = length, width of plate ω = angular frequency   f = natural frequency
w(x,y,t) = displacement   u(x,y)=static solution   m,n= integers
   g(t) =function that describes the temporal component (damping)

Basic Relations: $\quad \omega = 2\pi f, \quad I = \dfrac{bh^3}{12}, \quad D = \dfrac{Eh^3}{12(1-\sigma^2)}, \quad \rho' = \rho \cdot b \cdot h$

10.1 Model of the Plate:

Equation of plate's motion:

$$D\left(\frac{\partial^4 w(x,y,t)}{\partial x^4} + 2\frac{\partial^4 w(x,y,t)}{\partial x^2 \partial y^2} + \frac{\partial^4 w(x,y,t)}{\partial y^4}\right) + \rho h \frac{\partial^2 w(x,y,t)}{\partial t^2} = 0$$

Solutions for natural frequencies in two particular typical boundary conditions:

clamped along all edges   simply supported at all edges

$$f_{m,n} = 2\pi\left(\frac{m^2}{b^2} + \frac{n^2}{a^2}\right)\sqrt{\frac{D}{\rho h}} \qquad\qquad f_{m,n} = \frac{\pi}{2}\left(\frac{m^2}{a^2} + \frac{n^2}{b^2}\right)\sqrt{\frac{D}{\rho h}}$$

10.2 Model of the Beam:

Equation of beam's motion:

$$EI\frac{\partial^4 w(x,t)}{\partial x^4} + \rho' h\frac{\partial^2 w(x,t)}{\partial t^2} = 0$$

Solutions for natural frequencies in two particular typical boundary conditions:

clamped at both ends

$$f_n = \frac{n^2\pi h}{L^2}\sqrt{\frac{E}{3\rho}}$$

simply supported

$$f_n = \frac{n^2\pi h}{4L^2}\sqrt{\frac{E}{3\rho}}$$

11 Software Synthesis of Impact Sounds

So far we have designed an audio signal generator for "impact sounds". This generator consists of object libraries to support the modelling of the audio signals which arise from the interaction of standard structures. These objects can be used to build up an infinite number of real models whose parameters are mechanical material properties and geometric dimensions. The concept "impact sounds" covers also audio signals such as: "scrapping", "rolling", "bouncing", "breaking", etc. They can be modelled using the same object libraries.

The components which are briefly described below the block diagram (fig. 3) are suitable for the planned architecture of the audio-generator as a stand-alone product.

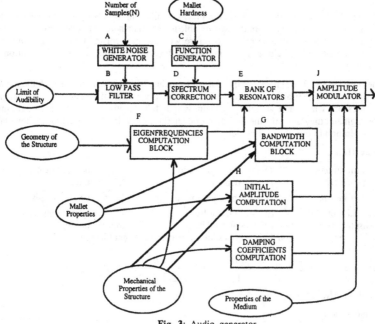

Fig. 3: Audio generator

A   *Random White Noise Generator*
B   *Low Pass Filter* cuts the frequencies above the audible range ($f_{cut\text{-}off} \approx 20$ kHz).
C,D   *Function Generator, Spectrum Correction Block.* The analysis of "impact sounds" from tapping with hammers of varying hardnesses has shown that the energy released by the hammer into the structure is distributed over a certain frequency range. A hard hammer (of steel) transmits force into the structure and quickly deforms it, thus supplying a large portion of high frequency energy. Whereas a soft hammer (made of rubber for example) deforms the

structure slowly and supplies mainly low frequency energy. This energy transmission function is calculated in Block C and drives the "spectrum correction" which is performed in Block D (see fig. 3).

E   *Bank of Resonators* is a bank of filters which only let through natural-frequencies. The bandwidths are calculated in Block G.

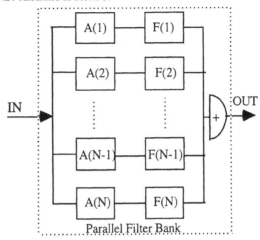

Fig. 4 Bank of Filters

This parallel implementation permits individual amplitude control for each natural frequency (Blocks A(1) - A(N)). The number of filters (N) is equivalent with the number of natural frequencies that are used in the model of vibrating structure. The transfer function of the bank of filters can be computed as follows:

$$H(z) = \frac{Y(z)}{X(z)} = \prod_{k=1}^{N} \frac{1 - 2e^{-2\pi B_k T}\cos(2\pi f_k T) + e^{-4\pi B_k T}}{1 - 2e^{-2\pi B_k T}\cos(2\pi f_k T)z^{-1} + e^{-4\pi B_k T}z^{-2}}$$

with f_k = the k-th natural frequency

         B_k = bandwidth of f_k

         T   = sampling rate

         N   = number of resonators (poles)

By applying the inverse z transform to each term of the product, we obtain, the filtered signal. Samples of the output of every resonator k are computed from the input sequence $x[nT]$ by the recursive equation:

$$y_k[nT] = C_k x[nT] + D_k y_k[(n-1)T] + E_k y_k[(n-2)T]$$

where $y_k[(n-1)T]$ and $y_k[(n-2)T]$ are the previous two sample values of the output sequence $y_k[nT]$. The constants C_k, D_k, E_k are related to the resonant frequency f_k and the bandwidth B_k of the resonator as follows:

$$E_k = -e^{-2\pi B_k T}, \qquad D_k = 2e^{-\pi B_k T}\cos(2\pi f_k T), \qquad C_k = 1 - D_k - E_k$$

F   The *Eigen-frequencies Computation Block* calculates the natural frequencies of the particular structure (see chapter 10). These natural frequencies are dependent only on the structure.

G   The *Bandwidth Computation Block* calculates the bandwidths of the bank of filters on the basis of the mechanical properties of the bodies which come in contact.

H   The *Initial Amplitude Computation Block* calculates the initial amplitudes of the frequency components which essentially comprise the interaction effect.

I   The *Damping Coefficients Computation Block* calculates the amplitude damping for the waves. It is dependent on frequency and the loss factor of the material of the structure. The following formula can be usefully applied for elastic materials:

$$\delta_n = \delta_0 \cdot \omega_n, \text{ where}: \omega_n = 2\pi \cdot f_n, \ \delta_0 = \frac{\tan \varphi}{2}$$

where tan φ = tangent of the loss factor

J   The *Amplitude Modulator*. The values calculated under I and H modulate the amplitude of the signals provided by the bank of filters (Block E).

12   Comparison of Physical Model and Experiments

In the evaluation of the output of these two approaches we have to consider the inherent errors of input parameters as well as the inhomogenities of the materials. We compared the respective natural frequencies through spectrograms (see Fig. 2 and Fig. 3). The output error was situated in normal expectations as follows below. The initial amplitudes of the vibrations and the damping coefficients were introduced qualitatively. We have in view a quantitative, theoretic-modelled description of these two parameters. We will also study the possibilities to find the influence of the sphere in the sound generating event.

Errors in our parameters are given as percentile deviations:

E: ~ 1% σ: ~ 1% ρ: ~ 1%

h: ~ 1%   a,b,L: ~ 1%.

Resulting errors in our solutions are given as percentile deviations:

- plate: ~ 4.5%
- beam: ~ 2.5%

Following activities should be carried out in the next steps of the project: (1.) description of a new model that contains all neglected aspects of interaction for impact sounds, (2.) implementation of the model, (3.) psycho-acoustical comparison studies. The subjects are asked to judge whether they can distinguish any difference between real and automatically generated sounds.

13   Conclusion

Having implemented our physical models in fast algorithms, we are now able to generate automatically the sound class of "spherical objects falling onto a beam or plate." It seems that our approach, to base our model on the physics of interacting objects is successful. The automatic generation of "impacted sounds" can be easily used to implement non speech audio cues for presenting objects and interactions in the non visual interfaces. The developed algorithms need low rate of storage and facilitate them to be incorporated in software systems.

References

[Blattner-92]   Blattner, M. M., Greenberg, R. M. and Kamegai, M. (1992) Listening to Turbulence: An Example of Scientific Audialization. In: *Multimedia Interface Design*, ACM Press/ Addison-Wesley, pp 87-102.

[Blattner-93]   Blattner, M. M., G. Kramer, J. Smith, and E. Wenzel (1993) Effective Uses of Nonspeech Audio in Virtual Reality. In: *Proceedings of the IEEE Symposium on Reaseach Frontiers in Virtual Reality*, San Jose, CA. (In conjunction with IEEE Visualization '93) October 25-26, 1993.

[Boyd-90]   Bloyd, L.H., Boyd, W.L., and Vanderheiden, G.C. (1990) The graphical user interface: Crisis, danger and opportunity. *Journal of Visual Impairment and Blindness*, p.496-502.

[Crispien-94]   Crispien,K. (1994) Graphische Benutzerschnittstellen für blinde Rechnerbenutzer. Unpublished manuscript

[Edwards-93]   Edwards, W.K., Mynatt, E.D. and Rodriguez, T (1993) The Mercator Project: a non-visual interface to the X Window system. *The X Resource*,4:1-20.(ftp multimedia.cc.gatech.edu /papers/Mercator /xresource).

[Gaver-86]   Gaver, W. W. (1986). Auditory icons: Using sound in computer interfaces. *Human-Computer Interaction*. 2, 167-177.

[Gaver-88]   Gaver, W. W. (1988). Everyday listening and auditory icons. Doctoral Dissertation, University of California, San Diego.

[Gaver-89]   Gaver, W. (1989) The SonicFinder: an interface that uses auditory icons. *Human Computer Interaction* 4:67-94.

[Gaver-90]   Gaver, W. & Smith R. (1990) Auditory icons in large-scale collaborative environments. In: D. Diaper, D. Gilmore, G. Cockton & B. Shackel (eds.) *Human-Computer Interaction - INTERACT'90*. (pp. 735-740), Amsterdam

[Gaver-91]   Gaver, W., Smith, R. & O'Shea, T. (1991) Effective sounds in complex systems: the ARKola simulation. in S. Robertson, G. Olson & J. Olson (eds.), *Reaching through technology CHI'91*. (pp. 85-90), Reading MA: Addison-Wesley.

[Gaver-93]   Gaver, W. (1993) What in the World do We Hear? An Ecological Approach to Auditory Event Perception. *Ecological Psychology*, 5(1).

[Momtahan-93]   Momtahan, K., Hetu, R. and Tansley, B. (1993) Audibility and identification of auditory alarms in the operating room and intensive care unit. *Ergonomics* 36(10): 1159-1176.

[Mynatt-92]   Mynatt, E.D. and Edwards, W.K. (1992) The Mercator Environment: A Nonvisual Interface to XWindows and Workstations.*GVU Tech Report GIT-GVU-92-05*

[Mynatt-92b]   Mynatt, E.D. and Edwards, W.K. (1992) Mapping GUIs to auditory interfaces. In: *Proceedings of the ACM Symposium on User Interface Software and Technology UIST'92*.

[Mynatt-93]   Mynatt, E.D. and Weber, G. (1993) Nonvisual Presentation of Graphical User Interfaces: Contrasting Two Approaches. *Tech Report/93*

[Rauterberg-94] Rauterberg, M., Motavalli, M., Darvishi, A. & Schauer, H. (1994) Automatic sound generation for spherical objects hitting straight beams. In: Proceedings of "World Conference on Educational Multimedia and Hypermedia" ED-Media'94 held in Vancouver (C), June 25-29, 1994.

[Rossing-90]   Rossing, T.D (1990) The Science of Sound 2nd Edition, Addison Wesley Publishing Company

[Sumikawa-86]   Sumikawa, D. A., M. M. Blattner, K. I. Joy and R. M. Greenberg (1986) Guidelines for the Syntactic Design of Audio Cues in Computer Interfaces. In: *19th Annual Hawaii International Conference on System Sciences*.

Stereo Sound Board for Real Time Auditory Coding of Visual Information

C. Faïk[1], C. Capelle[1&2], C. Halet[2], C. Trullemans[2], C. Veraart[1]

[1]Neural Rehab. Engng Lab., Catholic University of Louvain, UCL 54.46, 54 av. Hippocrate, B-1200 Brussels, Belgium.
[2]Microelectronic Lab., Catholic University of Louvain, 3 place du Levant, B-1348 Louvain-La-Neuve, Belgium.

This paper deals with the design of a stereo sound board for rehabilitation of blindness following the principles of sensory substitution. In this method, signals coding the lacking visual information are transmitted to an intact sensory organ. Moreover, real time functioning of the sensory substitution device has to be attempted to favor sensory motor interactions beneficial to the learning process. In the present study, we consider the feasibility of this conceptual model of sensory substitution and its implementation as a rough model of the retina connected to an inverse model of the cochlea.

The model of vision is limited to main features of the primary visual system, i.e. lateral inhibition and graded resolution. Lateral inhibition can be stimulated by filtering the initial image with an edge detection filter. Graded resolution is modeled using a multi-resolution artificial retina built on the filtered image. The inverse model of audition achieves a weighted summation of sinusoids (i.e. an inverse Fourier transform) whose amplitudes and phases depend on the corresponding ear, taking into account spectral sensitivity of the human ear. Coupling between the model of vision and the inverse model of audition consists of the association of a specific sinusoid to each pixel of the artificial retina; amplitude of each sinusoid is modulated by the gray level of the corresponding pixel.

A specific PC-plugged printed card board has been developed to meet follow the auditory specifications required by the prosthesis: the production of a weighted sum of 256 sinusoids whose phases and frequencies are loaded at card initialization, and whose amplitudes can be modified in real time. This complex sound has to be stereophonic, with different phases and amplitudes for the left and right signals. At this time, no low cost music generator meets these specifications. However, sound processors approach them more and more. Such a processor, the SAM8905 (DREAM s.a. manufacturer), can produce up to 64 monoral sinusoids. Hence, the printed card board contains eight SAM8905's (allowing the generation of 256 binaural sinusoids). The serial outputs of the SAM8905's are converted in parallel by serial-to-parallel shift-registers; then, they are added together. These shift registers and parallel adders are implemented in a FPGA which is followed by two Digital-to-Analog Converters. A control circuitry drives the whole data-path.

The conceptual model of sensory substitution of vision by audition has been implemented in a real time functioning experimental prototype, using this stereo sound board. This prototype is based on a Personal Computer which is connected to a miniature head-fixed video camera on the one hand, and to headphones on the other hand. In a second application, called acoustic screen, this sound board is used in an aid device for blind persons using computers with graphical user interface (Macintosh, Windows, etc.). This device transforms into sound an image which is captured on the computer screen, around the mouse.

The sound board: description and principle

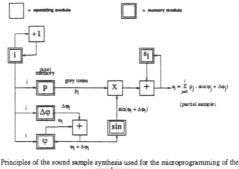

Principles of the sound sample synthesis used for the microprogramming of the sound processor.

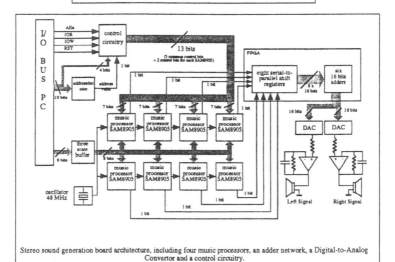

Stereo sound generation board architecture, including four music processors, an adder network, a Digital-to-Analog Convertor and a control circuitry.

Applications of the sound board:

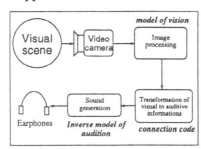

Visual prothesis of sensory substitution

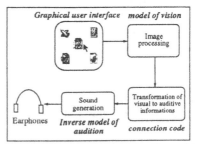

Acoustic screen for computers with graphical interface

DHT – Diary Handy Terminal – for Evaluating Fluctuations in Patients with Parkinson's Disease (PD)

M.M.Pinter, R.J.Helscher and H.Binder

Neurological Hospital Maria Theresien Schlössel
Vienna, Austria

Abstract. In order to permit immediate evaluation of fluctuations in advanced PD and corresponding modification of drug adminstration we developed a software package running on an Epson Handy Terminal.

In a prospective study of 38 PD patients we investigated the improved data evaluation and statistical evaluation of fluctuations registered by DHT as compared to hand-written entries. It was our main objective to investigate in principle the possibility of using a computer-assisted technique for the documentation of oscillations in Parkinson's disease.

The data acquired in the two different ways were evaluated for all 38 patients. As regards accuracy of data acquisition, DHT was superior to the handwritten version. Moreoever DHT also allowed a check of acutal drug intake time to the second. As regards the relationship between duration of drug action and occurence of fluctuations or dyskinesia, DHT provides rapid information for a modification of the therapeutical time schedule.

1 Introduction

With progression of Parkinson's disease, which phenomenologically does not present a straight course, motor fluctuations occur again and again; these are subdivided into short-term (seconds up to minutes), medium-term (hours) and long-term (days up to weeks) fluctuations. Parkinsonian symptoms fluctuate even without treatment, but they increase during long-term therapy and may develop into a major therapeutical problem (1-8). The initial therapeutic efficacy of oral L-dopa application in parkinsonian patients, therefore breaks down in the course of the first three two five years of treatmen (9, 10). "On-off" phenomena of motor symptoms occur in approximatelly 50% of parkinsonian patients receiving L-dopa and thus represent a limiting factor in the treatment (11).

It is well known that fluctuations of motor response - partly drug-induced - may occur in advanced stages of PD, which require a change of treatment strategies (12-18). A verified and generally accepted explanation for the reduction of drug efficacy does not yet exist. It might be connected with the decreased transformation of L-dopa to dopamine and the reduced storage capacity of dopamine due to progressive loss of dopaminergic neurons (19). Blockage of the L-dopa passage by accumulation of the metabolite 3-O methyl dopa is also being considered. It has been demonstrated that patients with a high plasma ratio of OMD/L-dopa have significantly more fluctuations (20-24).

Such fluctuations, either corresponding to drug intake or occurring independently, are usually documented every hour or every fifteen minutes by hand written entries in a motor diary, which serves as a basis for treatment modification and better symptom control. The only disadvantage of this method is the limitation in time of such a form of documentation. In order to overcome this obstacle and to permit immediate evaluation of fluctuations and corresponding modification of drug administration we developed a software package running on an Epson Handy Terminal.

We designed a comparative study of 38 parkinsonian patients demonstrating the improved data evaluation and statistical evaluation of fluctuations registered by developed a software package running on an Epson Handy Terminal as compared to hand-written entries.

2 Method

We have developed a software package called Diary Handy Terminal (DHT), written in Basic, which permits registration of "off"-, "on"- and "on" phases with dyskinesia while the patient is awake or is asleep as well as drug intake and meal times.

In principal, we differentiate two parts of the DHT programme: a module called "patients" to which only the examiner has access for recording demographic data such as name, birth date, onset of the disease, Hoehn and Yahr staging in the "on" phase, drugs prescribed and prescribed times of drug intake, - and a module called "service" to which the patient has access. Here the fluctuations during waking, drug intake and meal times are entered. The software package runs on an Epson handy terminal, which the patient takes home for documentation purposes. The patient himself enters on this terminal all changes of motor response and drug intake with accuracy to the minute. At the next follow-up at the hospital the data are entered into the SQL data base and are used for graphic processing and statistical evaluation.

For the purpose of this study the patient receives a Diary Handy Terminal - DHT (version 2) as described above and a movement diary (version 1), into which he enters in hourly intervals any changes of motor response as well as the time of drug intake. The patients were carefully instructed in the handling of the Diary Handy Terminal and received a short training. Patients were requested to complete both documentations in parallel. The data acquired in two different ways were checked for their accuracy, informative value and practical relevance.

3 Patients

We enrolled in the present study exclusively patients with idiopathic Parkinson's disease with a verified history of fluctuations. The patient populations of a total of 38 includes 24 males and 14 females, aged 42 to 72 years (mean 58.9 years). Mean duration of the disease was 11.2 years (3.2 to 15 years), mean duration of L-dopa treatment was 8.7 years (3 to 14 years), and the mean L-dopa dose amounted to 970 mg. First fluctuations occurred on the average 5.4 years (2.7 to 10 years) prior to study enrolment. Demographic data, Hoehn and Yahr staging, additive medication with dopamine agonists, anticholinergics and deprenyl, and a breakdown of the type of fluctuations are given in table 1.

age		58,9	(42-72) years
Hoehn & Yahr stage			
	- "on"	1,7	(1-3)
	- "off"	3,5	(3-4)
duration of PD		11,2	(3,2-15) years
L-Dopa / duration		8,7	(3-14) years
L-Dopa / dosage		870	(600-1300) mg
dopaminagonists			
bromocriptine			14 patients
lisuride			11 patients
deprenyl			21 patients
anticholinergic			10 patients
fluctuations / duration		5,4	(2,7-10) years
Typ	- wearing off		18 patients
	- komplex		10 patients
dyskinesia			7 patients
	- peak of dose		4 patients
	- biphasic		3 patients
dystonia			4 patients

table 1: Demographic data: 38 patients (f: 14; m: 24) with
idiopathic Parkinson's Disease

4 Results

The data acquired in the two different ways described above were evaluated for all 38 patients. As regards accuracy of data acquisition, DHT (version 2) was superior to the handwritten version. Version 1 permitted evaluation of changes in motor response in hourly intervals, while version 2 provided accurateness to the minute. Moreover version 2 also allowed a check of actual drug intake time to the minute (table 2 and 3).

	version1	version2
	hours	hours
"OFF"	4,5	5,12
	(1-6)	(0,88-5,98)
"ON"	9,2	9,43
	(6-14)	(6,22-13,98)
DYSKINESIA	2,3	2,12
	(1-4)	(0.98-4,68)

table 2:Fluctuations during the day.

	version1	version2
	minutes	minutes
time between drug intake / "ON"		31,2
		(12-57)
time between drug intake / DYSKINESIA		27,3
		(16-34)
time between drug intake / "OFF"		187
		(58-222)

table 3: Changes in motor response and relationship to drug intake.

As regards the relationship between duration of drug action and occurrence of fluctuations or dyskinesia, version 2 provides rapid information for a modification of the therapeutical time schedule. Version 1 on the other hand, which records fluctuations only in hourly intervals, allows only an approximate estimation of time relationships, even if the patient records drug intake to the minute (table 2).

From a practical point of view, version 2 is at first sight the more complicated procedure for the patient; however the majority of patients experience in the long run version 2 as an improvement, in particular since the accoustic signal , which reminds the patient that it is time to take the drug, is considered to be a positive aspect.

5 Discussion

There is no doubt that the diary handy terminal is superior to version 1 as regards data acquisition. The possibility of accurate evaluation of motor fluctuations reflected by drug intake opens the gate for better modification of drug therapy. It is possible to record rapidly principal data, such as onset and duration of action of the drug, in particular of L-dopa medication, which are not only determined by the progression of the disease but are also subject to individual flluctuations (9, 10). Moreover, the exact recording of time relationships between drug intake and occurrence of "on-off" phases or dyskinesia permits easy differentiation of the phenomenology of "on-off" phases and dyskinesia, which is an absolute necessity for adequate modificationof therapeutical strategies (12,13,16).

Since the software programme is very comfortable for the user and very simple, it causes certainly no problems with patient compliance. Our experiences lead to the following two conclusions:

- First: patients who complete accurate movement diaries have no problems whatsoever with the DHT, or vice versa, patients who are unable to operate the DHT, are also unable to complete correctly handwritten movement diaries.

- Second: on the basis of survey diagrams and the automatic calculation of various phases over the day and the relationships between drug intake and onset of action, the physician is more competent when correcting therapeutical strategies. Certainly, further, in particular randomized long-term studies are necessary to substatiae the latter argument, which will clarify the question of therapeutic efficiency for the patient provided by the data acquired with the diary handy terminal.

The present study is intended as a pilot study. It was our main objective to investigate in principle the possibility of using an EDV-assisted technique for the documentation of oscillations in Parkinson's disease and furthermore to evalulate to what extent, DHT is superior to conventional techniques.

References

1. C.D. Marsden, J.D. Parkes: "On-off" effects in patients with Parkinson's disease on chronic levodopa therapy. Lancet 292-296 (1976)

2. M.W.I.M. Horstink, J.C.M. Zijlmyns, J.W. Pasman et al.: Severity of Parkinson's disease is a risk factor for peak-of-dose dyskinesia. J Neurol Neurosurg Psychiatry 53, 224-226 (1990)

3. R.A.C. Roos, C.B. Vredevoogd, E.A. Vandervelde: Response fluctuations in Parkinson's disease. Neurology 40, 1344-1346 (1990)

4. A.E. Lang, K. Johnson: Akathisia in idiopathic Parkinson's disease. Neurology 37, 477-481 (1987)

5. M.A. Menza, J. Sage, E. Marshall et al.: Mood changes and „on-off" phenomena in Parkinson's disease. Move Disord 5, 148-151 (1990)

6. N. Giladi, D Mc Mahon, S. Przedborski et al.: Motor blocks in Parkinson's disease. Neurology 42, 339-339 (1992)

7. J. Jankovic, F. Nour: Respiratory dyskinesia in Parkinson's disease. Neurology 36, 303-304 (1986)

8. R.J. Hardie, A.J. Lees, G.M. Stern: On-off fluctuation in Parkinson's disease. A clinical and neuropharmacological study. Brain 107, 487-506 (1984)

9. W.H. Poewe, A.J. Lees, G.M. Stern: Low-dose levodopa therapy in Parkinson's disease: a six year follow-up study. Neurology 36, 1528-1530 (1986)

10. M.R. Luquin, O. Scipioni, J Vaamonde et al.: Levodopa-induced dyskinesia in Parkinson's disease: clinical and pharmacological classification. Mov Disord 7, 117-124 (1992)

11. A.J. Lees: The on-off phenomenon. J Neurol Neurosurg and Psychiatry. Special Supp. 29-37 (1989)

12. C.G. Goetz, C.M. Tanner, H.L. Klawans et al.: Parkinson's disease and motor fluctuation: long acting carbidopa/levodopa (CR4-Sinemet). Neurology 37, 875-878 (1987)

13. N. Quinn, J.D. Parkes, C.D. Marsden: Control of on/off phenomenon by continous intravenous infusion of levodopa. Neurology 34, 1131-1136 (1984)

14. S.T. Gancher, J.G. Nutt, W. Woodward: Response to brief levodopa infusions in parkinsonian patients with and without motor fluctuation. Neurology 38, 712-716 (1988)

15. J.A. Obeso, M.R. Luquin, J.M. Martinez-Lage: Lisuride infusion pump: A device for the treatment of motor fluctuations in Parkinson's disease. Lancet i, 467-470 (1986)

16. C.M.H. Stibe, A.J. Lees, P.A. Kempster, G.M. Stern: Subcutaneous Apomorphine in Parkinsonian on-off oscillations. Lancet 1, 403-406 (1988)

17. W.H. Poewe, B. Kleedorfer, F. Gerstenbrand, W.H. Oertel: Subcutaneous Apomorphine in Parkinson's disease. Lancet 1:, 943 (1988)

18. C.M.H. Stibe, A.J. Lees, G.M. Stern: Subcutaneous infusion of apomorphine and lisuride in the treatment of parkinsonian on-off fluctations. Lancet 1, 871 (1987)

19. G.F. Wooten: Neurochemistry. In: W.C. Koller: Handbook of Parkinson's disease. New York, Basel: Marcel Dekker Inc. pp. 237-251 (1987)

20. D.B. Calne, M.J. Zigmond: Compensatory mechanisms in degenerative neurologic neurologic diseases. Insights from parkinsonism. Arch Neurol 48, 361-363 (1991)

21. D.B. Calne: The free radical hypothesis in idiopathic parkinsonism: evidence against it. Ann Neurol 32, 799-803 (1992)

22. G. Fabrini, M.M. Mouradian, J.L. Juncos et al: Motor fluctuations in Parkinson's disease: central pathophysiologic mechanisms, Part I. Ann Neurol 24, 366-371 (1988)

23. M.R. Luquin, O. Scipioni, J Vaamonde et al.: Levodopa-induced dyskinesia in Parkinson's disease: clinical and pharmacological classification. Mov Disord 7, 117-124 (1992)

24. G.F. Wooten: Progress in understanding the pathophysiology of treatment related fluctuations in Parkinson's disease. Ann Neurol 24, 363-365 (1988)

Development of the system to teach the bedsore prevention method for wheelchair users

Hiroyuki Koyama, Takashi Komeda, Tateki Uchida, Masao Miyagi,
Kikuo Kanaya[1], Sadae Kuroiwa[2], Susumu Otsuka[3] and Hiroyasu Funakubo

Shibaura Institute of Technology, Saitama, Japan
1) Yokohama Image System Co., Kanagawa, Japan
2) National Murayama Hospital, Tokyo, Japan
3) National Rehabilitation Center for the Disabled, Saitama, Japan

Abstract. In this study, we are developing the system to teach bedsores prevention method for wheelchair users. This system can measure the distribution of pressure by the sensor sheet when a wheelchair user sits on it, and show the measured result on the monitor by the color image. Therefore, wheelchair users are able to learn the bedsores prevention method under recognizing their distributions of pressure with the therapist. We measured pressure distribution and got differences between SCI people and AB people using this system, and we confirmed that it is important to measure pressure distributions and this system is useful to use when therapist teach the bedsore prevention method to wheelchair users.

1 Introduction

For constantly bedridden people and wheelchair users, bedsores is one of the most horrible diseases. The medical term used for bedsores is "decubitus ulcer". "decubitus" is the Latin word for "recline". Thus, bedsores are ulcers which break out when bodies are reclining. However, bedsores is also caused to wheelchair users by reason of the continuous sitting. Because sitting is the same condition to reclining in concerning of the pressure to the body. When those people are continuously lying or sitting in the same posture, pressure,which is the physical factor, is continuously maintained upon the same area of the body and closes the capillary vessels in that area, leading to the blockage of the circulation. As the result, tissues in that area undergo irreversible changes leading to death and bedsores brake out.

It is usually said that prevention is the best strategy for bedsores. For example, restoration of healthy nutritional conditions or motive ability, keeping the area where bedsores often break out clean, reduction of the pressure, etc.. From a technical point of view, there are three ways to prevent bedsores, which are used singly or in combination.

(1) Use of a mat or bedding designed to support the weight equally and to prevent pressure from centering upon one local area of the body.

(2) To change the posture or to lift up the area under pressure at regular intervals by self-help or , if necessary, with the aid of helpers.

(3) Reducing the pressure by moving the bedding, mat, etc. in stead of moving the patient's body directly.

Normally, wheelchair users learn the bedsores prevention method from the therapist in hospital. For example, how to do the push-up, which is the best fit cushion etc.. However, there are no system and data to measure the distribution of the pressure, they teach it only by their experiences [1].

2 The aim of this study

In this study, we are developing the system to teach bedsores prevention method for wheelchair users. This system can measure the distribution of pressure by the sensor sheet when a wheelchair user sits on it, and show the measured result on the monitor by the color image. Therefore, wheelchair users are able to learn the bedsores prevention method under recognizing their distributions of pressure with the therapist. So this system belongs to the assist equipment when the therapist teach the bedsores prevention method.

3 System Configuration

3.1 The necessary conditions for System

In order to determine the mechanical relationship , measurement of the distribution of pressure between a body and a wheelchair seat is required. A number of methods have been suggested for it, such as pressure-sensitive films, load-cell matrix, pyramid-shaped matrix rubber sheets and switch arrays, but each method has its particular weak points to use this study. Most pressure distribution-detecting device are applied to flat surfaces only. If a device is applied to a flexible curved surface and each of the sensing transducers of that device is non flexible, the contact condition between a body and the transducer is poor. Also, as the sensors are placed at intervals of several centimeters, the spatial resolution of the device is fairly low. Moreover, since a large number of transducer necessitates many wires and amplifiers, the system is very bulky. Therefore, the measurement of pressure distribution between a body and a wheelchair seat has been impossible. The necessary conditions for measuring a moving body pressure distributions are as follows:
(1) flexibility of sensors
(2) availability of high-speed sampling
(3) availability of high-density measurement
(4) ease in processing detected data
(5) ease in installing equipment

3.2 System outline

We have developed a tactile imaging system which meets above conditions. This system transforms 23×24 matrix pressure distributions, which are detected by pressure-sensitive conductive rubber sheets, into video signals. This enables various applications of the video signals by using a variety of video equipment. Using this system, you can not only see the pattern of image pressure distributions on a video monitor but you can also easily store images, restore and record by using a video tape recorder. You can also process the images with a computer.

Fig. 1 shows the components of the tactile imaging system. A tactile image sensor receives vertical and horizontal digital address signals from an imaging controller. It returns analog pressure distribution signals to the controller.

The imaging controller forms a video signal of the pressure distribution analog signals by adding vertical and horizontal synchronous signals. It sends the video signal of a monochromatic image of pressure distribution to an image processor or a video tape recorder.

The image processor connects with not only a monochromatic video monitor which shows images from the imaging controller, but also a pseudo-color video monitor which displays pressure distribution images as color contour lines.

A personal computer, NEC PC-9801, and an additional image input memory board are used as the image processor. This makes it possible to store 4 successive images in a 640kb memory.

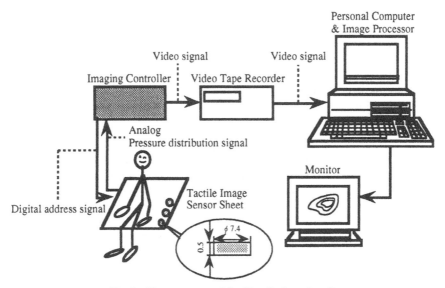

Fig.1 Components of the Tactile Imaging System

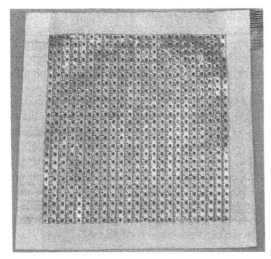

Fig.2 Sensor sheet overview   Fig.3 Detecting point overview

3.3 Sensor Sheet

Fig. 2 shows the overview of the tactile image sensor sheet. This flexible sensor sheet consists of flexible print circuit comb-shaped electrodes and pressure-sensitive conductive rubber which chances the electric conductivity continuously corresponding to the applied pressure. Each detecting point is placed in a 23×24 matrix with an 16mm pitch. The size of the sensing area is 352mm $\times$ 368mm. The detecting point, a pair of 16mm square comb-shaped electrodes and a pressure-sensitive conductive rubber in 7.4mm diameter and 0.5mm thickness, are shown in Fig. 3.

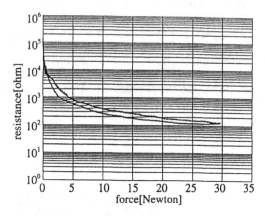

Fig.4 Typical pressure-resistance characteristics of a sensor

Fig. 4 shows an example of data characteristics of the pressure-sensitive conductive rubber . When no pressure is applied on it, it shows very low conductivity or very high resistance over M Ω , or it is almost isolated. Under a load of 30 Newton, the sheet becomes very highly conductive or has very low resistance. The resistance of the rubber sheet changes gradually and continuously, corresponding to the applied pressure. Fig. 4 also shows that hysteresis should be observed in the pressure-resistance characteristics, and therefore the tactile sensor is suitable for a relative pattern measurement, but is not recommendable for measurement seeking high accuracy of the absolute value [5].

3.4   Principle of Measurement for Pressure Distributions

A DC +5V current is put through a transistor and a current flows simultaneously into a row of inside electrodes, and then each outside electrode receives the current corresponding to the conductivity of the rubber sheet. At that time, a horizontal scanning circuit is transmitted to the outside electrodes through certain FET's, each in a 500ns time series. Subsequently, a time-serial signal of a horizontal row of the pressure distribution is given.

During this process, a DC +5V current is applied to the top row of inside electrodes for 64.5 μ s. Each gate of each FET connected to an outside electrode opens time serially from left to right during 0.5 μ s, driven by a horizontal address decoder and driver. A current corresponding to the row of the pressure distribution flows into an output line through each FET. Next, the 2nd line is indicated by the vertical address decoder-driver, and the time series current corresponding to the pressure distribution of the 2nd row is also transmitted to the output line. Successively, each row from the 3rd row down to the bottom row is time serially addressed by the vertical address decoder-driver, and a complete image of the pressure distribution is given on the output line in 16.7ms. Sixty images are produced per one second [2,3,4].

4 Experiments for Wheelchair Users

Using this system, we have measured pressure distributions of Spinal Cord Injured (SCI) people who use wheelchair and Able-body (AB) people when they sit on the wheelchair. Fig. 5 and Fig. 6 show examples of each data by the color image.

We got following results from this experiments.

(1) AB people have wide area to support the body pressure and have almost same shape distributions (only the density and the size are different). However, SCI people have small area to supportand the high pressure concentrate to one point. Furthermore, shapes of pressure distribution of SCI people are various.

(2) Pressure distributions of AB people are changed little by little while they are sitting on the wheelchair. This is quite natural thing. However, pressure distributions of SCI people are not changed under same conditions.

(3) When AB people slightly incline their upper body to right and left, the pressure distributions are changed according to their motion. In the other hand, pressure distributions of SCI people are not change even if they do same action.

From these results, it is important to measure the real-time pressure distribution of the wheelchair user when therapist teach the bedsore prevention method. Because their pressure distributions are variety and therapist must confirm that the prevention method, for example push-up etc., really release the high pressure or not.

 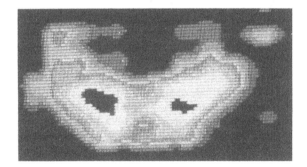

Fig.5 An example of the pressure distribution of Able-Body person

 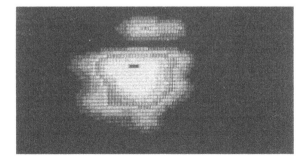

Fig.6 An example of the pressure distribution of Spinal Cord Injured person

5 Conclusions

We have developed the tactile imaging system using the flexible sensor sheet to measure and show the pressure distribution of wheelchair users in real-time. We measured pressure distribution and got differences between SCI people and AB people using this system, and we confirmed that it is important to measure pressure distributions and this system is useful to use when therapist teach the bedsore prevention method to wheelchair users. And we also got good estimations from therapists who used this system.

Next stage, we will try to evaluate various cushions which are on the market from the point of the pressure dissolution ability.

Acknowledgment

We wish to thank the Association for Technical Aids for support of this project, and Yuji Wakamiya for his graphic art work and editorial assistance.

References

1. H. Funakubo, T. Dohi, T. Komeda, T. Isomura: Development of a System to Prevent Bedsores. Journal of Faculty of Engineering, The University of Tokyo, Vol.38, No.3, pp.1-15 (1986)
2. K. Kanaya and M. Ishiskawa: Tactile imaging system and its aplication, The Society of Biomechanisms, Vol.13, No.1, pp.45-48 (1989)
3. K. Kanaya and M. Ishikawa: Dynamic measurement of foot-floor pressure distributions using tactile imaging system, Human Interface N&R, vol.3, pp.103-106 (1988)
4. K. Kanaya, M. Ishikawa, M. Shimojou: Tactile Imaging System for Body Pressure Distribution. Proceedings of the 11th Congress of the International Ergonomics Association, pp.1495-1497 (1991)
5. Yokohama Rubber Co.: Technical data of conductive rubber sheet (1984)

Development of the bedsore alarm system using microcomputer for wheelchair users

Takashi Komeda, Hiroyuki Koyama, Tateki Uchida, Masao Miyagi,
Kikuo Kanaya[1], Sadae Kuroiwa[2], Susumu Otsuka[3] and Hiroyasu Funakubo

Shibaura Institute of Technology, Saitama, Japan
1)Yokohama Image System Co., Kanagawa, Japan
2)National Murayama Hospital, Tokyo, Japan
3)National Rehabilitation Center for the Disabled, Saitama, Japan

Bedsores is one of the most horrible decease for wheelchair users. When those people are continuously sitting in the same posture, pressure,which is the physical factor, is continuously maintained upon the same area of the body, tissues in that area undergo irreversible changes leading to death and bedsores brake out. It is usually said that prevention is the best strategy for bedsores. Normally, wheelchair users learn the bedsores prevention method from the therapist in hospital and push-up is one of the most useful method to release the pressure. However, if they forget to do the push-up, they become dangerous conditions to occur bedsores. Therefore, they must learn the custom to do push-up in hospital.

In this study, we are developing the system to give a alarm when the wheelchair user forget to do the push-up, and they can learn the timing of push-up as the custom in their daily life after using this system one or two weeks.

This system consists of a flexible sensor sheet and a control box. The sensor sheet consists of flexible print circuit comb-shaped electrodes and pressure-sensitive conductive rubber which chances the electric conductivity continuously corresponding to the applied pressure. Each detecting point is placed in a 12×12 matrix with an 16mm pitch. The size of the sensing area is 176mm $\times$ 176mm. The detecting point has a pair of 16mm square comb-shaped electrodes and a pressure-sensitive conductive rubber in 7.4mm diameter and 0.5mm thickness. The control box has a electric circuit based on micro-computer (Z80), a LED display panel and switches. The electric circuit has a A/D converter to get the pressure value, address decoders to scan the sensor matrix, parallel I/O to put on LED and etc.. We use dry batteries which is attached to the control box to supply the electric power. The size of the control box is 200mm $\times$ 200mm $\times$ 70mm and the weight is 500g. Therefore, this system is a portable type and it is easy to use wheelchair users.

This system can measure the distribution of pressure by the sensor sheet when a wheelchair user sits on it, and show the measured result on the LED panel and also add the pressure value of each points to the memory of the electric circuit every 15 seconds. If the high pressure continuously applies to the same position, this system alarm to the wheelchair user by the buzzer. The level of the high pressure, the time interval of the alarm and the time length of push-up can be changed by three switches.

We confirmed the good operation of this system and will try to check the function through the experiment of wheelchair users.

A Case Study of Computer Analysis of the Arthritic User in Rehabilitation Engineering

G. Jeffries, D.K. Wright, N. Rogers and K. Leibrandt.

Dept. of Design, Brunel University, London, U.K.

Introduction

In this work we have combine the use of anthropometric data and mechanical analysis software to model a complete system in the form of a user combined with a product. Analysis of the system is then possible, to find the forces, moments, accelerations, and any other dynamic information. Applying existing maximum force and moment criteria, within an iterative process, we are able to evaluate different configurations of a product. This method of analysis can be used either to examine the quality of the interface on an existing product, or during the concept stage in the design of a new product.

Case Study

The subject of this study is a lady in her late seventies, with Rheumatoid Arthritis in her wrists, and also Osteo-arthritis in her back. An android (body segment model) was built to represent the user, corresponding to body measurements. A model of a cleaner was generated using a solid modeller, with the correct centres of gravity, mass distributions and moments of inertia. The two models were then combined by a connector at the hand-handle interface. The system was analysed with motion data taken from video images, driving the cleaner through space. The analysis data is then used to drive the Android in the form of an inverse kinematics analysis. Results are generated for the velocity, accelleration, and forces generated in the body segments and joints. From these it was possible to evaluate the effect of different configurations of a product, for example the texture, angle, size and shape of the cleaner handle. For example, in this user it was seen that the force generated in the shoulder could be reduced by increasing the angle of the handle to the vertical. Work is now being carried out to produce prototypes, as the next stage of the design process. These will be evaluated by a user group, and the results compared with that of the analysis.

Conclusions

From the data obtained by this method of analysis, and applying existing anthropometric and ergonomic principles, products can be evaluated with comparison to existing studies. This makes feasible the study of complex 3D systems, and also provides a valuable evaluation tool in the design process. Further development of this tool will incorporate joint range of motion and time dependent criteria such as fatigue.

Evaluation of ERGOLAB

Monique Noirhomme-Fraiture[1], Luc Goffinet[1], Clairette Charrière[2]

[1] Facultés Universitaires Notre-Dame de la Paix, Institut d'Informatique,
rue Grandgagnage, 21, B-5000 Namur (Belgium)
[2] Hôpital de Bicêtre, Rue du Général Leclerc, 78, F-94275 Kremlin-Bicêtre (France)

Goal

ERGOLAB is a software intended for *measuring* the abilities of users with special needs when they interact with a computer. It is mainly meant for *children with cerebral palsy.*

Principles

The exercises proposed to the user are *progressive*. Each level can consist of several exercises, ranging from the most simple to the most difficult ones. Each exercise can be done in two modes: *practice* or *test*. The latter enables *statistical data* about the user's performance to be *recorded*: response time, error rates, pressing time. As ERGOLAB was designed as an evaluation tool, and not as a learning tool, the screens have been designed with *simplicity and clarity*, so as not to distract children's attention from their task.

Evaluation

ERGOLAB is currently used by hospital Kremlin-Bicêtre in Paris, and occupational therapists find it useful for their work with children. However, the great diversity of disabilities and the slowness of children do not allow an evaluation of ERGOLAB itself. In order to get a greater number of homogeneous observations, we have tested ERGOLAB in a school with ordinary pupils. We have made 48 children work with ERGOLAB . They were between 3 to 7 years old, with little or no computer practice beforehand. Sorted by age category, children were given the same time to work, the same instructions, the same time for practice.

Conclusions

From our observations, we have gained information on the qualities that ERGOLAB and general software for young children should have. These qualities are:
1. Find a means to help young children *validate* their answers to the program.
2. The young children also need a way to *physically centre the mouse* on its board.
3. Software for the younger should take into account the fact that children need to express with words the actions they intend to perform.
4. There is an *age limit*, under which some specific actions cannot be carried out.
5. When someone interacts with the computer thanks to a switch and through a *scanning process*, the first item in the selection is often harder to choose than the others.

Evaluation of ERGOLAB (Poster contents)

1. Goal
2. Principles
3. Exercices

STAGE 1: PRESSING A MOUSE CONTACTOR

- *maintaining pressure on the contactor until an object reaches its target*

STAGE 2: NAVIGATING INSIDE THE SCREEN SPACE

- *linking up points on the screen*

STAGE 3: MANAGING HIDDEN INFORMATION

- *search for an element in different arrays*

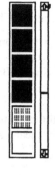

- *search for an element on a wheel*

4. Evaluation
5. Results

   for Ergolab
   for software in general

Dynamic Displays: the Changing Face of Augmentative Communication

Walter S. Woltosz

Words+, Inc.
Palmdale, California, 93550 USA

Augmentative and alternative communication (AAC) devices incorporating dynamic displays have been commercially-available since 1981 for text-based systems, and since 1986 for graphic-based systems. Beginning in about 1990, the advantages of dynamic displays became so overwhelming and so obvious that clinicians began recommending them more frequently and their use increased rapidly. This paper reviews the history of dynamic display AAC devices, describes their advantages and disadvantages with respect to static display systems, and discusses relevant research literature.

1 Introduction

"The purpose of a communication display is to arrange language in space so individuals can, by selecting from the available options, say what they wish to say as quickly as possible, and can do so with a minimal amount of effort." [1]

The above quotation from Sarah Blackstone is profound. For AAC users with sufficient visual skills to use visual feedback, the display of language symbols is often the primary factor that determines both the speed of communication and the amount of language available. From simple picture boards, to complex symbol boards, to letter/word boards, to electronic devices with fixed (static) symbols, to electronic devices with dynamic displays, those who have had the task of selecting the symbols to be displayed and their arrangement have struggled to provide access to large amounts of language with displays that are easy to use.

2 The Early Years - Static Displays

The earliest AAC devices were communication boards and books, and these remain in widespread use. Symbols used on such boards and books include small objects, tactile surfaces (sandpaper, cotton, cloth, etc.), photographs, pictographic symbols (line drawings, either in black and white or in color), abstract symbols, letters, words, and phrases. If the user can turn pages, then a communication book is often used to allow access to more than one page of symbols. If not, a single communication board is used with a reduced symbol set. For users with visual impairments and/or with limited pointing accuracy, symbols must be made large, further reducing the number of symbols that can appear on the display. Thus, language often has to be compromised in favor of visibility or accessibility.

2.1 Limited Symbol Sets

The greatest language limitation in early devices stemmed from the limited symbol set. This was especially true for users of pictographic symbols, but was also experienced by text users who used not only the alphabet, but complete words and phrases on their boards to save time.

Pictographic Symbols. Displays made up of pictographic symbols are used for nonspeaking persons who are able to see, but who are unable to spell or read. With these "low tech" devices, the user simply indicates (by pointing, or by some kind of signal when someone else does the pointing) a choice of one or more picture symbols in order to communicate a message. The symbols are selected to be easily recognized, and each is associated with a single language concept. With this method, the user relies on *recognition memory* - a relatively low cognitive function - in order to associate the picture with the language it represents [2].

Clinicians and teachers who make picture boards and picture books find them relatively easy to construct, inexpensive, and effective (at least for the symbols that are on the display. Note that the term "picture" is used here to mean pictographic symbols, as well as actual photographs.).

Adding speech output. During the early 1980's, electronic systems with synthesized speech output were developed for pictographic communication. Shortly thereafter, systems with recorded speech/sounds began to appear. These systems used keyboards and/or LED displays with picture symbols on or next to each key or LED. Most systems allowed no more than 128 pictures, although many users of such systems had much larger vocabulary and language.

Just as with earlier paper communication boards (but less so with communication books), there was a practical limit to the number of symbols a user could have (or see, or reach) within the size of the display area. The picture book got around this limitation to some extent by allowing the user to have many pages of symbols, allowing the same space to be occupied by various sets of symbols by turning pages; however, turning pages was not always practical, and the number of pages was usually limited by size, weight, and ease of finding the desired page when large numbers of pages were used.

Static display strategies. Static displays are those on which the language symbols do not change as the user operates the device. A static display is usually a paper or plastic sheet containing a number of language symbols arranged in some way - typically in rows and columns, but sometimes in a circular pattern, a single line, or some other arrangement.

The problem with static displays arises when the user's vocabulary (i.e., the number of language items in the user's repertoire) exceeds the number of locations for symbols on the display. In order to represent all of the user's language with the limited symbol set, some form of multiple use of symbols - an encoding scheme - is required.

Two such strategies have been employed: (1) levels, and (2) symbol sequences. Nearly every manufacturer of AAC devices has used both strategies. Some manufacturers have assigned special names to their particular implementation of these strategies for marketing purposes. Each of these strategies enables more than one action to be represented per symbol - millions of language elements can theoretically be represented with just 128 symbols. Both strategies are also often used together.

Levels. Using the concept of *levels*, the display appears as a single set of symbols, but there are actually two or more "levels" to the display, somewhat as though there were two or more devices, each with its own set of messages. Thus, a symbol has different meanings on different levels. In operation, the user first selects the desired level, and then selects the symbol(s) needed to communicate the message. As an example, a DRINK symbol might represent "I'd like a drink of water" on Level 1, "I'd like some milk" on Level 2, "May I please have some orange juice" on Level 3, and so on.

The primary difficulty with this approach is that the user had to employ *recall memory* to remember which level contained the desired message, then again use recall memory to remember how to get to the desired level, then select the level, and then select the symbol(s). Recall is a higher cognitive function than recognition [2], so the level strategy increased the cognitive load on the user. In fact, many devices capable of providing multiple levels are often actually used with only a single level - users are not always able to use the full capacity of the device because the cognitive load is too high.

In addition to the cognitive load, there is a high *visual perceptual* load with static displays resulting from the fact that all of the user's symbols (up to 128) are always in view. In this instance, the visual perceptual load refers to the quantity of visual information presented to the user. In a field of many symbols, the amount of information is high, and the user must search the dense visual field to find the desired symbol. Visual perceptual load is increased when the number of symbols is high, when symbols are very similar in appearance, when symbols are closely packed together, when symbols have multiple semantic meanings, and when symbols contain much fine detail and/or background information. For users with limited visual perceptual skills, the number of symbols may have to be reduced, and the size and/or spacing of the symbols may have to be increased, further limiting the number of symbols available to represent the user's language on a static display.

Sequences. The second strategy that is used to let a limited set of symbols represent a larger set of language items is *symbol sequencing*. This strategy was used thousands of years ago by the Chinese, Egyptians, and Mayans, among others. *Symbol sequencing* takes advantage of the many ordered combinations of symbols possible with a limited symbol set. For example, a set of only eight symbols can produce 64 possible ordered pairs of symbols. With 26 symbols (the number of letters in the alphabet) a total of 676 ordered pairs are available, while 128 symbols can produce 16,384 ordered pairs. With 128 symbols and allowing up to three symbols in sequence, over two million combinations are possible.

With pictographic symbol sequencing, the user might select a SUN symbol followed by a symbol for DRINK to represent their favorite hot drink - e.g., select SUN, then select DRINK, and the device would say "I'd like some hot chocolate". Or the user might select a TREE symbol followed by the DRINK symbol to say "I'd like some apple juice" (if there was not an APPLE symbol but there was a tree symbol).

These sequences probably seem logical to you, because you have the *world knowledge* to know that the sun is hot and that apples grow on trees (of course, so do lemons, oranges, pears, grapefruit, various kinds of nuts, Spanish moss, mistletoe, and lots of other things!). But for many users of pictographic symbols, world knowledge is still in an early developing stage. You need to have world knowledge to use the language system, but you need a language system to acquire world knowledge. Thus, this attempt to make it easier to recall symbol sequences actually can result in the requirement for rote memorization of what seem to be abstract sequences to the user.

Some developers have put a great deal of effort into coming up with associations that are supposed to be easy to remember, but which in practice have proved quite difficult and even less effective than simple letter abbreviations (for those who are capable of using letter abbreviations [3]). A picture of an elephant might carry the connotations of "big", "gray", "memory" (because "elephants don't forget"), "animal", and other meanings, depending upon the context in which the symbol was used with other symbols. A SUN symbol might mean "hot", "big", "round", "yellow", "far away", "morning", "day" and more. The tremendous amount of world knowledge required to make such associations, as well as the varying associational rules (size, color, shape, distance, temperature, time, cognitive characteristics, etc.), impose perhaps the most demanding cognitive load ever developed for augmentative communication system users, requiring hundreds of hours of training to achieve a reasonable level of communicative competence.

In the past, these demands on the user were necessary because of the limited symbol set - a restriction inherent in the available technologies associated with static displays. The computing power of early devices simply could not support anything more sophisticated, and so the user had to do more of the work. With enough computing power, as is now readily available, there is no longer any reason to impose these high loads on the user.

3 Dynamic displays - the future is now

A dynamic display is one which can present a changing set of symbols to the user.

Computer screens are dynamic displays, whether on a desktop CRT or on a notebook computer with an LCD (liquid crystal display).

The advent of dynamic displays has completely changed the preferred approach to augmentative communication for most AAC users. Modern systems allow rapid changing of the displayed symbolic elements in accordance with simple language rules. This makes possible a large symbol set, eliminating the need for multi-meaning symbols and allowing direct association between a symbol and the language or action it represents. At the same time, while the total number of symbols becomes unlimited (for all practical purposes on the most powerful dynamic display systems), the number of symbols displayed at any one time can be kept to a minimum in order to reduce the visual perceptual load. The user might have many thousands of symbols in their system, but might see only a dozen or two at any one time. The reduced cognitive load, reduced visual perceptual load, and reduced visual acuity load all mean faster and easier learning and faster and easier selection, which translate into faster and easier communication.

Large dynamic displays allow the system to behave like an electronic "communication book", much like the plastic-paged books often used for beginning picture communicators. For picture users of dynamic displays, for example, the software driving the display allows the user to select any of a large number of "pages", such as a food page, a drinks page, a places-to-go page, a people page, and so on. The large number of pictures allows more of a one-to-one association between the symbol and the language it represents - eliminating the need to memorize levels, as well as the need for multi-meaning symbols or abstract symbol sequencing.

Consider the DRINK symbol mentioned earlier in the discussion on levels. Rather than remembering that if Level 1 is selected and then the DRINK symbol is selected, the device will say "May I have a drink of water", and if Level 2 is first selected and then the DRINK symbol is selected, the device will say "I'd like some milk", and so on, when you use a dynamic display device you might simply choose the DRINK symbol and the screen would change to a page of drinks - with explicit symbols for each of the drinks you might want to select. If you want milk, you select the milk symbol. If you want orange juice, you select the orange juice symbol, and so on. The association is direct, and the process is self-prompting, relying on recognition memory, and eliminating the need for rote memorization and recall memory.

3.1 Symbols and the language they represent

With both static and dynamic displays, the choice of symbols for a particular AAC user, and their arrangement, is crucial. The "canned language" approach of providing a set of symbols and the language that goes with them, and then trying to teach this "language" to the user, is just the opposite of what published research indicates should be the preferred approach - to base the selection of symbols, and how you organize them, on the user's *associational* and *categorizational* strengths [4].

In a recent study of the vocabulary of preschool children, *not one single word* was found to be common to the vocabulary of the 90 test subjects (the word "Mom" was in 85 of the 90, and the top 10% of the items were only common to 18 of the 90 subjects) [5]. This illustrates the need to tailor the vocabulary (symbols) to the needs of the user, rather than using someone's preconceived idea of what the user's language should be. *There are no standard vocabularies for any population of AAC users.*

Cognitive science, a field only a few decades old, is investigating many aspects of how we think, including how we organize information in our brains [6]. People organize language in different ways, including *schematic, taxonomic, semantic-syntactic, and alphabetic* [1], and the specific organization that works best for one individual may be radically different from that for someone else. Thus, there are no standard categories.

If there are no standard categories, and there are no standard vocabularies, then what is a clinician to do to prepare a communication system for a user? The answer goes back to the earlier reference regarding the user's associational and categorizational strengths. *Clinicians simply must use their training and skills to determine the user's language, and then program that language into the AAC device.* We need to be putting users' language into devices, not devices' language into users.

3.2 Transition to literacy

One of the major issues in the field of augmentative communication today is the transition to literacy of users of pictographic communication systems. More abstract pictographic communication systems have been criticized for the detrimental effects they have been observed to have on the language development of their users, particularly with respect to learning literacy skills.

The dynamic display, properly implemented, can provide a system capable of using pictographic symbols and traditional orthography at the same time - mixing pictures and words in any proportion and any order. In fact, the technology of changing pages of symbols to which speech output can be assigned provides new opportunities for developing powerful tools to facilitate learning a variety of concepts, including literacy skills, mathematics, and more.

3.3 Dynamic displays and text-based communication

Dynamic displays are most often thought of in connection with pictographic communication; however, they were first used for text-based communication, and their advantages for text-based users have grown tremendously since their introduction in 1981. As with pictographic language, text-based language benefits from reduced cognitive and visual perceptual loads, expanded vocabulary, ease of learning, and ease of use.

The earliest use of the dynamic display for text was to offer word and phrase lists from which the user could select in order to minimize spelling. In the **Words+ Living Center** of 1981, for example, the user could select any of a set of high frequency words directly from the primary screen display, and could then further select any of about one thousand additional words by first selecting the first letter of the desired word, and then selecting from pages of words beginning with that letter. This early system, based on a 64K computer, provided single switch communication at rates up to ten words per minute for proficient users. Beginning in about 1990, with memory and disk storage measured in megabytes and hundreds of megabytes, text-based users have been able to access many thousands of words and many *hundreds of thousands or millions* of phrases with a few selections - and with very little need for recall memory beyond basic spelling skills. From second graders to Professor Stephen Hawking, text-based users are communicating more quickly and easily than ever with dynamic displays.

3.4 Technologies required for dynamic displays.

Effective use of a dynamic display requires much greater computing resources than for static displays. These resources are: display size, memory (chips), mass storage (e.g., disk drives), and speed. It is not enough to have a large display - you must also have the computing "horsepower" to drive it properly. Some early devices had only 48K of memory (49,152 bytes). On modern color displays, the memory required to represent *a single screen* of pictographic symbols can be over 160,000 bytes. And other resources are similarly taxed.

For example, the color **Talking Screen** pictographic communication software from **Words+**, requires approximately 15 million bytes of disk storage, at least four megabytes (over 4,000,000 bytes) of memory, and sufficient computing speed to allow drawing an entire screen of color pictures in a fraction of a second. Some "modern" dedicated devices with similar price tags have only a fraction of a percent of the computing capacity of such a computer-based dynamic display system.

The advances in technology are not just window dressing - they make dramatic differences in the kinds of augmentative communication strategies available to users, as well as for those who program the systems for the users. If the computer is not fast enough, then the user would have to wait too long before a new page of pictures would be drawn before making another selection. If there is not enough memory or mass storage, then the number of picture symbols available to the user is reduced, and the ease of programming the system is compromised. If the display size is not big enough, then the number and/or size of pictures the user can have on a page is limited. Color, which is now available on dynamic display devices, provides additional information making pictographic symbols more *transparent* (easily recognized), and which has been shown to be *necessary* for some populations to recognize some symbols [7].

4 Summary

Dynamic display AAC systems incorporate state-of-the-art technologies to reduce cognitive and visual perceptual loads, and to decouple the language aspects of the device from the motor and visual requirements, while simultaneously increasing the user's access to language and decreasing the learning costs of using the system.

All of these technologies are important in directly affecting the augmentative communication strategies available to the user (which results in making the machine do as much of the work as possible).

For both pictographic and text-based AAC, dynamic displays are the future, and the future is now!

References

1. Blackstone, S. (1993) Thinking a little harder about communication displays. Augmentative Communication News 6:1.

2. Light, J., & Lindsay, P. (1991) Cognitive Science and Augmentative and Alternative Communication. Augmentative and Alternative Communication (AAC), 7(3), 186-203.

3. Light, J., Lindsay, P., Siegel, L., & Parnes, P. (1990) The effects of three message encoding techniques on recall by literate adults using AAC systems. Augmentative and Alternative Communication (AAC), 6(3), 184-202.

4. Beukelman, D., Yorkston, K., & Dowden, P. (1985) Communication Augmentation: A casebook of clinical management. San Diego, CA: College Hill.

5. Fried-Oken, M., & More, L. (1992) An initial vocabulary for nonspeaking preschool children based on developmental and environmental language sources. Augmentative and Alternative Communication (AAC), 8(1), 41-56.

6. Lakoff, G. (1987) Women, Fire, and Dangerous Things, Chicago, IL. University of Chicago Press.

7. Mineo, B. (in preparation) Pictorial representation: An analysis of the abilities of two young adults with severe mental retardation.

BLISSVOX - Voice Output Communication System for Teaching, Rehabilitation, and Communication

G. Olaszy[1], S.L. Kálmán[2], P. Olaszi[3]

[1]Phonetics Laboratory of the Linguistics Institute, 1250 Budapest Pf. 19., Hungary
[2]Helping Communication Methodological Centre, 1071 Budapest, Damjanich u. 28/b, fszt. 7/a, Hungary
[3]Technical University of Budapest, Dept. of Telecommunications and Telematics, 1111 Budapest Sztoczek u. 2., Hungary

Abstract

Combining the text-to-speech system MULTIVOX and Blissymbolics and adapting them to the special needs of disabled children, outlined by the Hungarian Bliss Foundation, a speaking communication program using Bliss symbols has been developed for DOS environment. The special characteristics of this program and the preliminary results of its use will be described.

Introduction

It is well documented in the literature (see references) that, because of the type of the damage in the central nervous system, certain members of the severely speech impaired population are not able to acquire sufficient literacy skills. It is also proven that despite of this handicap, they can become effective communicators by use of other means, like different graphic or symbol systems (e.g. Picture Communication Symbols /PCS/, Oakland Schools Picture Dictionary, PICSYMS - Pictures Symbols, Pictogram Ideogram Communication /PIC/, Makaton Dictionary, etc.). One of these non-verbal, graphic systems is Blissymbolics, originally developed by Charles K. Bliss in 1949, and further developed to become an international communication system for the multiply handicapped non-verbal population by Blissymbolics Communication International (BCI) Toronto from 1971.

Present computer techniques provide the opportunity to become effective partners in communication for physically severely handicapped persons, who can be taught the use of Blissymbolics. As everywhere else in the world, most of them suffered cerebral palsy at the time of birth, and for a few of them there is no explanation for their condition.

Bliss symbols used in the BLISSVOX program were provided by the Hungarian Bliss Foundation. The Hungarian translation (Kálmán, Kassai, 1987) was based on the original vocabulary (Hehner, 1980), and the supplemented version (Reich et al., 1993). The translation was made possible by the translation agreement signed by the BCI.

The aim of this new program was to create a tool for educational and communication purposes for non-verbal students and their teachers. At present this is the only computer program in Hungary using Blissymbolics and a speech synthesiser for communication.

The basic design concepts of the BLISSVOX program

1. The program had to be made accessible either through two external parallel switches (for the disabled user), or from the keyboard (for the teacher).
2. The graphical organisation of the screen had to be simple and informative.
3. It was an important point that assembling messages using the Bliss symbols had to be simple and easy to understand for the handicapped users.
4. In order to provide a clearly understandable picture, there could not be more than twelve Bliss symbols on the screen to choose from at one time. The meaning of each symbol is displayed right above the symbol.
5. A highlighted frame indicates the selectable symbol. In User Mode the frame moves automatically, in Teacher Mode the frame can be moved using the cursor keys.
6. In order to accommodate the motor abilities of the user, the timing between two steps of the highlighted frame can be adjusted and readjusted easily at any time.
7. The Message Field contains the selected symbols. This will be the "text" of the communication.
8. The collected message must be saved automatically under the name of the user.
9. In order to provide opportunities for special exercises, it is possible to define special groups of Bliss symbols, and to create separate files for them.
10. The user had to be able to understand the symbols themselves, the use of the program, the meaning of communication, and must be able to handle two adapted switches.
11. The speech output is performed in Hungarian.

The BLISSVOX program

The following files constitute the BLISSVOX system:

The main program BLISS.EXE
The configuration file: BLISS.CNF
The picture files containing 2500 Bliss symbols (Copyright: C.K. Bliss 1949. BLISSIMBOLICS INTERNATIONAL exclusive licence, 1982.)
The text files containing the 2500 textual definition of the Bliss symbols
Page files with .PAG extension
Data files with .MSG extension
Multivox Text-To-Speech program for Hungarian

After starting the main program the screen shows three main parts (Figure 1.): the greatest part is engaged with the 12 actual symbols (this is called a "page"). The bottom part of the screen contains the message field with sufficient space for displaying eight symbols. The right part of the screen accommodates the command fields, where simple pictures are used to indicate the command (*Töröl* 'Delete the last selected symbol', *Új sor* 'Begin a new message', *Lap fel* 'One page up', *Lapok fel* 'Ten pages up', *Lap le* 'One page down', *Lapok le* 'Ten pages down', *Kimond* 'Say message', *Nyomtat* 'Print'). Under the Command Field the actual page number is shown. In the status row there is help information for the teacher. A highlighted square moves through the screen continuously, step by step. The time duration between the steps can be adjusted between 1-10 seconds according to the user's needs and abilities. Only the actually highlighted symbol can be selected for building the message. After selection, the symbol appears in the Message Field (at the bottom part of the screen). The messages can be of any length. At one time the last eight pictures of the message can be seen in the Message Field. After completion of the message, it can be pronounced by selecting the 'Say' command. In the meantime the message will also be saved.

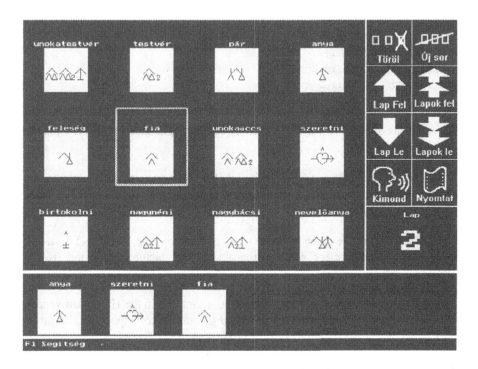

Figure 1. The main screen of the BLISSVOX program, User's Mode

The configuration file BLISS.CNF

In this file two starting parameters can be determined for the BLISS.EXE program: the default time duration between two steps and the .PAG file which will be used as a starting picture file.

The picture files

Ready-made (originally in English) picture files containing 2500 Bliss symbols (one file each in **64x64** pixel, PCX format) and a text file containing the textual meanings of the pictures were handed though BCI by Mr Henry Russel to the Hungarian Bliss Association for the purpose of using them in this development. Each picture file is identified by its name (maximum 8 characters). In most cases this name is identical with the meaning of the text file, i.e. the textual definition in the appropriate text file. For example, picture files beginning with the letter "f" are:

```
face.pcx, factory.pcx, falafel.pcx, fallto.pcx, family.pcx, etc.
```

The original English text files are in alphabetic order. The construction of one textual description of a Bliss symbol (after adaptation into Hungarian) is as follows:

```
maszk,1611,,0,falseface
család,1016,,38,family
család,2056,,20,family1
család,2057,,36,family2
családtervezés,3294,,40,familyplanning
```

The elements of every row are separated by commas. The meaning of the elements are as follows:

Hungarian meaning, Bliss symbol serial number, Reference to the main meaning (in case of synonyms), Width of the drawing in the picture, Picture file name (without the PCX extension)

Note: If the picture file name is longer than eight letters, (e.g. "`familyplanning`"), the superfluous characters will be truncated in the picture file name (result: "`FAMILYPL.PCX`").

The adaptation of the material into Hungarian meant that in the Hungarian version we had to replace the original English meanings with the corresponding Hungarian ones based on the Hungarian Bliss Symbol Dictionary.

The page files with .PAG extension

These files serve for teaching special topics, exercises etc.
The teacher can define symbols (using their serial numbers) in a file (with .PAG extension) from the vocabulary of 2500 symbols, she/he wants to choose for a special lesson or exercise. As an example the CSALAD.PAG file can contains the following pictures about the topic "family":

```
Család
200, 1134, 1092, 1012, 1013, 1014, 1015, 1016, 1017, 1018, 1019, 1020
1021, 1022, 1024, 1025, 1026, 1027, 1028, 1029, 1030, 1031, 1032, 1033
```

When choosing the CSALAD.PAG file the program will handle only these 24 pictures (two picture page with 12 symbols each), so there will be only two picture pages for the disposal of the user. Using this service of the program many .PAG files can be created and used in teaching and rehabilitation. Figure 2. shows an example of four page files: 'All Bliss symbols', 'Letters', 'To feel', 'Family'. The arrow points at the recently chosen file to be used.

Figure 2. Selecting a Page file

The message files with .MSG extension

The messages will be automatically saved (under the name of the actual user) when the user indicates that he/she wants to begin to construct a new message. The saved messages (i.e. the numbers of the symbols and the accompanying words) can be recalled to the screen in case of need. Thus the teacher can compare present and earlier works of his/her student. Figure 3. shows the names of four users, who already used the system, and constructed different messages. The arrow points at Rita, the chosen pupil, the earlier assembled messages of whom the teacher selected to be seen.

Figure 3. Selecting the messages of a user

Using the BLISSVOX program

The program can be used in two different modes: Teacher's and User's Mode.
The teacher can use the keyboard to control the program. Two main function keys are used for this work:

Enter selects picture or command (either in Teacher's Mode or User's Mode).
Tab button is used (either in Teacher's or User's Mode) for switching between the Command Field and Page Field.
A time sharing use for teachers can be performed by using the cursor buttons. For every strike the highlighted square will move further. The teacher can navigate the highlighted square on the full screen, i.e. to go through the 12 pictures (or the commands) quickly not waiting for the automatic step of the highlighted square.

F3 recalls the list of the former written .PAG files. By using the cursor, the desired file can be actualised by pressing Enter. Now the program works with this selected .PAG file.
F4 provides opportunity to overview the formerly written messages. After selecting the desired message and pressing Enter, the content of this message will appear in the Message Field. (Figure 4.) One can either listen to the messages by using the 'Say' command, or the student can go on to add further symbols to this message.

Figure 4. A message recalled by the teacher

When working on the user's level, only the two external switches are activated.
Switch 1 selects the appropriate (highlighted) symbol or command (same as Enter)
Switch 2 changes between the symbol field and the command field   (same as Tab)

Preliminary experiences with BLISSVOX

Since we had only a very short time for experimenting with the BLISSVOX, we can hardly talk about its real everyday use. In Hungary the use of computers in communication and generally in the handicapped's care, is not a routine. It means that first we had to convince the principal of the first user's school to participate in the program at all. It was important to consult the school about the purchase of the necessary equipment, to train the teaching personnel, to provide continuous consultation for the teachers and the students as well. The inexperienced teachers had many problems with the use of the computer itself, and were somewhat reluctant to include this special form of communication into their daily programs.

At this moment there is one 17 year old student, whose development looks promising. He has CP, he is athetotic, he has a serious speech impairment, but a remarkably good intellect. He is using about 800 Bliss symbols for communication, but has troubles with accessing the communication board. Considering his efficient use of the symbols, his good receptive language abilities, his already existing communication skills, he seemed a very good candidate for trying the BLISSVOX. Two different tasks were undertaken simultaneously. A trained teacher was working with him and with his personal assistant, to teach them the actual use of the computer, the handling of the switches, and other basic steps. Meanwhile work was being done to correct the small grammatical errors of the text, and the user's original vocabulary was turned into screen pages containing 12 symbols each. This latest step was a very slow and difficult job, because every symbol had to be chosen by its number, and compiled in a page. The new pages had to resemble partly the original Blissboard, but at the same time they had to be thematically sensible. (E.g. if we simply divide the original big Blissboard into 15 equal screen pages, a screen page can consist of numbers, letters, symbols for foods, clothing, and different activities etc. This way every screen would be a mixture of different topics. It is much better if a screen has a thematic approach, and there are screens with food or school items, clothing, moving, health care, feelings etc.) At this point it seems that the compilation of the individual vocabularies, which the users can choose their messages from, is the most crucial and time consuming part of the program. On the emotional level, our student already appreciates the ease which he can operate the program with, and despite of his/her restricted motor abilities, he/she can put together long and intelligent messages.

Further development plans

1. We intend to widen the program with a letter-to-text option. This means that the user will be free to create words letter by letter. The program will form words from the letters, so the synthesiser will pronounce correct words. So any kind of words, texts, and sentences can be created by the user and pronounced by the synthesiser.

2. A printing option is also planned to be added to give the teacher the possibility of printing the results of the work of the user.

3. A portable version of this system (based on notebook) will be designed for wheel chair users.

4. Adaptation for other European languages is possible, since Multivox speaks Italian, Spanish, German, Dutch, etc. The only thing to do is to translate the textual definition of the Bliss symbols to the given language.

References

G. Olaszy, G. Gordos, G. Németh: The MULTIVOX multilingual text-to-speech converter. In Talking Machines: Theories, Models and Designs, Ed.: G. Bailly, C. Benoit and T.R. Sawallis, Elsevier Science Publishers, B.V., Amsterdam, 1992.

Beukelman, D., Yorkston, K., Dowden, P.: Communication Augmentation: A casebook of clinical management, College Hill Press, San Diego, CA, 1985

Blackstone, S.W. /Ed./: Augmentative Communication: An Introduction, ASHA, Rockville, 1986.

Blackstone, S.W.: Thinking a little harder about communication displays, Augmentative Communication News, VI/1. 1. 1993.

Burkhart, Linda J.: Total augmentative communication in the early childhood classroom, Simplified Technology, Eldersburg, MD., 1993.

Hehner, B.: Bliss symbols for Use, Blissymbolics Communication Institute, Toronto, 1980.

Kálmán, S.L.: Kommunikáció Bliss - nyelven, (Communication by Blissymbolics), Bliss Alapitvány - Origopress, Budapest, 1989.

Kálmán, S.L.: A Bliss-nyelv bevezetése, oktatásának és alkalmazásának eddigi eredményei Magyarországon, (Introduction of Blissymbolics in Hungary), Kandidátusi értekezés, Budapest, 1989.

Kálmán, S.L., Kassai, I.: Bliss-jelképszótár, (Dictionary of Bliss symbols) Másokat Segítô GT - Táltos Kiadó, Budapest, 1987.

McNaughton, Sh.: Communicating with Blissymbolics, Blissymbolics Communication Institute, Toronto, 1985.

McNaughton, Sh.: Blissymbolic and Technology, Easter Seal Communication Institute, Toronto, 1989

Reich, P., Storr, J., Woods, C.: Bliss Reference Guide, Blissymbolics Communication International, Toronto, 1993.

Schiefelbusch, R.L. /Ed./: Nonspeech language and communication: Analysis and intervention, University Park Press, Baltimore, 1980.

Vanderheiden, G.C., Grilley, K.: Non-vocal Communication Techniques for the Severely Physically Handicapped, University Park Press, Baltimore, 1976.

Access to the Text Component of Multimedia Conversation Services for Non-speaking People with Severe Physical Disabilities

Hine N.A, Beattie W., McKinlay A., Arnott J.L.

MicroCentre, University of Dundee, Dundee, UK.

e-mail: nhine@mic.dundee.ac.uk

Abstract. This paper discusses an investigation of text communication as an element of interaction mediated by a broadband telecommunication system. This study is part of a wider investigation being undertaken by the EEC RACE IPSNI II project. The focus of the study was to determine if the typing rate achieved by non-speaking people with additional severe motor impairments could be improved by refining a scanning array. Whilst some improvement was achieved, the rate was still far lower than that of an able bodied typist. Other factors that affect the text production rate are discussed. The results suggests that a scanning text selection method could cause excessive expense for users seeking to undertake real-time text-based communication over broadband telecommunications networks, and alternative approaches are presented.

1. Introduction

The RACE IPSNI II project is a Pan-European collaborative research project investigating the issues governing accessibility of future broadband multimedia services by people with special needs. The goal of the project is to demonstrate that it is technically feasible to enable people with a wide variety of impairments and disabilities to use future multimedia telecommunications services. As such, the project is working with experimental services and terminals in order to ensure that the underlying infrastructure that is currently being developed throughout Europe will be able to meet the needs of people with disabilities.

The project partners identified a set of users that would be considered. These were people with blindness, deafness, motor impairments and those who were non-speaking. For users with these impairments, disability issues were identified, through a series of experiments, when using one or more of the following services: Video Telephony, Multimedia Database Access and Collaborative Working.

The target user groups considered by the team at the University of Dundee were non-speaking people and the service chosen was videotelephony. Experience in a series of preliminary studies confirmed that for non-speaking users the videotelephone needed to be adapted by including a text telephone service component. Various strategies were explored to enable these users to exchange text. An important consideration here was to investigate well established techniques for using computers, to see if they can be utilised in a situation where information is to be exchanged via computer-based systems, between remote users in a real time "conversation". These techniques included alternative keyboards, eye gaze tracking, on-screen keyboards and on-screen scanning arrays [1]. This paper will describe the study of the on-screen scanning arrays to illustrate the issues that are raised when these services available to these users.

2. Study

2.1 Goal

A number of different techniques have been tried and tested to enable people with motor impairments or people who are non-speaking to have conversations using a videophone adapted by the addition of a text telephone. The focus of this study is on those non-speaking people that have severe motor impairments with additional uncontrolled tremors or head movements. These people have a very limited set of possibilities for data input into the text telephone. One of the few techniques of data input available to them is to employ a switch driven scanning keyboard. An initial study at the beginning of the IPSNI II project found, however, that scanning is a very slow method of using a text telephone, where information is exchanged in real time. The results from that study are summarised in Table 1 below. [2]

	WPM
Able Bodied Typing	25.46
Foot Typing	20.59
Scanning Keyboard	0.58
Eye Gaze Typing	6.41

Table 1: The word per minute typing rate achieved by subjects

Because there are few alternatives available to severely disabled, non-speaking people, however, the technique was revisited and a revised scanning array was developed in an attempt to improve the data production rate.

A simple method that could yield useful results involved optimising the location of the letters so that the most frequently used letters were closest to the scan starting point. Alternatively, a method of reducing the effort involved in producing text that has been employed successfully with membrane keyboards to include bi-gram and tri-gram letter combinations [3]. A scanning array was constructed that incorporated bi-grams and tri-grams into the array.

2.2 Method

For the purpose of this study, three scanning array layouts were constructed and tested. The first had the letters of the alphabet arranged in alphabetic order. The second had the letters arranged with those most frequently used in the English language [4]] closest to the point where the scanning started. The third had an alphabetic arrangement of letters, with the 25 most frequently occurring bi-grams and tri-grams occurring in the English language [5] added to the array. The bi-grams and tri-grams were placed in a position in the array at a location close to their first letter. This array is shown in figure 1 below.

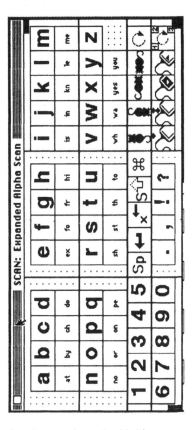

Fig. 1. Scanning Array enhanced with bi-grams and tri-grams

The underlying hypothesis was that by optimising the placement of letters relative to the point where the scans starts, the overall text production rate should improve. In addition, by providing bi-grams and tri-grams, scanning time would be further reduced since fewer characters would need to be scanned and selected.

The software used to construct the scanning arrays was the KE:NX software which allows the scanning to be broken up into blocks. First the rows are scanned, then, when a row is selected, the blocks on the row are scanned, and then, when a block is selected, the elements of the block are scanned, firstly across the top row of the block and then the next row of the block. Each array had a common set of numeric, punctuation and mouse control elements in addition to the letters.

The arrays were tested over a six week period at a cerebral palsy residential and day care centre, using the following procedure. The first array was installed on the host computers, and the subjects had two weeks in which to practice using them, the practice sessions being administered by the training staff at the centre. All of the subjects had previous experience of using KE:NX scanning arrays. The amount of time spent on practise was logged. At the end of two weeks, subjects held a scripted "conversation" via a text telephone, using the scanning array. The script represented an imaginary conversation between a patient and a doctor's receptionist. The time of each keystroke event was recorded by the computer, and the entire conversation was logged on each of the two machines being used for the conversations. Then the next array was installed and the procedure repeated. This was followed by the third array. In all cases the arrays were installed and examined in the order shown in the figures above. Although this did not allow order effects to be eliminated, it was considered that to try to have different subjects practising and being tested on different arrays at any one time would have added too much extra work to already busy centre staff.

2.3   Subjects

Four subjects took part in the study. Each subject was familiar with operation of the Ke:nx software. In addition, each subject had difficulty speaking and needed to enter text with a scanning array operated with a switch. Subject 1 pressed a switch fixed to the back of his wheelchair by moving his head, Subject 2 operated a foot switch, subject 3 held a switch box in one hand and pressed the switch plate with the other and subject 4 pressed a switch that was fixed to a desk. All subjects were adults.

2.4   Apparatus

The system used in the study consisted of two Macintosh LC II computers connected via an Appletalk/Localtalk link. The text telephone was developed using the SuperTalk project development environment. The scanning arrays were referred to as "conventional" where the elements were in alphabetical order, "optimised" where they were in most frequently used order and "enhanced" when bi-grams and tri-grams were added.

2.5   Measurements

The system recorded the time for each keystroke event, and recorded the complete conversation. From this, time between keystrokes and values for typing speed, expressed as words per minute (wpm) could be calculated. Because the scripts that were used were the same as those followed in the earlier study [1,2], the wpm figure was calculated taking the average number of characters-per-word figure from that study. This figure was 5.3 characters per word for these conversations. By using the same scripts for all three conditions, the three arrays could be directly compared. In addition, the performance could be compared with the earlier study.

In addition, the number of errors that were corrected by the subjects using the delete key and typing a preferred character were counted and the percentage of errors per total number of keystrokes were calculated.

3.   Results

The average time taken per character selected and the average word per minute (wpm) typing rate is shown in table 2 below, along with the percentage of errors that occurred in each session. The change in typing rate is shown in figure 2 below.

	wpm	errors (%)
Subject 1		
Conventional	0.83	11.89
Optimised	0.86	12.41
Expanded	0.91	6.99
Subject 2		
Conventional	0.39	10.20
Optimised	0.47	23.44
Expanded	0.54	20.18
Subject 3		
Conventional	0.52	16.67
Optimised	0.58	7.69
Expanded	0.70	23.26
Subject 4		
Conventional	0.52	2.60
Optimised	0.55	2.70
Expanded	0.57	5.97

Table 2: The word per minute typing rate and percentage of errors achieved by subjects

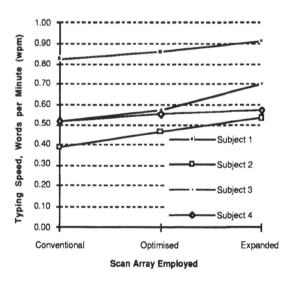

Fig. 2. Change in typing speed per subject when using the three different scanning arrays.

Because of the small sample size and its hetrogenous nature, it was not considered appropriate to analyse the results by means of statistical tests.

4.   Discussion

The empirical results show that there was a measurable improvement in the text input as the subjects moved from the conventional to the optimised and then to the enhanced scanning array. Whilst this is true, the improvements were small compared with the vast difference between the performance of an able bodied typist, or even a person typing with eye gaze.

Two trends in the proportion of selections that had to be corrected were observed. The first was that change from a conventional alphabetic layout introduced more errors. This was particularly problematic if the wrong bi-gram or tri-gram was selected as this introduced two or three characters that had to be removed. The second was that the addition of bi-grams and tri-grams reduced the number of errors because the second or third letter was supplied automatically and could not be miss-selected.

Three of factors were observed to be affecting the performance of the subjects which may have a confounding influence on the measured results.

The first factor was that the subjects had very poor ability to handle text, although all had been selected for the study on the strength of their apparent reasonable reading abilities. All subjects used a communication board or book. One pointed to the board with his foot, two used their hands to point to a board that was held for them and the last made noises to confirm or reject selections made from a book on his behalf by someone wishing to communicate. All subjects had exposure to Ke:nx scanning arrays and knew how to operate them. Because of this, they were considered to be suitable candidates for the study, and likely to benefit from it. The study exposed, however, that their use of a communication board was based more on a knowledge of a small set of words and phrases and the patterns necessary to generate those words and phrases rather than on a genuine ability to read or generate text. This poor text handling ability was most evident when the subjects were using the enhanced scanning array. On a number of occasions, the subject did not use a bi-gram or a tri-gram when it was appropriate to do so, particularly if the letters were not at the beginning of the word. It seems that the subjects were not sufficiently fluent in their ability to handle text to recognise and match letter pairs and triplets from the words that they were seeking to type.

It is possible that this problem was compounded by the fact that although the 25 bi-grams and tri-grams on the array were the most commonly occurring ones in the English language generally, they did not occur very frequently in the text used by the subjects. It may be that a larger set would have encouraged the subjects to look more carefully for suitable pairs and triplets to use. This solution is rather problematic, however, in the context of the experiment. The scanning array was only one of a number of function represented on the screen of the computer terminal. Space needed to be left for the text telephone, and in a more complete experimental set-up of the project, for a videophone window and a text prediction window. This limits the space available for a scanning array, which in turn limits the number of elements that can be represented in that array without the label on each scan cell becoming too small to be readable. An obvious solution would have been to use a larger screen, but, for cost reasons, none of the screens in the day centre are larger than 14". This is typical of the type of practical constraint that is encountered when investigating technological solutions: the eventual customer will often not have the resources to be able to afford an ideal solutions and is therefore forced to compromise.

When these observations were discussed with the care and training staff, they offered a further explanation for this poor text handling skill. Technology to assist in the learning of written language skills was not available when the subjects were young and so they had not received systematic training in this skill. Another explanation was that, when they were younger, these people were not considered ever to be likely to be able to read a newspaper and so training in this skill was not considered to have been of primary importance for them. The recommendation from the care staff was that extra attention is paid to the written skills training of children with disabilities so that they will not be handicapped to the same extent.

The second factor was the suitability of the switches being used by the various subjects. The switches that were operated by hand or by pressing with the foot were far from ideal, in that frequently errors were made and cell selections missed because the subject did not press the switch properly. The position of the person relative to the switch was critical. As the subject shifted position slightly their use of the switch could improve or deteriorate significantly.

The third factor that seemed to have a significant influence on the performance of the subject was their motivation and practical situation on a day to day basis. All of the subjects professed to have been interested in the experiments and enjoyed being involved. Over the duration of the study, however, the subjects had to continue to deal with the consequences of having severe disabilities. This meant that their level of concentration and application varied depending on other events that they were dealing with at the time.

5.   Conclusions

This study exposes the problems faced by non-speaking people who have an additional severe motor impairment as they seek to take part in real time conversations. Despite improvements in text production rates by all subjects, the rates achieved were very much slower than that of an average able bodied typist. In the context of telecommunications, this would mean that a conversation would take longer and consequently cost more. For this reason, three alternative approaches should be tried depending on the task to be accomplished.

1 Where conversation is possible by selecting from a board or a book, experiments should be conducted to see if it is possible to conduct a conversation with a videophone, perhaps with two cameras. One camera could show the board or book and the other show a view of the person.

2 Where conversation does not need to be in real time, electronic mail should be tested to allow conversation blocks to be created off-line and transmitted when complete.

3. Where a conversation would involve the exchange of a high degree of factual data, a form of computer based interview could be implemented, where the factual data is gathered off line, transmitted and then discussed. in this way, conversation duration could be reduced.

6.   References

1. IPSNI II, "Access solutions for people with special needs to telecommunication". Deliverable to the CEC from RACE Project R2009 IPSNI II, Workpackage (WP 1.4), CEC Deliverable Number R2009/IRV/WP1/DS/P/008/b1, 1992.

2   N. A. Hine, W. Beattie, A. McKinlay and J. L. Arnott, (1994) "Consideration of Scanning Keyboard and Text Prediction in the context of access to Telecommunications Services", ISAAC: 6th Biennial Conference of the International Society for Augmentative and Alternative Communication, Maastricht, The Netherlands, 9-13 October 1994.

3   Mathy-Laikko, P., West, C. and Jones, R., (1993) "Development and Assessment of a Rate Acceleration Keyboard for Direct-Selection Augmentative and Alternative Communication Users", Technology and Disability, 2(3), pp. 57

4   Ferguson, T.J. and Rabinowitz, J.H., (1984) "Self-Synchronizing Huffman Codes", IEEE Transactions on Information Theory, Vol. IT-30, pp. 687-693

5   Rubin, D.C. (1978) Word-initial and Word-final ngram Frequencies", Journal of Reading Behaviour, X, 171-183

Protocolling the TINATEL-System: A Contribution for Long Term Evaluation of an AAC-System for Speech Impaired Persons to Access the Public Telephone Network

Paul Panek

fortec - Working Group on Rehabilitation-Engineering
Vienna University of Technology

Abstract. This paper describes the long-term evaluation of the TINATEL-System, an Alternative and Augmentative Communication (AAC) device to be used for aided communication within the public telephone network. The system was especially developed for a single speech impaired User. An integrated logbook recorded a lot of data between 1991 and 1994 concerning the daily use of the system. These data are described and shown in different ways to keep in view the transferrate, the average daily duration of use, the social and therapeutical effects and so on.

Some general aspects of protocolling data by an AAC system are shown. It is stated that these data can contribute valuable parts to the evaluation of AAC-devices.

1 Background / Description of the TINATEL-System

The TINATEL-System, published in [10], has been in day by day use since November 1991. This paper gives a survey of the recorded data which have been collected by the TINATEL-System within 30 months. Recently an increasing amount of papers concerning the importance of evaluation in Rehabilitation Technology has been published ([4], [7], [14], [3], [11]). It is an aim of this paper to give an impression how the recorded data could be used to help evaluating AAC-devices.

1.1 Description of the TINATEL-System

The TINATEL-System consists of a PC/AT286, a speech synthesizer, an interface to the telephone network with an auto dialler, a hand-free talking device and a system software for building up the User interface. The input is done by the User with the help of a headstick and a keyboard with a keyguard. The system's output is realised by a VGA and a speech synthesizer.

The TINATEL-System was developed and implemented for a single User. Therefore it was possible to adapt the system to the individual and personal needs of the User. The User herself is severely physically handicapped in motorial control of her movements. She is not able to speak herself. She is doing the System's input with a headstick and an adapted keyboard. The keys pressed by the User are synthesized by the speech synthesizer and transferred to the communication partner via the public telephone network. In this way the counterpart can hear all the keys pressed by the User and is able to combine the single characters to whole words and sentences. There is also the possibility to use pre-stored phrases which are not spelled letter by letter but are synthesized as whole sentences.

With the help of the TINATEL-System the User is able to strike up a conversation with every member of the public telephone network. The things said by the counterpart get audible for the AAC-User by the hand-free talking device integrated in the TINATEL-System. The principle of the aided communication is shown in Fig. 1 with reference to the work of C. Bühler et al. [6].

The User lives in a family environment and uses the TINATEL-System for communication with her friends. From the start the TINATEL-Project had very good working conditions. The User has had high interest and motivation to get into contact with High-Tech aids. Also there has been a great need to find a more effective way to communicate with other persons. M. Scherer describes the importance of a good relationship of environment, personal and technology aspects in her "Matching Person and Technology" model, published in [15].

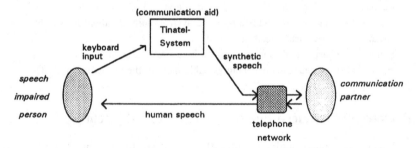

Fig. 1. Principle of the aided communication realised in the TINATEL-System.

2 Collecting the Data / Methods of Recording

The data described in the following sections were recorded in two different ways: automatically and manually. The automatic recording offers information about the number of calls and the duration of these calls. Manual recording allows to analyse the internal structure of the User's calls.

2.1 Automatic Recording

The TINATEL-System is automatically recording the system events which occur during use of the system. The recorded data consist of date and time of the daily start up and termination of the system, time of the beginning and termination of a telephone call (only calls initiated by the system!) and the telephone number dialled by the system. The data covers the period from November 1991 until April 1994, these are 30 months.

2.2 Manual Recording

14 telephone calls initiated by the TINATEL-User were recorded manually. These calls took place in three periods: January-Juny 1992, March-May 1993 and Feber-April 1994. The recording was done by manually taking notes of all the information sent by the system. The actually recording of the data was done by the communication partner[1]. During the 14 recorded calls only the spelling mode was used (the system spells letter by letter as the keys are pressed by the User). Prestored phrases were not used. In general the topics of the calls came from the private area. The recorded data consist of the number of keys pressed by the User and the number of characters predicted by the communication partner during the telephone call.

3 Presentation of the Recorded Data

3.1 Data from the Automatic Recording

Preparation of the Primary data. First the data which had been primarily recorded were transformed off-line into records. Each of these records describes one telephone call. A record contains the following information:
- Date of the call,
- Duration (T) of the call and
- Dialled number (= communication partner).

These records of data are describing a period of 30 months. Within this period a number of 1815 calls had been recorded by the TINATEL-System. During the off-line preparation the data records of 48 calls (2.6%) had to be eliminated because of incompleteness[2].

The system does not verify the status of the telephone line. Therefore the recorded data do not include any information concerning the question if the communication partner really had picked up the receiver. To handle this a limit of time (2 minutes) is introduced. Only those calls which lasted for longer than two minutes are stated to be "real" calls, all the others are eliminated because the communication partner probably did not pick up the receiver. In the following only the 534 calls which lasted longer than 2 Minutes are used (Fig. 2).

Total number of calls initiated by the TINATEL-System (November 1991 - April 1994)	1815
completely recorded calls	1767
completely recorded and longer than 2 minutes	534

Fig. 2. Number of automatically recorded calls.

---

1 Restriction: all 14 calls were done with the same communication partner.
2 Their data records did not include the termination time. Therefore it is not possible to calculate the duration of the call.

Presentation of the Automatically Recorded Data. The data can be shown in different ways. In Fig. 3 there is a presentation concerning the duration of the calls within each month. The total duration of all 534 calls is 224 hours, the average is 7.5 hours per month.

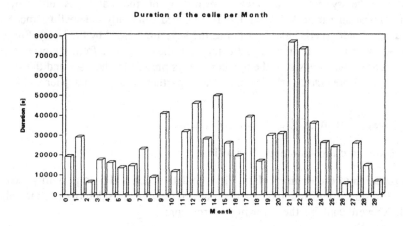

Fig. 3. Total duration per month of the calls initiated by the TINATEL-System. (only calls with T>2 minutes, total duration: 224 hours, total number of calls: 534).

The same data can be presented in order to show the monthly amount of calls build up by the system as well. This is done in Fig. 4. The average number of calls is 534/30=17,8 calls per month.

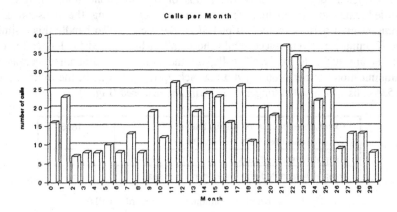

Fig. 4. Number of calls per month initiated by the TINATEL-System (only calls with T>2 minutes, total number of calls: 534).

3.2 Data from the Manual Recording

14 calls have been recorded manually in order to get the following data (Fig. 5):
- Date and duration (T) of the call,
- Number of the correctly pressed keys (characters) (C),
- Number of mistyped keys (M), immediately corrected by the User with the help of the delete key,
- Number of times the delete key was pressed (DEL, with DEL=M),
- Number of the mistyped but not corrected characters (Mnc) and the
- Number of letters predicted by the communication partner (P).

Date	T [min]	C [char]	P [char]	M [char]	DEL [char]	Mnc [char]	NTR [char/min]	NTR_max [char/min]
210292	30	189	26	46	46	0	7.16	10.23
130392	135	1524	330	123	123	40	13.73	15.85
240492	32	300	46	45	45	8	10.81	13.88
190592	63	755	49	37	37	9	12.76	14.08
90692	89	1602	75	188	188	52	18.84	23.65
200393	70	1324	239	122	122	56	22.33	26.61
30493	24	272	96	9	9	1	15.33	16.12
90493	58	647	81	55	55	13	12.55	14.67
140493	38	644	107	57	57	12	19.76	23.08
230493	35	402	107	19	19	14	14.54	16.03
80593	28	484	119	51	51	11	21.54	25.57
110294	24	623	17	14	14	0	26.67	27.83
180394	39	430	54	28	28	7	12.41	14.03
40494	29	573	51	25	25	6	21.52	23.45

Fig. 5. Manually recorded calls.

Explanation. When the User types with her headstick a wrong key, then this key will be transmitted via speech synthesizer and telefon line, too. If the User notices the mistyped key, she can make a correction by pressing the delete key which would transmit the message "Wrong key typed!" to the communication partner or she can believe in her communication partner's ability to recognise and correct the mistyped letter by his own. In the last case she will not press the delete key but continue in typing the word she wants to say. The communication partner is able to predict a word by guessing which letters might follow those which have already been transmitted.

It seems to be interesting how this contribution of transferred characters changes during the period of 30 months. Therefore all 14 manually recorded calls have been put into a diagramm (Fig. 6) showing the relationship between correct, predicted, mistyped and corrected, mistyped and not corrected characters.

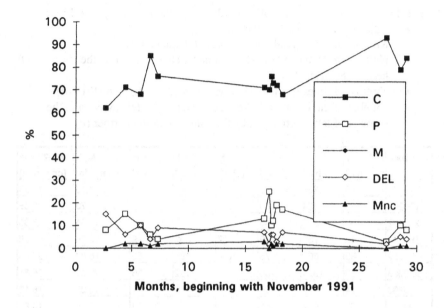

Fig. 6. Ratio of the keys pressed by the TINATEL-User.

Transfer Rate. Another point of view is the transfer of information from the AAC-User towards the communication partner. A first step was done in [10]. The Netto-Transferrate is introduced. It describes the amount of characters transmitted to the communication partner related to the duration of the communication.

$$NTR := \frac{C+P}{T} \qquad (Eq.\ 1)$$

It is to say that only C characters are really transmitted via telephone line. P characters had been predicted by the communication partner. The quantities of DEL, M and Mnc do increase the number of transferred characters but do not increase the transferred information *(Eq. 1)*.

As a second variable

$$NTR_{max} := \frac{C+P+M+DEL+Mnc}{T} \qquad (Eq.\ 2)$$

is defined. NTRmax would be reached if the User made no mistakes any more. Then every pressed key would carry information to the communication partner *(Eq. 2)*. Both variables, Netto-Transferrate and NTR_max are measured in characters per minute. They are shown in Fig. 7 within a period of 30 months.

Transferrates

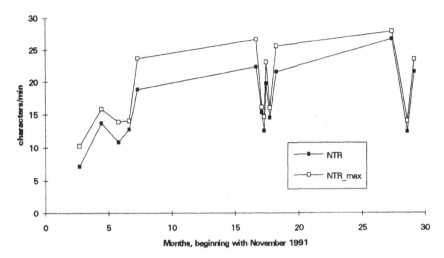

Months, beginning with November 1991

Fig. 7. Netto-Transferrate and its theoretical maximum (NTR_max) of 14 calls with the TINATEL-System.

4 Interpretation of the Recorded Data

The recorded data show that the system has had success in getting a good acceptance by the User. The number of telephone calls initiated by the User had an increasing trend within the first months after installation of the system. This fact allows to state that the system is able to meet the most important needs of the User and that it is accepted as an AAC-device by the User.

The manually recorded data of the 14 calls show the effect of training: After having got some practise in using the system the User was able to increase effectiveness of communication. On the other hand the NTR also shows great differences even within short periods of time. This gives a hint of the fact that many extern parameters are influencing the actual transfer rate and effectivness of the system. For example: condition and disposition of the User, abilitiy of the communication partner to interact and to predict characters or words, percentage of communication time spent by the User and spent by the counterpart, and so on. Nevertheless there is a slowly increasing trend recognisable.

The absolut quantity of the NTR variable is much smaller than the transfer rate of unimpaired speech[3]. Even if the average duration of daily use is about the same as

---

3   The transfer rate of not impaired speech is about 120-200 words per minute [9]. A. Kraat states a rate between 2 and 10 words per minute to be representative for a

that of a not impaired person using the telephone network, the transferred information is much less. The low input rate of the User seems to be the limiting factor. With the concept of an AAC-device as realised in the TINATEL-System it is not possible to reach the transfer rates of not impaired speech. Therefore alternative ideas for increasing the transferred information are necessary, e.g. published in the work of N. Alm et al. ([1], [2]).

5 The Significance of Recording Data for the Evaluation of an AAC-device

The data presented in this evaluation of the TINATEL-System give an example of the possibilities that can be realised by recording the events of daily use. Certainly there are much more things which are worth to be recorded than it is actually done in the system. Some information, for example about the incoming calls is not recorded, also there is no detailed recording of the percentage of time available for the AAC user in comparison with the time used by the communication partner. This important subject is described in the evaluation of the AAC-device "MultiTalk II" done by P. Raghavendra et al. [12].

The long-term evaluation of the TINATEL-System offers information about the long-term use of an AAC-System. In general there are a lot of possibilities created by recording all important events during the use of the system. Questions to be asked during evaluation could be:

- Acceptance of the system: is it really used?
- Suitability: does the system meet what it was planned to meet?
- Transfer rate: in which way does the transfer rate of the evaluated AAC-device differ from the transfer rate which can be reached by other methods?
- How does the way of communication and human interact change?
- Effect of training: does the efficiency of use increase?
- Daily life: is the configuration of the system really adapted to the situation of daily life?

In this way an automatic recording of user events can be a valuable source of information for the evaluation of AAC-devices. It is not able to produce data as objectively as an Assessment Center (see [16], [7], [11]), but gives information of the real life environment. Nevertheless it can not be more than a contribution to an evaluation. The experiences and situations of the users [5], their familiar partners and therapists are essential.

The recording function of the TINATEL-System is a background job. It goes without saying, that the user must be agree to the recording procedure of data.

---

communication with the help of an AAC-device [9]. P. Raghavendra et al. report a communication rate with Multi TalkII of 11.3-18.8 words/minute [12]. W. Roßdeutscher reports 0.4-5.5 characters per minute for severly handicapped persons who have to use scanning methods to interact with the AAC-device [13]. The User of the TINATEL-System reaches rates of about 20 characters (about 4-5 words) per minute.

6 Future Aspects

It is planned to integrate the experiences gained with automatic data recording into the implementation of an assistive system to support the independence of elderly and handicapped persons described in [8] and [17]. This system will be installed in a special training-room of a support centre for physically and multiple handicapped persons in spring 1995. The data which should be recorded there are provided to give an overview of the acceptance of a flexible system for differently impaired users.

References

1. Alm, Norman; Waller, Annalu; Arnott, John L.; Newell, Alan F.: Improving Assisted Communication with Narrative Texts, in: Proceedings of the Second European Conference on the Advancement of Rehabilitation Technology, ECART2, Stockholm: Swedish Handicap Institute, 1993, p.26.1.

2. Alm, Norman; Newell, Alan F.; Arnott, John L.: An Integrated Research Strategy for Improving Communication Systems for Severely Physically Impaired Non-speaking People, in: Ballabio, E.; Placencia-Porrero, I.; Puig de la Bellacasa, R. (Eds.): Proceedings of the 1st TIDE Congress (Technology for the socio-economic Integration of Disabled and Elderly people), Amsterdam: IOS-Press, 1993, p.249-253.

3. Batavia, A.I. and Hammer, G.S.: Towards the Development of Consumer-based Criteria for the Evaluation of Assistive Devices, in: Journal of Rehabilitation Research and Development, Dept. of Veterans Affaires, Vol.27, No.4, (1990), p.425-436. (referred to by [12]).

4. Besio, Serenella and Ferlino, Lucia: Software and Hardware for Mobility Disorders: A Proposal for Evaluation, in: Zagler, W. (Ed.): Proceeding of the 3rd International Conference on Computers for Handicapped Persons, Vienna: Oldenbourg, 1992, p.22-30.

5. Bühler, Christian and Schmidt, Michael: User Involvement in Evaluation and Assessment of Assistive Technology, in: Proceedings of the Second European Conference on the Advancement of Rehabilitation Technology, ECART2, Stockholm: Swedish Handicap Institute, 1993, p.30.1.

6. Bühler, Christian and Heck, Helmut: The versatile communication aid BASKO helps people with speech impairment, in: Journal of Microcomputer Applications (1993) 16, London: Academic Press, 233-241.

7. Craig, Ian; Nisbet, Paul; Odor, Phil; Watson, Marion: Evaluation Methodologies for Rehabilitation Technology, in Ballabio, E.; Placencia-Porrero, I.; Puig de la Bellacasa, R. (Eds.): Proceedings of the 1st TIDE Congress (Technology for the socio-economic Integration of Disabled and Elderly people), Amsterdam: IOS-Press, 1993, p.238-243.

8. Flachberger, C.; Panek, P; Zagler, W.: AUTONOMY - A Flexible and Easy-to-Use Assistive System to Support the Independence of Handicapped and Elderly Persons, to be printed in: Zagler, W. (Ed.): Proceeding of the 4th International Conference on Computers for Handicapped Persons, Springer, 1994.

9. Kraat, A.: Communication Interaction Between Aided and Natural Speakers: A State of the Art Report, Toronto: Canadian Rehabilitation Council for the Disabled, 1985. (referred to by [2]).

10. Panek, Paul: Tinatel - A Talking Text-Editor with Telephone Interface for Speech Impaired Persons, in: Zagler, W. (Ed.): Proceeding of the 3rd International Conference on Computers for Handicapped Persons, Vienna: Oldenbourg, 1992, p.397-402.

11. Persson, Jan; Brodin, Håkan; Hass, Ursula: Technology Assessment in Rehabilitation: Conceptual Issues and Two Applications, in: Proceedings of the Second European Conference on the Advancement of Rehabilitation Technology, ECART2, Stockholm: Swedish Handicap Institute, 1993, p.20.1.

12. Raghavendra, Parimala and Rosengren, Elisabet: Effectiveness of Multi-Talk II as a Voice Output Communication Aid, in: Ballabio, E.; Placencia-Porrero, I.; Puig de la Bellacasa, R. (Eds.): Proceedings of the 1st TIDE Congress (Technology for the socio-economic Integration of Disabled and Elderly people), Amsterdam: IOS-Press, 1993, p.50-54.

13. Roßdeutscher, Wolfram: Kommunikationshilfen für Schwerstbehinderte, in: Boenick, Ulrich (Ed.): Biomedizinische Technik Forschungsberichte für die Praxis, Bd.4, Berlin: Schiele und Schön, 1992

14. Sandhu, Jim; Mckee, Ian; Carruthers, Stuart: The Role of Evaluation in the Development of Rehabilitation Technology Products, in: Ballabio, E.; Placencia-Porrero, I.; Puig de la Bellacasa, R. (Eds.): Proceedings of the 1st TIDE Congress (Technology for the socio-economic Integration of Disabled and Elderly people), Amsterdam: IOS-Press, 1993, p.174-178.

15. Scherer, M. J.: Living in the State of Stuck - How Technology Impacts the Lives of People with Disabilities, Cambridge, MA: Brookline Books, 1993.

16. Spens, K.-E.; Plant, G.; Gnosspelius, J.: Controlling Time Parameters in Connecting Discourse Tracking, in: Proceedings of the Second European Conference on the Advancement of Rehabilitation Technology, ECART2, Stockholm: Swedish Handicap Institute, 1993, p. 4.2.

17. Zagler, W.L. and Flachberger, C.: Autonom - A Remote Control System: An Example for what technology can do, but what technicians don't know, COST A5 Workshop on Gerontechnologies, Vienna, 1993.

The Conventional Braille Display
State of the Art and Future Perspectives

Dipl.-Ing. Bernhard Stöger and Mag. Klaus Miesenberger

Educational endeavour "Computer Science for the Blind"
Johannes Kepler Universität
Altenbergerstr. 69, A-4040 Linz

Abstract. The conventional one-line Braille display is explained and discussed in great detail, the emphasis being laid on the ergonomic and software-technical aspects rather than the electronic or the electromechanical ones. Especially closely studied are the deeper aspects of text-based Braille display operation such as video attribute viewing and lightbar handling. In addition, some suggestions to improve present Braille display software are given, especially concerning the recently developed programs to access graphical user interfaces.

1 What is Braille?

The Frenchman Louis Braille (1809-1852) invented a writing system that is used by blind and visually impaired people and that is based on tactile rather than on optical perception. In original Braille, characters are generated by embossing small raised dots into a sheet of paper. Every Braille character occupies a small section of the sheet that is organized as a 2.3 grid and that can therefore take up to 6 dots. Every character (letter, number, punctuation mark etc.) is a certain selection within such a 2.3 arrangement. If one includes the space - the character with no dot at all -, one thus obtains 2 to the 6th = 64 possible characters; it is therefore possible to represent the letters of the Roman alphabet together with the numbers, the punctuation marks and several special characters.

Since its invention toward the end of the first half of the past century, Braille has been used by blind and strongly visually impaired people in two main ways: Firstly, special machines were devised that allowed a blind person to make personal notes - this made possible written communication between blind persons, however, at least in general, without the possibility to include sighted people. Secondly, by special printing methods literature was produced in Braille.

2 What is a Braille Display?

When, by the end of the seventies and in the beginning of the eighties, the computer became more and more the central medium of information processing in all areas of society, attempts were made to make the computer accessible for the blind by means of the Braille system. In these efforts, the conventional way to write Braille dots on paper proved totally inadequate; for most of the time the computer is operated interactively, presenting much information to the user that is relevant only for the moment. The problem was to devise an output medium for the blind user that replaced the screen, the "refreshable display" used by the sighted. To this end, in the middle seventies electromagnetic display elements were developed. Each display element was able to move a small metal pin up and down between two positions, whose distance was about 1 millimeter. Every pin is furnished with a soft plastic top that can be felt as a Braille dot when in the raised position. Six such elements are arranged in a 2.3 grid, thus forming the matrix for a complete Braille character. Such a unit consisting of 6 or 8 (see below) pins together with the electromechanical elements for their motion is also referred to as a Braille module.

Theoretically, it would be possible to form a "tactile screen" from such Braille modules by arranging them in a rectangular manner, e.g., in a 25.80 matrix. However, both the electromagnetic and the later developed piezo electric modules are so expensive that a machine consisting of more than 80 modules is practically unaffordable. Until the time when a cheaper technology will be available, one must therefore be satisfied with representing one, one half, or even only one quarter of a line at a time. Such a machine consisting of 20, 40, or 80 linearly arranged Braille modules is called a Braille Display.

As mentioned above, the elements of a Braille display are arranged in a horizontal row. In most cases, to the left of this row there is a smaller row consisting of 3 or 4 Braille modules called Status Modules. These extra modules represent some additional information about the status of the display in encoded form, such as the present position of the Braille Window on the screen (see next section) or the position of the cursor.

Most Braille displays have a flat design. If they consist of 40 modules, their width is that of a PC keyboard. The depth is normally such that one can position the keyboard onto the display, the surface with the tactile pins being in front of the keyboard. From this ergonomically very advantageous connection between display and keyboard many sighted people gain the impression that the blind user would work with a special keyboard for the blind. However, this is completely wrong: Off-the-shelf PC keyboards are normally well suited for use by a blind person, the special thing is only the display.

There is a strong trend to design Braille displays in a portable form (weight less than 2 Kilogram). Since the dimensions of a notebook PC are much the same as the dimensions of a PC keyboard, one can position such a computer on top of the display. A combination of this kind, although already somewhat bulky and heavy, can still be considered portable, thus making the computer fully available to a blind user even when (s)he is on tour. The rechargeable batteries built into a portable Braille display grant 3 to 4 hours of independent operation, a time generally longer than that granted by the batteries of a notebook PC.

3 The Braille Window. 40 vs. 80 Character Braille Display

The blind computer user working with a Braille display never sees the whole screen at one glance: (s)he is limited to one line, in many cases only one half or a quarter of a line of the screen at a time. For sighted people it is hard to imagine that under such restricted conditions efficient use of modern software is still possible, and, yet, it is: The art is to move the Braille Window, that is, the one-dimensional portion of the screen presently displayed by the Braille modules, quickly and efficiently across the screen to places where relevant information is located. Such movements of the Braille display can be performed in two different ways:

User-controlled movement: On every Braille display the user finds certain keys (or key combinations) to move the Braille window line by line or, on a 40 character Braille display, half line by half line.

Software-controlled movement: Although the above mentioned functions allow complete access to every spot on the screen, work would be extremely cumbersome if the user were not supported by a set of automatic jump functions. The by far most important capability of this kind is the Cursor Binding function discussed in the next section.

4 How the Cursor is Handled by a Braille Display

There is probably no interactive, text-oriented software program that would not in the one or in the other form make use of the Cursor. Although today there are more and more situations where the cursor is replaced by a lightbar (see section 8.), the cursor still plays an essential part on the screen: It is present wherever text has to be input by the user. To deal with the cursor correctly is therefore an absolute necessity for every Braille display.

As soon as the Braille Window covers a portion of the screen containing the cursor, the actual position of the cursor is displayed by the corresponding Braille module. To do this, there are several different ways in use:

Display by the Full Braille Cell: The module corresponding to the cursor position shows the Braille character consisting of all eight dots.

Representation by Dot 7 and Dot 8: These two dots are added to the character at the cursor position.

Representation by Vibrating Cells: Some or all dots forming the character at the cursor position are put into a vibrating state.

Associated with the cursor are two important functions, one of which user-controlled, the other software-controlled:

Jump to the Cursor: This user-controlled function lets one move the Braille window instantly to the cursor position, whatever its original position may have been. This becomes important if one wants to convince oneself about the present cursor position, or if the surroundings of the cursor on screen are to be explored.

Automatic Cursor Binding: This software-controlled capability moves the Braille window automatically to the cursor whenever its position on the screen changes. One consequence of this function, at first sight a rather trivial one, is the fact that, whenever the user inputs text from the keyboard, then the Braille Window is at the position of the input text, loosely speaking, it follows the input.

There are circumstances where automatic Cursor Binding has disturbing effects: These are situations where the screen is updated continuously and where a piece of information apart from the cursor has to be watched, whereas the cursor itself moves constantly on the screen.

5 Cursor Routing

In order to correct text written by any editor it is necessary to quickly move the cursor to a place where an error is found. Since the error was detected using the Braille window, the task is to move the cursor to a certain spot covered by the Braille window. It would be rather cumbersome if one had to use the cursor arrow keys to perform such a movement. In order to ease the work, most Braille displays are furnished with special buttons to perform what is called "Cursor Routing": Above every Braille module there is a knob which, when pressed, causes the cursor to move to that point on the screen presently covered by the Braille module. This mechanism which, in a sense, can be viewed as a tactile substitute for the mouse, makes it possible to easily correct texts processed by a computer.

Cursor routing keys exist both as mechanical buttons and as optical sensors. Sensors have the advantage that they require absolutely no physical pressure, but their disadvantage is that one can trigger unwanted actions by inadvertently touching them. This drawback does not appear with the mechanical variant, but there are some cases where very firm pressure is needed to trigger the cursor routing buttons. Another crucial advantage of the sensor variant is pointed out in the next section.

That the cursor can be routed only to those spots on the screen where it is allowed by the current application program is obvious. However, with some less developed implementations there are situations where a cursor routing cannot be performed although it would be allowed by the running application.

6 Representation of video attributes

The text characters and the position of the cursor are not the only items of information that are relevant within a text-oriented environment: An essential component are the video attributes that are assigned to every character on the screen. From the software-technical point of view, a video attribute is just a sequence of 8 bits that is associated with every screen character in addition to the 8 text bits. From the user's viewpoint, these attributes are visible in terms of foreground and background colors and of certain highlightings such as blinking, underlined or boldface characters. Hereby, the special form of an attribute is often of little relevance for a blind user. Rather, it is important to notice changes in attribute within a text and to grasp the information for whose sake the change was performed.

For the representation of attributes by means of a Braille display, there are several common possibilities:

Binary Representation: The Braille display is switched into a special attribute mode where every Braille module represents the attribute bits rather than the text bits of the corresponding character. Here, in contrast to the customs in the Braille writing system, one normally establishes a one-to-one correspondence between the bits of an attribute and the dots of the representing Braille cell. Since each of these bits represents a unique foreground colour, background colour or highlighting, the blind user can feel the actual colours or highlightings from the bit pattern displayed on the Braille line.

Encoded representation by the status modules (see section 2): With displays that have cursor routing buttons sometimes a special mode can be enabled where the attribute of a character is displayed by the status cells once the cursor routing button above this character is pressed or touched, respectively. For this representation, a code is employed that uses easily remembered, three or four letter abbreviations for the colours and the highlightings.

Representation of Certain Attributes by Using Additional Braille Dots: In most applications, only very few attributes are relevant to the user: In this case (and in similar cases) some Braille displays allow to define the relevant attribute as a "special attribute" and to have such a special attribute represented by adding dots 7 and 8(or dot 8 alone) to each character with the attribute in question.

7 Handling Lightbars (Soft(ware) Cursors)

The system cursor (or hardware cursor) discussed in section 4 is not the only object on the screen that has to be automatically followed by the sighted user's eyes (and hence also by the Braille display).In modern application programs, selections in pull-down menus, in listings like directories etc. are very often marked by a video attribute (a lightbar) rather than by the system cursor. If one of the arrow keys is pressed, then the position of the video attribute in question changes on screen, and the selected item can be viewed.

Theoretically, a Braille display user can use the methods discussed in the previous section to detect the presence of a lightbar attribute. However, efficiency and speed in working with modern software would dramatically decrease if such a method were applied. It would be desirable that, whenever an arrow key is pressed, then the Braille window automatically jumps to the place where the lightbar attribute is located, establishing an automatic following mechanism completely analogous to the cursor binding discussed in section 4.

Contrary to the system cursor which is also referred to as the Hardware Cursor, spots of the screen carrying a lightbar are called Soft Cursors (or Software Cursors) in the world of blind users. The addressed problem will therefore be referred to as the Soft Cursor Problem.

Before we attempt to sketch the presently available methods to cope with the problem, we must remark that there is hardly a system on the present market that would solve the problem in a completely satisfactory way. Although today's Braille displays all are able to follow every soft cursor, it either requires much configuration or even programming work to install the mechanism, or it can be easily installed, but it causes trouble to switch to an alternative method of cursor following within the current application. It is certainly not exaggerated when we call the soft cursor problem the canonical weakness of the present Braille display.

The reason why different methods of soft cursor following were developed is because the spot on the screen where a lightbar attribute appears is not always unique, such that an algorithm to decide which occurrence should be displayed is needed. The most important example is the classical pull-down menu as is commonly used within the Microsoft and Borland programs. If, for example, in Microsoft Word no submenu of the horizontal menu "file - process -layout -insert - ..." is selected, then the place where the highlight attribute is located is still unique - it only moves across the top line of the screen when the left or right arrow key is pressed. However, as soon as one of the menu items, say "File", is selected, then the attribute appears not only on the "File" selection, but also on one of the vertically arranged sub-menus "new- open - close - ..." and so on.

The following strategies to overcome this problem were developed:

7.1 Movement-oriented Soft Cursor Handling

With this method, the user first defines the attribute to be followed. When the application in question is running, the (normally unique) place on the screen where the attribute has moved is calculated in regular time intervals, and the Braille window is directed to that location. For instance, in our above example of the pull-down menu, this method always presents that occurrence of the lightbar attribute currently relevant for the user: For in the first case where still no submenu is open, hitting a horizontal arrow key can cause a movement of the soft cursor only within the horizontal menu line, whereas in the second case where a vertical submenu is selected, hitting a vertical arrow key leaves the horizontal line unchanged, and a movement of the soft cursor attribute takes place only within the vertical section where the submenu resides.

The movement-oriented method is very simple to install, and in most cases it provides the desired results immediately. However, in order to use it efficiently, it has to switch back automatically to the normal cursor binding (section 4) in cases where a lightbar to follow is no longer present on the screen. Moreover, it should be possible to switch automatically between different attributes for movement-oriented lightbar handling. However, both automatisms are presently implemented within very few systems. Since in many applications situations where a soft cursor has to be followed and situations where the hardware cursor is relevant coexist and since very often more than just one lightbar attribute has to be watched, the afore-mentioned drawback kills much of this method's attractivity and efficiency.

7.2 Window-oriented Monitoring

Here the problem of multiple occurrence of the same attribute is faced by confining the monitoring process to a rectangular portion of the screen, a so-called "Window", within which the attribute occurs only once. The main disadvantage of this approach is apparent: The above stated need for automatic switching mechanisms appears here already in situations where the first method still works perfectly without them: In order to stick to our example: In the first case (no sub-menu open), the soft cursor window can be the entire screen. In the second case, however, when a sub-menu is opened, we shall exclude the top line of the screen in order to attain uniqueness. So, already in this simple situation, we need two different soft cursor windows, and we need an automated mechanism to switch between them unless we want to kill ease of working by an endless series of key hits for manual switching.

Especially within systems that utilize the third method, automatic switching procedures are already quite common. The idea behind the mechanisms is that the system regularly monitors the apparition of specified strings on the screen which are unique indicators for the necessity of an automatic switching. However, implementations of this kind have three crucial disadvantages:

- Complicated Installation
- Noticeable Loss of Performance
- High Memory Consumption

The problems pointed out above can probably be completely solved only by furnishing the Braille display software by artificial intelligence that analyses the Video Memory in order to automatically manage lightbar handling. Although there are already a few systems with such a software, it does not yet belong to the set of standard equipment for a Braille display.

8 Computer Systems Accessible with a Braille Display

Since the (IBM)-compatible PC is by far the most common computer in modern working life, Braille displays have been devised almost exclusively for this computer platform. Since, however, the PC can be used as a terminal for a vast variety of computer systems by terminal emulation software, the Braille display opens, via the PC as a connecting link, access to virtually every text-oriented computing environment to a blind user. Workstations with a UNIX (or a similar) operating system, VAX Computers, or mainframes with VM or MVS as their operating systems are only a few examples.

9 Attaching a Braille Display to a Computer; Hardware and Software Solutions

To attach a Braille display to a computer, there are two completely different ways:

9.1 The Software Solution

This is the more common variant: Here a TSR program is loaded in the PC that manages the monitoring of the Video Memory and the control of the Braille display, and the display is connected to the computer via the parallel or a serial port. The advantages of the software solution are:

- Portability of the Braille Device: Since no interface card has to be utilized, it is relatively easy to operate a Braille display with different computers.
- Possibility to use with a notebook PC
- Portability: Since it is still hardly possible to integrate an interface card into a portable PC, a software solution is required to employ a Braille display for such a computer.

9.2 The Hardware Solution

In the PC, there is installed an interface card that is connected to the Braille display and that is furnished with a special firmware that monitors the Video Memory and sends its contents out to the Braille display. The chief advantages of the hardware solution are the following:
- Considerable Independence from the Underlying Operating System
- No Memory Occupied by the Driver Software
- No Conflicts With Other TSR's

10 Braille Displays and Graphical User Interfaces

It is completely obvious that a conventional one-line Braille display is not suited to furnish a tactile representation of a screen in graphics mode. However, in the last two years the development of software products was begun that make certain classes of graphically oriented environments accessible to the blind by means of synthetic speech. This is done by means of so-called "Off Screen Models", these are textual descriptions of elements on a graphic screen. With such off screen models it is indeed possible to describe standard controls such as pull-down menus, list boxes, check boxes, radio buttons, etc., as they are common within Microsoft Windows or OS/2. Icons can be made accessible at least inasmuch as it is possible to assign a verbal label to an icon that is heard when the icon is met by the mouse pointer. Of course, this method completely fails when it is attempted to make maps, technical drawings or photos readable by a blind user.

Although, as already mentioned, most of these new programs were originally developed with a speech synthesizer as an output medium in mind, presently a strong trend can be felt to adapt them for a Braille display afterwards.

In doing so, some difficulties have to be overcome, many of which arise from the significant differences between a speech and a Braille system: While in a speech system the various items of information are conveyed sequentially - one item after another -, the information presented by a Braille display is in a sense two-dimensional: Although there is only one physical display line, the blind user sees the screen contents line by line, and, even more important, (s)he gets a complete tactile image of the geometrical arrangement of items within one line. In many cases, this image can be extended much beyond the current line.

Such geometrical views of the screen are nearly illusive to the user of a synthetic speech device: Although most speech-based screen review programs incorporate facilities to retrieve the screen coordinates of a character, these tools are much harder to use than the parallel ones on a Braille display.

This problem has, at least at present, a very negative impact on Braille software for GUI's: Since so little geometrical information is immediately encompassed within a speech-oriented GUI reviewer, the same is true for the Braille versions of these products. There have to be undertaken considerable efforts to make Braille-based GUI review software as "geometrically aware" as their textual counterparts are.

To work toward this aim, an extended, Braille-oriented concept of an Off Screen Model seems to be necessary.

The Concept of a Full Screen Tactile Display (FSTD) Driven by Electrochemical Reactions

Ryszard Kowalik, Irena Postawka

Department of Optoelectronics, Technical University of Gdańsk,
Gdańsk, Poland

Abstract:
A concept of a full screen tactile display driven by electrochemical reactions is presented. It is based on theoretical considerations of electrochemical reactions which occur during electrolysis. The basic calculations of electrochemical equations are discussed. A model of one cell and full size tactile display is proposed. A project of a driving and controlling system of a tactile display is presented.

1. Introduction

The blind computer users due to braille displays and speech synthesisers have had a good opportunity to work with sighted people. But nowadays more and more software is designed in graphic environment such as f.e.Microsoft Windows. For sighted people it is a great advantage because they do not need to type long and difficult to remember commands and instead of that they only manipulate graphical object on the screen clicking or dragging with mouse or trackball. This kind of man-computer interaction requires good hand and eye co-ordination what is impossible for the blind. Solution of a problem full screen tactile display is still incomplete although a lot of efforts have been undertaken [1], [2]. The main barrier to overcome in a tactile displays is a driving mechanism of a system which is always very complex, large and expensive. Although the several projects of electrotactile, thermal and mechanical displays was presented the problem of a full size tactile display is still unsolved [3], [4], [5].

The concept of a tactile display driven by electrochemical reactions is a new aproach to the problem of driving system. It is based on theoretical considerations of electrochemical reactions which occur during electrolysis. A preliminary basic calculations let us to assume that products of electolysis could be a good medium to drive the tactile points of a display.

2. The size and resolution of a FSTD

The main assumption of presented model is that tactile display will represent full monitor screen e.g. 80 columns and 25 rows of text and it will be able to present a simple graphic images as plots, schemes and maps. All points will be placed regularly in distance about 2,5-3 mm from each other. ASCII signs will be representing by 8-point braille code formed into 4x2 points cells with one point wide break between them. So, full screen size requires 239 points in each row (160 points for 80 ASCII signs and 79 breaks between them) and 124 points in each column (100 points for 25 rows and 24 breaks between them). For presentation of images all points will be active together with breaks between braille cells. Assuming that size of one point is about 2 mm and distance between them is about 1 mm the size of a full display is about 370x720 mm.

3. Driving system of a FSTD

To avoid a problem with mechanical part of a tactile display the idea of driving points by products of electrochemical reactions is proposed. The main advantage of this idea is that driving medium of a tactile point is placed inside the point. Therefore no more space is needed for the driving system. Theoretical considerations and calculations convinced about the reliability of that approach.

The passage of an electric current in electrolyte causes an electrochemical reactions. The oxygen and hydrogen mixture is produced as a result of electrolysis. If that process takes place in limited volume the gas mixture causes an increasing of a pressure inside an electrolytic cell. Making an assumption that cell is cylindrical a force arising during electrolysis can be calculated.

$$F = S * P \qquad\qquad (1)$$

F – *force*
S – *cross- sectional area*
P – *gas pressure*

In according to Dalton's right:

$$P = P_{H2} + P_{O2} \qquad\qquad (2)$$

P_{H2} – *hydrogen pressure*
P_{O2} – *oxygen pressure*

then from (1) and (2) :

$$F = S * \frac{2}{3} * \frac{E}{V} * (n_{H2} + n_{O2}) \qquad (3)$$

E – average kinetic energy
V – gas volume
n_{H2} – hydrogen molecule quantity
n_{O2} – oxygen molecule quantity

Since:

$$E = \frac{3}{2} * \frac{R * T}{N_A} \qquad (4)$$

and

$$n = \frac{m}{\mu} * N_A \qquad (5)$$

then:

$$F = \frac{S * R * T}{V} * \left(\frac{m_{H2}}{\mu_{H2}} + \frac{m_{O2}}{\mu_{O2}} \right) \qquad (6)$$

T – temperature $°K$
N_A – Avogadro constant
R – gas constant
m_{H2} – hydrogen mass
m_{O2} – oxygen mass
μ_{H2} – hydrogen molar mass
μ_{O2} – oxygen molar mass

Hydrogen and oxygen mass can be calculated from Faraday's right:

$$m = k * Q \qquad (7)$$

$$k = \frac{\mu}{v * N_A * e} \qquad (8)$$

k – electrochemical equivalent
Q – electric charge
v – amount of electrons to obtain one gas molecule
e – electron charge

then:

$$m = \frac{\mu * Q}{v * N_A * e} \qquad (9)$$

Because in (6) a ratio $\frac{m}{\mu}$ is calculated then from (7) and (8):

$$\frac{m_{H2}}{\mu_{H2}} = \left(\frac{Q}{v_{H2} * N_A * e} \right) \qquad (10)$$

$$\frac{m_{O2}}{\mu_{O2}} = \left(\frac{Q}{v_{O2} * N_A * e} \right) \qquad (11)$$

and because an electrolytic cell is cylindrical then:

$$V = S * H \qquad (12)$$

S – $\quad$ cross - sectional area of cylinder
H – $\quad$ hight of cylinder

Finally, the calculated force is:

$$F = \frac{R * T * Q}{H * N_A * e} * \left(\frac{1}{v_{H2}} + \frac{1}{v_{O2}} \right) \qquad (13)$$

When process of electrolysis takes place in an elastic cylindrical cell the force could cause an increasing in size of a cell. As it is seen from (13) the force is not depending on cross-sectional area of cylinder but on the height. Because for the tactile display the increasing in height of a point 1 mm is enough to be perceptible and electric charge of 10 mC is enough to cause electrolysis then estimated force for:

$H = 1$ mm
$Q = 10$ mC
$T = 300$ °K

is equal:

$F = 0.194$ N

That force is strong enough to sustain a tactile point of a display.

4. A model of a tactile cell.

A model of one cell of a tactile display is presented below as an example of utilisation of a force arising during electrolysis. A tactile point has a form of cylinder 2 mm in diameter and 5 mm height. It should be made of elastic material with internal surface covered with catalyst which enables hydrogen to oxidise in room temperature. The cylinder is filled with weak water solution of sulphuric acid and two electrodes are dipped into that liquid. The amount of 29636 cells are mounted on a non-conductive surface with an array of 124 row collection lines and 239 column collection lines. During the passage of current through the electrolyte inside a single cell the mixture of hydrogen and oxygen is produced and the pressure inside a cylinder increases. Because cylinder's walls are elastic the pressure causes increasing of size of a tactile point. Simultaneously due to presence of catalyst the oxygen and hydrogen molecules forms the water molecules again. The amount of catalyst should be fitted to the time of oxidation to keep a pressure during several seconds. For a longer time the active tactile points must be refreshed periodically.

5. Controller of a tactile display

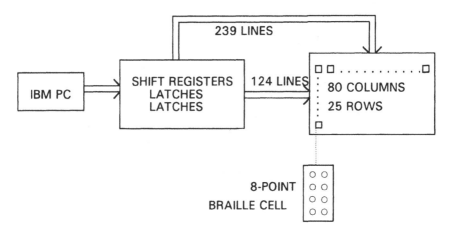

Fig.1. Block diagram of a control system.

The block diagram of a control system is presented on the figure 1. Tactile display is controlled by IBM PC computer via the interface. That interface consists of 124-channel latch connected with rows of FSTD and 239-channel shift register connected with columns of FSTD. Information regarding each consecutive column is latched in a set of latches and proper tactile points in that column are excited by passing an electric current and starting an electrochemical reaction. That cycle repeats 239 times column by column until full tactile display will be activated. The time of 239 cycles should be short enough to keep all excited points in high position. After it the new information about the status of a display could be passed to the first and next columns. Even if information does not change the display must be activated at regular intervals to sustain the outline of a display.

6. Conclusions

Tactile display presented in this paper is a theoretical model which has not been constructed yet. Although the results of calculation and simplicity of a controller are very encourage the problem of selection of elastic material and type of catalyst is still unsolved. We are looking for a co-operation with specialists in chemistry for better recognition of possibility of practical realisation of our project.

7. References

[1] Gill J.: Access to Graphical User Interfaces by Blind People, RNIB, London, 1993
[2] Fricke J., Bähring H.: A Graphic Input/Output Tablet for Blind Computer Users, Proc. of 3rd ICCHP, Vienna, 1992
[3] Brümmer H.: Elektrotaktiles Blindenschrift-Display mit Sprachaussgabe, Proc. of EuroDisplay Conference, Frankfurt, 1989
[4] De Baetselier E., Du M., De May G.: A Thick Film Resistor Circuit as a Prosthesis for Blind Persons, 9th European Hybrid Microelectronics Conference, 1993
[5] Shinohara M., Saida S., Shimizu Y., Mochizuki A., Sorimachi M.: Development of a 3-D Tactile display for the Blind: System Design, Proc. of 3rd ICCHP, Vienna, 1992.

Displaying Laterally Moving Tactile Information

Joerg Fricke, Helmut Baehring

Department of Computer Science, FernUniversitaet Hagen
D-58084 Hagen, Germany
e-mail joerg.fricke@fernuni-hagen.de

Abstract. A movable dynamic tactile display has been developed presenting information to one or several fingertips resting on the display. As a main goal, the virtual line or plane of information to be displayed should be read using the same perceptual and cognitive resources as with real objects like paper braille or tactile graphics. This is achieved by a nonvibratory display comprising an array of tactile pins having a spacing of about 1 mm, at least in the x-direction. These pins can be lifted by piezoelectric bending strips to a variety of heights. A scanned braille dot, for example, is presented by a smooth lateral "wave" of lifted and lowered pins. A special design resulting in a negligible power dissipation even at high bandwidth allows the integration of the bending strip drivers into the display mechanics. First experiences with a prototype are reported, and future research topics are outlined.

1 Introduction

For blind or visually impaired computer users, dynamic tactile output devices are useful besides speech output, depending on the application and on the preferences of the user. Surely, the most convenient solution is to provide a real line resp. a real screen of braille or graphics. However, if size, weight, or costs are critical factors, then a virtual line or a virtual screen presented only partially at a time by a small movable display could be a satisfactory compromise. This is especially true if the information to be read does not contain complex graphics but text enhanced by a limited set of graphic symbols and providing some relevant information by its twodimensional structure, as the mathematical notation Dotsplus [1], for example.

Virtual objects displayed by movies to the visual sense can be recognized without training. This is due to the fact that looking at a movie screen involves the same perceptual and a subset of those cognitive resources which are engaged in looking at real world objects. Our goal was to develop an equivalent display for the tactual sense, for the present restricted to the presentation of braille characters to one or a few fingertips. Each braille reader should be able to use this device achieving his or her normal reading performance without any special training. Such a dynamic braille display can be mounted on a laterally moveable carriage [2] or on some kind of mouse similar to the Optacon puck [3].

To outline the background, section 2 presents some fundamentals on tactual signal processing, and section 3 gives a survey on state-of-the-art devices. After introducing the principles of our "Braille Movie" approach in section 4, we describe the features of the laboratory devices in section 5. Section 6 presents first experiences made by informal testing of a prototype, section 7 deals with the design of devices comprising a Braille Movie display, and section 8 is concerned with future research topics.

2 Perceptive and cognitive processing of tactile signals

Braille and tactile graphics can be considered as texture providing information by a spatial structure. For this reason, many results of research on texture perception apply as well to tactual reading [4]. In the skin of the fingertips, there are receptors responding to perpendicular indentation of the skin (SA I), to tangential displacement by friction (SA II), to vibration in the range of 5 to 40 Hz (RA), and to vibration in the range of 40 to 400 Hz (PC) [4]. In spite of the fact that scanning a rough surface should excite always SA I and SA II units and, depending on the surface pattern and the scanning speed, RA or PC units as well, it was shown that lowering the response of the SA II, RA, or PC units does not affect the perception of roughness [5, 6]. The respective cognitive process seems to take only, or mainly, the SA I signals into account. Since the SA I units allow also a sufficient localization of the stimuli, tactile structures like braille can be read without any friction and within a wide range of scanning speed. Even more, the absense of friction as a source of "noise" should improve the reading performance [7].

Although Braille readers commonly use several fingers of both hands in order to track the current and the following line and to explore in advance the structure of the text, e.g. the length of words and sentences, the actual reading is performed by just one finger of one or both hands each [8].

Navigating through a complex text is eased by dealing with a mental image of the text structure, and constructing such images is facilitated by some proprioceptive feedback reporting the position of the hand during the reading.

To summarize, "natural" tactile reading involves at least the stimulation of the SA I receptors by indentation, rather of several fingertips than of only one, and some proprioceptive feedback concerning the position of the reading fingers.

Vibrotactile displays offer an advantage mainly on the engineering side: The PC units can be stimulated by skin displacements of a few μm, i.e. by transmitting a small amount of energy. However, the user has to develop by training a pattern recognition process based on the PC signals. For this reason, results obtained by experiments based on vibrotactile displays apply not, or only partially, to braille reading and dealing with static tactile graphics.

The spatial resolution of the skin of the fingertips is different depending on whether recognition, localization, or distinction of perpendicularly tapped or tangentially scanned tactile stimuli are concerned: A single point stimulus can be localized with an accuracy of about 1 mm. Two simultaneous tactile point stimuli are felt by tapping as two distinct objects if their distance is larger than about 2 mm. Structure widths of 0.1 mm are well perceived by scanning the object. Likewise, a movement is already recognized if a single stimulus is moving laterally for about 0.1 mm [9].

Consequently, a braille dot or a raised line composed of several narrow dots or pins is felt as a single object when touched without tangential movement but its rough structure is perceived by scanning. A slow sequence of lateral "jumps" of an tactile object can be felt as a smooth motion if the width of each jump is only a fraction of 1 mm.

As for the visual sense, one apparently moving object can be perceived if two stimuli are applied to distant points of the skin sequentially, but it feels different from an actually moving stimulus [10] - perhaps due to the high temporal resolution of the tactual sense.

Due to the adaptation of the SA I units, the structure of complex static information is well recognized only by scanning. Additionally, it is reasonable to assume that the determination of the structure is based not on the SA I signals itself but on their changes, i.e. on the movements of the edges of the indentations. In this case, tapping on a structure or popping up some information under the resting finger provide a perceptual pattern that did not match any pattern out of the temporal sequence obtained by scanning the same structure because the progressive indentation during the first phase of tapping causes only "leading" but no "trailing", i.e. releasing edges, and the edges move perpendicularly to their own local tangent instead of unidirectionally on the whole fingertip as during scanning.

3 State-of-the-art devices

There are some proposals how to display moving braille characters by a wheel [11] or by a belt [12] carrying balls or pins inserted or removed by an electromechanical display controller. Certainly, such devices would provide the same sensations as static braille does but they would be too heavy and too bulky to be integrated in a mouse, for example. The well known vibrotactile Optacon display [13] is not designed to show laterally moving Braille characters but enlarged ink print characters and graphics. Of course, with a modified pin matrix geometry it could do so but even a skilled braille reader would have to learn to process the vibrotactile sensations. Furthermore, some devices displaying a virtual braille line contain one or a few usual braille cells [2], [14]. During scanning the line, the characters are "popped up". Again, the user has to undergo some training because instead of being provided with the usual temporal sequence of spatial patterns he has to recognize a single unfamiliar pattern, as mentioned in section 2.

4 Providing the impression of moving dots

Obviously, laterally moving tactile objects on a horizontal surface can be obtained by transversale waves, i.e. by lifting and lowering parts of the surface in an appropriate sequence without moving any material laterally. Smoothly moving very small pieces of the surface would result in a virtually noisefree data presentation to the skin resting on the surface. The distinctness of the perception would be better than by scanning the static information by the skin. By choosing a coarse partitioning of the surface and by limiting the number of intermediate levels of the surface parts, the display becomes producable and affordable but some noise is introduced. Fortunately, braille readers and users of static tactile graphics are accustomed to a certain amount of noise by scanning the surface with the skin. So, the noise should be limited just to the "normal" level.

While the static spatial resolution of the display is given only by the partitioning of the surface, the dynamic spatial resolution, i.e. the number of steps the information is doing to move along a given distance, is determined by the distance between the surface parts and by the number of heights the parts of the surface can be driven to.

Laterally moving 8 dot braille characters results in 4 "dot tracks". Hence a dynamic braille display can consist of a solid surface with 4 rows of vertically moveable tactile pins. In the direction perpendicular to the movement, the width of the pins should just equal the width of the presented dots. In the direction of the movement, the width of the pins can be determined by the following considerations. During the movement of a dot for one pin width, the height of the dot should not change considerably in order to yield a nonvibrating dot. This can be achieved by holding one pin at full height as long as one neighbouring pin is lifted and the other neighbour is lowered. Consequently, one dot has to be presented by at least two or three pins depending on the phase of movement. Since there must be a gap between two dots in the same row, the maximal pin width plus spacing is a third of the lateral center-to-center distance of the braille dots. Figure 1 shows the arrangement of pins in a braille display. Figure 2 is a side-view of pins presenting two moving dots in four phases. The shown dot spacing of 3 mm could be enlarged to improve the separation of neighbouring dots.

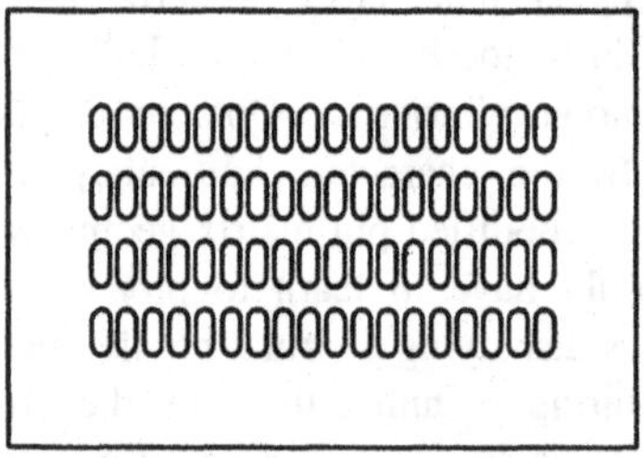

OOOOOOOOOOOOOOOOOOO
OOOOOOOOOOOOOOOOOOO
OOOOOOOOOOOOOOOOOOO
OOOOOOOOOOOOOOOOOOO

Fig. 1. The arrangement of pins in a braille display surface (drawing enlarged)

Fig. 2. 1 mm spaced pins displaying two braille dots moving laterally by steps of 0.25 mm

Graphic displays should comprise a pin array having the same spacing in x- and y-direction. On principle, presenting graphics using a frictionless display as described could lead to a difficulty: a long horizontal or vertical stroke would perceptually vanish during a scanning movement parallel to its axis because the contents of the display would not change. Of course, the display controller could recognize such situations and introduce small movements of the display contents perpendicular to the main movement. However, having a sufficiently high dynamic spatial resolution, this problem will virtually never arise because, as during scanning real structures, the user will never carry out exactly straight movements. As long as the amplitude of the wavy line he moves along is larger than half the spatial quantization caused by the dynamic resolution, the display contents will vary and the stroke will stay perceivable.

Both braille and graphic displays of the kind described above have a peculiarity: With the fingertips resting on the moving display, the scanned objects are felt as smooth and the tactile pins itself are not distinguishable. However, if the user starts to scan the display surface the smooth objects turn into rough ones because the gaps between the pins becomes perceivable although not localizable.

5 The first laboratory displays ("Braille Movies")

Till now, two displays are built. The first display contains 4 rows of 18 pins each. The center-to-center distance of neighbouring pins is 1 mm in lateral direction and 2.5 mm from row to row. The horizontal cross-section of each pin is nearly rectangular with a size of about 0.7 mm by 1.7 mm. So, a braille dot represented by two adjacent pins has a basis of 1.7 by 1.7 mm. The angles on top of the pins are smoothed. The geometry of the second display differs in having a row-to-row spacing of 3 mm, the remaining measurements equal those of the first display.

Each pin is driven by one piezoelectric bending strip. In order to provide sufficient forces and to match the distance of 1 mm, the strips being arranged in three layers for each row of pins have a width of 2.5 mm but narrow ends of 0.8 mm. 12 layers of bending elements are glued within a stack of 13 printed circuit boards (PCBs).

In the second version, the 11 inner PCBs of the stack are replaced by two thinner PCBs each resulting in a decomposable stack of 12 modules. As shown in figure 3, each module carries also the electronic drivers of the piezoelectric benders and a shift register. Both the volume and the profile of the display including these drivers match approximately that of an assembly of 4 usual braille cells.

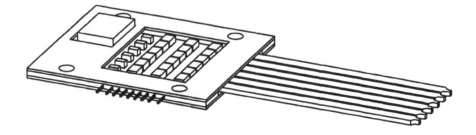

Fig. 3. A perspective view of a module carrying bending strips, drivers, and a shift register

The capacitances of the piezoelectric benders are not switched to one out of two DC supply voltages by means of open collector or push-pull output stages, as usually. Instead, in order to achieve a low power dissipation within the drivers even during fast movements of the displayed information, the electrodes are charged from a sinusshaped AC voltage of up to 500 Hz by means of controlled halfbridge rectifiers. Given a reading speed of 14 characters per second, a carriage return time of 1 second, characters with 3 dots on an average, a capacitance of 40 nF per bending strip, and a control voltage range of 200 V, we had an average heat dissipation within the 72 compactly arranged drivers of about 6 W with push-pull outputs but we have less than 0.1 W with controlled rectifiers. Each electrode can be charged to an arbitrary value within the voltage range of the AC voltage by changing the state of the corresponding driver each time the AC voltage reaches the desired value. So, an arbitrary force within the given range can be exerted on each individual tactile pin.

A microcontroller on an additional PCB is executing the following tasks: Communications with the attached personal computer using a serial interface, determining the position of the display unit and hence the section of the virtual braille line to be displayed, conversion of the supply voltage of 5 V DC to 200 V DC and to 200 Vpp AC by means of switching converters, and controlling the rectifiers which are driving the bending strips. So, except for the geometry of the display, the way the text is displayed may be altered rather easily by software changes.

6 First experiences testing the Braille Movie

We presented the prototype (first version) during an exhibition. No questionnaire nor any schematic way to process the testing of the display by the visitors of the exhibition was prepared. So we just gave some hints to the visitors how to use the device, and the persons testing the display reported in an informal way the recognized characters and words and the difficulties they discovered during reading. Obviously, such a procedure cannot yield any numerical results but first impressions and hints about which problems should be faced during the next steps of the development.

About 50 persons tried to read using the Braille Movie. Two stated that they would refuse to use such a device. About 95 % succeeded in reading the single characters and words presented by the test programs. Their general attitudes were in the range between relevant criticism and enthusiasm. Topics critized by many were:

a) There was some tactile noise in the background, i.e. though the display should be nonvibrating sometimes some pins were actually vibrating.

b) Neighbouring dots appeared not distinctly separated from each other, i.e. a "C" could be taken for a horizontal stroke, for example.

c) Braille dots 2 and 5 were perceived weaker than the rest of the dots.

Topic a) was due to a software bug we could not fix before the beginning of the exhibition. Of course, this is not an inherent problem.

b) should be solved or at least considerably improved by changing the shape of the pins. Using pins with more narrow ends in the direction of the information movement, the gaps between neighbouring dots will be better perceivable. Furthermore, as mentioned in section 4, the horizontal distance of the braille dots can be enlarged. The consequently enlarged width of the virtual line can be compensated by moving the virtual line contrary to the direction of the movement of the display unit [2].

It seems rather unlikely that problem c) was caused by generally weaker bending strips in the second row. Perhaps this is a general effect with this kind of displays. We have enlarged the row-to-row distance to 3 mm in the second display in order to avoid dots 2 and 5 to be hidden by the other dots.

Having in mind that this was the very first approach and that the display is certainly improvable, we feel that the basic principle will become a sufficiently convenient way to display Braille when costs or size and weight of the output device are critical factors.

7 Possible features of devices containing a Braille Movie

To provide some proprioceptive feedback, a device presenting a virtual screen can be designed as a free moveable unit like a mouse or with the display mounted on a guided carriage. A mouse would be less bulky and more lightweight and allows arbitrary wide movements, on principle. However, its use requires a flat support, the user has to care for not confusing the cable, and tracking lines of characters has to be supported by acoustic or tactile signals. A mouse employing an optical position detector running on a pad with a coarse pattern would provide a virtually errorfree absolute modus, like a digitizing tablet. However, an optical mouse is smaller, less weighty, and less expensive than a tablet. The working area can be easily adapted to the current application either by changing the pad or by folding it like the board of a board game. A large but foldable pad can well be employed with portable equipment.

A device guiding a carriage is easy to use and provides space for additional control knobs and keys. It could be placed partially under the keyboard like conventional braille lines. An unusual but promising approach could be a "flying mouse" on a virtual pad. That could be achieved by carrying the mouse by some rods with angle encoders and electric controlled brakes at each joint of the rods.

Generally, some coarse tactile elements on the right of the high resolution display would allow a prerecognition of the word boundaries. Besides functions supporting the navigation and orientation in structured texts and tables [2], features concerned with reading plain texts could be valuable, too. For example, a fast movement of the display to the left end of the line could cause an automatic line feed. In this way, a large text could be read just by moving the display.

8 Future research topics within the Braille Movie approach

The Braille Movie render possible various display modi. For example, the spacing between dots, characters, and words can be varied, different attributes of characters can be indicated by different low vibrating frequencies, and the presented virtual braille line can be resting or moving contrary to the movement of the display unit.

The reading performance of both skilled and unskilled braille readers should be compared using paper braille, conventional braille lines, and a Braille Movie with combinations of the mentioned display modi. Learning braille using a Braille Movie from the beginning could be advantageous because it may help to concentrate on just one fingertip, and since the computer can track the reading finger a teaching system could provide some individual help by speech.

Also, it would be interesting to display ink print characters and plain graphical elements using a "Graphic Movie". Compared to vibrotactile displays, we expect the users to show a similar performance but to become skilled after a considerably shorter period of training.

References

1. W.A. Barry, J.A. Gardner, T.V. Raman: Accessibility to Scientific Information by the Blind: Dotsplus and ASTER could make it easy. To be published in: Proceedings of the 1994 CSUN Conference on Technology and Person with Disabilities, Los Angeles 1994
2. A. Parreno, P.J. Magallon: Teresa'80: An 80 Character Single Cell Braille Line. In: W. Zagler (ed.): Computers For Handicapped Persons. Proceedings of the 3rd Int. Conference, Vienna 1992, pp. 403-408
3. G. Vanderheiden et. al.: A dual information class model for providing access to computers with graphic user interfaces for people who are blind. Proceedings of The First World Conference on Information Technology, Washington D.C. 1991, Vol. III, pp. 77-89
4. S.J. Lederman: The perception of texture by touch. In: W. Schiff, E. Foulke (eds.): Tactual perception. Cambridge University Press 1982, pp. 142-155
5. M.M. Taylor, S.J. Lederman: Tactile roughness of grooved surfaces: A model and the effect of friction. Perception & Psychophysics 17 (1), 23-36 (1975)
6. S.J. Lederman, J.M. Loomis, D.A. Williams: The role of vibration in the tactual perception of roughness. Perception & Psychophysics 32 (2), 109-116 (1982)
7. S.J. Lederman: "Improving one's touch" ... and more. Perception & Psychphysics 24 (2), 154-160 (1978)
8. J.S. Lappin, E. Foulke: Expanding the tactual field of view. Perception & Psychophysics 14 (2), 237-241 (1973)
9. J.M. Loomis, C.C. Collins: Sensitivity to shifts of a point stimulus: An instance of tactile hyperacuity. Perception & Psychophysics, Vol. 24 (6), 487-492 (1978)
10. C.E. Sherrick, R. Rogers: Apparent haptic movement. Perception & Psychophysics 1, 175-180 (1966)
11. German patent application DE 3033078 (1980)
12. European patent application EP 0123205 (1984)
13. J.C. Bliss, M.H. Katcher, C.H. Rogers, R.P. Shepard: Optical-to-Tactile Image Conversion for the Blind. IEEE Transactions on Man-Machine Systems, Vol MMS-11 (1), 58-65 (1970)
14. J.T. Ohsann: New role for 'mice'. IBM Research Magazine (publ. date unknown)

A New Architecture Conception for a Two Dimensional Tactile Display

Bertold Schulz

Universität Karlsruhe, Studienzentrum für Sehgeschädigte,
Engesserstr. 4, D-76128 Karlsruhe

The design of new solutions for dynamic access to graphic information for the blind requires new kinds of mechanisms on the one hand and a systematic approach to the construction of the whole display on the other hand. The information transfer in the tactile-haptic way from machine to man can be described by a seven layer reference model. The seven layers are labeled "application (7)", "presentation (6)", "communication control (5)", "transport (4)", "addressing (3)", "conversion (2)" and "transmission (1)". The new concept deals with the lower four layers, which are also called the mechanism-oriented layers:

Layer 1: the kind of stimulus: The transmission layer is denoted by single pins made of plastic or metal which convey a sprung sensation.

Layer 2: the control of stimulus: The conversion layer describes the kind of pin-mechanism used. In this concept, the mechanism works with a wire of shape memory alloy which transforms - when electrically heated - electrical into mechanical energy activating a pneumatical valve. The pneumatic energy (excess or below atmospheric pressure) drives and holds the pin in the upper or lower position. Because no (mechanical) driving parts are needed at the side of the pin, a close arrangement of mechanisms in a two-dimensional way is possible.

Layer 3: the addressing of mechanisms: The addressing layer manages the selection of the single pins. This is done by collecting a quadratic number of pins into a display module which is internally controlled by a microprocessor. For the display area several display moduls are arranged in a rectangle form.

Layer 4: the control of the display: The transport layer is realized by a special communication module which serves in one direction as interface to the computer and in the other direction as controlling unit for the communication within the display. For conveying the information some additional bus modules are needed. The communication is realized as a ring, it starts in the communication module, goes through the different display modules and back to the communication module.

Advantages of the architecture: The new patented pin-mechanism allows a high resolution and a two-dimensional arrangement. The parallelism of the information processing within the display modules results in short picture modification times. The modular design of the display with few types of modules is advantageous for production and maintenance. The replacement of a single module will be simple.

A New Architecture Conception for a Two-Dimensional Tactile Display

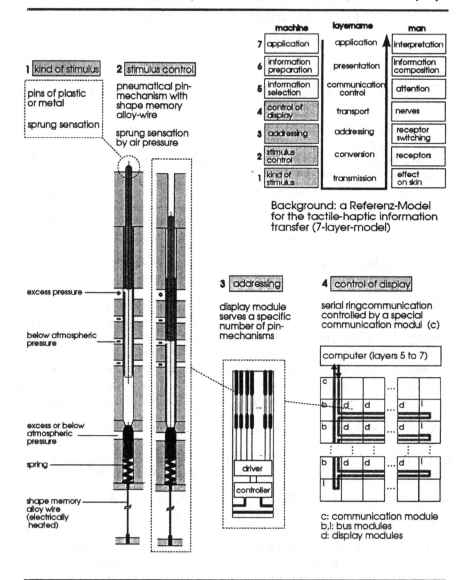

	machine	layername	man
7	application	application	interpretation
6	information preparation	presentation	information composition
5	information selection	communication control	attention
4	control of display	transport	nerves
3	addressing	addressing	receptor switching
2	stimulus control	conversion	receptors
1	kind of stimulus	transmission	effect on skin

Background: a Referenz-Model for the tactile-haptic information transfer (7-layer-model)

1 kind of stimulus

pins of plastic or metal

sprung sensation

2 stimulus control

pneumatical pin-mechanism with shape memory alloy-wire

sprung sensation by air pressure

excess pressure

below atmospheric pressure

excess or below atmospheric pressure

spring

shape memory alloy wire (electrically heated)

3 addressing

display module serves a specific number of pin-mechanisms

driver

controller

4 control of display

serial ringcommunication controlled by a special communication modul (c)

computer (layers 5 to 7)

c: communication module
b,l: bus modules
d: display modules

UNIVERSITÄT KARLSRUHE   Studienzentrum für Sehgeschädigte
Engesserstr. 4 - D-76128 Karlsruhe - Tel.: ++49-721-608-4301 - email: schulz@ira.uka.de

Tactison: a Multimedia Learning Tool for Blind Children

Burger Dominique, Bouraoui Amina *
Mazurier Christian, Cesarano Serge, Sagot Jack **

* INSERM-Creare - Université Pierre et Marie Curie, Paris, France.
E-mail : Dominique.Burger@snv.jussieu.fr

** CNEFEI, Suresnes, France.

research supported by grant n° 89D0168 from the Ministère de la Recherche, and a research grant from the CNAMTS, Paris

Abstract : This paper introduces a tactile and auditory interactive material, Tactison, that was developed to teach blind or visually impaired children. The principles and design of the system are described. Some applications in education are presented and prospects for future developments are discussed. The purpose of this paper is to demonstrate how technology can bring about metaphorical environments which may be as useful for the blind as images are for sighted people.

1. Introduction

Images on paper play a central role in the education of sighted children, mainly because images provide useful substitutes for real objects. Pictures give children many opportunities to explore, identify, analyse, classify, and verbalise about things or scenes. Pencils, scissors, paste and other low cost tools allow them to transform and build up images.

In contrast, there are few educational materials available for visually handicapped children, and those thar are poorly-adapted, scarce and expensive. Blind children suffer from a lack of rich educational and recreational documents, even before they have learned to read and count.

This paper describes and discusses a computer interface designed to do two things : 1) enriching tactile learning support by embedding sounds, and 2) allowing the direct manipulation of data within a 2-D space. It was developed as part of a research project that was put in place by the Institut National de la Santé Et de la Recherche Médicale (INSERM) and the Centre National d'Etudes et de Formation pour l'Enfance Inadaptée (CNEFEI) to evaluate the potential of multimedia techniques in the education of blind children [Burger et al., 1990; Burger, 1991; Burger et al., 1991].

2. Tactison

a) Metaphor

Tactison was developed from the following metaphor used to devise : Imagine a tray containing objects which you cannot see because they are covered by a sheet of paper or cardboard, an overlay. You can, however, hear them since they emit a sound as soon as they are touched. They also produce different sounds, depending on the way you touch them, on whether you click, double-click or press. You can also move, cut and copy them. Overlays carry raised marks that can help locate, identify and retrieve objects and thus contribute to the understanding of the overall organisation. Some overlays are divided into areas, like windows on a screen. In fact these areas can be understood as outlining boxes on the tray in which the objects are or can be arranged. Boxes represent another type of object that can also utter messages when the finger clicks, double-clicks or presses them. But these boxes are stuck to the back of the tray. They therefore cannot be moved.

Obviously, this metaphor will never fully match the characteristics and functions of computer systems. Nevertheless, it seems to be fairly consistent with the everyday experiences of the blind, who perceive objects by hearing, reaching, manipulating and palpating. It may therefore help to create a representation of the system using intuitive knowledge and concepts.

b) Hardware Implementation

Tactison inherited an interaction technique previously explored at INSERM that combined a touch device and a sound production system, under the control of a desktop computer [Liard & Burger, 1987]. A Concept Keyboard ^{TM} was used as touch device. This device has a 21x29.7 cm, A4-format and counts 256 active contacts whose lay-out is organised in 16-contact lines and 16-contact columns. Sounds are produced by either a PSOLA^{TM} or SYNTHE3^{TM} French speaking text-to-speech synthesiser or a Sound Blaster^{TM} sampling system. The minimum computer configuration is a 286 PC with a 20Mo hard disk.

c) Commands

The basic operating concepts are: reading, page turning, marking, cutting, moving and copying. Each can apply to various objects, in various situations.

A *read* command makes it possible to get information about the contents of a line, the contents of a column, the contents of a box and all the contents on the tray

A *turn page* command allows users to change exercise by loading the contents of another tray

A *mark* command is used to make an object special or noticeable

A *cut* command removes an object from the tray

A *move* command changes the position of an object on the tray

A *copy* command creates a clone of an existing object in a specified position on the tray

d) Design Considerations

Tactile Overlays

Some empirical rules of tactile design have been followed :
• very simple shapes for both abstract and figurative items,
• tactile hints and guidance
• symmetrical shapes as often as possible in order to make the pattern recognition process independent of the direction of finger exploration
Overlays are frequently revised after they have been used by the students

<u>Lay-out (Fig. 1)</u>
• Objects are always presented in the central of the overlay,
• Commands are presented at the periphery.
• If possible, things are presented in rows and columns in order to facilitate exploration. Once readers have understood this principle, they can guess the general organisation from only partial exploration. This can compensate for the loss of global perception. Such a regular arrangement also facilitates item retrieval.

Actions

Three types of physical actions can be carried out on the surface of an overlay: click, double-click and press. Each is precisely defined in time. A beep sound is emitted when a pressed action has been detected (time over 1.1 sec.).

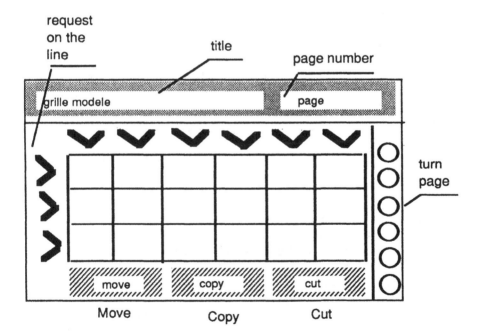

Fig. 1 The general lay-out adopted for the design of overlays.

Direct Manipulation

All commands are accessible by means of keys on the overlay. Simple rules were adopted to allow an intuitive understanding of the commands and to facilitate their memorisation. For instance, the location of a read command corresponds to the objects to be read. As shown in figure 1, all buttons on the left part of the overlay are *read-the-line-in-front-of-me* commands, whereas buttons on the top are *read-the-column-above-me* commands. Clicking, double clicking or pressing the read command buttons address the different sounds that objects can emit. The cut, move and copy commands are activated by

1- pointing and clicking on an object,
2- pointing and clicking in the right location - if necessary,
3- pointing and clicking on the command button.

The system responds by stating the action to be performed. The user can then confirm the command by double-clicking the command button.

Sounds

Both sampled sounds and synthesised spoken messages can be used. Their duration must be carefully chosen, depending on the type of activity, to allow clear identification or comprehension, but also to avoid being a load. We adopted the principle that if an action is to involve a sound utterance, any sound in progress is to be stopped.

Semantic Organisation

The messages are organized in a systematic semantic fashion, which means that the message associated with the click action can usually be described as giving a concrete, immediate aspect of evoked reality. The double-click sound generally provides more sophisticated information. The pressed sound can be a meta-message. For instance, let us imagine that the object to be evoked is a cat. The messages associated with its location could be:

click action: "miow" resulting from a sampling operation, double-click action: "My name is Pussy"

press action: "A cat is a domestic animal, it lives in a house with people".

3. Discussion

a) Use in the Classroom

An experiment was carried out for about a year wit carried out for about a year with both visually impaired and sighted children in two schools in the suburbs of Paris. It involved about 20 students ranging in age from 6 to 10 years (CP, CM2 in the French system). Several of the visually impaired children were totally blind. Students worked in small groups of 3 or 4. Training sessions took place once a week and lasted about 40 minutes. Figure 2 shows an exercice in which students are asked to classify objects - a collection of animals - by moving them from one box to another. Two image boxes, *Domestic Animals* and *Wild Animals* have been dropped into the trash. The student must put them back into their original boxes.

b) The Students' Point of View

The first point to come out of the experiment was the eagerness with which children participated in the weekly Tactison training sessions.

• Children learned to operate the device very rapidly. Children differentiated perfectly between the three pointing gestures on the touch device, clicking, double-clicking, pressing. (It is worth noting that gesture control does not necessarily imply the use of sophisticated or expensive devices.)

• The situations created with TactiSon entailed animated debates among students.

• The metaphor of mobile objects underneath the overlay was accepted without any difficulty.

• Students were able to work quite autonomously most of the time.

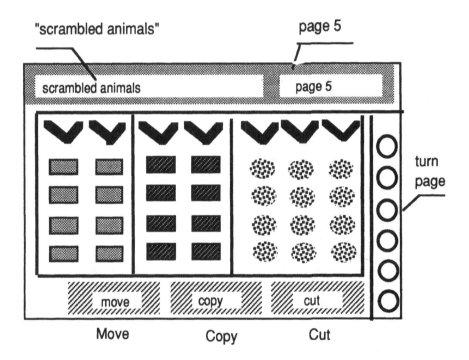

Fig. 2. The Scrambled Animals overlay illustrates how messages can give indications to the users. Message were uttered when an actions involved the corresponding objects.

c) The Teachers' Point of View

• Teachers appreciated the facilities dealing with different presentations of the same concept. It illustrated that transient auditory and tactile sensations can be used to contribute to the construction of more general and permanent representations of a concept. This is of great importance for the education of the blind, particularly since the overuse of verbal exchanges without connection to sensory experiences can lead to inadequate attitudes, known as verbalism, when facing real situations.

• They also pointed out that this type of device offers rich opportunities to make children aware of spatial organisation and for training their ability to think about space. The use of a touch device proved to be an efficient way of retrieving and manipulating data, which confirmed an experimental study by Hill and Grieb [1988], in which subjects were given a stylus that could be used to access or manipulate auditory data organized on the surface of a pad device. They were asked to perform two tasks. One was to locate an area on a page, the other was a more classical editing task. The spatial device performed almost 50% better than a conventional keyboard-based access product.

• The device was considered to be "more practicable than manipulatives since it does not weigh 2 kg and since objects cannot be lost or thrown down".

• Many applications were suggested, including exercises and games which involve various types of material, such as letters, words, numbers, notes and melodies.

• Activities were principally organised in groups.

d) The Designers Point of View

• The design rules that emerged from this study were very specific and rarely obvious. Once a solution had been tested, it became a kind of standard for future interface design. Such rules also concerned tactile diagrams, sounds and interaction methods. Three concrete examples can be given:

a) the localisation and identification of tactile symbols often appears to be quite different from what visual experience suggests.

b) regular layout in rows and columns does not evoke such an orderly organisation when explored by hand as it does for vision.

c) as explained above, feedback messages are emitted before actions have been performed, while in visual interaction feedback is obtained by observing the moving image on the screen. This exemplifies how non-visual interaction sometimes has to be designed in a very special style.

• Despite the fact that speech production was obtained through a high-quality speech synthesiser, the variety of voice timbres appeared very poor, presenting some difficulties for some exercises. On the contrary, pre-sampled sounds were greatly appreciated by children.

e) Future Prospects

• We are now developing of an authoring tool that should satisfy the following need : the creation of tactile overlays, sound recording and editing, and the design of exercises, i.e. audio-tactiles and functions.

• New input/output peripherals should be added. For instance, a braille output would be easy and would enrich opportunities to develop reading and spelling skills.

• Automatic identification of the overlays, possibly by means of bar-coded marks or other techniques, could improve the interface by making the change of page automatic.

• The addition of speech input and the implementation of multimodal interaction techniques would minimize the work load and avoid the frequent disruption of motor tasks involved in using a command buttons for the edition commands and the manipulation of data within the 2D-space [Salisbury, 1991; Martin & Béroule, 1993, Bellik & Burger, 1994].

4. Conclusion

This experiment leads to encouraging conclusions for the development of learning environments based on non-visual modalities, i.e. audition, touch and proprioception. It has confirmed that space provides a good support for the dynamic process of data organisation, comparison and classification. It is a way to help the user quickly find objects he/she needs. Semantic information, such as relative importance, similarity, or belongingness can also be communicated by the location of the objects in relation to each other.

Such multimedia environments appeared to be rich enough for teachers to consider them useful complements to existing techniques. It is hoped that they will help close the gap between the richness of learning materials available for the sighted and the relative scarcity of those accessible to the blind.

Finally, we feel that the interaction techniques that have been designed and tested in Tactison might also contribute to the design of non-visual interfaces for other computer applications.

5. References

1.   Y. Bellik & D. Burger : Multimodal interfaces: new solutions to the problem of computer accessibility for the blind. In : *Proceedings of CHI'94*, Boston (1994)

2.   D. Burger, E. Beltrando and J. Sagot : Sound Synthesis and Bar-code Technology to Develop Learning Environments for Blind Children. *Journal of Visual Impairment and Blindness*, 84, p.565-569 (1990)

3.   D. Burger : *Technologies hypermédias: Implications pour l'enseignement aux jeunes déficients visuels.* Editions INSERM, Paris. 87p (1991)

4.   D. Burger, J. Sagot et S. Cesarano : Technologie et outils d'enseignement spécialisés : Réflexions à partir du projet Polyson. *Handicaps et inadaptations - Les Cahiers du CTNERHI*, 54, pp. 53-64 (1991)

5.   D. R.Hill, and C. Grieb : Substitution for a Restricted Visual Channel in Multimodal Computer-Human Dialogue,*IEEE Transactions on Systems Man and Cybernetics., vol.* 18, 2, pp. 285-403 (1988)

6.   C. Liard et D. Burger : Composant audio-numérique et tactile et dispositif informatique en comportant application. *Brevet INSERM* n°8703340, 11 mars 1987 (1987)

7.   J.C. Martin and D. Béroule : Trends in human-machine multi-modal interaction. In: *Non-Visual Human-Computer Interactions,* D. Burger and J.C.Sperandio, Eds., John-Libbey Eurotext, Montrouge, France, pp. 145-166 (1993)

8.   M.W. Salisbury, J.H. Hendrickson, T.L. Mammers, C. Fu and S.A. Moody : Talk and Draw : Bundling Speech and Graphics, *IEEE Computer*, vol. 23, pp. 59-65 (1991)

fortec's Efforts to Support Mainstream Education through Research and Technology Development

F.P. Seiler
J. Haider, P. Mayer, W.L. Zagler

fortec - Rehabilitation Engineering Group
Vienna University of Technology
Gusshausstr. 27/359-B, A-1040 Wien-Vienna, Austria
Tel.: +43/1/504 1830-21
FAX: +43/1/504 1830-12
email: seiler@fortec.tuwien.ac.at

Abstract. Mainstream education of visually impaired pupils and students depends heavily on the accessibility of the same information than those available for sighted colleagues. These information are: **printed text** like books, lecture notes and transparents; **graphics and figures** are often used to illustrate or support the understanding of a verbally described procedure; and **access to information** available in electronic form like library catalogues, information services (e.g. gopher) and electronic texts.

fortec developed **HotDot**, a printing device that allows the production of Braille and/or inkprint within the same unit and on the same page. Another project is **RELIEF**, a new system to produce graphics and figures as hardcopy materials in tactile (three-dimensional) form. And the third project described in this paper is the conceptual design and set-up of the multifunctional **VIP-Workplace** for visually impaired students at the Vienna University of Technology.

Introduction

The "Working Group on Rehabilitation Engineering" (fortec) was established in 1986 at the Institute of Electronics, Vienna University of Technology, to intensify and consolidate efforts related to research and development of new technical solutions for handicapped and elderly persons.

The expertise and know-how amassed by fortec's members during the past years has made it possible to branch off in different directions. Firstly, fortec initiated numerous R&D projects to improve the independence of disabled persons by technical solutions in the fields communication and orientation, safety aspects and daily living. Secondly, projects were started to support mainstream education on primary and university level and to develop technical-organisational concepts for special and mainstream education. Thirdly, fortec's know-how in the field of image processing and optical character recognition led to some industry related projects which deal with aspects of document analysis, automated document processing, scene analysis and optical process control. And finally, fortec tries to introduce rehabilitation technology in Austria and to change the society's opinion about acceptance and integration of disabled persons.

In this paper three R&D activities concerning mainstream education will be presented:

* The development of **HotDot**, a printing device that allows the production of Braille and/or inkprint within one single unit and on the same document. The Braille production is based on a new principle described below. Also a German language speech-output is implemented.

* The project **RELIEF**, a new system to produce graphics and figures as hardcopy materials in tactile (three-dimensional) form. A drawing program was developed to meet certain demands for producing tactile graphics.

* And the description of the conceptual design of the multifunctional **VIP-Workplace** for visually impaired students. The set-up at the Vienna University of Technology will be illustrated.

1. HotDot - a New Technology for Braille Printers

Usually Braille producing is based on mechanical dots which are set and unset according to the represented Braille character. These dots are embossed into sheets of paper, usually cardboard in order to have a good reading quality material. Disadvantages of common Braille printers are their weight, the produced noise and vibration/motion during embossing and the restriction to have only one output medium, namely Braille.

The need to have a multimodal output device and to produce Braille and inkprint within one device and on one and the same document which can be used by sighted as well as by blind persons initiated the project HotDot.

1.1 Braille producing technique

The HotDot Braille printing unit operates on a new principle, utilising heated dots which are pressed into sheets of thermoplastic material, thereby producing very little noise. The form of the Braille dots is produced by the shape of the heated dots and a mould which is positioned behind the sheet [3].

By this new Braille producing technology three goals could be achieved:

* The Braille producing device becomes very compact and lightweight so that it can be attached to an ordinary dot-matrix or ink-jet printer. Within one single unit, inkprint and Braille material can be produced, reducing cost and saving desk space.

* Due to the thermal operation the Braille producing unit works silently. Noise is caused by the motion of the sheet and, if used, by the matrix printer. If an ink-jet instead of the matrix printer is used the noise could be reduced. Additionally the printer needs little force to produce Braille, as the forming is done mainly thermal and not only mechanical.

* The integration of the Braille producing mechanism into a state-of-the-art matrix printer offers the option to place Braille and inkprint on the same page. This technology makes it possible to have interline Braille material, where the translation into inkprint is placed beneath every line of Braille. This helps to lower the communication barrier between e.g. sighted teacher and blind student, if the teacher does not know Braille. Teacher and student can read from the same document.

1.2 Features

The "WineTU" translation software is directly implemented into the HotDot printer's control processor. It provides readable interline inkprint, even if the Braille text was entered in German Grade I (often used character combinations are represented by a single Braille sign) or Grade II Braille (context dependent meaning of one or two Braille characters) [6]. This occurs very often, as usually one of these forms of Braille (Grade I or II) is chosen in order to increase the text input frequency. Using Grade I Braille saves about 10 %, Grade II 30 % in average compared to plain text entry.

In addition status information from the printer's front panel and pressing of one of the printer's function keys as well as error messages are conveyed to the user by a synthetic speech generator. This also permits the use of the HotDot printer as a speech output device instead of printing a given text. Combining tactile (Braille), audio (speech output) and inkprint, HotDot can be considered as a multimodal output device for VIPs.

1.3 Future aspects

A prototype model was developed. Currently we are looking for a possibility for easy and cheap production of the thermoforming elements.

Some efforts have to be done to implement the graphic mode. This would enable the printing unit to produce "primitive" tactile graphics as known from other Braille printers [5].

2. RELIEF - CAD/CAM Production System for Tactile Graphics

The most common way to produce tactile graphics is to build a full scale three-dimensional positive model by hand and to make copies from the model (usually positive) by vacuum thermoforming. Disadvantages of this method: The manual production is very expensive as a person with experience has to build the model. Additionally this process takes a relative long time. For only one or few copies this way will not pay.

A second, very popular way is to use swell-paper, a special coated material which has the property that all black lines or areas drawn or copied onto the paper will rise when the paper is exposed to infrared heating (Minolta sells a product named Swell-Paper). Disadvantages of this method: The costs per copy are linear, that means independent of the amount of produced copies. For one or few copies this is an advantage. Furthermore swell-paper offers only two different layers (ground and raised), so that more effects cannot be presented to the blind user. (For an overview see [1, 8].)

These facts lead us to find a new solution for producing more effective, easier and cheaper tactile graphics [7]. We designed RELIEF, a CAD/CAM (Computer Aided Design / Computer Aided Manufacturing) system that consists of three main components:

* a CAD-like drawing program for the design of the graphic: The needed hardcopy material is created using the specially designed and easy to use drawing program. The program has minimal hardware requirements.
* a Numeric Controlled (NC) milling machine to produce the wooden 3D-model: A negative three-dimensional model is shaped using the HP-GL (Hewlett Packard Graphics Language) data exchange interface. The use of negative models has been chosen because lines and Braille labelling can be accomplished much more easily and quickly with this approach. Each available NC machine with HP-GL interface can be used.
* a deep-drawing equipment for vacuum thermoforming of the foils: Using the 3D-model, as many foils as needed can be produced.

2.1 How tactile graphics are produced using RELIEF

The sighted teacher uses the CAD-program installed on the normally available PC at her/his school to make drawings. The data diskette is sent to the Supply Centre for Educational Material in Vienna. Here the NC machine and the deep-drawing equipment is installed. The data diskette is fed into the PC connected to the NC machine which produces a negative model of the desired drawing. In the following vacuum thermoform process, sheets of thermoplastic material are heated and deep drawn into the model.

2.2 Features

The heart of the entire RELIEF system is the CAD software by which sighted teachers create their drawings. As these teachers are usually inexperienced in designing tactile graphics, the CAD software supports them with a lot of special features to ensure acceptable results:

* Tactile graphics should not show too much detailed information. The drawing area is DIN A3 (or two times DIN A4 if desired). This is the optimal space for the perception of tactile graphics.
* The object size must have at least the size of a single Braille dot. Objects smaller than that could not be pulpated.
* It is ensured by implemented functions that two neighboured objects have sufficient distance from one another so that they can be separated by the haptic sense.
* Tactile graphics must have Braille lettering. As the teacher in most cases will not be familiar with Braille, the text can be displayed on the screen or later on

the printout in Braille, as well as in inkprint characters which use the same space as the Braille characters.

* The CAD program offers the option of producing tactile graphics with as many as 7 distinct horizontal layers. The program, however, will make sure that the incline between elements placed in different layers will not exceed the maximum slope so that the thermoplastic material can be formed without tearing during the deepdrawing process.

* The graphic can be plot on a conventional matrix or laser printer for proof-reading and for making inkprint copies for sighted pupils. Thus, it is guaranteed that the teacher, both sighted and blind pupils use identical material in the lessons.

* A standard library with often used elements and objects is available within the program. Elements can be chosen and placed on the drawing area. This library will be extended through the collected data sent to the Support Centre. Updates are distributed.

Once the teacher got used to the program, graphics can be drawn very quickly. The production of the 3D model lasts - depending on the number of objects and used layers - only about 10 minutes. The thermoforming process takes about 2 minutes per foil. The costs are very low, as standard materials (pressed wood, PVC or Polystyrol) are used. The basic equipment (PC, program, NC machine, deepdrawing equipment and first material) is available from a Viennese company. Two systems were already installed (Vienna and Berlin) and some more requests are pending.

The use of this new system by teachers is only one possibility. The easy production offers ways to more independent living for blind persons: Orientation maps of buildings or public transportation connections increase the mobility of blind travellers. Also additional tactile graphic information in user guides or manuals for technical products increase the perception of the given information.

The program won the "Deutsch-Österreichischer Hochschul-Software Preis 1993" (German-Austrian Academic University Software Award) for the best software to support education of disabled persons.

3. VIP - Concept and Set-Up of a Hi-Tech Workplace for Visually Impaired Students

World-wide there is a trend toward the integration of disabled students into common education. For visually impaired students the access to literature and to university infrastructure has to be provided. In many universities outside of Austria there exist support centres where students with special needs find the necessary adaptive technology and human advise [4].

Since 1991 the University of Linz (Upper Austria) offers a curriculum in computer science for blind and vision impaired students. For all other curricula, there are no special provisions to support blind and visually impaired students in Austria. Though e.g. the University of Karlsruhe (Germany) has set up a good infrastructure to support visually impaired students [2], in Austria the realisation of this concept (including psychological support) has not been possible up to now.

3.1 Aim of the Project

The aim of the project VIP (which stands for 'Visually Impaired Persons') is to find a general concept for a technical support centre to allow visually impaired student to
* write texts (reports, papers, ...),
* print texts in Braille and/or ink-print,
* access information on CD-ROM or from Networks (e.g. gopher),
* browse the library catalogue,
* communicate with other students and teachers (e.g. via e-mail),
* read printed material,
* take tests and examinations,
* access available lecture notes.

After information collection about already existing support centres the first step was the selection and purchase of the necessary adaptive technology. The hardware, special developed software and organisational concept will be documented and available in order to stimulate the setting up of VIP-like workplaces at other universities within the next few years. At the Library of the University of Vienna a workplace with similar equipment was set-up in February 1994.

3.2 Components

VIP is a high-tech conceptual workplace for blind and visually impaired students. The VIP-workplace consists of:
* PC with CD-ROM and Magneto-Optical drive,
* Braille display,
* scanner and OCR software,
* Braille keyboard (additional to the common keyboard),
* screen review software,
* speech synthesiser,
* Braille and laser printer,
* 20" monitor with screen enlarging software,
* software to scan documents and display magnified on the monitor,
* software for large print output on the laser printer,
* audio unit with tape deck, head phone and indexed tape recording,
* easy access to the different PC-interfaces.

Students with other or additional disabilities will profit from the adjustable desk (suited for wheelchairs) and the monitor platform, which can be moved into any desired working position. Also the use of the audio unit could be of profit for hard of hearing students e.g. to listen once again to recorded lectures.

In order to have maximum flexibility in providing different levels of authorised access and to interact with peripheral units (printers, data communication lines, etc.) from one or, if necessary, from more user PCs, a client/server architecture has been chosen.

3.3 Conclusion

To increase the mobility of visually impaired students we suggest to install VIP-like workplaces at other universities. Being familiar with one of the VIP-Workplaces should enable the visually impaired student to immediately use any other VIP-Workplace without additional training.

The technical support centre should allow to be run on a self-service basis as far as possible. In addition to the technical equipment it is necessary to have human advise. In the last year in Austria counsellors were installed at some universities. This trend should be completed in order to have personal support at Austrian universities for students with special needs.

4. Acknowledgements

The projects mentioned in this paper have been supported by the Austrian National Bank (Oesterreichische Nationalbank) and by the Austrian Federal Ministry of Education and the Arts (Bundesministerium für Unterricht und Kunst).

References

1. Emiliani, P.L.: Production of Hardcopy Materials for the Blind. In: Proceedings of the European Workshop; Florence; (1989).

2. Klaus, J.: Integrating Blind and Visually Handicapped Students into University Learning and Living: A Pilot Project at the University of Karlsruhe. In: Proceedings of the 6th Annual Conference "Technology and Persons with Disabilities", Los Angeles; 525-535; (1991).

3. Mayer, P., Busboom, M., Ehrenfels, G., Zagler, W.L.: HotDot - A Combined Braille- and Inkprint Printing Device. In: Proceedings of the Third International Conference on Computers for Handicapped Persons, Oldenbourg, Vienna; 338-343; (1992).

4. Murphy, H.: The Use of Computers by University Students with Disabilities. In: Computers for Handicapped Persons; Oldenbourg, Vienna; pp. 61-68; (1989).

5. Nater, P.: DOTGRAPH - a Drawing Program for a Conventional Braille Printer. In: Proceedings of the Third International Conference on Computers for Handicapped Persons, Oldenbourg, Vienna; 373-381; (1992).

6. Seiler, F.P., Oberleitner, W.: WineTU, German Language Grade 2 to ASCII Braille Translator. In: Journal of Microcomputer Applications, Academic Press, Vol. 13; 185-191; (1990).

7. Seiler, F.P., Grünfelder, R., Deisenhammer, H.: Producing Hardcopy Graphics for Blind or Visually Impaired Persons Using a Special Drawing Program Called RELIEF. In: Journal of Microcomputer Applications, Academic Press; Vol. 16; 301-306; (1993).

8. Witte, R.F.V.: Production of Hardcopy Materials for the Blind; Proceedings of the European Workshop; Toulouse; (1989).

Providing Assistive Technology Training to a Rural School of Education Through an In-Direct Service Strategy

Melissa Salem Darrow

W. Scott Thomson

School of Education, East Carolina University
Greenville, NC 27858 USA

Abstract. A strategy is described for staffing and equipping an assistive technology training laboratory within the constraints of a rural environment. The acquisition of appropriate hardware and peripherals is described, as well as a model for staff training and the coincidental delivery of service to a disabled population. A discussion of the effectiveness of the project is included.

1 Introduction

The use of microcomputers and other generic technologies equipped with specialized adaptive peripheral devices is revolutionizing the education of students with disabilities. Through the use of the growing array of available systems, persons with sensory, physical, and/or intellectual disabilities can achieve previously unobtainable levels of personal independence and freedom. As these technologies become increasingly available in public schools and residential programs serving children and youth with disabilities, special educators are expected to demonstrate competencies required to use them effectively. Increasingly, even regular classroom teachers are expected to enter their profession armed with the knowledge and skills necessary to provide children with disabilities full access to the educational experiences other children enjoy. In today's schools, meeting this expectation often includes demonstrating competency in the use of adaptive technology.

Specifically, educators and related service personnel need skills in the following areas: (a) assessment of students in order to provide the appropriate peripheral match for physical and/or cognitive needs; (b) selecting peripherals in relation to specific types of applications such as environmental control, vocational needs, leisure/recreation or cause and effect training; (c) interfacing peripherals with the computer; (d) customizing the specific function of the peripherals to meet individual student needs; (e) accessing electronic augmentative communication devices that utilize microcomputer technology; and (f) advocating for students in relation to procuring devices and effectively integrating them into students' environments [1, 2, 3, 4].

In 1991, the East Carolina University Special Education Department applied for, and obtained, internal funding to support a small Assistive Technology Laboratory to be housed within the School of Education. Prior to its inception, there was no access to equipment or software needed to adequately train educators to specialized technology with individuals with disabilities. The Department of Special Education had acquired limited samples of adaptive devices and a small quantity of software, in addition to video tapes demonstrating uses of technologies to which there was no access for hands-on practice. The existing collection proved to be grossly inadequate for addressing the training needs of over 249 graduate and undergraduate special education majors, as well as the other 1,713 students majoring in elementary and secondary teacher and administrator preparation programs, who also sought this important knowledge and training. Once funding became available, a limited set of equipment and software was purchased, a small staff was assembled and trained, and purposes of the laboratory were outlined.

2 Method

Discussion of the methods for using the Assistive Technology Laboratory necessary includes descriptions of equipment and software that was purchased, purposes defined for the laboratory, and the staffing methods that were used. Of particular interest was a volunteer training project that began as a method of addressing staffing needs and has since become one of the core purposes of the laboratory.

2.1 Physical Description of the Assistive Technology Laboratory

Hardware. Two IBM DOS^{TM} platform machines, two Apple G S^{TM} and 1 Macintosh LC II ^{TM} were purchased. In order to make the computers accessible to the special needs of a wide variety of children and youth, a full array of adaptive devices was added to each machine. Each "prototype station" was equipped with specialized peripheral appliances, which included Touch Windows^{TM} , Muppet Learning Keys^{TM} , Power Pads$^{T M}$, Intellikeys^{TM} , Unicorn Expanded Keyboards^{TM} , Speech Synthesizers and single switches. The intent was to represent as many as possible of the types of machines and peripheral devices that teachers might encounter in school settings. The five stations were placed within a wheelchair accessible environment, central to the School of Education.

Software. An emerging variety of specialized software is devoted to the needs of special education populations. This software is equally useful for use by the regular student population, due to its tendency to break down complex tasks into more easily learned linear sequences. A representative sample of this software was purchased that represented the needs of students with mild to severe cognitive limitations, learning disabilities, sensory impairments and physical disabilities. The most difficult disability to address specifically with currently available software appears to be behavior disorders. All curriculum domains were represented by the approximately 250 software packages purchased, including personal/social skills, vocational skills, language arts, leisure and recreation, cause and effect, and so on. Additionally, the software was selected to serve students across age categories so that software for students from birth through adult could be represented.

Goals of the Laboratory. It became evident from the outset that before any activities or training could begin in the Laboratory, it would be necessary to define some very specific purposes of its use. These simply defined goals became a blueprint for all laboratory activities. The goals were also set into a prioritized order, according to importance, so that later the staff were able to prioritize projects and activities according to this order. Five prioritized goals were defined, as follows.

Goal 1: Develop special education majors' competency in the use of technology with exceptional children and facilitate the use of appropriate software and hardware in departmental courses and practica.

Goal 2: Provide training to undergraduate and graduate students from other departments in the School of Education in the use of adaptive computer systems with students who have disabilities.

Goal 3: Provide computer access to students with disabilities attending East Carolina University.

Goal 4: Secure external funding for technology-related projects.

Goal 5: Provide a community resource for persons seeking information on assistive technologies.

Staffing. The staff was composed of graduate research assistants and a professor in the ECU Department of Special Education. When students came to use the lab in groups, classroom teachers and assistants (or sometimes parents) remained in the lab with visiting students, and participated in service delivery. This allowed the laboratory staff to provide direct service, in the form of evaluation and one-on-one remediation on the appropriate hardware/software combination. At the same time, it allowed teachers and/or parents to preview software and adapt software and hardware respective to each child's individual needs.

Although the lab staff were capable, innovative and enthusiastic about their work, there were obstacles due to the lack of time that could be devoted to actual laboratory management, including individual . One issue was the lack of a full-time Director. This meant that all lab activities, including purchasing, set-up and maintenance of equipment, had to be accomplished during the "spare time" of responsible faculty members. The other staff members were either graduate students in the School of Education or undergraduate, student workers - all employed on a temporary basis. We began to realize that there would have to be a system in place that would train special education teachers in use of assistive technology while providing the children and youth visiting the lab with appropriate services. With the intent of accomplishing these tasks, the volunteer training program was developed.

The Volunteer Training Program. A structure for the volunteer training program was developed by Laboratory staff. The program included a two hour intensive training commitment, an eight hour direct service provision component, documentation procedures and evaluation measures.

Volunteer students were recruited from special education as well as other teacher education courses. Classes were brought into the laboratory, and given a brief equipment/software demonstration, as well as information on how assistive technology equipment was used. Students were then given information on the new volunteer training program, and given the opportunity to enroll for one of the initial two hour training sessions, at the beginning of which they could sign up for a total of ten volunteer hours.

At the two hour training sessions, students were given contracts to sign. The use of contracts was one of the features that facilitated the volunteer program's success. Students who participated by signing contracts could receive a number of extra credit points in courses they were taking in the School of Education (this had been prearranged with course instructors). The credit was set up on an "all or nothing" basis. If they completed ten hours or more, as specified on a contract, they received a certificate that documented that they had earned a pre-determined number of extra credit points. If they did not complete at least the full ten hours specified in their contract, they received no points. No partial credit points were awarded.

After the contracts were signed, students received instructions on how to use the volunteer time documenting materials. After these initial business items had been addressed, the rest of their two hours was spent on intensive training time with laboratory staff on use of the assistive technology equipment and software in the laboratory that they would be using. They were each assigned to a time slot when their volunteer hours would be fulfilled, as well as a computer station, upon which they would focus their training.

All volunteers completed eight hours of work directly with students with disabilities in the lab, at an assigned station. They were not randomly assigned to students as they showed up, but instead assigned to specific times and students on a consistent basis. We felt this would increase chances of success for both teachers in training and students with disabilities.

All student volunteers documented their participation after each session. Each volunteer had a folder in which they kept an ongoing log of what had occurred during each of their volunteer sessions, along with any questions or concerns that came up. They were also asked to document any evaluative remarks on the volunteer system or the lab itself. On the same form, a member of the laboratory staff would sign to document that the volunteer had indeed completed that day's hours. This documentation system served us well, providing an ongoing description of lab activities, as well as ongoing formative and summative evaluation measures. Furthermore, this system provided a structure for students so that they could mark their progress and note their accomplishments as volunteers.

3 Results

3.1 Achievement of Training Goals

By the end of the first academic year using the Volunteer Training Program and using the Assistive Technology Laboratory, over eighty-five children and youth with special needs received direct assistive technology services in the form of evaluations and practice with equipment. Over five hundred students within the School of Education were able to experience short demonstration sessions provided by Laboratory staff. Over ten students' families used the Laboratory to find information and to try out equipment that would be most beneficial to their children.

At least twenty-five special education teachers who came to the Laboratory with their classes or individual students, or on their own, received intensive instruction on currently available assistive technology, and many were given assistance in ordering systems and software for their own classrooms, and given training in set-up, use, and maintenance of equipment.

Finally, the volunteer training program was completed by twenty-five special education and School of Education students, many of whom enjoyed the work so much that they volunteered for far more that the required ten hours. In fact, a number of volunteers who had previously selected other majors switched their majors to special education after completing the volunteer program.

Overall, the evaluation data showed that services in the Laboratory were received with high levels of satisfaction. One comment that came up repeatedly was that the Laboratory needed more equipment and more software (we have actually been able to purchase more items since that time). Additionally, Lab staff evaluations called for a consistent manager - a permanent staff position to coordinate all Laboratory activities. The School of Education has recently placed the attainment of this staff position high in their priorities for action for the next year.

The Laboratory was able to accomplish Goals 1, 2, 3, and 5 (described in Methods, above) very successfully during its first year. The programs put into place at that time have evolved and continued, and the focus of the new Directors at this time is upon Goal 4, to obtain external funding.

3.2 Comparisons of Hardware and Peripherals

Computers. Of the machines purchased, the Apple II GS^{TM} was the most used during the first year, because of the wide array of special education peripherals and software available for that machine, at the time. The Macintosh^{TM} slowly moved into the "most popular machine" slot over the course of the year, as more software and peripherals became available. Its "user friendly" nature and its built in capability for digitized speech made it especially useful with younger children and those with communication impairments. The IBM^{TM} machines were probably used the least in the Assistive Technology Laboratory for two reasons. First, the adaptive peripherals that were available at the time for these two systems were extremely unreliable in terms of staying in working order. Second, because Apple Computers^{TM} had traditionally led educational software development while IBM^{TM} had traditionally been a business computer, there was very little software available for use on the IBM^{TM}, and much of what was available was more easily adapted for special needs when used on one of the other systems.

Overall, across disability categories, as well as age groups, we have found the Macintosh^{TM} systems and their accompanying adaptive peripherals to be the most versatile in terms of serving persons with a wide variety of disability types as well as a wide age range of students.

Peripherals. The Muppet Learning Keys^{TM} have by far been the most popular adaptive keyboards for the early childhood age range, with a wide variety of disabilities. Its digitized speech and music, as well as clear graphics when used on the Macintosh make it extremely engaging to the young learner. Additionally, it can be used with various input methods. The Touch Window^{TM} can be used for direct selection, or even a single switch can be used for scanning selection.

For students at the elementary level, we found the Unicorn Expanded Keyboard^{TM} as well as the Intellikeys^{TM} to be very versatile in customizing programs for a number of curriculum areas, from basic vocabulary and communication skills to accessing word processors or mathematics programs in an alternative fashion. These peripheral devices tended to be trouble-free as far as predictability of day to day working order.

At the high school to adult levels, we werevery pleased at the adaptibility of a number of peripheral devices for persons with various types of disabilities. For example, the Intellikeys^{TM} large, high contrast letters made it easier for a person with low vision to access a word processor, while Ke:nx^{TM} made it possible for lab staff to customize nearly any type of conventional software for various types of selection devices, from single switch, to direct selection with the Touch Window^{TM}.

The Echo^{TM} Speech Synthesizer was also a very helpful tool, across age categories, for those programs that could not be accessed using digitized speech. Unfortunately, various software packages call for various specific types of Echo^{TM} devices, so to be able to use it with a large number of educational programs, the user must have several versions of this peripheral device on hand. Finally, the Touch Window^{TM} peripheral device and software became a favorite with all ages and across disability types because of its capabilities for allowing direct selection. This device was especially powerful with very young children or with persons whose cognitive or physical capability levels made use of the mouse or keyboard or scanning systems difficult or frustrating.

4 Discussion

This project was born out of the need to provide a great deal of equipment and services to a rural area under conditions that offered few resources. As a vehicle for magnifying the efforts of a few competent people and few resources, the authors recommend replication of the methods described above to professionals who find themselves in similar situations, with the following cautionary statement.

A weakness of the project was that what began as an indirect service project with a primary purpose of training educators gradually threatened to become a direct service resource available to the regional special education community. Any agency considering adoption of a similar plan must guard against this inherent desire of the surrounding community to convert the Laboratory to a direct service resource. This desire of the community is very understandable in an environment which has so few opportunities for similar direct services. Unchecked, such a demand necessarily forces direct service to the point where training functions become secondary.

References

1. G. Church, S. Glennen: The handbook of assistive technology. San Diego: Singular Publishing Group, Inc., 1992.

2. M. Male: Technology for inclusion: Meeting the special needs of all students. Needham Heights, Mass: Allyn and Bacon, 1994.

3. M. Darrow, J. Darrow: Preparing special educators in eastern North Carolina to use assistive technology: A multimedia approach to addressing training needs unique to rural areas. In Proceedings of the eighth annual international conference "Technology and Persons with Disabilities". Northridge, Ca: California State University, Northridge Center on Disabilities, 1993.

4. E. Jacobs: Providing assistive technology assessments for school districts: A rural model. In Proceedings of the eighth annual international conference "Technology and Persons with Disabilities". Northridge, Ca: California State University, Northridge Center on Disabilities, 1993.

The CORES Project

P.A. Cudd[+], M. Freeman[+], R.B. Yates[+], A. J. Wilson[+], M.P. Cooke[+], M.S. Hawley[*]

+ University of Sheffield, UK   * Barnsley District General Hospital, UK

Abstract. Discussion paper of a proposed project that is the initial phase of a far reaching research programme. The CORES project aims to investigate the development of a speech-only-input based Human Computer Interface (HCI) which will lead to suitably skilled disabled users being able to operate any commonly available commercial personal computer or workstation. The long term aim is to generalise this to a portable device with an adaptable HCI (both in hardware and software terms) suitable for disabled and able-bodied people alike.

1   Introduction

The UK lags North America and Scandinavia in establishing multi-disciplinary research and development centres in the fields of Rehabilitation and Human-Machine Interfacing. There is a direct correlation between the higher levels of this type of research and the degree of productive employment and social integration of disabled people in these geographical regions. It is of note that the industrial sector has also recognised that applications of technology for disability has mass market applications among the general population[1].

The technology required to achieve rehabilitation becomes more complex when those with severe physical disabilities are considered[2,3,4].   For such individuals a very limited number of controllable movements are available to operate devices which replace the motor and communication functions. Current assistive devices clearly benefit disabled people, but they do not provide communication or motor function at the speed or response that is required for the activities of daily living.

Electronic and computer technology has a major role to play in the process of optimising the control of devices to substitute impaired function, both in its ability to control flexible displays for presentation of options and control information to the user, and, to process historical sequences of actions to predict those which are most likely to be selected next. The potential of Automatic Speech Recognition to enhance the HMI is great, but many issues have still not been fully investigated, e.g. safety for control applications; automatic recognition for impaired speech; and tailored Human-Computer Interfacing, in terms of both software and hardware[2].

The CORES project aims to go beyond current investigations and initiate a five to ten year research programme. The name 'CORES' is derived from 'COmmunication and Rehabilitation Engineering at Sheffield'. The project will contribute to the long term goal to develop a Universal Human-Machine Interface (UHMI), i.e. a portable device that would facilitate the operation of any type of computer or industrial/domestic electronic control system by either able-bodied or disabled individuals. Thus the concept goes beyond existing research[2,3,4].

Many disabled people have both limited and uncontrolled limb movements while still having some speech, but that may also be severely impaired. Nonetheless, speech offers a useful alternative to other input modalities. Thus the CORES project will aim to result in a design framework for the UHMI and a demonstrator with impaired-speech input that will facilitate the use of commercial computers.

2   The Universal Human Machine Interface

For more than a decade the cognitive processes associated with human tasks have been analysed to improve the effectiveness of the HCI.   Through fundamental research, this branch of systems development has now established a well founded theoretical framework in which computer interfaces can be designed. Unfortunately, little of this work has either been applied to the development of generic electronic systems for disabled users or to include consideration of the optimum hardware. So currently commercially available state of the art HCIs such as Microsoft Windows™ and X-Windows™ require an input modality transducer for non-standard input devices. Interaction (i.e. control of) computers by disabled users is an area that has received some attention. However, the HCI aspects of the existing systems to be used, i.e. the standard hardware input devices and the operational characteristics of the software application, have been accepted as a starting specification. So, problems, or at least awkwardness of use, appear because the input device and the feedback needs of the user were not part of the original HCI. The CORES project demonstrator system aims to provide a tailored interface for the chosen input modality (speech) which maximises independence of the application-user interface. Implementation of the demonstrator based on user- and application-adaptable state of the art hardware gives the CORES project a significant edge over previous approaches to HMI for the disabled. The work of CORES therefore points to the possibility in the future of bespoke user interfaces for everyone; in the more immediate future this may only be justifiable for specialist applications.

In industrial and business applications increasing amounts of computer system processing power is devoted to the user interface, viz. Graphical User Interfaces, multi-media, speech recognition and virtual reality. Current hardware implementations are not tailored to these input/output (I/O) tasks, and consequently the implementations of even well- researched and designed HMIs are frequently slow. When such interfaces are considered for use by the disabled community, they are not sufficiently adaptable to cope with the extra-ordinary needs. These factors have led to the recognition of the need for a new approach in designing a Human Machine Interface (HMI). Future implementations of HMIs should be portable and be conceived as a quite separate I/O device to the 'application tool'. The latter 'application tool' could be a computer or an industrial/domestic electronic system. Of particular interest, therefore, is a framework for the development and evaluation of a modular and integrated Universal Human Machine Interface (UHMI). This would include software, operating system and hardware, and be modular in terms of its I/O capabilities, these modules being tailorable to the appropriate requirements of the user and the attached 'application tool'. Such a framework would bring together the host application (e.g. word processor) with components of communications technology (e.g. speech recogniser) and the user-application interaction.

3   Work to be carried out

The first task is to create a requirements specification for the framework, using information from related work such as in the area of telecoms[5]. Specification of hardware for the demonstrator will also be initiated. Next, the framework will be developed using available communications technology resulting in a demonstrator. Preliminary evaluations would be carried out and reported. Lastly, investigation of more specific day to day and long term needs of disabled individuals would be addressed, e.g. casual communication, and, facilitating education and employment. It is difficult at to give more precise details on the work to be carried out until the requirements specification has been achieved, but we expect to consider the following themes taking full advantage of existing HMI tools and experience:

- Existing speech recognisers and impaired speech
- The parameters of impaired speech
- Gesture recognition based on recent advances in machine vision
- Input systems based on movement analysis
- Actuator feedback and cognitive issues
- Use of parallel input and output modalities
- Adaptive HMI
- Commonality with applications using processing intensive user interfacing.

It is envisaged that the user will effect control through supplying input to a device which 'connects' this input to the computer system in such a way that manipulation of the processes on the computer is possible. It is planned that computer platform independence will be achieved through use of those input/output connections that change little with time, e.g. mouse, keyboard and display ports. It is intended to use recent advances in 2D object recognition and ASICs to achieve automatic recognition of screen activity.

4   Conclusions

Commonality with other processing intensive user-interfacing applications, such as Virtual Reality, means that the future holds a greater opportunity to achieve more powerful, bespoke and hence more appropriate user interfaces for disabled individuals. The complexity of augmenting or assisting impaired functions will, by necessity, mean that the approach to the technology required to realise user-friendly and use-efficient systems be both complex and innovative. Development of bespoke user interfaces in the Rehabilitation field has useful implications and indeed may lead the way for the general Human-computer/machine-interfacing of the future.

Acknowledgement : The authors are indebited to Dr. P. Courtney.

References

1. The Apple Macintosh and Disability Access Syllabus, 1994.
2. Hawley, M.S., Cudd, P.A. and Cherry, A.D. : 'Implementation of a PC-based integrated control system for children', Med. Eng. Phys., May 1994, Vl. 16, 237-42.
3. Buhler, C. : 'Uniform user interface for communication and control', Proceedings ECART2, Stockholm, May 1993, pp22.3.
4. van Woerden, J.A. : 'M3S A General Purpose Interface for the Rehabilitation Environment', Proceedings ECART2, Stockholm, May 1993, pp22.1.
5. von Tetzchner, S. (Editor) : 'Issues in Telecommunication and Disability', CEC, EUR 13845 EN, ISBN 92-826-3128-1, 1991

Real Time HCI and Limits of Human Performance

V. Risak[1]

Summary: Real-time-systems impose demands concerning *complexity* and *reaction-time* onto the user. The limits of human performance can be compared with these demands in a special diagram. Special types of handicaps and the result of countermeasures by modifying the task or training can be shown.

Introduction:

The difficulty of real-time tasks is essentially influenced by *complexity* and necessary *reaction-time*. Both components alone or in combination have to be compared with the limits of human performance. Examples are: driving a racing-car (reaction-time), playing chess (complexity) or controlling an industrial plant (complexity and reaction time).

Handicaps can cause longer reaction-times and-or reduce the information-processing ability. Countermeasures try to compensate these handicaps by *lowering the real-time demands* (e.g. by automating some functions like ABS in cars), by *reducing the complexity* (e.g. automating routine tasks like automatic switch-gear, intelligent-help with operators-guide) or by *special training* (e.g. with simulators) to relief the scarce resource of conscious information-processing.

Complexity-Velocity-Diagram

We propose a diagram, which allows us to compare the human performance-limits with the difficulty of the task. The effect of different types of handicaps relative to a given task can be shown. If this task is too difficult, possible countermeasures can be derived.

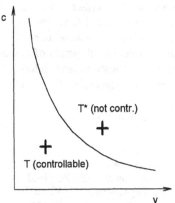

Fig. 1 c-v-Diagram

We will assume, that the performance-limit P of a given person depends on his velocity v and his fitness to handle complexity c.

$$P(v,c) = k.(v^a.c^b)$$

$$a, b, k > 0$$

(1)

We use this product-form, because $P = 0$ either if the velocity of reaction $v = 0$ or the ability to manage complexity $c = 0$.

The exponents a and b make it possible to give different weights to both components of human performance.

[1]Siemens Austria PSE1, University of Salzburg, risak@siemens.co.at

If $a = b$ both components have equal weight. If $a>b$ $(a<b)$ than the reaction velocity is better (worse) than the management of complexity. k is a measure of overall performance, whilst a and b enhance selectively one or the other performance component.

(1) takes the form of hyperbolas[2], which by k, a, b describe the abilities of a person.[3] The area below the hyperbola is controllable by him (e.g. a task marked by T). The task T* above the hyperbola is too hard.

Types of Handicaps

Handicaps reduce the performance in some types of tasks. In the diagram the corresponding hyperbola lies below the original one. We distinguish:

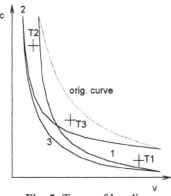

Fig. 2. Types of handicaps

- **Reaction-velocity handicaps:** (Fig. 2, curve 1) The velocity-parameter a is lowered. As a consequence performance on time-critical tasks is impaired, whilst the ability to manage complexity is normal. (This corresponds to peripheral handicaps with intact intelligence.)

- **Complexity Handicaps:** (Fig. 2, curve 2) The complexity-parameter b is lowered. The management of complexity is reduced, but reaction-velocity is normal. That means, easy tasks can be handled as before, but growing complexity early cause overload. (This corresponds to reduced intelligence with normal peripheral reaction-velocity.)

- **Global Symmetrical Handicaps:** (Fig. 2, curve 3) The global performance-parameter k is reduced. The corresponding hyperbola lies nearer to the origin. Both reaction-velocity and handling of complexity are reduced.[4]

The consequences for mastering tasks can be seen from the relative position of the corresponding points describing their difficulty.

---

[2] It could be better to use a log-scale on both axes, because the hyperbolas then look like straight lines. But there is the problem, that the complexity of tasks varies for many orders of magnitude, whilst reaction-velocity does not vary so much.

[3] For more realistic purposes we could define an absolute upper limit on reaction velocity caused by anatomical conditions, e.g. reaction-time > 0,1 sec. For complexity, given enough time, we see no such limit.

[4] I think this type of handicap is not very realistic, because velocity- and complexity-handicaps follow different mechanisms.

Counter-Measures:

After describing different types of handicaps, we will discuss compensating measures.

One possibility is to *make the task easier,* so that the task-point lies below the performance hyperbola. This can be accomplished by (see Fig. 3):
- *reducing the complexity* (arrow 1) for example by automating routine-tasks, intelligent help, expert-systems, working on a higher abstraction level, ...
- *reducing reaction-velocity demands* (arrow 2) for example by automating time-critical sub-tasks like ABS, ...

Another way is to *enhance the capabilities of the user:*
This can be done e.g. by systematic training. After sufficient training we can perform actions unconscious, which before had to done conscious step by step. This relieves the load on the very scarce resource conscious-thinking. This free capacity now can be used otherwise, e.g. for managing complexity.

An example is learning to drive a car in heavy traffic:

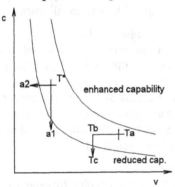

In the beginning this task (point Ta) is without reach of the learner. Therefore the first steps are performed slowly (reduced reaction-velocity needed, point Tb) on an empty place (reduced complexity) The task-point is now moved below the hyperbola (point Tc). After some experience the individual global performance-parameter k grows, so that in the end the demands of real heavy traffic (point Ta) now can be mastered.

Fig. 3. Counter-measures

Summary:

A qualitative complexity/velocity-diagram gave us the possibility to display and compare limits of human performance at the man-machine-interface. We described different types of handicaps and discussed the effect of possible counter-measures.
Perhaps this diagram gives us the possibility to locate main problems in real-time situations and to help in selecting the proper measures.

Computer and Computer Communication Guidance Centre for the Disabled

Dr. P.D. Bhalerao

Project Leader, Dept. of Computer Science, Institute of Science, R. Tagore Rd, NAGPUR INDIA 440001.

Abstract. Computer and Computer Communication Guidance Centre for Disabled is started at the Institute of Science, Nagpur India with the financial assistance from UNCSDHA Vienna and infrastructural facilities from State Govt. of Maharashtra. This is a highly motivated project that focusses on the upliftment of disabled to the status of economic independence through free of charge high tech. education in the field of computers. In fourteen months fifty disabled have been trained and referred for job placement. Other objectives include Computer aided diagnosis of medical and psychological health of disabled, adoptions and attachments for regional languages, training in D.T.P., FAX and EPABX as well development of incidental software.

1.   Introduction

Self relience and respectable status in profession/career for the physical handicapped has been as a noble goal in various civilization and cultures of the world. In the last decade in India and the South-East Asian countries awareness for computer and computer communication systems in on the increase. A wide range of new professions are being thrown open in this field. It is, therefore time that adoptions and training in this field for the handicapped of different categories is worked out. The centre is located at the Govt. Institute of Science, a prime educational institute in central India since last eight decades with higher education in Physics, Electronics, Computer Science, Maths, Chemistry, Botany, Zoology, Statistics and Environment science. Presently the centre is equipped with 486 AT, a LAN with four 286 nodes, 4 XT's, 3 DMP's, Speech System from COVAX U.S.A., Language Card from CDAC for regional languages, DTP facilities and related software. An offer is received from Robotron Australia for lending a braille computer and text reader. We are approaching funding agencies for obtaining the facilities permanently.

2.   Objectives

A)   Vocational evaluation and adjustment of handicapped persons to the growing world of personal and mini computer and computer communication world.

B)   Development of computer and computer communication systems with suitable attachments for adoption of disabled persons to take computer training and help them rehabilitate in approprite vocational/selp employed jobs.

C)   To set up computer aided diagnosis of the medical and psychological health for the disabled.

D)   To constitute an R&D Base for incidental hardware & software development.

E)   Adoptations of attachments for regional language so that disabled can record better pick-up of training.

3.   Activities

The Project is started with the resources provided by United Nations(US$ 20,000) and the basic infrastructure and support from the State Government of Maharashtra. This is a highly motivated project that focuses on the upliftment of disabled to the status of economic independence through free high tech education in the field of computers. We have trained fifty disabled persons in computer use during a period of fourteen months. Ten of them have been employed. Some more students are referred for job placement and some are starting their own business with computer related jobs. With the hardwork put in by our dedicated team the project is successful in creating basic infrastructure for training of disabled during the very first year even though its tennure is of three years.

Since disabled students are drawn mainly from the lower middle class and poor families, who cannot affored costly education in new technologies like computer, the centre provides free education to all disabled students as a policy matter. A new batch of ten employed disabled has also started from 1st Jan. 1994 to improve their promotional chances in service. The centre is presently training deaf and dumb student to use the speech system for communicating their thoughts. The centre gives four weeks short term computer training free to Maharashtra Government employees deputed from various departments. Senior batch disabled students help in this training. A software has been developed to solve the non linear auto regressive time series (ARTS) which generates various patterns. These patterns ARTS simulated are useful in textile·Industry. Progress is made in the development of software to translate English text into regional languages with limited vocabulary. A Project on OCR is in pipeline in collaborations with IIT, Bombay.

4.   Conslusions

In order to meet the growing demand of educating more disabled students we need to update and increase the infrastructural facilities at the centre. Similarly there is a requirement to constantly train our staff in keeping pace with the latest technology as well as make new technologies available at our centre for the benefit of the disabled.

5.   Acknowledgements

Our Acknowledgement are due to United Nations Social Development Division Vieena, Govt. of Neitherlands and State Govt. of Maharashtra for their aid in this project.

Assistive Technology in the Public Schools

M. Shannon McCord

Pajaro Valley Unified School District, Special Education Department,
Watsonville, CA 95076 USA

Abstract. Providing assistive technology and/or augmentative communication devi ces to students with disabilities ranging from severe cognitive delays to orthopedic handicaps can drastically increase their ability to participate to their potential in the public school system and improve self-esteem at the same time. Our Special Education Local Plan Area has established a new lab to facilitate exposing as amany students as possible to the latest technology and to provide a space for training the entire team that works with the students including the family.

Introduction

We, Shannon McCord and Valerie Benito are two specialists in the field of technology and special education who reside in Santa Cruz County, California, U.S.A.. We work in the Pajaro Valley Unified School District which is a multi-cultural, multi-lingual district located in central California. We are only hours from San Francisco and the technology rich silicone valley. Our diverse student population consists of 17,000 students from a wide range of ethnic backgrounds. We have programs for 2,200 special education students from 0 to 22 years of age. Many of our students come from families with limited economic resources.

The Pajaro Valley Unified School District is committed to providing appropriate inclusive educational programs for all students. We have established programs for physically disabled, hearing or visually impaired and most recently, severely emotionally disturbed and autistic children. These programs are supported by itinerant teachers who work collaboratively with general education teachers to facilitate the mainstreaming of special education students with unique needs. This allows us to serve the majority of our students in their neighborhood schools.

Overview of Assistive Technology Program

Purpose

The Pajaro Valley Unified School District (PVUSD) recognizes that one of the barriers to equal access for all students is the availability of technology in the classrooms. Students with special needs often require the use of assistive technology devices to reach their full potential in general education classrooms. The provision of assistive devices aides in increasing communication, mobility, and independence in daily living skills for many students. Collaboration between parents and teachers in the use of assistive devices for children with special needs also significantly modifies the class learning environment so that segregated placements for individuals with severe disabilities no longer needs to be the norm.

Our full inclusion programs are successful, in part, because the district uses assistive technology to supplement and support the curriculum.   The staff and administration of PVUSD realizes that, in order to create schools where all students flourish in their natural settings, it is necessary to take full advantage of the current technological advances that are making the world more accessible to all people today.

The recently established Assistive Technology Program is the vehicle by which PVUSD meets the technical needs of our special education students. The following Concept Attainment data set will help the audience to understand our purpose by categorizing the terms:

YES (Access to devices)	NO (Without access)
-Independent Living	-Isolation
-Communication	-Dependence
-Establishing Peer Relationships	-Misunderstood
-Increase self-esteem	-Negative Personal Regard
-Increase Performance	-Communicate personal needs only
-Develop fine and gross motor skills	-Unable to complete assignments
-Computers	-writing skills to assess potential
-Augmentative Devices	

Augmentative Communication and Assistive Technology Lab

Components

We will use an Inductive Lesson Data Set to have the audience explore the materials and discover the categories of our lab. The set includes:

-Wheelchair mounting bar
-Switch Kit
-Augmentative Communication Devices
-Computer Training Program
-Books, Catalogs
-TDD
-Language Games
-Community Skills Cards

The participants will look at the material and list the attributes of each one. They will then discuss the attributes in a small group and discover the common themes. This will help them find that we have organized our lab into the four following areas:

A. Assessment
B. Training of students, staff, and parents
C. Resource Area
D. Social/Pragmatic Area

Conclusion

In conclusion, we would like to explain the benefits that we have seen from having a specialist and a lab available in the district. It is not only the special education students who benefit from the use of the equipment. The general education students, school support staff (secretary, custodian) and teachers all benefit from the experience of having a more diverse student population. In the long run, all of society will benefit from seeing that more people can be productive members of society. We would like to share some personal stories of the people whose lives were affected. [Read quotations and excerpts from collected stories.]

One amazing example of the way technology can enrich the lives of people with significant disabilities is a demonstration of "Switch Ensemble". This is a music based program that allows students with severe cognitive and/or physical delays to perform high quality concerts independently. [Video and hands-on experience.]

ADAMLAB
Educational Agency Designs Voice Output Communication Aid

Gregory A. Turner

Adaptive Devices Applied Methods Laboratory (ADAMLAB)
Wayne County Regional Educational Service Agency
Wayne, MI 48184

Abstract. This paper gives a thumbnail sketch of the ADAMLAB project. The project has pioneered an entrepreneurial model in the governmental (public agency) sphere for the design and delivery of low-cost electronic assistive technology products to handicapped individuals for whom the otherwise high cost of the technology is prohibitive.

1 ADAMLAB- a Unique Project for Special Education Technology

ADAMLAB (Adaptive Devices Applied Methods Laboratory) is an innovative project for the design and manufacture of low-cost electronic and microcomputer technology for special education students who are mentally and physically challenged. ADAMLAB's particular specialty is voice output systems, in particular Voice Output Communication Aids (VOCA).

ADAMLAB personnel include engineers, programmers, and other technical and data management staff. Responding to the perceived and voiced needs of special education teaching staff, ADAMLAB designs equipment from the micro-component level up and then contracts local assembly firms for its manufacture. Revenues from the distribution of ADAMLAB products nationally and internationally balance all expenses and provide funds for the provision of free equipment and services to students locally. Thus, custom engineering services are available to the local community at no cost to the taxpaying public.

2 Wayne County Regional Educational Service Agency

ADAMLAB's parent organization is the Wayne County Regional Educational Service Agency (RESA). The RESA is the level of educational administration and support services at the county level. Wayne County, which includes metropolitan Detroit, USA, is one of the nation's most populous counties. As an example of the services provided, WCRESA's Data Processing operation supports the thirty-four local school districts in the county for their finance and student record needs--one of the largest such operations for education in the whole country.

Data Processing's field engineering service was the birthing place for the RESA's special education technology engineering activities in the late 1970's. At that time, WCRESA was collaborating with Michigan State University's Artificial Language Laboratory in the development of synthetic voice applications for students in WCRESA's programs for the Severely Mentally and Severely Multiply Impaired. After several years, the engineering program was transplanted to WCRESA, eventually developing into the full blown ADAMLAB project in 1986.

3 The Wolf- Pioneer Low Cost VOCA

From 1978 to 1984, several generations of talking devices were prototyped, resulting finally in the development of the Wolf Voice Output Communication Aid. Hand held and battery-powered, the Wolf has a membrane touchpanel, on which overlays are positioned bearing pictures and symbols meaningful to the student user who presses these to activate corresponding synthetic voice messages--so, for example, a picture of a television could have the voice output: "I want to watch TV." The Wolf's electronics consist of the ADAMLAB-designed single board 8-bit microcomputer, with banked memory to augment the fundamental architecture in order to accommodate the data storage requirements for programmed vocabulary and for the installed software synthesizer. The synthesizer, the commercial *Provoice* product from First Byte Inc. (Torrance, CA), has a kinship to diphone systems in that its atomic units are digital samples. Besides English, the synthesizer can also generate Spanish, German, and French and we intend these languages to be available in the Wolf in the near future.

The principal ideas behind the Wolf device are low-cost, durability, and simplicity of use. As a case in point, the Wolf's original 1984 $250 cost was ten times less than the then $2,500 average cost of comparably used equipment from private manufacturers--and indeed, only since 1990 are there available some commercial VOCAs in the one thousand dollar and under price range. Low cost has made the Wolf available and practicable for use to all the speech disability groups, including those in the severe categories for whom the purchase of multi-thousand dollar devices will always be controversial. As of mid 1994, over *fifteen thousand* Wolf units have been distributed.

4 ADAMLAB as an Economic Model

The Wolf is priced to recover direct costs (components and the cost of the contracted manufacturing, and miscellaneous "raw" costs like postage), associated ADAMLAB staff costs (including the one-time, at purchase custom vocabulary programming service), and pro-rated costs to cover loss, breakage, repair under warranty, on-going R&D costs, and costs associated with equipment re-capitalization.

In addition, a charge is added to provide funding for Wayne County-specific special education activities. So, for example, in 1992 the Assistive Technology Resource Center (ATRC) project was established with funding provided from these designated revenues. ATRC's evaluation, assessment, and consulting activities are carried out by a three person team, consisting of speech and occupational therapists and a computer systems consultant. Besides assisting local school districts in critical programs such as IEP, inclusion, vocational education, and transition, ATRC staff also engage in research-related activities. In 1993, a collaboration between ATRC, ADAMLAB, and students and faculty at Wayne State University's Department of Electrical Engineering resulted in the first place design win at the RESNA student competition. The design, called the Sequential Task Trainer, uses sensors and lighted and voice-output feedback to prompt and correct low-cognitive students in manual assembly tasks as typically found in sheltered workshop contexts. This field, technology products for vocational education, is fast emerging as one of the exciting new areas of application for assistive technology and rehabilitation.

ADAMLAB's positive revenue situation has allowed for the provision of no-charge repair services. Repair costs are typically not factored in to the cost of assistive technology products but these can be substantial. ADAMLAB's ability to provide repair at no-charge means that long-term maintenance of product by consumers is economically neutral to them.

ADAMLAB is a "win-win" situation: appropriate technology is provided at very low costs to adequately meet the demands of the consuming public, at the same time yielding revenues sufficient to fund long-term maintenance of the equipment, to provide custom engineering and consulting services to local consumers, and to support on-going research and development to practically apply advances in technology to the needs of the handicapped.

5 ADAMLAB Assistive Technology in the Nineties

ADAMLAB's research agenda in the mid-nineties has resulted in a set of new products that utilize modern digital voice technology and highly integrated microchip architectures. The Hawk and Lynx VOCA devices provide the ultimate simplification in voice synthesis programming: just talk into the microphone. These devices continue the tradition of the Wolf: low-cost, minimalistic design for increased reliability and ease of use, and maximized availability to all speech-disabled populations. By their nature, these digital voice products also expand the potential market to take in non-English language applications and indeed, the demand for these products for use overseas is on the upswing, with Hawks and Lynxes currently in use in Israel, Lithuania, Hungary, and Denmark.

Large Print Desktop-Publishing by PC for the Partially Sighted

Ulrich Zeun

Department of Special Education, University of Dortmund, Germany

Abstract. This paper emphasizes the need of large print text-books for partially sighted readers as a alternative reading medium. Research showed that there are almost no production facilities for large print, too little large print titles, and widely spread photocopying does not fit the perceptual needs of low vision people in all aspects. First experience of a large print project working with regular PC-equipment are stated, and guidelines are given concerning technical equipment, large print layout and typography. Though image editing is a more time-consuming and and sophisticated job than text editing, adapted pictures should be included in large print books.

Introduction – Starting point of research

Though electronic texts become more and more available, screen reading is not the ideal reading situation for the partially sighted. This is due to physiological conditions as well as disadvantages of screen enlargement software compared to black print reading techniques such as browsing, skipping from leaf to leaf, getting a full page overview etc.

Software enlarged screens only show a fraction of the regular 25 line and 80 columns screen.

In spite of all discussion, whether reading large print or reading normal print with optical aides is preferrable [6], large print still has its justification. This is even more true, if the large print is adapted didactically. Enlarged photocopies bear disadvantages: Flaws in print such as hard-to-read typefaces, a too small spacing, blurred and broken strokes of letters cannot be altered. On the contrary, flaws are sometimes emphazised [9]. Moreover, photocopying often results in unhandy and bulky formats [7]. Colour copiers are still expensive as well as color copies made in a copy shop. So, colour copies are seldomly done. Colour information is lost.

This was the starting point of our idea to find out how large print including coloured graphics can be adapted near to optimally for low visioners by taking advantage of modern PC-technology for large print production. Our project is named "Large Print Service for the Partially Sighted" (German abbreviation is *GrUsS* = **Gr**oßdruck-**U**msetzungs-**s**ervice für **S**ehbehinderte).

Two questionnaires one for teachers for low vision students, the other for publishing houses, and specialized adaptation services for the visually impaired should reveal, whether and if yes how large print is made. Here are some results of the situation in German speaking coumtries:

Schools for the partially sighted / Teachers' methods:
- teachers mainly use photocopiers, but colour copiers are only available in 5 of 45 German schools for visually impaired pupils;
- computer und printers are used only by a few teachers;
- a service producing large print materials for partially sighted students not only would relieve the teacher from time-consuming material adaptation but is also welcome by a majority of the teachers.

Publishing houses – special services
- there are only some publishing houses that have book series in large print. But the type size is seldomly more than 12 points [1], a size I consider too small. Larger type sizes can rather be found amongst school book publishers, especially for primary grade readers;
- their large print books cover only novels but no school or university textbooks;
- only two specialized institutions produce fitting large print: the "Schweizerische Bibliothek für Blinde und Sehbehinderte in Zurich" (Swiss Library for the Blind and Partially Sighted) enlarges print with a photocopier, but also produces textbooks, whereas the "Deutsche Zentralbücherei in Leipzig" (German Central Library for the Blind) started a computer aided reproduction, but scientific books are not included.
- existing large print material are one time productions, and partly out-of-date,

---

[1] I do not distinguish here betwenn American and Western-European point measure.

– existing and newly produced large prints do not include coloured graphics.

This big lack of textbooks for partially sighted students needs improvement by establishing a production and dessimination center. A concept has already been elaborated for supplying study material. This concept was developed by the visaully impaired students themselves and their "Federal-wide Workgroup on Access to Literature for Visually Impaired Students" [2].

Remark:
Again, according to the publishers demands for camera-ready typesetting, this article is reproduced contrary to some typographical needs we consider to be adequate for the partially sighted. A large print sample is added at the end of the article.

Adapted books and demand for large print material

Who are the addressees?
There are two groups that should be supplied with large print books: pupils and university students.

The project *GrUsS* has not yet adapted university textbooks, because the partially sighted at the University of Dortmund have not demanded for large print material or contacted us, partly because they had yet not known about the GrUsS project or hesitated to demand large print as long as they can manage reading somehow – not necesarily better. We did adapt material for partially sighted in the past, though. Adapted materials were conference brochures and some on-campus material, such as newsletters or the menu-card of the cantine [12].

Examining study material, however, shows that scientific books comprise rather less than too many graphics and colored images compared to modern school books. Thus, the problems we will mention below take place less often with university textbooks. Experiences we gathered from adapting school books can be transferred better to university books than vice versa.

What textbooks are needed?

Teachers called for dictionaries, vocabulary lists, and indexes. Above all, a demand for lavishly pictured textbooks in geography, mathematics or foreign languages were uttered. Maps are needed, too. Those latter books and texts can all be counted among books with colored illustrations which can not be copied in the school without loss of quality and didactical expression.

Technical aspects

What technical PC equipment do we use?

The project is equipped with the following hard- and software:

Input devices
- a greyscale flatbed scanner (Ricoh RS632, 300 dpi) for scanning texts and line graphics,
- a colour flatbed scanner (Microtek Scanmaker II Xe, 400 dpi or more) for scanning images, *
- a graphics tablet (Genius),
- keyboard and mouse
- triple-speed CD-ROM drive *

Processing and editing
- two PCs (80386 and 80486 * cpu)
- an OCR/ICR software (Omnipage Professional 5.0),
- an image processing software (PhotoStyler 2.0) *,
- other picture and painting software on trial (e.g. CorelDraw, Windows-Paintbrush, Harvard Graphics),
- word processing / DTP software (Word for DOS 5.5, Ami Professional 2.0, PageMaker 5.0 *).

Storing, back-up
- gigabyte hard disk drives,*
- gigabyte magneto-optical disk drive,*
- gigabyte streamer system.*

Output and telecommunication
- a PostScript laser printer (NEC Silentwriter, 300 dpi),

- a colour PostScript inkjet printer capable of DIN A3 outputs (IBM Lexmark 4079 PS),*
- a 24 pins matrix colour printer capable of DIN A3 outputs (NEC P70c),
- a high-speed modem for transferring formatted data to schools and others *.

From my point of view, it is important to use regular PC-products (low and medium cost) to find out, how the average user, teacher or smaller production facility can carry out production processes on their own. Therefore, using the Apple Macintosh, as many professional publishers and DTP services do, was left out for the Apple system is not as wide spread as IBM-compatible PC systems in schools and among teachers or visually impaired users. The same holds true for T_EX. It is only used at universities and by its members. We make use of the standardised PostScript language and compatible printers to make large print outputs.

Results about shortcomings of the used system can be expected. Additions will be and were already neccessary (marked with an astericks in the equipment list above). High end setting and print machines are surely rather commendable for bigger production centres.

First experiences

As coloured textbooks were demanded, we had to use a colour scanner. First experiences – we started in 1993 – revealed that immense storing capacities are needed for colour scans. An image can use up to twenty megabytes or more depending on its original size and scanning resolution. To set no limits, we raised funds for purchasing large storing media in 1994.

Handling pictures within texts made it also neccessary to buy a so-called desktop publishing software (i.e. PageMaker). This or other similar software is more suitable for importing graphics, rotating and editing images within the text layout than word processing software running under Windows. However the DTP software has other cutbacks compared to editors, such as no footnote management or no editor for scientific formulae (we use the Ami Pro math editor; the WinWord math editor can be used with PageMaker).

Perceptual and diddactical aspects

The following remarks concern perceptual aspects on typography for partially sighted readers, and didactical needs of an adapted layout. I will differentiate betwenn mere text, scientific formulae or graphic symbols, and graphics.

Text

We did some research on typographical layout for the partially sighted by
a) studying relevant literature [1, 2, 10, 11],
b) applying a perceptual test on partially sighted readers – readers were given text samples of different layout, typefaces and with different point sizes -, and
c) our first experiences during adapting material.

From that, we drew some guidelines for large print typography and layout. To number all, would make up a seperate paper. Only some old and new guidelines shall be mentioned here (for further details feel free to contact me). Some of the guidelines are contrary to typographical rules often stated for normal visioners [2, 8].

1) Sans-serif typefaces are all in all better readable for partially sighted readers than serif fonts – an average of 18pt typesize suits many low vison readers.
2) For low visioners with problems of resolution sans-serif typefaces should be used that are highly distinguishable in terms of letter differentiation. Typefaces for reading beginners, for example, show characteristic differences between the small "l" and the capital "I", or the capital "J".
3) Head column titles should be contrasted from the text body through bigger and bold letters, thus allowing a good orientation within a book.
4) The paging should be at the outside top margin of the page and be set in huge pointsizes so that the partially sighted reader can perceive it at first glance even from a wider distance. Moreover doing this, the reader does not need to open the book fully while browsing for a certain page.

5) Scientific textbooks and those used in mainstreaming programmes must have references to the original print page numbers. This enables the reader to quote correctly or to refer to the page to be read. We mark page number by special non used characters (black triangles) within the text as well as on the botton margin of the page set in larger print and in lined frames.

6) A line spacing of five typografical points is advantageous (compared to 2 or 3 points).

7) The standard paper format (i.e. DIN A4 or letter) should be used for reasons of handling and weight.

To comply with these guidelines for large print formatting, you can use so-called style-sheets which every versatile word processor offers, and thus allows quick formatting. This function defines the format of text, paragraph, and page layout.

Formulae and graphic symbols

As semigraphical and mathematical symbols cannot be scanned and recognized, they must be typed anew. We use Ami Professional's math editor to set the scientific figures of a mathematical textbook (Ami uses T_EX for encodeing the figures!).

It is neccessary to set mathematical symbols in larger type sizes. This is due to two reasons. First, math symbols are not as uniformally characteristic as letters. This worsenes perception. Second, keeping the regular large print point size (average of 18 pt.) would let numbers of fractions or exponents appear much too small. The base size therefore must be increased. Similar results are to be expected for musical notation. Though there was yet no demand for musical textbooks, a larger typesize for the musical symbol set should be used. Presumably, a musical editor will have to be used for it.

Coloured Images

Problems of adapting material can rather occur with images than with text. Black and white or line art graphics can still be scanned quite easily, and edited afterwards. In these cases, it is most of all important to simplify the graphics structure. A process we know from preparing tactile graphics for the blind. Simplifying can sometimes mean to draw the graphic newly. Editing coloured images, however, is a much more sophisticated job. Time for training and handling the image editing software is higher. Working on the images is also more time-consuming than it is when editing line art.

What adaptation must be used upon coloured graphics?
Coloured graphics sometimes must be ● enlarged, ● simplified, ● labelled anew, ● changed in colour contrast.

We use two mehtods of enlarging. Either you can keep the regular portrait format of a DIN A4 page, or you can print the picture in landscape format. Landscape paging enables a higher enlargemnet.

Results are: pictures or photos that are clearly structured and are unambigious need to be enlarged less (e.g. a agricultural country-side photo with clear-cut meadows and fields of green, yellow and brown). Complex images or photographs, however, demand higher enlargement (e.g. a bird's view of an industrial town). Enlargement will partly depend on the perceptual skill and his or her environmental pre-experiences of the partially sighted reader. The first picture could be printed regularly in portrait format, a landscape enlargement was appropriate for the second one. The low resolution of the landscape enlarged photograph – due to the printers standard resolution of only 360 dpi – was not found to be inadequate by the partially sighted reader.

Mere enlargement of graphics and images will not suffice. Typefaces of images are partly serif fonts, partly set on coloured backgrounds which lead to low reading contrast. Adaptation is a must (but is not done by adapting services shrinking from the plus of editing work). So images must be labelled anew. Labelling should mostly be done with vector orientated painting software for pixel-based painting software reproduces zigzag outlines of the letters. For example we used Corel-Draw to reset words rather than using the image editing software PhotoStyler. To change reading contrast either the background colour has to be altered to a lighter hue (e.g. light yellow or light blue) or the text is set into a white framed box. Negative contrast, i.e. white labeling on black background frames means optimal contrast. Positive and negative contrast can be used altenatively for different categories (e.g. country names vs. capital town names on a map).

Colour contrast must be adapted especially for readers with colour perception problems or colour blind people. Adjacent planes should be coloured far from each other on terms of satuaration, e.g. deep blue contrasting to light yellow. After this principle, adjacent colours reproduced or seen in greyscale will also be differntiable for the colour blind. In case more than two planes meet, optimal greyscale and colour contrast for all adjacent planes may be impossible. Colour changes can be made as long as the colours do not carry certain meanings as they do on topographical maps, or as long as they do not signalize meanings (e.g. red stands for danger, red stop sign) [4]. Natural colours within photographs must not be estranged, but you can change a dark blue of the sky to a lighter hue or a dark brown of an earth layer within a sectional view to beige. Colour editing tools such as the "colour pick" (eyedropping tool) or the "bucket fill" to catch a hue and to colour a whole plane enable us to do these changes.

Contour lines (black and/or white) between planes can effect in better defferentiation. Simple line art paintings such as wood engravings make use of these perceptual advantages. That is why they are often preferred as illustrations in large print books (e.g. books from the Library in Leipzig). We have yet not tested perceptual pros and cons of hatched planes.

Conclusion and outlook

We have seen that large print production especially of textbooks with coloured images is neglected. There are only a few services that already provide some books. Our project on PC-based large print editing shows that though adaptation is quite time consuming – but this is also true for braille adaptations – it can be done with low-cost or medium cost DTP systems. These experiences must be carried on further. Efforts to supply large print must be intensified. Adaptation guidelines and methods should be elaborated further. Perhaps some adapting processes such as colour changes could be automatically done by a software still to be developed.

I would be thankful for every idea or cooperating partner. From my personal point of view as a partially sighted reader, I would welcome every institutional effort to produce large print as an alternaive reading medium to optical aids.

contact: Universität Dortmund – FB 13 – GrUsS – Ulrich Zeun – Emil-Figge-Straße 50 – 44221 Dortmund – phone: 0231/755-4579 — FAX: 0231 / 755 4558

Sources and Reading proposals:

[1] **Barraga, Natalie C./ Morris, Jane E.**: (1978) Program to Develop Effeciency in Visual Functioning (Source Book on Low Vision), Ed.: American Printing House for the Blind, Louisville, .

[2] **Baumann, Hans D./ Klein, Manfred**: (1990/2) Desktop-Publishing – Typografie und Layout (Seiten gestalten am PC – für Einsteiger und Profis), Niedernhausen.

[3] **BAG-L** (Bundesarbeitsgemeinschaft zur Literaturbeschaffung für sehgeschädigte Studierende): unpublished concept paper.

[4] **Boldt, Werner:** (1969) "Über die Bedeutung von Lehr-, Arbeits- und Hilfsmitteln bei der Erziehung und Rehabilitation Blinder und Sehbehinderter", in: die aula, pp. 156-161.

[5] **Burtt, Harold, E.**: (1949) "Typography and Readability", in: The Sight-Saving-Review, 19. vol, No. 3, pp. 147-157.

[6] **Corn, Anne L./ Ryser, Gail R.**: (1989) "Access to Print for Students with Low Vision", in: Journal of Visual Impairment and Blindness, 83. vol, pp. 340 – 349.

[7] **Fonda, Gerald:** (1965) Management of the patient with subnormal vision, St. Louis.

[8] **Hochuli, Jan**: (1987) Das Detail in der Typografie; Wilmington

[9] **Shaw, Alison:** (1969) Print for Partial Sight, Ed.: The Library Association, London.

[10] **Tanner, Margarete:** (1971) "Schriftgut für sehbehinderte Kinder", in: Zeitschrift für das Blinden- und Sehbehindertenbildungswesen, 91. vol, pp. 175 – 181.

[11] **Tinker, Miles A.**: (1965) Bases for Effective Reading, Minnesota, .

[12] **Zeun, Ulrich**: (1993) Aufbereitung hochschulinterner Materialien für sehgeschädigte – Abschlußbericht, Dortmund

---

Credits: our thanks for donations and support go to "Sieglinde - Hildebrandt-Stiftung", Aldus Software, Fa. Frank Audiodata

Example for a adapted large print page

24 Drei schwarze Katzen

25

Großmama tut so,
als gehe sie einkaufen.
Sie verriegelt die Tür.
Dann geht sie
den Gartenweg hinunter
und versteckt sich
hinter der Mauer.

Im Park setzt Großmama sich auf eine
Bank und hört ▶13◀ der Musikkapelle
zu.
Es ist ein schöner, sonniger Tag.
Großmama gefällt das sehr.

13

A new Approach in Designing Low Vision Aids (LVA)

Berry P.L.M. den Brinker

Department of Psychology
Faculty of Human Movement Sciences
Vrije Universiteit van Amsterdam
van de Boechorstraat 9
1081 BT Amsterdam, The Netherlands

Abstract. In reading text, two processes can be discriminated: 1) the search for desired information on the page, and 2) the process of processing information once the desired spot on the page has been found. A global overview is given about the research on the structure of the visual system and how this system is used in normal reading and reading by people with low vision (LVP). It is concluded that research has been concentrated at the second process of the reading process and that no knowledge is available on how LVP can use their residual visual function to enable search. It is argued that visual search is of increasing importance in our modern society and that low vision aids (LVA) should support visual search. It is assumed that betters LVA can be developed on the basis of an *'Ecological approach to visual perception'* (Gibson (1979).

1 Introduction

Today, our modern society requires more processing of visual information than ever before. Visual information is presented in various ways via books, papers, magazines, television, high definition computer monitors, LCD control panels, and so on. The expanding flow of visual information places an increasing demand on the visual system in occupational as well as daily life situations. As a consequence, people with reduced vision will be confronted more quickly with their disabilities, which can result in a handicap. More than in the past, rehabilitation is aimed at using the potentials of the visually impaired person (Welling, 1994).

In training low vision people (LVP) a shift has taken place from substitutional/compensatory training to utilisation of the residual vision (Backman, 1994). From the 1970es onward LVP are trained to use magnifiers and other low vision aids (LVA) to enable or support reading. It no longer necessary to blindfold LVP during Braille training. New electronic devices are developed, the most prominent being the closed circuit television (CCTV) magnifier and programs to enlarge the characters on the computer screen (LEP). Nowadays the use of these LVA is wide spread in occupational situations and they are also becoming more and more popular in daily life situations. Moreover, the need for LVA will grow because the number of age related cases of low vision will increase in the near future.

However, there are several reasons to reconsider the design of reading aids. First of all reading with a CCTV magnifier is slow, and even more important, tiring. As a consequence, LVP tend to avoid its use (den Brinker e.a., 1994) or stop using it at all (Buijk, 19986). Secondly, the present generation of letter enlarge programs (LEP) is becoming out-of-date since the introduction of graphical oriented window systems (Vanderheijden, 1989).

Problems connected with the LVA can be solved by determining in practice what the complaints are and engage in a trial-and-error procedure for minimizing inconveniences for the actual users. This approach is at present indispensable. However, good engineering should rest on solid insight into the functions that the to be developed devices would have to fulfil to avoid unacceptable situations (Bouma, 1980). Therefore insight in the reading process and visual search is necessary for designing LVA.

In this presentation an overview is given of the reading process as it occurs in normal-sighted and low vision people. It is followed by a critical look at the design of the presently available electronic devices for reading and computer use. Finally, suggestions are given about tests to be developed for evaluating reading performances in both normal and low vision people.

2 The Visual System

From a biological perspective, the visual system has to support the organism in the basic functions of navigation and object-recognition under varying conditions of illumination. These tasks led to conflicting demands for the 'biological engineer'. For example, the requirements of high acuity and high sensitivity cannot be met simultaneously. The present situation, with a small retinal region of high acuity and a decreasing acuity with eccentricity is a good compromise between acuity and sensitivity: an eye with full retinal acuity would require 150 times more fibres and thus lead to an unacceptable large blind spot (Van der Grind, 1994). The lack of full retinal acuity is compensated for by an ingenuous control system by which all parts of the surrounding world can be focused into the central region (fovea and parafovea). In other words, it is the combination of a small retinal region of high acuity and a eye movement control system that enables us to get sharp images of every detail in our visual environment.

3 Normal Reading

In reading texts two processes can be distinguished (Bouma, 1980; Van Nes, 1986). First the search for desired information on the page, and second, the processing of that information. To optimize legibility (the extend to which visual information can be processed during reading) the structure of the page should enable rapid search and subsequent reading of the interesting passages. While searching, the eyes scan the page, guided by text attributes such as words that have specific first letters, length or printing style (bold face), etc or whole areas that are conspicuous by there layout.

During reading of connected text the eyes make rapid jumps, saccades. Between saccades, the fixation pauses, information is extracted from the visual reading field (about 10 to 20 characters). During this process both letter recognition and word contour recognition play a role. Words in lower case have a high legibility because of characteristic contours from ascenders (b,d,f,h,k,l,,t) and descenders (g,j,q,y). While reading the eyes proceed along the line with rightward saccades of 4 to 12 characters, the length being determined by both display and content variables. This leads to the typical 'staircase' pattern of eye movements (see Figure 1). Small backward or correction saccades are made when comprehension of the text lags behind the recognition process during the fixation pauses. Line saccades, long leftward eye jumps, are made when the end of a line is reached. During a line saccade, the beginning of the next line has a peripheral retinal projection and therefore cannot be seen clearly. Hence, line saccades are often misdirected. Therefore the left margin should be a straight line and sufficiently wide to prevent under- and overshoots in horizontal direction. Errors in vertical direction occur when the angle between the line saccade and the line is to small (less than 2 degrees), which happens when lines are to long or to close.

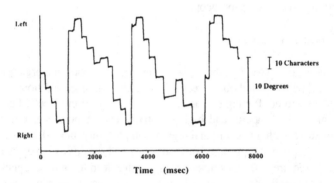

Fig. 1. A typical 'staircase' pattern of eye movements in normal reading.
(Adopted with permission from Bowers & Ackerley, 1994)

4 Reading with Magnifiers

Perception can not be studied without reference to movements. As shown above, this is also the case for 'pure' perceptual tasks such as reading. For people with reduced vision movement control is even more important. While reading, they have to hold the magnifier and synchronize the eye movements with those of the magnifier. Little is known about the particular difficulties of reading with a loupe compared to normal reading. Investigations should be directed at the effect of magnification, reading-field width, lens aberration, reflection of lens-surface, and how these factors relate to the control of the movements of the eyes and loupe. The study of Blomnaert & Neve (1987) shows the complexity of these problems. They calculated the theoretical maximum reading-field width of three kinds of looking through loupes (monocular, binocular and a composite method). Experimentally they tried to identify these styles and effective field widths in five normal subjects and in one subject with moderate low vision. All three styles were identified and the effects were discussed in relation to other parameters, such as spherical and chromatic aberrations and reflection. It was assumed that loupes should not be used as eye glasses and that for severely impaired readers the absence of aberration is more important than field of view or magnification. These ideas, described in an information brochure (Korpel, Tebak & de Vette, 1989), are contrary to what is sometimes found in practice. People with poor visual acuity often prefer to use loupes as eye glasses to compensate for the severe loss of the reading-field width caused by the small diameter of the strong loupe. Furthermore, it can be shown (see below) that aberrating lenses, when used as eye glasses, need not disturb the perception process.

An important other class of magnifiers is that of the closed-circuit television magnifier, CCTV magnifier or video-loupe. Studies about the field of view, magnification, contrast, polarity of the magnified image, etc are easier to be carried out using these electronic devices. However, the quality of the electronic parts may have an aversive effect on the observed behaviour and makes it difficult to draw general conclusions. This is exemplified by the research of Lowe & Dresdo (1990). While discussing the optimal strategy for moving the text (on a X-Y platform) along the camera, they speculated that it is better not to move the X-Y platform during the recognition phase to prevent blurring of the image (p.232). This would not be a good advise using modern CCTV magnifiers. Their blur was caused by the inferior quality of camera tubes that were used at the time of their experiments (before 1980). Modern CCTV magnifiers, equipped with a CCD camera, don't have this problem and enable the same movement patterns (eye and text) as those found with loupes.

From the literature it is clear that LVP don't have the typical 'staircase' pattern of eye movements. While moving the magnifier smoothly along the line, they fixate on the same location in the image. As soon as the recognition process is completed, the eye jumps to the next fixation point in the moving image (opto-kinetic nystagmus: OKN) (see Figure 2). The resultant 'saw-tooth' pattern has been found in LVP (Legge e.a., 1985; Legge, 1991) and in normal-sighted subjects using magnifiers (Fotinakis & Dickinson, 1994).

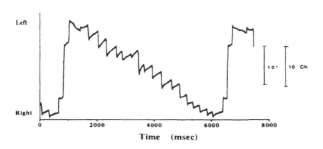

Fig. 2. A typical 'saw-tooth' pattern of eye movements while reading with a hand hold magnifier. (Adopted with permission from Bowers & Ackerley, 1994)

Efforts have been made to find parameters that determine reading performance using LVA (hand-hold magnifiers, spectacle-mounted magnifiers and CCTV magnifiers). In general, character size (or magnification) was found to be negatively correlated with reading rate (Fotinakis & Dickinson, 1994; Lowe & Drasdo, 1990; Legge, 1985). However there is no agreement on the minimal number of characters in the viewing field. Legge e.a. (1985) found optimal reading with a viewing window of only 4 characters, while Lowe (& Drasdo, 1990) claimed 20 to 30 were necessary.

In any case, the two parameters are representative for the research into the use of LVA; all research is directed at parameters that are directly or indirectly responsible for the quality of the display. The relevance of these parameters is determined on the basis of the reading rate of a continuous text of 100 to 200 words. By doing so, no information is collected about the way LVA are used for the search process, which was distinguished by Bouma (1980) as one of the two basic ingredient of the reading process.

5 The Ecological Validity of Reading rate Tests

In a recent review on the comparison of reading from paper and screens, Dillon (1992) criticized the use of reading rate as a test for reading performance. Such tests are based on the assumption that textual information consists of a sequence of words that has to be recognized and comprehended in a fixed order. In real life, that is only the case with prose. Papers, magazines, telephone book, manuals, flyers, study books, etc, are not meant to be read from the beginning to the end. They are all designed to help the reader to find the desired information. Books have contents, index registers, glossaries, etc to help the reader to find his way through the pages. As soon as the reader has reached the page on which he expects to find information, the layout may help him find it.

As mentioned in the introduction, our modern society requires its participants to digest loads of visual information. The search for desired information is at least as important as the processing of that information. So, if we want to support people with reduced vision, we have to help them find that information. The equipment that has been developed so far was not designed for that purpose. It's suitable for processing the information that was found otherwise. In a recent study (den Brinker e.a., 1994) 22 LVP were interviewed about activities of daily live. None of the interviewed CCTV magnifier owners used the apparatus for tasks that require search (numbers in a telephone book). It is almost a tragedy that the present CCTV magnifiers only support the part of text processing that probably will be replaced in the future by speech-generation (on the basis of opto-electronic character recognition).

6 Future Developments in Research and Design

In the last fifteen years a correspondence is found between research in (the improvement of) the quality of video display units (VDU) and research in the use of low vision aids. In both research lines display characteristics are of major concern and were tested with the same kind of reading performance tasks.

Dillon (1992) was one of the first authors who questioned the importance of *manipulation* of the text in determining the usability of computerized information systems. Most people still prefer books over computerized information systems in which people easily get lost. In discussing the usability the concept of the *'navigation problem'* is often mentioned as the major factor determining the unpopularity of hyper text based information systems.

LVP using LVA have similar problems. While reading with a magnifier, the biggest part of their visual field is filled with only a few words. During the search for desired information they have to switch back and forth between an overview and an enlarged image. This process is made even more complex by the need to refocus the magnifier when the search is shifted to another part of the page or the book.

It is clear that something has to be done to attack the problem of manipulation and navigation. It is wise not to start with a trial and error search for parameters that may influence the usability of modern information systems. I have the idea that there is a correspondence between navigation in 'the real world' and navigating in information systems, virtual reality, and the use of CCTV magnifiers. Therefore the work on locomotion and manipulation by Gibson (1979) is very relevant for research in ergonomics.

His *'Ecological approach to visual perception'* makes clear that perception and action have to be considered complementary, tightly coupled subsystems of the perceptual system. Gibson rejects the idea that it is possible to understand how we move around in an environment, by considering the eyes as cameras, connected by nerves to transport images to the brain. Instead, he suggests that natural vision depends on *the eyes in the head on a body supported by the ground* with the brain as the centre of the visual system. He describes how such a system is able to detect the invariant aspects in the *ambient optic array* necessary to distinguish changes in the environment from changes caused by eye, head and body movements. The sequence of stimulation is not a sequence of discrete snapshots, but a sequence that is converted into a (stable) scene. The optical flow is continuously sampled by the visual system and the invariants contribute to a persistent environmental scene in which co-existing parts (objects) and events are all perceived together (p. 222). With such a system it can be understood that our visual system *interprets* straight lines as such, although the retinal projection of that line isn't linear at all.

With this theory in mind an earlier presented problem in the use of lenses can be understood. When handling a loupe with spherical aberrations on some distance of the eye, conflicting images will emerge: the lines seen through the loupe are more or less curved while the same lines outside the border of the loupe remain straight. This situation will disturb the reading process as was stated by Blomnaert & Neve (1987). When using the same loupe as an eye glass these image distortions will, after a while, not be noticed. While moving the head along the lines of the text, the eye glass will consequently represent the lines as curves and still be interpreted as straight lines because of the absence of conflicting visual images.

This is only a minor example of how Gibson's theory may contribute to the understanding of the problems that LVP face when handling LVA. If, as I have said before, a major problem for LVP in our modern society is to find the desired information, we have to know more about visual search and navigation by those people.

If navigating in an environment, according to Gibsons view, can be described as a continuous extraction of invariant features from the ambient optical flow to contribute to the *building of a permanent scene*, one might imagine that the use of some LVA may disturb this process of the visual system. Since we know from the literature (Kooijman e.a. 1994) that LVP are able to navigate in their living environment in spite of major losses of visual acuity, there are reasons to believe that tools can be developed to profit from this capability while searching for desired information to read.

When designing new aids for LVP, the engineer has to know which cues, to state it in more traditional terms, are available for people with reduced vision to support him in the search for desired information. Finally, more relevant, *ecological valid* assessments of the usability have to be developed as well.

References

1. O. Backman: Reading skills, reading training and technology for the visually handicapped, Prospects for the 1990 es. In: A.C. Kooijman, P.L. Looijstijn, J.A. Welling & G.J. van der Wildt (eds): Low Vision, Research and new developments in rehabilitation. Amsterdam: IOS Press 1994, 251-254

2. J.J. Blomnaert, J.J. Neve, J.J.: Reading fields of magnifying loupes. Journal of the Optical Society of America 4, 1820-1830 (1987)

3. H. Bouma: Visual reading processes and the quality of text displays. In: E. Grandjean, E. Vigliani: Ergonomic aspects of Visual Display Terminals. London: Taylor & Francis Ltd 1980, 101-114

4. A. Bowers, R. Ackerly: Reading characteristics of normal observers using Low Vision Aids. In: A.C. Kooijman, P.L. Looijstijn, J.A. Welling, G.J. van der Wildt (eds.): Low Vision, Research and new developments in rehabilitation. Amsterdam: IOS Press 1994, 235-238

5. B.P.L.M. den Brinker, K. Bolder, K. Mollevanger, P. Tummers: The use of Low Vision Aids (LVA) in daily life activities. In preparation (1994)

6. C.A. Buijk: Slechtziendheid en hulpmiddelen. Amsterdam: LTP 1986

7. A. Dillon: Reading from paper versus screens: a critical review of the empirical literature. Ergonomics 35, 1297-1326 (1992)

8. V.P. Fotinakis, C.M. Dickinson: Reading with Hand Magnifiers. In: A.C. Kooijman e.a. (eds.): Low Vision, Research and new developments in rehabilitation. Amsterdam: IOS Press 1994, 259-268

9. J.J. Gibson: The ecological approach to visual perception. Boston: Houghton Mifflin Company 1979

10. W.A. van de Grind: Limits and mechanisms of vision. In: A.C. Kooijman e.a. (eds): Low Vision, Research and new developments in rehabilitation. Amsterdam: IOS Press 1994, 28-37

11. A.C. Kooijman, G.I.J.M. Kempen, F.W. Cornelissen, M.J.G. Heuvelen, A. van de Wege, P. Fritsche, W.A. Houtman: Screening of visual function compared with self-report visual disability. In: A.C. Kooijman, P.L. Looijstijn, J.A. Welling, G.J. van der Wildt (eds.): Low Vision, Research and new

developments in rehabilitation. Amsterdam: IOS Press 1994, 11-14

12. L.M.H. Korpel, N.E. Tebak, M.E. de Vette: Met een loep pakt u de draad weer op! Eindhoven: IPO 1989

13. G.E. Legge, C.S. Rubin, D.G. Pelli, M.M. Schleske: Psychophysics of Reading-II, Low Vision. Vision Research 25, 253-266 (1985)

14. G.E. Legge: Glenn A. Fry Award Lecture 1990: Three Perspectives on Low Vision Reading. Optometry and Vision Science. American Society of Optometry, 763-769 (1991)

15. J.B. Lowe, N. Dresdo: Efficiency in reading with closed-circuit television for low vision. Ophthalmology Physiological Optics 10, 225-233 (1990)

16. F.L. van Nes: Space, Color and typography on visual display terminals. Behaviour and Information technology 5, 99-118 (1986)

17. C.C. Vanderheijden: Nonvisual alternative display techniques for Output of Graphics-Based-Computers. Journal Of Visual Impairment and Blindness 83, 383-390 (1989)

18. J.A. Welling: Foreword. In: A.C. Kooijman, P.L. Looijstijn, J.A. Welling, G.J. van der Wildt (eds.): Low Vision, Research and new developments in rehabilitation. Amsterdam: IOS Press 1994, XI-XII

Multimedia Authoring Systems For Constructing Education Packages For Special Needs Education

J. Fowler and S.Swales

School Of Computing And Information Systems, University Of Sunderland
Priestman Building, Green Terrace, Sunderland, Tyne & Wear, United Kingdom, SR1 3SD.

Abstract. There are many problems involved with using "off-the-shelf" educational packages in Special Needs Education. For instance, commercial packages have , in the past, been found to accomplish only about half the function requires, or are found not to meet the needs of the pupils at all. An additional problem, is that these pupils often require special hardware which caters for their individual needs. There seems to be a complete lack of software which can be configured for the use of these special devices, which would enable the individual pupils to use the various programs.

This paper contains details of proposed research, which is currently underway, looking into specifying, designing and developing a system, which would allow teaching staff at such Special Needs Schools to construct their own customised software for teaching purposes. With the use of such a system, software would be individually tailored to meet the needs of the pupils, and more accurately adjusted to the material being used in the curriculum of the time.

The proposed system would consist of a multi-media authoring system, which together with an easy-to-grasp user interface, would allow teachers to build their own stand-alone packages without the need to know a programming language.

Introduction - Computers in the Classroom

The use of computers as an aid to teaching in the classroom has become well established in recent years. They are widely used throughout the education system from kindergarten to higher education. Most subject areas employ computer applications to some extent and they have proved to be of particular benefit in special needs education [1],[2],[3].

There have been many initiatives to establish the use of computers in teaching . In the early 1980's the British government aimed to provide every school (including Special needs schools) in the country with at least one computer.

Many schools have been able to grasp the opportunity to use computers in teaching. In other schools, however, their use has been limited. The reasons teacher resistance to computer use are varied [4],[5] but will include a lack of resources, time to develop the software, resistance to change [6],[7], and a lack of appropriate educational programs.

Where the potential of computers has been recognised by teachers, (special school teachers in particular could see the benefits) the lack of educational software still has had to be addressed.

This could be done in a number of ways:

1. Software packages could be bought in. The drawback of this approach is that schools have a very limited budget and buying the wrong software could often be an expensive mistake.

2. Teaching staff could develop their own programs based on a their expert subject knowledge. This approach has a high probability of producing appropriate software with a sound educational value. Unfortunately in order to achieve this the teacher has to devote an enormous amount of time to developing such programs, in terms of both the teaching subject content and in their having to master the computer systems and software. They have to learn everything about the computer system from scratch, and for many the task has been too much.

3. A better approach was to employ computer experts to work in collaboration with the teachers to produce educational software[8]. The end product would usually be much better because the teacher avoided the need to learn how to program and was free to concentrate on the teaching material content. Again although this was highly successful there was still a high financial cost involved in this type of collaborative project.

A compromise solution to the problem of educational software production was to use packages to produce CAL courseware[9],[10]. Such systems claim to provide a user friendly interface which takes the pain out of programming[11]. Whereas it is the case that developing courseware through this type of system requires less programming than a conventional language there is nevertheless still a programming language to learn.

The aim of this project is to produce an authoring package which will enable teachers to easily produce computer based teaching materials without the need to directly write computer programs.

The Development System

It has been decided that we should use the Commodore Amiga 4000 multimedia workstation as a base for the development system[15]. The grounds for the use of this system are given below:

Ease Of Use:

The Amiga series of microcomputers are about the most user-friendly systems that we have encountered so far. It has been observed that a user, new to this particular system took less than half an hour to familiarise themselves with how the machine operated and had a word processing package up and running and in use in under an hour from first plugging the machine in and turning it on.

Hardware:

The Amiga series of computers are all based around the Motorola 680x0 family of microprocessors. The development system, the Amiga 4000 is available with either a 68030 or 68040 32-bit microprocessor. As well as this the Amiga systems have a number of custom support microprocessors which specifically handle things such as graphics, sound, memory and I/O functions. In short all the main processor actually contributes to this setup is the maths functions and provides the base instruction set. This combination of microprocessors adds up to an impressive machine, capable of running virtually any type of application at more or less peak efficiency.

Graphics:

The graphics capabilities of the Amiga are well known as being some of the best available on a low cost computer system. With a wide range of graphics modes and resolutions, with a 16.8 million colour palette available, and the provision of a graphics animation co-processor which can animate objects at high speeds.

Sound:

The sound capability of these machines features full voice synthesis, and sampling of real life sounds in four channel stereo. One of the most useful features of the sound system is the speech synthesis facility. This has been employed on another project called Art Master, which was an art package for use with special needs education. This employed the speech synthesizer to act as a computerised "instructor" which taught the children how to use the package with the minimum of teacher interaction. This proved to be very effective.

Operating System:

The Amiga is equipped with a highly efficient DOS known as AmigaDOS which is a fully multitasking system i.e. more than one program can be executed at once. AmigaDOS has the facility for recognising, reading and writing disks from other operating systems such as PC or Macintosh as well as its own formats.

Compatibility:

The Amiga is practically unique as far as considering compatibility between systems. This particular computer system has the ability to be given multiple "personalities." With the addition of low-cost expansion cards, it is possible to make the machine completely IBM PC compatible, right up to 486 standard, or make it completely Apple Macintosh compatible, BBC micro compatible or because of its superb multitasking abilities it is possible to have it running applications for all three personalities at once as well as its own native mode. It is even capable of running UNIX with the addition of an AMIX card.

Because of this unique feature, it is envisaged that the proposed multimedia system could well be used to produce programs which are IBM PC, Macintosh or BBC micro compatible as well as those which would run on Amiga systems. This would be particularly useful as it has been observed that there are plenty of schools in the U.K. which have a mixture of machines available to them. In short, a single Amiga system could be used to produce classroom software for all their systems.

Availability:

There are many schools which have adopted the Amiga as a classroom machine. This in many cases seems to be a growing trend. Also, the low-end Amigas are very popular in homes all over the country, this means that if a teacher wished to, the children who had these machines could take the classroom programs home to work on them. In the case of special needs children, this could be very important, as the child might not be in a position to be able to come into school. In which case a low-cost low-end system could be provided, equipped with programs put together by the teachers at the school.

All the Amiga range of computers from the low-end Amiga A500 right up to the high-end Amiga 4000/040 would be able to run the software created with this multimedia based authoring system. The authoring system itself should be useable on any of the "big box" Amigas equipped with a CD-ROM drive i.e. Amigas A1500, A2000, A3000 and A4000. As can be seen the above features make the Amiga the ideal machine for setting up the authoring system on.

The Proposed System

There is a need within special needs education for some way to customise software, so that it is truly usable in the classroom, as opposed to some package being bought "off-the-shelf," which may do some of the job or none of it at all.

The idea being that a system would be developed, which would enable staff within special needs education schools (or mainstream schools for that matter) to produce their own educational programs for use in the classroom.

One of the main problems teachers have in developing their own systems, is the time which is required to learn computer programming languages. The proposed system is designed to take away the need to learn any of these languages, and so shortens the time which is needed to learn enough about their computer system in order to use it, is reduced to an absolute minimum. It is envisaged that all the teaching staff would need to learn to use this program building tool, is how to use a mouse controller and how to make selections from a graphical user interface (GUI) driven icon and menu system.

This lays a heavy emphasis on a user interface design which should be both easy to use and easy to understand[12][13][14]. It would be ideal if most of the operating manual could be reduced to a few pages telling the user how to get the package running, and then the package should be easy enough to use without needing the manual.

Over the years this has seemed to many people as being a very difficult thing to achieve. However, if the package is designed to operate in a very logical and sequential manner, then theoretically it should be quite difficult to make mistakes while using it. If the user had missed something out, which would prevent the finished classroom program from running, the development system should be able to tell the user this, and give the user an appropriate indication as to what it is that is missing, before the final product is put together and made into a stand-alone, self-running program.

There are several different authoring systems available on Amiga systems. This includes packages such as Scala MM300, AmigaVision, CanDo and the newly released Mediapoint system[16]. All of these systems allow users to construct "presentation" style applications. Some do allow the production of stand-alone programs, but all the ones which do this, require the user to use a script language or write some program code to do different things. This can be obstructive as far as the time necessary to learn them goes. The exception to this is the new MediaPoint system which uses a point and click graphical user interface..

The system that has been proposed, is somewhat different to these packages, in that the programs it would produce will be stand-alone, i.e. they will run by themselves. This will mean that there need only be one development machine equiped with the authoring system. All the programs produced should be runnable on all models of Amiga computer systems, so the classroom machines could be lower cost systems such as the Amiga A1200.

The system would use a set of module library CD-ROMs which would contain a large amount of program "segments" which can be added together via a specially designed program editor, to construct the final stand-alone program.

The authoring system therefore, would consist of the following parts:

The Program Editor:

This together with its easy-to-use user interface, would be the main driving program for the system. This would allow the teacher using the development system to actually plan out and create the classroom software that is required.

The Program Compiler:

This part of the system takes the program design taken created with the program editor and constructs the stand-alone program from the program modules libraries on CD-ROMs.

The CD-ROM module libraries:

These CD-ROMs would hold the program modules, as mentioned above. The CD-ROMs would contain program segments which can be used to cover the whole curriculum.

Conclusions

There is clearly a need for the authoring system outlined above in Special Needs Education. There are many possible benefits. For instance, an authoring system which can be used for multi-machine format development has obvious benefits, i.e. most of a particular school's equipment could be utilised. Classroom software produced with such a system, rather than becoming obsolete when a curriculum change occurs, can simply be brought back into the development system and edited accordingly. The classroom software can also be tailored exactly to the requirements of the teachers concerned.

The major part of this work in developing the authoring system, will be the user-interface design. This process should be useful in establishing a methodology for constructing "intuitive" user interfaces for multimedia applications as a whole. The modular CD system is open ended, so new subjects and new program modules can be added to the development system with relative ease.

Research and development work on this system will be continuing with the emphasis on the construction of the user interface first. Once this has been completed, a generic development system will be produced which can be used to write classroom software within a limited subject area. This generic system will be used in field trials in a local Special Needs School, in order to evaluate the system. If the evaluation is successful then further subject areas will be added to the system.

References

1. Berg M., 'Computerised system for special needs', Computer Education, p.30, Feb. 1993.

2. Bailey J., 'Curriculum approaches in special education computing', Journal of Computer-based Instruction, p.1-5, Winter 1992.

3. Wood D. L., 'The Characteristics of intrinsically motivating early childhood and special education software', proc. IFIP TC 3 fifth world conference on Computers in Education, July 1990.

4. Hannafin R., Savenye W., 'Technology in the classroom: The Teacher's new Role and Resistance to it', Educational Technology, p26-31, June 1993.

5.   Drew D., 'Why Don't all professors use computers?', Academic-Computing, p12-14, 58-60, Oct 1989.

6.   Kolehmainen P., 'The Changes in Computer Anxiety in a required computer course', proc. European conf. on Educational Research, The Netherlands, June 1992.

7.   Crowe B., 'Computers in the Secondary Art Curriculum', Annual meeting of the Mid-South Educational Research Association, Lexington USA, Nov. 1988.

8.   'Marketing Education Computer Curriculum. Final Report.', Pittsburgh Univ., School of Education, 1988.

9.   Pyzdrowski A., DeNardo A., 'Creating a computer simulator package for a hypothetical computer architecture', proc. Ann. conf. Eastern Educational Research Assn., March 1992.

10. McCluskey C., 'Interactive Video in the Classroom', proc. Nat. Staff Dev. Conf. Nat. council of States on Inservice education', Nov. 1985.

11. Motteram G., 'Using Standard Authoring packages to teach effective reading skills', p. 15-21, System, V18 n1, 1990.

12. Waterworth J., 'Multimedia technology and application', Ellis Horwood 1991

13. Tway L., 'Welcome To Multimedia', MIS Press 1992

14. Maybury. M. T., 'Intelligent Multimedia Interfaces', American Association for Artificial Intelligence 1993.

15. Fowler J., Swales S., 'Art Master - A Package For Special Needs Education (Paper)' Proc. AETT 29th International Conference, Edinburgh 1994

16. Amiga Shopper Magazine, Future Publishing Ltd., Issue 37, May 1994

Computer-Aided Instruction with Blind Persons on an Audio-Tactile Basis

by Paul Nater and Thomas Thäle

Dep. of Special Education and Rehabiltation, University of Dortmund

Abstract. A hardware configuration to realize Programmed Instruction (as a partial aspect of Computer-aided Instruction) on an audio-tactile basis is discribed. In order to enable teachers without special EDP-knowledge to program teaching-programs as interactive (branched) systems with Braille interaction and speach-output, an author-system is explained. Contours of current and future research are outlined.

1 Programmed Instruction (PI) as a Partial Aspect of Computer-Aided Instruction (CAI)

1.1 The Concept of PI

CAI stands for a generic term including all processes in the field of planned instruction where computers are used actively by learners. We basically distinguish between two categories of computer application: Computer as a tool (e. g. for text processing or for checking actors like model robots) and computer as a presentation medium for "programmed instruction". By "PI" we understand a form of objectivated instruction characterized by permanent learner-software-interaction precisely fixed by an educational expert before the teaching software is written by a programmer, (which means a translation into computer-comprehensive commands). Such a "teaching program" has to be looked upon as an anticipatation of a teaching dialogue realized by a sequence of learning steps ("frames") in a fixed logical and psychological order called the teaching algorithm. The verbally and/or symbolically fixed "teaching dialogue", including references to the chaining of frames as well as to special outputs like sound, we call the program script, in analogy to film script.

1.2 The Function of an Author-System

As mentioned above, this didactic script must be programmed with the help of an EDP-programming language. Unfortunately, educators usually are not acquainted on the use of a programming language. On the other hand programmers are not familiar with didactic reasoning. Cooperation of the two specialists is one solution of the problem; another, giving the educators (teachers) far-reaching independence of assistance by programmers, constitutes an author-system for programming.

It is most important that the handling of such an author-systems is not too complicated. There is the danger, otherwise, that educators without special EDP-training are not willing or have not enough time to deal with them.

2 PI for Blind Students on an Audio-Tactile Basis

2.1 PI and Special Learning Needs of Blind Persons

Experts argue that PI, because of its permanent demands for reactions, compensates for a tendency of passivity not seldom to be observed in learning behaviour of blind individuals. Immediate experience of success after every learning-step, is expected to motivate for independent and continuous learning.

Learning groups in special school settings usually show rather heterogeneous prerequisites concerning intellectual and/or motor abilities. In the seventeenth we proved that PI (presented by an electronical teaching device) tended to even out the effect of heterogeneous learning conditions. When students were allowed to make individual use of learning aids and worked at their own pace and rhythm, they were able to compensate for deficiencies in learning disabilities, e. g. lower degrees of intelligence [1].

Visually impaired pupils in mainstream settings need a substantial amount of practice in special skills. Individualization of teaching may be achieved more easily and effectively if PI can be applicated.

In social and vocational rehabilitation people not seldom have to wait after the loss of their sight until they can attend to rehabilitation courses e. g. in Braille learning. If they desire measures of rehabilitation, waiting time usually makes more difficult to cope with their stroke of fate. Teaching programs may be put at disposal, together with the hardware required, by local associations of the blind and thus bridge the waiting period.

2.2 Abilities and Requirements of our PI-System

Hardware Necessities. The PI-system that has been developed at the University of Dortmund in cooperation with F.H.Papenmeier, Schwerte. The auther system, written by Thomas Thäle, consists of three main programs: (1) a user interface that helps making development easy, (2) a module for verifying program syntax, (3) an interpreter for running programmed lessons.

The required PC should be an AT-386 with two megs of ram at least. The development kit supports EGA and VGA both. The interpreter itself needs no special graphics adaptor because there is no special visual output on the screen; all program outputs are displayed via a NOTEX486 on its tactile display. (NOTEX486 is a notebook-PC with a Braille-display and a Braille-keyboard.) Sound and voice are given out by a SoundBlaster. For having a good quality it is necessary to have a SoundBlaster 2.0 or better and a high capacity hard disk. Depending on the quality of sound about 11.000 bytes/s (for low-quality-recordings) to about 90.000 bytes/s (for CD-quality-recordings) are needed. For that reason, the our teaching programs which are in progress, will be available on Compact-Disk in the future. For selfmade lessons, there is the possibility of using the hard disk, or to have a CD manufactured. To use such a CD at least a Doublespeed CD-Rom is required.

Speech-recording can be done with any software supporting a SoundBlaster.

Functions and Facilities of the Author-System. Programming a lesson is easy to do because there is only quite a handful of commands to be known to the teacher who writes the programs. This special programming language makes use of structures known from BASIC and PASCAL and is easy to learn.

The programmer has the ability to
(1)   write text to the Braille display;
(2)   send recorded voice, music, etc. to the speakers;
(3)   wait for a defined or undefined keyboard or Braille input;
(4)   program conditional and absolute jumps (branching of frames);
(5)   assemble subroutines for often used procedures;
(6)   create a case-sensitive help-system;
(7)   influence the level of tolerance in regard to inputs;
(8)   switch on/off a braille echo for inputs;
(9)   define variables to store inputs or a system status;
(10)   include libraries of already written procedures or constants that keep complex dot combinations e. g. used in Braille II.
(11)   Above all the option should be left open to integrate the embossing of tactile drawings developed by the aid of our drawing program DOTGRAPH and put out by a modified Braille printer or a plotter [2].

2.3   Programming with the Author-System

At the beginning stands the didactic sketch, the program script, as we called it. The next step to EDP-programming is the representation of the formal chaining of the frames by a flow chart. Its algorithm can be easily translated into a programming language which is explained by the following example:
The example deals with a common problem in German spelling whether a noun ends with a "p" or "b". As pronounciation gives no direct hint at the correct spelling a solution to the problem is to form the plural.

F	Speech & Sound	Braille Display	Input & next F	Program code	Comments
				REMARK b or p ?;	Comments name of the program.
				VARIABLE name, a, b;	Declares variables.
				PROCEDURE Enter;	Procedure ENTER begins.
				a :=echo;	a receives the contents of echo.
				echo :="OFF";	echo gets the contents "OFF". ("OFF" means that there is no Braille representation on the display when the student is writing.)
				READ(b);	Fetch Braille input and wait for Enter
				echo := a;	Restore echo status
				ENPROC;	End of procedure
				PROCEDURE CD; PRINT("");	Clears Braille display. Prints nothing on the Braille display as there isn´t any letter indicated between the quotation marks; effects clearing display.
				ENDPROC;	
				MAIN;	Here starts the interpreter with its work.
1	Hello, I am Nicki, the computer worm. I like to work with children, and children like to do exercises with me. Would you like to work with me ? Fine, so write your name for me, please. After writing, press ENTER.			REMARK Frame1;	Comments beginning of frame 1.
				CD;	Procedure CD (see above) is called.
				VOICE(f01.voc);	Output of the speech file belonging to frame 1, stored under the name of f01.voc.
				echo :="OFF";	No "echo" of student´s input on the Braille display.
			name of the student	READ(name);	Reads the string of the letters (name of the child) which is assigned to the variable "name".

Table 1. Frame 1 of the teaching program *"b" or "p" ?`*

F	Speech & Sound	Braille Display	Input & next F	Program code	Comments
2	This is a nice name, indeed! I wish to write it down for myself. Please look at the Braille display!	Name of the student		REMARK Frame2; VOICE(f02.voc); PRINT(name);	Prints the name the student had entered on the Braille display.
3	To write without mistakes is not easy,..... We will learn now, whether we spell a word with "b" or "p" at the end. I give you an example: **Der Die̱b klaut Geld.** (The thief pinches money.) (Pause) Do you already know whether you spell Dieb with "b" or "p"? I give you another example. **Die Die̱be klauen Geld.** (The thieves ...) **Die̱be - Dieb,** what have I done here?... I print you a word with the last letter being missing. Please write the last letter. ... The word is **Kalb** (calf).	Kal_		PRINT("Kal_"); HELP :="HELPf03.voc"	Prints Kal_ A helping function. The auditive contents of this file is: "You can fill in only b or p." This file will be played after having made five mistakes or after a request for help.
			"b" ⇨·F4 "p" ⇨ F41	READSTRICT(DV1);	The interpreter reads the file DV1 on the hard disk and compares the student´s input letter by letter. Thus it "forces" the student to a correct spelling.

Table 2. Frames 2 & 3 of the Teaching Program *"b" or "p"* ?

F	Speech & Sound	Braille Display	Input & next F	Program code	Comments
4				LABEL Frame4;	Defines a location for program branching.
				CD;	Clear display
	Fine, this was correct. You probably found out you can determine the last letter by lengthening the word. Read again, please and press Enter.	Kälber-Kalb		VOICE(f04.voc);	Play Voice-file
				PRINT("Kälber-Kalb");	Print text
				Enter;	Branch to Enter-procedure
				F5;	Jump to frame 5
41		Clear display		LABEL F41;	Defines a location for program branching.
				CD;	Clear display
	I´m sorry, that wasn´t quite correct. Please, listen closely. **Kälber - Kalb**, fill in the missing letter!	Kal_		VOICE(f41.voc);	Play Voice-file
				PRINT("Kal_");	Print text
			"b"⇨f4 "p"⇨f41	READSTRICT(DV2);	Check answer of student and branch correspondingly
5				LABEL F5;	Defines a location for program branching.
		Clear display		CD;	Clear display
	So keep in mind: You can find out whether a word is written with "b" or "p" by lengthening the word... Press Enter to finish the lesson.			VOICE(f05.voc);	Play Voice-file
				Enter;	Branch to Enter-procedure

Table 3. Frames 4, 4.1, 5 of the Teaching Program *"b" or "p" ?*

Within the above example, not all facilities of the author-system have been exhausted. We have not made use of the system variable ERRORCOUNT. With the help of ERRORCOUNT it is possible to determine when the help function is activated. The predifined value for ERRORCOUNT is five. In addition the author system takes down a record of the students´ actions which gives the teacher detailed information about the learning progress of the student. A further facility is to influence the number of repeated speech outputs when the student presses the REPEAT-button at NOTEX486. Furthermore speed and loudness of speech output can be adapted to individual needs.

3 Aspects of Future Development and Research

Three topics will be to the fore: (1) Modification of the author system so it will support a standard Braille display which is normally available in schools. For economical reasons a seperate low-cost Braille keyboard should be possible when Braille inputs are didacticly convenient.

(2) It must be investigated whether teachers are interested in working with the author-system. Eventually occuring difficulties in its use must be analized and removed as far as possible.

(3) Teaching programms should be developed to find out for what kind of teaching stuff and aims PI, realized with the aid of our equipment, is appropriate. These investigations are done with special reguard to the conditions of learning in mainstream settings and self-initiated courses e. g. prior to official rehabilitation measures.

References

1 P. Nater 1982. An Electronic Teaching Device for Blind Students. Journal of Visual Impairment and Blindness, 76, 274-279
2 P. Nater 1993. Tactile Graphics with the Aid of a Conventional Braille Printer. Journal of Microcomputer Applications, 16, 307-314.

Authoring Software in Special Education

Panayiota G. Smirni and Pearl Brereton

Department of Computer Science, Keele University
Keele, ST5 5BG, UK

Abstract. The limited quantity and quality of existing software (course-ware) restricts the use of computers in today's special educational environments. Special educators are often reluctant to become involved with the development of new courseware because of the high costs associated with courseware development. Therefore in this paper we are focussing on procedures for the development of Computer-Assisted Instruction (CAI) lessons. Three primary techniques to help authors produce CAI lessons are the use of traditional programming languages, authoring languages, and authoring systems. These techniques are defined and compared. For our study we concentrated on those authoring systems which require no programming from the user and which provide a courseware generator for special teachers to enter their own content. These authoring systems can be divided into three categories according to the type of CAI lesson they support. Criteria are also given for selecting between the authoring systems.

An Authoring Courseware Development Model (ACDM) is proposed to guide the development of authored lessons. According to this model the development of special CAI lessons is separated into four phases: lesson design, lesson authoring, lesson testing and lesson documentation. It is hoped that by using this model from beginning to end, teachers will be rewarded for their time and effort with lesson products that can be used over time with students with learning difficulties.

1 Introduction

The diffusion of New Information Technology (NIT) in an ever increasing number of sectors of human activity within society, including education, special education, science and technology, as well as the workplace has shown the usefulness and effectiveness of NIT, and also its potential as an agent of change. In the educational environments this has yielded a vast amount of software packages aimed at supporting student's learning. As Flake, McClintock and Turner in [9] note, "The quantity of educational software, in particular, varies because most programmers who have produced educational software are without a conceptual background of instructional design".

The prospect of computer applications for children with learning difficulties is an exciting area, with great potential, but it is an area of research just beginning to be explored. There are many software packages available to the special teacher for teaching specific skills. Guidelines and sources of knowledge about selecting quality software are limited. Thus, many teachers experience frustration after purchasing poorly designed software packages which fail to help students achieve the desired learning outcome [21]. Some checklists use terms that are too technical for special teachers; some are disorganised and hard to follow; and some are too simplified to handle the wide array of software now on the market. None of the rating systems now available are systematic, comprehensive, and easy-to-use by special teachers. More importantly, existing evaluation scales do not have adequate self-instructional training to aid the user becoming a proficient software critic [25].

As teachers gain aptitude with computers in special classrooms, many become interested in creating CAI lessons, referred to as 'courseware' to input their own content and modify program presentation features to meet local needs and seek advice about methods and media for use in such a project. Anyone who has ever developed a piece of CAI software knows that such an activity is a major undertaking, and decisions about which tools to use in the production of the program are crucial.

Software to help special teachers write their own instructional CAI program is available in the form of **authoring software**. There are a number of different types of authoring software however, and there is a great deal of confusion about the capabilities and purposes related to each of these. We have considered the advantages and disadvantages of each type and have examined factors such as ease of learning, ease and speed of use, power and efficiency, and support of various instructional strategies. Based on this analysis we advocate the use of those authoring systems which, basically, require no programming ability on the part of the user or author, and provide a lesson shell structure into which special teachers enter their own content. Additionally, technological and cognitive considerations are given for selection among different level of authoring systems.

Having selected an authoring tool special teachers have to face the process of developing CAI lessons. This process consists of four separate but related phases: 1) the design and creation of the instructional text (lesson design); 2) the development of the computer code so that the text might be offered via microcomputer (lesson authoring); 3) the testing of the designed lesson; and 4) the courseware documentation. A planning model that can guide the development of both CAI lesson design and lesson authoring is given. By using a systematic design approach from beginning to end, special teachers will be rewarded for their time and effort with lesson products that can be used over time with multiple learners.

2   Computer-Assisted Instruction in Special Education

There are many different and varied reasons why CAI has been used for students with special needs. Hogg in [16], listed the following features which are associated with students with learning difficulties (LD): a) difficulty making and extending associations; b) restricted ability to interpret abstractions; c) lack of intellectual curiosity; d) inability to generalise from observations; e) short attention span; and f) impoverished sensory perceptions.

According to Conners et al in [5] CAI is used because it can provide: 1) individualisation; 2) motivation; and 3) active learning. There are also indirect advantages to using computers. For example generating programs for computers provides an opportunity to examine teaching materials in depth [10].

There are conflicting views concerning the effectiveness of CAI in Education. Several authors have commented that CAI is most effective when it is used to supplement traditional teaching methods rather than when it is used to replace it [23], [5]. According to Rude-Parkins (1983) the studies evaluating CAI are not unanimously favourable. Edwards et al in [6] say that in a review of the literature 45% of research studies are in favour of CAI, 40% find no difference between traditional and CAI methods of teaching and 5% produced mixed results.

The available software is generally of disappointing quality and the use of research-based components of instructional design and of the capabilities of microcomputers for colour, sound, and graphics is frequently lacking. The features of sound and colour may also be used inappropriately as Goldman and Pellegrino in [13] explain: 'Software packages that feature bells and whistles when students give wrong answers create at least two negative conditions: 1) they draw attention to the students and the activity becomes a punishing rather than a non-punishing environment; 2) students may prefer the consequences for incorrect responding more than those for correct. The software ends up motivating the student to respond incorrectly rather than correctly'. Often the software is not age appropriate and according to Ridge in [22] the age group of 16 years and over is being neglected. He advocated that the software used by young adults should be specifically designed for them.

Now that there is a wide range of software available to teachers of students with learning difficulties, it would be helpful if they had some criteria for determining in advance which CAI systems would be most effective for teaching specific knowledge, skills and concepts to particular individual student. Although the teacher may have some choice in selecting hardware and software for particular teaching purposes, at present there is little available research which would help with the selection of CAI systems to suit particular children.

3 Authoring techniques for writing CAI lessons

There are three categories of techniques used to help produce CAI lessons. These are: (a) **traditional programming languages**; (b) **authoring languages**; and (c) **authoring systems**.

The term **traditional programming languages** refers to the development of courseware through the use of programming languages, such as Basic, Fortran, C, Pascal and so on.

The term **authoring languages** refers to a high-level computer language (similar in nature to the language of traditional programming) that enables the easy construction of courseware for use in an instructional environment [2]. An authoring language is enriched with simple commands supporting procedures typically needed for courseware development, such as presenting text, judging the accuracy of students' responses, presenting feedback, and maintaining students' records and a list of multiple-choice and 'essay' questions. The developer using an authoring language must construct the courseware by writing computer code. Sophisticated authoring languages like IPS, PILOT, MICROTEXT, COURSEWARE, TUTOR and STAF are commonly used over the past years.

The term **authoring systems** refers to a development environment which is much more restricted than the systems described above. It is a program or a set of programs which allow an instructor or instructional developer (teacher) to create courseware without programming. The teacher specifies the content to be taught and usually the instructional logic or strategy to be used. The authoring system automatically generates the debugged code which corresponds to these specifications[17].

In general, authoring systems are easier to use than authoring languages and, in turn, authoring languages are easier to use than traditional programming languages. However, traditional programming languages are usually more powerful and more efficient in their use of the microcomputer's capabilities than the authoring languages. Authoring languages, in turn, are usually more efficient and powerful than authoring systems.

The importance of these differences depends on the circumstances surrounding the development of CAI lessons. If limited time is available for CAI lesson development or the developers are naive in regard to computer programming, then he/she has to know that the more powerful the software, the more difficult and time consuming it will be.

Although very powerful, traditional programming languages such as Basic, or Fortran are so difficult that most teachers do not use them, unless they simply enjoy programming. Authoring languages will suit more teachers than will traditional programming languages, since they retain a good deal of power and flexibility while simplifying the programming task. However, teachers who choose an authoring language will still need programming aptitude and expertise, and will still find lesson development to be quite complex and time-consuming.

Authoring systems is a third choice. Such systems provide prompts for the teacher, usually making use of menus. The teacher fills in the content to be presented in response to the software prompts. Authoring systems are much easier and faster to use than are traditional programming languages or authoring languages. Their disadvantage is in their comparative lack of power and flexibility. Many educational decisions are made by the developer of the authoring system, and these decisions may not be to the liking of the teacher. Although this is a serious problem, authoring systems are the developing option that is best for the largest number of teachers.

Although there are considerable differences among authoring systems in terms of what they are capable of doing, they can be grouped into three primary categories [15]: 1) First-level authoring systems, which support the development of CAI lessons that are primarily drill and practice; 2) Second-level authoring systems, which support the development of CAI lessons that are more tutorial in nature; and 3) Third-level authoring systems, which support the development of CAI lessons based on a cognitive orientation to instruction, allowing learners to have a more active role in sequencing instructional content and selecting from a variety on instructional displays [20].

4 Selecting an Authoring system

Much current work focusses on the development of more sophisticated authoring systems [7]. Some authoring systems, such as HyperCard [11], are being enhanced and becoming more powerful, so that most instructional features can be included in CAI lessons. These authoring systems are capable of supporting a wide variety of instructional displays and place fewer restrictions on the instructional logic[19]. These authoring systems take advantage of more hardware options including synthesised speech, higher resolution graphics, and touch screens. Some of them provide a lesson shell structure (courseware generator) into which special teachers enter their own content. In this paper we will only be considering authoring systems that offer this facility.

Authoring system selection is an evaluation process involving description and judgement. Selection should be undertaken on the basis of local needs and, generally authoring systems will be needed if a substantial amount of courseware development is to be done by persons lacking programming skills, time, or interest. However, the identification of local needs should be more specific, since the focus of the selection effort will be to find one or more systems that match them [18].

There are several problems peculiar to authoring system evaluation. When researchers began investigating the technology in 1984, they were aware of half a dozen systems. A few years later, over sixty have been identified and undoubtedly more will appear. Their quicksilver nature makes selection especially difficult, since new systems often have innovative features and existing ones change constantly. In addition, selection is complicated because systems must be judged by their capabilities as authoring tools and by the products they produce. As more intelligent programs or those based on new learning theories appear, another generation of authoring tools will emerge [1]. While both such systems might not exactly fit existing criteria, most can be presumed to apply. In fact the criteria are probably more stable than the technology.

4.1 Selection criteria

There are technological and cognitive considerations in the selection of the authoring systems proposed. These considerations fall into the following categories:

1. authoring environment (hardware requirements, training requirements, and ease of use);
2. lesson content creation (text, graphic, and sound);
3. lesson definition (structure of lessons, display strategies, student response processing, and branching sequences); and

4. course management (student management, scoring data, summary information or student performance).

The criteria given above are not exhaustive and are not all likely to be universally applicable but they hopefully illustrate the range of factors that need to be considered when investigating authoring systems. Any reasonably objective assessment will involve setting up a rating sheet so that each authoring system under consideration can be evaluated against established criteria. It may then be necessary to assess the different criteria to reflect the relative importance of each.

To illustrate the point a subset of the above criteria is used to examine some of the features in which two authoring systems, ToolBook and HyperCard 2.0 differ.

- Graphics: The most common types of graphic images are bitmapped (paint) graphics and object-oriented (draw) graphics. Using HyperCard, developers can create and edit bitmapped graphics using the paint tools provided, but there is no provision for creating or manipulating object-oriented graphics. In ToolBook, as there are no paint tools, bitmapped graphics must be created in other paint programs and imported into ToolBook. However, ToolBook does support the creation and editing of draw objects. It is generally desirable to use draw graphics rather than paint graphics, since it uses less space.
- User Interface: In HyperCard there are five levels of interaction (browsing, typing, authoring, painting and scripting). In ToolBook there are two (reader and author) which makes it easier for the user.
- Printing: HyperCard's printing capabilites are much more powerful than those in ToolBook.
- Other differences:
  - In ToolBook commands to control keyboard input are available. In HyperCard external commands have to be used to obtain the same results.
  - In ToolBook, all objects can be in colour, including fields and buttons. HyperCard 2.0 only supports colour graphics displayed in additional viewing windows which are manipulated by external programming commands.
  - Additional memory is also required to display HyperCard's colour graphics.

5 Development of CAI Lesson

To produce quality CAI lessons, competence is needed in the subject matter, skill with an authoring program, and knowledge of systematic instructional design [24]. While most guidelines espouse a systematic approach to courseware design, the successful designer often depends as much on personal experience and intuition as she/he does on any systematic approach. This occurs because: a) we do not have a clear concept of the uniqueness of the computer-assisted learning experience or of the computer as a medium; b) instructional systems design principles do not map easily or directly into CAI; c) learning theories and research do not always produce obvious principles for practice. Most novice authors of courseware understand neither the planning time nor the process required for creating CAI materials. Because the tools offered by authoring programs have specified the process of development, the complexity of design can easily be overlooked [14]. Estimates for developing interactive CAI materials range from 15 to 400 hours, depending on their type and complexity [3]. Experienced developers suggest that between 60% and 80% of courseware development is taken up in planning time [24].

A variety of formal instructional design and development (IDD) models exist that are based on the systems approach suggested by Gagne and Briggs in [12]. An effective approach for the special teacher is to adapt an IDD model and systematically implement the steps of pre-planning, designing, authoring, testing and revising as the courseware product is developed. The Courseware Authoring Process (CAP) model illustrates this sequence [8]. In this paper an alternative approach to creating effective CAI courseware for special students is proposed.

5.1 Authoring Courseware Development Model

The research on CAI has demonstrated that the use of microcomputers does not necessarily enhance the quality of the instructional text [4]. Therefore it is important to consider what factors might enhance CAI lessons. Although these factors are involved in the design of CAI lessons, they have implications for authoring.

Based on the characteristics which are bound to the CAP , the proposed Authoring Courseware Development Model (ACDM) (see Fig. 1.) consists of four separate but related phases:

1. the design and creation of the instructional text;
2. the development of the computer code so that the text might be offered via microcomputer; and
3. the testing of the designed lesson and
4. the courseware documentation.

The first phase is called "lesson design"; the second phase is called "lesson authoring"; the third phase is called "lesson testing"; and the last phase is called "lesson documentation". When carefully and appropriately designed instructional text is turned into CAI lessons the results are usually encouraging. It seems a truism that the quality of the final CAI lesson is more a function of lesson design than lesson authoring or lesson testing or lesson documentation.

In the "lesson design" phase the teacher has to provide the exact plan for how the lesson will operate by giving the: a)definition of target population; b) goals for the program; c)organisation and orientation of content toward objectives; d) definition of prerequisite skills; e) appropriateness of the content for intended users; f) presentation of the content; g) effectiveness and appropriateness of the

A C D M

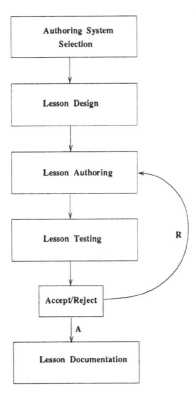

Fig. 1. Authoring Courseware Development Model

feedback (confirmational, motivational, instructional); and h) learners interaction with the program.

In the "lesson authoring" phase the teacher has to: a) select an authoring system and learn the mechanics of using an authoring system; b) learn the use of the courseware generator (editing existing activities and writing new activities) as part of the database courseware program; and c) begin creating the lesson (assessment activities).

In the "lesson testing" phase the teacher has to prepare a pilot test (a peer review process followed by a pilot-tested with students) to find out whether or not the lesson works as intended.

If the lesson does not work smoothly the teacher has to search for another authoring system and she/he has to restart from the "lesson authoring" phase, otherwise she/he can proceed to the next phase, -the "lesson documentation" phase-, where the courseware should be considered complete and she/he has to write a courseware documentation including: a) description of the objectives and content; b) users groups; c)prerequisite skills; d) implementation guidelines; and d) supportive materials.

After all the phases are completed the system is ready for use.

6 Conclusions

Powerful authoring systems, which provide customised courseware generators, offer special educators the means to create CAI lessons to fit student needs. Developing a courseware requires curriculum expertise, skills with an authoring system and knowledge of CAI design. Using the Authoring Courseware Development Model (ACDM) to guide the development process we hope to improve the efficiency and quality of the final product and increase significantly the cost-effectiveness of courseware development.

References

1. Allen, M.A.: A new approach to authoring CBE courseware. Paper presented at the Sixth Interservice/Industry Training Equipment Conference Washington D.C. (1984)
2. Barker, P.G., Singh, R.: Authoring languages for computer-based learning. British Journal of Educational Technology 13(3) (1982) 167–196.
3. Barron, A.: Instructional design for computer-based instruction. Paper presented at a faculty workshop West Virginia University Morgantown (1990)
4. Clark, M.M.: Educational Technology and children with moderate learning difficulties. Exceptional Child 33(10) (1986) 28–34
5. Conners, F.A., Caruso, D.R., Detterman, D.K.: Computer-assisted instruction for the mentally retarded. In: N.R. Ellis, N.W. Bray (eds.): International Review of research in mental retardation. Academic Press Inc New York XIV (1986) 105–134
6. Edwards, J., Norton, S., Taylor, S., Weiss, M., Dusseldorp, R.: How effective is CAI? A review of the research. Educational Leadership 22 (1975) 25–34.
7. Fairweather, P.G., O'Neal, A.F.: The impact of advanced authoring systems on CAI productivity. Journal of Computer-Based Instruction 11(3) (1984) 90–94.
8. Fitzerald, G.: Authoring systems for higher education. Postdoctoral training session presented at CEC Project Retool. New York: Long Island University (1989)
9. Flake, J.L., McClintock, C.E., Turner, S.V.: Fundamentals of Computer Education. Belmont, CA: Wadsworth Publishing (1985)
10. Fleischner, K., Nuzum, M.B., Marzola, E.S.: Devising an instructional program to teach arithmetic problem-solving skills to students with learning disabilities. Journal of Learning Disabilities 20(4) (1987) 214–217
11. Friedler, Y., Shabo, A.: Using the HyperCard Program to Develop a customised courseware generator for school use. Educational Technology (1989) 47–51
12. Gagne, R.M., Briggs, L.J.: Principles of instructional design. New York: Holt, Rinehart, and Winston (1979)
13. Goldman, S.R., Pellegrino, J.L.: Microcomputer: Effective Drill and Practice. Academic Therapy 22(2) (1986) 133–140
14. Hannafin, K., Mitzel, H.: CBI authoring tools in postsecondary institutions: A review and critical examination. Computers and Education 14(3) (1990) 197–204

15. Hannum, W.H.: Techniques for creating Computer-Based Instructional Text: Programming Languages, Authoring Languages, and Authoring Systems. Educational Psychologist **21**(4) (1986) 293–314

16. Hogg, B.: Microcomputers in special needs: A guide to good practice. National Council for Special Education 1 Wood Str. Stafford Upon Avon CV37 6JE (1984)

17. Kearsley, G.P.: Authoring systems in computer-based education. Communications of ACM **25**(7) (1982) 429–437

18. Locatis, C.N., Carr, V.H.: Selecting authoring systems. Journal of Computer-Based Instruction **12**(2) (1985) 28–33

19. Locatis, C.N., Carr, V.H.: Authoring systems and assumptions about them. Journal of Biomedical Communication **13**(2) (1986) 4–9

20. Merrill, M.D., Wood, L.: Computer guided instructional design. Journal of Computer-Based Instruction **11**(2) (1984) 60–63

21. Preece, J.: Selecting CAL Packages: Helping teachers to recognise quality software. Computer Technology (1984) 20–21

22. Ridge, V.: Computers in Special Education. Teaching and Training **24**(2/3) (1986) 216–230

23. Rude-Parkins, C.: Microcomputer and learning disabled adolescents. The Pointer **27**(4) (1983) 14–19

24. Sampath, S., Quaine, A.: Effective interface tools for CAI authors. Journal of Computer-Based Instruction **17**(1) (1990) 31–34

25. Wright, E.B., Forcier, R.C.: The Computer: A Tool for the Teacher. Belmont, CA: Wadworth Publishing (1985)

Radio Computer Communications Network for DisABLED People

András Arató, Teréz Vaspöri

KFKI Research Institute for Measurement
and Computing Techniques

Abstract. Communication is essential for people with all kinds of disabilities. Blind people can access more information, deaf people can have conversation with others, mobility impaired people can also access information easier. What to do in a country like Hungary which has a shortage of telephone lines? This article describes a possible solution through extending two-way radio to the internet.

1 The Importance of Computer Communications:

Prof. Norman Coombs a blind history teacher at the Rochester Institute of Technology NY USA made a presentation about telecommunication and education of disabled students at the 2nd ICCHP in Zurich [1]. This meeting played an important role in modifying our activity in the development of assistive devices. Our BraiLab talking computers [2] can be used more effectively by blind users if they have communication facilities. During a short visit of prof. Coombs in Hungary in 1993 we demonstrated the usefulness of computer communication not only for blind people but also for the community of deaf and mobility impaired people.

Using the BraiLab PC Hungarian visually impaired users can have access to information from the Teletext broadcast of Television. Several data bases are also available on CD-ROM (e.g. Hungarian Laws, Telephone Book) with special application environment of the intelligent BraiLab screen reader program. Many data bases are accessible only via internet. A late development of talking telex could have helped blind people but the use of telex is decreasing in Hungary too.

Deaf people in Hungary use only text telephones as electronic communication devices. The level of education of hearing impaired persons is rather low unfortunately. This is not due to their intelligence level but due to our limited possibilities. We hope that if we will use computer communication for education it will help greatly.

Mobility impaired people have already been using computers for their rehabilitation. There were organized working places for data entry. Only floppy disks are used for "data transfer".

A normal way for connecting users to network resources would be telephone modems. Unfortunately there is a shortage of telephone lines in Hungary so you often have no phone line for voice transmission to say nothing about data transfer. To overcome this situation we decided to build a radio communications network.

2 The Center for Disabled Students Services

Prof. Laszlo Varga initiated the education of visually and mobility impaired students at the Budapest Eotvos Lorand University from the 80s till the present. He is the head of the Computer Science department of the Faculty of Natural Sciences.

Digital Equipment Corporation helped to build a computer center for blind students with its European Contributions Program. A VAX computer is the main resource while 7 PC-s equipped with DECtalk speech synthesizers serve as terminals. All computers are connected to the Ethernet of the University. From the University Local Area Network there is an access to the internet too. This University center will serve as the nucleus of radio communications network for disabled students.

Blind users have already learned how to access the internet with Telnet, FTP (File Transfer Protocol), Finger, Ping etc. They enjoy it very much. There is a Braillo braille printer with Hungarian braille publishing system and the Recognita OCR for their services [3]. As all the students have their own PC-s with BraiLab PC talking adapters they would like to have access to network facilities from home.

3 The Packet Radio Principle

The authors of this article are radio amateurs (our callsigns are HG5BDU and HG5BDR) so we are familiar with AX25 packet radio techniques. Packet radio was first created by Vancouver amateurs in Canada. They used fixed addressing of possible 256 different stations. American amateurs built the AX25 standard with extended addressing and similar features to X25 packet switching standards. Callsigns are used for station addresses. There is also the possibility to use several callsigns for designating packet repeaters showing the route in the header.

Later special node software was developed (NET/ROM, TheNet Node) for the 3rd level of ISO OSI model. Protocols are implemented in 8 bit computer codes mostly for Z80 microprocessor so devices are very cheap. A typical packet radio terminal consists of a PC, Terminal Node Controller (TNC), radio transceiver and antenna. The TNC is an intelligent modem containing the AX25 protocol implementation and the modem hardware. TNC does the packet assembling disassembling so it is actually a PAD for AX25.

The most commonly used modem is 1200 baud Audio Frequency Shift Keying (AFSK) which is a standard used in telephony. For higher speeds Frequency Shift Keying (FSK) is used. AFSK modems can be plugged in the speaker and microphone connectors of the radio while FSK requires special plugs for modulator and demodulator of VHF or UHF FM transceivers.

A milestone occurred in packet radio development when Phil Karn developed his first TCP/IP software for personal computers and AX25 in 1989. His callsign is well known not only among radio amateurs but at universities too. The Technical University of Vienna also used KA9Q tcp/ip package for their routing purposes. This software is free for educational and amateur use. There are several variants of this software. Descriptions will be found further in this article.

Edwin Brownrigg and Dewayne Hendricks made a packet radio demo in Budapest in the buildings of the Hungarian Academy of Sciences in October 6, 1992. The goal of the Budapest project was to demonstrate the technical feasibility of using packet radio as an interface to the Internet, thus establishing the potential for low cost international connectivity for the Central European Agricultural Libraries. Unfortunately the authors of this paper did not know about this demo at that time.

4 The First Experimental Radio Network in KFKI

A PC gateway has been set up in KFKI research center since March 1990. This firs gateway could be crossed only from radio side to Ethernet. A radio amateur software SP (made by S. Kluger DL1MEN) was modified to accept special command implementing CTERM protocol for DECnet. CTERM is a remote terminal protocol in Digital's network. The //KFKI command contained the DECnet hostname, accountname and password for connecting to the proper host.

The schematic diagram of the KFKI radio Ethernet gateway experiment looks like:

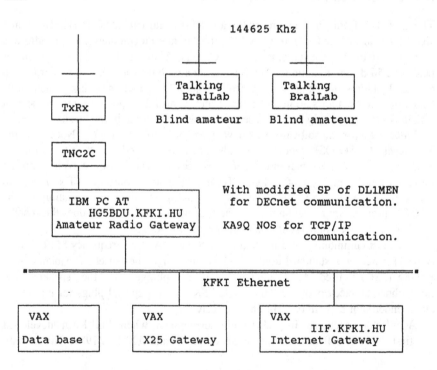

After internet connections were established the SP software was changed to KA9Q. At present the so called JNOS version of gateway software is running. The developer of this version is Johan K. Reinalda (WG7J/PA3DIS). The features of this Gateway and Bulletin Board System (BBS) are very rich. You can go not only from the radio side to the internet and vice versa but it is a full service amateur BBS with internet Simple Mail Transfer Protocol (SMTP), Network News Transfer Protocol (NNTP), FTP, Post Office Protocol (POP) etc.

JNOS can serve as a router from and to the radio side and the mail gateway too. JNOS is developed from KA9Q NOS (Network Operating System) [4]. NOS means that all client and service processes are handled by an operating system under MS-DOS. From radio side you can use simple AX25 protocol or TCP/IP protocol. TCP/IP can be routed through existing AX25 VHF/UHF radio networks. With AXIP protocol, the internet is transparent for the AX25 and for TheNet protocol. When KA9Q is working in a PC, there is a very simple protocol is loaded in the TNC (KISS Keep It Simple Stupid). AX25 protocol implementation is written in C in NOS.

The amateur society has the large A class 44.x.x.x internet address. This is a very special network which is distributed all over the world. Therefor a special routing called encapsulating is developed for routing 44.x.x.x addresses. The whole internet is viewed as transparent network for the 44.x.x.x addresses.

There was a unique feature developed for NOS: the Converse. All gateway systems form a large on line conference network. They use the converse protocol for exchanging lines all over the world. If you can not meet your partner on line you can of course write letters, bulletins or network news.

5 The Plan of the Full Duplex Radio Network

As a next step we would like to build a PR radio network using a simplex 9600 baud radio channel. The KFKI research center is on the top of a 500 meter high hill in Csilleberc. It can be reached from the hill. As the number of users grows, we should change the simplex channel to full-duplex one. We will use G3RUH's 9600 baud FSK modem for full-duplex operation.

For this solution two 25 KHZ step channel is required for the radio communication. We would gladly widen this network for other countries, where handicapped persons need computer communications as an equalizer factor in their learning. We have experimented with NOS in radio amateur band. The Hungarian Ministry of Transport and Communications promised a free channel for blind people in the professional band. We do hope that later we can realize the usefulness of our proved technique for the wider handicapped user community.

Why full-duplex operation is so important? The answer is in the "hidden transmitter" phenomenon. On simplex channel station A sends a packet for B, addressed to C, B decodes the packet and hands it on to C on the same radio channel. The disadvantages are that each retransmission after collision by the repeater station B blocks the single radio channel. Also, A and C and perhaps other stations on the channel cannot hear each other's transmissions. As a result, their packet may collide and get lost. All this affects the throughput. Networks based on single radio channel digipeaters are a waste of time, especially when one expects heavy traffic.

In regenerating repeaters the data signal is decoded into a bit stream, which get immediately re-encoded and retransmitted on another frequency. Good regenerating repeaters also regenerate the TX clock, i.e., the rate at which the bits come in. This permits a near-perfect output signal stripped of almost all noise. If the packet was decodable at the repeater site, it will almost certainly be decodable at its destination as well [6].

User stations work in half-duplex mode with shifted frequencies for transmitting and receiving. All stations have to be compatible only with the central repeater station and can use directional antennas still they can detect a carrier from every station for proper CSMA mode of operation (Carrier Sensing Multiple Access).

Terminals of the system in KFKI will use 434.200 MHZ for receiving and 432.600 MHZ for transmitting. This 1.6 MHZ shift is rather small so special filters and separate antennas have to be used at the full duplex repeater.

The system schematics diagram with full duplex repeater will look like:

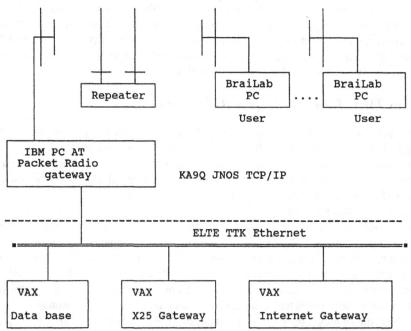

Users of this system will be able to reach packet radio gateway as BBS with Telnet function or as a mail gateway with SMTP. They will be able to use internet sources from their transportable radio terminals equipped with small directional antennas even from home or from anywhere in the town. This will be a small step towards personal communication. Ten packet radio tcp/ip terminals will be given to blind, deaf and mobility impaired radio amateurs to test and learn their new possibilities.

There is an Information Program for Handicapped radio- Amateurs to help in satisfying special needs for people to pass exam and work as HAMs. I.P.H.A. is coordinated by A. Tobbe (PA3 ADR) in the Netherlands.

6 Conclusions

People with disabilities have more need for the digital communications for their studying and integration into the society than able persons. The computer communications and assistive devices equalize them with the able bodied. When you can not use land line cables you can try to use packet radio networks.

Network communication can help in distributing free software, computer documentation, tutorials for the handicapped persons. A blind computer programmer can discuss problems with a deaf colleague in different countries using remote computer conferencing. The amateur radio development in this field could change the life of many handicapped people in Central and Eastern Europe.

7 Acknowledgements

The radio communication project was funded be IIF ˙ program. Assistive devices research was funded by OTKA. Thanks for Norman Coombs for helping to write this article.

Literature

[1] Norman Coombs, Telecommunications, Education and the Handicapped. 2nd ICCHP Zurich 1990. p 51-54.

[2] Andras Arato & Terez Vaspori, Synthetic Speech for the Blind Integrated with Intelligent Screen Reader. 3rd ICCHP Vienna 1992. p 8-13.

[3] A. Arato, P. Molnar, T. Vaspori, Computer Aided Hungarian Contracted Braille. 2nd ICCHP Zurich 1990. p 1-6.

[4] Ian Wade, NOSintro TCP/IP over Packet Radio An Introduction to the KA9Q Network Operating System. Dowermain Ltd. Bedfordshire United Kingdom 1992. p 356.

[5] A. Tobbe Information Programme for Handicapped radio- Amateurs. I.P.H.A. 1990 I.A.R.U. Region 1.

[6] Ulrich Guenther ZL1DDL, 10 Feb 94 06:29:25 GMT From: news-mail-gateway@ucsd.edu

An Investigation of Global Positioning System (GPS) Technology for Disabled People

Paul Blenkhorn, David Gareth Evans and Stephen Pettitt

Technology for Disabled People Unit, Systems Engineering Group,
Department of Computation, UMIST, Manchester, M60 1QD, England.

Abstract. There has been a good deal of both interest and confusion regarding the capabilities and use of the Global Positioning System (GPS) to assist people with disabilities. The confusion has resulted mainly from the uncertainty regarding the resolution of the system in determining the position of a user. The Technology for Disabled People Unit (UMIST) has examined this problem in two ways: by purchasing a GPS development system for field trials; and by undertaking a search of relevant information in an attempt to clarify the situation. This paper reports on the results of these investigations and also highlights potential applications, problems, and, where known, possible solutions.

1   Introduction

The Global Positioning System (GPS) is a radio navigation system with world-wide coverage, originally implemented by the United States military. The specifications of the system were released in 1978, and subsequently a number of commercial systems have been produced. Basically the system gathers information from satellites and delivers an accurate fix of the position of the receiver. As well as its military applications, GPS has proved to be particularly valuable for marine navigation systems where a number of systems are now commercially available [7]. Research interests are also very strong in the area of navigation systems for automated vehicles [8].

The Technology for Disabled People Unit (TDPU) is a research unit in the Computation Department at UMIST that is interested in the use of microelectronic systems to assist people with disabilities. It was thought that GPS could prove to be a valuable 'assistant' to blind people [2][4], providing information on a user's position, and also may prove to be useful for automating systems such as 'intelligent' wheelchairs. During discussions with professionals in the field it became clear that there was a great deal of confusion regarding just how GPS could be used by disabled people especially with regard to the level of positional accuracy. To gain some experience with GPS the TDPU purchased a Rockwell NavCore V [6] and has been undertaking some field trials. At the same time the TDPU has been undertaking a search of relevant literature to determine the current state and future direction of commercially available systems, particularly with respect to their positional accuracy.

2   How does GPS work?

As stated above, the Global Positioning System was originally intended for military use, it consists of 24 satellites (including 3 spares) orbiting in circular 20,200km orbits with a 12 hour period. Each satellite transmits unique location information in the same frequency band (1575MHz) using a spread spectrum technique. To calculate a position on the ground information is required from 4 satellites (or 3 if the altitude of the user is known). Users have a receiver (with aerial) that receives and decodes the signal from each satellite and uses this information to calculate the user's position from a matrix of four simultaneous equations. This requires considerable processing. The derivation of a user's position using 3 satellites is shown in Fig.1. The position of the user is determined were the three wavefronts propagating from each of the satellites intersect.

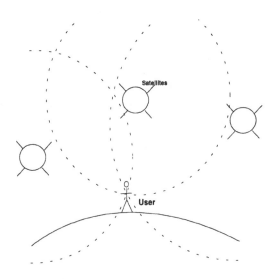

Fig.1. Position of user relative to 3 GPS satellites

Two services are currently provided by GPS: the Standard Positioning Service (SPS) and the Precise Positioning Service (PPS). The PPS is only available to US Department of Defence authorised user. The SPS was made available to all users on a continuous, world-wide basis with no direct charge in a 1983 Presidential Proclamation. The accuracy of SPS is stated by the US Department of Defence as being 100 m for 95% of the time and 300 m for 99% of the time. This level of accuracy is useful for many applications, notably marine navigation. However the PPS is very much more accurate, around 18m. The SPS accuracy is downgraded by adding small, random perturbations to the navigation orbit data and the satellite clock frequency. This added 'noise' reduces the precision with which an SPS derived location can be calculated. The methods by which the noise is applied is highly secret, of course. This is known as Selective Availability and by this technique SPS has lower accuracy than DPS. However, during the Gulf war the lack of sufficient DPS receiving sets caused the removal of Selective Availability. This meant that SPS receivers obtained the higher level of accuracy for a period of time. This is responsible for some of the confusion that surrounds the accuracy of these systems.

There are several factors which can affect the accuracy of a GPS system, namely signal obscuration (i.e. the blocking of the signal from the satellite to the receiver by, for example buildings or natural features), spurious reflections and the fact that the satellites may be decommissioned at will by the US. Within a city, buildings may either obscure and reflect transmission, and, although reflections can be minimised by suitable choice of more directional aerials, in the general case signal obscuration is potentially much more serious.

3   How can the accuracy be improved?

A relatively simple way to remove the effects of Selective Availability is to use a fixed receiver at a known position. From a known position the perturbations added to the satellite data can be determined and transmitted to the mobile receivers which can then apply the corrections to their own GPS calculations (see Fig.2). This system is known as Differential GPS and the accuracy is reported to be 5 to 10 m although some claim better encoding of the difference information might increase this to 2.6 m [3]. Note that the user requires two receivers, one for the GPS signals, and the second for the differential information from the fixed receiver.

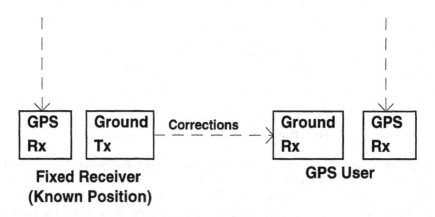

Fig. 2. The Configuration for Differential GPS

The US Coast Guard has a programme, due for completion in 1996, implementing a Differential GPS by adding the difference signal to its existing marine radio beacons operating on the Longwave band. These marine transmitters have various ranges - typically 125 Nautical Miles (approximately 230 Km), and are intended to aid shipping in the Great Lakes area and the coastal areas of the USA., however, they can be received inland. The US. Coast Guard has liaised with the International Association of Lighthouse Authorities (IALA) to provide a uniform system world-wide and some implementation has taken place in Europe [1]. If this system is further implemented 5 to 10 m accuracy positioning may be achieved by land based users in coastal districts.

A further improvement in accuracy has been claimed by determining the phases of the carrier signal [5]. The carrier frequency of the satellites is about 1.5 GHz, a wavelength of about 200 mm. It is possible to determine the phase of this carrier wave and hence ascertain position to this resolution; accuracy of 1 cm + 1 mm for each kilometre of separation between the two receivers can be obtained. However, this requires considerable processing power and, using current technology, takes 10 minutes to compute the result.

During periods of signal loss from whatever cause, dead-reckoning may be used by using only the last received data from the GPS system, since both course and speed can be determined from two consecutive readings. Information for dead reckoning can be augmented by a compass to provide directional information, although magnetic compasses can be affected by geological magnetic anomalies or man-made anomalies such as large buildings or buses. These disadvantages could possibly be overcome by using gyroscopic compasses, but these are not absolute devices and thus require frequent calibration. Similarly, the use of accelerometers can provide data for dead-reckoning, but since their outputs must be integrated to obtain the new position, errors are also integrated. The use of such techniques is application dependent, subject to safety and accuracy requirements.

4   Potential of GPS technology for people with disabilities

There are two groups of disabled people for whom it is thought that GPS technology can be of assistance, namely blind people and wheelchair users. In the case of blind people it should be made clear that the use of GPS is to be considered very much as an assistant to the current methods of navigation using a combination of cane, guide dog and tactile maps. The detailed requirements of such systems for blind have been discussed elsewhere [4], however, in short there are requirements for the blind person: to find out their current position; to be given routing information and advice; and to have the information presented in a suitable manner, whether this be tactile, or acoustic, whilst they are moving around.

The use of the system for wheelchair users would be to enhance existing 'intelligent wheelchairs' so that they could be told where to take a user, and then be left to get on with it. In this case there are clearly issues to do with the safety critical aspects of the system, particularly with respect to obstacles. In addition it is clear that the resolution of the positioning is critical, even though it can be aided by dead-reckoning of the wheelchair's movement.

In both cases the GPS system needs to be complemented by an electronic encoding of a map from which suitable position and routing information can be determined, and, of course, the system needs to be small enough to be wheelchair mounted, or carried by a blind person.

It should be noted that the accuracy of the GPS system plays a major role in determining the potential usefulness for disabled people. If we consider such a system for blind people, it is clear that a resolution of 100m would permit a user to know the area of the country and town where they are located, and in which direction they are heading. However such a level of accuracy is insufficient to determine which street or road they are travelling along. A resolution of 10m would, in many cases, permit a user to know the street or road name but not the side of the road they were on. It is considered vital that GPS systems for disabled people clearly identify which mobility needs they are attempting to address, and how they deal with the issues relating to accuracy.

5   GPS accuracy on the UMIST campus

An experiment has been undertaken to investigate the accuracy of a GPS system in a built up area, particularly with respect to see if the position deterioration (due to Selective Availability) could be reduced. The experiment was undertaken on the UMIST campus which has a number of multi-storey buildings as can be seen in Fig.3.

On a number separate occasions during a six hour period, sets of sixty readings were taken at each of three sites on the UMIST campus: on the benches to the front of the main building, from the corner of a roof on top of a multi-storey car park at the side of the campus, and on the lawn between the Ferranti Building and the Maths and Social Sciences Building.

The results support the accuracy level predicted in the GPS specification. Whilst the sixty readings in each set were clustered closely together indicating in the short term (around 2 minutes) a stable signal, the sets of readings taken at different times differed by up to 100m. This limited testing on the campus also showed that despite the large numbers of multi-storey buildings satellite visibility was generally good and signal loss due to signal obscuration was rare.

6   Concluding remarks

The Global Positioning System offers great potential to assist disabled people in the area of orientation and mobility. Although there is considerable interest in GPS perhaps the greatest obstacle to it becoming available to disabled users will be the cost. However, the hope is that with the considerable interest in GPS for automated vehicles and cars that the GPS hardware will become a commodity device and hence low cost.

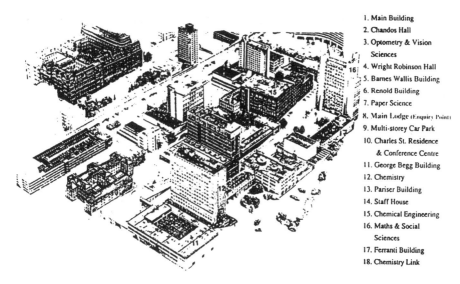

1. Main Building
2. Chandos Hall
3. Optometry & Vision Sciences
4. Wright Robinson Hall
5. Barnes Wallis Building
6. Renold Building
7. Paper Science
8. Main Lodge (Enquiry Point)
9. Multi-storey Car Park
10. Charles St. Residence & Conference Centre
11. George Begg Building
12. Chemistry
13. Pariser Building
14. Staff House
15. Chemical Engineering
16. Maths & Social Sciences
17. Ferranti Building
18. Chemistry Link

Fig. 3.. The UMIST campus

7 Acknowledgements

The authors would like to acknowledge the work of Sartaaj Rihal who has developed a prototype evaluation system as part of his undergraduate degree in Software Engineering from the Department of Computation at UMIST. He has contributed greatly to the practical evaluation of GPS.

This project has been carried out within the Technology for Disabled People Unit at UMIST. The authors would like to acknowledge the grant funding for this unit by both The Guide Dogs for the Blind Association and the UMIST Millennium Fund.

References

1. D.H. Alsip, J.M. Butler, J.T. Radice: The Coast Guard's Differential GPS Programme. Journal of Navigation, 46, 78-94 (1993)
2. D.A. Brusningham, M.G. Strauss, J.M. Floyd, B.C. Wheeler: Orientation Aid Implementing the Global Positioning System. In: Proceedings of the Fifteenth Annual Northeast Bioengineering Conference, 1989, pp. 27-28, 33-34
3. P.K. Enge: Forward Error Correction for Radiobeacon Broadcast of Differential GPS Data. IEEE Transactions on Aerospace and Electronic Systems, 29, 223-232 (1992)
4. R.G. Golledge, J.M. Loomis, R.L. Klatzky, A. Flury, X. L. Yang: Designing a personal guidance system to aid navigation without sight: progress on the GIS component. Int. J. Geographical Information Systems, 5, 373-395 (1991)

5. P. Mattos The GPS Message on the Hardware Platform. Electronics and Wireless World, February, 146-151 (1993)

6. NavCore ® V Global Positioning System Receiver Engine for High-Volume OEMs and System Integrators, Operations Manual. Rockwell International, (1992)

7. S. Parry: Flexible Transputer based satellite positioning sytem. New Electronics on Campus, Summer, 20-22 (1992)

8. D.H.M. Reekie, E.R. Case, J. Tsai, J. (eds.): Vehicle Navigation and Information Systems. Conference Record of Papers presented at the First Vehicle Navigation and Information Systems Conference (VNIS '89), Torronto Ontario, Canada, Sept. 11-13, 1989.

TeleCommunity
Telecommunication for Persons with Mental Retardation - A Swedish Perspective

Jane Brodin

Department of Education, Stockholm University
S-106 91 Stockholm, Sweden.

Abstract. A study of the use of telecommunications for persons with moderate mental retardation has revealed that videotelephony may provide possibilities of participation in society and social life for persons with special needs. The Swedish ACE (Advanced Communications Experiments) is part of the European project TeleCommunity and based on data collected from a minitrial with two participants, and background information, questionnaires, interviews and observations with 24 adults with moderate mental retardation living in group homes. The results show that the effects of the impairments can be diminished, that communication and independence increase and that the quality of life may increase by using a videotelephone which is based on both visual and auditory impressions.

I Introduction

The goal of the Swedish handicap policy is to avoid special solutions for people with disabilities as far as possible and instead make society as a whole accessible to all citizens. New technology offers many possibilities to facilitate daily life and to offer opportunities for development and independence provided that the technology is adapted to the persons with disabilities and made available. The goals are equality, participation, mutuality and communication, and the keywords are integration and normalization.

Most people consider it as natural to be able to participate in different activities in society and to use facilities offered. To have access to TV and to be able to use telecommunications are basic needs today. Most people regard it as impossible to live without having access to a telephone and today telefax machines are used not only at working sites, but also as a possible way to use telecommunications in private homes. In the near future, different telecommunication modes will be accessible to persons with disabilities, and telecommunication will be a natural part of daily life for all. Studies have revealed that still picture telephones and telefax machines can be used as support in communication for persons with different kinds of disabilities [1, 3, 6, 7, 8]. Persons who have never been able to communicate via an ordinary telephone have thus been able to send messages with different kinds of symbols to friends, parents and staff via the telenetwork.

Persons with mental retardation are individuals in need of special support for their daily living. In order to have access to ordinary services in the community and to be able to participate in social activities at 'normal' living conditions, people with mental retardation somtimes require more support than other groups of disabled persons due to intellectual, cognitive, motor and social factors, as well as the comprehension of additional disabilities. Mental retardation is an intellectual disability caused by a brain damage at an early developmental stage and it has no connection with mental illness. About 70% of this population also have multiple disabilities as motor disability, language and/or communication disorder, visual impairment and epilepsy, in addition to the mental retardation, which makes the situation extremely complex.

In Sweden the most commonly used graphic symbol system among persons with mental retardation is the Pictogram system. This symbol system is an augmentative and alternative way of communication and consists of about 650 symbols in white on a black background. The system is used mainly by persons with non-verbal communication and to support communication in persons with poorly developed spoken language.

However, technical development seems to proceed more and more rapidly, not least within the telecommunication area. During the eighties a number of devices that facilitate communication have been introduced on the market e.g. automatic dialling and loudspeaking telephones. Three studies with still picture telephones for persons with moderate mental retardation, with profound mental retardation and with traumatic brain damages [3, 5] and one study with telex communication [2] were effected and make the basis for the Swedish minitrial and ACE (Advanced Communications Experiments) in the European project TeleCommunity. The results from these studies revealed that the frequency of use and the motivation and involvement increased, the ability to take initiatives increased, and the pictures transmitted became more relevant and functional over time. The still picture telephones also increased the possibilities to establish and develop social contacts.

Nine countries are involved in TeleCommunity, RACE 2033 (Research in Advanced Communications Technologies in Europe). The areas of disability covered in the study are visually impaired, deaf and hearing impaired, elderly and persons with mental retardation. Ireland, Norway, Portugal and Sweden have projects with participants with mental retardation.

A minitrial with two men with moderate mental retardation was carried through in 1993 [4]. The study focused on user aspects, technical aspects and staff aspects and formed the basis for the main study. The results showed that the quality of sound and image had to be improved, that the participants were positive and interested in using the equipment and that the staff found the task stimulating, but time-consuming, and stressed that the use of the videotelephones was a good support for communication for the participants. The empirical study with the 24 participants with moderate mental retardation (12 women and 12 men) started in March/April 1994 and the data collection will continue till December 31st, 1994.

2 Aims of the Empirical Studies

The overall aim of the studies carried through in the telecommunication area in Sweden has been to find out if children, adolescents and adults with different degrees of mental retardation may benefit from the use of still picture telephones, videotelephony and telefax communication in their daily lives.

The concrete questions were:

- Can transmission of pictures via the telecommunication network stimulate, facilitate and support communication?
- Can communication with pictures on the telenet contribute to increased potential for social contacts?
- Can picture telephones and telefax be considered as individual communcation aids for persons with mental retardation.

The overall aims of the Swedish ACE are:

- to support and establish social relations
- to stimulate and encourage individuals to communicate
- to facilitate, support and improve interaction
- to have access to telecommunications in an ordinary way
- to increase social integration
- to extend the social network.

The main research interest is to study the communicative interaction and the social network for persons with moderate mental retardation. Another interest is to evaluate the user requirements and to investigate the need for support services for this population. The Swedish ACE has a socio-economic as well as an individual and society-oriented approach.

3 Methods

The methods used in TeleCommunity to perform the empirical study are background descriptions of the participants based on information from medical journals, questionnaires, semi-structured interviews with the participants, parents, staff from group homes and staff from day centers, telephone records completed by the staff, and assessment of the communicative ability of the the participants. Individual goal setting has been effected and the degree of goal attainment will be measured at several occasions and over time.

The study is based on a close co-operation between the participants with mental retardation, their parents and staff from group homes and day centers. Different sources and different contexts are used for the data collection.

3.1 Equipment used

The equipment used in the Swedish ACE is a videotelephony equipment, consisting of several different parts. The basis is an IBM compatible multimedia PC-terminal, an industrial type of CCD-camera and a document camera. The videotelephone software is designed for a Window environment. The public ISDN (integrated service digital network) is used for connections between the videotelephones. A microphone and a loudspeaker are included in the audio system. The outgoing audio and video signals are fed directly to the codec, which is a standard H.261 type codec from the Norwegian company Tandberg. The incoming audio signal is fed to the loudspeaker. The incoming and outgoing video signals are both visible on the PC-monitor. The user interface is a 20" colour screen and the modified concept keyboard has a built-in optimal sheet detecting facility. The screen shows the graphic Pictogram symbols received and transmitted during the call. The concept keyboard is used to start and finish calls as well as for the graphic symbol communication. The equipment also includes a camera with a built-in camera switch. A laser printer is included for printing the Pictogram symbols transferred during the call. For the awareness of incoming calls a paging system is used. Every user is equipped with an own tactile receiver.

3.2   Subjects

Six day centers, three in the Stockholm area and three in the Jönköping area are included in the study. Three of the day centers are thus situated in the south and three in the middle of Sweden within a distance of 500 km. The participants are consequently divided into two separate groups. Twentyfour persons with moderate mental retardation are involved in the study. Twelve women and twelve men aged between 23 and 60 years participate. From each day center four persons with mental retardation are involved.

The staff involved in the project are occupational therapists, speech therapists and care nursers. The videotelephony training and calling are effected as part of their daily jobs which means that no extra staff have been engaged for the project. The staff (one main responsible and at least two or three other as co-trainers) have to fulfil certain criterias such as:

-      be interested in learning how the equipment works
-      be motivated and positive to teach and train the participants
-      be willing and able to spend time on training
-      be willing to document the work in writing
-      produce diary notes according to a special scedule.

The specific task they have to carry out are to be the "helping hand" of the participants with mental retardation. The maximum time for using the videotelephone for each individual has not been restricted, but each participant has to be involved in two telephone calls a week. In the introduction phase one day´s staff education about communication in general and about telecommunication was conducted at each day center.

The participants have several disabilities in addition to the mental retardation. All of them have severe speech and communication disorders and are in great need of support for communication. The modes of communication are gestures, body language, sign communication, Pictogram symbols and a poorly developed spoken language. More than 50% of the participants have also visual impairments, hearing impairments and motor difficulties. Only eight of the participants had used a telephone before the project start. Today they live in group homes, this being a result of the abolishing of institutions for this population in Sweden. They have lived most of their lives in institutions and some of them have never been to school. All of the participants have a limited social network and many of them have no longer contact with their families.

4 Results

Although the TeleCommunity project will not be finished until December 1994, the presentation will give the very first results from the empirical study. Videosequences of the equipment and of the use of the videotelephones with some of the participants with moderate mental retardation will illustrate the promising results.

An early impression is that the participants are positive to the use of the videotelephones and that they are interested in getting in touch with other peers and in establishing new relations. This was also an experience from previous studies of the use of still picture telephones and telefaxes [1, 2, 3]. It is also remarkable to note that the participants have started to change their behaviour in some respects. Many of the participants are today, after some training, able to run the equipment by themselves and some of them also take initiatives to make calls and to chose communication partner. The reports from the staff illuminate that the use of the videotelephones has stimulated and supported the communicative ability and according to information from the parents the participants have extended their social network and made new friends of importance for them. The participants have for instance met at leisure time at special dances arranged for persons with mental retardation and they have recognized each other.

TeleCommunity seems to be a great challenge and opportunity for the participants and one assumption is that videotelephones may be a good communication aid for persons with special needs, and especially for persons with mental retardation..

References:

1.   J. Brodin: Still Picture Telephones as Communication Aids for Persons with Mental Retardation. EuroRehab 3/1993, 163-168 (1993a)

2.   J. Brodin: Telefax för personer med utvecklingsstörning [Telefax communication for persons with mental retardation]. Stockholm: Telia AB (The Swedish telecom) (1993b)

3.   J. Brodin: Ny teknik för personer med i vuxen ålder förvärvade hjärnskador. [New technology for persons mental retardation. International Journal of with traumatic brain injuries] Stockholm University: Department of Education.(1994)

4.   J. Brodin: Videotelephony for two persons with moderate mental retardation. International Journal of Rehabilitation Research, 17(3) (1994)

5.   J. Brodin, E. Björck-Åkesson: Evaluation of still picture telephones for persons with mental retardation. Stockholm: Telia AB (The Swedish telecom) (1991)

6. E. Hjelmqvist, E. Winroth Hallqvist:Slutrapport från Hemtelefax-projektet. Lässervice för synskadade personer. [Final report from the Hometelefax project. Reading service for visually impaired persons]. Göteborg University: Department of Psychology (1991)

7. S. von Tetzchner, F. Hesselberg, H.Langeland: Supervision of Habilitation via Videotelephone. In S. von Tetzchner Issues in Telecommunication and Disability, COST 219, Brussels (1991)

8. L.M. Pereira, M. Matos, J. Purificaçao, P.Lebre: Videotelephony and People with Mental Impairment.The Technical University of Lisbon, Tudor 1988(1992)

Tactile–Audio User Interface for Blind Persons

Hiroki Minagawa, Noboru Ohnishi, Noboru Sugie

Department of Information Engineering,
School of Engineering, Nagoya University, Japan
e–mail: minagawa@sugie.nuie.nagoya–u.ac.jp

Abstract. We are developing a communication media for blind persons which enables blind persons to represent diagrams freely using only their tactile and auditory senses. We conducted psychological experiments in which blind students used and evaluated our prototype system, tactile–audio display (TAD). As a result, some problems on the user interface for blind persons were revealed. These included "troublesome keyboard operations", "rasping voice menu" and "difficulty in simultaneous use by three or more persons". We considered how to resolve such problems.

1. Introduction

Diagrams are very useful media that can support our thinking, communication with others, and so on. However, blind persons can not use visually represented diagrams. There are thus few means by which blind persons may obtain diagrammatical information.

In daily life, blind persons use tactile diagrams (plastic sheets) in which figure elements such as lines are embossed by foaming ink. However, it is difficult for blind persons to recognize diagrams only with the tactile sense because the tactile sense has lower resolution than the visual sense.

In recent years, tactual and auditory representation of diagrams has been proposed and used in some systems [1], [2]. The idea is that coarse information of diagrams is represented by the tactile sense, and fine information, by the auditory sense. In NOMAD [1], auditory information (voice data) is stored and linked to each location on the tactile diagram in advance. Users touch the tactile diagram and hear fine information describing the detail of objects by selecting a location on the diagram. In this way, users can interpret diagrams by integrating information obtained through the auditory and tactile senses. With this system, users can read diagrams, but they can not write diagrams by themselves.

Our aim is to develop a communication media for blind persons by which blind persons can represent diagrams freely using their tactile and auditory senses. In this paper, we consider the possibility of our system, especially its user interface.

2. Tactile–Audio Display (TAD)

2.1 Hardware

The system consists of a tactile display with digitizer, a voice recorder, a voice synthesizer, a keyboard, a disk unit and a personal computer [2] (see Fig. 1).

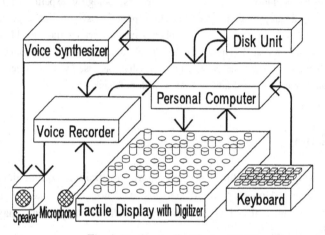

Fig. 1. Tactile–Audio Display (TAD)

The tactile display has an 8x8 pin matrix, and each pin can take one of three states. Furthermore, the display can detect the position of the user's finger because a small switch is embedded in the top of each pin.

The voice recorder is used for recording voice data from a microphone. The data can be played back from a speaker whenever users need. The voice synthesizer transforms the character data to audible voice data.

The keyboard is used for inputting commands, and the disk unit saves diagrams.

All devices are controlled by the personal computer.

2.2 Software

Blind persons can represent diagrams using only their tactile and auditory senses. That is, blind users can set each pin's height and link voice data to a specified pin on the tactile display. Each diagram is saved with a voice label with which users can recall saved diagrams.

A voice menu enables for users to select such data as voice data and diagrams with voice labels. Users can easily operate the voice menu by such simple commands as "listen to the previous term", "listen to the next term", and "select this term". The voice menu is also used to input commands for system operations.

3. Evaluation by Blind Students

We conducted out psychological experiments at the Nagoya School for the Blind. Subjects are seven blind students (nine to twelve years old). We asked subjects to use our prototype system in their classroom work. We describe below the observed behaviors of the subjects and their subjective impressions.

•**Keyboard operation** While using TAD, subjects had to move their hands frequently between the tactile display and keyboard because their hands must do two different jobs, recognize tactile patterns and operate the keyboard. They thus sometimes made mistakes in repositioning their hands on the tactile display or the keyboard.

•**Voice menu** Subjects said that the voice menu for command input was easy for novice users to operate TAD, but repeated messages were rasping and unpleasant for users accustomed to TAD. The reason is, we think, that they can memorize the order of menu items while they repeat operations. While using TAD, subjects recorded their voice into the system as voice data and eventually stored more than 20 voice items. It therefore took much time for users to select desired data because they had to sequentially search a menu of voice data with more than 20 items.

•**Auditory noise** The subjects seemed to be very sensitive to slight sounds. For example, they could perceive faint noises in the voice data recording phase, and could understand the system status based on this auditory noise. From this unexpected fact, we can conclude that even noise is very important feedback for blind users.

•**Hand-in-hand instruction** When a sighted teacher instructed a blind student, the teacher usually held the student's hand and guided it on the tactile display or keyboard. Such hand-in-hand instruction was observed between two blind students as well. Such operation seems to be a basic behavior for communicating among blind persons. However, when four blind students attempted to use TAD together, it was difficult for each student to understand the information represented on the tactile display because of interruption by other students' hands. To prevent hand collisions, we tried another approach, in which the location selected by a student was reported to the other students by voice message. However, we found that this was more difficult for them to understand than hand-in-hand instruction.

4. TAD User Interface

4.1 Command Input

Blind persons use their hands not only to obtain tactile information, but also to manipulate the TAD; that is, their hands are an input-and-output device. To increase tactile performance in recognition, it is necessary to reduce keyboard operation loads.

Using a speech recognition device is one solution for the above problem, but there are reliability problems.

Users' feet are another motor organ available for command input. That is, the user steps on foot switches to input commands while touching the tactile display. It is difficult to input complex commands with foot switches, but a standard or braille keyboard may be used in such situations.

A voice menu is an important blind users' interface, however, as the number of menu items increases, it becomes more difficult to locate the desired item. A hierarchical structure with submenus may be an effective means of coping with the above problem. However, there are many problems in implementing such a structure, so this is a subject for future study.

It may also be useful to present the menu on the tactile display. The merit of this is that the user can memorize the items associated with the two-dimensional location.

4.2 Auditory Output

Voice messages are useful for conveying information to blind persons. Even novice users can use our system by relying on voice messages. However, when the users become accustomed to TAD operations, monotonous, tedious messages become unpleasant and rasping. It is thus necessary to reduce tedious output according to users' experience.

Earcon [3], a menu of natural sounds such as cries of animals or sounds of machines, can be used to reduce voice messages. Moreover, this may enhance users' motivation for learning.

Artificial sounds such as synthesized music can also be used to reduce voice messages. Human hearing, especially blind persons' hearing, is very sensitive to slight changes of sound. Expert users may operate TAD rapidly relying on just a short music menu.

A problem related to earcon and music menus is how to associate each function with earcon or music.

4.3 Tactile Output

In blind persons' communication, hand-in-hand instruction is very important. One person can guide the other's hand to a specific location or path on a map. In non-contact communication, it is difficult to instruct location or path. However, it is difficult for three or more persons to touch one tactile display at a time in contact communication. If many displays are linked with computer networks, all persons can access the tactile display simultaneously. This is, however, non-contact communication, and presents a paradox.
It is interesting to note that human-computer communication is also non-contact communication. The need for blind persons to instruct location or path in non-contact communication presents an interface problem.

Our tactile display can change the displayed pattern according to the situation. It is thus possible to direct users' attention to a specific location or path by repeating on and off cycles. However, how to simulate "hand-in-hand" communication by this method remains a problem.

5. Concluding Remarks

We considered the possibility of a tactile–audio user interface based on some knowledge obtained by a preliminary field test in a school for the blind. There are many problems to be overcome before we can realize our aim. User interfaces for blind persons have many problems which differ from those of visual user interfaces. We must establish the foundation of a user interface for blind persons based on the blind users' advice.

We would like to thank Mr. A. Mizutani, Mr. A. Onoda and other members of the Nagoya School for the Blind for valuable discussions.

References

1. Parkes, D.: "NOMAD 2, Interactive Audio–Tactile Graphics System", Version 4.0, Workshop at Tomteboda Resource Centre, Sweden (1992).

2. Minagawa, H., Ohnishi, N. and Sugie, N.: "A Vision Substitution System for Reading and Writing Diagrams Using Tactile and Auditory Senses", Proc. of 3rd ICCHP, pp.353–362 (1992).

3. Glinert, E. P., Kline, R. L. and Wise, G. B.: "UnWindows: Bringing Multimedia Computing to Users with Disabilities", Proc. of IISF/ACM Japan International Symposium, pp.34–42 (1994).

Computer-aided Access to Tactile Graphics for the Blind

Jürgen Lötzsch

INNOVATIVE TECHNIKEN des BSVS e.V.
Weissbachstrasse 5, D-01069 Dresden, Germany

Abstract. Every day sighted people use 2D graphic representations of informations for communication and documentation. At school and work but also in the daily life they bring a lot of advantages especially efficiency and speed. Now we see all of them on computer screens. But how can blind people manage the access to such 2D representations used in computers ? The experiences, gained during the author's involvement in projects dealing with audio-tactile pictures, are presented in this paper.

1. 2D Representations of Informations

Every day sighted people use 2D graphic representations of informations for communication and documentation. 2D representations bring very many advantages. They are needed to achieve the aims of efficiency and speed.

You can find numerous types of graphic representations, particulary at school, at work and during the studies. Beside the various graphics from basic disciplines as for example mathematics, physics, chemistry, biology, geography, astronomy and anatomy they are also used for building civil engineering drawings, arrow diagrams, structured programs, flow charts, circuit diagrams, piping network diagrams for drinking and heating water among others.

Beside these types of 2D representations related to education and job you can also find a lot of interesting pictures, graphics and diagrams in the daily life as e.g. city maps (historical, modern and referring to development); network plans of buses, trams and so on; maps for different purposes (tourists, weather, economy, ...); surveys of museums, exhibitions, parks and gardens; ground plans and elevations of historical buildings (churches, theaters, castles, fortresses, etc.), representations of the functional structure of administration and service institutions (townhalls, banks, insurance companies etc.); surveys of the situation of departments in shopping centers, supermarkets; schematic representations of railway stations with their platforms, counters and service; surveys of medical institutions (hospitals, health centers); schematic representations of sports facilities, grounds for ball games etc.

Whereas in former times these 2D representations usually were available only on sheets of paper now we see all of them on computer screens. Furthermore computer science itself created a lot of new ones e.g. graphic user interfaces for operating systems and application programs.

But how can blind people manage the access to 2D representations used in computers ?

Following VANDERHEIDEN [13] there are three tasks of different types:
  a) Graphical user interfaces (GUI) on the computers (operating systems)
  b) Graphical user interfaces on public information systems
  c) Access to graphics.

The theme of the paper is "Acces to graphics" where "graphics" is used in the sense of the examples above without any consideration of GUI.

2. From Graphics to Tactile Graphics for Blind People

Blind people are able to compensate seeing by feeling and listening. Therefore it is necessary to "translate" the given 2D graphic representations of informations into tactile and/or audible ones.

Of course it would be very pleasant if one could get the tactile and/or audible graphic for the blind in a 1-to-1 manner from the original graphic. But usually this "translation" process is very complicated and the portion of manual work is considerably which has to follow certain design rules (see e.g. [5]). Only in some cases you can write a translator which automatically transforms a certain class of graphics for sighted people into graphics for the blind. This has been done for instance for special business charts [6].

But usually it is impossible to do so because of the complexity of the picture. An impressive example for such a graphic is a city map.

But problems arise already when considering texts. "Scientific literature is usually presented to sighted readers in a multi-dimensional format. It is multi-dimensional in the sense that the information is contained not just in the words themselves, but also in the positions of the words and in the fonts used in printing the words." [1]

Examples for that are two-dimensional mathematical notations, chemical formulas, and so on. Sighted people use this kind of representations because they possess the advantage of a clear arrangement of the semantic structure of the formula. Why transforming it into a linear braille form when its clarity is lost by doing this? This is the basic idea of DotsPlus and ASTER developed by BARRY, GARDNER and RAMAN for scientific documents [1].

In such 2D formulas only a few very simple graphic elements arise such as horizontal lines, symbols for sum, integration and so on, which have a very close relationship to the alphabets of formal grammars [7]. It seems to be an interesting approach to apply translator writing techniques to the problem of transforming general pictures into audible and tactile ones.

But the bigger the portion of graphic elements is in the picture the greater are the problems to be solved when preparing the picture for the blind.

Therefore in many cases it is a long way from the prototype of a graphic to its equivalents for blind people. And although this process can be supported by the computer it remains a lot of manual work for which you have to have the right feel. Not too much objects in the graphic means e.g. you have to concentrate on the essential content, you have to leave out the unnecessary details, you have to split the graphic into several ones, you have to enlarge it, and so on.

One big problem is text on graphics. Why?

The first reason is that braille text is also a tactile object. All textual objects must be touched in addition to the objects of the pure underlying graphic. They increase the complexity of the picture and decrease the threshold of its recognizability. Furtheron must be taken in consideration that only 15-25 % of the blind people are able to read braille.

One piece of text gives an explanation to a certain object of the graphic. As the braille text must have a minimum size it is very often difficult to place it in the right position to the corresponding object. In such cases you can
- replace the full text by a braille label and integrate all labels into an appendix with the full texts,
- or you can place the text in the surrounding of the picture and draw an arrow to the belonging to object (but this arrow is an additional tactile object again that must be recognized including at which graphic object the arrowhead is pointing)
- or you can remove the texts completely from the picture and write a guide through the picture which can be printed in braille or be recorded on tape
- or you can leave out the text assuming that a partner will explain the graphic objects to you when you are asking him.

Therefore we can distinguish between the following types of tactile graphics
1. Full text graphics possibly with pointers
2. Labelled graphics (with additional legend) possibly with pointers
3. Textual guided pure graphics (with an additional guide in braille or on tape)
4. Pure graphics (requires help by a human being or by a computer) .

Undoubtedly the pure graphics posses an extraordinary importance when they are combined with a computer as dialogue "partner".

A pure graphic contains only the graphic objects and no additional braille or additional arrows to be touched. Therefore in one graphic you can place more graphic objects until the threshold of recognizability is exceeded.

Pure graphics which can be explained by the computer are called
audio-tactile graphics.

From the computer partner is expected that it will guarantee the independent navigation through the graphic by the blind.

3. Audio-Tactile Dialogue Systems

An audio-tactile dialogue system offers blind people as the user of the system the access to tactile graphics:
- A blind person explores a tactile graphics in the usual manner using its fingers.
- If he/she wishes to get informations about a certain object in the graphic he/she requests them.
- He/she listens to the informations given on the audio channel.

Unfortunately until now it was not possible to find a safe and cheap solution of a graphic display for the blind, where the contents of the screen is displayed in tactile form. First steps in the right direction have been done by Schweikhart, Fricke/Bähring, Shinohara et al., Schulz and others.

Therefore at present only one solution seems to be reasonable: the efficient design and production of tactile graphics on paper or foil and the preparation of them for the dialog between the blind users and the computer.

The general scheme of an audio-tactile dialogue system is the following:
1. There must be a place where the tactile graphic can be touched.
2. When putting the graphic there it must be identified by the system.
3. It must be possible to feel the graphic in the usual manner and furtheron to point to a chosen graphical object.
4. The system must be able to identify the pointing position and the chosen object.
5. The system has to react by generating an information and sending it through the audio channel.

Hardware. You can access the objects of a graphic when you place it on a digitizing tablet or a touch window which are commercially available.

The audio information can be generated using a sound card. Text can be handled in two different ways: sending digitized speech to the sound card or alphanumerical text to a text-to-speech synthesizer. The synthesizer itself is either software working on a sound card or an electronic device.

Especially for use in a audio-tactile system PARKES developed his Nomad board about in 1988 [10, 11]. It is a touch board combined with an integrated speech synthesizer. Since 1991 it is produced by Quantum Technology Pty. Ltd. Rydalmere, Australia. The American Printing House for the Blind (APH) took a licence and since March 1993 they make Nomad too [4].

Software systems. Some attempts have been made to design and implement audio-tactile dialogue systems.

The first one was PARKES's Nomad system especially working with the Nomad board connected to a MS-DOS computer with the Nomad software.

The Dresden AUDIO-TOUCH system Version 1.0 was ready in 1992 [8]. It can be configured for different digitizers and Touch Windows and for different text-to-speech synthesizers as well as for SoundBlaster cards with software synthesizers. It is working also on the Nomad board. The authors prefer to use a sound card with talking blaster because of the the speech quality and the integration of sound.

BLENKHORN reported in March 1994 the principal features of the Talking Tactile Maps System [2]. The hardware used is an IBM compatible computer with a Touch Window and a text to speech synthesizer. Evaluations have been undertaken to date in a school.

VANDERHEIDEN illustrated in [13] a technique for accessing the picture on the computer screen. You need a tactile copy of the screen picture, put it on a Touch Window and explore it supported by a screen reader.

4. Audio-Touch

Visually impaired persons use the AUDIO-TOUCH system with the traditionally media for tactile information. Such media exist in different types such as
- relief of foil
- swelling paper with mechanically produced graphics
- paper embossed with a braille printer
- foil embossed with an embossing plotter
- textile materials embroidered with a sewing machine etc.
AUDIO-TOUCH can be operated with different materials.

Graphics for AUDIO-TOUCH are designed using standard software such as Designer, CorelDraw and others. The implementation for AUDIO-TOUCH is then done automatically. Furtheron there is an integrated component for scetching audio-tactile graphics.

Each graphic consists of a set of graphic objects. The simplest form of a dialogue is to point to an object and to listen to the objects name spoken by the speech synthesizer. Demanding discourses can be designed on further talking levels. On each talking level sequences of text and sound can be assigned to the graphic objects. Each talking level represents certain semantics of the underlying graphic.

Series of graphics have been prepared for AUDIO-TOUCH from different fields of application: dialogue on mathematical functions and planar geometry, information about touristics and sightseeing, maps in geography, mobility training using tactile maps of railway stations and traffic networks, course on Windows graphical user interfaces, anatomy course for blind masseurs.

5. Conclusions

The application of systems like AUDIO-TOUCH in the area of education or in the tourism field or as an information system for exhibitions is "both enjoyable and useful" [2]. There is no doubt that audio-tactile dialogue system have a wide application field. They will improve the access to 2D representations of informations by blind people considerably.

References

1. Barry, Gardner, Raman: Accessibility to Scientific Information by the Blind: DotsPlus and ASTER could make it easy, CSUN'94 "Technology and People with Disabilities", Los Angeles, March 16-19, 1994
2. Blenkhorn, Evans: A System for Reading and Producing Talking Tactile Maps and Diagrams, CSUN'94 "Technology and People with Disabilities", Los Angeles, March 16-19, 1994
3. Burger et al.: The design of interactive auditory learning tools, in: Burger, Sperandino (eds.), "Non-Visual Human-Computer Interactions", INSERM 1992, pp.97-114
4. Duennes: Putting Puff to Work for the Visually Impaired, SCREEN Printing, 58-62, Dec 1993
5. Hinton: Tactile and audio-tactile images as vehicles for learning, in: Burger, Sperandino (eds.), "Non-Visual Human-Computer Interactions", INSERM 1992, pp.169-179
6. Krämer: Automatische Übersetzung von Lehrgangsunterlagen in tastbare Dokumentationen für Blinde, Programmdokumentation, Innovative Techniken, Dresden 1993

7. Lötzsch: Ebene Fachsprachen (Planar Specialized Languages), Thesis, Mathematische Kybernetik und Rechentechnik, Technische Universität Dresden, 1982

8. Lötzsch: Audio-taktiler Dialog über Graphiken und Diagrammen insbesondere für Blinde und Sehbehinderte, in: Mehnert (ed.), Proc. Konferenz "Elektronische Sprachsignalverarbeitung in der Rehabilitationstechnik", 22.-24.11.1993, Berlin, Studientexte zur Sprachkommunikation, Heft 10, Humboldt-Universität Berlin

9. Lötzsch: Auditory Feedback from Tactile Pictures on Digitizing Tablets, Symposium on "High Resolution Tactile Graphics", Los Angeles, March 15, 1994

10. Parkes: Nomad, an audio-tactile tool for the acqustion, use and management of spatially distributed information by visually impaired people, in: Tatham (ed.), Proceedings of the "Second International Symposium on Maps and Graphics for Visually Handicapped People", A.F.&Dodds, London 1988

11. Parkes: Nomad: enabling access to graphics and text based information for blind and visually impaired and other disability groups, in Proceedings of the world congress on Technology for People with Disabilities, Washington DC, December 1-5 1991, pp.689-716

12. TIDE 103: Textual and Graphical User Interfaces for Blind People, in "TIDE - Pilot Action, The Synposes", CEC March 1992

13. VanderHeiden: Update on Access to Graphic User Interfaces by People who are Blind: Current Progress and Future Issues, CSUN'94 "Technology and People with Disabilities", Preconference session, Los Angeles, March 16-19, 1994

Braille reader

— Old braille text for young —

Yasuhiko Ogawa[t],   Yoshinobu Kikuchi[tt],   Nobuyuki Ohtake[t]

[t] Tsukuba college of Technology, Japan.
[tt] Tokyo Kaseigakuin Tsukuba college, Japan.

Abstract

A braille reader is developed as an input device on a personal computer. This mechanism is direct touch for embossed point on braille paper by an isolated thin metal wire. We designed a braille reader considering standard input/output interface[3] of general computers, then this can connect any other large/small computers. Not only a braille reader is used by the blind and volunteer, but such a useful machine should be set up in public offices and libraries. Furthermore, this braille reader makes many copies of an old braille document which exists only one.

1 Introduction

When we think about education for the blind and social independence of a blind person, an input device of computer[1], which reads braille and tactile patterns, is increasingly required for (1) a regeneration or a reproduction of braille document or text, (2) a speech synthesizer, (3) a translation from braille text to some printed materials (reverse conversion), (4) a reading check for some important braille documents after writing, (5) a proof reading of tactile pattern and (6) an assistant/compensative equipment for someone who does not know about braille. Then these items are more and more necessary for the blind themselves and also an administration office of government or a related place from this time forth.

In an observation of braille information circulation, a writer records their documents to a floppy disk by using a personal computer or a word processor in recent years, and he uses this floppy disk as a distribution medium. Or someon· perhaps directly inputs a braille text or braille information (which contain tactile data) to a computer by using an on-line computer system. But all of the blind do not have a personal computer or any other machines. Then there are many cases that braille documents, which are written on a thick paper by hand using a braille board, are circulated for daily use generally. A braille hand writing tool (a board and a stylus set) is very convenient for carrying when we think about its weight, handling, no electric power supply and its size compare with a personal computer. Furthermore, a hand writing tool is extremely cheap in comparison with various kinds of other electronic information devices. Then such a hand writing tool is obviously utilized as a note taking tool of the blind from this time forth. In this fact, for example, there are some chances that the blind submit a document which is written by braille to a municipal office, a bank or any other reception offices. In other cases, some teachers may read a braille document written by students. In such cases, a small and simple braille reading device is necessary as a handy tool for a receipter who can not read braille. If such a device or machine exists, it is very easy to make many reproductions from an old braille document which remains only one in a library or personal collections.

2 Development goal

A braille reading device, which mechanism is an "optical method", has already been developed. For example, braille reproduction/copy device "Braille Master" is a famous commercial product. An optical method is as follows. When optical light from irradiated angle is applied to a braille sheet, the shade of embosses is fell upon the paper. These convex points or concave points of braille from oblique direction are read by an image scanner. A shortcoming of this method is against some dirt on the paper causes misreading. This is an unavoidable point in an optical method. Especially, old braille documents contain such weak points. In the case that braille is printed on both sides of the paper, each shade of the convex and concave points appears on one side at the same time. Very advanced processing is required to distinguish convex and concave points in such an optical approach. Currently it is very difficult to recognize the surface and reverse side braille points on one sheet by such optical method. A principle of this experimental reading device is that "convex points of braille are detected mechanically" at first, then analyzing braille or tactile figure by opening and closing a contact point of an electronic circuit[4].

We set up a development goal in the following manner.

1. A reader is not influenced by the dirt of braille sheet or tactile paper.

2. A reader is not influenced by the size of the braille character.

3. A reader can recognize weakly destroyed convex points.

4. A reader does not damage the original sheet and paper while the braille is reading.

5. A reader is not influenced by some inclination of the braille sheet.

6. A reader can correspond to A4 size, letter size and Japanese braille paper size.

7. Reading speed is at least less than 10 seconds for A4 size paper.

8. Small size and low price are required for personal use.

3 Mechanical principle and internal structure of a braille reader

Our method is led by various experiments. A project point of braille is converted to mechanical movement of a touch sensor, this movement opens and closes an electric contact point. We judged that this way have high possibility of realization, because this mechanism is very simple. One physical touch sensor is made by a spring wire, this wire is bended to a right angle about 10 millimeters apart from the end (Figure 1 and Picture 1 show the touch sensor). This bended part is the mechanical contact point for a convex point of an embossed point and the opposite side of this wire is fixed. Bended wires guide a moving wire to a vertical position when it is rising up by a convex point. It can express equivalent circuit for one wire in Figure 1, positive logic output for the convex point is obtained from this.

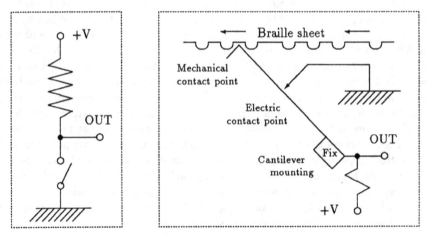

Figure 1. Positive logic output circuit & its application.

Only concave points can be detected by changing a sensor position with the same mechanism. General demands from a user for standard devices are summerized in the following items, but detail requirements are not listed.

- Simple operation and high reliability for the machine.
- Easy trouble shooting.

Easy handling (it also includes pre/post process), the reliability and stability of a machine are essential elements. Then we materialized these items by the following methods in this research. (1) All controls for the braille reader are executed by a personal computer, then all operation switches are omitted from this device. If a braille manuscript is inserted to the reader, the sheet is detected, then a motor trigger works and the reading is started automatically. Even if the sheet reading finishes, the reader is in operating condition for a specified time and can read the next manuscript continuously. This operation time is variable, of course, if it does not insert the next manuscript within a specified time, the reader suspends. (2) There is high possibility of paper jamming during operation in such a machine that handles paper like a document copy machine. The sensor of the convex point, an electronic circuit relates to this sensor, a motor drive for input paper etc., these control functions are arranged inside the braille reader. When the paper is jammed, you can take it out easily by opening the top board in this design. (3) Pre/Post processing. We chose method that the manuscript is read with face down. The manuscript is stacked up on the discharge part after reading. The order of input sheets do not reverse, then a replacement of input sheets are not necessary for this operation. Thus, no complex operation is required for pre/post process.

Picture 1. A sensor part.

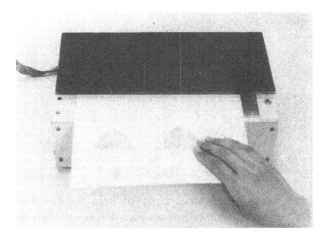

Picture 2. A braille reader.

4 Braille recognizing algorithm

The next functions are necessary for automatic braille character recognition from an image data that is obtained from the braille reader.

- Detection of line position.
- Decision of braille character size.
- Pattern matching and skew processing.

In the decision process of line position, the image of braille points is projected in the horizontal direction at first, a line position is determined by searching the mode from the histogram. Vertical direction is the same as the horizontal way. Figure 2 indicates these horizontal and vertical histograms. Figure 3 shows outline of a character position decision way from these histograms.

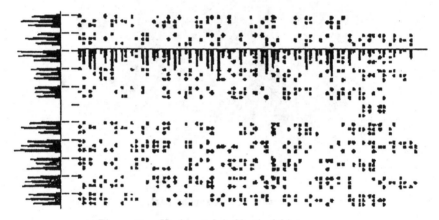

Figure 2.   Horizontal & Vertical histograms.

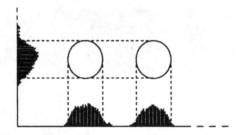

Figure 3.   Logical hole.

The size of a braille character is obtained from the distribution of width direction. Both horizontal and vertical analysis in these histogram search methods, the distance between the braille letters and the braille character size can be decided automatically. In the case that a histogram search area is defined the whole of the input sheet, when a piece of paper is inserted at an angle of some degrees for the touch sensor, it is very difficult to solve the mode from the histogram by this searching method. Because such a histogram has no good peak (data is flat). Accordingly, several lines that are at a specified length from the upper end of input sheet and some numbers that are at a designated length from the left end of the input, are the restricted target areas which are analyzed. Figure 4 shows relation between whole area and the defined region.

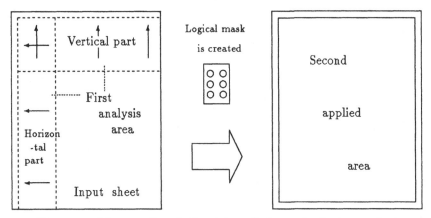

Figure 4.   First analisys & Second applied area in the input sheet.

This is a characteristic of this braille reader, thus decision of braille character size and a line space are treated statical research by restricted horizontal and vertical directions in this method. A statical analysis box area, which defines horizontal and vertical length, is justly variable. In the case that a numerical value which shows a page number does not appear in the histogram of vertical projection, because the page number is near the right edge of the braille sheet. Then a line position, which is placed in distant location, is determined to co-ordinate correction in estimation from horizontal analysis in this algorithm. At last a logical mask which has 6 holes is created from braille character size that is determined by this algorithm. At this time, the next three values have been defined from the restricted area.

- Distance between lines.
- Braille character size.
- A logical mask of 6 holes.

It should analyze the full area of the braille sheet as a second step by using this data and for a previous estimation. Overlapping this logical mask upon image data, it finds a good position which matches this logical pattern. If there exists some point which is bigger than regular value compared with the logical mask hole size, these points create a correspond braille code. This operation is iterated from left to right and top to bottom on full image data, and then this pattern matching finishes. In this pattern matching, this logical mask can move not only in a straight line but also in a wavey line, then it can analyze some inclined image data.

5 Actions

A reader part consists of 430 sensors, these are arranged 2 sensors per millimeter. This dissolution ability is sufficient for small Japanese braille size compared with other countries' braille scale. Full image of the input sheet, which has braille and tactile patterns, is read by a moving the sheet, this minute transfer is a synchronized electronic pulse. Reading speed is 8 seconds for a A4 size sheet, when a MS-DOS personal computer (NEC : PC-98RL, CPU : Intel 80386, Clock : 20 MHz) is used. It takes about 8 seconds to transform to braille and Kana[1] letter (or English/number/symbol/Greek/Russian letter etc.,) from recognized image data. Recognized braille and Kana letters can be transformed from internal data to standard disk/floppy files, and print out directly to a braille printer and a normal printer respectively. And it is possible to read braille aloud into a machine by a combination of a voice synthesis device. When an irregular pattern is found in analyzed braille, it can add/delete one point of a 6 dot pattern by an editor which is contained in this control software. It is possible to add/delete/move one braille character, and modification of Kana letter is also easy by this editor. It can only express 64 kinds of character (contains space character) by 6 dots braille method, then digits, large/small English letter, Greek, Russian letter, etc., are needed several distinguished marks before individual words when the context is changed. There exists 8 dots braille method in Japan, but this is an unusual way. Although these marks switch a context, several previous marks are sometimes omitted in some mathematical expressions and computer program descriptions, thus humans can understand omitted marks from the context. But it is very difficult to recognize the hidden mark for this braille reader which is controled by software. When a previous mark is omitted, if a special description (for example, chemical expression and it's symbol) is read as a general sentence, it will become a meaningless character set. Then we provided an interactive mode which can change the reading pattern. Braille patterns contained in tactile figure are recognized as braille characters by designating partially, and these characters are also transformed to print characters on display. This braille reader is a prototype product which reads braille and tactile figure patterns by arranging many mechanical sensors, this is the pursuit of its possibility and ability. Detailed contrivances are omitted in the first development step, therefore, only a flat sheet is passed though this sensor part continuously. This braille reader is weak at processing correctly a broken or distorted sheet. However the solution of this problem currently remains, materializing process has become clear. It will be scheduled about this weak point after this. Furthermore, recognition rate of this braille reader is 99.8% for a flat sheet which does not have a broken part or distortion.

---

[1] "Kana" is Japanese phonetic alphabet.

6 Conclusion

We proved "an input of braille and tactile pattern to a computer" by simply using a hand made touch type braille reader. It is very easy to convert from braille to Kana string, because Kana and Japanese braille have one to one correspondence like alphabet and its braille code. There is no difficult point in this Japanese conversion technically, then it can make braille reading software by voice synthesizer[2] without any problem. Although we developed an automatic "Kana to Chinese character conversion"[6], this conversion program is currently an isolated software from this braille reader. Using this software, the blind can write a general document or print a text "by themselves" from braille to sentences mixed with Kana and Chinese character[5]. And it is also espected to convert from a tactile sheet to a visible print automatically. These are the applications of this braille reader in our research. Though there remained co-ordinate correction in estimation, smoothing method, and other problems (a treatment of Japanese, high performance, etc.), each problems are solved in visible prints and materials, an application for braille reading method is not difficult by improvement and combination of our technology and commercialized products.

References

[1] Margaret R. Barker, *"Computer input devices for physically disabled people"*, IEEE, 26th COMPCON, 1983, pp.175-178.

[2] R.Marsden, L.Tanne and N.Durdle, *"Computer-aided speech prosthesis"*, Proceedings of the SID, Vol.30, No.1, 1989, pp.45-49.

[3] Elliot Cole and Parto Dehdashti, *"Interface design as a prosthesis for an individual with a brain injury"*, SIGCHI Bulletin, Vol.22, No.1, 1990, pp 28-32.

[4] Yasuhiko Ogawa, Yoshinobu Kikuchi, Nobuyuki Ohtake, et.al., *"Technical report No.63880035"* by a Grant-in-Aid for Scientific Research, Ministry of Education, Mar., 1990. (in Japanese)

[5] Nobuyuki Ohtake and Yuji Takano, *"Japanese braille"*, The British Journal of Visual Impairment. Vol.10, No.3, Nov., 1992.

[6] Nobuyuki Ohtake, *"Japanese braille translation system"*, The Journal of Visual Impairment and Blindness, 1994. (to be published)

Yasuhiko Ogawa	†	Tsukuba college of Technology Kasuga 4–12, Tsukuba, 305, Japan.
Yoshinobu Kikuchi	††	Tokyo Kaseigakuin Tsukuba college Azuma 3–1, Tsukuba, 305, Japan.
Nobuyuki Ohtake	†	Tsukuba college of Technology Kasuga 4–12, Tsukuba, 305, Japan.

Computer Camp

for the Handicapped and their Family Members

Vanja R. KISWARDAY, spec. pedagog

Department for applied mathematics, "Jožef Stefan" Institute,
Ljubljana, Slovenija

Abstract. With the rapid development of information technology and its increasing in all fields of life and work, there are practically no more workplaces without computer possibilities. In Slovenija everyone but the handicapped has a chance to join a computer class satisfying his interests. At the "Jožef Stefan" Institute, we made appropriate modifications to existing computer literacy programs to meet the special education needs of some children. We prepared a computer camp for handicapped children and their family members. The aim of this camp was to link the knowledge and first experience in computer use with their everyday needs. We found that it is important to introduce children's family members to various possibilities as to how the computer can become a useful tool in study, creative work and daily life. By inviting family members to join the camp, we encourage them to involve themselves in this process.

1. Introduction

The "Jožef Stefan" Institute is a research organization for pure and applied research in the natural sciences and technology. Both are closely interconnected in research departments composed of different task teams. Emphasis in basic research is given to the growth and education of young scientists, while applied research and development serve for the transfer of advanced knowledge, contributing to the development of the national economy and society in general.

The department of applied mathematics (OUM) has paid special attention to education: more than 40,000 participants have attended OUM education programs. In the field of youth education, OUM has organized various classes and work groups with regard to the different interests the students have in using the computer. In preparing of the programs we pay special attention to age, previous knowledge and the special interests of students.

2. Experimental computer camp

I started working at the Institute as a student of special pedagogy and gained some experience teaching children computer literacy. I realized that the computer has a significant motivation effect on children. They do not accept it as a complicated machine where you need a lot of knowledge and experience - as some adults do, - but as an interesting tool for creating, playing and studying. I saw their enthusiasm and good will to do anything with the computer. Time had no effect on their concentration at work, they were listening, working, enjoying and they did great jobs admired by adults.

In the publications "Computer and education" and "Educational computing", I read about the great results that special-needs children had with computer support. I saw that the computer can give those children more and new possibilities for study and creative work, opportunities in getting jobs and integrating into society.

I took up this challenge of introducing computers to children with special needs for my diploma work. With the help of the Institute - special support of my mentor Bojan Rovtar, 86 children with special needs and some of their teachers we realized an experimental one-week computer camp for special school pupils. The results were very good. Children at the camp have been very interested in working with computers and they learned a lot. Their teachers noticed increased motivation in other activities like drawing, writing, communicating. We had many observations at this camp made by professors from the Faculty of Education, teachers from special-program school's, journalists, and we proved to them that computers are not only accessible for these children but can be, by a creative approach, also the key to their's activity.

3. Family computer camp

After the first camp, we organised other camps organized for hearing and speech impaired, visually impaired and children with brain damage. All camps were highly successfull. Many parents showed interest in introducing themselves with programs and contents of the camp and occasions to include computers in their children's education and work. They showed interest in learning how to use computers themselves, too. Considering these requests, we prepared a FAMILY COMPUTER CAMP by including a "family members'" program.

Work at camp was oriented around the project of publishing a camp review. There were four activities for young journalists: Writing for readers, Getting to know yourself, Excursions and Working with computers. For youth and adult's groups, we included contents related to the market economy and management. We divided participants into three groups based on their previous knowledge (some of children were in the camp for the third time), age and interests:

- Younger child group - pupils of elementary school,
- Youth group - mostly secondary school students,
- Adult group.

4. Activities at the camp

4.1. Writing for readers.

In this part, children got an insight into journalists work; they were visited by a well-known Slovenian journalist who told them about his work and showed them how to do an interview. Considering this information they prepare their own interview questions to get some answers about where people usually use computers. How can they write an interesting article - it seemed not to be a problem - at least not at camp, where their imagination is enormous. Anyway, they listen to some rules about the best way to transfer ideas on paper.

4.2. Getting to know yourself.

This activity touched them with titles: My life story, Ways of getting know myself, The body, Feelings and my responses, My relationships, Masculinity and femininity, What should I do with the talents I possess?

Our intention was to invite young people to co-operate actively. First they examined their existing understanding of a given subject (photo-talk, poster drawing, discussion in pairs, etc.), then they tried to find its true significance (lectures) and evaluate it within our lives (life stories, stories, slides,...). All the notes and texts the young people worked with were compiled in his or her own "book".

4.3. Excursions

Our camp location was Zgornje Gorje near Bled. It is a small village under the Alps with many natural attractions and interesting tourist points. The beautiful surroundings inspired us with new ideas, and gave us an opportunity to lose all superfluous energy. One more important thing: we always met interesting people prepared to respond to our interview questions - in this way children integrated themselves in society and gained more self-confidence and courage in contacting other people.

4.4. Market economy

We animated the program for Youth and Adult's group with some contents from the area of market economy. They tried to earn some money on computer business simulations, then they made some calculations to find the best possibility to enrich that money by investing it in the bank, stock market or somewhere else. Those two groups also watched video films about successful managing in different situations, mistakes we usually make without noticing them and problems that appear as a consequence.

4.5. Working with computers.

It was a mix of learning how to use computers and, because of their enthusiasm, almost a real publishing office in the end.

In computer classes, we introduced them to:

- computer (basic components, how to maintain computer),
- basic commands in DOS - how to load programs,
- simple program for desk publishing (News Master),
- word processor,
- spread sheets and databases,
- computer games for evening fun.

News Master is a simple program but very impressive and attractive for children. It has around 250 pictures and 34 different fonts. Almost all commands are present as icons and knowledge of English is not necessary. As a result, children learn how to work with this program almost immediately. For younger children this program was basic during this camp. They made a camp poster, a cover for a review, writings, riddles, cartoons, crosswords.

The next program they we introduced them to was a word processor. The youth group and adults used it to write all the reports, abstracts and other writings.

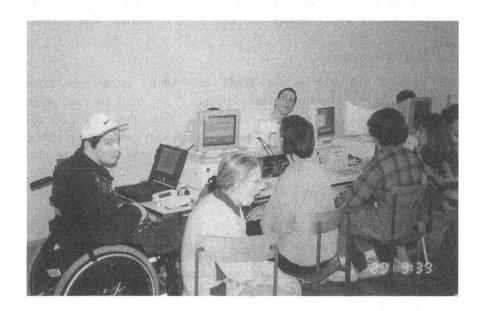

Fig. 1 Creating with computers

We also learned about spreadsheets and how to prepare them to make a calculation of our assets. Younger children learned something about databases and made a directory with the names, addresses, telephone numbers and birth-days of all participants in the camp.

The last day we prepared a presentation of all we did during the week and we presented them a review published the last evening. We invited all family members and friends that could not participate in our camp. They were all most satisfied and shared the opinion that applying computers in their life can have a significant influence on their children's education and integration into society.

5. Conclusion

In this group of children the computer was not only a tool for writing, drawing, calculating and publishing the review. It also became a substitution for a skillful hand, communication aid, trigger for otherwise restrained abilities and a possibility to recognize the opportunity of equal integration in professional life that is now presenting itself as a future full of barriers and doubts for those young people.

These camps have an important role in the process of education and they give a unique opportunity for socialization and integration of children with special needs. For many of those children, this was their first experience of camp life; they gained more self confidence and confidence in friends and mentors. We were happy to hear from children's parents how grateful they were for this concrete way of helping them in educating their children for an independent life.

References

1. Goldenberg P. Computers, education and special needs, Addison Wesley publishing company, 1984

2. Heermann B. Teaching and learning with computers, Jossey-Bass Publishers, 1988

3. Kiswarday V., Rovtar B. Uvodni seminar za uporabo računalnika kot orodja Introductionary seminar: Using computer as a tool), "Jožef Stefan" Institute, Ljubljana 1991

SMLLSTPS: the Software Version of the Macquarie Program, a Computerized Child Assessment System

Erik de Graaf

Director, Stichting Down's Syndroom
Wanneperveen, the Netherlands

Abstract. This paper describes an application of DataPerfect, which was designed to accommodate the early intervention programme from Macquarie University in Sydney. Not only will its use save time, it can also be used as a powerful tool to monitor the development of children with developmental disability in
a way which was not possible before.

1 Introduction: an Early Intervention and a Computer Program

Present day practice of professional support in the field of early intervention (early,
structured support of children with developmental disabilities), carries with it quite
some administrative fuss. This is particularly so for professionals, or professional
organizations, that support a larger number of children. Just think of the amount of
writing involved per child e. g. in producing a detailed activity chart once a week
with all the necessary background information. Furthermore, the experiences of the
professionals concerned, per task of the program as well as per direction to every
single child, have to be administrated, of course, at a central point. This has to be
done in such a way that these data are directly available for at least all co-workers
of the same organization. Sometimes, particular activities, which are necessary for
the assessment of a child, are considered to be so laborious that they are never
executed. Drawing up a developmental profile for a differentiated assessment (see
below) is an example of that. Finally, a direct comparison between children is not
easy with the materials available. The computer program SMLLSTPS (small steps),
which is to be presented here, the software-version of the well-known Australian
Macquarie Program, is meant to aid in the alleviation of these kinds of problems.
As opposed to the Macquarie Program itself, SMLLSTPS is a completely Dutch
development.

Before giving a description of the *computer* program SMLLSTPS some words
must be said about the *early intervention* program named after Macquarie University in Sydney [1]. The version of the Macquarie Program that has been built into
SMLLSTPS not only makes use of all five developmental domains that were originally distinguished, but of four others, that were originally presented in a different
way [2,3,4], as well. Besides:

GM = gross motor
FM = fine motor / cognitive development
RL = receptive language
EL = expressive language and
PS = personal and social skills
the 'new' domains
VS = pre-requisite skills
RP = reading program
DP = drawing and pre-writing program
NP = number skills program

are included as integral components of the Developmental Skills Inventory (or DSI for short) and the Manual of the Macquarie Program. This means that the total number of tasks is no longer 665 but has increased to 786. The unacquainted reader is referred to the screen prints further on in this paper, to get a feel of the set up of the Macquarie Program.

2 Hard and Software Requirements

The computer program SMLLSTPS is an application of DataPerfect. The latter program, as well as its applications, runs on every PC, XT as well as AT and up. However, the production of a number of reports of the application SMLLSTPS, particularly drawing a developmental profile (see below), will take so much time at an XT that moving to an AT might become desirable. But when extensive reports like these are produced at a central place on a faster machine, it is still very well possible to even work with an XT in field.

SMLLSTPS was originally written as an application of version 2.1 of DataPerfect but runs just as well as an application of the so-called Runtime-version of the same program. This last option is much cheaper. However, in that case the support organization of the children concerned cannot adapt the program on its own (although it still can adapt the reports!) and cannot, of course, develop other databases either. One has to think of that before purchasing one of the aforementioned database programs which will enable one to install SMLLSTPS.

Both the aforementioned database programs come from the same WordPerfect-'stable'. This means that all kinds of key-stroke combinations, which are known by heart by experienced WordPerfect users, can be applied directly within the Data-Perfect environment. E. g. here, too, Shift-F7 means printing and F2 searching, while this program also has to be exited with F7, etc. Another advantage of this close family relationship is the easy transfer of data from DataPerfect to WordPerfect. For example, a developmental profile made with SMLLSTPS (see below) can be imported rightaway into a WordPerfect document.

3 Personal Data

Upon starting up the program one enters the panel with personal data (depth 1), called 'NAMECHLD' (name of the child). In this panel every child gets its own record. In addition to his or her personal data it can accommodate data of the responsible professionals or professional organizations.

By means of a so-called 'door' ('panel link') to depth 2 the panel 'ASSESSMT' (assessment, Screen 1) can be reached. Moving the cursor to that door and pressing arrow-down leads the way to the results of one particular child on the DSI. In this case the results of the child with AI-number 1, which has Down's syndrome, are shown (AI = auto increment). Once in the ASSESSMT panel, the individual results of all children can be recorded there, in conjunction with the remarks which are applicable to a particular child for that particular task. Therefore, this panel is the translation into computer terminology of the right hand part of the pages of the original DSI, notably the columns with pluses and minuses for every single task.

All DataPerfect applications, and therefore also SMLLSTPS, show a type of screen in which the top part is used alternately for the lookup list of the database concerned (see Screen 1) and a help function belonging to that particular application (so-called 'custom help', see Screen 2 below). The bottom part of the screen shows the data within the individual records.

The ASSESSMT panel is shown below in the lookup situation in front of the NAMECHLD panel. In the top part one can see a small portion of the list of 786 tasks of the present version of the Macquarie Program. With the aid of the keys from the cursor block, one can scroll very fast through this list until the required task has been found. In this example that is FM 78.

```
                                                        ┌─15/04/92─14:45─┐
FM   77    13/05/88    50 -     1
FM   78    26/06/87    40 +     1
FM   79    10/05/88    50 +     1
FM   80    13/05/88    50 +     1
FM   81    02/03/88    48 +     1
FM   82    14/12/91    93 -     1

┌─NAMECHLD─5──────────────────────────────────────────────────────────────
1st name: Dolf          Fam. name: De Groot         Diagnosis: Down's syndrome
─ASSESSMT─2698──Depth 2─
Task:♦FM  78  Dat: 26/06/87 Mnth.:      40 State: + No.:      1 a:g A:A I:    7:0
Rem.: Only with his mother.

Service:    Early Intervention Service         Phone no.: 08889-266166
Address:    North Sea Drive 11
Zcode:      7777 XX Place: ROTTERDAM
```

Screen 1

The field 'Dat' in Screen 1 can accommodate the date of the particular assessment. Via an automatic link with the panel containing personal data, the child's age at that particular date will be included in the field 'Mnth.' immediately. The term 'Stats' stands for the status of the child with respect to that particular task. Three levels are distinguished, notably: '+' (yes) for a child that has met the criterion from the Manual of the Macquarie Program, '±' (nearly) for a child that has almost mastered the task and finally '-' (no) if the child cannot do that particular task. The field 'Rem.' for remarks speaks for itself.

In the lookup list of Screen 1 only the results of child number 1 are shown (see the figures 1, at the right). Had the door to depth 1 not been opened by arrow-down but by F5 (function key 5) then one would have seen corresponding tasks of the various children. In that way, at a glance, one can see how a particular child performs in relation to the others within the database.

While entering data into the ASSESSMT panel, what if you no longer know what is the exact task description belonging to the abbreviation FM 78? Is it still necessary to look into the original books? No, certainly not! For that purpose the field 'Task' in the ASSESSMT panel again forms a door (this time a so-called 'data link'), notably to depth 3, the 'DSI' panel with the descriptions from the DSI of the Macquarie Program (Screen 2). As in all DataPerfect applications, arrow-down means a path to the description of one particular task and F5 a path to all tasks of the DSI. By organizing all available information in this way, task descriptions from the Macquarie Program, which, of course, are equal for all children, are recorded on disk only once. That is a main feature of this application.

```
                                                     ─15/04/92──14:46┐
Task code in the terminology of the "DSI" of the Macquarie Program.

To look for another record give arrow up or function key 8.

For more about this task (materials, method, criterium) give arrow down.
For more about all tasks (ditto) function key 5.
└BROWSING RECORD   ↑Panel-F7   Create-F9   Edit-F6   Lookup-↑   Help-F3┘
┌NAMECHLD─5┐
1st name: Dolf       Fam. name: De Groot       Diagnosis: Down's syndrome
┌ASSESSMT─2698──Depth 2 ┐
Task:♦FM  78  Dat: 26/06/87 Mnth.:     40 Stats: + No.:     1 a:g A:A X:   ?:0 ⠿
Rem.: Only with his mother.
┌DSI─786──Depth 3 ┐
Task code:♦FM  78                                              Mark:
Task:        Matches pictures, choice of 2.
```

Screen 2

In exactly the same way one can walk from depth 3, the DSI panel, again via a data link, to depth 4, the 'MANUAL' panel, containing all the extra information belonging to the tasks within the Macquarie Program (Screen 3, next page). As such, it gives the unacquainted reader a good impression of the set-up of the Macquarie Program as well.

Finally, at the extreme right in the MANUAL panel one sees another panel link, this time to depth 5, the 'EXTRAINF' panel, the note book of the professional concerned. In that panel extra information per task, which is relevant for all children, can be administrated. In this way, one can record e. g. references to particular articles, experiences with certain task analyses as well as cross references with other intervention programmes.

The way back to higher levels is found, as always with programmes from the WordPerfect stable, by pressing F7 one or more times. It just depends how far one wants to go back.

```
                                                    ─15/04/92──14:47┐
 Door to the panel with (room for) extra information per task.

 For the information to this task code give arrow-down.
 (If required pressing function key 5 twice will produce a new record.)
 For all extra information give function key 5.
└─BROWSING RECORD    ↑Panel-F7    Create-F9    Edit-F6    Lookup-↑    Help-F3─┘
┌─NAMECHLD─5─
 1st name: Dolf        Fam. name: De Groot        Diagnosis: Down's syndrome
 ░MANUAL─786─Depth 4
 Task code: FM  78 Equiv. age. (mnth):          (year):          Mark:      Inf: :
 Sequence:  Matching and sorting (objects and pictures)
 Task:      Matching pictures, choice of 2.

 Materials: Two sets of two identical pictures, 5 cm square or larger.
            Or lotto board with two pictures and matching cards.
 Method:    Place one picture from each set on table in front of child and
            say "Look, I can put the ... on the ...". Demonstrate. Hand
            picture to child and say "Put the ... on the ...". Repeat
 Criterion: Pass if the child places picture on identical picture without
            physical or verbal prompting in three out of four trials.
```

Screen 3

4 Reporting

A very favourable quality of DataPerfect is the enormous range of possibilities to export data from a database, 'reporting'. Within SMLLSTPS extensive use is made of that, too. At the present time the application contains nine standard reports:

1. *Built-In Short Reports* offers a variety of possibilities to specify all kinds of different reports very quickly, as well as for the production of back-ups and checking of entered data. In addition, data can easily be exported from one computer (teacher, therapist) to another (central place).

2. If large groups of data have to be imported from the DSI of a particular child, which was filled-in by hand, or a pre-existing file has to be updated, this can best be done by using the report *Edit a record in ASSESSMT (updating a file)*. Upon entering the search criteria the computer is able to deal with a whole series of tasks in the desired way in just a few key strokes.

   In addition, this option offers the simple possibility of having the same 'correction' automatically entered into the data as often as required. This is needed e. g. at every update for tasks which remain at 'no' at the new date. Furthermore, it might be necessary when data for particular children have to be exported from one computer into another. Clearly, one then has to take into account that two different children in those two computers could, in principle, have received identical AI-numbers. If nothing is done this will most certainly lead to problems. Such an operation can only be carried out without mixing up data by 'correcting' AI-numbers before transferring.

3. In the *Personal report* tasks are reproduced in such a way that within all nine separate developmental domains first all 'yes' (+) are printed, followed by all nearly's' (±) while finally the no's' (-) are given. Within these three groups the tasks are furthermore sequenced according to the date of mastery and finally according to number. In this a way it can be made very clear what that child 'is doing' at that particular time. To avoid this report becoming unreasonably long, particularly with younger children, the report itself 'asks' for the maximum

number of 'no's' that will be printed. In fact, this report is the equivalent of a completed DSI, including the remarks per task for that particular child.

4. The *Personal report of 'no's' and 'nearly's'* is a particular case of the previous one. This time tasks for which the child has reached criterion are not reported, but only those tasks that have not been mastered by the child. However, in contradiction to the foregoing report, all available information for the tasks will be printed, also the data from the Manual. As such, this report can be looked upon as a collection of relevant tasks, or rather a plan of work for the interme-diate term. There are two different types:

a) a report that is differentiated according to the nine developmental domains from the early intervention programme and

b) a report that is differentiated according to all 29 sequences as a finer subdi-vision of the developmental domains.

To avoid the reports concerned becoming unreasonably long and parents disap-pointed because of the number of 'no's' in relation to their child, in both types of report the number of tasks with a 'no' that will be presented can be limited to any specific number entered beforehand. The reports simply 'ask' for its value.

5. The *Activity chart* contains a description of the 'homework' of one child for the coming intervention period of e. g. one week. If an X is placed into field 'X' of panel ASSESSMT upon activating this report, the printer will automatically produce the activity chart belonging to that task for that child, with all relevant data.

6. The *Mutual comparison of various children* shows per DSI-task how long speci-fic children took to reach mastery. In addition an average value is computed.

7. A bit more needs to be said about the *Developmental profiles with MDF*. The advances in a child's development can be followed exactly on the basis of the results of his or her periodical assessments according to the DSI. That develop-ment can further be quantified by calculating the percentage of tasks for which the criterion from the Manual to the DSI has been reached. If a child at an age of e. g. four years shows a '+' for about three quarters of all tasks of the DSI and a '-' for the rest then, obviously, that four year old child in that particular domain 'functions on the level of a child of three years' (popular terminology to relate to the concept mental age). That is all the more plausible when one reali-zes that the child will have mastered the more early tasks in particular, but most probably not the latest ones. By calculating that percentage for every one of the original five developmental domains and by plotting the results, one gets a so-called developmental profile. Upon studying that, one can see at a glance, what the child is good at and also what are the weakest domains that will need most attention. As such, this kind of profile gives a much more differentiated image than the in itself fairly meaningless term 'mental age' without anything more, as is frequently used by professionals. Upon calculating the aforementioned per-centages a problem is encountered. Even within the various developmental do-mains the numbers of tasks per year vary considerably. To accommodate for these differences in numbers one has to use the following formula:

$$\sum \left(\frac{\text{number of tasks with a } +}{\text{total number of tasks}} \times 1 \text{ year} \right)_{\text{per year}}$$

The developmental profiles in this paper are calculated according to this formula. Furthermore, per developmental domain, the report computes the so-called partial fractions: the percentage of tasks scored in relation to the total number in that domain. These partial quotients are of particular interest when one wants to see whether a child gradually starts deviating more or less from the standard after, say, a certain number of months. Next, these quotients are averaged into what has been called the Macquarie Developmental Fraction (MDF). That can be interpreted as a (nonvalidated) measure for development, very much in the sense of IQ. The program does the same calculation again, after exclusion of the language components, to arrive at a non-verbal MDF.

8. Besides the aforementioned report for the production of gross developmental profiles, there is a corresponding report *Partial profile GM, FM, RL and PS*. Using this, four separate profiles in the developmental domains concerned, which are differentiated into the sequences that make up the domain concerned, are calculated. These last reports in particular can be used very effectively as a diagnostic instrument, for they provide a very accurate image of the development of a child, much more accurate than a test, because of the fact that a developmental quotient is calculated for every separate sequence within every developmental domain.

   Both reports prompt the user for the reference date of the desired profiles, so enabling him to produce a report for an earlier age afterwards by simple means, e. g. for a child which is now five for a particular date in its third year of life.

9. In the *Personal report in ascending order of tasks, with average time to criterion,* all items with a "yes" (+) are presented in chronological ascending order, within all five separate developmental domains. In addition, the report shows the number of months it has taken the child to reach criterion on every particular task. In this way, it immediately becomes clear which tasks in the programme have caused the child concerned particular difficulties.

5 Further Possibilities

It is impossible to describe all aspects of SMLLSTPS in full detail here. Therefore, only a very brief description of some other important aspects will be given. Whether the program runs as an application of DataPerfect or of its Runtime-version, for computers with a colour monitor the user can adapt the screen colours himself.

The search function is very important. To produce a report, the child concerned has to be chosen in the NAMECHLD screen. For a report which compares different children one can search for e. g. diagnosis to exclude comparisons of little relevance, e. g. between children with motor limitations due to cerebral palsy and children with Prader-Willi-syndrome.

It is furthermore important to know that the user of SMLLSTPS can easily adapt all reports by himself, or can define his own reports, whether the program runs as an application of DataPerfect or of its Runtime-version.

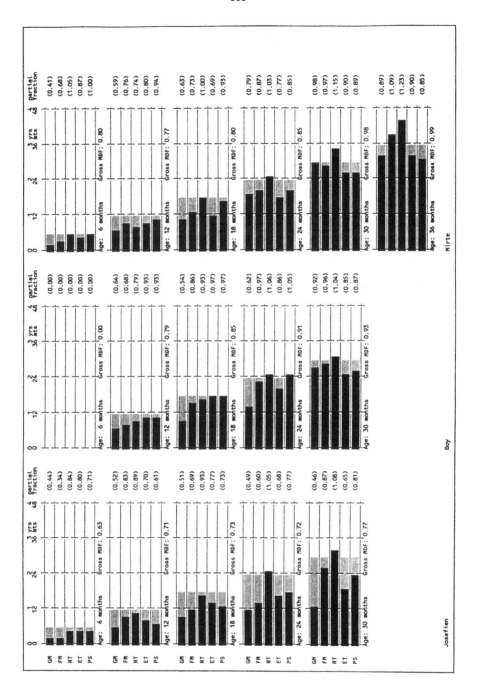

Apart from the application for which the computer programme is offered here, it can also accommodate all kinds of other comparable intervention programmes, or child assessment systems, which work with a checklist (here the 'DSI') on the one hand, and per task in this checklist an amount of additional information (here the Manual) on the other. Programmes like e. g. Portage can be entered into SMLLSTPS to be used subsequently in the way proposed here.

6 References

1 M. Pieterse, S. Cairns, and R. Treloar: The Macquarie Program for developmentally delayed children. Manual to be used in conjunction with the Developmental Skills Inventory (DSI). Sydney: Macquarie University, Special Education Centre 1986
2 S. Cairns and M. Pieterse: The Macquarie Program for developmentally delayed children. Reading Program. Sydney: Macquarie University, Special Education Centre 1979
3 M. Pieterse and S. Cairns: The Macquarie Program for developmentally delayed children. Drawing and Prewriting Program. Manual. Sydney: Macquarie University, Special Education Centre 1981
4 Anonymous: The Macquarie Program for developmentally delayed children. Number Skills Program. Sydney: Macquarie University, Special Education Centre 1981

Acknowledgement

The author wishes to express his thanks to Mrs. Susanne Tonkens-Hart who corrected the English.

Captions for figures on next two pages

Developmental profiles with MDF for three children with Down's syndrome, notably Josefien, Boy and Mirte, at different ages. The profiles have been produced one by one by SMLLSTPS and were subsequently imported in a WordPerfect text frame.

Partial profiles in the gross motor domain at subsequent age levels for one child with Down's syndrome. The profiles have been produced one by one by SMLLSTPS and were subsequently imported in a WordPerfect text frame.

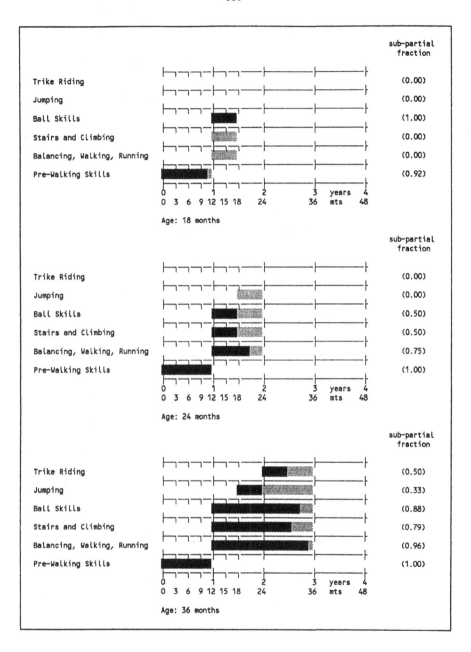

Development and Use of a Speech Recognition System for Physically Handicapped Users

James Monaghan & Christine Cheepen

University of Hertfordshire, England, UK

Abstract This paper reports on the impact of the implementation of a totally hands-free work station based on an automatic speech recognition (ASR) user interface management system in a school for disabled children with learning difficulties. It focusses on two major areas of impact - firstly the general effects of the introduction of a speech input computer system into the organisational context of a school, and secondly the educational benefit to the student users which arose from the introduction of the system.

1   Introduction

The CALE project[1] had as its aim the provision and implementation of a totally hands-free computer system based on a standard workstation for disabled school children. The research team worked with a particular group of target users at Lonsdale School in Stevenage, Herts., UK, using the school's existing hardware platform - a Nimbus 386, and IBM's VoiceType^{TM} as the speech recognition software base[2]. The school caters for disabled children from 3 to 18 years old, all of whom have some degree of learning difficulty, and the particular group of users involved in the research and development project were taken from the 16-18 age bracket. Some work was done with sufferers from cerebral palsy, but in the main the target user group were disabled due to muscular dystrophy - a fatal disease which causes sufferers to become progressively weaker, so that they are unable to walk, and ultimately lose any manual ability.

---

[1] The CALE project was partly funded by a substantial donation from Save and Prosper Educational Trust.

[2] VoiceType provides a pre-set dictionary of 5000 words and allows the user to add a further 2000 words, which can be repeatedly updated.

2   Organisational Matters

Clearly in any school situation the smooth running of the day is dependent on observing the timetable and having an overview of where teachers, individual pupils and classes are at any given time. In a school for pupils with special needs this is exacerbated by the pupils having to engage in therapeutic bed rest periods, swimming and the like at specific times of the day. Any technology has to be made available in this context. An ASR based system also has special aspects such as the sound of the user talking possibly disturbing parallel speech-based activity in the same room, and, conversely, the possibility of noisy classroom activities interfering with the speech recognition. As a consequence, the system was installed in a separate computer room with three other computer sytems.

All computer systems create tensions in that they represent a significant deskilling of all but specialist computing staff, and in the present environment the primary agenda of most staff is the care for the pupils as a whole. Any difficulties with such a system, due to inexperience, present a very strong temptation to abandon the experiment and substitute it by very hands-on supportive work such as taking dictation. While this approach can be beneficial in terms of creating and maintaining social bonds between staff and students, it inevitably creates an ever increasing dependence of the disabled child on the able-bodied adult. This can - and only too often does - result in deteriorating motivation in the student, and, as we will illustrate in section 4 below, a consequent drop in educational performance, particularly in terms of written language skills.

In order to ensure that this kind of avoidance of the system does not occur, it is necessary, particularly in the initial stage of development, to have support personnel from the research project on site to pick up on obvious teething problems until staff and at least some pupils find it worth while to solve problems using the ASR system rather than to revert to less efficient but more familiar solutions. It is also important to aim at a spread of competence among staff because uneven skill development causes frictions and tends to raise a perception that the technology is 'owned' by specific departments rather than by the school as a whole.

3   Physical Access to a Speech Input System

For pupils with conditions such as muscular dystrophy, numerous difficulties must be overcome. As well as the physical problems which characterise the disease, there is often poor morale and lack of motivation. This, coupled with a life-long physical dependence on able-bodied help, often results in a general lack of concentration and application, so that pupils are unwilling to cooperate in activities requiring any sustained effort. This problem of user attitude became particularly apparent in the matter of providing the users with physical access to the system.

The VoiceType speech recognition system, which is the core of the CALE development, provides a headset for use with the microphone, and this clearly militates against user independence, as it seriously constrains the severely disabled user, who needs help getting in and out of it. To cope with this, we provided a gooseneck microphone stand which they could simply approach in their wheelchairs, thus allowing them total independence when using the system.

Although effective in providing user independence, this created problems in the case of some users. Because of their dependence on teachers and helpers they accepted the constraints of the headset without complaint, but, given the freedom of the gooseneck stand, and having no experience of self-discipline, they simply stopped working whenever they were inclined to do so, and wheeled away, leaving their work unfinished and unsaved. When this was observed, the research team considered removing the gooseneck stand and returning to the headset, but in time, as the users became more proficient, and their satisfaction with the system increased, they became willing to work for longer and to enjoy completing word processing tasks. Our recommendation for future installations in schools is to provide the headset in the early stages, and, when the users have begun to experience considerable success with the system, to introduce the gooseneck stand in order to allow them full independence.

4   Users' Educational Problems and some Solutions

As we have indicated above, severe permanent disability frequently leads to poor morale and lack of motivation in those afflicted. The pupils at Lonsdale School all have some degree of learning difficulty, this being primarily evident in terms of their reading age (which was in most cases some five years lower than their chronological age) and associated written language skills. The reason for this poor level of literacy is, however, often difficult to establish, as experts in special needs education have no way of determining whether the problem is due to a cognitive disability in addition to the physical disability, or simply a consequence of the lack of practice and impoverished feedback which are due to the constraints of the physical disability.

The speech input system which we introduced to the pupils at Lonsdale School proved to be an important diagnostic and remedial tool in this area of literacy skills. In some cases, it became clear that poor literacy levels were not merely apparent, but a fundamental educational problem. This was most certainly the case with a 17 year old girl who suffered from a form of deteriorating cerebral palsy. She appeared to have great difficulty using the system, and was reluctant to come to grips with the effort required to learn how to use it, employing a variety of techniques to distract the researcher who worked with her, such as incessantly chattering, displaying new jewellery etc. After some weeks of attempting (unsuccessfully) to teach this pupil to use the system, it became evident that her level of literacy was extremely low, so that, when faced with the system's 'offers' of candidate words on the screen in response to her voice input item, she was unable to read them, and was therefore unable to choose the right one. For her, and other such users, a speech input system such as VoiceType, used to access a standard word processing package, such as Word, was totally inappropriate. Any attempts to proceed with this kind of user would be likely to result in demotivation, due to the experience of repeated failure rather than success in using the system. Our recommendation for these users - and a problem currently under consideration - is to use speech input for special software packages which provide for high age, low ability education in literacy.

However, in other cases the introduction of a speech input system dramatically improved users' satisfaction, and, as a consequence, their observable literacy skills. Three boys who suffered from muscular dystrophy showed substantial progress after a few months of using the system, showing that their previously observable level of literacy had been artificially depressed by poor morale due to deteriorating ability in using conventional input methods.

One boy, a 17 year old called Glen, had particularly outstanding success with the system. At the beginning of our work with Glen he was causing the staff some concern, as his deteriorating condition had resulted in him becoming severely demotivated, not only regarding his school work, but in the social aspects of his life as well, so that he would not enter into conversation with team members, with the staff, or even with his fellow pupils. He had an apparent reading age of about eleven, and his last written work with a pen was very poor indeed, with badly spelt, and often incomplete words.

Glen's progress over approximately 6 months was remarkable, both in terms of his attitude, which improved enormously, so that he began to communicate with people again, and, very dramatically, in terms of his literacy skills. It became clear that in Glen's case most of his learning difficulties (certainly in terms of literacy skills) were due to lack of feedback and reinforcement. Because, in his later stage, he was unable to produce much written work (in a typical half-hour session of writing he would produce an average of 18-25 words), he was missing out on the practice of writing lengthy pieces of text, and the reinforcement of seeing lengthy texts which were his own work. After six months of using the CALE system, he was able to produce around 150 words of text in a half-hour session, and because using speech as an input medium was less tiring, was able to continue working enthusiastically for much longer. The improvement was not only in the amount of work done, but also in the range of vocabulary used and (as our detailed analyses of a wide range of his work revealed) in his sentence length. When using a pen, Glen's average sentence length was 7-9 words, but with the CALE system his sentence length rose to around 16 words, which is the average sentence length for normal, literate adults.

5   Customisation of Software

VoiceType is a functionally very powerful system, which allows full voice access to any standard, pc based software package which can normally be accessed by the keyboard. This functionality can, however, be rather overwhelming for new users of low educational ability. For the pupils at Lonsdale School we were concerned to ensure that the CALE system would be sufficiently simple so that they could quickly achieve success, in order to encourage their further use of it. This consideration was particularly important in Glen's case, as it was a matter of some urgency to grant him some independence with the system in order to improve his confidence and general morale.

Many of the spoken commands provided by the VoiceType system were unsuitable for Glen, because they were too long for him to remember, for example the sequence which is the default way of loading personalised voice files:

Example 1   **voice console**
                   wake up
                   new user
                   golf
                   lima
                   echo
                   november
                   enter key
                   yes please

With this kind of sequence, when the voice recognition is less than perfect (a fact of life with any speech input system in the early stages) the number of errors necessitating correction (without access to the keyboard for a disabled user) can be very discouraging to a novice user of the system. We therefore developed customised commands so that he and his teacher, Sonia, could easily access their own voice files. We set up the system to boot up in a general voice file, and provided Glen and Sonia with their own, trained voice files. They were then able to simply say:

Example 2

change to glen   or   **change to sonia**

to carry out the lengthy procedures of Example 1 above, but without the need to make each step explicit by a command word. To unload their voice files and return to the general file, they said:

Example 3

get general

This was a very successful improvement for Glen, as it avoided most of the problems of misrecognition while trying to begin work, and it allowed him to experience early success with the system rather than early failure. The resulting boost to his motivation meant that he was able to tackle the business of using a word processing package by speech with confidence and the expectation of success. We built in several similarly simplified commands for him to use for basic word processing, and provided him with a set of instructions to use instead of the VoiceType manual, so that he would not be discouraged by having to use commands which were lengthy or difficult to say.

6   Summary and Recommendations

With any computer system and any group of users there is inevitably a tension between the provision of full functionality and the human factors requirements of the user. A balance must be achieved between these often competing needs in order to make the system properly usable on a day-to-day basis. The problems are most acute in the case of novice users, as they can be discouraged only too easily from using the system, and in the case of disabled users - particularly in a school context, where there are many able-bodied helpers on hand - the possibility of simply ceasing to use the system is very real indeed.

As preceding sections have shown, our solution to this potential problem was to provide access to the full functionality of the system by gradual stages. In terms of the users' direct interaction with underlying speech software, we initially catered only for their most basic requirements, hiding facilities and functionality, so as not to create confusion. This was done largely by producing customised user documentation and requiring the users to operate according to that, without any reference to more sophisticated instructions and information, such as the VoiceType manual. As the expertise and confidence of the user increases, more facilities can be made available to them, permitting more comprehensive functionality of the system.

With regard to users' physical access to the system, our work at Lonsdale School showed very clearly that special problems tend to occur when the users suffer from life-long, severe disabilities, as they have little self-discipline, and are disinclined to commit themselves to the lengthy periods of sustained effort which are necessary if they are to become proficient with a speech input system. Again, our approach is to allow them fully independent access only in gradual stages, either by restricting novices to using a microphone headset, or, where appropriate, by ensuring that there is close supervision of the user during the early stages of learning how to use the system.

This process of gradually introducing the users to the full power of the system inevitably has a beneficial result in the area of the impact of the new system on the organisation as a whole. Because the progress of disabled school children from full dependence on the teaching staff and helpers to independent use of the system is completed in stages over a period of months, the staff also become increasingly familiar with the system, willing to promote its use, and confident of their new role in relation to pupils who are newly independent of able-bodied help.

Bibliography

Cheepen, C. & J. Monaghan (1993) *Speech interfaces and their effects on written language skills,* <u>Proceedings of Eurospeech '93,</u> Berlin

Gilchrist, P. (1994) *An Evaluation of the CALE System at Lonsdale School,* unpublished BA dissertation, University of Hertfordshire

Head Mounted Accelerometers in the Control of a Video Cursor

E. Gallasch, D. Rafolt, T.Kenner

Department of Physiology, University of Graz
8010 Graz, Harrachgasse 21, Austria

Background

Spinal disabled persons often have limited movement capability in lower and upper extremities but some cerebral innervated muscles are still intact to move the head. It is therefore obvious to use head movements for man - machine control. In this paper a head mounted triaxial accelerometer, is used as an input device to control a video cursor in interactive software applications. Two transducer mechanisms of piezo-resistive accelerometers are available to calculate cursor position from the accelerometric signal: double integration and inclination in the gravity field. The first mechanism is considered in this study.

Realization

To use accelerometers for full cursor control three basic functions have to be realized, (1) - get the zero position of the cursor before movement, (2) - move the cursor from one position to an arbitrary position on the screen and (3) - perform a prompt to do an action in the software. Zero position (1) was obtained by a twitch-like turning of the head in the horizontal axis. Peak acceleration is used to dicriminate between functions 1 and 2. For cursor movement (2) the accelerometric signal is continuously integrated two times to calculate velocity and distance. Both distance and velocity are used to calulate the cursor trajectory. Prompt (3) was obtained in the same way as (1) but with turning the head in vertical axis.

Miniature triaxial accelerometers were used in this study (Type EGAX-5, Entran Inc., France). Cursor positioning software was implemented in „C" on a labtop (Toshiba T 3100 SX) with an integrated 12-bit A/D-card (TADA, IBP Inc., BRD).

Results and Conclusions

The results had been obtained on non disabled. As in contast to the hand the head has considerable mass and head movement further acts as an input to the vestibulo-occular system, the display gain (ratio of head movement to cursor movement) should be less than 0,5. If the values become smaller than 0,1 cursor position control becomes less accurate due to some tremors and the integration drift. Peak acceleration for discrimination between smooth cursor movement (2) and functions (1) and (3) was found optimal in the range between 0,5 and 2 g.

This study also shows that a twoaxial accelerometer (x and y-axis of the triaxial sensor) will be sufficient to realize the three basic functions, as fore and back movements (z-axis of the sensor) of the head are unphysiological. A disadvantage is the cable supporting the sensor. By the use of micro-machined sensor technology realization of a telemetric wireless sensor will be possible in near future. In combination with a speech recognition system the keybord and the mouse of a traditional computer system may be totally replaced by contactless head functions.

Computer Assisted Training Programme for Early Intervention for Children with Mental Retardation

Air Vice Marshal V. Krishnaswamy (Retd.)

Indchem Research and Development Laboratory
Madras 600 017, India

Abstract. Mental retardation is the worst of all human handicaps. An estimated 2% of the population suffer from this handicap. The earlier the intervention the greater is its effectiveness. There is hardly any systematic programme of early intervention suited to the cultural milieu and socio-economic conditions of India. Noting the need for an indigenous programme suited to the country, Indchem Research and Development Laboratory developed a computer assisted programme of training for children with mental retardation. The curriculum of training was developed by an interdisciplinary team of experts in the field. A logic was developed to relate the pre-requisite skills in different developmental areas to those in the area of Self-Help. The programme called *Upanayan* (To lead along) is confined now to children with mental retardation in the age group 0-2 years. The mothers are trained on this programme to train the children.

The computer assistance for the training programme was developed in Microsoft 'C' and operates on an IBM compatible PC/AT. A programme for recording the data on children under training and their progress facilitates the setting of goals and the monitoring of progress.

Parents of children at Madhuram Narayanan Centre for Exceptional Centre, Madras, use this programme for early intervention. The programme for the children has been documented and the results of training using it are satisfactory and encouraging.

1. Introduction

1.1 Indchem Research and Development Laboratory is a scientific association recognised by Government of India and dedicated to research and development in the field of electronics. As a part of its societal responsibility, the laboratory took up a project in 1987 for the developmental training of children with mental retardation in the age group from birth to two years.

1.2 In a survey prior to this, the Laboratory had noted that mental retardation was the worst and the most neglected of all human handicaps and that the services to persons with this category of handicaps, were poor in this country. The estimated number of persons with this handicap is about 1.8 million i.e. about 2% of the country's total population which is nearing 900 million. Out of these only about 70,000 persons receive the services needed. This is because of the paucity of trained teachers and the lack of suitable material for imparting training. There are only about 5,000 special educators and there will never be a situation when there are enough teachers to serve the vast population with mental handicap. There has been practically no worthwhile standard material produced in the country as there has been hardly any research in the field because of limited resources. Whatever programmes have been used are drawn from western sources not quite suited to the socio economic conditions and cultural milieu of the country.

1.3 Early Intervention

The organisation also noted that earlier the intervention in the case of the handicap, the better the chances of reducing its impact as established by a number of pioneering studies in India and abroad [1,2,3,4]. It noted that there was an urgent, felt need for a standard, systematic tool for providing early intervention services appropriate to the conditions in the sub continent.

1.4 The potential of the micro computer

The organisation took note of the potential of the micro computer in this area, its capacity to receive, store and enable retrieval of, a large amount of information/data and its capability to be the platform for an expert system. It was envisaged that the computer will enable provision of services to a much larger population than the traditional methods of training.

2. The Upanayan Project And The Early Intervention Programme

2.1 The Laboratory took up a project for the development of a programme of early intervention which could be understood and implemented by mothers of children who need such services. The programme named *'UPANAYAN'* to signify the 'leading to progress' of the child by the mother was evolved by an interdisciplinary team of experts in the field, comprising, amongst others, a neo-natal pediatrician, developmental psychologists, special educators, a speech therapist, a physiotherapist and an occupational therapist. [5]

2.2   The interdisciplinary team identified 250 discrete skills in the five developmental areas - Motor, Self-Help, Language, Cognition and Socialisation - as the optimal ones for the training of children with the handicap.

2.3   The intervention system consists of (a) a developmental check list of skills for assessment and programming, (b) a profile to record the observation and (c) intervention strategies in the form of activities to train the mother/ professional to train the children in all the skills in the check list. Formats to evaluate the efficacy of the programme and the methodology of activity-oriented intervention strategies for the acquiring of the skills by the child were developed. The programme was field-tested and its workability and suitability established.

2. 3.1 To give the necessary visual impact, the activity modules were illustrated with over 600 photographs of children performing the various skills.

2.3.2 The are of Self-Help was considered as the priority goal by the parents. The related skills in the other developmental areas which are pre-requisites for the achievement of a particular Self-Help skill are shown as `Linked Skills' at the end of the module for each Self Help skill.

3.   Computer Assistance To The Training Programme

3.1   The text of Upanayan Early Intervention Activities corresponding to the 250 skills are stored in the hard disk of a personal computer along with the photographs illustrating these activities. Any desired skill and activity could be called and displayed.

3. 1.1 The training package comprising the text and photographs was developed in Microsoft 'C' (version 6.0.). the text of the instructions on the intervention activities was edited using the Northern Editor (NE). An IBM compatible PC/AT with a hard disk capacity of 10 MB, along with an VGA monitor, is used in the system operated.

3. 2.2 Relevant particulars of the child and his parents, his medical history and his performance on the skills are recorded in the computer. His performance on the skills appropriate to his age at the initial assessment and at the subsequent quarterly assessments are also recorded. The mother sees the performance profile of her child on the screen after every periodical evaluation, after which new goals and objectives are set by the teacher in consultation with the mother, based on the the child's achievements and his priorities. An Individual Programme Plan is then worked out for the child and implemented.

3. 2.1 The process of training and evluation mentioned in para 3.2 continues.

3. 2.2 The programme for recording the data on children and the progress of their training was developed using the 'Clipper'.

3.3 The mother goes ahead with the programme till the child acquires the necessary skills.

4. Application

The programme is in use at Madhuram Narayanan Centre for Exceptional Children established at Madras, India, in 1989, as a division of Indchem Research and Development Laboratory for providing early intervention services using the Upanayam programme. The Centre has been using the programme effectively over the last 5 years, with nearly 340 children on its rolls now. It is noted that the parents and the teachers were particularly motivated by the novelty of the computer assisted programme which displays the programme graphically on the monitor apart from the efficacy of the training itself and the progress acheived in the child's development.

The centre has trained teachers from 16 institutions in the country on the Early Intervention Programme in the print form. As these institutions do not have the computer facility, they were not trained on the computer version of the programme. The centre plans to train teachers from other institutions on the computer assisted programme when computer facilities are made available in the various district headquarters in the neighbourhood of these institutions.

5. Future Plans

We propose to convert the basic modules developed in the computer into an Interactive Visual Training Programme. This interactive visual training programme will enable the linking of the related skills in different developmental areas to facilitate correction in the training activity, where necessary, and re-training, as needed.

Multi-media tools will be used for developing the above said visual training modules. The training modules will employ step-by-step approach with digitized pictures of the actions in the training process and voice explanation of the same. Facility will be provided for retracing the steps and the related pre-requisite skills for any specific activity. By developing interactive visual tools to aid training, we plan to make learning more enjoyable and rewarding. This will also eliminate the need for experts to be available in all places where training is given.

Indchem Research and Development Laboratory is presently engaged in the development of a multimedia tool. This tool will be utilised for the purpose mentioned above.

The future plan also includes providing computer aided on-line interaction with different groups by employing state-of-art technology and development and implementation of performance contoured programme of training.

6. Conclusion

6.1 Computer assistance to the Upanayan Early Intervention Programme has facilitated the easy implementation of the programme, assisted in monitoring the progress of the children and enhanced the effectiveness of the system of training.

6.2 The computer assisted programme has the potential of the extension of the services to a much larger population than the traditional methods and of enhancing the quality and effectiveness of these services.

References:

1.   Brazelton, T B (1973) Neonatal behavioural assessment scale. Philadelphia: Lippincott.

2.   Bronfenbrenner (Ed.), Influences on human development. Hinsdale, IL: Dryden.

3.   Boaz P D, Jeyachandran P., etal - Feasibility of Training Mothers of the Mentally Retarded in Day Care Centers. 1968, Bala Vihar, Madras.

4.   Schaefer, E.S.,& Aaronson, M.(1972). Infant education research project: Implementation and implications of the home-tutoring program. In R.K.Parker (Ed.), The preschool in action. Boston: Allyn and Bacon.

5.   Jaya Krishnaswamy, (1992) Group Training of Parents - Fifth National Annual Seminar on Mental Retardation by National Institute for the Mentally Handicapped, Bhuvaneswar, India.

ICCHP 94 PRECONFERENCE SEMINARS

**The following list shows the titles of the Preconference Seminars,
the authors and the addresses of the authors mentioned first**

Utilization of the Internet for Communication Among Rehabilitation
Facilities
George W. Kessinger

Goodwill Industries of Orange Country
410 North Fairview
Santa Ana, CA 92703
USA

SGML Up-to-Speed
Tom Wesley, F. Evenepoel

Dept. of Computing, University of Bradford
Bradford, BD7 1DP
United Kingdom

The Conventional Braille Display - State of the Art and Future
Perspectives
Bernhard Stöger, K. Miesenberger

Modellversuch Informatik für Blinde, Univ. Linz
Altenbergerstr. 69
A-4040 Linz
Austria

The AbleProfessionals Seminar: Strategies and Techniques for Employing People with Disabilities
Darcy Painter, J. H. Ramseur, L. S. Gardner

Center for Rehabilitation Technology (CRT), Inc
490 10th Street, N.W.
Atlanta, Georgia 30318
USA

Access to MS Windows for Blind Users
Gerhard Weber, D. Kochanek, H. Petrie

Universität Stuttgart, Inst. f. Informatik
Breitwiesenstr. 20-22
D-70565 Stuttgart
Germany

Access to Electronic Information for Visually Impaired Persons
Franz Peter Seiler, N. Vigouroux,
M. Truquet, P. Bazex, C. Decoret,

fortec - Rehabilitation Engineering Group
Gusshausstr. 27/359-B
A-1040 Wien
Austria

INDEX OF AUTHORS

Lecture Notes in Computer Science

For information about Vols. 1–786
please contact your bookseller or Springer-Verlag

Vol. 824: E. M. Schmidt, S. Skyum (Eds.), Algorithm Theory – SWAT '94. Proceedings. IX, 383 pages. 1994.

Vol. 825: J. L. Mundy, A. Zisserman, D. Forsyth (Eds.), Applications of Invariance in Computer Vision. Proceedings, 1993. IX, 510 pages. 1994.

Vol. 826: D. S. Bowers (Ed.), Directions in Databases. Proceedings, 1994. X, 234 pages. 1994.

Vol. 827: D. M. Gabbay, H. J. Ohlbach (Eds.), Temporal Logic. Proceedings, 1994. XI, 546 pages. 1994. (Subseries LNAI).

Vol. 828: L. C. Paulson, Isabelle. XVII, 321 pages. 1994.

Vol. 829: A. Chmora, S. B. Wicker (Eds.), Error Control, Cryptology, and Speech Compression. Proceedings, 1993. VIII, 121 pages. 1994.

Vol. 830: C. Castelfranchi, E. Werner (Eds.), Artificial Social Systems. Proceedings, 1992. XVIII, 337 pages. 1994. (Subseries LNAI).

Vol. 831: V. Bouchitté, M. Morvan (Eds.), Orders, Algorithms, and Applications. Proceedings, 1994. IX, 204 pages. 1994.

Vol. 832: E. Börger, Y. Gurevich, K. Meinke (Eds.), Computer Science Logic. Proceedings, 1993. VIII, 336 pages. 1994.

Vol. 833: D. Driankov, P. W. Eklund, A. Ralescu (Eds.), Fuzzy Logic and Fuzzy Control. Proceedings, 1991. XII, 157 pages. 1994. (Subseries LNAI).

Vol. 834: D.-Z. Du, X.-S. Zhang (Eds.), Algorithms and Computation. Proceedings, 1994. XIII, 687 pages. 1994.

Vol. 835: W. M. Tepfenhart, J. P. Dick, J. F. Sowa (Eds.), Conceptual Structures: Current Practices. Proceedings, 1994. VIII, 331 pages. 1994. (Subseries LNAI).

Vol. 836: B. Jonsson, J. Parrow (Eds.), CONCUR '94: Concurrency Theory. Proceedings, 1994. IX, 529 pages. 1994.

Vol. 837: S. Wess, K.-D. Althoff, M. M. Richter (Eds.), Topics in Case-Based Reasoning. Proceedings, 1993. IX, 471 pages. 1994. (Subseries LNAI).

Vol. 838: C. MacNish, D. Pearce, L. Moniz Pereira (Eds.), Logics in Artificial Intelligence. Proceedings, 1994. IX, 413 pages. 1994. (Subseries LNAI).

Vol. 839: Y. G. Desmedt (Ed.), Advances in Cryptology - CRYPTO '94. Proceedings, 1994. XII, 439 pages. 1994.

Vol. 840: G. Reinelt, The Traveling Salesman. VIII, 223 pages. 1994.

Vol. 841: I. Prívara, B. Rovan, P. Ružička (Eds.), Mathematical Foundations of Computer Science 1994. Proceedings, 1994. X, 628 pages. 1994.

Vol. 842: T. Kloks, Treewidth. IX, 209 pages. 1994.

Vol. 843: A. Szepietowski, Turing Machines with Sublogarithmic Space. VIII, 115 pages. 1994.

Vol. 844: M. Hermenegildo, J. Penjam (Eds.), Programming Language Implementation and Logic Programming. Proceedings, 1994. XII, 469 pages. 1994.

Vol. 845: J.-P. Jouannaud (Ed.), Constraints in Computational Logics. Proceedings, 1994. VIII, 367 pages. 1994.

Vol. 846: D. Shepherd, G. Blair, G. Coulson, N. Davies, F. Garcia (Eds.), Network and Operating System Support for Digital Audio and Video. Proceedings, 1993. VIII, 269 pages. 1994.

Vol. 847: A. L. Ralescu (Ed.) Fuzzy Logic in Artificial Intelligence. Proceedings, 1993. VII, 128 pages. 1994. (Subseries LNAI).

Vol. 848: A. R. Krommer, C. W. Ueberhuber, Numerical Integration on Advanced Computer Systems. XIII, 341 pages. 1994.

Vol. 849: R. W. Hartenstein, M. Z. Servít (Eds.), Field-Programmable Logic. Proceedings, 1994. XI, 434 pages. 1994.

Vol. 850: G. Levi, M. Rodríguez-Artalejo (Eds.), Algebraic and Logic Programming. Proceedings, 1994. VIII, 304 pages. 1994.

Vol. 851: H.-J. Kugler, A. Mullery, N. Niebert (Eds.), Towards a Pan-European Telecommunication Service Infrastructure. Proceedings, 1994. XIII, 582 pages. 1994.

Vol. 852: K. Echtle, D. Hammer, D. Powell (Eds.), Dependable Computing – EDCC-1. Proceedings, 1994. XVII, 618 pages. 1994.

Vol. 853: K. Bolding, L. Snyder (Eds.), Parallel Computer Routing and Communication. Proceedings, 1994. IX, 317 pages. 1994.

Vol. 854: B. Buchberger, J. Volkert (Eds.), Parallel Processing: CONPAR 94 – VAPP VI. Proceedings, 1994. XVI, 893 pages. 1994.

Vol. 855: J. van Leeuwen (Ed.), Algorithms – ESA '94. Proceedings, 1994. X, 510 pages.1994.

Vol. 856: D. Karagiannis (Ed.), Database and Expert Systems Applications. Proceedings, 1994. XVII, 807 pages. 1994.

Vol. 857: G. Tel, P. Vitányi (Eds.), Distributed Algorithms. Proceedings, 1994. X, 370 pages. 1994.

Vol. 858: E. Bertino, S. Urban (Eds.), Object-Oriented Methodologies and Systems. Proceedings, 1994. X, 386 pages. 1994.

Vol. 859: T. F. Melham, J. Camilleri (Eds.), Higher Order Logic Theorem Proving and Its Applications. Proceedings, 1994. IX, 470 pages. 1994.

Vol. 860: W. L. Zagler, G. Busby, R. R. Wagner (Eds.), Computers for Handicapped Persons. Proceedings, 1994. XX, 625 pages. 1994.

Vol: 861: B. Nebel, L. Dreschler-Fischer (Eds.), KI-94: Advances in Artificial Intelligence. Proceedings, 1994. IX, 401 pages. 1994. (Subseries LNAI).

Vol. 862: R. C. Carrasco, J. Oncina (Eds.), Grammatical Inference and Applications. Proceedings, 1994. VIII, 290 pages. 1994. (Subseries LNAI).

Vol. 863: H. Langmaack, W.-P. de Roever, J. Vytopil (Eds.), Formal Techniques in Real-Time and Fault-Tolerant Systems. Proceedings, 1994. XIV, 787 pages. 1994.

Vol. 864: B. Le Charlier (Ed.), Static Analysis. Proceedings, 1994. XII, 465 pages. 1994.

Vol. 865: T. C. Fogarty (Ed.), Evolutionary Computing. Proceedings, 1994. XII, 332 pages. 1994.

Vol 867: L. Steels, G. Schreiber, W. Van de Velde (Eds.), A Future for Knowledge Acquisition. Proceedings, 1994. XII, 414 pages. 1994. (Subseries LNAI).